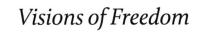

*Visions of Freedom*

THE NEW COLD WAR HISTORY
Odd Arne Westad, editor

# Visions of Freedom

*Havana, Washington, Pretoria, and the*
*Struggle for Southern Africa, 1976–1991*

PIERO GLEIJESES

The University of North Carolina Press
*Chapel Hill*

Designed and set in Calluna by Rebecca Evans
Manufactured in the United States of America

The paper in this book meets the guidelines for permanence and
durability of the Committee on Production Guidelines for Book
Longevity of the Council on Library Resources.

The University of North Carolina Press has been a member of the
Green Press Initiative since 2003.

Library of Congress Cataloging-in-Publication Data
Gleijeses, Piero, author.
Visions of freedom : Havana, Washington, Pretoria, and the struggle
for southern Africa, 1976–1991/Piero Gleijeses.
pages cm. — (New Cold War history)
ISBN 978-1-4696-0968-3 (cloth : alk. paper)
1. Africa, Southern—History—1975- 2. Cold War—Political aspects—
Africa, Southern. 3. Africa, Southern—Politics and government—1975-1994.
4. Africa, Southern—Foreign relations—1975-1994. 5. Africa, Southern—
History—Autonomy and independence movements. I. Title. II. Series:
New Cold War history.
DT1165.G54 2013
968.0009048—dc23 2013024964

Portions of this work have appeared earlier, in somewhat different form,
as "Moscow's Proxy? Cuba and Africa 1975-1988," *Journal of Cold War Studies*
8:4 (Fall 2006): 98–146, © 2006 by the President and Fellows of Harvard
College and the Massachusetts Institute of Technology, and "A Test of Wills:
Jimmy Carter, South Africa, and the Independence of Namibia," *Diplomatic
History* 34:5 (Nov. 2010): 853–91 (John Wiley & Sons, Ltd., publisher), and are
reprinted here with permission.

17 16 15 14 13   5 4 3 2 1

*To Setsuko Ono*

# Contents

# Maps and Illustrations

# Acknowledgments

Setsuko Ono has stimulated me along my journey with her probing and frank comments, and she has inspired me with her intelligence, her courage, and her art. Her sculptures adorn Havana, Washington, Baltimore, Tokyo, and Shibukawa. The paintings that she exhibited at the 2009 Bienal of Havana—*For Our Beautiful Earth: Resistance to Overwhelming Force and Dreams of Peace*—express with exquisite sensitivity her longing for a more just world. They challenge me to be relentless in seeking the truth in my chosen field.

For the past decade, I spent at least two months every year in Havana doing research for this book. Gloria León, one of Cuba's most gifted intellectuals, has helped me understand her country and saved me from countless gaffes and faux pas. Jorge Risquet, a key protagonist of the events analyzed in this book, made it possible for me to gain access to the closed Cuban archives. He has become a close friend while remaining a harsh and very intelligent critic. I was fortunate to be able to count on Hedelberto López Blanch—Cuba's foremost investigative journalist—and on the help of Rodrigo Álvarez Cambras, Juan Carrizo Estévez, Gisela Castellanos Castro, Nancy Jiménez Rodríguez, Antonio López López, Fernando Remírez de Estenoz, and Jorge Risquet Valdés Jiménez. Migdalia León is my Cuban doctor and a dear friend.

My research in Pretoria, Windhoek, and Luanda was enriched by the help of six good friends: Claudia Uushona, Paulo Lara, Isabel Martín, Emiliano Manresa, Pedro Ross, and Rosa Fonseca. Thenjiwe Mtintso, Aziz Pahad, and Ronnie Kasrils helped convince the National Archives of South Africa to declassify the documents of the State Security Council that were critical to my research.

At the Johns Hopkins School of Advanced International Studies, where I teach, Associate Dean John Harrington, a lover of history, is a good friend and has helped me in every possible way. I also owe a special debt to Senior Associate Dean Myron Kunka and to Kelley Kornell, the best coordinator that the U.S.

foreign policy department has ever had. Kelley holds our department together, and she has assisted me with intelligence, grace, and skill. I also benefited from the assistance of Brian Wingfield, Willy Shield, Thomas Field, David Fowkes, Elizabeth Wente, and Raphaël Guévin-Nicoloff. Three brilliant research librarians—Linda Carlson, Kathy Picart, and Barbara Prophet—tracked down even the most outlandish publications. They performed miracles with good cheer.

I greatly appreciated the intelligent criticism of Professors Lars Schoultz and Odd Arne Westad, who reviewed my manuscript for the University of North Carolina Press. My good friend Isaac Cohen offered, as always, incisive and wise comments, as did Professor Jim Hershberg. I thank Anna-Mart van Wyk for her insights on South Africa. Bringing this manuscript to press was greatly eased by the professionalism of Chuck Grench, Ron Maner, and Sara Cohen at the University of North Carolina Press. For more than three decades Doctor David Berler has safeguarded my eyesight—a challenging task—and Doctor Marwa Adi has now joined the effort. I am deeply grateful to them.

My research took me to archives in the United States, Cuba, Europe, and Africa. I thank all the archivists, but I feel a particular debt to Teresita Muñoz at the military archives in Havana and to Neels Muller at the Foreign Ministry Archives in Pretoria. And, above all, to my dear friend Ivys Silva Jomarrón, at the Central Committee of the Cuban Communist Party. Her wisdom and efficiency were invaluable.

Maja Murisic searched the Yugoslav archives for me and translated the documents she gathered. Jan Krzewinski did the same in the Polish archives. All other translations are mine.

Four protagonists read the manuscript: Jeff Davidow, the director of the Office of Southern African Affairs of the U.S. State Department in 1984–86; Eeben Barlow, a senior officer in the South African Defence Force in the 1980s; Jorge Risquet, Castro's point man for Angola in the period covered in this book; and General Paulo Lara, a senior officer in the Angolan army in the 1980s. All were forceful critics of my manuscript. To them, and to all who agreed to be interviewed for this book, I give my sincere thanks. And I also thank the John Simon Guggenheim Memorial Foundation, the American Philosophical Society, and SAIS for their financial assistance.

Nancy Mitchell is much more than the foremost expert on Carter's foreign policy. Her forthcoming book, *Race and the Cold War: Jimmy Carter in Africa*, illuminates U.S. foreign policy with unsurpassed intelligence. She generously set it aside time and again to read my manuscript, and I greatly benefited from her literary skill and her penetrating criticism. I depend on the intellectual collaboration we began many years ago.

# Abbreviations

The following abbreviations are used in the text. (For source abbreviations used in the notes, see p. 527.)

| | |
|---|---|
| ANC | African National Congress of South Africa |
| ATN | Agrupación de Tropas del Norte |
| ATS | Agrupación de Tropas del Sur |
| CIA | Central Intelligence Agency, United States |
| COMECON | Council of Mutual Economic Assistance |
| DCI | Director of Central Intelligence, United States |
| DIA | Defense Intelligence Agency, United States |
| DTA | Democratic Turnhalle Alliance |
| EPG | Eminent Persons Group |
| FAPLA | People's Armed Forces for the Liberation of Angola |
| FAR | Revolutionary Armed Forces (Fuerzas Armadas Revolucionarias), Cuba |
| FLEC | Front for the Liberation of the Enclave of Cabinda |
| FLS | Front Line States |
| FNLA | National Front for the Liberation of Angola |
| FRELIMO | Liberation Front of Mozambique |
| GDR | German Democratic Republic |
| INF | intermediate-range nuclear forces |
| INR | Bureau of Intelligence and Research, Department of State |
| JCS | Joint Chiefs of Staff, United States |
| JMC | Joint Monitoring Commission |
| MI | Military Intelligence, South Africa |
| MINFAR | Ministerio de las Fuerzas Armadas Revolucionarias, Cuba |
| MK | Umkontho We Sizwe |

| | |
|---|---|
| MPLA | Popular Movement for the Liberation of Angola |
| NSC | National Security Council, United States |
| OAU | Organization of African Unity |
| PRA | People's Republic of Angola |
| RENAMO | Mozambique National Resistance |
| SA | South Africa |
| SACP | South African Communist Party |
| SADF | South African Defence Force |
| SAG | South African government |
| SALT II | Strategic Arms Limitation Talks |
| SCC | Special Coordinating Committee of the U.S. National Security Council |
| SWA | South West Africa (Namibia) |
| SWAPO | South West Africa People's Organization |
| SWATF | South West Africa Territory Force |
| UNITA | National Union for the Total Independence of Angola |
| UNSC | United Nations, Security Council |
| UNTAG | United Nations Transition Assistance Group |
| USG | United States Government |
| ZANU | Zimbabwe African National Union |
| ZAPU | Zimbabwe African People's Union |

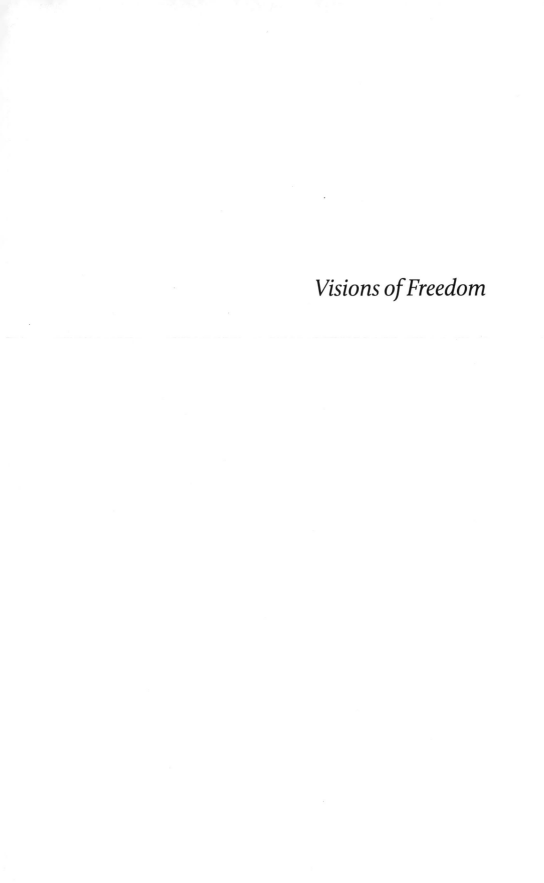

*Visions of Freedom*

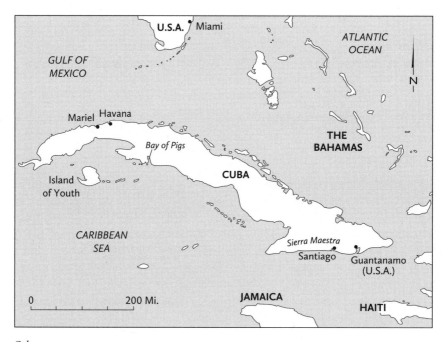

Cuba

Africa

Angola

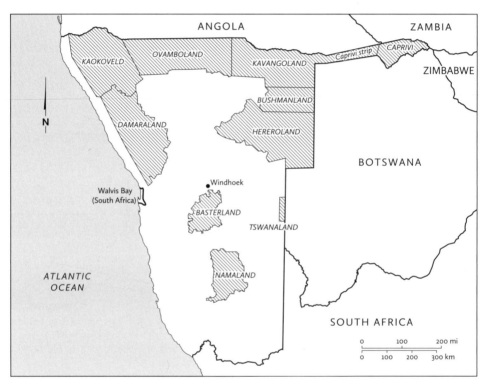

Namibia, showing the homelands and "White Area" (adapted from *Rand Daily Mail*
[Johannesburg], July 13, 1978)

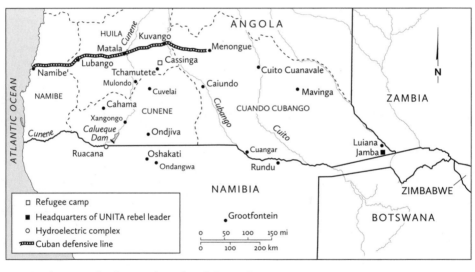

Southern Angola, showing the Cuban defensive line

Angola's eleven military regions

# Prologue

Until 1974 southern Africa was a backwater of the Cold War. The guerrillas who fought against Portuguese rule in Angola and Mozambique, against white minority rule in Rhodesia, against Pretoria's rule in Namibia, and against apartheid in South Africa seemed impotent. The stage was dominated by Washington's friends—apartheid South Africa and Portugal.

The collapse of the Portuguese dictatorship in April 1974 opened the first fissures in the dam that protected white rule, but Secretary of State Henry Kissinger was confident that the damage could be contained. He zeroed in on Angola, where Pretoria and Washington worked together to crush the left-wing Popular Movement for the Liberation of Angola (MPLA) and install instead friendly leaders. They almost succeeded.

Between November 1975 and April 1976, 36,000 Cuban soldiers poured into Angola. They were proxies of the Soviet Union, the outraged Ford administration proclaimed. Fidel Castro countered that they were internationalists helping the Angolans repel the South African troops who had invaded the country with Washington's collusion.

By April 1976 the Cubans had pushed the South Africans out of Angola. The MPLA ruled the country. Southern Africa had been hurled into the vortex of the Cold War. For the next fifteen years—until 1991—tens of thousands of Cuban soldiers remained in Angola. Their number peaked at 55,000 in 1988.

The Cuban role in Angola is without precedent. No other Third World country has projected its military power beyond its immediate neighborhood. Brazil's mighty generals had gone as far as the Caribbean, sending a small troop to the Dominican Republic in 1965 as the United States' junior partner; Argentina's generals briefly helped Anastasio Somoza's defeated cohorts in 1980–81 as they sought to regain a foothold in Nicaragua. Vietnam's soldiers never ventured beyond Indochina; China's military activities outside Asia were limited to the supply of weapons and the dispatch of a few hundred instructors to Africa. During the Cold War, extracontinental military interventions were the preserve of the two superpowers, a few West European countries, and Cuba.

I studied the Angolan events of 1975–76 in an earlier book, *Conflicting Missions: Havana, Washington, and Africa, 1959–1976*. Now, in *Visions of Freedom*, I investigate what happened over the subsequent fifteen years. These were the last years of the Cold War, a convulsed period with dramatic ups and downs in relations between the two superpowers. When the curtain opens, President Gerald Ford has frozen détente with the Soviet Union, largely because of the Cuban intervention in Angola. President Jimmy Carter revives détente, but it never blossoms, in part because of the presence of the Cuban troops in Angola. In 1979, the Soviet invasion of Afghanistan plunges the Cold War into one of its most bitter phases. But several years later Ronald Reagan would preside over an epochal change in U.S. relations with the Soviet Union—from the "evil empire" of the first term to the deepening détente with Mikhail Gorbachev in 1987–88.

Many have analyzed how these changes affected the high politics of superpower relations. But how did they affect events in those areas where the Cold War was actually being waged, where it was hot? As historian Nancy Mitchell writes, "The Cold War was a contest that consisted of shadow-boxing in areas of marginal significance because real war in places that really counted—Berlin, Washington and Moscow—was unwinnable."[1] After the Cubans' arrival in Angola, that shadowboxing occurred in southern Africa. Africans, Americans, Cubans, and Soviets jostled in a confusing landscape. They fought over the future of Angola and the decolonization of Namibia, Africa's last colony. Beyond lay the great prize: South Africa.

In Angola, throughout this period, the MPLA government faced two enemies bent on its destruction: the charismatic rebel leader Jonas Savimbi, and the South African government. Pretoria was well aware of the MPLA's commitment to help those who fought for the eradication of apartheid; therefore, the MPLA had to be destroyed. The South Africans bolstered Savimbi with economic and military aid. "We are working with South Africa to shape a common destiny," Savimbi pledged.[2] He was brilliant, he was eloquent, and he was without scruple. He was, a British ambassador in Luanda explained, "a monster whose lust for power had brought appalling misery to his people."[3] The South Africans did more than help Savimbi: they waged war on Angola for longer than a decade, sending their troops at will into the south of the country.

Sandwiched between Angola and South Africa is Namibia, a sprawling, underpopulated country. It had been a German colony before falling under a South African mandate at the close of the First World War. South Africa had ruled it as its fifth province. In 1971 the International Court of Justice and the UN Security Council had decreed Pretoria's occupation of the country illegal and ordered it to withdraw immediately. South African officials knew that if Namibia were ever truly independent, it would have "an extremely negative impact on every front" for the apartheid regime. It would encourage "black militant groups in South Africa . . . [and] lead to a decline in white morale."[4] They were willing to give Namibia independence, therefore, in name only. For its future leaders, they handpicked malleable men who scurried across the stage, eager for power and money but unable to garner popular support or legitimacy. Over them loomed the shadow of the South West Africa People's Organization (SWAPO), the Namibian guerrilla movement that challenged Pretoria's rule. SWAPO, a U.S. ambassador to South Africa wrote in 1977, "has, over the years, in the mind of the [Namibian] population come to symbolize independence, equal rights, and freedom from South Africa."[5] SWAPO, South African officials lamented, would win any free election; therefore, the UN-supervised elections that the international community demanded were a nonstarter. The war continued.

Namibia and Angola were more than neighbors; their struggles in the last years of the Cold War were intimately related. The SWAPO guerrillas were based in Angola, where the MPLA government gave them what, a South African general wrote, "is virtually a prerequisite for a successful insurgent campaign, namely a border that provided safe refuge."[6] In Angola, the SWAPO guerrillas were trained by Cuban and Soviet instructors.

South Africa, the region's powerhouse, was "prepared to go to any length, break any promises, threaten any alliance in order to protect what she regards as her own legitimate interests," a conservative British newspaper commented.[7] Among these interests one was paramount: apartheid. Beginning in 1984 the South African government faced "the most prolonged and intensive black uprising" in the country's history.[8] "The protests and violence," the Central Intelligence Agency (CIA) noted, "catapulted the African National Congress (ANC) . . . into the forefront of the antiapartheid movement."[9] Like SWAPO, the ANC had its military camps in Angola where its fighters were trained by Cuban instructors and armed by the Soviet Union.

South African officials agreed on the need to preserve apartheid, but they disagreed about the best way to do it. The "doves" within the South African government—Foreign Minister Pik Botha and his aides—were skeptical about the generals' plans to install Savimbi in Luanda and maintain sway over Namibia, but they kept their misgivings to themselves because they were intimidated by the country's strong-willed prime minister (then president) PW Botha, who shared the generals' views. Furthermore, they had no alternative to offer: like the generals, they loathed the MPLA government in Luanda and opposed free elections in Namibia. They were simply more aware than the generals of the dangers lurking ahead.

Thus there was a complex and deadly interplay between Angola, Namibia, and South Africa. The MPLA helped SWAPO and the ANC, which fought against South Africa. The South Africans, in turn, wanted to topple the MPLA and hold on to Namibia.

Had these African protagonists been left to themselves, the South Africans would almost certainly have brought down the MPLA government and enthroned Savimbi in Luanda. Savimbi would have ejected SWAPO and the ANC from Angola, and South Africa's control over Namibia would have been strengthened. This turn of events would have demoralized the black masses in South Africa and, Pretoria believed, "strike a blow against the revolutionary onslaught against South Africa."[10]

Instead, the Cuban soldiers, armed by the Soviet Union, protected the MPLA government and thereby protected SWAPO and the ANC. Even the CIA acknowledged that the Cuban troops were "necessary to preserve Angolan independence."[11] Nevertheless, their presence there was intolerable to both the Carter and Reagan administrations. It was, simply, an affront.

Both Carter and Reagan faced two interrelated challenges in southern Africa. The first was a Cold War problem: how to pry the Cubans out of Angola and reduce Soviet influence in the region. The second had domestic implications: how to deal with South Africa. In the United States, racial segregation— America's own brand of apartheid—was not long past, and racial tensions simmered. Should apartheid South Africa be a partner in the U.S. efforts to force Cuba out of Angola? And how should the United States deal with Pretoria's ally, Jonas Savimbi, Angola's rebel chieftain?

Figuring out how to address these two challenges opened schisms in each administration. Nancy Mitchell's study, "Race and the Cold War: Jimmy Carter in Africa," demonstrates that Secretary of State Cyrus Vance and National Security Adviser Zbigniew Brzezinski could work harmoniously on some important foreign policy questions. But on Angola, Namibia, and Cuba they were far apart, and their differences reflected contrasting visions of what U.S. foreign policy should be. Carter did not waver between them, unable to reach a decision, as happened in other instances (notably during the agony of the Shah's regime). He sided with Brzezinski, because he shared his views—and also because, unlike Vance, the national security adviser spiced his recommendations with an eye to electoral politics.

Deep divisions also rent the Reagan administration. They pitted the pragmatists, led by Secretary of State George Shultz, against the "true Reaganites," who claimed to represent the president's instincts. Southern Africa was one of their major battlegrounds. How tightly should the administration embrace South Africa? Should it simply push the Cubans out of Angola, or should it help South Africa bring Savimbi to power? And should the United States defy the international community, including its West European allies, and oppose free elections in Namibia? Reagan, after all, had deemed SWAPO "a Marxist terrorist band."[12] In answer to all these questions, Shultz and the pragmatists advocated moderation; the true Reaganites, on the other hand, brooked no compromise.

By Reagan's second term, the clash reverberated loudly in Congress and in the press. "Mr President: Why Is [Assistant Secretary of State for African Affairs] Chester Crocker Trying to Sell 20 Million Black Africans into Communist Slavery?" the leaders of the country's most prominent conservative organizations inquired in a December 1984 open letter to Reagan.[13] Chester Crocker, their bête noire, was the most influential assistant secretary of state for Africa during the Cold War. He enjoyed Shultz's trust, and he ably led the pragmatists on African issues. "I think he sympathizes with the communist government [of Angola]," Howard Phillips, chair of the Conservative Caucus, groused—a demented statement that reflected the views of an important segment of the Republican establishment.[14]

Angola was, by far, the most important foreign policy initiative of the Cuban revolution. It illuminates the aims and the motivations of Cuban foreign policy. It is also a rich laboratory to study the relationship between Cuba and the Soviet Union. Documents from the Cuban archives, complemented by the memoirs of former Soviet officials and the testimony of senior Angolan military officers, reveal an authoritative "inside" view of Cuban-Soviet relations during the last fifteen years of the Cold War. The interaction between the two countries took place at two levels: among top government officials in Havana and Moscow, and between the Cuban and the Soviet military missions in Angola. The Cubans knew very well that they were dependent on the Soviet Union. They were keen to avoid quarrels, but when necessary, they stood up to the Kremlin. In Angola, the Cuban generals challenged the recommendations of the Soviets, often vehemently. No one who reads the minutes of the exchanges between General Polo Cintra Frías, head of the Cuban military mission in Angola, and his Soviet counterpart, General Konstantin Kurochkin, can have any doubt about how obstreperous the Cubans could be.

Fidel Castro had defied Leonid Brezhnev by sending troops to Angola in November 1975, and he defied Gorbachev in November 1987 when he decided to send important reinforcements to Angola to push the South Africans out of the country once and for all—at the very moment Gorbachev wanted desperately to foster détente with Washington. "You know that our General Secretary will soon go [to Washington] to sign the INF [Intermediate-range Nuclear Forces] treaty," Soviet defense minister Dmitry Yazov complained to the chief of the Cuban General Staff. Havana's escalation in Angola was "undesirable from the political point of view. . . . We don't want to do anything that the Americans can use against the Soviet Union and Cuba."[15]

In his memoirs Gorbachev writes that "the Cuban government got us involved in, to put it mildly, difficult situations, such as Angola." In Moscow, opinions about Havana's African ventures were divided. "Our military was interested in establishing a reliable bridgehead in Africa, and so it supported Cuba's involvement in Angola . . . with enthusiasm. At the same time, Cuba's excessive engagement, which dragged in the Soviet Union, provoked serious objections in our political circles. In our 'corridors of power' many said openly that the Cubans 'were saddling us with a second Afghanistan.'"[16] The doubts increased as Gorbachev engaged in a search for détente with the United States. Nonetheless, Moscow loyally supported the Cuban engagement in Angola, even when it disagreed with Castro's decisions.

What did the Soviet Union gain from its long involvement in Angola? The CIA summed it up: Moscow got "a reliable supporter of Soviet positions in international forums" and the use of naval and air facilities in Luanda.[17] It sold vast amounts of weapons to Angola—approximately $6 billion between 1976 and 1988[18]—but the Angolans paid in cash only for 10 to 15 percent of the amount; the rest was given on credit, and the debt was not paid during the lifetime of the Soviet Union. Far from being a source of profit, the sale of weapons was, Soviet deputy foreign minister Anatoly Adamishin writes, a "black hole."[19]

In their memoirs, most former Soviet officials are critical of Moscow's involvement in Angola because it hurt relations with the United States and diverted resources that should have been used at home. It was "a serious mistake," wrote Marshal Sergei Akhromeyev. "It did not . . . serve the national interest of the Soviet Union," stressed Deputy Foreign Minister Georgi Kornienko. "Why, with all our problems, did we have to get involved?" Adamishin asked. "Whether it was just or not, we could not afford it, we had too many problems of our own."[20]

Vladimir Shubin, a former Soviet official and now a prominent scholar, offers a rare contrast to this litany of lamentations. He is proud of what the Soviet Union did in southern Africa. The achievements justified the costs—Moscow helped protect Angola from South Africa and lent crucial assistance to the liberation movements of southern Africa. Armed struggle was a key element in the collapse of white rule in southern Africa, he argues, and it would not have been possible without the weapons provided by the Soviet Union.[21]

Without Moscow, Cuba could not have kept tens of thousands of soldiers in Angola for more than a decade. Without Moscow, the Angolan army would have been virtually without weapons. "The two great achievements of the USSR in Angola," a senior Angolan officer remarked, "were to give the weapons to our army and to aid Cuba." Angolan president José Eduardo dos Santos told Castro in December 1988, "The Soviet Union helped Angola and helped Cuba to help Angola."[22]

The engine was Cuba. It was the Cubans who pushed the Soviets to help Angola. It was they who stood guard in Angola for many long years, thousands of miles from home, to prevent the South Africans from overthrowing the MPLA government. It was they who in 1988, with the reinforcements Castro sent against Gorbachev's wishes, forced the South African army out of Angola. It was they who forced Pretoria to abandon Savimbi and hold free elections in Namibia—which SWAPO won. In the words of Nelson Mandela, the Cuban victory over the South African army in southern Angola in 1988 "destroyed the myth of the invincibility of the white oppressor . . . [and] inspired the fighting masses of South Africa."[23] This was Cuba's contribution to what Castro has called "the most beautiful cause"[24]—the struggle against racial oppression in southern Africa. Humiliating one superpower and repeatedly defying the other, Cuba changed the course of history in southern Africa.

## My Sources

*Visions of Freedom* is the first international history of the conflict in southern Africa based on archival sources. It relies primarily on a triptych of documents: from Cuba, from the United States, and from South Africa.

The Cuban archives for the post-1959 period are closed. I am the only foreign scholar who has been allowed to enter them—after years of effort and failure. Over time, my access has improved, in quantity and in quality. I gathered 3,500 pages of Cuban documents for *Conflicting Missions*, but 15,000 for *Visions of Freedom*, including more than 3,500 pages of conversations of Fidel Castro with his closest aides or with foreign leaders, among them Gorbachev. The same rules that governed my research in Cuba for *Conflicting Missions* applied for this book. I never used a document unless I was given a photocopy of the original. Therefore, I have photocopies of all the Cuban documents I use in *Visions of Freedom*.

Christian Ostermann, the Director of the Cold War International History Project at the Woodrow Wilson International Center for Scholars, has created a website on which I have posted a large selection of the Cuban documents I use in this book. This will allow scholars, wherever they are, to have access to them. It is available at digitalarchive.org. I want to thank Christian Ostermann, James Hershberg and Laura Deal for making this possible.

The U.S. archives are, without question, the best-organized and richest that I have used in my professional career. But the pickings get slimmer when the researcher ventures into the Reagan years, because fewer documents have been declassified.

Fortunately for my research, there was a powerful remedy: the South African archives. They are brimming with documents that shed light on U.S. policy in the region. For example, they include the minutes of a great many meetings between U.S. and South African officials that are still under lock and key in the United States.

Other archives add insight and information, especially on the 1970s. Yugoslavia was a close friend of the MPLA; the Yugoslav documents shed light on Angola's relations with Cuba and the Soviet Union at critical moments in the 1970s. British documents are particularly helpful in understanding U.S. policy toward Namibia in the Carter years. The archives of the Communist Party of the former German Democratic Republic are open through the 1980s and provide important information about Angola, as well as about Cuban and Soviet policy toward southern Africa. The Zambian archives include useful dispatches from Zambian diplomats, and the French archives house the reports of the French chargé in Luanda in the late 1970s; he was an intelligent and knowledgeable observer. The Canadian archives include little relevant to this book. I had hoped to find valuable documents on southern Africa in the archives of the Italian Communist Party, but I had overestimated the party's interest in the region. I was also disappointed in my hope that the Polish archives would provide an interesting window on developments in Angola—only two documents rewarded the effort. The Angolan archives are closed, but I managed to collect several documents from private collections in Luanda. The Russian government has declassified very little relevant for this book, but the Gorbachev Foundation has released useful documents. Former Soviet protagonists—among them two former ambassadors to Cuba, as well as several generals and senior party officials—have written memoirs with valuable information.

I have also interviewed more than 150 protagonists from South Africa, Namibia, Angola, Cuba, and the United States. Interviews add color and texture; they complement the documents.

## CHAPTER 1

# The Cuban Drumbeat

## The Last Hurrah: Gorbachev in Havana

Mikhail Gorbachev visited Cuba in April 1989. Some of his closest aides had urged him not to go: Fidel Castro was a political dinosaur, they argued, his policy in the Third World was reckless, and going to Cuba would irritate the United States. Other aides disagreed. In a memo to Gorbachev accompanying a draft of the speech the Soviet leader would deliver to the Cuban National Assembly, Georgi Shakhnazarov noted Cuba's economic crisis and added: "I have attempted to include warm words about the significance of the Cuban revolution . . . to give moral support to the Cuban government in this moment that is so difficult for them."[1]

Gorbachev did not consider Castro a relic of the past. He wrote in his memoirs, "I had and have a high opinion of this man, of his intellectual and political abilities. He is, without doubt, an outstanding statesman. . . . In my conversations with Castro I never had the feeling that this man had exhausted himself, that he, as they say, 'was a spent force,' that his worldview was cast in cement, that he was unable to absorb new ideas. It was possible to have a constructive dialogue with him, to attain mutual understanding, to count on cooperation."[2]

In Havana, Gorbachev was a tactful and respectful guest. The Cubans appreciated that he did not try to lecture them, give them advice, or criticize them. At the press conference after the talks, when a journalist asked "What advice did the charming Gorbachev give the Cubans?" Castro quipped, "Gorbachev is charming precisely because he does not tell other countries what to do."[3]

The Soviet leader assured the Cubans of continuing support. "Cuba—it is our revolutionary duty, our destiny to help her," Gorbachev wrote after leaving the island.[4] His promises rang hollow, however, against the backdrop of the rapidly deteriorating situation in the Soviet Union and in the Soviet bloc. Seven months later, the Berlin Wall fell. Throughout Eastern Europe, Communist regimes crumbled.

Castro had told Angola's President José Eduardo dos Santos in late 1988, as détente between Washington and Moscow blossomed, "We don't know how the United States will interpret peace and détente, whether it will be a peace for all, détente for all, coexistence for all, or whether the North Americans will interpret 'coexistence' as peace with the USSR—peace among the powerful—and war against the small. This has yet to be seen. We intend to remain firm, but we are ready to improve relations with the United States if there is an opening."[5]

There was no opening. For the next three years, as the Soviet Union teetered on the brink of collapse, U.S. officials pressured Gorbachev to cut all aid to Cuba.[6] The collapse of the Soviet Union in December 1991 meant that Havana was alone, and in desperate economic straits. Washington tightened the embargo, making it as difficult as possible for third countries to trade with Cuba. U.S. officials hoped that hunger and despair would force the Cuban people to turn against their government.

## The Burden of the Past

Why such hatred? The answer lies, in part, in Castro's betrayal of the special relationship that had existed between the United States and Cuba since the early 1800s, when President Thomas Jefferson had longed to annex the island, then a Spanish colony. Jefferson's successors embraced the belief that Cuba's destiny was to belong to the United States. No one understood this better than José Martí, the father of Cuban independence. In 1895, as Cuba's revolt against Spanish rule began, he wrote, "What I have done, and shall continue to do is to . . . block with our [Cuban] blood . . . the annexation of the peoples of America to the turbulent and brutal North that despises them. . . . I lived in the monster [the United States] and know its entrails—and my sling is that of David."[7] The next day he was killed on the battlefield.

In 1898, as the Cuban revolt entered its fourth year, the United States joined the war against an exhausted Spain, ostensibly to free Cuba. After Spain surrendered, Washington forced the Platt Amendment on the Cubans, which granted the United States the right to send troops to the island whenever it deemed it necessary and to establish bases on Cuban soil. (Today, the Platt Amendment lives on in the U.S. naval base at Guantánamo Bay.) Cuba became, more than any other Latin American country, "an American fiefdom."[8] Until 1959, that is, when Fidel Castro came to power and tweaked the beak of the American eagle.

When Americans look back at that fateful year of 1959—when it all began—

they are struck by their good intentions and by Castro's malevolence. The United States had offered its friendship, only to be rebuffed. Indeed, President Dwight Eisenhower had sought a modus vivendi with Castro—as long as Cuba remained within the U.S. sphere of influence and respected the privileges of the American companies that dominated the island's economy. Castro, however, was not willing to bow to the United States. "He is clearly a strong personality and a born leader of great personal courage and conviction," U.S. officials noted in April 1959, and, a few months later, a National Intelligence Estimate reported, "He is inspired by a messianic sense of mission to aid his people."[9] Even though he did not have a clear blueprint of the Cuba he wanted to create, Castro dreamed of a sweeping revolution that would uproot his country's oppressive socioeconomic structure. He dreamed of a Cuba free of the United States. Eisenhower was baffled, for he believed, as most Americans still do, that the United States had been the Cubans' truest friend, fighting Spain in 1898 to give them independence. "Here is a country," he marveled, "that you would believe, on the basis of our history, would be one of our real friends." As U.S. historian Nancy Mitchell has pointed out, "our selective recall not only serves a purpose, it also has repercussions. It creates a chasm between us and the Cubans: we share a past, but we have no shared memories."[10] Ethnocentrism and ignorance are the pillars of the City on the Hill.

The United States responded to Castro's challenge in the way it always dealt with nuisances in its backyard: with violence. On Eisenhower's orders, the CIA began planning the overthrow of Castro. In April 1961, three months after John Kennedy's inauguration, 1,300 CIA-trained insurgents stormed a Cuban beach at the Bay of Pigs—only to surrender en masse three days later.

Flush with this victory, Castro tendered an olive branch. On August 17, 1961, Che Guevara told a close aide of Kennedy that Cuba wanted to explore a modus vivendi with the United States. Kennedy was not interested. A few months later, on the president's orders, the CIA launched Operation Mongoose, a program of paramilitary operations, economic warfare, and sabotage designed to visit what Kennedy's aide Arthur Schlesinger has called the "terrors of the earth"[11] on Fidel Castro.

## Relations with Moscow

Castro enjoyed widespread support among the Cuban population, as the CIA acknowledged, but he understood that only strong Soviet backing could protect his fledgling revolution from the wrath of the United States. The fate of Guatemala's President Jacobo Arbenz, overthrown by the CIA in 1954, was a bitter reminder of what befell errant presidents in the U.S. backyard. In January 1959, the Soviets knew very little about Castro. For several months their only contact was through leaders of the Cuban Communist Party visiting Moscow to vouch for the revolutionary credentials of the new government. In October 1959 a KGB official arrived in Havana, establishing the first direct link between the Kremlin and the new Cuban leadership. Soon, the tempo accelerated: in March 1960 Moscow approved a Cuban request for weapons. Diplomatic relations were established the following May. In 1961, the relationship grew close and even ebullient as Soviet bloc arms and economic aid arrived. Castro was charismatic, he seemed steadfast, he worked well with the Cuban communists, and he had humiliated the United States at the Bay of Pigs. The Soviet Union would transform the island into a socialist showcase in Latin America.

It was the Missile Crisis that brought the romance to an abrupt end. Thirty years later, in 1992, Kennedy's defense secretary, Robert McNamara, finally understood why the Soviets and the Cubans had decided to place missiles in Cuba: "I want to state quite frankly with hindsight, if I had been a Cuban leader, I think I might have expected a U.S. invasion. . . . And I should say, as well, if I had been a Soviet leader at the time, I might have come to the same conclusion."[12] Kennedy's reckless policy meant that Castro had legitimate concerns for his country's security. Added to this was the Kremlin's desire to close the "missile gap," America's well-publicized overwhelming superiority in strategic weapons.

Kennedy learned that there were Soviet missiles in Cuba on October 16, 1962. On October 24 the U.S. Navy quarantined the island. Four days later, when Nikita Khrushchev agreed to remove the missiles, he did not bother to consult Castro—"I don't see how you can say that we were consulted in the decision you took," Castro wrote Khrushchev.[13] The honeymoon was over.

In the wake of the Missile Crisis, the United States continued paramilitary raids and sabotage operations against Cuba, trying to cripple its economy and assassinate Castro. U.S. officials were no longer confident that they could topple Castro, but they were determined to teach the Latin Americans that the price of following Cuba's example would be high. "Cuba was the key to all of Latin America," the Director of Central Intelligence told Kennedy. "If Cuba succeeds, we can expect most of Latin America to fall."[14]

While Kennedy promoted subversion in Cuba, Castro promoted revolution in Latin America. Castro argued that "the virus of revolution is not carried in submarines or ships. It is wafted instead on the ethereal waves of ideas. . . . The power of Cuba is the power of its revolutionary ideas, the power of its example." The CIA agreed. "The extensive influence of 'Castroism' is not a function of

Cuba's power," it noted in mid-1961. "Castro's shadow looms large because social and economic conditions throughout Latin America invite opposition to ruling authority and encourage agitation for radical change."[15]

Cuba, however, did not rely just on the power of its example. "By 1961–1962, Cuban support [for revolution] began taking many forms," the CIA noted, "ranging from inspiration and training to such tangibles as financing and communications support as well as some military assistance." Most significant was military training. The CIA estimated that between 1961 and 1964 "at least" 1,500 to 2,000 Latin Americans received "either guerrilla warfare training or political indoctrination in Cuba."[16]

By 1964 the guerrillas in Latin America had suffered a string of setbacks, and Cuban support for them had become a source of discord between Havana and Moscow. The Cubans resented the Soviets' growing antipathy for armed struggle in Latin America, and the Kremlin was unhappy because Castro's policies complicated its relations with the United States and Latin American governments.

Castro was unbending. At a meeting of communist parties in Moscow in March 1965, Raúl Castro, Fidel's brother and minister of defense, stressed that it was imperative "to organize a global movement of solidarity with the guerrillas in Venezuela, Colombia, and Guatemala who . . . are fighting heroically for the independence of their countries."[17] By 1968, however, the guerrillas had been crushed in Bolivia, virtually wiped out in Guatemala, and brutally punished in Colombia and Venezuela. These defeats, and Che's death, taught Havana that a few brave men and women could not by themselves ignite armed struggle in Latin America. "By 1970 Cuban assistance to guerrilla groups . . . had been cut back to very low levels," U.S. officials concluded.[18]

This removed a major irritant in Cuba's increasingly strained relationship with the Soviet Union. In the late 1960s, while U.S. policy makers publicly lambasted Castro as a Soviet puppet, U.S. intelligence analysts quietly pointed to his open criticism of the Soviet Union and his refusal to accept Soviet advice. "He has no intention of subordinating himself to Soviet discipline and direction, and he has increasingly disagreed with Soviet concepts, strategies and theories," a 1968 study concluded, reflecting the consensus of the U.S. intelligence community.[19] Castro criticized the Soviet Union as dogmatic and opportunistic, niggardly in its aid to Third World governments and liberation movements, and overeager to seek accommodation with the United States. He made no secret of his displeasure with the inadequacy of Moscow's support of North Vietnam, and in Latin America he actively pursued policies contrary to Moscow's wishes. "If they gave us any advice, we'd say that they were interfering in our internal affairs," Raúl Castro later remarked, "but we didn't hesitate to express our opinions about their internal affairs."[20]

To explain why the Soviets put up with "their recalcitrant Cuban ally," U.S. intelligence reports noted that Moscow was "inhibited by Castro's intractability."[21] The Soviets still saw advantages in their relationship with Cuba, a 1967 study observed; it proved their ability to support even "remote allies," and it had a "nuisance value vis-a-vis the US." Above all, Moscow drew back from the political and psychological cost of a break: "How could the Soviets pull out of Cuba and look at the world or themselves in the morning? It would be a confession of monumental failure—the first and only Socialist enterprise in the New World abandoned—and it would seriously damage Soviet prestige and be widely interpreted as a victory of sorts for the United States."[22]

By the early 1970s, however, reeling from the twin failures of his revolutionary offensive in Latin America and his economic policies at home, Castro softened toward the Kremlin. Cuban criticism of Soviet policies ceased, and Havana acknowledged Moscow's primacy within the socialist bloc. At the same time, Havana's new approach to armed struggle in Latin America—more subtle, more discriminating—eased relations with the United States. In 1974 Secretary of State Henry Kissinger concluded that the U.S. embargo of Cuba had become counterproductive. West European and Latin American governments increasingly resented Washington's heavy-handed pressure to join its crusade against Cuba, and U.S. public opinion, spearheaded by businesses eager to corner the growing Cuban market, now favored peaceful coexistence with the island. Kissinger proposed secret negotiations aimed at normalizing relations, and in a meeting on July 9, 1975, Cuban and U.S. representatives discussed steps that would lead to an improvement in relations and, eventually, full bilateral ties. Four months later, however, Cuban troops landed in Angola.

## Africa: The Beginnings

I was among those stunned by the sudden outpouring of thousands of soldiers from a small Caribbean island which, in 1975, seemed more like a tropical Bulgaria, a well-behaved Soviet client, than a fiery revolutionary outpost. "You can't understand our intervention in Angola without understanding our past," a Cuban official later told me. He meant that the Cubans who went to Angola were following in the footsteps of those who, over the previous fifteen years, had gone to Algeria, Zaire, Congo Brazzaville, and Guinea-Bissau.[23] He also meant, very gently, that my mental construction of Cuba as a tropical Bulgaria was, simply, nonsense.

History, geography, culture, and language made Latin America the Cubans' natural habitat, the place closest to Castro's and his followers' hearts, the first place they tried to spread revolution. But Latin America was also where their freedom of movement was most circumscribed. Castro was, the CIA observed, "canny enough to keep his risks low" in the U.S. backyard.[24] Hence, fewer than forty Cubans fought in Latin America in the 1960s, and Cuba exercised extreme caution before sending weapons to Latin American rebels.

In Africa, Cuba incurred fewer risks. Whereas in Latin America Havana challenged legal governments and flouted international law, in Africa it confronted colonial powers and defended established states. Above all, in Africa there was much less risk of a head-on collision with the United States. U.S. officials barely noted the Cubans in Africa—until 36,000 Cuban soldiers landed in Angola.

Moreover, the Cuban leaders were convinced that their country had a special empathy for the Third World beyond the confines of Latin America. The Soviets and their East European allies were white and, by Third World standards, rich; the Chinese exhibited the hubris of a great and rising power and were unable to adapt to African and Latin American culture. By contrast, Cuba was nonwhite, poor, threatened by a powerful enemy, and culturally both Latin American and African. It was, therefore, a unique hybrid: a socialist country with a Third World sensibility. This mattered, in a world that was dominated, as Castro said, by the "conflict between privileged and underprivileged, humanity against imperialism,"[25] and where the major fault line was not between socialist and capitalist states but between developed and underdeveloped countries.

If this were a play—"Cuba's African Journey"—the curtain would rise at Casablanca where a Cuban ship, *Bahía de Nipe*, docked in December 1961. It brought weapons for the Algerian rebels fighting against French colonial rule, and it departed with precious cargo: wounded Algerian fighters and war orphans from refugee camps. This represented the dual thrust of Cuban internationalism: military aid and humanitarian assistance. In May 1963, after Algeria had gained its independence, a fifty-five-person Cuban medical mission arrived in Algiers to provide free health care to the Algerian people. ("It was like a beggar offering his help, but we knew that the Algerian people needed it even more than we did, and that they deserved it," explained the minister of public health.)[26] In October 1963, when Algeria was threatened by Morocco, the Cubans rushed a force of 686 men with heavy weapons to the Algerians, jeopardizing a contract Rabat had just signed with Havana to buy Cuban sugar worth $184 million, a considerable amount of hard currency at a time when the United States was trying to cripple Cuba's economy.

Havana's interest in sub-Saharan Africa quickened in late 1964. This was the moment of the great illusion when the Cubans, and many others, believed that revolution beckoned in Africa. Guerrillas were fighting the Portuguese in Angola, Guinea-Bissau, and Mozambique. In Congo Brazzaville, a new government proclaimed its revolutionary sympathies. Above all, there was Zaire, where armed revolt threatened the corrupt pro-American regime that Eisenhower and Kennedy had laboriously put in place. To save the Zairean government, in the summer of 1964 the Johnson administration raised an army of 1,000 white mercenaries in a major covert operation that provoked a wave of revulsion even among African leaders friendly to the United States. In December, Che Guevara went on a three-month trip to Africa. Thomas Hughes, the director of the State Department's Bureau of Intelligence and Research (INR), noted that this "trip was part of an important new Cuban strategy" to spread revolution in Africa: it would win Havana new friends and challenge U.S. influence on the continent. Che explained that he offered the Zairean rebels "about thirty instructors and all the weapons we could spare," and they accepted "with delight." Che left with "the joy of having found people ready to fight to the finish. Our next task," he wrote, "was to select a group of black Cubans—all volunteers—to join the struggle in Zaire."[27] From April to July 1965, 120 Cubans, led by Che, entered Zaire. In August, 250 Cubans, under Jorge Risquet, arrived in neighboring Congo Brazzaville at the request of that country's government, which feared an attack by the CIA's mercenaries; the Cuban column would also, if possible, assist Che in Zaire.

But Central Africa was not ready for revolution. By the time the Cubans arrived in Zaire, the mercenaries had broken the resolve of the rebels, leaving Che no choice by November 1965 but to withdraw. In Congo Brazzaville, Risquet's column saved the host government from a military coup and trained the rebels of Agostinho Neto's MPLA before withdrawing in July 1967.

The late 1960s were a time of deepening maturity in Cuba's relationship with Africa. No longer deluded that revolution was around the corner, the Cubans were learning about the continent. In those years the focus of Havana's attention in Africa was Guinea-Bissau, where rebels fighting for independence from Portugal asked for Cuba's assistance. In 1966 Havana sent military instructors and doctors, and they remained until the end of the war in 1974—the longest and most successful Cuban intervention in Africa before the dispatch of troops to Angola in 1975. In the words of Guinea-Bissau's first president, "we were able to fight and triumph because other countries helped us . . . with weapons, medicine, and supplies. . . . But there is one nation that in addition to material, political and diplomatic support, even sent its children to fight by our side, to shed their blood in our land. . . . This great people, this heroic people, we all know that it is the heroic people of Cuba; the Cuba of Fidel Castro."[28]

Not once did U.S. intelligence reports in the 1960s suggest that Cuba was acting in Latin America or Africa at the behest of the Soviet Union. Instead, they consistently stressed that self-defense and revolutionary fervor were Castro's main motivations. They were correct. The United States had repeatedly rebuffed Castro's offers to explore a modus vivendi, and Castro had concluded that the best defense was offense. Attacking the United States directly would be suicidal, but assisting revolutionary forces in the Third World would gain friends for Cuba and weaken U.S. influence. "It was almost a reflex," Che's second-in-command in Zaire remarked. "Cuba defends itself by attacking its aggressor. This was our philosophy. The Yankees were attacking us from every side, so we had to challenge them everywhere. We had to divide their forces, so that they wouldn't be able to descend on us, or any other country, with all their might."[29]

To explain Cuban activism in the 1960s merely in terms of self-defense, however, would be to distort reality—a mistake U.S. intelligence analysts did not make. There was a second motive force, as CIA and INR freely acknowledged: Castro's "sense of revolutionary mission." Report after report stressed the same point: Castro was "a compulsive revolutionary," a man with a "fanatical devotion to his cause," who was "inspired by a messianic sense of mission." He believed that he was "engaged in a great crusade" to help free the people of the Third World from the misery and the oppression that tormented them.[30]

These, then, were the dual motivations of Cuban activism in the 1960s: self-preservation and revolutionary idealism. They ran along parallel tracks, until Angola.

## Angola

In 1974 Angola was Portugal's richest colony. Almost twice the size of Texas, it was the fourth-largest coffee producer in the world, the sixth-largest diamond producer, an important exporter of iron ore, and sub-Saharan Africa's third-largest oil producer. Its population was approximately 6.4 million, including 320,000 whites. There was only one large city, Luanda, with more than 500,000 residents.

Angola's mulattoes—estimates range from 60,000 to 100,000—were not a homogeneous social group. They were the great majority of Angola's nonwhite elite, but they were also found among the most destitute. For most black Angolans, however, the mulattoes were the willing auxiliaries of the Portuguese, ready to serve the white man and betray the African. As John Marcum, one of Angola's keenest observers, pointed out, "a legacy of mistrust between mulatto and African" had developed over the centuries.[31]

At the bottom of Angola's society were the blacks, more than 90 percent of the population. They were the unlucky charges of Europe's most backward colonial power. Most of Angola's black population belonged to the country's three major ethnic groups: the 2 million strong Ovimbundu in the central highlands; the 1.3 million Mbundu in the north-central region; and the 400,000 Bakongo in the northwest. Angola's ethnic and racial composition helps explain the divisions among its rebel movements—each was based on one of the three major ethnic groups: Agostinho Neto's MPLA on the Mbundu; Holden Roberto's National Front for the Liberation of Angola (FNLA) on the Bakongo; and Jonas Savimbi's National Union for the Total Independence of Angola (UNITA) on the Ovimbundu.

Each of the three movements was led by an authoritarian leader. All three leaders were black. However, unlike their rivals, the leaders of the MPLA, some of whom were mulattoes, thought in terms of class rather than race. Neto's top military aide, Iko Carreira, was a light-skinned mulatto, as was his closest aide, Lúcio Lara. The MPLA's "largely Mulatto character helps it to transcend tribal divisions and to render its appeal multiracial," the British consul in Luanda remarked in 1965.[32] The movement also included whites. Both Neto and Lara were married to white women. "Let's not reject people who can help us just because they're white," Neto urged. "All that matters is that they're progressive and honest."[33] This attitude caused the rank and file to grumble, and it deepened the rift between the MPLA and its rivals. The leaders of both the FNLA and UNITA were suspicious of mulattoes and hostile to whites, and they accused the MPLA of selling out to the exploiters of Angola's black population.

Whereas the top echelons of the FNLA had no more than a secondary education, many UNITA leaders had university degrees. None, however, had attained the intellectual prominence of the MPLA leadership. President Neto and several of his colleagues were, the CIA noted, "distinguished intellectuals who have studied in Europe." Neto was "a well-known doctor and poet. . . . Brilliant student; led his class at the University of Lisbon," INR director Hughes wrote. "As a distinguished intellectual," Hughes's predecessor stated, "Neto commands widespread admiration from politically aware Africans and mulattoes in Angola."[34] He was an honest man who asked little for himself in the way of material comforts. After his visit to East Berlin in May 1963, East German officials remarked that "Dr. Neto was modest and unassuming. He asked for no special treatment of any kind." A journalist wrote that he was "a strong character, built stronger by adversity, little given to words, often finding words a waste of time (even when they might not have been) . . . a poet and a scholar who had made himself into a revolutionary. Uninspiring as a public speaker . . . though witty and persuasive in private talk, a man whose mildness of manner concealed a tough, unyielding stubbornness, Neto combined an unbending devotion to his cause with a corresponding moral power."[35] This omits the fact that Neto was an authoritarian leader, acting at times, as one of his circle wrote, "without even informing his closest aides."[36]

Neto, Lara, and several other MPLA leaders espoused an eclectic interpretation of Marxism-Leninism that was, a Yugoslav official noted, "adapted to the specific conditions and needs of Angola."[37] A few intellectuals, none in a senior position, supported orthodox socialism oriented toward the Soviet Union. Most military commanders had no ideological compass, beyond a vague belief that independence should be followed by deep changes in Angolan society. However murky the MPLA's ideological commitment may have been, it set it apart: the leaders of the FNLA and UNITA espoused no political doctrine. Jonas Savimbi, who led UNITA with an iron hand, was a warlord whose consuming passion was absolute power and who was ready to inflict any sacrifice on his countrymen to attain that goal. The FNLA, the U.S. consul general in Luanda observed, "was totally corrupt." The CIA station chief in Luanda agreed: "This organization," he wrote, "was led by corrupt, unprincipled men who represented the very worst of radical black African nationalism."[38]

None of the three rebel movements developed an effective fighting force. The MPLA almost succeeded, in the vast, thinly populated areas of eastern Angola. Through the early 1970s, the Portuguese considered the MPLA their "most dangerous foe [in Angola]," the U.S. consul in Luanda called it "the single most significant threat for the future," and INR concluded that it was "the best disciplined and most effective" of the three rebel groups. "We were at our peak," Lara recalled, in 1970 and early 1971.[39] Then a series of Portuguese offensives battered the eastern front, inflicting heavy blows on the MPLA. This inflamed latent ethnic tensions and led to a serious challenge to Neto's leadership, further weakening the movement.

By April 1974, when the Portuguese dictatorship collapsed, the MPLA had come full circle militarily. It was once again weak and ineffectual. Nevertheless, it "remained the most important movement in Angola," as the chief of the general staff of the Portuguese armed forces remarked.[40] Over the years, the

MPLA's shortwave broadcasts had kept its name alive for hundreds of thousands of Angolans who had never seen an MPLA fighter or read an MPLA tract. The movement's emphasis on class rather than ethnicity had gained it supporters throughout Angola's urban centers and had made it, in the words of U.S. consul general Everett Briggs (1972–74), "the only Angolan [rebel] organization that had any national representativeness, that could be considered an Angolan-wide organization." Furthermore, as the State Department noted in 1975, the MPLA commanded "the allegiance of most of the best educated and skilled people in Angola." It was, Briggs's successor Tom Killoran explained, "head and shoulders above the other two groups in terms of skills, education, and knowing what to do and how to do it."[41]

## From Local Conflict to Cold War Crisis

The new Portuguese government and the three Angolan movements agreed that a transitional government would rule Angola until independence on November 11, 1975. Civil war erupted, however, in the spring of 1975. That July, Pretoria and Washington began parallel covert operations in Angola, first supplying weapons to both the FNLA and UNITA, then sending military instructors. South Africa and the United States were not pursuing identical ends in Angola, but both wanted to crush the MPLA. Pretoria's motivation was to shore up apartheid at home and eliminate any threat to its illegal rule over Namibia, sandwiched between South Africa and Angola. South African officials feared the MPLA's implacable hostility to apartheid and its promise to assist the liberation movements of southern Africa. (By contrast, UNITA and the FNLA had offered Pretoria their friendship.) Although U.S. officials knew that an MPLA victory would not threaten American strategic or economic interests, Kissinger cast the struggle in stark Cold War terms: the freedom-loving FNLA and UNITA would defeat the Soviet-backed MPLA. He believed that success in Angola would provide a cheap boost to U.S. prestige and to his own reputation, pummeled by the fall of South Vietnam a few months earlier.

The first Cuban instructors for the MPLA arrived in Luanda at the end of August 1975, but Soviet aid to the MPLA was still very limited—Moscow distrusted Neto and did not want to jeopardize the SALT II arms control negotiations with the United States. By September, Washington and Pretoria realized that the MPLA was winning the civil war, not because of Cuban aid (no Cubans were fighting in Angola) or superior weapons (the rival coalition had a slight edge, thanks to U.S. and South African largesse), but because, as the CIA station chief in Luanda noted, the MPLA was "more effective, better educated, better trained, and better motivated."[42]

Washington urged Pretoria to intervene. On October 14, South African troops invaded Angola, transforming the civil war into an international conflict. As the South Africans raced toward Luanda, MPLA resistance crumbled; they would have seized the capital had not Castro decided on November 4 to respond to the MPLA's appeals for troops. The evidence is clear—even though many scholars continue to distort it—the South Africans invaded first, and the Cubans responded.[43] The Cuban forces, despite their initial inferiority in numbers and weapons, halted the South African onslaught. The official South African historian of the war writes, "The Cubans rarely surrendered and, quite simply, fought cheerfully until death."[44]

As the South African operation unraveled and credible evidence surfaced in the western press that Washington and Pretoria had been working together in Angola, the White House drew back. It claimed, loudly, that it had nothing to do with the South Africans, and it condemned their intervention in Angola. Hence the cry of outrage of South Africa's defense minister, who told the South African parliament: "I know of only one occasion in recent years when we crossed a border and that was in the case of Angola when we did so with the approval and knowledge of the Americans. But they left us in the lurch. We are going to retell the story: the story must be told of how we, with their knowledge, went in there and operated in Angola with their knowledge, how they encouraged us to act and, when we had nearly reached the climax, we were ruthlessly left in the lurch."[45] Betrayed by the Americans, pilloried as aggressors throughout the world, and threatened by growing numbers of Cuban soldiers, the South Africans gave up. On March 27, 1976, the last South African troops withdrew from Angola.

U.S. officials responded to the humiliating defeat with fury. They blasted the Cubans as Moscow's mercenaries. Perhaps they believed it. In any case, the image of Castro as Moscow's proxy was comforting: it simplified international relations and cast Cuba's extraordinary actions in a squalid light. In other words, it sidestepped difficult questions. As former under secretary of state George Ball has written, "Myths are made to solace those who find reality distasteful and, if some find such fantasy comforting, so be it."[46]

With the passing of time, the evidence that the Cubans sent their troops to Angola "on their own initiative and without consulting us [the Soviets]," as a Soviet official writes, has become too compelling to deny. The intervention "was a unilateral Cuban operation designed in great haste," the CIA noted in

1981. Even Kissinger was forced to reconsider. "At the time we thought he [Castro] was operating as a Soviet surrogate," he writes in his memoirs. "We could not imagine that he would act so provocatively so far from home unless he was pressured by Moscow to repay the Soviet Union for its military and economic support. Evidence now available suggests that the opposite was the case."[47]

What motivated Castro's bold move in Angola? Not Cuba's narrow interests, not realpolitik. Castro's decision challenged Soviet general secretary Leonid Brezhnev, who opposed the dispatch of Cuban soldiers to Angola, and it risked a serious military clash with Pretoria, which, urged on by Washington, might have escalated. The Cuban soldiers would have then faced the full South African army without any guarantee of Soviet assistance. Indeed, it took two months for Moscow to begin to help the Cubans to airlift their troops to Angola.[48] Furthermore, the dispatch of Cuban troops jeopardized relations with the West at a moment when they were markedly improving: the United States was probing a modus vivendi; the Organization of American States had lifted the sanctions it had imposed in 1964; and West European governments were offering Havana low-interest loans and development aid. Realpolitik required Cuba to rebuff Luanda's appeals. Had he been a client of the Soviet Union, Castro would have held back.

Castro sent troops because of his commitment to what he has called "the most beautiful cause,"[49] the struggle against apartheid. He understood that the victory of the Pretoria-Washington axis would have tightened the grip of white domination over the people of southern Africa. It was a defining moment. As Kissinger observed later, Castro "was probably the most genuine revolutionary leader then in power."[50]

The tidal wave unleashed by the Cuban victory washed over southern Africa. Its psychological impact and the hope it aroused are illustrated by two statements from across the political divide in apartheid South Africa. In February 1976, as the Cuban troops were pushing the South African army toward the Namibian border, a South African military analyst wrote: "In Angola, Black troops—Cubans and Angolans—have defeated White troops in military exchanges. Whether the bulk of the offensive was by Cubans or Angolans is immaterial in the color-conscious context of this war's battlefield, for the reality is that they won, are winning, and are not White; and that psychological edge, that advantage the White man has enjoyed and exploited over 300 years of colonialism and empire, is slipping away. White elitism has suffered an irreversible blow in Angola, and Whites who have been there know it."[51] The "White Giants" had retreated, and black Africans celebrated. "Black Africa is riding the crest of a wave generated by the Cuban success in Angola," noted the *World*, South Africa's major black newspaper. "Black Africa is tasting the heady wine of the possibility of realizing the dream of total liberation."[52] There would have been no heady dream, but, rather, the pain of crushing defeat, had the Cubans not intervened.

## Circling the Wagons

"The credibility of our military is being questioned in many circles," the South African Defence Force lamented in the wake of the Angolan fiasco. "This is certainly one of the reasons that . . . the morale of the revolutionary movement has improved."[53]

The collapse of the Portuguese dictatorship in April 1974 had opened gaping holes in the buffer zone that separated South Africa from the hostile continent to the north. The Portuguese colonies of Mozambique and Angola had been part of South Africa's forward defense, protecting two other white-ruled countries, Rhodesia and Namibia. Of the two, Namibia was, by far, more important to South Africa. This vast, underpopulated country had been a German colony before falling under a South African mandate at the close of the First World War. South Africa had ruled it as its fifth province. In 1971 the International Court of Justice and the UN Security Council had decreed Pretoria's occupation of the country illegal and ordered it to withdraw immediately. The mounting international clamor against South Africa's occupation of Namibia was accompanied by growing unrest among the territory's African population, chafing against Pretoria's harsh rule, and by the rising influence, at home and abroad, of the South West Africa People's Organization (SWAPO). Though SWAPO had begun guerrilla activity in 1966, it had been hamstrung by geography. Only Zambia offered it safe haven, which meant that its fighters had to traverse either southeastern Angola or Namibia's Caprivi strip, a 250-mile panhandle squeezed between Angola, Zambia, and Botswana that was dotted with South African military bases.

The Portuguese had been neighborly to the South Africans, allowing them to conduct search and destroy operations against SWAPO in southeastern Angola. The overthrow of the dictatorship in Lisbon changed this. In September 1974, the Portuguese informed Pretoria that its patrols would no longer be allowed in Angola. "On October 26, the last South African liaison officers left the territory," a South African military historian writes. "In November SWAPO camps of up to 70 men were already in place." Unrest increased in Namibia.[54]

## The Turnhalle Conference

Pretoria responded to the Portuguese revolution by embarking on a policy of détente with black Africa, dangling economic aid and trade concessions and launching a flurry of diplomatic activity. Peaceful coexistence would be based on absolute respect for the internal system of each state, particularly, that is, for South Africa's own apartheid regime. "Domestic politics must not obstruct international cooperation," Prime Minister John Vorster told *Le Monde*.[55]

Détente required that Vorster modify his policy toward Rhodesia. Nine years earlier, on November 11, 1965, Rhodesian prime minister Ian Smith had unilaterally and illegally decreed the British colony independent in order to prolong white rule. Stoutly refusing to use military force against the white rebels, London promised to bring down Smith through sanctions. But the mandatory sanctions imposed by the UN Security Council proved ineffectual, in part because Pretoria defied them. South Africa also sent Ian Smith 2,000 paramilitary policemen, as well as helicopters and spotter planes with their pilots, to help his regime fight the black insurgents who assailed it.[56] It was the Portuguese coup, in 1974, that shattered this status quo: henceforth Mozambique, Rhodesia's eastern neighbor, would be ruled not by the friendly Portuguese, but by the Liberation Front of Mozambique (FRELIMO), a bitter foe of apartheid and of white Rhodesia. Adapting to the new times, Vorster concluded that it would be in South Africa's interest to encourage majority rule in Rhodesia. This would reduce the risk of ending up with a radical government in Salisbury, and it would demonstrate Pretoria's newfound goodwill toward black Africa.

Détente also required a change in South Africa's policy toward Namibia, where Pretoria would have to adjust the policy of "separate development" it had been pursuing. Separate development meant the establishment of separate homelands for each of the ten ethnic groups into which it had divided the territory's nonwhite population. The problem was that these homelands were not economically viable. The CIA remarked that even though the Ovambos made up about half of Namibia's population of 900,000, Ovamboland was "inadequate for the expanding Ovambo population. Some of the smaller tribes . . . have been restricted to 'homelands' that are virtually barren."[57] Moreover, the ten homelands, which held approximately 90 percent of Namibia's people, were only half of the territory. The remaining half—with the richest mines and best land—was reserved for Namibia's whites, who were 10 percent of the population. Pretoria's intention was to incorporate this white area into South Africa, while the ten destitute nonwhite homelands would receive nominal independence and exist as Pretoria's tributary states. Entirely dependent on the goodwill of the South

African regime, they would serve as reservoirs of cheap labor for "White Namibia." As a black headman said, "We are the mat on which the white man stands."[58]

In late 1974, this policy—which was an open slap to black Africa, the international community, and the United Nations (UN)—changed. Part of Vorster's détente offensive was to create a single Namibian state. This was signaled on September 24, 1974, when, under instructions from Pretoria, the all-white National Party of South West Africa (South Africa's name for Namibia), called for a constitutional conference in which the territory's ethnic groups would jointly consider the country's future. A year later, on September 1, 1975, 154 duly screened delegates from Namibia's ten nonwhite ethnic groups plus the National Party delegates (representing the whites) assembled at the historic Turnhalle building in Windhoek.[59]

Violence and intimidation marked the opening of the Turnhalle conference. "Significantly," the historian of the conference, André du Pisani, writes, "the talks were preceded by a wave of arrests of black opposition leaders." Du Pisani points out that "the conference was initiated and intended to run under the control of white minority political leadership." The nonwhite delegates were "dominated," the CIA reported, "by old-line tribal chiefs who usually have gone along with South African tutelage." It is therefore not surprising that SWAPO dismissed the conference, deeming it South Africa talking to its "puppets in the silence of a political graveyard."[60]

Responding to the changed circumstances wrought by Portugal's revolution, Pretoria's method had changed, but its goal was the same: to retain control over Namibia and salvage what it could of the cordon sanitaire that had once protected the apartheid state. Furthermore, unlike Rhodesia's 275,000 Anglos, white Namibians were "kith and kin" to the voters of South Africa's ruling National Party: approximately 60 percent of them were Afrikaners. Abandoning them to hostile black rule would have been demoralizing for white South Africans and politically costly for the government. Conversely, a SWAPO government in Windhoek—the most likely alternative to a Namibia dominated by Pretoria—would have given hope to blacks in South Africa. "The way in which self-determination and independence are achieved in Namibia," a U.S. Presidential Review Memorandum noted, "will have significant consequences for South Africa's domestic situation."[61]

There were also economic considerations underlying South Africa's determination to hold onto Namibia. As the CIA stated, "South Africans regard Namibia as a substantial economic asset as well as a buffer." South Africa derived annually some $250 million in foreign exchange from the territory's mineral, fish, and agricultural exports; South African private investment in Namibia amounted to at least $500 million; and South Africans owned some 70 percent of the mines, which provided, by far, the territory's most important exports.[62]

## Castro's Army

The Turnhalle conference had just finished appointing a committee to draft a constitution when, in late March 1976, Cuban and Angolan troops reached the Namibian border. By early April there were 36,000 Cuban soldiers in Angola. As Fidel Castro explained,

> When we accepted the risk of fighting against the South Africans, we decided to send enough troops to prevail in a major clash. Given the distance between Cuba and Angola, our motto was: if we need one regiment, let's send ten. We sent 36,000 men because if we had to fight South Africa, which is a strong military power, we wanted to be prepared to defeat them. This was our philosophy. When they got wind of how many troops we were sending they got scared. Because theirs is a regime based on bravado: outwardly aggressive, but inwardly—morally and politically—weak. So instead of rising to the challenge, when the South Africans saw that wall of tanks, artillery and men advancing from different directions, they began to withdraw. We kept advancing, but we gave them an opportunity [to withdraw]. We kept pushing, pushing and pushing until they withdrew completely from Angola, without fighting. This is the battle that we won without bloodshed. Because we gave them time, and kept applying psychological pressure . . . and they withdrew.[63]

After this victory, Castro was in no hurry to withdraw his troops from Angola. The new Angolan government did not have an army yet. The MPLA's weak guerrilla units had been joined by thousands of untrained recruits during the civil war, but this was not an army. It was just an illiterate, poorly armed rabble. The South Africans had withdrawn from Angola, but they remained across the border, in Namibia. Implacably hostile, they represented a potential, deadly threat to the new regime in Luanda. Therefore, Castro explained, "We thought that we should stay until the Angolans and ourselves were satisfied that we had created a strong Angolan army."[64] Furthermore, he added, "we wanted to apply pressure on South Africa to see if we could obtain the independence of Namibia."[65] It is unlikely that Castro had a clear idea of how this pressure would be exerted; certainly there were no plans to send Cuban troops into Namibia.

Castro's desire to keep his army in Angola met a formidable obstacle: Leonid Brezhnev. In the spring of 1976, the Soviet leader sent Castro "a letter asking, almost demanding, that we begin withdrawing our troops [from Angola]."[66] The Soviet government, Castro said, "was insisting that we proceed to a rapid withdrawal, because it was worried about the possible reactions of the Yankees."[67]

There was no way that this small, underdeveloped island could maintain a large army in faraway Angola for several years against the will of the Soviet Union. Castro had to reconsider. He met Brezhnev halfway. In Castro's words, Brezhnev "sent a letter . . . and I replied with another letter, a long letter explaining why it was not possible to withdraw as quickly as he wished. . . . In my letter I told him that we were taking his concerns into account . . . and I explained that we had developed a withdrawal plan, which was gradual."[68] The Cuban troops would leave over the next three years—1976, 1977, and 1978—"until only military instructors remained."[69]

As Castro said, "Because of the delicate situation this created, Comrade Raúl [Castro], Minister of Defense, went to Angola in April 1976 to discuss with President Neto the necessity of gradually withdrawing the Cuban troops over the course of the next three years."[70]

On April 20, 1976, Raúl Castro arrived in Luanda. In his second conversation with Neto, on April 22, the Angolan president accepted the Cuban timetable with only minor changes, including that "the Cuban military doctors remain and continue to offer their valuable services." In response, Raúl Castro "thanked the Angolan leadership for its openness to the Cuban plan. As for Angola's proposed changes, they would be referred immediately to Fidel and the political bureau, but he could already say in advance that he found them reasonable."[71] Within a few days, Havana agreed to Neto's modifications.

The issue appeared to have been settled amicably, but the Cubans received a report that the Angolans were upset. The head of the Cuban civilian mission in Angola, Jorge Risquet, told Raúl Castro: "If this is true, only time and our steadfastness toward Angola will dispel whatever doubts our decision to gradually withdraw our troops may have stirred in Neto."[72]

## Kissinger's Legacy

Kissinger's Angolan debacle spurred him to pay attention, at long last, to southern Africa. He wanted to foreclose any more opportunities for the Soviets and—as he deemed them at the time—their Cuban "proxies." He sought, therefore, to resolve the war in Rhodesia by prodding the white regime into negotiations with the guerrillas. "If the Cubans are involved there, Namibia is next and after that South Africa itself," he told the National Security Council (NSC) before leaving for his first official visit to sub-Saharan Africa in April 1976. "On my African trip, I will identify with African aspirations." *Newsweek* surmised that "dropping Washington's traditional, if unstated, support for the white regimes seemed a reasonable price to pay for thwarting the Communists." It was painful but necessary, Kissinger told the NSC on his return. "I have a basic sympathy with the white Rhodesians but black Africa is absolutely united on this issue, and if we don't grab the initiative we will be faced with the Soviets, and Cuban troops."[73]

Kissinger, however, was undercut by his own president: looking nervously at Ronald Reagan's challenge in the presidential primaries, Ford was loath to do anything that might antagonize the Republican right, which howled with indignation at Kissinger's intended betrayal of fellow whites. The South African Embassy reported from Washington, "The reaction to Dr. Kissinger's Africa trip and his newfangled policy is paradoxical: it is welcomed by the Democrats, but it has split the president's own party. . . . It is clear that Dr. Kissinger personally has become a factor in the struggle for the nomination between Mr. Ford and Mr. Reagan. Because Dr. Kissinger is the object of criticism and disapproval from the conservative wing of the Republicans, this favors Mr. Reagan."[74]

Kissinger's new policy also embraced Namibia. Following the 1971 International Court of Justice ruling on Namibia, the United States had dutifully endorsed UN resolutions demanding that South Africa withdraw from the territory, but it had consistently vetoed resolutions that imposed sanctions on Pretoria for its refusal to comply. In January 1976 the Ford administration supported UN Security Council Resolution 385, which demanded independence for Namibia through free elections "under the supervision and control of the United Nations." The resolution set a deadline of August 31, 1976, for South Africa to agree to comply.[75] When South Africa failed to do so, a majority of the Security Council voted in favor of a mandatory arms embargo, but the United States, together with France and Britain, vetoed the resolution with the lame explanation that negotiations were under way.[76]

The collapse of the Portuguese empire in 1974 shattered the oppressive status quo in southern Africa. The following year Cuba's successful intervention in Angola dealt a major blow to apartheid South Africa, humiliated the United States, and transformed the region into a major Cold War theater. Henceforth, for the first time, the United States would have to focus on southern Africa. The departure of the Cuban troops from Angola became an urgent priority for Washington, and the possibility that the Cubans might intervene in Rhodesia and Namibia spurred U.S. officials to seek peaceful solutions in those countries. Pretoria grew increasingly nervous.

## CHAPTER 2

# Neto, Castro, and Carter
## *A New Beginning?*

## Carter and Southern Africa

Jimmy Carter assumed office in January 1977 determined to reestablish the prestige of the United States in Africa, shattered by the Angolan fiasco. The appointment of civil rights leader Andrew Young as U.S. ambassador to the United Nations with cabinet rank—the first African American to be appointed to a senior foreign policy position in the U.S. government—was a symbol to Africans of the new administration's priorities.

In no other region of the world did U.S. interests appear as threatened as in southern Africa. One of the first Presidential Review Memoranda of the new administration (PRM 4) was devoted to Rhodesia, Namibia, and South Africa. "Violent resistance by blacks against efforts by whites indefinitely to maintain their domination in Rhodesia, Namibia or South Africa," it warned, "would increase the chances of increased Communist influence, major power confrontation in the area and a kind of involvement on our part which the American people do not want and do not support. Our policies for southern Africa . . . will have a major impact on our relations with Africa and will affect our position in the United Nations and other international forums."[1] Carter and his principal advisers intended to push Rhodesia toward majority rule, help achieve independence for Namibia, and "promote a gradual transformation of South African society"[2] that would lead to the end of apartheid.

"In terms of urgency, the Rhodesian problem is the highest priority," PRM 4 stated.[3] It was there that the guerrillas were strongest, and they faced an intrinsically weak regime (fewer than 300,000 whites among more than 6 million black Africans). Rhodesia received the immediate attention of the president, and his point man for Rhodesia was none other than Young himself.

Namibia, on the other hand, had a weaker insurgency, and it faced the South African Defence Force, not the Rhodesian army. But, as Secretary of State Cyrus Vance wrote, "Even though the Namibia conflict was not as urgent or inflammable as the escalating war in Rhodesia, there were important reasons for revitalizing the flagging negotiations." One reason was to forestall a South African fait accompli. "The South Africans," PRM 4 noted, "have given increased priority to an 'internal solution through the Turnhalle framework.'"[4] The committee appointed by the Turnhalle conference to draft a constitution had almost completed its work by the time Carter was inaugurated. The next step would be countrywide elections under South African control followed by the establishment of a government that would lead Namibia to independence in name only. This was Pretoria's "internal settlement": elections and independence under South African, not UN, supervision. It "would preserve white control," Vice President Walter Mondale said, "and in our view result in prolonged civil war."[5] It would also, U.S. officials feared, lead to greater Soviet and Cuban involvement in the war and heighten international pressure on Pretoria's major commercial and financial partners—the United States and its West European allies—to impose sanctions on South Africa. Sanctions would hurt important Western economic interests and anger many Americans and West Europeans. Opposing sanctions, however, would precipitate "an early confrontation between Western countries and black African governments."[6] In order to escape this dilemma the United States needed to devise a Namibian solution that would be acceptable to both South Africa and SWAPO and that would also provide for free elections under UN supervision. At a March 3, 1977, National Security Council (NSC) meeting, Andrew Young offered a proposal: the representatives of the five Western members of the UN Security Council—West Germany and Canada in addition to the United States, France, and England—would begin meeting to "develop a common strategy and set up a committee to talk to the South Africans about Resolution 385."[7]

Thus was born the Contact Group, also known as the Western Five or, more simply, the Five. Young's deputy, Ambassador Donald McHenry, became the group's de facto chairman. The Contact Group negotiated with Pretoria, with SWAPO, and with the Frontline States (FLS)—Tanzania, Zambia, Mozambique, Angola, and Botswana, plus Nigeria. "We wanted to keep them [the FLS] informed and to enlist their support to apply pressure on SWAPO," McHenry recalled.[8]

The administration also intended to move toward establishing diplomatic relations with Angola. It was part of a more general approach that included establishing relations with Vietnam and Cuba. Vance and Young, in particular, argued that better relations with Angola could benefit the United States. Luanda could exert a moderating influence on the Namibian and Rhodesian movements it helped (SWAPO and the Zimbabwe African People's Union [ZAPU]). In February 1977, the United States responded to Angolan overtures by agreeing to begin talks on April 1 in New York.[9]

But within the administration the initial consensus on the Angolan question was shallow, and it was swept away by what became known as Shaba I: on March 8, 1977, 1,500 Zairean exiles living in Angola—the Katangans—invaded the southern Zairean province of Shaba. They were assisted by the Angolan government, which was retaliating against Zaire's support for insurgents launching raids into Angola from bases in Zaire. The Angolan government had initially restrained the Katangans, a close aide of Neto told Yugoslav officials, but "the raids from Zaire did not stop" and Neto decided to unleash the Katangans.[10]

The leaders of the Katangans "were eager to go home and challenge Mobutu," the CIA reported. "They knew that [Zaire's president] Mobutu [Sese Seko] was unpopular, his army inept, his treasury virtually bankrupt. . . . The invasion turned out to be 'a piece of cake . . . a walk,' in the words of one military observer in Zaire. The exiles walked into Zaire and were welcomed by the Shabans, who hoped Mobutu's misrule of their region was about to end." The report continued: "The venture could well have served as a catalyst, bringing about the collapse of Mobutu's shaky economic and political structure. . . . Mobutu, who owes his long tenure to his political adroitness, redressed the threat of collapse by converting his personal peril into an international one. He conjured up the 'red threat' portraying the armed Zairians in Shaba as a Cuban-led surrogate invasion force in a Soviet offensive against his weak country."[11] And he sent urgent appeals for military aid to his Western patrons.

Among these was the United States. To an administration that had come to power promising to make the United States "a beacon of light for human rights throughout the world,"[12] Mobutu's request was not welcome. His army's pitiful performance in 1975, when it had invaded Angola to crush the MPLA, and the collapse of his country's economy had stripped away the aura of a successful strongman to reveal a corrupt, repressive, and bumbling thug. The Carter administration, which considered Mobutu an embarrassment, felt more sympathy for men like Julius Nyerere of Tanzania and Kenneth Kaunda of Zambia, who appeared more in tune with American values.[13]

Nevertheless, on March 15, the United States announced that it would send supplies worth $2 million to Mobutu. "Reports of an invasion of Zaire have brought an immediate but so far cautious response from the Carter administration: nearly $2 million in military supplies, but no arms or ammunition,"

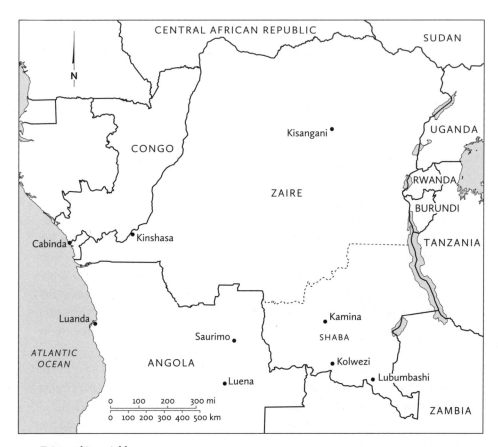

Zaire and its neighbors

noted the *New York Times* five days later; "both the swiftness and restraint of last week's action were significant."[14] Swiftness and restraint reflected the tension between Carter's human rights policy and the instinctive Cold War reflex to support an imperiled anticommunist client.

On April 7, when the Katangans were poised to capture Kolwezi, the economic lung of Shaba, the announcement that Mobutu had long expected finally arrived: urged on by Washington and Paris, Morocco would send troops to rescue him. The soldiers flew to Zaire two days later on military aircraft provided by France, which had already supplied Mobutu with weapons and spare parts, and with military advisers attached to the troops fighting in Shaba. (The United States gave a modest contribution to the joint effort, sending Mobutu an additional $13 million in nonlethal military supplies.)

The Katangans fell back when the Moroccans arrived. By late May they had returned to Angola. Shaba I was over.

In the United States, while Carter was criticized both for doing too little and for doing too much, a majority in Congress and the press supported his policy toward Mobutu. As long as other governments were willing to help the Zairean dictator, the U.S. administration needed to give him only limited aid.

Carter's explanation of his policy, however, was not always graceful. Asked at a press conference how he could justify the aid he had sent Mobutu in view of his commitment to human rights, he replied: "I know that there are some problems in Zaire with human rights as there are here and in many other countries. But our friendship and aid historically for Zaire has not been predicated on their perfection in dealing with human rights." When asked whether Cuba had been involved in the Katangans' attack, he was cautious: "Our best information is that the Katangans have been trained within Angola by the Cubans. We have no direct evidence at all that there are Cubans within Zaire."[15] This was an understatement. As a State Department official who dealt with Cuban affairs has recorded, "There was no credible evidence at all of Cuban complicity."[16] In fact, the Cubans had neither trained the Katangans nor given them any assistance. They had been surprised by the attack.[17]

Carter appeared to respond with equanimity to Shaba I. Realizing that Cuba was not involved, he chose not to make an issue of "Cuban complicity" with the Katangans. He sent nonlethal materiel to Mobutu and encouraged the Moroccans to send troops, but he also supported a Nigerian effort to mediate between Angola and Zaire. U.S. officials were aware, as Vance noted in his memoirs, that Luanda was retaliating for Mobutu's support for Angolan rebels. Nevertheless, in late March the United States notified Luanda that the talks about normalization would be suspended because of Shaba.[18] The Nigerian government sought to spur Washington forward: Foreign Minister Joe Garba urged Vance and National Security Adviser Zbigniew Brzezinski to "review US policy toward Angola. He said Nigeria had pressed the Angolans hard 'to be flexible and not blindly follow ideology. . . .' Nigeria believes that US and others should avoid actions that might drive Angola further into the hands of the Cubans and the Russians. . . . Nigeria believed the time was ripe for Neto and the US to get together."[19]

Andrew Young attempted to nudge things forward. In a May 4 memo to Carter, Mondale, Vance, and Brzezinski, he noted that he and Mondale would be in Lisbon on May 15, and wrote: "I also wish to inquire whether we might consider inviting the Angolan foreign minister to meet with the Vice-President and me while we are in Lisbon. I believe such a meeting might provide a useful opportunity to discuss questions of mutual disagreement and to pave the way for the establishment of diplomatic and economic relations." There was no meeting, remarked Paulo Jorge, who was Angola's foreign minister.[20] On July 7, an aide told Vance: "Peter Tarnoff [the executive secretary of the State Department], [Policy Planning Director] Tony Lake and I have discussed your breakfast tomorrow morning [with Carter, Mondale and Brzezinski] and suggest that you consider raising and discussing the following points." Among the eleven points was Angola: "We are receiving two messages from the White House [on Angola]. First, get tough with the Cubans; second, show sympathy to [Savimbi's] UNITA." Savimbi, with South African support, was still waging a guerrilla war against the MPLA. "We are developing a strategy and would prefer to continue to seek normalization with the Neto regime, using the leverage we acquire to urge it towards a settlement with UNITA."[21]

We do not know whether Vance raised the issue in his breakfast with the president, but one thing is certain: the secretary and his senior aides were sympathetic to normalization with Angola. The problem was that for them Angola was not a priority. "It was certainly secondary," Tony Lake observes, "to Rhodesia, the Horn, South Africa and Namibia." Richard Moose, who became assistant secretary for Africa in June 1977, recalls that "up to 75 percent of my time was spent on the Horn. Rhodesia came second." And when, after the early months of 1978, "my concentration eased on the Horn, I spent more time on Rhodesia." Lake, who was very close to Vance, "spent more time, energy and capital on Africa than on other areas," notes Marianne Spiegel, the Policy Planning Africa specialist, "but he focused on Rhodesia and South Africa." Young led the effort on Rhodesia. Young's deputy McHenry, also very close to Vance, was the administration's point man on Namibia. No one was ready to pick up the Angolan ball and run with it. Nor was there much room to run. In mid-

October 1977, Brzezinski informed Vance that Carter had "stated that he does not intend to recognize the Neto government." There was no great urgency. U.S. economic relations with Angola were good, and Angola was being helpful in the Rhodesian and Namibian negotiations. More important, for the administration, were the possible openings with Vietnam and Cuba. "I don't remember discussions on Angola," Lake said. "On Vietnam, there was a lot of discussion." And on Cuba.[22]

## Negotiating with Castro

On March 15, 1977, Carter had signed Presidential Directive/NSC-6 stating, "I have concluded that we should attempt to achieve normalization of our relations with Cuba. To this end, we should begin direct and confidential talks in a measured and careful fashion" with the Cuban government.[23] "It was understood on both sides that after eighteen years of hostility and given the magnitude of the problems which stood between them, the process of normalizing relations would be protracted and often painful," a 1978 State Department analysis noted.[24] For the Americans, a key condition for normalization was the withdrawal of the Cuban troops from Africa—that is, from Angola—but Havana would not budge. "In our first talks with the Cubans in March 1977," the State Department noted, "they showed no give at all on Africa. Their only response to our reference to their military presence in Angola was to say that this was not a subject for negotiation." Cuban foreign minister Isidoro Malmierca told Assistant Secretary of State Terence Todman that "Cuba's agreements with Angola were not open to negotiation [with the United States]." In Luanda, the head of the Cuban civilian mission in Angola, Jorge Risquet, assured President Neto that U.S. pressures and blandishments would not change "the firm and categorical position of Cuba: the Cuban presence in Angola concerns only our two countries and cannot be the object of any negotiation between Cuba and the United States."[25]

In mid-1976, however, the Cubans had begun withdrawing their soldiers from Angola, as agreed with Neto, and by March 1977 almost 12,000 had returned home.[26] Washington took note. In the spring and summer of 1977, relations between Cuba and the United States slowly improved: Carter halted reconnaissance flights over the island and lifted travel restrictions; Havana released ten U.S. citizens imprisoned on drug-related charges; a fishery agreement was signed and on September 1 the two countries opened Interests Sections in each other's capitals. In early August, Senator Frank Church (D-Idaho), who had just visited Havana, told Carter, "President Castro asked me to pass on to you the following messages: 1. He understands that the process of normalizing relations between Cuba and the United States has to be slow and that 'a spectacular thing can't be done over night.' He expects to continue to work in the direction of normalization. 2. He recognizes that the Panama Canal problem is of number one priority to President Carter in this part of the world and that the President 'can't do both at once.' 3. He is pleased at what the President has done so far."[27]

The courtship, however, was already faltering. The Cubans had been surprised by Shaba I. They had known nothing of the plans of the Katangans, whom they had always kept at arm's length, believing their leaders to be adventurers with "a tainted past."[28] They had condemned the invasion of Shaba for two reasons: it increased tensions on Angola's northern and eastern borders at a time when the real threat came from South Africa, and it triggered the arrival in Zaire of Moroccan troops on French planes to defend Mobutu. The Moroccans were close friends of the West, and France was a North Atlantic Treaty Organization (NATO) country. Nor were the Cubans pleased that the Angolans had acted without so much as informing them. Nevertheless, they responded not with recriminations but by agreeing to suspend the phased withdrawal of their troops from Angola. The Franco-Moroccan intervention in Shaba "has reinforced the psychosis of encirclement here," the French chargé reported from Luanda. The Cubans agreed with the Angolans that more troops would be needed because, Castro explained, "we saw that a new threat had arisen."[29]

Washington drew back. The State Department reported that "toward the end of 1977, Cuba's continuing military presence in Angola began to obstruct significantly the measured progress in US-Cuba relations." In December, two U.S. congressmen who favored improving relations with Cuba had a lengthy meeting with Castro in Havana. They told him that "though President Carter was 'eager' to normalize relations, some indication of a willingness to deescalate Cuban involvement in Angola was needed." Castro gave no ground. Angola was threatened by South Africa and Zaire, he said. "The Cuban mission in Angola was the defense of the country." The congressmen insisted: "President Carter simply wanted a statement of Cuba's intentions to deescalate." Castro replied that "this could not be done unilaterally. . . . The Angolan government had to decide this, since the Cubans were not there on their own account. . . . If the restoration of relations [with the United States] was presented in the Angolan context, things would not advance. On this basis, no matter how important or convenient, Cuba could not be selfish . . . 'Regarding our policy in Africa we cannot negotiate that.'"[30]

This was the constant refrain: Cuba would not let the United States determine its policy in Africa. What this meant would soon be clear.

## The Horn

In Ethiopia, less than two weeks after Carter's inauguration, the military junta that had overthrown Emperor Haile Selassie in 1974 turned further to the left, quashing any lingering U.S. hope of retaining influence there. In July 1977 the junta was rocked by Somalia's invasion of the Ogaden, a region in eastern Ethiopia inhabited by ethnic Somalis. The attack had been encouraged by ambivalent signals from Washington. As the NSC specialist on the Horn wrote in 1980, "The crucial decision [to invade] seems to have been taken only . . . when the Somalis concluded they had a good chance of securing American military aid."[31] The Somalis made swift progress, and by late August 1977 Vance told the Chinese foreign minister, "I think they [the Somalis] will succeed. . . . They . . . will be in control of the Ogaden."[32] Ethiopia's leader, Mengistu Haile Mariam, turned to Cuba, which had begun sending military instructors and doctors to Addis Ababa in April. He asked for troops.

Castro's reply was negative. A secret Cuban military history notes, "It did not seem possible that a small country like Cuba could maintain two important military missions in Africa." In an August 16 cable, Castro told the head of the Cuban Military Mission in Addis Ababa, "We absolutely cannot agree to send Cuban military forces to fight in Ethiopia. You must convince Mengistu of this reality. . . . Despite our sympathy for the Ethiopian revolution and our profound indignation at the cowardly and criminal aggression to which it has fallen victim, it is frankly impossible for Cuba to do more in the present circumstances. You cannot imagine how hard it is for us to constantly rebuff these requests."[33]

However, as the Ethiopians' military situation deteriorated, the Cubans reconsidered. On November 25, 1977, Castro decided to send troops to Ethiopia to help repel the Somalis. Two days later, Brezhnev wrote Castro a warm message expressing "our complete agreement with your policy. We are pleased that our assessment of events in Ethiopia coincides with yours, and we sincerely thank you for your timely decision to extend internationalist assistance to Socialist Ethiopia."[34] Over the next three months, 12,000 Cuban soldiers arrived in Ethiopia. As a 2000 study of the Russian Ministry of Defense noted, "many of them had already had combat experience," and the troops "were notable for their high degree of discipline and organization."[35] By March 1978, the Cubans and the Ethiopians had repulsed the Somali invaders.

The contrast between the Soviet reaction to the dispatch of Cuban troops to Ethiopia and its response to the Cuban intervention in Angola two years earlier is stark: in Angola, Cuba acted without even informing the Soviet Union, whereas in Ethiopia there was close consultation; in Angola, for two harrowing months the Cubans operated without any logistical support from the Soviet Union, whereas in Ethiopia Moscow supported the airlift of Cuban troops from day one; in Angola, the Cubans planned military operations without any Soviet input, whereas in Ethiopia the Soviets and Cubans worked together to help the Ethiopians plan military operations. As Castro told Neto, "In Angola we took the initiative, we acted on our own. . . . It was a decision full of risks. In Ethiopia, our actions were coordinated from the very beginning with the Soviets."[36]

That Havana and Moscow agreed about what policy to pursue in Ethiopia does not mean that the Cubans were subservient to the Soviets. Arguably, the key to explaining Cuban motivations is provided by Brzezinski, who told Carter, "Castro ended up more favorably impressed by the Ethiopians. He found the Somalis, who pressed their longstanding territorial demands on Ethiopia, more irredentist than socialist." Castro had been very impressed by the Ethiopian revolution, and by Mengistu, whom he had met in March 1977. He told East German leader Erich Honecker that "a real revolution is taking place in Ethiopia. In this former feudal empire the land has been given to the peasants. . . . Mengistu strikes me as a quiet, honest and convinced revolutionary leader."[37] Hundreds of Cuban documents covering the critical period from late 1976 through the spring of 1978 make clear that Castro's feelings were shared by the three top Cuban officials in Addis Ababa: the ambassador, the head of the military mission, and the head of intelligence.[38]

With hindsight, we know that Mengistu's policies resulted in disaster, but this was not clear in 1977: though the process was undeniably bloody, the Ethiopian junta had decreed a radical agrarian reform and taken unprecedented steps to foster the cultural rights of the non-Amhara population. Even the U.S. government had been impressed. The CIA noted "the new rulers' efforts to improve the lot of the disadvantaged," and the State Department reported that the government was focusing on "improving living standards for all" and that "much has been accomplished."[39] The evidence indicates that the Cubans intervened because they believed, as Cuban intelligence stated in March 1977, that "the social and economic measures adopted by Ethiopia's leadership are the most progressive we have seen in any underdeveloped country since the triumph of the Cuban revolution."[40]

U.S. officials claimed that the Cuban intervention represented a gross violation of détente and an unjustifiable interference in African affairs, but it is difficult to follow their reasoning. Mogadishu had violated the most sacred principle of the Organization of African Unity (OAU)—the respect for the borders inherited at the time of independence. Without this principle, there could be no peace in Africa. As the NSC specialist on the Horn told Brzezinski, "The Soviets and Cubans have legality and African sentiment on their side in Ethiopia—they are helping an African country defend its territorial integrity and countering aggression."[41] The Cubans helped the Ethiopians repel the Somali invaders. They refused to fight against the insurgencies that beset Ethiopia. They were instrumental in preventing the country's dismemberment at Somalia's hands.

In January 1978, when they became aware that Cuba was sending combat troops to Ethiopia, U.S. officials engaged in a loud campaign of denunciations of Cuba's intervention and urged African countries to join in condemning the aggression. In a courageous cable, the U.S. ambassador to Nigeria, Donald Easum, sought to inject a dose of sanity:

> We suggest consideration be given to linking our criticism of Soviet/
> Cuban intervention with "equal time" given to the importance of Ethiopia's belief that the Somalis have crossed a recognized border. We surmise that, while embarrassed that extracontinental military assistance once again had to be requested by an independent African state, most African countries support the OAU principle of territorial integrity and believe Somalia has transgressed it. We must not be seen to ignore that principle.
>
> While fully recognizing the obvious elements of difference between the two cases, we are struck by the parallels between Moroccan/French/ Egyptian/Saudi assistance to Zaire when it was "invaded" from Angola and the Soviet/Cuban assistance to Ethiopia when invaded by Somalia. In the first case we quietly approved. In the second we loudly object. The parallels and the difference cannot be expected to go unnoticed.[42]

## An Anemic Détente

By the time the Cubans intervened in the Ogaden, relations between Washington and Moscow were strained. Carter's vigorous attacks on the Soviet Union in the name of human rights offended the Soviet leaders who had grown used to Kissinger's restraint. The administration's silence about the human rights violations in Iran and China showed that Carter's concern for human rights was selective.[43]

Carter resumed the SALT negotiations that Ford had frozen, but with a twist. In March 1977 the United States presented a new proposal. As historian Raymond Garthoff writes, "The proposal was raised suddenly and publicly. . . . The substance of the proposal, while it might have been acceptable for normal bargaining purposes, was so fashioned to American advantage as to ensure a negative Soviet response. . . . [This] not only doomed the proposal to failure, but made the Carter approach a new obstacle in the path of American-Soviet relations." The negotiations stalled. "The heart of the matter for the Soviets is that the new Administration has changed the framework and terms of reference which they have been negotiating for over two years," Vance told Carter in late August 1977. "They argue predictably that they have made important concessions since [the December 1974 meeting between Ford and Brezhnev in] Vladivostok while we have pressed them for even more. While they overstate their case and exaggerate what had been agreed to, they have a point. Our March proposal went well beyond past negotiations in an effort to achieve a more far-reaching arms control agreement. The Soviets proved unready to match this vision." Deputy Foreign Minister Georgi Kornienko vividly describes the Kremlin's anger and frustration with Carter's new proposals. They were skewed against the Soviet Union, and they scrapped the Vladivostok agreement that Brezhnev had painstakingly sold to his military leaders. And, as if that were not enough, Carter had revealed them to the American public before showing them to the Soviet leaders. This was interpreted in Moscow "as a clear indication that Carter was not serious about negotiating, but only sought a propaganda victory."[44]

Beyond the tensions about human rights and the fractious negotiations on SALT II, Washington and Moscow engaged in one cooperative venture in 1977: the convening of a conference in Geneva on the Middle East. The two superpowers would co-chair the conference, and all the parties to the Arab-Israeli conflict would be invited to attend. Washington and Moscow explained in a joint communiqué on October 1, 1977, that "a just and lasting settlement of the Arab-Israeli conflict" would require the establishment of a comprehensive peace that would include not just an end to belligerency, but normal relations between Israel and its neighbors; the withdrawal of the Israeli army from territories occupied as a result of the 1967 war; and a settlement of the Palestinian question "including insuring the legitimate rights of the Palestinian people."[45] The communiqué was a compromise. It did not call for—as Moscow wanted—a Palestinian state, or for the participation of the Palestinian Liberation Organization at the conference, or for Israel's return to its exact pre-1967 borders. On the other hand, for the first time, the United States signed a document that recognized the "legitimate rights" of the Palestinian people.

The two countries had been able to achieve, Kornienko writes, "what had not been achieved through the previous decade . . .: they had elaborated and agreed upon the principles for common and parallel actions of the USSR and the U.S. that could lead to a comprehensive solution in the Middle East."[46] But the wonder was short-lived. The communiqué triggered the wrath of Israel and Israel's supporters in the United States. The American Israel Public Affairs Committee had a prodigious fund-raising capacity, Carter's chief domestic affairs adviser warned, an "unsurpassed" ability to mobilize political pressure across the country, thirty-one "hard" votes in the Senate and forty-three others that could be counted on in a showdown. There was "no political counterforce" to agitate for the Arabs or Palestinians. "The political reality," another aide writes, "was that Carter was under great pressure from the friends of Israel, and Israel played with his discomfort with extraordinary skill." Chastened, Carter retreated, and the Geneva conference never met.[47]

Détente between Washington and Moscow never blossomed under Carter, not even in the first year of his presidency, before the Cuban troops arrived in the Ogaden. Clearly, Cuba's actions in Ethiopia damaged the anemic détente that existed. Brzezinski's famously claimed that "SALT lies buried in the sands of the Ogaden."[48] But what sparked America's outrage? U.S. ambivalence had encouraged the Somalis to invade Ethiopia, threatening the principle of the inviolability of the territorial integrity of African states. The Cuban troops upheld that principle. What died in the sands of the Ogaden was the delusion of a one-sided détente, in which the enemies of the United States did not have the right to send troops anywhere, whatever the provocation, whatever the violation of international law, whereas the friends of the United States did, as, for example, when the South Africans invaded Angola in 1975 and the Moroccans sent troops to Zaire in 1977.

## Punishing Castro?

U.S. officials knew that Cuba had intervened in the Ogaden at the request of the Ethiopian government, which was recognized by the entire international community, including the United States, and they knew that it had helped repel a foreign aggressor. "The conundrum in the Somali problem is that they [Cubans and Soviets] are fighting an aggressor," Vice President Mondale observed.[49] But the fact that the Cuban intervention had met every requirement of international law did little to assuage the anger felt by many Americans. The fact that many African states, including close friends of the United States, had welcomed the arrival of the Cubans in the Ogaden made their success more galling, as did the ease with which they had won. Brzezinski fanned Carter's anxieties: "It is only a matter of time before the right wing begins to argue that the above [the failure to respond to the Cuban intervention in the Horn] demonstrates our incompetence as well as weakness. This will have a negative impact politically." Carter's frustration spilled out in a major foreign policy address on May 17, 1978, in which he assailed the "ominous inclination on the part of the Soviet Union . . . to intervene in local conflicts, with advisers, with equipment, and with full logistical support and encouragement for mercenaries from other Communist countries."[50] And it spilled out, as Carter's own word ("mercenaries") indicates, in the tired accusation that the Cubans were proxies of the Soviet Union. Once again, as so often, there was a gap between the policy makers' words (and actions) and the more subtle, balanced views of U.S. intelligence. A few months after the Cuban victory in the Ogaden, an NSC interagency study explained, "Cuba is not involved in Africa solely or even primarily because of its relationship with the Soviet Union. Rather, Havana's African policy reflects its revolutionary ethos and its determination to expand its own political influence in the Third World at the expense of the West (read U.S.)." Robert Pastor, the NSC expert on Latin America, told Brzezinski: "Let me suggest that we try to use a different term to refer to the Cubans than that of 'Soviet puppet.' The word 'puppet' suggests that the Cubans are engaging in revolutionary activities because the Soviets have instructed them to do it. That, of course, is not the case."[51]

The Horn episode not only harmed détente; it also damaged the relationship between Brzezinski and Vance. In Brzezinski's words, "I could sense that personal tension was entering into our relationship."[52] Press leaks about the clash between Brzezinski and Vance added to the impression of disarray. The steady and successful campaign by Brzezinski to diminish Vance in Carter's eyes began in earnest. After Vance's resignation in April 1980, Brzezinski penned a memo to Carter that is an accurate reflection not of Vance's record but of the depth of the national security adviser's vindictiveness. "It is particularly important," he told Carter, "that the new Secretary [of State] speak often to the American public and convey to it a strong case on behalf of your policies. Cy never did it, and the people around Cy continuously conspired either to dilute your policy or to divert it into directions more to their own liking. The so-called zig-zags in our past policies have been more apparent than real and have been exaggerated by an absence of a strong public voice by the Secretary and by leaks and a lack of discipline in the State Department ranks."[53]

The clash between Vance and Brzezinski intensified with the arrival of the Cuban troops in Ethiopia. Brzezinski ineffectually sought ways to "make the

Soviets and Cubans bleed,"[54] but Vance argued that there was nothing the United States could do to counter the Cubans in the Horn. Washington was not willing to invade Ethiopia to help the Somalis against the Cubans, nor were any of the U.S. allies in the region—Iran, Saudi Arabia, and Egypt—willing to send troops. Supplying weapons to the exhausted Somali army would not have been enough. Many Americans, however, condemned Carter's weakness, and within the administration a debate raged as to how tough the United States ought to be.

Unable to find ways to punish the Cubans in the Horn, Brzezinski turned to Angola. At a February 23, 1978, NSC meeting that was attended by only a handful of top officials, including the president, he "raised the issue of other responses to the Soviets and Cubans, and noted that the president favored some additional aid to Savimbi in Angola." A few days later, at a March 2 meeting of the Special Coordinating Committee, he urged covert operations to help Savimbi. Vance disagreed: "Another alternative would be to open some discussions with Neto. We should think of this. He has no place to turn but to the Soviets and the Cubans. This is worth thinking about. We should think of all sides of these problems. Suppose we start helping Savimbi, and he takes back a few more towns, are the Cubans not going to send more people in then?" Brzezinski considered this the wrong question. "The issue is not whether we get more Cubans in Angola," he explained, but whether covert aid "increases their casualties and the cost of their involvement. . . . Why not make them increase their involvement in Angola? Let them be pinched by it." The discussions continued through a series of high-level meetings until, on April 7, 1978, at a meeting attended by Vance, Defense Secretary Harold Brown, Director of Central Intelligence (DCI) Stansfield Turner, and the acting chairman of the Joint Chiefs of Staff (JCS), the Special Coordinating Committee "agreed that the possibility of support for Savimbi, with the aim of complicating the Cuban position in Angola, would be desirable to explore. In light of the importance of Congressional attitudes it was decided that key Congressmen should be discreetly consulted on their attitudes, e.g., on provision of communication equipment or other non-lethal help." A handwritten note specified, "not to be initiated until after the conclusion of the Vance trip to Africa"—obviously for fear of leaks that might mar the secretary's reception in the African capitals he would visit.[55]

On May 15, the Special Coordinating Committee met again. "Based on Admiral Turner's consultations on the Hill, all agreed that this would not be the time to try for repeal of the [Clark] amendment [which forbade U.S. covert operations in Angola]. It was decided to leave the issue alone for now."[56] A few days later, the probe became public knowledge, as the *Washington Post* reported that Turner had approached Senator Dick Clark (D-Iowa), chair of the Foreign Relations Subcommittee on Africa, with a plan to supply covert aid to Savimbi.[57]

Carter claimed that he knew nothing of the entire affair.[58] Wryly, columnist Tom Wicker remarked, "Either Mr. Carter in fact knew of the arms-to-Angola plan and is now ducking responsibility, which is bad enough; or else he doesn't know what his own National Security Council is proposing to high-ranking senators, which is downright scary."[59] Wicker need not have worried: Carter had read the April 7 minutes of the Special Coordinating Committee, as indicated by an "OK" in the margin of the relevant paragraph. Two other documents indicate that Carter's dissembling went deeper. The minutes of the February 23, 1978, NSC meeting state unequivocally that Brzezinski "noted that the president favored some *additional* aid to Savimbi." Furthermore, on March 3, Brzezinski wrote to Carter, "I have proposed at the SCC [Special Coordinating Committee] *more direct* assistance to Savimbi in Angola."[60] The English is clear: *additional* indicates that some aid was already flowing, and *more direct* means that indirect assistance was already being provided. Therefore, when the administration contacted key members of Congress, it was already funneling some aid to Savimbi and was considering increasing it. Andrew Young's deputy, Ambassador Donald McHenry, remarked, "Even though we had a law and a policy that precluded us from covert operations in Angola, we did it. I came to believe, I still do, that the US government got around that in two ways— but I have no proof. One way I know, but I cannot prove: we were supplying UNITA with communications equipment—and claiming that by so doing we weren't giving aid to Savimbi, but allowing us to spy on him. The second is more deadly. It is like what happened under Reagan with the [Nicaraguan] Contras: we would tell selected governments: 'We are precluded from giving aid, but you Saudis or Moroccans would be doing us a great favor if you did what we cannot do.'" When I read McHenry's statement to Carter's under secretary of state David Newsom, he responded, "I have no direct information, but the mindset of those who were determined to help Savimbi was, 'if we cannot do it, we will ask someone else.'"[61] Some light is shed by Carter himself. In a June 19, 1978, memo to the president, Vance wrote that McHenry would assure the Angolans "that we are providing no support to Angolan dissidents, and that 'we are discouraging others from providing such support.'" In the margin, Carter wrote, "This is not true."[62]

I sent the February 23 NSC document ("some additional aid") and the March 3 document ("more direct assistance") to Brzezinski. When we talked, he was straightforward. "There was some aid going to Savimbi," he said. "I cannot remember what exactly our aid was. Probably telling third countries to help Savimbi."[63]

South African general Chris Thirion, who was a senior military intelligence officer in the Carter and Reagan years, told me that the CIA was helping Savimbi in the late 1970s with "items of a better quality than we could provide," but he refused to elaborate, saying that he did not want to embarrass the agency.[64] The details may never be known, but clearly, as Brzezinski wrote in plain English, by early 1978 the administration was giving at least indirect aid to Savimbi.

## Shaba II

Toward the end of the Katangans' March 1977 invasion of Zaire (Shaba I), a prominent expert on Zaire had written, "In the last few years the United States' considerable influence in Zaire has been used to open the country to American investments . . . and to persuade Mr. Mobutu to accept some control over foreign currency exchange. Would it not be possible to press instead for an effective improvement in the lot of the common people, with the clear implication that failure to produce would result in an end to United States aid?"[65]

There was no such pressure. Following Shaba I, Mobutu unleashed a wave of terror. A well-informed journalist reported that "the behavior of the Zairean army in Shaba was even more hateful than usual. Tens of thousands of Zaireans sought refuge in Angola, and all their testimonies agree: 'The army has looted, robbed and raped. They have burned our villages and perpetrated wholesale massacres.'"[66] Throughout Zaire there were purges, trials for treason, and executions of army officers and civilians accused of plotting. Any sign of resistance was met with an orgy of brutality. Western diplomats and Amnesty International reported that after quelling a local disturbance in the region of Idiofa, 600 kilometers east of the capital, the army had gone on a rampage, burning villages and killing between 500 and 3,000 people.[67]

Buffeted by the crisis in the Horn, the Carter administration was learning to appreciate stalwart friends of the United States, irrespective of their peccadilloes. Deputy Assistant Secretary of State for Africa Lannon Walker told skeptical members of the House Committee on International Relations in March 1978 that "we do not consider Zaire to be a gross consistent violator of human rights." Mobutu, he stressed, had implemented political and economic reforms: thus, "the process has begun within that country." As the *New York Times* pointed out, the economic reforms were merely concessions to lure foreign capitalists back to Zaire. As Mobutu opened more and more of his country to expatriate control, foreigners sang his praise, loudly: in the spring of 1978 an international consortium of sixty banks was in the final stages of approving loans totaling $200 million to Zaire.[68]

The West might avert its eyes as Mobutu massacred his people, but Luanda could not ignore his continued backing of the insurgents attacking Angola. Neto prepared to retaliate. In February 1978, after receiving intelligence reports that the Katangans were planning another attack, Castro sent the head of the Cuban civilian mission in Angola, Jorge Risquet, who was on home leave in Cuba, back to Luanda with a fourteen-page memorandum for Neto. Risquet met with Neto on February 20, 1978, the day after his arrival. "Our conversation lasted approximately one and a half hours," he told Castro. "I presented our position based on the written document. Of course, my reading [of the memorandum] was interrupted by conversation."[69] Risquet reminded Neto that the first invasion of Shaba had taken Havana by surprise:

> During the first week of March 1977, I was not in Angola but in Libya, where I had gone to see Fidel. Had I been in the PRA [People's Republic of Angola], perhaps I would have been told by you or by another comrade in the Angolan leadership—to the extent that you knew what was going to happen—about the imminent attack. As you know, in the military briefing after I returned, I asked whether there had been prior knowledge of the invasion or whether, on the contrary, the Katangans had acted without authorization and behind the back of the government of the PRA.
> You asked Comrade [Defense Minister] Iko Carreira to answer my question, but his response was vague and unsatisfactory. I decided, however, that it would not be correct to insist, particularly since many Angolan, Cuban, and Soviet comrades were present.
> I later thought about it and concluded that perhaps my question had been inappropriate, given where I asked it, but I do not think that it was unreasonable, given the potential impact on the Cuban troops of war breaking out in Angola, the territorial integrity of which is, for Cuba, a sacred cause.[70]

Risquet told Neto that Havana had learned from several sources that the Katangans were "prepared to renew action against Mobutu in the near future." Courteously but firmly, he relayed Castro's opposition to such an operation. However, even though Havana was providing vital aid to the Angolans, the memorandum contained no threat of retaliation if Angola failed to restrain the Katangans. Nor was there even a hint of condescension. It did contain lucid warnings, however, about the likely consequences of a second invasion of Shaba: "The imperialists will in all likelihood intervene, as they did on the previous occasion. Indeed, they will probably intervene more forcefully, even directly, not just with Moroccan, but with imperialist forces—from France, for example." Castro worried about the security of Angola:

In southern Africa, Angola is today, even more than a year ago, the pillar in the struggle against the racists, and it is, without question, the revolutionary vanguard. The imperialists know this. The imperialists must know what Angola is doing for Zimbabwe, what Angola is doing for Namibia, what Angola is doing for South Africa. Bravely, Angola is extending real support to the liberation movements of Namibia, Zimbabwe, South Africa. It does so in concrete terms, training on its territory 20,000 fighters from these three countries oppressed by the racists.

In so doing, Angola runs a risk, but it is a risk worth taking. It is an unavoidable duty of solidarity and internationalism. In this case, the imperialists are politically cornered; they cannot openly defend the cause of the racists, so they seek solutions that will tame the raging volcano with some concessions. The international assistance to these three movements—SWAPO, ZAPU, and the ANC—has been well planned; the coordination among Angola, Cuba, and the USSR is well oiled. The carefully executed plan of the three governments is achieving good results and will be decisive in the victory of the three movements in the short, medium, or long term.

This excites the imperialists' hatred of Angola. The imperialists seek a pretext, a political "justification" to launch an open attack on Angola. The renewal of the Shaba war could provide this pretext.

"President Neto," the memorandum concluded, "we could delay no longer conveying these concerns to you. They are not new. We have had them for some time. If we have not talked as frankly in the past as we do now, it is because we wanted to refrain from doing anything that could be interpreted as interference—even if only in form—in the internal affairs that are properly the concern of only you and your government."[71]

Risquet reported to Castro that Neto had "declared that he agreed fully with us." The next day, Neto sent Risquet a handwritten letter in which he said, "As was clear in our conversation, I am in full agreement with the views expressed by the Cuban leadership and by Comrade Commander in Chief Fidel Castro."[72]

Neto's actions, however, did not match his words. He ignored the Cubans' advice. On May 13, 1978, the Katangans struck again, suddenly. Whereas in 1977 they had invaded Zaire directly from Angola, about 500 kilometers west of Kolwezi, this time they traveled undetected through Zambia, and invaded closer to the city. "Some 2,500 rebels crossed into Shaba," the head of the French military mission in Zaire reported; "once there, they immediately raised a militia and increased their number to 4,000."[73] The West responded more promptly than it had in 1977, in part because of the deterioration of détente and in part because the threat was more serious: the Katangans were better organized, Kolwezi fell at once, and Mobutu's army collapsed. On May 18 the Carter administration supplied France and Belgium with eighteen C-141 transport planes to move troops to Zaire. By May 20, the French and Belgian soldiers had taken control of Kolwezi with little fighting. During the next two weeks, as the rebels retreated into Zambia and Angola, there were no serious clashes. Before the end of the month, Shaba II was over.

The invasion, which occurred three months after Neto had categorically promised Risquet that he would not allow the Katangans to attack again, surprised the Cubans. "We were stunned," Cuba's ambassador in Angola, Manuel Agramonte, recalls.[74] On May 19, in Luanda, General Senén Casas, Cuba's first deputy minister of defense, conveyed his government's reaction to Neto:

> Within hours, because of the Katangans' action and because of the propaganda machine of the imperialists, Angola went from being seen as the victim of the brutal aggression of the racists [on May 4 the South Africans had attacked a Namibian refugee camp deep inside Angola] to being called the launching pad for an "invasion" of its neighbor. The Katangans have given a great gift to the imperialists.
>
> More than once, we have expressed our concern that the Katangans could create problems for the PRA. After our last conversation about it, when Risquet made a special trip to Luanda in February, you said that you shared our views, and this reassured Fidel and the leadership of our party. You can therefore understand how surprised and upset they were when they learned that thousands of Katangan fighters had penetrated into Shaba. . . .
>
> We trust in your honesty, Comrade President, and therefore we do not doubt that you are true to your word. But we don't understand how entire battalions, thousands of men based in Angola, could enter Zaire without the approval of some Angolan authorities. We do not know whether this approval was at the provincial level or at a higher level.[75]

Neto's reply was evasive: "The Katangan matter was very unfortunate. Because of this, the enemy will attack in the north, perhaps in Cabinda." After addressing other issues, he returned to the subject: "In the case of the Katangans, there was much sentimentality [sentimentalismo] on the Angolan side. After the previous war [Shaba I, 1977] we decided that they should not launch another attack from Angola, but we took no measures to stop them. Under everyone's eyes (FAPLA, DISA [Angolan intelligence], ODP [militia]) they were able to move battalions from one point to the other. I knew nothing of this until the Cubans [Risquet] informed me." He added, "We are taking measures," to prevent it from happening again.[76]

This was the extent of Neto's explanation. Casas did not press the issue, nor did Havana raise it again, even though the Katangan invasion meant that it felt obliged to send additional troops to protect Angola, which further strained relations between Washington and Cuba.

On May 17, 1978, two days before Casas's meeting with Neto, Castro summoned the head of the U.S. Interests Section in Havana, Lyle Lane, to give him his word that Cuba had not taken part, directly or indirectly, in the invasion of Shaba. This was the first time Castro had met Lane, who had been stationed in Havana since September. The State Department seemed pleased: "Please deliver the following message as soon as possible to Foreign Minister Malmierca from Secretary Vance," Vance cabled Lane on May 19. "We have noted President Castro's assurances that Cuba is in no way involved with the Katangan forces in Shaba. We trust that this is the case, since such involvement would be viewed with greatest concern here. We have also read with deepest interest President Castro's expression of . . . his concern that further external involvement might widen the conflict there. . . . Please also inform Foreign Minister Malmierca that Secretary Vance hopes to meet with [Cuban] Vice President [Carlos Rafael] Rodríguez in New York at the special [UN] session on disarmament."[77]

However, a few hours after Lane delivered Vance's message, the State Department's spokesperson, Tom Reston, acting "on orders from the White House," announced that Cuba had trained the Katangans and equipped them with Soviet weapons.[78] That evening, Cuba's deputy foreign minister protested to Lane: "It is truly irritating that after leaking the news about Comrade Fidel's words to you, there should now appear a public declaration making these imputations which present the Government of Cuba as making false affirmations. We consider the declarations of Reston absolutely dishonest and an act of bad faith. We cannot understand why a constructive gesture on our part should be met in this way."[79]

A bitter war of words followed, as Castro angrily denied the White House's accusations, as did Rodríguez when he met Vance in New York. Carter then called both Castro and Rodríguez liars, telling members of Congress that the evidence of Cuban complicity had been collected over a "long time" and came from "many . . . top-sensitive" sources. On Meet the Press Brzezinski stated flatly that the invasion of Shaba "could not have taken place without the invading parties having been armed and trained by the Cubans." Behind the scene, many administration officials disagreed with the national security adviser. "We all joked about the smoking cigar," mused Policy Planning Director Lake, referring to the large number of skeptics within the administration. "I thought we were hyping a crisis that should not have been hyped—unless you had reliable intelligence."[80] The White House, however, stood firm. Its spokesperson told skeptical journalists, "We are willing to place the records of veracity [of Carter and Castro] side by side and let the American people decide for themselves."[81]

Americans stood by their president. His accusations squared with their perception of Cuba as an aggressive, rogue state whose troops controlled Angola. Furthermore, between the word of the president of the United States and that of Castro, how could an American hesitate? Kissinger put it well: "This tells us something about the level of our public discourse. All the evidence is on the President's side, yet here we are engaged in a public argument questioning the honor of the President of the United States."[82]

In August, the NSC Cuba specialist, Pastor, told Brzezinski's deputy David Aaron that a memo prepared by the State Department for Vance "on the veracity of Cuban official statements has concluded that other than statements related to the Shaba invasions, Cuban officials have told the truth and, at times, stretched it, but very infrequently to the breaking point. Castro has made something of a cult about not lying." Pastor also noted that "a report prepared by the CIA . . . agrees with State's that lying by Cuban officials is unusual, and explains the Shaba case as being sufficiently serious as to justify Castro's lie and after that, sharp reaction, when we called him on it."[83]

In fact, Castro was indignant because he had told the truth, and Carter had called him a liar. The Cubans had been taken by surprise by the Katangans' attack in 1978, just as they had been a year earlier. And they never received a satisfactory explanation from Neto. In 1984 Fidel Castro told Neto's successor, José Eduardo dos Santos, "The Shaba wars have always been a mystery to us, because we were taken by surprise. This is the truth."[84]

Secretary Vance, who had publicly supported Carter's accusations, was on the defensive when talking to Soviet foreign minister Andrei Gromyko at the end of May 1978: "As for the sources of our information, it was the commander of Katang [sic] armed forces, General Nathanaël Mbumba, and Cuban sources in East Germany. We considered these sources reliable." When Gromyko expressed disbelief, Vance added lamely: "Evidently it does not make much sense to continue this argument. I mentioned these facts only to illustrate difficulties in receiving trustworthy information." In his memoirs, Brzezinski, who had been categorical in asserting Cuba's complicity in Shaba II, said merely that the Katangan attack was "apparently fomented with some Angolan and *probably* Cuban assistance." Vance admitted in his memoir, "We did have some ambiguous and, as it turned out, not very good intelligence."[85]

Walter Cutler, the U.S. ambassador in Zaire, soberly assessed the intelligence: "It was very difficult to get information from the ground. Getting intelligence was tough, very difficult. In both Shaba I and Shaba II there was a lot of flying blind. It's so difficult to get reliable intelligence. There was a fear of putting U.S. human resources on the ground for fear that they might be captured, and this affected the quality of the intelligence."[86] The United States had no evidence of its own that Cubans had joined the Katangans in Zaire or helped them in Angola. What it did have were second- and thirdhand reports about people who were said to look like Cubans. Murky evidence that had been discounted during the first invasion became credible in the second.

The difference was not the quality of the intelligence but the domestic and international environment. Shaba II occurred against a grim backdrop. The Cubans had intervened successfully in Ethiopia, and the U.S. attitude to Cuba had hardened. Brzezinski was in the ascendant. Unlike Vance, he peppered his arguments with one item to which the president was very sensitive: the polls. Carter's popularity was declining—between November 1977 and mid-April 1978 by 18 percent. Being "too soft" on Communism in general and failing to check "Cuban-Soviet adventurism" in Africa were cited as key reasons for the president's slide.[87] As the *New York Times* later noted, "Asked why the administration went out on a limb late in May [1978], some officials said it reflected the inevitable White House tendency to shape intelligence to fit policy. 'The Cuban thing came along just at the right time,' one explained.... 'The President was in trouble in the polls for not standing up to Moscow and Havana while Brzezinski and others were getting increasingly upset by events in Africa.'"[88] This helps explain the clumsy volte-face: on May 19 Vance had cabled a constructive response to Castro's assurances to Lane; a few hours later, the White House denounced the Cubans. No new evidence had been uncovered. Carter had simply decided to read the evidence as Brzezinski suggested.

The challenge to Cuba was applauded in the United States, but it carried a price, as Lane's successor as the head of the Interests Section, Wayne Smith, notes: "The Carter administration beats the drums, the Cubans are behind this! Perfect! But the next question is: What are you going to do about it? You paint your adversary as a ravenous beast. Then the pressure builds: What are you going to do about it?"[89] By its gratuitous accusations, the administration limited its ability to achieve a more normal relationship with Cuba. Arguably, the cost was minimal, because Carter did not intend to move forward with normalization unless the Cubans bowed to his demands on Africa. But his accusations dealt another blow to détente. If Cuba was a Soviet proxy, then the Soviet Union was also the aggressor in Shaba. It was a repetition of the Ford-Kissinger antics during the 1975–76 Angolan debacle: accusing the USSR of violating détente, calling its behavior unacceptable, yet being unable to devise a way to punish it. What made the whole performance pathetic, in 1978 as in 1976, was that the Cubans and Soviets were not the guilty parties.

The Americans' major European allies—the French, British, and West Germans—shared Washington's one-sided view of détente. The leaders of these countries—the social-democrats Helmut Schmidt and Jim Callaghan and the conservative Valéry Giscard d' Estaing—lambasted the Cubans and the Soviets as aggressors for intervening to defend Ethiopia from the Somali invasion, yet they applauded when the French and Belgians sent troops to save Mobutu from the Katangan exiles.[90]

## Cassinga

At daybreak on May 4, 1978, a few days before Shaba II began, South African planes flew low over Cassinga, a Namibian refugee camp in southern Angola, 260 kilometers north of the Namibian border. As Claudia Uushona, a young refugee living in the camp, recalls of that May day, "We were gathered outside to salute the flag when we saw white things falling from the sky. We thought it was candy that our president [SWAPO's President Sam Nujoma] was sending us. We were eager to see him. We said, 'The president is coming! And he is bringing us candy!' We were living in a refugee camp; we were all dreaming of the candy the president would bring us. But," she paused as she remembered, "they were bombs."[91]

The air strike, South African general Edward McGill Alexander writes, "was a finely coordinated movement, delivering an awesome total of 1,200 anti-personnel bombs, 20,000 pounds . . . of high-explosive bombs and a devastating two-aircraft strafing run with 30mm high-explosive fragmentation shells. . . . [It] sowed death, destruction and terror amongst the occupants of Cassinga." And it was only the beginning: after the bombs came the paratroopers.[92]

In the words of Jorge Risquet, head of the Cuban civilian mission in Angola, the assault on Cassinga marked the first time "that Cubans and Namibians shed their blood together fighting against the South African racists."[93] A Cuban military unit based at Tchamutete, an Angolan village sixteen kilometers south of Cassinga, advanced to confront the paratroopers despite being strafed and bombed by the South African planes. Sixteen Cubans were killed and more than eighty were wounded.[94] Willem Steenkamp, author of the standard account of the operation from the perspective of the apartheid regime, wrote that "the South Africans who monitored their [the Cubans'] approach with such foreboding that day pay tribute to the courage of the Cubans who pushed forward in spite of the imminent danger of being knocked out by aircraft against which they had no defenses at all." Using documents from South Africa's military archives, General McGill Alexander described the reaction of the paratroopers when they "began to hear the low rumble of armoured vehicles' engines, the clanking of metal tank tracks" heralding the arrival of the Cubans. "The Cuban vehicles were old (the tanks were of Second World War vintage)," but the Cubans had "caught the paratroopers unprepared and badly organized," McGill Alexander explained. "The Cuban advance . . . resulted in a panic among the paratroopers. . . . All order evaporated in a chaotic every-man-for-himself scramble."[95]

"The [Cuban] comrades of Tchamutete were very brave," President Neto commented, noting that no Angolan troops had been able to help. He added, "We are convinced that the South Africans will launch more raids like the one against Cassinga. They have no intention of leaving Namibia. . . . We will continue to help SWAPO. We won't pull back just because it is difficult."[96]

More than 600 Namibians were killed at Cassinga by the South African planes and paratroopers. In an article datelined "Cassinga, 9 May 1978," the London *Times* reported, "Foreign journalists were yesterday shown an open mass grave packed with the decomposing bodies of 460 people who the Angolan authorities said were massacred by South African troops. . . . The dozen foreign correspondents flown to Cassinga by the Angolan authorities could make out the brightly coloured dresses of a large number of women among the dead, said to be Namibian refugees . . . Another 122 bodies were buried in a separate trench. . . . Most of the town, built of wood or dried mud, was razed."[97]

A bitter debate ensued: the South African government claimed that Cassinga had been a major SWAPO military base, whereas SWAPO said that it was a refugee camp. All the evidence indicates that Cassinga was indeed a refugee camp, administered by SWAPO with the assistance of the United Nations and protected by a small SWAPO military force, which included a senior SWAPO commander. The testimony of the representatives of the UN High Commission for Refugees and the World Health Organization who visited Cassinga three weeks after the raid is eloquent:

It was with profound shock that the representatives of the United Nations verified, on the ground at Cassinga, the extreme savagery, the attempted annihilation, and the systematic destruction wrought upon a group of refugees who were under the protection of the High Commission for Refugees. . . . That these people were civilians is attested to by all the evidence that this UN mission has been able to gather. . . . The village of Cassinga—which had a population of approximately 3,000 Namibian refugees and was a well organized place with houses, schools, health centers, warehouses, and other social centers for its people who were mostly children, teenagers, women and old people—has been completely destroyed. . . . All the facts that this UN delegation has been able to verify reveal that what happened in Cassinga must be described as criminal in legal terms and savage in moral terms. It reminds us of the darkest moments of modern history.[98]

Brzezinski told Carter that Pretoria's raid "provides a striking example of its insensitivity to international reactions."[99] He failed to add that the Western reaction reinforced South Africa's insensitivity. The Western press reported the massacre but dropped the story after one or two days.[100] Western governments barely reacted. In the UN Security Council, the United States and its allies opposed sanctions against South Africa.[101] President Carter, self-styled champion of human rights, told reporters, "The South Africans claim that it was just a retaliatory raid against the SWAPO forces who had invaded Namibia with small strikes, and they've claimed to have withdrawn and have not left any South African forces in Angola. So we hope it's just a transient strike in retaliation and we hope it's all over." Risquet, the Cuban point man on Africa, astutely explained to SWAPO president Nujoma the significance of this reaction: "If the South Africans were ever going to be held accountable for their aggression, well, they would have been made to pay for Cassinga—and they weren't. This means that they are free to repeat acts of aggression like this again and again."[102]

## Cuban Reinforcements

A few days after Cassinga, amid the furor caused by Shaba II, the U.S. press reported that the administration intended to seek the repeal of the Clark Amendment and to embark on a new policy in Africa that would "permit the United States to funnel sophisticated arms and funds clandestinely to African guerrilla forces fighting Soviet-backed Cuban troops in Angola and Ethiopia." Washington was abuzz with rumors that there was a connection between this new

African policy and the "international rescue mission" that had brought French and Belgian troops to Shaba. Administration officials insisted that no such connection existed, "but that disclaimer," the *Washington Post* wrote, "left untold numbers of skeptics in Washington."[103]

Not surprisingly, the Cubans, too, were skeptical. The CIA wrote: "Castro has always been concerned that Western powers, aligned with Mobutu, might use evidence of Cuban involvement in the Shaba invasion as justification for a retaliatory strike into an already extremely insecure Angola. Havana's concern on this point was no doubt considerably heightened by the South African raid into Angolan territory on 4 May of this year as well as by the rapid Western response to last month's Shaba invasion." The Cubans' concern was further heightened by the fact that they knew that the allegations of their involvement in Shaba II were lies. They wondered what would happen next. In Risquet's words, "Cassinga happens and at the same time there is the second Shaba war, and this time [the West intervened] not only with Moroccans but also with Belgian and French paratroopers, that is, two NATO countries. The situation [for Angolan security] became even more serious."[104]

Neto agreed. "I want to announce here," he told the Fifteenth Summit of the Organization of African Unity in July 1978, "that I will not order the Cuban troops to leave Angola while the military, political and diplomatic aggression against my country continues. The Cubans will remain for as long as the aggression persists. If necessary, their numbers may increase."[105] At Luanda's request, Havana began sending reinforcements to Angola.

The Cuban planes that brought these reinforcements refueled at Sal Island, Cape Verde. The U.S. Embassy in Praia reported in July 1978 that the number of Cuban flights had "increased dramatically" during the last few weeks. "The Portuguese ambassador, the Brazilian consul, the U.S. Chargé and the Vice Consul all were at the airport at different times when the Cuban passengers disembarked and entered the transit lounge of Amilcar Cabral airport. The Cubans would remain in the transit lounge for at least ninety minutes while their aircraft took on fuel and was serviced. . . . [They] were generally a homogeneous group (young, trim, curious, short hair, good physical condition, good discipline, uniforms in excellent conditions) . . . There always seemed to be several older men who were in charge of the group."[106]

Shaba II brought French and Belgian troops to southern Zaire, near the border with Angola, and provoked a first-class row between Washington and Havana. It was, the Cubans believed, a foolhardy adventure. But was this true from Luanda's perspective?

Did Neto unleash the Katangans despite his promise to Castro, or was the operation organized by other Angolan officials without his knowledge? There is no smoking gun—no Angolan documents are available—but the logic of the situation seeps into this void: Neto was a strong president, in control of his government, and it strains credulity to believe that the invasion could take place without his approval. His own answer to General Casas—that he "knew nothing of this" until Risquet had informed him in February—reveals an artful avoidance of saying what he knew and when he knew it.

If Neto had hoped that the Katangans would overthrow Mobutu, then he was sorely misguided—the Western powers had shown in 1977 that they would not allow the Katangans to succeed, and to think that they might relent in 1978, after the Cuban intervention in the Horn, was naive.

Yet the operation was not as foolhardy from Neto's point of view as the Cubans believed. True, it entailed costs: French and Belgian troops entered Zaire and deepened Luanda's sense of insecurity; Washington was inflamed, and Havana was irritated. But the French and Belgians departed, Washington directed its wrath at the Cubans, and Havana swallowed its irritation. Shaba II had no significant long-term costs for Angola. It had, moreover, one significant, long-term benefit: Mobutu was intimidated. Before Shaba II, he had allowed rebels to attack Angola from Zaire. After Shaba II, that threat to Neto's regime was extinguished.

## CHAPTER 3

# The Cubans in Angola

## Jonas Savimbi

Friend and foe alike acknowledged the intelligence and charisma of Jonas Savimbi. "Savimbi is an impressive figure," the U.S. ambassador in Zambia reported after meeting him in January 1975. "Savimbi is very intelligent," MPLA leader Lúcio Lara agreed. He was also a gifted military commander. Unlike Neto, who spent very little time with his guerrillas inside Angola during the war of independence, Savimbi, as a South African journalist observed, "spent most of his time leading his troops in the field." Savimbi himself boasted, in a clear swipe at Neto, "I alone remained in the bush for six years."[1] He failed to mention, however, that he had spent several of these years working with—not against—the Portuguese.

"Jonas Savimbi was a very ambitious man, and he led a small group [in eastern Angola]," recalled General Francisco da Costa Gomes, the Portuguese commander in chief in Angola from May 1970 through August 1972. In early February 1972 Savimbi proposed that UNITA and the Portuguese "cooperate" against the MPLA, which had established a strong presence in eastern Angola. "We would be willing to provide guides to enemy zones," Savimbi wrote to the Portuguese authorities. "I am sure that with our cooperation the MPLA . . . would be eliminated from the East."[2] He proved to be a valuable ally: UNITA, a Portuguese officer remarked, "gave the Portuguese forces the decisive weapon in that kind of war: information about the guerrilla base camps [of the MPLA]."[3]

The arrangement came to an abrupt end, however, when a Portuguese general exceeded his authority. "In the last quarter of 1973," Costa Gomes writes, "we broke the agreement [with Savimbi]." Joaquim da Silva Cunha, who was Portugal's defense minister, explains what had happened: in September 1973 a new Portuguese commander in eastern Angola, General Abel Barroso Hipólito, launched an offensive against UNITA, "despite his instructions."[4] This was what transformed Savimbi, the collaborator, into the freedom fighter. "It was sheer lunacy," another Portuguese general laments. "UNITA was on our side, but Barroso Hipólito said that for him all the Angolan rebels were the same." Barroso Hipólito was recalled to Lisbon. "I sacked him," says Costa Gomes, who had become the chief of the general staff of the Portuguese armed forces. Contacts between Savimbi and the Portuguese authorities were reestablished early in 1974. "Things were, therefore, on the way to returning to the previous situation and negotiations were under way," Silva Cunha writes, when Prime Minister Marcelo Caetano was overthrown on April 25, 1974.[5]

UNITA was far weaker than the country's two other rebel movements—the MPLA and the FNLA. "Unlike the other two main groups, UNITA had only a small armed force (600–800 men) on April 25 [1974]," U.S. consul general Tom Killoran reported from Luanda. "These men had much less combat experience than FNLA or MPLA troops."[6] A few days after Caetano's ouster, however, Savimbi took advantage of the festive mood of the Portuguese troops to carry out his most successful military operation. UNITA captured an entire company of Portuguese soldiers, disarmed and stripped them, so that they returned completely naked to their barracks.[7] With that brilliant stroke, Savimbi burnished his credentials as a freedom fighter.

Without wasting time, the freedom fighter turned to Pretoria for help. With increasing zest, he regaled wary officials from South Africa's Military Intelligence and Bureau of State Security with his vision of an independent Angola that would join South Africa in an anticommunist bloc. He told them that he knew where SWAPO's camps in southern Angola were and that he was "absolutely ready" to help the South African Defence Force (SADF) "attack, detain or expel" SWAPO from the territory. In return, he wanted South African military aid to help him seize power in Luanda.[8] Pretoria obliged and launched Operation Savannah. First came weapons, then instructors, and finally, on October 14, 1975, South African troops invaded Angola to crush the MPLA.

The Cuban intervention forced the South Africans to leave Angola, but they left with a high regard for Savimbi. They were dazzled by his personality and his eloquence. He had proved his loyalty: UNITA detachments had clashed with SWAPO and he had honored his pledge "to supply guides in order to move against SWAPO." He had worked well with the SADF commanders and had been willing to listen to their advice. "The climate of cooperation between the South African army and UNITA is very good," the SADF noted.[9]

## Savimbi's Friends

When the South Africans had informed Savimbi, on December 25, 1975, that they were going to withdraw from Angola, they had promised to help him if he continued to fight against the MPLA.[10] General Chris Thirion, who was then a colonel in South African Military Intelligence (MI), recalls that as Operation Savannah drew to a close, "we [MI] infiltrated into Angola to tell the UNITA chiefs, 'Regroup, we will support you.' And we started training UNITA." Savimbi established his headquarters in northeastern Namibia, at Camp Delta, in the Caprivi strip. South African instructors trained UNITA guerrillas at Delta and at other small bases in the Caprivi, and inside Angola.[11] Furthermore, as Colonel Jan Breytenbach, a renowned leader of South Africa's Special Forces, writes, "Small operations north of the border continued after our withdrawal from Angola." They were carried out by Special Forces and by a unique unit under his command—the Buffalo Battalion, black Angolans who were opposed to the Neto regime and were led by South African officers. Some of the attacks were directed against SWAPO; others against Angolan targets. Breytenbach explains, "[We were] lending clandestine support to or executing operations on UNITA's behalf. Such operations were always conducted with the troops disguised as UNITA forces." As a former officer from Buffalo Battalion writes, "All the whites in the team were to blacken their faces with the Black is Beautiful camouflage cream that the army provided. This horrible cream was used on a daily basis while on operations."[12]

South Africa was "UNITA's only reliable window to the outside world," Brzezinski noted in 1977, but other countries "friendly to us continue to aid Savimbi."[13] China sent weapons; as the Zambian Embassy in Beijing said, "China in her global policy wherever Russia and Cuba appear, they will do the opposite."[14] The Safari Club joined the fray. This shadowy organization had been created at France's initiative. In the words of Prince Turki Al-Faisal, who was the Director of Intelligence of Saudi Arabia, in late 1974 the Director of French Intelligence, Alexandre de Marenches,

> made a visit to four countries in our area. He visited the Shah of Iran, he came to visit King Faisal . . ., he went to visit President Sadat and he then went on to visit with King Hassan of Morocco. His proposition was that our American friends were in trouble, their intelligence collection and capability had been diminished to say the least and literally they didn't have any money left to do anything. So we . . . should get together and try to

do something to face the Communist threat on our doorstep in Africa. . . . So the leaders of these four countries agreed to set up what was then called the Safari Club. . . . The Safari Club included. . . . Iran, Egypt, Morocco, Saudi Arabia, plus France. We actually engaged in countering Soviet expansion in all of these areas. Whether by money, by human resources, by intelligence work. . . . The Safari Club also initiated the support for . . . Savimbi . . . by giving him financial aid, intelligence, training and things like that.[15]

Iran's aid ended with the fall of the shah in early 1979, but the other members of the Safari Club soldiered on. According to Savimbi's biographer, France, Saudi Arabia, Egypt, and the Gulf Emirates gave cash. Morocco gave weapons and "offered training for selected UNITA guerrilla specialists." The French "also helped in another way," recalls UNITA general Nunda: they stiffened the resolve of some African countries sympathetic to Savimbi—the Ivory Coast, Senegal, Gabon, and Togo gave UNITA diplomatic and logistical support. Mobutu, who loathed the MPLA, offered UNITA military facilities and logistical support. It was through Zaire that China's weapons reached Savimbi. Mobutu also allowed the FNLA and a separatist movement, the Front for the Liberation of the Enclave of Cabinda (FLEC), to have bases in Zaire and use its territory as a springboard for raids into northern Angola.[16]

But Shaba II sobered Mobutu—Zaire had "to eat at the same table with the MPLA," a Zairean intelligence officer explained to Savimbi's envoys. A deal was struck. Neto disarmed the Katangans, and Mobutu ended his aid to FLEC and FNLA. "Mobutu threw us out," recalls the FNLA's chief of staff, General Tonta.[17] UNITA received better treatment. Unlike the FNLA and FLEC, it had performed well during the 1975–76 civil war, and Savimbi, a gifted military leader, enjoyed the support of Zaire's friends—including South Africa, the United States, and Morocco. Mobutu continued to give Savimbi some diplomatic and logistical assistance, but he closed UNITA's military facilities and no longer allowed his country to be used as a conduit for weapons. This worried the Chinese. "The Chinese have told UNITA that Peking would continue its aid," the CIA reported, "but was concerned about how it would reach UNITA if Zaire was no longer able to act as a transit area." South Africa offered to help. Beijing held its nose, and with Pretoria's assent in 1979 it delivered "550 to 600 tons of weapons" to Savimbi through Namibia.[18]

U.S. intelligence struggled to understand who was supporting UNITA. In July 1978, Intelligence and Research of the State Department (INR) wrote that "South Africa is no longer UNITA's major arms supplier. . . . Most of UNITA's external aid is now funneled through Zaire and originates from European and Arab sources."[19] This statement turned reality upside down and is an example of the poor quality of CIA and INR reporting on Angola in the Carter and Reagan years. South Africa remained through 1988 Savimbi's main benefactor.[20] For Savimbi, it was a marriage of convenience, just as his dalliance with the Portuguese colonial authorities had been. While he was very dependent on Pretoria's aid, he was never Pretoria's lackey. "They [UNITA] have a fierce desire for independence and will not be dictated to, nor will they allow anyone to rule their lives for them," the South African officer who was in charge of day-to-day contacts with UNITA noted in 1988.[21] For Pretoria, Savimbi was a valuable ally in the defense of apartheid—or, to use Pretoria's lingo, in its struggle against the Soviets and their MPLA puppets.

## Moscow and Agostinho Neto

In fact the MPLA was not, and had never been, anyone's puppet. During the war of independence, its relationship with Moscow had been difficult and at times strained. The Soviet Union had helped the MPLA during the liberation struggle, but this support had been tempered by its distrust for the leaders of the movement, particularly Neto.

Oleg Nazhestkin, a KGB officer who worked on Angola, writes that "our relations with Neto were complicated. . . . We worked with Neto and the movement he led, we helped him, but at the same time we did not trust him. . . . He was not a pliant figure in the hands of our apparatchiks. He always had his own views, his own ideas about what to do, about how to carry out the struggle. His views did not always—to put it mildly—coincide with ours, and he was more than willing to defend his point of view."[22]

Soviet suspicions that the MPLA was pro-Chinese had been fanned by an ephemeral thaw in the MPLA's tense relations with Beijing after Neto visited China in 1972. "This rapprochement with China inevitably creates problems with the USSR," Neto's close aide Iko Carreira complained to Yugoslav officials, while a Soviet report warned, "Neto has always looked with suspicion . . . on the cadres who have trained in the USSR, seeing them as agents of Soviet influence."[23]

In 1973 Soviet aid to the MPLA, which was reeling from the Portuguese assault in eastern Angola and was torn by internal crisis, "virtually ceased," writes Nazhestkin. In Lúcio Lara's words, "The Soviets dropped us. We assumed it was all over." Some vitally needed aid continued to come from Yugoslavia, which had become, by the early 1970s, the MPLA's closest friend.[24]

The Soviets resumed aid to the MPLA in 1975, as Angola plunged into civil war, but they continued to distrust Neto and his aides. "A Soviet source has informed me," Cuba's ambassador in Brazzaville, Arquimedes Columbié, cabled Havana in December 1975, that Moscow "is presently very worried because Sweden has recognized the MPLA [government]. While on the one hand they consider it a positive step, on the other hand they consider it dangerous, because of . . . the influence they [the Swedes] could acquire over President Neto and other MPLA leaders." The Soviets were also wary of Brazil, which had recognized Neto's People's Republic of Angola with what they considered suspicious speed. The Soviet ambassador in Brazzaville, Yevgeny Afanasenko, told Columbié that "Even though it seems that the initiative came from them [the Brazilians]," one could not exclude the possibility that they had done it at the behest of the United States, "which knows that it would be fairly easy for the Brazilians to manipulate the MPLA leadership." Moscow considered Neto's close aide, Lúcio Lara, a particularly weak link. Afanasenko told Columbié "that the fact that Lara played an important role in the party [MPLA] worried him." Furthermore, the Soviets continued to distrust Neto. Before 1975 they had suspected him of being pro-Chinese; by 1976, they worried that he might be swayed by the Americans. "It is very important to be aware," they told Columbié, "of Neto's relations with the Yankees."[25]

In November 1975 the Kremlin had been angered by the dispatch of Cuban troops to Angola. General Secretary Brezhnev was focused on the SALT II negotiations with the United States and the February 1976 Congress of the Soviet Communist Party. "He knows that it is his last Congress—they occur every five years—and he doubtless sees it as the occasion for securing his place in history," DCI William Colby told the NSC. "He wants to go before the congress proclaiming the success of detente."[26] But when the Congress met, in February 1976, the Soviet leaders embraced Castro's daring exploit as their own. The Cubans had won in Angola, and Ford, caving to conservative pressure, had frozen the SALT II negotiations. Castro's victory and Ford's volte-face strengthened the hard-liners in Moscow. As Soviet ambassador Anatoly Dobrynin writes, they asserted that "the United States was . . . busy consolidating its positions in Egypt and elsewhere, and had actively overthrown a socialist government in Chile that came to power legally, so how could the Americans see our support for the newly formed government of Angola as a violation of detente? Must we yield to American arrogance and their double standard?" Brezhnev, who had hoped to crown the Party Congress with a SALT treaty, instead used the Cuban victory in Angola to burnish Moscow's claims to be the champion of Third World liberation. A few months later the CIA concluded that the MPLA's "victory in Angola was one of Moscow's most important and visible foreign policy successes in the past few years. It refurbished the Soviets' revolutionary credentials, enhanced their status among the radical black African states, and gave them an important win over their Chinese competitors in Africa [who had supported the anti-MPLA coalition]."[27]

Eager to obtain full Soviet cooperation for their Angolan operation and for the MPLA government, the Cubans went to great lengths to assuage Moscow's sensitivities. "The Soviet representatives [in Angola]," a knowledgeable historian writes, "often expressed a certain degree of surprise to Moscow at how harmonious were relations with the small Caribbean ally. . . . Soviet diplomats and officers lauded the Cubans for their bravery and for their ability to function as a link between Moscow and Luanda while at the same time 'respecting' the paramount role of the CPSU [Soviet] leadership. The overall Cuban-Soviet relationship improved significantly in the wake of the Angolan operation, up to a point which had not been reached since the 1962 missile crisis."[28]

This improvement was possible because Castro agreed to withdraw the Cuban troops from Angola, albeit at a slower tempo than Brezhnev had wished. And he accepted, indeed asked, that the Soviets play the leading role in the creation of the new Angolan Armed Forces (FAPLA). He told East German leader Erich Honecker, "Neto wanted us to take charge of the entire Angolan army. This might have been the best in practical terms, but not politically. The Soviet Union is the major provider of weapons and the Angolans must work with the Soviets."[29]

Raúl Castro emphasized this point during his visit to Angola in the spring of 1976: "I insisted on the importance of coordinating with the USSR everything to do with planning, with the training and preparation of cadres, and with the armament of the FAPLA. . . . Cuba will cooperate with the Soviets to the fullest extent possible."[30]

Moscow agreed to provide the weapons and to help create the FAPLA. It established a large military mission in Angola, but it is impossible to determine the exact size of the mission. A study by the Russian Defense Ministry states that 10,985 Soviet military advisers and specialists served in Angola from late 1975 to January 1, 1991, but it gives no yearly figures. Senior Angolan and Cuban officers believe that in the late 1970s the figure was a little less than 1,000 and that it increased by a few hundred by the mid-1980s.[31] Soviet military officers served as advisers to the Angolan Ministry of Defense, the Angolan General Staff, the commanders of the country's eleven military regions,[32] and the commanders and senior staff of many of the regular brigades that constituted the bulk of the fledgling Angolan army. Soviet military specialists instructed the

Angolans in the use of the weapons sent from the Soviet Union and helped maintain them. Soviet officers taught in the military schools that were being created. In their free time, Soviet officers tried to teach the Angolans about the Soviet Union, a country that was, for the immense majority of Angolans, distant, nebulous, and overshadowed by Cuba. Lieutenant Colonel Vladimir Barganov, who was in 1977 the adviser of the political commissar of the FAPLA in the Fifth Military Region, spoke one evening to the students of the University of Lubango. "Even though they were, on the whole, educated people, their knowledge of the USSR was virtually nonexistent," he recalls. "They were stunned by the size of our country when I showed them the USSR and Cuba on the map. They thought it was the other way around."[33]

But when it came to the FAPLA, Havana was Moscow's junior partner. Cuban military advisers helped train lightly armed counterinsurgency units, but the Soviets advised the Angolan minister of defense and the top military commanders and helped organize the new army. Here was the rub. The Soviet advisers and the Angolan military leaders wanted to create a regular army that could fight a conventional war against a foreign enemy, including South Africa. Havana, however, believed that the FAPLA should concentrate on fighting the insurgency—UNITA—at home, leaving the Cuban troops to protect the country from a foreign invasion. Castro expressed his concern about this to Neto when he visited Angola in March 1977. He insisted in their first meeting: "It is important to develop the army, to organize the regiments, the military academies, but you don't have to worry about foreign aggression. In my opinion what you need to do now is to focus on liquidating the bandits [UNITA]. This is the critical task."[34] This concern became almost an obsession for Castro during his visit, as he talked with Cuban officers in Angola and gained a firsthand impression of the situation in the country. In a letter to the first deputy minister of defense, the head of the Cuban military mission was eloquent. "Senén," he wrote,

> A brief note to tell you about the visit of the Commander in Chief here in Angola.
>
> He arrived [from Mozambique] on the 23d in [the city of] Huambo. . . . He took time . . . to talk with us. . . . I told him my worries about the war against the bandits, that it was mired in chaos . . . because of the FAPLA's lack of organization, commitment, attention, etc. etc. Then we left for Luanda. And from that first night, when he met the Political Bureau [of the MPLA], he insisted that they should focus on the war against the bandits. . . . This was the issue that concerned him most and on which he was most adamant with Neto: the need to create units to fight the bandits. . . .

On the 25th we visited Namibe and Lubango . . . and the day after that we went to Benguela and Lobito. . . . We were back [in Luanda] on the 27th. . . . On the 28th he met with Neto and went to a dinner in the [Presidential] Palace, where he kept hammering away on the need to fight the bandits. . . . On the 29th he visited a fishery with Neto and in the evening he met with the liberation movements, the ANC [African National Congress of South Africa] . . . ZAPU [Zimbabwe African People's Union] and . . . SWAPO. It went on until very late in the night. . . .

In the morning of the 30th, he met with the staff of our military mission. . . . He explained to us that the fight against the bandits was necessarily and without question the responsibility of the Angolans, that we could not wage this war, that it was their war. He put immense stress on this problem of the war against the bandits. He did it constantly. . . .

On the 31st, he met again with Neto and once again he kept hammering away about the importance of fighting the bandits.[35]

When he stopped in Berlin, on his way home, Castro told Honecker about his impressions of Angola: "In one matter we have . . . worries. This has to do with the creation of the army." The FAPLA and the Soviet mission were neglecting the fight against UNITA. "Regular Angolan troops are not employed against the bandits. The Soviet advisers are focusing on organizing a conventional army and are not very interested in fighting the bandits."[36]

The Cubans advisers in the light counterinsurgency units of the FAPLA fought beside their Angolan charges against UNITA, and a Cuban regiment joined the FAPLA in operations against UNITA, but Havana continued to insist that this was a struggle that had to be fought by the Angolans themselves.[37] These were the first hints of a tug-of-war between Cubans and Angolans that would continue through the end of 1987: the Angolans wanted the Cuban troops to remain in the country and fight with them against UNITA, while the Cubans believed that the war against UNITA was the responsibility of the FAPLA and that they should remain in Angola only as long as there was a foreign threat.

## Nito Alves

On May 27, 1977, two months after Castro had left Angola, there was an attempted coup in Luanda led by Nito Alves, a former member of the MPLA's leadership. The plot included key members of the army, the police, the MPLA, and the administration throughout the country. But on May 27, only the plotters in Luanda acted. Those in other cities remained passive, waiting for the outcome in the capital, where Cuban forces—although few in number—would play a decisive role. It was the Cubans who forced the main rebel military unit (the 9th Brigade) to surrender, without fighting, as Lúcio Lara told a Soviet officer.[38] It was a Cuban, Colonel Rafael Moracén, who led the group that retook the government radio station, which had been seized by the rebels, and it was Moracén who seized the microphone to announce that the radio was again in loyalist hands. *Le Soir* of Brussels noted that "when the studios of the radio were invaded by the pro-Neto group, one could clearly hear on the waves the characteristic accent of Cuba." In the emotion of the moment, Moracén had spoken in Spanish.[39]

The revolt had been defeated almost without bloodshed, and the aftermath might have been less harsh, had the leaders of the coup not murdered, before fleeing, seven high-ranking loyalists whom they had captured earlier in the day. As Amnesty International wrote, Neto had initially indicated "that some clemency would be shown towards the members of the *Nitista* faction," but after the murders were discovered a wave of repression engulfed the country. "This remains one of the most grim pages of the history of independent Angola," a biographer sympathetic to Agostinho Neto wrote in 2005.[40]

Westerners as well as Africans, scholars and bureaucrats cite this coup attempt as a glaring example of the divergence of Soviet and Cuban policy in Angola. Ambassador Andrew Young told a Senate subcommittee in 1978, "The Cubans and the Russians haven't been always united in Angola. . . . When there was a recent coup attempt against Neto, it was pretty clear from African sources that the Russians were behind that coup. Yet the Cubans sided with Neto." Five years later, the London *Times* reported that in Luanda "it is said sotto voce" that Alves had acted "with Russian support."[41]

While the Soviet role remains murky, clues about it can be gleaned from Cuban, Angolan, and Yugoslav sources.

Nito Alves had not been considered an admirer of the Soviet Union—he seemed instead to be sympathetic to China—until he went to Moscow in February 1976 to attend the Congress of the Soviet Communist Party as a delegate of the MPLA. "After his return, Nito Alves was literally obsessed with the USSR," writes the foremost authority on the MPLA. "From that moment forward, he seemed to have only one point of reference: Moscow." Neto told the Yugoslav ambassador that "Nito Alves used to carry around brochures of Mao's writings, but after he attended the last Soviet Congress he swapped them for Soviet works and cast himself as a great Leninist and supporter of the Soviet path." Nito Alves "spoke about the Soviet Union from morning to night," a senior FAPLA officer recalled.[42] Soviet officials in Luanda took note, in a manner that concerned Angolan officials. On May 21, 1976, Prime Minister Lopo do Nascimento told Raúl Castro, who was visiting Angola: "To be frank, I don't know whether in my forthcoming trip to the Soviet Union I should say that some people in the Soviet Embassy here are trying to enhance the importance of some individuals." He was referring to Nito Alves. Two days later, Nascimento told the head of the Cuban civilian mission in Angola, Jorge Risquet, that "President Neto had decided to write a confidential letter to Brezhnev on the problem with the Soviets."[43] The following July, in Belgrade, Nascimento told Tito, "What we ask from other countries is simple cooperation, not the importation of their dogmas. . . . We think that since the Soviet Union is the biggest and economically strongest socialist country, it should bear some burden in the development of our country and provide us aid, but in no way does this mean that they can do whatever they want in Angola."[44]

The tension between Neto and the Soviets was apparent during the Angolan's visit to Moscow in October 1976. "He meets with Brezhnev," recalled Foreign Minister Paulo Jorge, who was present, "and Brezhnev begins to reproach him, saying 'We have helped you [Angolans] so much, we are helping you, but you have done this and that!' Neto, who was a zealous defender of our national sovereignty, zapped a sharp reply. This tension between the USSR and Angola explains the Soviet attitude on May 27 [the day of the coup]. There was a huge difference between them and the Cubans. The Soviets wanted to tell us what to do."[45]

In March 1977—two months before the coup attempt—the Yugoslav ambassador in Luanda, Nikola Šašić, informed Belgrade about "the deterioration in relations between the Soviet Union . . . and the leadership of the MPLA." He wrote that the Soviet Embassy suspected that President Neto and his associates were "not committed to the Soviet system and its solutions" and that they might strike a deal with the West—or even China. The Soviet Embassy, Šašić concluded, was using Nito Alves "as a means of pressure and blackmail against Neto and the Angolan Political Bureau . . . and Nito [Alves] himself counts on Soviet support in his struggle [against the Angolan leadership]."[46]

One week after the failed coup, Raúl Castro visited Angola. His report is worth quoting at length:

From the moment we arrived in Luanda we were told about the mood of hostility toward Soviet officials, diplomats and security officers in Luanda among the top leaders of the MPLA. We already knew about Risquet's conversation with Neto, in which the latter had recalled with some bitterness that "the Soviets have been wrong about us several times; at one time . . . they refused us all aid." . . .

Even before the coup, the Angolan leadership had been keen to deny the Nitistas' accusation that it was anti-Soviet. . . . At the same time, our military mission became aware that Soviet military interpreters and military specialists had openly expressed support for Nito [Alves] and Bakalov [a leading plotter]. I gave instructions to investigate whether these had been isolated, personal views or whether they reflected a common opinion among the Soviet military in Luanda.

As is clearly indicated in a later report . . ., while the nuances may vary, the common assessment was that Nito, Bakaloff and the other plotters "are friends of the Soviet Union."

Some of the Soviets are actively partisan, others say they are neutral. There is also the case of Colonel Grishin . . . who hid one of the rebels in his car and helped him escape. Knowing the Soviets, and above all their military, it is clear that behavior and attitudes like this, even if they are spontaneous and reflect the personal views of an individual, must be explained, in the final analysis, by the fact that these individuals know that their views are consistent with those of their superiors.[47]

Until more evidence surfaces, this is the most persuasive explanation of the Soviet role: several Soviet officials probably knew of the plot and welcomed it. They were encouraged by Moscow's distrust of Neto, a distrust that fed on many years of strained relations and that approached paranoia—how else to explain Moscow's wariness when Brazil and Sweden recognized the People's Republic of Angola?

Agostinho Neto had no doubts: Moscow had connived with Nito Alves. Nevertheless, he could not quarrel openly with the Soviet Union, his only supplier of weapons at a time when his country faced Pretoria's implacable hostility and Carter refused to establish diplomatic relations. Four days after the failed coup, Brezhnev sent a message of support to Neto, who commented to the Yugoslav ambassador that "it said the right things, but in a vague, imprecise, and unconvincing way."[48]

In late September 1977 Neto traveled to Moscow. The French chargé, Jean-Jacques Peyronnet, wrote, "The chill in relations with Moscow that has persisted since May 27 thawed with President Neto's trip." Ambassador Šašić reported, "Angola needed this visit in order to clear the air and get an apology for everything that was going on during the coup. . . . This step [Neto's visit] was necessary for the continuation of normal relations and it was a precondition for asking additional military aid, which Angola had to do."[49] But Neto's willingness to turn the page did not mean that he was willing to make any concession to Moscow. He told Šašić that he was determined to follow an independent domestic and foreign policy. He expressed doubts about the ability of the Soviets to adjust to Angola's position. And he stressed, "We are not going to change."[50]

Neto appreciated what Cuba had done to defend his government during the coup. He told Šašić that "Cuba had behaved well, unlike the Soviet Union." But notwithstanding the proofs of loyalty that Havana had given—during the recent coup and in November 1975, when it challenged Brezhnev to come to the MPLA's assistance—Neto's trust was not absolute, because of Cuba's very close ties with the Soviet Union. "The question of Cuban constancy and trustworthiness is left to the future," he said, according to Šašić.[51] In the meantime, he stressed, Cuba's relations with Angola "are good."[52]

Probably Neto would have felt most comfortable with Yugoslavia—a country that kept the Soviet Union at arm's length—but Yugoslavia could not help him, not enough. When Neto visited Belgrade in April 1977, Yugoslav officials reviewed the aid they had provided Angola since independence: $14 million in military aid (of which $4 million had not yet been disbursed); forty-six scholarships for Angolan students; training in Belgrade for twenty-eight future Angolan diplomats, fifty-six security personnel, and twenty-five factory workers; and a few Yugoslav aid workers were in Angola.[53] This paled in comparison to what Cuba was doing. "The Cuban presence is indispensable to the country's security," a Yugoslav report noted, "and it is becoming more and more important in the economic sphere as well."[54]

## Castro's "Mercenary Army" in Angola

"A great percentage of the country's [Angola's] foreign exchange is spent to provide for the Cuban soldiers," former U.S. Senator John Tunney (D-Calif.) wrote in February 1977, after a five-day trip to Angola. This was a view that would be repeated ad nauseam, to the present day, in the Western press and by Western scholars who asserted that the Cuban troops—"the rental army from Cuba"—cost Angola a fortune, possibly as much as $500 million a year. For example, the *Economist* announced, "Cuba itself is well paid for its mercenaries," while *New York Times* columnist William Safire wrote, "Castro's Cuba desperately needs to continue to rent out its troops." Havana "had been receiving up to $1,000 per month from the MPLA government for each soldier it sent to Angola," J. E. Davies wrote in a 2007 book published by Ohio University Press, an assertion so widely accepted that he apparently felt no need to provide a source.[55]

The Cuban documents debunk these assertions. On May 18, 1976, in Luanda, Raúl Castro raised financial matters for the first time during a visit to the Angolan Defense Ministry. "I spoke with my friend Iko [Carreira, the minister of defense] about the complex problem of supplies for the FAPLA. I explained that we are feeding some 25,000 men, in addition to the Cubans, as well as the population of Cabinda. I told him that the last shipment of food for our troops sent from Cuba to Angola was supposed to last for six months, but it had lasted only three. . . . As I spoke, both Iko and those with him pulled a face as if to ask, 'OK, but what can we do?'" And so Raúl decided that he had to raise the issue with Neto, something he clearly was reluctant to do. "The best solution," he suggested, "is that we promise to feed the FAPLA, or some of it, until a given date, sometime later this year."[56]

On May 26, 1976, Raúl reminded Neto that "at present some 25,000 Angolan soldiers are being fed by the Cuban military mission." He asked when the FAPLA might be able to start feeding its own troops and whether the Angolan government could eventually supply the Cuban troops with "fresh food."[57]

Neto's reply was courteous and noncommittal: "He explained that he had never raised the possibility of helping defray these expenses because he thought it was a delicate subject and he didn't want to offend the Cuban comrades by raising it. The Angolans were ready to study the matter, and they would make some proposals."[58] Nothing happened. Finally, in May 1978—two years later—General Casas, Cuba's first deputy minister of defense, again raised the issue with Neto. "There is a subject that is very awkward for us," he said. "It pains us, but we have to raise it. It is the cost of maintaining our troops here. . . . The problem is that Cuba cannot afford to pay for anything in hard currency. We will pay all those expenses that we can defray with our own currency, for instance the salaries of our officers and our soldiers. But we are not in a position to spend even one cent in foreign currency, because, quite simply, we don't have it." After describing the difficult economic situation facing Cuba, General Casas explained that his request was not an ultimatum: "The fact that we say this does not imply, in the least, that we are thinking of withdrawing or reducing our troops. We will maintain them even if you cannot satisfy our request."

Neto's reply was similar to that he had given Raúl Castro two years earlier: "If it is awkward for you to raise this subject, it is even more painful for us to broach with you our concern about the heavy burden that Cuba is bearing and our desire to help. . . . We cannot let Cuba bear this burden alone. We must help."[59]

The issue was finally settled in a military agreement signed in September 1978. The agreement stipulated that Cuba would continue to pay the salaries of its military personnel in Angola and the Angolan government would defray all other expenses.[60]

This was the only military agreement ever concluded between the two countries. It was extended tacitly—that is, neither side asked that it be terminated or modified—until the Cuban troops left Angola in 1991. In Risquet's words, "It lasted forever!" Fidel Castro told Angola's president José Eduardo dos Santos in March 1984, "The Angolans know that we have never charged for our military aid; we cannot pay all the expenses, such as feeding our troops, but we pay their salaries, and no one knows how many millions of pesos our military assistance has cost us. . . . Our soldiers are internationalists; they are not mercenaries."[61]

## Cuba's Technical Assistance to Angola

"The abysmal lack of basic skills within the Angolan population" struck every observer.[62] The exodus of 90 percent of the 320,000 Portuguese living in Angola in 1974 had deprived the country of its skilled labor force, from managers to taxi drivers, leaving behind a population that was 90 percent illiterate. Four days after arriving in Luanda in April 1976, Raúl Castro informed Havana that the Angolan government had requested aid from other communist countries, "but everyone, from President Neto and the other leaders down to the ordinary people in the most remote corners of the country, is hoping for Cuban assistance. This is natural, given our participation in the war, the fact that our languages are so similar, our ethnic background, and the prestige of our revolution."[63]

The aid had already begun to flow. The first Cuban doctors had arrived in Angola in late November 1975, a few days after the first troops. The following July *Jeune Afrique*, not a friend of Havana's policy in Africa, reported: "Huambo [Angola's second city] lives in fear that the Cuban doctors may leave. 'If they go,' a priest said recently, 'we'll all die.'. . . [When] a Cuban medical team arrived on March 7, only one Angolan doctor and a Red Cross mission were left [in Huambo]. The latter . . . left at the end of June. The Cuban medical teams play a key role throughout the country." A year later, the Angolan delegate to the World Health Assembly told Carter's special assistant for health, "[The] most important contribution [in health care] has been from Cuba with no strings attached. We only had 14 doctors, but now we have more than 200, thanks to Cuba."[64]

By the end of 1976, more than 1,000 Cuban aid workers were in Angola, and more were arriving. "Seventeen years of revolutionary rule under Fidel Castro had made them a tight, disciplined and well 'groomed' lot," a correspondent of the major black South African newspaper wrote from Luanda. "Monday through Saturday they can be seen working industriously. . . . The impression is indisputable. The Cubans not only won the war for the MPLA, they are now intent on pulling the country back together for them through a dozen different reconstruction programs." U.S. intelligence agreed: "Havana provides the vast majority of the foreign military, technical, and social welfare personnel currently engaged in supporting the Neto government," a memorandum said in September 1976. "At present it faces little competition and no other government is likely to supplant the Cubans. Portugal, because of its own political and economic uncertainties and the strained state of relations with Luanda, is in no position to offer assistance." Nor was any other Western government going to step forward. Furthermore, "with the exception of its contribution of military assistance, even the Soviet Union has not yet made a significant direct contribution to Angola's post–civil war development." The Cubans were everywhere, trying to fill the void left by the Portuguese—"Cubans are supervising port operations in Luanda and Lobito, running airports and communications facilities, and rebuilding roads and railroads. They are restoring Angola's once lucrative fishing industry, building up its modest sugar industry, and providing a broad array of administrative support. . . . Neto, an ardent nationalist, probably wants to lessen the Cuban presence in his country as rapidly as possible, consistent with national stability. On the other hand, Cuban advisers are in key positions at all levels of the Angolan administration and military power structure, and Neto undoubtedly realizes he cannot do without them."[65] Cuba was footing the bill. "We are paying for the food for our aid workers," Risquet reported, "for their salaries in Cuba, and for the cost of bringing them to Angola." The French chargé in Luanda wrote, "Since its creation, the People's Republic of Angola has received expressions of support only from the socialist countries, combatants and aid workers only from Cuba, arms only from the Soviet Union."[66]

Neto asked the Cubans to increase their aid. "It was stipulated," in agreements signed in June and December 1976, "that the cooperation during 1977 would continue to be free of charge and that the Angolan government would provide the board and lodging for the Cuban aid workers, and would give each of them US$30 in the Angolan currency every month [roughly 1,000 kwanzas at the official exchange rate] as pocket money. Beginning in the second half of 1977, Angola would also pay for the international transportation of the aid workers."[67] By November 1977 there were 3,355 Cuban aid workers in Angola.[68] Contrary to the agreement, it was Cuba, and not Angola, that provided them with pocket money, 1,000 kwanzas per month.[69] "It was peanuts," remarks Gina Rey, a young architect who worked in Angola for two years beginning in late

1976; "but there wasn't anything to buy anyway." In late 1977 the Cuban Embassy opened a small shop in Luanda where the aid workers could spend their kwanzas before returning to Cuba, if they had any left. "The pickings were very slim," says Aleyda Escartín. "1,000 kwanzas didn't go far," Isabel Martín remembers. "One guayabera [a shirt] could cost 700 kwanzas."[70]

The aid workers spread through Angola's cities, living in buildings that were often in disrepair as a result of the war. They ate in community dining halls. In those first years, everything was organized on the run. The meals were at best monotonous. "What Angola contributed was very little," Emiliano Manresa, the embassy's economic attaché, points out. "There were many difficulties that the Angolan side could not overcome . . . the fundamental burden fell on Cuba." Aleyda Escartín remarks, "You had to eat whatever they gave you, because there was nothing else." Gina Rey recalls, "The food we ate arrived from Cuba. We ate whatever the ships brought. If a ship arrived with canned sardines—it was sardines all the time. Another time, it was SPAM from the Netherlands." The aid workers remember the SPAM with particular vehemence. "They gave it to us very often; we ended up hating it," muses José Antonio Choy. "It was canned ham, very fatty, no one liked it," remarks Guillermo Domínguez. "We ate SPAM for lunch, for dinner, it was never-ending," adds Rolando Carballo.[71]

The aid workers were volunteers. Most were in their twenties, and many had left behind spouses and children, though in a few cases couples went together. "I was married and had two children, aged two and four," Serena Torres, a nurse who arrived in Angola in May 1976, told me. "My husband and I agreed that I should go." She had volunteered for a year. In those first years, some aid workers went to Angola for twelve months, others for 18, a few for two years. According to Angola's needs, some groups of volunteers were asked to extend their stay by six months, or by one year. "At the end of the year they asked us to stay longer. Some agreed. Others didn't and returned home." Serena chose to stay. Like all who decided to remain a second year, she returned to Cuba for a one-month vacation. At the airport in Havana her husband and her two children were waiting for her. "I explained to them that I had not come back to stay."[72] The Cuban government continued to pay aid workers the salaries they had been earning before leaving for Angola. (The money was either paid directly to their families or deposited in a bank account under their name.) The pocket money was minimal and the same for all. There was no financial benefit. Some volunteers were doubtless motivated by the desire to impress their neighbors or their government. Curiosity, and a sense of adventure, may have influenced many. But, the CIA said, they represented the new generation that had grown up under Castro and "are instilled with a high degree of nationalism, motivation and self-esteem."[73] Internationalism—the duty to help others—was at the core of the Cuban revolution. For Castro's followers, and they were legion, this was not rhetoric. Aleyda Escartín wrote to her child, "We are in good health and working hard to help the Angolans carry out the revolution to overcome misery, ignorance and backwardness."[74] It may sound like propaganda—but the letter was not in a government archive or on public display when I found it; it was in a box in Aleyda's apartment, among the letters she had sent her child from Angola and other family mementos. Of course, some might argue that she wrote these words thinking that a government official might read them. But there was no doubt about the pride with which she spoke of her Angolan experience when I interviewed her thirty years later. Her name had not been suggested to me by a government official; she was merely the friend of a friend. The most reasonable explanation is that her words reflected what she and many of those who volunteered to Angola sincerely believed. In late 1979 the CIA concluded, "Service in Angola remains popular with the youth."[75]

## The November 1977 Agreement

Since its beginnings in 1963—when the first Cuban medical mission had gone to Algeria—Cuba's technical assistance had been free of charge. By 1975, approximately 1,000 Cuban aid workers had gone to a dozen African countries, South Yemen, and North Vietnam.[76] In 1976–77, technical assistance was extended to Jamaica and Guyana in the Western Hemisphere; to Angola, Mozambique, and Ethiopia in Africa; and to Laos in Asia.[77] The CIA noted: "The Cuban technicians are primarily involved in rural development and educational and public health projects—areas in which Cuba has accumulated expertise and has experienced success at home."[78]

By 1977 there were more than 3,000 Cuban aid workers in Angola, far more than in any other country, yet Neto wanted their number to increase. Under these circumstances, Havana argued, the technical assistance could no longer be free. The negotiations about compensation began in Luanda in August 1977 and were supervised by Jorge Risquet, the head of the Cuban civilian mission in Angola. Risquet was a figure of the first rank—he was a member of the Communist Party's Secretariat, he had a close working relationship with Fidel Castro, and a close personal friendship with Raúl Castro. He had long-standing ties with Neto and the MPLA: for eighteen months, beginning in August 1965, he had headed the Cuban mission in Congo Brazzaville, which had been the main rearguard base of the MPLA. "He knows Africa and is an old friend of many of us," Neto told Raúl Castro in April 1976.[79] As head of the Cuban civilian mission, Risquet ranked above the ambassador. His task was to maintain a close contact with Neto and the top Angolan officials, take care of the most difficult issues, work closely with the head of the Cuban military mission, and report directly to Fidel and Raúl Castro.

In late September 1977, Risquet wrote to Fidel Castro, "As soon as comrade Levy Farah [a senior Cuban aid official] arrived with your instructions, we analyzed what would be the best way to present Cuba's position to the Angolans. I decided to prepare a detailed memorandum."[80] The memo, which Farah presented to the Angolans, explained,

> Cuba offers technical assistance to several countries free of charge. But the assistance involves only a limited number of aid workers. Our technical assistance to Angola could continue to be free of charge, as it has been in 1976 and 1977, if it involved only a few hundred aid workers. But if we are talking of thousands, our economy cannot bear the burden.
>
> These constraints on our economy did not prevent us from extending military assistance [in 1975–76], because what was at stake was the freedom of a people, the independence of a nation, and preventing one more crime of the imperialists. We did not hesitate. Nor did we stop to consider the costs. The greatest cost of military aid is in human lives, which are priceless. But in monetary terms, our military effort in Angola cost us several hundred million dollars in 1975 and 1976 and now it represents more than one hundred million dollars per year. This is a very heavy burden for our economy, but we consider it a sacred duty toward the Angolan Revolution. . . .
>
> But we cannot afford on top of these military expenses the cost of sending ten thousand aid workers whose salaries would be entirely paid by Cuba.

Cuba sought, however, to make the burden for Angola as light as possible:

> We have asked our people to accept the greatest sacrifice: that they travel without their families, for twelve months, that they share a bedroom with another aid worker, and that they eat in communal dining rooms. . . .
>
> The aid workers who go to Angola receive no personal benefit, only the satisfaction of having done their internationalist duty. Unlike other countries, we do not offer material inducements to those who participate in internationalist missions. We merely pay the aid workers their full salary in Cuba, the same amount that they were earning when they left on the mission. . . .

We provide all aid workers with the same lodging, food and pocket money, be they high-level specialists or skilled workers. . . . Of course, in Cuba a medical doctor earns more than a carpenter, but here in Angola they all receive the same treatment.[81]

On November 5, 1977, the two countries signed a cooperation agreement that took effect on January 1, 1978. It established seven categories of salary, ranging from $1,200 to $250 monthly. Most aid workers belonged to the middle categories: engineers, doctors, and economists who earned $815; midlevel technicians, high school teachers and nurses who earned $630; and skilled workers who earned $470. The top earners were the advisers to senior officials; the lowest were a handful of unskilled workers.[82]

Angola agreed to pay these salaries to the Cuban government, 50 percent in hard currency, and 50 percent in kwanzas, which were nonconvertible. Cuba would use half of the kwanzas to defray the living expenses of the aid workers, and the other half to import Angolan products.[83] But Angola's exports went to Western countries that could pay in hard currency. Risquet recalled, "I had a room full of kwanzas. I didn't know what to do with them. There was nothing we could buy—I think that on one occasion we used them to buy a shipment of coffee." In late 1983, Risquet told President dos Santos, "We have a lot of kwanzas that we have received for the technical assistance, and we have nowhere to spend them. Our ambassador is a millionaire."[84] In February 1984, the Cuban Embassy had 572 million kwanzas.[85]

In 1978 there were almost 7,000 Cuban aid workers in Angola, including 1,199 women. They were present in every province. The largest groups were teachers, construction workers, and health personnel.[86] In his visit to Angola in March 1977, talking with a group of senior aid workers, Castro had expressed a dream: that by 1980 there would be 1 doctor for every 10,000 Angolans—this meant 500 Cuban doctors, 150 Angolans, "and about 60 from other countries. Medicine is the most important sector for the consolidation of the Angolan revolution. . . . It is the revolutionary weapon par excellence in the construction of socialism."[87] The number of Cuban doctors in Angola continued to increase, from 112 in 1976 to 223 in 1977, 324 in 1978, and 336 in June 1979.[88] Cuba also helped train Angolan doctors and specialists. "Cuba's medical aid was exceptional," recalls Angolan general Tozé Miranda, a doctor who headed the FAPLA's medical services. Testifying before a U.S. House subcommittee in late 1980, one of the few Americans who had an intimate knowledge of Angola— Professor Gerald Bender, not noted for his Cuban sympathies—said, "I think in certain sectors the Angolans are extremely pleased with the Cuban help and they have good reason [to be]. . . . Particularly in the medical field, where they [the Cubans] have been very, very successful, and in construction. . . . Since construction was completely paralyzed with the departure of 300,000 Portuguese the Cubans went in and sort of finished up the buildings that were started and began building many new ones. You could not find a single Angolan that would criticize the Cubans for doing that."[89]

## The Island of Youth

In Cuba an experiment was under way. In the late 1960s the government had decided to build boarding schools in the countryside for high school students. The students would combine their studies with light agricultural work for three hours a day to learn the value of manual labor. The government decided that the Island of Pines, lightly populated and beginning to be cultivated with citrus groves, would become a center for these high schools. In his speech inaugurating the first school on the Island of Pines in June 1971, Castro said, "When we have 30,000 students here in schools like this, then this will truly be, in every way, the Island of Youth."[90] In August 1978, the Island of Pines was officially renamed the Island of Youth.[91]

The previous year, in Luanda, Raúl Castro had told Agostinho Neto that the Cuban government wanted to open four schools for Angolan students on the Island of Youth. Each school would house 600 students. Raúl Castro "explained at length what steps would be taken to ensure that the young students did not lose touch with their native land. He stressed that it was necessary that they be accompanied by several Angolan teachers who would hold classes on the history and geography of Angola and the Portuguese language, as well as by Angolan political cadres who would be responsible for the students' political education." Angola should send students who had completed fourth grade, so that they would not be too young to leave home. They would study on the Island of Youth until they had completed high school. Upon graduation, they could remain in Cuba to attend a university, or technical school, or military academy.[92]

In Maputo, President Samora Machel learned of Cuba's offer and "asked Fidel if Mozambique could also send some of its children to this island." Castro agreed, and "Mozambique acted with lightning speed. A few weeks later the Mozambican students arrived."[93] The first two schools for 1,200 Mozambican students opened their doors in September 1977. The CIA reported, "The students are subjected to basically the same curriculum as Cuban students, including part-time labor in the isle's citrus industry."[94]

A second group of 1,200 Mozambican children arrived in March 1979. They were accompanied, the Zambian Embassy in Maputo reported, by sixteen Mozambican teachers "who will give them lessons in Portuguese, history, geography and political education." With their arrival, the number of Mozambican students on the Island of Youth rose to 2,400.[95]

Angola lagged behind. The first Angolan school on the Island of Youth was opened in November 1977 with 421 students. By the end of 1978 there were only 1,200 students, filling two of the four schools Cuba had offered.

## Cuba's Aid to the Liberation Movements: ZAPU

Agostinho Neto had told Raúl Castro in April 1976 that just as Cuba had fulfilled "its internationalist duty by extending such generous aid to the Angolan people, . . . Angola will in turn . . . offer its support to others, especially the peoples of Africa oppressed by the racists."[96] These were not empty words. On December 20, 1976, Risquet wrote to Fidel Castro that Neto would allow SWAPO, the African National Congress of South Africa (ANC), and the Zimbabwe African People's Union (ZAPU) to have military camps in Angola and that he would grant them "every facility" to receive help from other countries, especially Cuba and the Soviet Union.[97]

Castro was eager to help. "The struggle for liberation is the most righteous endeavor," he said.[98] Helping SWAPO, the ANC, and ZAPU became a tripartite effort: the Cubans provided most of the instructors, the Soviets the weapons, and the Angolans the land.

ZAPU was one of Rhodesia's two guerrilla movements and the only one that had close relations with the MPLA through the decade preceding Angola's independence. In April 1977 the Cubans began preparing a large training center for ZAPU at Boma, in eastern Angola, near the border with Zambia. Then, on June 25, Operation Z-4 began: a column of Cuban trucks left Luanda for a trek of 4,622 kilometers. They drove over dirt tracks and bridges in disrepair to the ZAPU camps near the Zambian capital, where they delivered Cuba's gifts: ten trucks, thirty tons of blankets, and forty tons of other supplies. They returned to Angola with 2,000 ZAPU trainees. On July 24, the column reached Boma.[99] On August 1, the first training course began. The Cubans had promised ZAPU's leader Joshua Nkomo that they would train 6,000 ZAPU guerrillas in Boma in three courses over an eighteenth-month period. This was "possibly the largest school of this kind in the world," Risquet told the Soviet ambassador in Luanda.[100]

After the first training course had ended, Operation Z-5 returned the guerrillas to their camps in Zambia, and brought back a new batch of 2,000.[101] A third group followed. On October 21, 1978, the third course concluded, "and with this," the head of the Cuban military mission informed Havana, "we have fulfilled our promise to ZAPU to train 6,000 of its combatants. Actually we have trained 168 more."[102]

The Soviet Union had provided the weapons and the uniforms.[103] It also sent ten instructors when the camp opened in July 1977. "We remember our Cuban comrades with affection," recalls one of these instructors. "They were efficient, good humored, honest, and friendly."[104] The Cubans directed the training center, and most of the instructors were Cuban. When the third course ended, in October 1978, the Cuban roster included 154 officers, 4 sergeants, and 26 soldiers.[105] "The training they gave our soldiers," Nkomo writes, "was better and more realistic than that offered by almost any other country, and I am deeply grateful for it."[106] At Nkomo's request, a Cuban "medical mission" of about twenty went to work in the ZAPU guerrilla camps in Zambia. Half of them were indeed medical personnel, the others were military instructors and advisers under cover. Zambia's President Kenneth Kaunda knew of the ruse and had given his blessing.[107]

When Rhodesian planes struck Boma, on February 26, 1979, there were 1,552 ZAPU guerrillas, 125 Cubans, and 6 Soviets in the camp. For the Rhodesians, it was a good day: they killed 207 (including 6 Cubans) and wounded 533.[108] But Boma had already accomplished its mission: 6,168 ZAPU guerrillas had been trained there.

Cuba had kept its promise, but it had little impact on the course of the war in Rhodesia. Very few ZAPU guerrillas actually fought there. Nkomo kept most of his forces in Zambia, in part for geographic reasons—entering Rhodesia from Zambia was difficult because of the mighty Zambezi River that separated the two countries. Those who bore the brunt of the fighting were the guerrillas of ZANU (Zimbabwe African National Union), who entered Rhodesia from their bases in Mozambique. Cuba had no military ties with ZANU.

But if Cuba's impact on the war on the ground was slight, much more important, as we shall see, was its impact on the Rhodesia policy of the Carter administration. This was its major contribution to the independence of Zimbabwe.

## Cuba's Aid to the African National Congress

For the ANC, Neto's victory had been a key turning point. Until 1976, most of the guerrillas of its military wing, Umkontho We Sizwe (MK), had been trained outside of Africa. "Most of us received our training in the Soviet Union, some in China, a few comrades . . . went to Cuba in the 1960s," recalled Che Ogara, a senior MK commander.[109] After the detention of Nelson Mandela and other MK leaders in 1962, ANC activity in South Africa virtually ceased. By the early 1970s, a few hundred guerrillas vegetated in camps in Tanzania and Zambia, and the ANC's influence among the South African population was greatly diminished. But Mozambique's independence in 1975 signaled the victory of a black liberation movement over white overlords; a few months later Cuba humiliated South Africa in Angola. This "was very much on the minds of his 700 students," the principal of a black school in Soweto told a *New York Times* journalist in February 1976. "It gives them hope."[110] Three months later, Soweto exploded. Young black students defied their parents and their teachers to challenge the apartheid state in waves of strikes and demonstrations that were met with extreme brutality.

Che Ogara noted that "what emerged from Soweto was . . . a completely new generation that understood, all of a sudden, the need for armed struggle. They had grown up without knowing much about the ANC." Many left South Africa and sought out the ANC. The movement political headquarters were in Lusaka, but its military camps were now in Angola, and it is there that the new recruits would be trained, by Cuban instructors. "In 1976–77, approximately 1,000 young people joined us," Che Ogara recalled. "We had the immense advantage of our base in Angola, and we also had the advantage of having Cuban comrades by our side." The ANC's main camp was at Novo Catengue, forty-five kilometers southeast of the city of Benguela. "There were over 500 MK recruits undergoing training and a large contingent of Cuban officers and men in the camp," writes Ronnie Kasrils, an MK leader who worked at Novo Catengue in 1977. The Cubans "were in charge of the training programme and the logistics supply. . . . It was pleasant being in a camp with the Cubans. They were full of fire and passion and reminded me of the Red Army officers who had trained us in Odessa [in 1964]." As Cosmas Sechaba, an MK guerrilla who arrived at Novo Catengue for training in 1977, remembers, "There were Cuban doctors in military uniform living at Novo Catengue. The Cubans ate what we ate, slept in tents like us, lived as we did." An ANC commission of inquiry later noted, "Military instruction (by Cuban comrades assisted by MK stalwarts) was of a high quality."[111]

Initially, all the instructors were Cuban, but in October 1978 the ANC requested that the Soviets join in the training. As Vladimir Shubin, the foremost authority on Soviet relations with the ANC, explains, "The initiative to involve the Soviets came originally from Havana. The matter had been raised with ANC leaders by Jorge Risquet. . . . The Cubans had become involved in training ANC cadres as soon as they arrived in Angola. . . . When they raised this new issue the Cubans either wanted to lighten their own burden, or to have the Soviets more deeply involved. Or—the most likely option—they wanted a combination of both." A Cuban document tells the story: in August 1978 Risquet had told ANC president Oliver Tambo that "because of our economic situation it was necessary for the Soviets to join in the training and help defray the costs. . . . Tambo agreed in principle, and he asked Risquet to help prepare a report itemizing the needs of the ANC that he would give the Soviets during his forthcoming visit to Moscow."[112] It worked. In late 1979 three Soviet military instructors and an interpreter arrived in Angola.[113] "So," Shubin writes, "seventeen years after the first discussions in Moscow in 1961, the participation of Soviet instructors in the training of Umkhonto [MK] fighters on African soil was at last possible."[114] The three instructors and their interpreter joined forty-four Cuban instructors at Pongo, near the little town of Quibaxe, in central Angola, where the major ANC training camp had been relocated following a South African air strike against Novo Catengue on March 14, 1979. Other Soviet instructors followed, but it is unlikely that there were ever more than half a dozen at any given time. After the sudden influx of recruits to the ANC following Soweto, the flow dried up. Tambo told a Cuban official in September 1979 that the ANC faced great difficulties "taking a militant out of South Africa. Of course these departures are illegal. At times his men are captured before they reach the border."[115]

Nevertheless, MK was by the late 1970s active again in South Africa for the first time since the early 1960s: small teams of guerrillas who had been trained by the Cubans in Angola infiltrated into South Africa. Its reappearance was dramatically underscored in June 1980 when in a single night MK guerrillas attacked three strategic fuel installations in the Johannesburg area, "igniting fires that could be seen nearly fifty miles away." As a South African scholar writes, "The ANC's revival as a political force inside South Africa was also an effect of the resumption of Umkhonto's military operations."[116]

## Cuba's Aid to SWAPO

Until 1975, SWAPO had been based in Zambia.[117] From there, small groups of SWAPO insurgents had entered the eastern districts of northern Namibia by trekking either through southeastern Angola—where Portuguese and South Africans hunted them—or directly from Zambia into the narrow band of the Caprivi strip, Namibia's eastern panhandle, where the South Africans awaited them.

After the MPLA's victory in Angola, SWAPO moved its political headquarters from Lusaka to Luanda and established its military headquarters near the city of Lubango in southern Angola. SWAPO guerrilla units, based now in Angola, began crossing into northern Namibia. "Our geographic isolation was over," SWAPO's president Sam Nujoma wrote. "It was as if a locked door had suddenly swung open. . . . For us . . . [it] meant that . . . we could at last make direct attacks across our northern frontier and send in our forces and weapons on a large scale." The South African military commander in Namibia agreed: "For the first time they [SWAPO] obtained what is virtually a prerequisite for a successful insurgent campaign, namely a border that provided safe refuge."[118] SWAPO lost no time. In late April 1976 South African Military Intelligence reported that "more than 400" insurgents had entered the Ovambo region of Namibia from Angola and that "more than 70 percent of the local population supported them." Two months later, Military Intelligence warned that SWAPO was "a formidable enemy. Freedom of movement in Angola, growing international support, a relatively high standard of training and a well organized propaganda machine, are all factors that contribute to the fact that SWAPO's morale is good." The report assessed SWAPO's military strength at about 2,400 trained fighters; two years earlier, by contrast, there had been "only a few hundred of us at most," a SWAPO commander recalled.[119]

Whereas Cuba's relations with the ANC and ZAPU dated from the early 1960s, contacts with SWAPO had been established only in late 1975, after the arrival of the first Cuban troops in Angola. In March 1976 groups of SWAPO fighters were flown from Zambia to Angola. They landed at Luanda's military airport. "It was the first time I had seen a Cuban," recalls General Charles Namoloh, who belonged to one of these groups. "I said, 'What kind of people are they? They aren't black, and they aren't white!'" Like several of his friends, Namoloh had received military training in the Soviet Union, and it was the Soviets who took the lead in providing military training to SWAPO in Angola. Soviet instructors arrived before their Cuban colleagues, and in larger numbers.[120] The Cubans welcomed the Soviet initiative: "Regarding the Soviet training center for SWAPO, give it our enthusiastic support so that we will be able to invest fewer resources," General Casas, first deputy minister of defense, told the head of the Cuban military mission in Angola in January 1977.[121]

But if the Soviets took the lead in military training, it was the Cubans who provided medical assistance. Cuban doctors worked at SWAPO's main training center and also visited small guerrilla camps in the Angolan countryside. Haydée del Pozo, a wisp of a woman who was then in her early thirties, was one of these doctors. "We would drive for two or three hours in a jeep," she recalls. "Me, the SWAPO guide, a Cuban soldier and sometimes a male nurse. We were armed. We were our own escort." At small SWAPO camps, she treated mainly men, a few women, and some malnourished children. Malaria and anemia were rampant. "The malaria ate them up. I saw people suffering from extreme anemia, who were very weak, and yet they were on guard duty. It took heroism to shoulder a gun when suffering from such acute malaria and anemia."[122]

In late 1977 Cuba agreed, at Nujoma's request, to bring Namibian children to the Island of Youth to study there. It also agreed to open a school in Angola where the young Namibians chosen to go to Cuba could first learn Spanish.[123] "We went around looking for a suitable place for the school," recalls Mwetufa Mupopiwa, who was SWAPO's liaison officer with the Cubans for this project. They finally found some abandoned buildings near Chibia, a village forty-two kilometers south of Lubango. "The Cubans had to do a lot of work to repair that place; they were all very old buildings." In January 1978, the school opened with more than 100 students from age eleven to seventeen. Cuba provided the teachers. "It also supplied the food, the furniture, the household necessities and so on," Mupopiwa remembers. "It was my little grain of sand—my contribution—to Namibia's independence," remarks Feliberto Fortun, the school's director and also a teacher.[124]

In May 1978 the South African massacre at Cassinga added new urgency to SWAPO's desire to educate Namibian children in Cuba. Risquet told Nujoma, "I am worried about the Namibian refugees in southern Angola. I'm afraid that at any moment the racists might launch more surprise attacks and again slaughter children, women, and old people."[125] In late 1978, 600 Namibian children arrived on the Island of Youth to study and grow up far from the South African bombs. "Cuba took the majority of the children who survived Cassinga," recalls Claudia Uushona, who was one of those children. The German Democratic Republic took about eighty, Czechoslovakia and Yugoslavia took a few.[126]

The Namibians who went to the Island of Youth brought with them the trauma of Cassinga. And the fear of white faces. "We thought of white people as South Africans. When you saw white people you were scared," explains Marcus Nixon, who was five years old when the South Africans attacked Cassinga. "The first Cubans I ever saw were the soldiers who came to Cassinga," recalls Sophia Ndeitungo, another Cassinga survivor who was twelve years old at the time. Among them were whites. "We thought they were South Africans. Later, we understood that not all whites are bad."[127]

Like the Angolan and Mozambican students who had preceded them to the Island of Youth, the Namibians were accompanied by a few teachers from their own country, who would teach them English, and the history and geography of Namibia. The other teachers were Cubans. Claudia Uushona remarks, "It's incredible what those professors did for us. They were mothers and fathers to us, not just professors."[128]

Uushona's words showcase Cuba in a very favorable light, as does the account of Havana's aid to ZAPU, the ANC, and SWAPO presented in these pages. I have looked for criticism of the Cuban aid program to these liberation movements but have found none. The Cuban documents on which I rely might be self-serving, but they are consistent with the testimonies of members of the three liberation movements—what they have written and what they have told me—as well as the recollections of Soviet participants. Cuban aid to ZAPU, the ANC, and SWAPO—its training for the guerrillas and its scholarship program for youth—was well run and effective.

## The Namibian Negotiations

While the Cubans helped SWAPO, the South Africans were trying to construct a puppet regime in Namibia. In March 1977 the Turnhalle conference approved a constitution for an interim government that, under South African supervision, would lead the country to independence in name only. The document provided for a three-tiered system of government: a central administration with a national assembly and a council of ministers; provincial governments for the country's "White Area" and each of the ten homelands; and local administrations. The U.S. State Department explained that "at the bottom line, ethnic divisions will be the controlling principle . . . [this system] gives whites the power of veto over all actions of the national government." It was, the CIA said, an "uneven compromise" between the whites' determination to retain their privileges and black expectations expressed, however timidly, by some of the tribal chiefs who had been shepherded to the Turnhalle conference; it preserved the existing "extreme disparities in economic conditions." U.S. ambassador William Bowdler reported from Cape Town: "South Africa will continue to exercise considerable influence over South West Africa [Namibia] during the interim government period and well beyond. . . . A South African military presence will also remain in Namibia as long as the threat of outside attack continues." He added, "No powerful personalities have emerged to take the lead among the non-white Turnhalle delegates. The delegates have shown themselves to be cautious and willing to bow to white pressure."[129]

It was to derail South Africa's unilateral initiatives in Namibia—the internal settlement—that the Carter administration had created the Contact Group in March 1977. In April, in Cape Town, the ambassadors of the Contact Group—the United States, Great Britain, France, Canada, and West Germany—delivered a forceful message to Prime Minister Vorster: "in the absence of early South African agreement to pursue a settlement" based on Resolution 385—which demanded independence for Namibia through free elections under UN supervision—their governments "will be obliged to reconsider their previous positions regarding proposals for stern action against South Africa by the United Nations." The note "was a work of art," U.S. ambassador McHenry muses. "We did not say it explicitly, but the South Africans understood what we meant: don't count in the future on a veto to protect South Africa from sanctions in the Security Council."[130]

Vorster was willing to talk—except about one point: the 436-mile enclave of Walvis Bay, which included Namibia's only deep-water port and was the site of a major South African military base. The South African government asserted that Walvis Bay belonged to South Africa, not to Namibia, because it had been annexed to the Cape Colony in 1884 and its status as a British enclave had been recognized by the Anglo-German agreement of 1890. But all colonial powers could justify their arbitrary rule by referring to a treaty, imposed on cowed natives or negotiated with other colonial powers. As UN secretary-general Kurt Waldheim told President Carter, Walvis Bay was "not a legal problem, but a matter of decolonization. It must be part of Namibia."[131]

Walvis Bay was Namibia's vital link with the outside world. The country's limited rail system connected the capital and major mines with Walvis Bay, and with only one neighbor, South Africa. Therefore, writes a knowledgeable scholar, "Closing the harbor to Namibia would imply severing the rail link with the interior, vital for the export of mineral products and the import of bulk material, petroleum and consumer goods." If South Africa also closed the border, Namibia would be virtually cut off from the outside world. "By retaining Walvis Bay, South Africa would thus be able to retain Namibia in a state of dependency and economically to destabilize the country, if she decided to do so."[132] As Pretoria's powerful State Security Council noted, "On psychological, political, economic and military grounds Walvis Bay is a trump card for South Africa."[133]

At the Contact Group's insistence, Vorster shelved the constitution that had been approved by the Turnhalle conference. Instead, he appointed a retired South African judge to the new post of administrator general of Namibia. Vorster had not renounced the internal settlement. He had simply adopted a two-track strategy: while appearing to negotiate with the Contact Group about an international settlement under UN auspices, he continued to jockey behind the scenes for an internal settlement. The administrator general's first task would be to forge a Namibian political system that would carry out Pretoria's will—that is, the CIA explained, "a coalition of conservative elements from each ethnic group that would continue to welcome the South African counterinsurgency forces" and would be adorned "with sufficient trappings of Namibian nationalism" to create an illusion of independence.[134] On November 6, 1977, the day before the Turnhalle conference ended, a loose grouping of eleven ethnically based parties—one white (the National Party of South West Africa), two mulatto, and eight black—established the Democratic Turnhalle Alliance (DTA). "Nonwhite participants," the CIA noted, "are mostly traditional tribal chiefs."[135] The National Party included "moderates" who were willing to make some concessions to black aspirations as long as the whites maintained the bulk of their privileges. This was too much, however, for the white hard-liners. The National Party split: the moderates, led by Dirk Mudge, a rich farmer, created their own party, which became the engine of the DTA. The rump National Party, led by Abraham du Plessis, was isolated. The *Windhoek Advertiser* drew a sympathetic portrait of du Plessis. "Perhaps . . . [his] most striking feature," it wrote, "is the considerable degree of sadness, of disappointment, that he expresses. . . . The country, which he so dearly loves, . . . is, in his opinion, drifting in the direction of a dangerous unknown."[136] But Namibia was not drifting toward the unknown: it was being pushed by South Africa in a very clear direction. Mudge and his "moderates" were Pretoria's chosen instrument. The administrator general's task was to ensure, through whatever means, that the DTA become Namibia's dominant political force, able to defeat all opponents in a UN-supervised election, should one be held.

The threat to the DTA's dominance was not the white hard-liners, impotent without South Africa's support, but SWAPO. SWAPO, the U.S. ambassador to South Africa said in March 1977, "has, over the years, in the mind of the population come to symbolize independence, equal rights, and freedom from South Africa."[137] The South African security forces and the tribal constabularies that had been created under South African tutelage responded to SWAPO's growing guerrilla actions by unleashing a reign of terror. Terror was most fierce in the northern districts, home to more than half the population, where SWAPO was particularly active.

While the fighting escalated, the Contact Group continued its efforts. It spoke with South Africa and with the Frontline States—Tanzania, Zambia, Mozambique, Angola, and Botswana, plus Nigeria. There was a division of labor: the Frontline States, three U.S. officials wrote, "assumed the responsibility of obtaining SWAPO's agreement to a reasonable settlement plan while we [the Contact Group] assumed the same role vis a vis South Africa."[138]

SWAPO president Sam Nujoma sought the Cubans' advice about the ongoing negotiations. "We do not criticize Nujoma in any way for negotiating with the West, we simply warn him about the dangers and urge him to be very careful," Risquet reported to Castro after meeting with Nujoma in early September 1977. The Cubans encouraged SWAPO to strengthen its hand by intensifying the armed struggle and to be flexible, except on key points. "There are two issues that I think are not negotiable," Risquet told Nujoma: "The total withdrawal of South Africa's armed forces . . . [and] Namibia's sovereignty over Walvis Bay. . . . Everything else is open to discussion. Summing up: do not give in on these two points, do not refuse to negotiate, and, meanwhile, keep intensifying the armed struggle."[139]

In mid-September 1977 Steve Biko, one of South Africa's most charismatic black leaders, died in police custody after being savagely beaten. This was nothing unusual for the apartheid regime—Biko was the twentieth detainee to die in police custody since March 1976.[140] But his prominence transformed his death into an international scandal and set off a storm of protest and outrage throughout Africa and even in the West. Then, on October 19, the regime banned eighteen opposition organizations and shut down the *World*, South Africa's most important black newspaper. Finally, the Western governments responded. On November 4 the UN Security Council unanimously approved an arms embargo against South Africa. It was the first time that the council imposed mandatory sanctions against Pretoria. "We wish good relations," the South African secretary for foreign affairs told Brzezinski a few days later; "we want to know whether this is possible." He added, "Prime Minister Vorster has no intention of going back on his assurances concerning Zimbabwe and Namibia, but undoubtedly a shadow has been cast over those two issues. We will still try to carry out our promises on them." Brzezinski was sympathetic, but he offered no solace: "The death of Steve Biko and the events of October 19 pose an international issue. It [*sic*] provoked a considerable amount of US moral and political opposition to South Africa. . . . This has occurred in a process that is both national and international over which we have little control."[141]

In late March 1978, the Contact Group presented its proposals to South Africa and SWAPO. Its plan called for free elections under UN supervision for a constituent assembly, and it included several concessions to Pretoria. Resolution 385 had demanded that South Africa leave Namibia before the elections to preclude any possibility of intimidation. The CIA had warned, in May 1977, "The mere presence of South African police and troops during an election would probably discourage voting for SWAPO, even though international supervision would restrain them from coercive practices."[142] The Contact Group, however, stipulated that the elections would be held with the South African administrator general still in office, working with the UN special representative;

the South African police would retain primary responsibility for law and order, albeit under UN supervision; and 1,500 South African soldiers would remain in the country, although restricted to one or two bases, until the certification of the elections. Namibia would become independent by December 31, 1978. Walvis Bay was not included in the plan, and this meant that it would remain in South African hands.[143]

On April 25, 1978, South Africa accepted the plan. SWAPO, however, objected to several of its provisions. Talks between Nujoma and the Contact Group to address these issues had been scheduled for May, but on May 4 the SADF launched its devastating assault on Cassinga.

Perhaps the South Africans did not realize, as they planned the attack, that Cassinga was a refugee camp; perhaps they really believed that they were targeting a major SWAPO military base. The answer may be in an unopened file in the South African archives, or the relevant documents may have been destroyed. But one thing is certain: as Vance writes in his memoirs, "Given the size of the attack and the prior intelligence work and military planning required, it seemed that Pretoria must have been preparing the raid even as Vorster was agreeing to our . . . [March] proposal [about Namibian independence]."[144] Certainly, Pretoria understood that SWAPO would respond to the attack by backing out of the negotiations—and one of the raid's objectives, if not its main objective, was, as a foremost Namibian scholar writes, "to induce SWAPO to reject the Western proposals (at least temporarily) to allow South Africa to get its internal option in place in Namibia."[145]

It worked. SWAPO did suspend the talks. The United States enlisted the aid of the Frontline States to nudge Sam Nujoma back to the table. Among the Frontline States, Angola was the key. "Neto has much more influence with Nujoma than any of the other frontline presidents," Tanzania's foreign minister pointed out, "because SWAPO must operate from Angolan territory. While other frontline presidents can 'tell Nujoma off,' only Neto has sufficient leverage on SWAPO to compel acceptance of Western Five [Contact Group] Initiative."[146]

In early 1976, flush with victory over South Africa, Castro had intended to keep his army in Angola until the MPLA had created a strong FAPLA—a task that would require at least several years. But the Soviets had insisted "that we proceed to a rapid withdrawal," Castro recalled, because they "worried about the possible reaction of the Yankees."[147] The Cubans had eventually agreed to withdraw their troops in three years. This eliminated a source of strain not only with the Kremlin but also with the incoming Carter administration. In

1977 Havana's relations with Washington improved, and the first steps toward normalization were taken. But after Shaba I, Cuba halted the withdrawal of its troops, and after Shaba II it sent reinforcements to Angola—a decision triggered by the arrival of French and Belgian troops in Shaba, the South African massacre at Cassinga (and the lack of a Western response), and the talk in Washington of repealing the Clark Amendment.

There is no indication in the reams of Cuban documents I have examined that Havana consulted the Soviets in 1978 before deciding to reinforce its troops in Angola, or that the Kremlin objected to the decision. By then it was obvious that there was a growing South African threat against Angola, and it was equally clear that the Cuban troops were Angola's only defense against it. Moscow was committed to the survival of the Angolan regime. It maintained an important military mission in the country, it was Angola's sole arms supplier, and it had been given access to naval and air facilities in Luanda. A Soviet general who served in Angola wrote that three of the eleven ships of the 30th Brigade of the Soviet navy were based there and that "Soviet reconnaissance planes Tu-95RZ landed regularly in Luanda."[148]

Furthermore, Neto had opened his country to the ANC, SWAPO, and ZAPU, three movements that had long enjoyed Moscow's support, and he had invited Cuba and the Soviet Union to train these movements in Angola.

The South Africans knew all of this. The reasons to defeat the MPLA in 1975 were even more compelling in 1978 when Angola had become a rear base for their worst enemies—the guerrillas of the ANC and SWAPO. Either they crush the MPLA, or the threat against apartheid would grow.

South Africa's wrath posed a deadly menace to the MPLA regime. Through 1977 Neto had relied exclusively on the Soviet Bloc, but by 1978 he was eager to develop relations also with the West. His country's economy was in shambles, and recovery required more than a few thousand Cuban aid workers. Angola needed foreign capital, and this could come only from Western Europe and the United States. Above all, Angola needed security from foreign—that is, South African—aggression, and the best way to achieve this was for Namibia to gain its independence, creating an essential buffer between Angola and South Africa. But only the United States and its allies had the leverage to make Pretoria loosen its hold on Namibia. Closer relations with the West would have the added benefit of lessening Angola's dependence on the Soviet Union, which had proved to be a dubious ally during the Nito Alves coup, and on Cuba—a loyal friend but too close to the Soviet Union for comfort. By mid-1978, Neto was ready to approach the United States.

## CHAPTER 4

# Strained Relations
## Cuba and Angola

## The U.S.-Angolan Minuet

Carter "was of two minds about Angola," Vance writes. "His instinct was to work with the Angolans to help them reduce the insecurity problems that had caused the introduction of the Cubans into Angola and that now served to justify their retention. . . . But politically Carter was sensitive to Cuban activities and the impact they would have at home if we appeared too soft in dealing with them. This led us to step back from the brink every time we came close to establishing diplomatic relations."[1]

On June 1, 1978, UN ambassador Andrew Young and his deputy Donald McHenry met with Angolan prime minister Lopo do Nascimento and foreign minister Paulo Jorge, who were in New York for the special UN session on disarmament. The Americans expressed their concerns—namely, the Katangan invasion of Zaire, the Cuban troops in Angola, and the negotiations on Namibia. The Angolans, in turn, expressed theirs: Zaire's support for the Angolan insurgents and, above all, the threat from South Africa. Young reported, "Nascimento said that everyone seemed to be complaining about the Cubans while ignoring the attacks of South Africa on Angola. . . . He said that attacks from the South Africans and indirectly from Zaire made it difficult for Angola to maintain non-alignment. . . . He expressed a desire for continuing communication with the U.S. There was a sense of helplessness about Nascimento. He seemed resigned to attacks by South Africa and Angola's inability to control its territory. It was also emphasized that Angola needed U.S. help if it was to avoid alignment, i.e., dependence on the Soviets. This is the same plea we have heard since 1975. It is uttered without bitterness or frustration but clearly a plea for help."[2]

A few days later, the Angolan representative to the United Nations conveyed to Young and McHenry an urgent message from Neto, "asking if it is possible for 'someone' from the United States to visit Luanda." Neto's message "spoke of the importance of U.S.-Angolan relations on a range of issues, including Namibia, Zaire, Cuba," and expressed the hope that the meeting "would occur soon. . . . Angola did not wish to dictate who should represent the U.S. side but felt that Ambassador McHenry, with a suitable mandate, would be acceptable to Angola."[3]

On June 22 McHenry and an aide, Don Junior, arrived in Luanda for three days of talks. McHenry, who was the administration's point man on Namibia, had already traveled several times to Luanda with the Contact Group to discuss the Namibian negotiations with the Angolan leaders, but, the State Department noted, "this will be the first time since Angola's independence that U.S. officials have visited Luanda outside the context of the Namibia Contact Group."[4]

McHenry's instructions were straightforward. On June 14, Brzezinski had sent Vance a memo that said, "The president has been informed that Angolan President Neto is anxious for a U.S. official to visit Luanda to discuss U.S.-Angolan relations. The president has determined that we might consider an unofficial visit focusing on these issues: 1. Namibia; 2. Neto and Savimbi; 3. Withdrawal of Cuban troops; 4. Recognition." In a later memo, the White House elaborated: "Our strategy in meeting with the Angolans is to open the prospect of an expanding dialogue with us, which could in time and depending on Angolan actions on key issues, lead to normalization of relations. Specifically, we will seek their cooperation in reaching a Namibia settlement; progress toward internal reconciliation with Savimbi; willingness to improve relations with Zaire; and withdrawal of Cuban combat troops."[5]

During eight hours, on June 22–25, Nascimento and Pascual Luvualu, the MPLA official in charge of foreign relations, met with McHenry and Junior. According to McHenry's report, Nascimento "said he wished to lead his remarks on specific issues, by sketching the principles which drive Angolan policy. He would arrange for his visitors to tour Luanda to see the harsh realities which his government faces: the fundamental need for food, housing, clothing and medical care for the Angolan people. It was those realities which shape Angolan policy. Years of struggle for independence had created in Angola a vision of what independence means. The Angolans look to the government to fulfill its promises. The Angolans have opted for socialism. Usually the socialist experience in Africa has been associated with governments which have not been successful in solving their economic problems. But the Angolans were determined that their socialism would be one of welfare, not of misery. . . . This theme," McHenry remarked, "was the core of the Angolan presentation, and colored the Angolan view of every issue: the need for peace, for security, for freedom from multiple external and internal threats in order to devote Angolan resources to resolution of the massive developmental and social problems of the Angolan society."[6]

In reading McHenry's report, one can sense that he was sympathetic to the Angolans' plight, but he had his instructions. The issue of Zaire was quickly disposed of: the Angolans were willing to improve relations with Mobutu, even though they did not trust him. But U.S. demands for a negotiated settlement with Savimbi were met, predictably, by a flat refusal. "This is an internal problem," Nascimento said, "one for us to solve without outside intervention."[7]

McHenry noted: "During course of discussions, delegation found it necessary to emphasize . . . that . . . the United States government is providing no assistance, direct or indirect, to Angolan dissident groups, including UNITA, and that we are prepared to discuss the point of such aid with others." The words "we are prepared to discuss the point of such aid with others" were underlined by Carter, who wrote on the margin: "This seems to contradict my instructions."[8] In fact, Carter had good reason to complain, given that his government was providing assistance to UNITA.

On the need for the Cubans to withdraw from Angola, the Americans were categorical. McHenry reported: "We did make clear, on a number of occasions, that the indefinite presence in Angola of large numbers of Cuban troops will continue to be a very real and difficult problem for progress in our relationship."[9] Nascimento was equally firm. Stressing that Angola was threatened by South Africa and Zaire, he said, "It is no bargain, for us or for the Cubans, to maintain large numbers of Cubans here. But they are here to secure our territorial integrity. Our preferred solution is political, to remove the threat from our borders." The presence of the Cubans was not negotiable: "We could not accept conditions which would remove the Cubans from here in order to achieve diplomatic relations with you. . . . The Cubans are here and will remain here. There is no other way to maintain our independence, as costly as the burden may be."[10]

Reflecting on the visit, a State Department cable noted, "No 'breakthrough' was sought or achieved. No arrangements were made or date set for subsequent bilateral discussions, but we anticipate they will occur as need arises."[11]

The trip's most important result was to enlist Angola's support with SWAPO. McHenry reported that Nascimento "made no commitments but said, 'We must work fast and together' on Namibia." McHenry concluded, "We have impression GOA [government of Angola] will use its influence favorably with SWAPO." (Carter's skeptical comment on the margin was, "We'll see.") A few days later, on July 12, SWAPO accepted the Western plan for Namibia's independence without changes. "Angola had played key role in pressuring SWAPO to agree to settlement," a State Department official noted.[12]

Summing up McHenry's visit, Vance wrote Carter that the talks "were cordial, frank and comprehensive. The Angolans are clearly motivated by a pervasive sense of insecurity based on the perceived external threat, primarily from South African forces in Namibia, but also from Zaire." The two sides had "essentially agreed to disagree" on two issues: the Cuban presence and reconciliation with Savimbi. "On Namibia, the Angolans showed recognition that they and we have a mutual interest in finding a settlement. . . . On Zaire, the Angolans showed strong interest in cooperating to bring about a solution"— provided Mobutu too was willing.[13]

McHenry's June visit to Luanda was followed by another, again at Neto's request, in late November. In Brussels, on November 8, Luis de Almeida, Angola's ambassador to Belgium, gave his government's draft agenda for the talks to the political counselor of the U.S. Embassy, Arthur Olsen. Almeida was, Assistant Secretary of State for Africa Dick Moose noted, "Angola's senior European ambassador . . . [and] at present our principal channel to Neto."[14] The agenda focused on Angolan security, Namibia, normalization of relations with the United States, trade, and technical cooperation. "When I noted that this was a comprehensive and substantive list," Olsen reported, Almeida replied that Neto "would be pleased to spend an entire week" with the U.S. delegation "to review these central objectives." Almeida stressed "strong Angolan interest in normalization with U.S. . . . [and] spoke of urgent need for technical assistance, trained personnel, capital and project support, and foreign investment. . . . I noted . . . broadly based American concern at Cuban troop presence . . . Almeida seemed so eager for rapid normalization that I thought it best to suggest on personal basis that a modest step by step progress toward better understanding might prove more realistic. . . . The recurrent theme [of Almeida] was deep concern for security."[15]

On November 21 Assistant Secretary Moose arrived in Angola, accompanied by McHenry and Jerry Funk, an NSC staff person for Africa. ("Jerry was sent by Brzezinski to keep an eye on us and make sure we didn't do anything we shouldn't," Moose remarks.)[16] "Dick Moose and Don McHenry met with the Angolans for two and one-half hours this afternoon in Luanda to discuss Angola's security concerns," Deputy Secretary of State Warren Christopher told Carter. "The Angolans said they . . . are deeply concerned about the situation along the Namibian frontier. They asked for our help in restraining South Africa." The Americans expressed their deep concern about Cuba's presence in Angola. Christopher reported that "the Angolans related Cuban withdrawal from

Angola to a Namibia settlement and left no doubt that the removal of South African forces from their southern border is their basic security objective."[17]

But a Namibian settlement seemed less and less likely. In September, South Africa had flatly rejected UNSC Resolution 435, which spelled out the provisions for Namibia's independence. The Angolan government, Foreign Minister Jorge remarked drily, "doubts that [the] Group of Five will exert sufficient pressure on SAG [South African government] to bring about SAG cooperation with UNSC resolutions on Namibia."[18] As events would prove, he was right.

When one pieces together Moose's and McHenry's recollections of their 1978 trips to Luanda with the available documents, a split picture emerges. On Namibia, there was a fruitful exchange. "Namibia—that was the main point," Moose recalls, "to seek the Angolans' assistance with SWAPO. The Angolans were very cooperative on the subject of SWAPO." On relations between Angola and the United States, however, the two governments were at cross-purposes.

The Angolans wanted to establish diplomatic relations with the United States, and they worried about South African aggression. The Americans wanted the Cuban troops to withdraw but offered no substitute to shield Angola from the South Africans. When Foreign Minister Jorge asked "in a very pointed form, 'If we were convinced that the SAG was about to carry out further aggression against Angola, what would the US do?'" the Americans' reply was not reassuring. Moose said that "much would depend on the circumstances of such an event. Origins of and responsibility for violence are often difficult to determine with so many armed forces in the area. In any event we would take back to Washington the question raised by Jorge." Jorge remarked, "Despite a variety of contacts at various levels, GPRA [the Angolan government] believes USG [the U.S. government] had not given serious consideration to normalization." This was accurate, since the precondition was the departure of Cuban troops. He pointed out the inconsistency in the U.S. demand that Cuba withdraw its troops. "Jorge asked rhetorically whether US in recognizing Djibouti [the former French colony that had just become independent] had taken into account the presence of some 7,000 French troops there at this time." What was the difference, he implied, between Djibouti being defended by French soldiers and Angola being defended by Cuban soldiers? It was a fair question, but the answer was obvious: Cuba was not France. Washington believed that France, a U.S. ally, had the right to keep troops in Africa while any Cuban military presence was, by definition, an act of aggression. There is no indication, in the U.S. report, that Moose bothered to answer.[19]

A few days later, on December 11, Senator George McGovern (D-SD) arrived in Luanda, where he met Neto. It was the first visit by a member of Congress in more than two years, the *New York Times* reported. On his return to Washington, McGovern told Vance that he "found Neto 'loud and clear' in his desire for normalizing relations with us and genuinely interested in reducing Angola's dependence on the Soviets and Cubans. McGovern believes we should move promptly toward recognition," Vance wrote Carter.[20]

## Neto Searches for a Way Out

Neto wanted to improve relations with the United States, to receive Western economic aid, and to lessen his dependence on the Soviet bloc, including Cuba. He indicated his feelings at a press conference that he gave to a group of American journalists who had accompanied McGovern to Luanda. "There was a moment," he told them "when it seemed to us as though the leadership of our party was not following our own ideas, but was following ideas that came from outside." And when a journalist asked "where did these ideas come from?" Neto answered, "From all sides."[21]

The stumbling block to a rapprochement with the United States was the presence of the Cuban troops. As Neto said, "The Americans promise that they will come in when the Cubans get out."[22] But it was not the Cubans who insisted that they stay. It was Neto himself. Even more than U.S. recognition and aid, Neto wanted to protect his country from South African aggression. Pretoria's attack on Cassinga and the Western response in the second Shaba crisis made him feel more vulnerable. He wanted to reduce the danger by supporting a negotiated settlement in Namibia, and he was pressuring SWAPO to make concessions. This earned him repeated praise in Vance's memoirs: Neto and the Angolan leadership "proved to be vigorous supporters of a negotiated solution," Vance writes; they "were making [in the spring of 1978] an exceptional effort to dissuade Nujoma from blocking the Contact Group proposal."[23]

Neto, however, would also continue to support SWAPO and armed struggle until the negotiations succeeded. And he was not optimistic that they would ever succeed. Pretoria's bad faith, and the Contact Group's unwillingness to resort to sanctions, deepened his pessimism. On December 2, 1978, he reiterated that he supported "complete freedom of action for SWAPO on Angolan territory, so that it can infiltrate as many fighters as possible into Namibia and intensify the armed struggle to the greatest possible extent."[24] He told Castro, when they met in Havana the following January, that the South Africans "are not willing to leave Namibia. They want to stay there." When Castro asked, "What do you think SWAPO should do?" Neto replied, "Fight. I see no alternative to war." He told East German leader Erich Honecker, in February 1979,

"We believe that Angola, together with the other progressive countries, must continue to help SWAPO as much as possible."[25]

Neto supported the Contact Group's negotiations on Namibia, but he was acutely aware of Pretoria's intransigence. Nor were the U.S.-led talks on majority rule in Rhodesia faring any better, and so Neto agreed to ZAPU leader Nkomo's request for greater Angolan logistical aid to his rebel movement—"We will make one more sacrifice," he told Risquet on December 5, 1978. In a major speech five days later, Neto was accompanied, as guests of honor, by SWAPO president Nujoma and Nkomo, and he expressed his total support for their struggle, "which is also our struggle."[26] And he continued to support the ANC.

Neto knew that these policies provoked Pretoria, but he saw no alternative: the MPLA had the duty to assist in the liberation of southern Africa, just as it had been helped in its struggle for the liberation of Angola. He believed that South Africa, which was supporting Savimbi, was determined to destroy the MPLA. "They will attack us in any case," he told Risquet. He was right. Pretoria's State Security Council concluded in March 1979: "The aim of the strategy of the SA government is to further the establishment of a well-disposed or at least neutral government in Angola and to perpetuate its existence after it has come to power. Angola must eventually form part of a community of states in Southern Africa." Clearly, that government could not be the MPLA. In Washington, an NSC Africa specialist summed it up well: "The big boogy man in Angola is 'our' South African forces on their southern border."[27]

## Luanda and Havana: The Bloom Fades

As Neto's statement decrying influences "that came from outside" indicates, there was tension in Cuban-Angolan relations. Neto was searching for a way to appease the United States and enlist U.S. aid to restrain South Africa. From this perspective, the Cuban troops in his country were an obstacle. And it was human to forget at times why they were in Angola and focus instead on the problem they presented. Furthermore, after the agreement with Havana of September 1978, the Cuban presence entailed an economic cost for the Angolan government, which had grown used to having the Cubans pay all expenses.

Neto was also trying to improve relations with America's allies in Western Europe. In September 1978, Brzezinski had told Carter, "In recent months, several West European countries have received overtures from the Angolan government for diplomatic links and economic cooperation." Neto was looking "toward the green pastures of the West," the French chargé in Luanda reported.[28] The Angolans set particular hope on Portugal. Relations with Lisbon, strained since independence, had finally improved after the two countries had signed an agreement in June 1978 that provided, in principle, for Portuguese technical assistance.[29] Many Angolan officials preferred this to relying on the austere Cubans. The ethos of Cuban assistance had been epitomized by Fidel Castro during his March 1977 visit to Angola, when he met with a group of senior aid workers. Addressing the role of Cuban advisers in the Angolan Foreign Trade Ministry, Castro said: "Help them to buy well, to buy cheap. . . . They should buy food, books, clothes, soap, toothpaste, etc. Eliminate all luxury products. . . . Our duty is to give them advice, to advise them well, and to make sure that they don't get cheated, even if they are negotiating with a Cuban firm." Two months later, a few days after the Cubans had helped defeat Nito Alves's coup, Raúl Castro stressed the same message to the same group in Luanda: "Do not abuse their trust. Be even more careful because this trust is greater today."[30] This was very ethical, very uplifting, but also frustrating for enterprising Angolan officials eager to improve their personal circumstances, to provide for their own and their families' welfare. The Cubans offered no bribes and no expensive gifts. The contrast between this rectitude and the allure of Western culture, in a country that had been used to Portuguese ways, was stark. "The Portuguese and the Westerners promise them [Angolan officials] holidays in their countries," Neto's successor, José Eduardo dos Santos, later noted. "They [Westerners] offer good hotels, . . . perks, gifts, and they corrupt them."[31]

There was another, pervasive, factor, a grievance against the Cubans that was shared by many Angolan officials. Neto had said something very insightful to Raúl Castro in the spring of 1976, when Raúl had brought up the behavior of an Angolan commander in Cabinda who was very aggressive in his dealings with the Cubans. Neto "explained that it is very important to remember that the Angolan cadres are itching to decide everything about their country, after so many centuries in which they couldn't decide anything."[32] In the first years after independence the pervasiveness of Cubans in Angola was extraordinary— because of the lack of skilled Angolans at every level of the bureaucracy. This bred resentment. As Manuel Agramonte, who was Cuba's ambassador in Luanda in 1976–79, points out, "We were mature enough to be in Angola without undermining the country's sovereignty, but you can't ignore the fact that the extent of our role created resentment."[33]

There were Cuban advisers who were arrogant and patronizing, but the evidence—documents and interviews—suggests that they were atypical. What is striking is the respect with which the Cubans treated the Angolan government. Nothing illustrates this better than the two Shaba crises. The Angolans had known about the Katangans' plans to invade Zaire in March 1977, but they did not inform the Cubans. After the invasion, the Cubans expressed their disapproval, but they neither lectured not punished the Angolan government. Instead, they agreed to Neto's request that, to protect Angola from possible retaliation, they suspend the phased withdrawal of their troops, even though this meant straining relations with Washington. In February 1978, after learning that the Katangans were preparing to attack again, Castro sent Risquet to Luanda with a memorandum urging Neto to restrain them. Neto promised Castro that the Katangans would not be allowed to launch a second invasion, but three months later invade they did, with obvious Angolan complicity. Once again, Cuba's response was not to lecture, but to come to Angola's assistance sending reinforcements to protect it.

The interaction between Angola and Cuba during the two Shaba crises shows clearly that Neto was at no moment a Cuban client—and at no moment did the Cubans try to treat him as one. On the contrary, the Cubans bent over backwards to treat Neto with respect and deference. It is striking that, even when provoked, they did not threaten to withdraw their support, on which Neto depended; instead, they consistently respected Angolan sovereignty. This is rare in international relations.

## Neto and Castro

In January 1979 Neto visited Havana, where he had two lengthy tête-à-têtes with Castro. In the first, they surveyed the situation in southern Africa. Then Neto said, "I think it is better to end this meeting now, before we start talking about our bilateral relations." Castro agreed. "Right, Comrade Neto. It is important that we discuss our relations, Cuba's technical assistance, your opinions, the complaints and criticism you might have, and your wishes. It is important that we talk about the Cuban troops in Angola, your views, your opinions, the ideas that you have about this."[34]

In their second tête-à-tête they began with military matters. Neto suggested that some Cuban troops could be withdrawn to save money. He noted that relations with Zaire had improved (thereby reducing the threat from the north) and that "when we talk with the Americans the number one problem is how many Cuban soldiers are in Angola and when they will leave." Castro readily agreed. "Fine," he said. "Tell me, then, what's your plan: How many soldiers should we withdraw? Where do you think we should start reducing personnel?" He unfolded a map of Angola with the location of the Cuban troops. When Neto replied that he was thinking "of the regiment based in [the city of] Uige [in the north]," Castro continued: "Let's see exactly how many soldiers this regiment has. It has 1,370 men. Do you want us to withdraw the entire regiment, or only a part of it? We should analyze what's more effective—to withdraw the entire regiment or to leave some men to take care of the weapons and serve as a symbol [of our presence] there. What do you think?" Neto replied: "I think you should leave some men behind to take care of the materiel that will be left there, like tanks, antiaircraft weapons, and communication equipment."

> *Castro*: "Right, a drawdown, but not a complete withdrawal of the personnel."
> *Neto*: "Yes, not a complete withdrawal."
> *Castro*: "What other troops do you want us to withdraw?" . . .
> *Neto*: "None."

Castro then noted that a few more troops could be safely withdrawn. When he asked, "How many soldiers would you like us to withdraw, more or less?" Neto replied, "I don't have a precise figure." He had no concrete suggestions beyond Uige. When Castro asked, "Would you like us to analyze whether we could withdraw other troops without weakening our defenses in the south and in Cabinda?" Neto stressed the need for caution: "We must study it carefully," he warned. He did not trust Mobutu and his Western allies, who could use Zaire as a base against Angola; and he was clearly ambivalent about how to deal with Washington's pressure. While on the one hand it was the main reason he wanted to withdraw Cuban troops, on the other hand he stressed, "when I speak of the possibility of reducing the personnel of a [Cuban] regiment, if we don't proceed with great caution it might seem that it is a concession to the American imperialists, because they are pressuring us on this issue." Castro suggested that it might be possible to reduce the number of Cuban troops in Angola "by 2,000 or 3,000 . . . leaving between 20,000 and 21,000 men." Neto listened, without expressing either approval or disapproval.

While Neto remained silent, it was Castro who continued to speak. His impassioned words to a man he deeply respected are worth quoting at length.

> I tell you in all sincerity that you must intensify your training of the FAPLA, because, look, Comrade Neto, you pay a price for our presence, and it is also a great sacrifice for us. I am not speaking of the economic cost. . . . When we helped Angola [in 1975–76] we didn't even think about the money. It was a critical juncture in history and we sent the troops. . . .
>
> The problem is not just economic. We have to ask tens of thousands of our men to leave their country for a year, eighteen months, two years. The cost in human terms is enormous. . . .

For us, therefore, it is important that you strengthen the FAPLA as quickly as possible so that you will be able to assume the responsibility of defending your country. I understand that this is not possible now, because South Africa is there, and it is a very powerful country; Zaire is also there—today it is behaving, but this could change tomorrow.

Therefore, I urge you to do everything you can to prepare the FAPLA, so that one day, Comrade Neto, we will be able to withdraw our troops. Our presence [in Angola] limits our ability to help other countries, because we have 40,000 soldiers abroad. . . . If some day it were necessary to help Mozambique . . . Right now, with the effort that we are making in Angola and in Ethiopia, we are stretched to the limit. . . .

This is why I think that you must do whatever you can to speed up the preparation of the FAPLA. . . . So that in the future we will be able to reduce our troops.

Castro stressed that its commitment to Angola represented an economic burden for Cuba but that he worried above all "about the human cost, the demands upon the energy of the population, and the people's willingness to sacrifice. I believe that in the right circumstances the people are willing to do anything . . . but one must not abuse this. Otherwise some day you might encounter mission fatigue, a kind of exhaustion, because this effort requires great sacrifice for tens of thousands of families who have a son, or a father, or a brother abroad. I know that it is necessary sometimes to make this effort, but I also know that it has to be done sparingly."[35]

The two leaders also discussed Cuba's technical assistance. Neto asked Castro to withdraw the Cuban advisers to ministers, department directors, and other key officials. Castro encouraged Neto to reduce his country's dependence on Cuban technical assistance. "Please study this issue," he said.

Examine it, and then tell us: "We want 3,000 aid workers, or we want 2,500." And if you ask us for fewer than 1,000, we will provide them free of charge. . . . You must ask for as few aid workers as possible. . . . If you cut the number from 6,000 to 3,000, I am happy. . . . In all the other African countries, except for those that are rich and export oil, we don't charge for our technical assistance. . . . We will have almost 1,000 aid workers in Ethiopia, and it will be free of charge; we have about 600 in Mozambique . . . it is free. . . . In São Tomé we have more than 100 . . . it is free. And in Guinea Bissau, Congo Brazzaville, Tanzania, in all the countries of Africa our technical assistance is free of charge. But in Angola we can't afford it, because we have thousands of aid workers. We can't; we really can't. . . . If we had the same number of aid workers in Angola that we have in Ethiopia or Mozambique, then we wouldn't charge you. The day that you cut the number we will be glad. . . . There will be fewer problems, fewer sources of disagreement—we will have fewer worries, Comrade Neto. I will be more relaxed, much more relaxed. . . .

You must determine how many aid workers you really need. . . . I think that it is proper that your country seek to train its own cadres. I think that this is an internationalist duty of Angola, the internationalist duty to try to train your cadres, civilian and military. . . . This will help us. . . . One way for Angola to fulfil its internationalist duty is to depend as little as possible on the assistance of Cuba, in both civilian and military matters.[36]

Over the next few months, the two governments agreed to reduce the number of Cuban aid workers, which decreased from almost 7,000 in early 1979 to less than 4,000 by late 1980.[37] In their stead, came Western experts, particularly Portuguese. The Zambian ambassador in Lisbon reported in April 1979, "Several high-powered delegations have visited Luanda mainly in order to resume economic ties. . . . The Portuguese overtures for trade [and] cooperation are apparently being received warmly." Senior Portuguese and Angolan officials met in Lisbon the following July "in an atmosphere," *Jornal de Angola* said, "of frank fraternity and genuine sincerity."[38] By 1984, 6,000 Western experts hired by the Angolan government worked in the country.[39]

Cuban senior advisers had provided a bulwark against corruption. As they departed, "the control of the economy became looser, corruption and waste increased, the efficiency in the administration decreased," Neto's successor observed.[40] Looking back at those early years, Julio de Almeida, who was Angola's deputy minister of transportation from November 1976 to December 1983, remarked, "The Cubans were extremely valuable. We couldn't have done it by ourselves; we had no experience whatsoever." When I asked whether he had problems with his Cuban advisers, he smiled. "The Cuban believes that he knows everything; he has a very high degree of self-confidence; in some situations they made mistakes, but what they did was extraordinary. . . . The Cubans accepted their role as advisers. They offered advice, but they did not impose their opinions."[41]

## Changes in Angola

In 1979, after three years in Angola, Cuba trimmed its sails. The Cuban civilian mission disappeared; and Risquet returned to Havana, where he resumed his work as a top government official. Henceforth, the senior Cuban civilian representative in Angola would be the ambassador, who ranked lower than Risquet.

The battlefront was also changing. In January 1979, Cuba stopped participating in the fighting against UNITA. The military mission informed Angolan defense minister Carreira that the Cuban advisers in the counterinsurgency units would be withdrawn. The FAPLA, the Cubans argued, had received sufficient training in counterinsurgency operations, Savimbi had been weakened, and Cuba's task was to defend Angola from foreign aggression.[42] (Whereas the assessment of the FAPLA's counterinsurgency skills was wishful thinking, there is no doubt that Savimbi had been weakened and that, from the outset, Havana had insisted that its role was to defend Angola from foreign aggression, not internal enemies.)

Havana also decided to withdraw its forces in the extreme south of Angola. It would instead create strong positions some 250–300 kilometers north of the Namibian border along a line that stretched from the port of Namibe on the coast to the town of Menongue in the east—a distance of 700 kilometers. The reason was simple. The South African air force was much stronger than the Cuban air force in Angola (to say nothing of the puny Angolan air force), and it flew from modern airports in northern Namibia, close to the border. The airports that the Cubans could use, on the other hand, were far from the border, and the Cuban troops lacked powerful antiaircraft weapons. Castro told Neto in January 1979:

> As you know, Comrade Neto, after [the South African attack on] Cassinga [in May 1978] we spoke with the Soviets, and we told them that we had to strengthen our position in the south. . . . We have developed a plan to strengthen our position along this line. . . . The enemy has control of the air. . . . Therefore, we want to create conditions in Lubango [the major city of southern Angola, 250 kilometers north of the Namibian border] that will allow our air force to operate. We propose to place surface-to-air missiles, so that the enemy air force will not be able to operate there with impunity. We will send as many antiaircraft weapons as possible . . . as well as planes to this region. Our air force there will not be strong enough to take the offensive, but . . . I believe that we can create a strong defensive line there . . . around Namibe, Lubango, Matala and Menongue . . . a line that the South Africans will not be able to cross even if they arrive with great strength.[43]

This Cuban defensive line barred the easiest and most direct access to the heartland of Angola and, by extension, to Luanda. To its south was a wide strip of territory that was scarcely populated and of limited economic importance. East of the line was the province of Cuando Cubango. For the South Africans to have invaded there with the intention of attacking Luanda would have required a long detour through a region crisscrossed by rivers and saddled with a very poor road network, even by Angolan standards—a region that was not suited to modern warfare.

Once the Cubans established the defensive line, the only military forces south of it were FAPLA units and SWAPO guerrillas on their way to Namibia. These FAPLA units were strong enough to keep UNITA at bay. Savimbi's guerrillas had no significant presence in the southwest. The real test would come if South Africa launched a major incursion in the territory.

## Neto Still Seeks a Way Out

One question remained. In Havana, in January 1979, Neto had proposed to Castro that the Cuban regiment in Uige, or part of it, be withdrawn, and Castro had asked Neto to determine other Cuban forces that could depart without endangering Angola's security. After Neto returned to Luanda, he received a memo from the Cuban military mission proposing the withdrawal of 4,500 Cuban soldiers. Neto backtracked. He told General Menéndez Tomassevich, the head of the Cuban military mission, that in Havana he had floated the possibility of withdrawing some Cuban troops but that he "does not consider it opportune—for Cuba or for Angola—to reduce troops at this time."[44] And so matters stood. "Comrade Fidel Castro rightly thinks," noted a Soviet official, "that it would be easy to withdraw the Cuban troops, but that this might precipitate the fall of the progressive regime."[45] Castro also believed that it was the Angolans' call. This is what General Casas, Cuba's first deputy minister of defense, told Neto in Luanda on May 4, 1979. Casas had not expected to see the president—as he noted in his report, he had gone to Angola to visit the Cuban troops; "taking advantage of this trip," he planned to discuss some technical matters with Angolan defense minister Carreira. However, "during my visit, no leader of the FAPLA was in Luanda; the minister of defense was in Rome, and the others were attending a four-month course in Huambo or on vacation, and therefore I could not meet with any of them." Neto learned that he was in town and invited him to his office. There was no formal agenda, and the conversation rambled, but Neto never mentioned the possibility of reducing the Cuban troops in Angola. This worried Casas. "It was the only outstanding issue," he wrote in his report, "and I was concerned that if I did not raise it the Angolans might infer that we don't want to leave. With hindsight, it is clear that I should have asked for instructions before leaving Cuba but I didn't." And so he improvised: when Neto failed to bring up the issue, Casas volunteered "that 'when' [Cuban troops would leave] and 'how many' was something that Neto alone should decide, as he and our Commander-in-Chief had agreed. Neto told me that he had not agreed to reduce the troops, only to study the matter. Laughing, he told me, 'I'll go to Cuba in September, I hope that by then the international situation will be more clear.' 'Well,' I said, 'this is something that you, the Commanders-in-Chief, decide; I want only to reiterate that my government's policy is that this is your decision.'"[46]

The problem was that Neto could not make up his mind. "The People's Republic of Angola, caught in a pincer at its independence by the Zairean and the South African troops, has since then developed a siege mentality," the French chargé reported from Luanda.[47] Neto was tempted by the benefits normalization with the United States would bring, but he did not trust the United States and its Western allies to restrain South Africa. And with good reason. President Félix Houphouët-Boigny of Ivory Coast, an ardent anticommunist and bitter foe of the Cubans, gently reminded the U.S. ambassador that "it was natural that Angolans . . . would be distrustful of Europe and the US" since neither had made "any real effort to convince Portugal of the importance of facilitating progress toward independence of its African colonies."[48] Then, in 1975, the Ford administration had joined with South Africa to crush the MPLA. The Carter administration had seemed to want better relations with Angola, but had done nothing. As UN ambassador Andrew Young pointed out to Carter in March 1979, "Angola has been very helpful in our attempts to find a UN solution for Namibia. They brought SWAPO along even when it required real pressure. . . . But . . . the Angolans find themselves humiliated by the bombings of their territory by South Africa and only *pro forma* criticism from the West."[49]

In a speech on the third anniversary of Angola's independence, on November 11, 1978, Neto vented his frustration: "We know the routine. After each savage act of aggression by the racists, the western powers wring their hands, launch new diplomatic offensives, and pretend that they disagree with their [South African] protégés. Time passes; the peoples of southern Africa bury their dead amid suffering, humiliation and pain. This is what happened after Cassinga." And he repeated, a few days later, "In all truth we can tell the Americans that we do not accept diplomatic relations with conditions. . . . They want us to ask our internationalist friends to leave so that the South Africans can attack us."[50]

Neto knew that the remedy was to bolster the FAPLA, but he also knew that this would take time. He told Risquet in December 1978 that he was aware of "the lack of discipline, the disorganization and the lack of fighting spirit of the

FAPLA, its general staff and the Ministry [of Defense]." He shared the belief of the Soviet and Cuban military missions that "the FAPLA's ability to respond [to an attack] was less than zero."[51] Therefore, his country needed the Cubans. The Namibian negotiations were stalemated, and the South African threat to Angola was increasing. In March 1979, the South Africans launched a major raid in southern Angola, advancing eighty kilometers beyond the border. The Western response confirmed Neto's fears. Together with France and Great Britain, the United States abstained on the Security Council resolution "strongly" condemning South Africa's raid, because it threatened sanctions.[52]

Through the spring and summer of 1979—in the last days of his life—Neto continued to search for a negotiated solution for Namibia. Seeking to appease the Americans, he again considered withdrawing some Cuban troops; the Cubans were consistently receptive.[53] Neto wanted the war in Namibia to end, he wanted relief from South Africa's attacks, and he wanted to devote his country's resources to economic recovery. Neto had "indicated," Vance told Carter, that a Namibian settlement would lead to a withdrawal or a "significant reduction" of the Cuban troops in Angola.[54] If the negotiations made no progress, it was not due to Cuban or Soviet interference. It was because of South African intransigence. Pretoria wanted a client government in Windhoek, and it doggedly opposed true independence. "The process is blocked by Pretoria's refusal to implement the Waldheim plan [UNSC Resolution 435]," the French chargé in Luanda remarked. "Angola is impotent and depends on the Western powers to make South Africa come around. [Foreign Minister] Paulo Jorge . . . said on September 26: 'The serious consequences that will inevitably result both in Namibia and in the region [from the failure of the negotiations] . . . will be the direct and full responsibility of the governments of the Five [the Contact Group]. This will be especially so if they decide not to use all the means at their disposal to apply pressure on South Africa.'"[55] Pretoria's growing aggression against Angola strengthened Neto's desire for a negotiated solution in Namibia, and it simultaneously made the Cuban shield more necessary. The CIA conceded, "Angolan officials can claim with some justification that 'the Cuban presence is necessary to preserve Angolan independence.'"[56]

On August 30, 1979, Neto received the new head of the Cuban military mission, General García Peláez, and the head of the Soviet military mission, General Vassily Shakhnovich. Neto was battling cancer, and he saw the generals at his house. "I have to receive you here and not in my office," he explained, "because my doctors have recommended that I stay in bed as much as possible." He wanted to broach two issues: the first "one is about the two regiments that we have planned to withdraw. There is a confusion about the origin of this decision." Rewriting history, he said that it had been Raúl Castro—not he—who had first raised this issue when he had visited Havana the previous January. "I said that the moment was not opportune. . . . That is, the proposal comes from Raúl Castro, not from us."

He had planned to discuss it again with Fidel Castro at the Non-Aligned Movement summit in Havana in September, but he was too sick to travel. "I can't go to Cuba now. It would have been a good moment to talk about this. However, I think that we can discuss it in other ways."

A brief exchange followed. "Comrade President," García Peláez said, "as you know it is a great sacrifice for Cuba to keep its troops here. We would be happy to withdraw some of them, but the Angolan government—you, Comrade President—must tell us which troops, when, at what speed." Neto replied that Defense Minister Iko Carreira "could work on these plans. Well, have we decided that two regiments will be withdrawn, or should we examine this again?" Iko Carreira, who was present, was cautious. "Comrade President," he said, "my proposal was that we study . . . what units could be withdrawn without endangering our defenses, examine the situation of the FAPLA, and analyze this with [García] Peláez and Vassily [Shakhnovich]. I think that this would be sensible. To simply assert that we will withdraw troops is not a good idea. We must get down to specifics."

Neto then said that there was a second issue he wanted to raise: Namibia. Angola needed peace. "We have a dire economic situation . . . we have been at war since 1961 [when Angola's war of independence began] and our people . . . especially the most poor, have such yawning needs. We cannot solve their problems . . . because of South Africa." He would continue to seek a peaceful solution in Namibia, but he had little hope that he would succeed. Therefore, the war would go on. He suggested that Cuba, the Soviet Union, and Angola work hard to better coordinate their efforts in support of SWAPO. This was important, he insisted.

García Peláez and Shakhnovich said very little. The conversation lasted only thirty minutes. Neto was tired. "We will talk again about all these problems in a few days," he said.[57]

Neto died eleven days later, on September 10, 1979. The person most apt to succeed him, his closest aide, the best prepared intellectually, and a man of extreme probity, was Lúcio Lara. Lara, however, was a light-skinned mulatto, and most Angolans distrusted and resented the mulattoes. Eager to avoid a divisive battle among the party leaders, Lara withdrew from consideration, a selfless act that robbed the country of the man most qualified to lead it.[58] Instead, the MPLA leaders chose thirty-seven-year old José Eduardo dos Santos, a close aide of Neto and a black. Dos Santos was a compromise candidate, the lowest common denominator, on whom all could agree. When he assumed the presidency, he was at best a primus inter pares. The result was, as Chester Crocker, Ronald Reagan's assistant secretary for Africa, writes, "a weak and fragmented regime. . . . Dos Santos had a healthy awareness that his presidency rested on the premise that he would respect the baronies around him and work for compromise among them." It would be years before dos Santos would consolidate his position. But the MPLA, as Crocker writes, "never recovered" from the death of Neto.[59]

## Cuba and Neto's Succession

A Cuban delegation led by Juan Almeida attended Neto's funeral. Almeida was one of the most prominent Cuban leaders, a hero of the revolution, but he was not closely involved in Angolan issues. He brought with him a letter from Castro. Addressed to the Political Bureau of the MPLA, it read:

> Dear comrades:
>
> During these sad days I have been wrestling with my desire to lead the Cuban delegation to the funeral of our beloved Comrade Neto. But I have decided that it would not be advisable, because you must now focus on the crucial selection of the person who is going to assume the immense responsibility of leading your country. The enemy is already alleging that Cuba is trying to influence your choice. My presence in Angola would fuel this slander.
>
> I believe that this moment of sorrow is also the supreme proof of Angola's complete independence and the maturity of its leadership. We, your friends, must do everything we can to draw attention to this reality.
>
> If I may take the liberty of suggesting one word, it is: Unity! Remain united so that the Angolan Revolution will triumph over the formidable obstacles that it faces, so that the life, the work and the revolutionary ideals of Comrade Neto become a beautiful and indestructible reality.
>
> We face several important decisions about our military and civilian cooperation. I had begun a profound analysis of these issues with Comrade Neto. . . . I repeat to you as a group what I had told Comrade Neto during our last encounter: Cuba cannot indefinitely continue to offer military cooperation on the scale it now does in Angola. It limits our ability to help revolutionary movements in other parts of the world and to defend our own country. Furthermore, the great sacrifices that it demands of our

people erode our reserves of strength. The most urgent internationalist duty of Angola at the present moment is to develop its defensive capacity to the utmost and without delay, so that all the Cuban soldiers—down to the last one—can return home. . . .

This is why I implore you to send a delegation of your Political Bureau with the power to discuss these issues to Cuba as soon as possible. We would be pleased to extend this invitation to the comrade whom you elect president, if he wishes to come.

Our future relations will be solid and indestructible as long as we uphold our principles and are mutually honest, frank, and sincere with each other.

I want to assure you, above all, that in this sad and bitter time Cuba will stand at your side unconditionally.[60]

After reading the letter, Lúcio Lara said on behalf of the Angolan leadership that they "had no doubt whatsoever" that they could continue to count on Cuba's solidarity. He noted that "indeed, as Neto had said, the circumstances might allow Cuba to withdraw some troops," and agreed "about the need to discuss some important questions."[61]

One month later, on October 16, Castro sent a message to the Cuban ambassador in Luanda, Jaime Crombet. "Jaime," he wrote, "Ask for a meeting with José Eduardo [dos Santos], and tell him that I have received no reply to my September 15 message asking the Political Bureau to send a delegation [to Havana] to discuss important problems that are pending. I need to know when they plan to send the delegation because these problems cannot be postponed indefinitely." That same day, October 16, 1979, Defense Minister Carreira informed the head of the Cuban military mission that the Angolan government had concluded that "no Cuban troops" should be withdrawn "for the time being."[62] The decision had been made against a backdrop of increasing South African attacks: in late September, South African planes had attacked Lubango, 250 kilometers north of the Namibian border, and the town of Xangongo, killing scores of people and wounding more than 100; then, on October 28, South African Special Forces, arriving in helicopters, blew up the bridge on the Serra de Leiba Pass and also the Humbe railway tunnel, killing FAPLA soldiers and civilians and disrupting rail and road traffic for several weeks along the important route from Namibe, the major port of the south, to Lubango.[63]

The Angolan government blamed South Africa for these assaults, but UNITA claimed credit for the attacks on the bridge and the railway tunnel, and Pretoria claimed to have had no involvement. The air strikes on Lubango and Xangongo, however, were harder to explain, since UNITA had no air force.

Nevertheless, the Western press did not investigate, and the Carter administration said nothing.

On January 1, 1980, dos Santos fired Iko Carreira as defense minister. The Cubans learned of the decision only "by listening to the news on radio and television."[64] This clearly indicates that dos Santos intended to continue Neto's independent policy. And, like Neto, he was in no hurry for the Cuban troops to leave. He told the Cuban ambassador that, given the intensifying military threat from South Africa, "the subject had to be analyzed again."[65]

The Angolans were not exaggerating the threat. In February 1980, the Secretariat of the South African State Security Council had summarized its government's policy toward Angola: "South Africa is not satisfied with the present Angolan government and works clandestinely to achieve its overthrow."[66]

Dos Santos arrived in Havana on March 17, 1980. The minutes of his conversations with Castro have not been declassified, but it was during these talks that the issue of the withdrawal of the Cuban troops was settled. As General Casas later told Soviet defense minister Dmitry Ustinov, "dos Santos spoke with Fidel and told him, 'Please, don't even think of withdrawing troops in the coming years.'"[67]

## South Africa Flexes Its Muscles

Their Angolan fiasco in 1975–76 had been a severe shock for the South Africans. For the first time since its creation, the South African Defence Force (SADF) had met a strong enemy—the Cubans. After Angola the apartheid regime faced new challenges: a stronger SWAPO, a resurgent ANC, and a harsher international climate, including a very unsympathetic Carter administration. But there were also positive signs. The bloody raid against the Namibian refugee camp at Cassinga provoked no outcry in the West. The Carter administration, which had come to power intent on pushing South Africa to renounce apartheid, soon lost its missionary zeal—relations were cold, but there was no significant pressure from Washington on Pretoria. In late 1978 Defense Minister PW Botha, a politician particularly close to the military establishment, became South Africa's prime minister. Under Botha, the influence of the military within the ruling councils grew. The State Security Council—a committee chaired by the prime minister that included the ministers of foreign affairs, defense, and police as well as the heads of the SADF and of the National Intelligence Service—replaced the cabinet as the dominant institution in the formulation of foreign policy. Its powerful secretariat was headed by a general and staffed by military officers.

In April 1979, PW Botha approved a "more pro-active stance for the SA Defence Force"[68]—"pro-active," that is, against South Africa's neighbors and, in particular, Angola. For Angola this was ominous. Cassinga had demonstrated the West's immense tolerance for South Africa's violence, the Cubans had withdrawn from Angola's far south, and no one expected the FAPLA to be able to repel an invasion. Small-scale SADF raids and air strikes into Angola became more frequent, provoking no reaction from Washington and its Western allies. Then, in June 1980, the SADF launched another major raid, advancing 180 kilometers into southwestern Angola.[69] The UN Security Council responded with a tough resolution condemning the invasion, and the U.S., French, and British representatives on the council minced no words in their speeches chastising South Africa. When it came to vote on the resolution, however, all three abstained because it included language that suggested that, if South Africa launched another attack, the Security Council might impose sanctions.[70]

Testifying to a congressional committee a few weeks later, Professor Gerald Bender said,

> My most recent visit to Angola this past June and July vividly dramatized the full extent of the South African threat to Angola today. During our 650-mile trip by road through two southern provinces, my wife and I saw continual evidence of South African air and ground attacks against the country. . . .
>
> We experienced the fear which grips every Angolan in the area, the fear of being hit by a bomb from one of the South African planes which fly over southern Angola almost every day and night. Dozens of carcasses of burned-out trucks and cars lie along the roads. Three were hit while we were in the area; one, in fact, was still smoking. Especially prejudicial to Angola has been the South African bombing of Government trucks carrying food, seeds, and other essentials to the starving people in the south.[71]

## CHAPTER 5

# The Fronts Harden

*The United States and Cuba, 1978–1980*

## Flowers in Cuernavaca

Cuba's intervention to defend Ethiopia from the Somali invasion ended the tentative rapprochement between Washington and Havana. Castro sought, however, to keep a channel of communication open. In February and March 1978, at the height of the crisis in the Horn, he proposed that the two countries hold informal talks.[1] Castro did not intend to make any concession about what the United States most wanted—the withdrawal of the Cuban troops from Angola and Ethiopia—and he was not going to budge on Cuban aid to the liberation movements of Namibia and Rhodesia. "But we want, without making any concessions, to get rid of the embargo," he told Neto, "to end the embargo against Cuba. Therefore we will talk to them, we will receive them, we will debate with them."[2]

As Under Secretary David Newsom recalls, when Castro's proposal for talks "was placed before Carter and Brzezinski, they were very reluctant to have any kind of contacts with the Cubans. They were apprehensive about Carter's domestic position and feared that any publicity about contacts with the Cubans that might have suggested normalization would damage Carter's political position." Finally, at Vance's urging, Carter relented.[3] Five secret meetings ensued, in New York on April 14 and June 15, 1978, Washington on July 5, Atlanta on August 8, and Cuernavaca, Mexico, on October 28.

According to Wayne Smith, who was Director of Cuban Affairs at the State Department, the NSC and the Department of State viewed these talks very differently. "From . . . Vance on down, State saw them as positive, dynamic and open-ended. They offered an opportunity to address the problems between us. The NSC's perception, on the other hand, was essentially negative and static. We would listen to (but not hear) the other side only as the price we had to pay to reiterate our refusal to take any additional steps toward improving relations until Castro withdrew his troops from Africa." Brzezinski's aide Robert Pastor sharply disagrees. "There was no real difference between State and the NSC about the talks—not any more. Ethiopia had been clearly perceived by everyone—and especially by Carter—as military intervention, a new kind of imperialism. As a result, everyone was on the same page. There was disagreement about what to do about it, but we all condemned the Cuban intervention. By the summer of 1978 the State Department's and NSC's positions on Cuba were similar: there were bureaucratic and personality tensions, but not a significant difference anymore."[4]

Both Smith and Pastor are right. As Smith suggests, the State Department was much more open than the NSC to the idea of talks with the Cubans. It wanted to explore what steps Castro might be willing to take on issues other than Africa that were of interest to the United States. On one point, however, it agreed with the NSC: there could be no significant improvement in relations, no real step toward normalization, unless the Cuban troops left Africa. Furthermore, if anyone in the State Department had been inclined to disagree, one thing was clear: this was Jimmy Carter's position. In Under Secretary Newsom's words, "Carter was uneasy about his ultimate reelection; very conscious of the problem he had with the Soviets and especially the Cubans. Brzezinski felt that part of his job was that the president show firmness on international issues and especially issues related to the Soviets." Therefore, the State Department "would have had to move more forcefully than I think Vance was prepared to do if he wanted a real dialogue with the Cubans. It was too hot an issue for political reasons. Even the very limited discussions we had [with the Cubans] were held in great secrecy."[5]

The senior Cuban representative in these talks was José Luis Padrón, a close aide of Fidel Castro. The Americans fielded two teams. At Brzezinski's request, Carter established two separate tracks: the State Department, that is, Under Secretary Newsom, would deal with Padrón on humanitarian matters. The NSC, that is Deputy National Security Adviser David Aaron, would deal with Padrón on "broader political matters"—this meant, above all, Africa. "Our role [State] was very much confined to talking about the prisoners—Cuban political prisoners and Americans in Cuban jails. Brzezinski just didn't trust us," Newsom muses. "He worried that we would make too many concessions."[6]

At first the Cubans believed that the two-track approach was a negotiating ploy to confuse them: "We thought they were playing good cop, bad cop," Padrón recalls, "but bit by bit we understood that we were in fact seeing two positions that were to some extent in conflict with one another."[7]

It was an artificial division of labor that could not last. Padrón was blissfully unaware, or pretended to be, of the intricacies of U.S. diplomatic rules when, on June 15, in New York, he spoke to Newsom about both humanitarian matters and Africa. Newsom responded. He told Padrón that he understood that Cuba's policy in Africa was "separate from Soviet policy, although not all [in the U.S. government] see it that way." However, he added, Cuba's policy was inimical to U.S. and Africa's interests; therefore, it must withdraw its troops from Africa and use its influence to support U.S. negotiating efforts in Rhodesia and Namibia. Newsom's words provoked a storm in Washington: Brzezinski complained to Carter and to Vance, while Aaron bristled: "Newsom exceeded his mandate (which was to talk only about prisoners)," he told Brzezinski. Furthermore, Newsom's comments on Africa had been "bad for two reasons. First, my line, which you and the president approved, is that regardless of their motivations they [the Cubans] are in effect serving as tools." This was a bizarre point: if the Cubans were Soviet tools because their intervention also served Moscow's interests, then the French, by intervening in Shaba, had been tools of the United States, a notion that would have stunned French president Valéry Giscard d'Estaing. "Secondly," Aaron went on, Newsom "openly acknowledged differences with the Administration and putting [sic] himself on the side of being more pro-Cuban."[8]

Carter faced an impossible choice: to insist that the State Department could not discuss political matters with the Cubans, as Brzezinski urged, would have meant a resounding vote of no confidence in Vance. In late July he handed down a Solomonic verdict: the two tracks were merged, henceforth Newsom and Aaron would jointly meet with Padrón.[9]

One issue had already been settled by the time the two tracks merged. On June 15, when Newsom asked what Havana intended to do about those Cubans "who are political prisoners in some sense or other," Padrón replied that his government had decided to free most of them; and that they and their families would be granted exit permits to leave the country, as would former prisoners and their families. He added that "an estimate . . . of the numbers [who might want to emigrate to the United States], including family members, is 4,000 at most." The United States could, of course, refuse to accept them, but this would not influence Cuba's decision to free the prisoners and to grant the exit visas: "We have already decided. We do not need the opinion of the United States to start issuing the exit permits." Padrón was blunt: "In other words, the decision has been made. There is nothing to negotiate. We are here to inform you of the decision and express the hope that the families wishing to come to the US would be accepted. We look at this as something which can improve the climate between the US Cuban community and Cuba, and also something which can create a propitious climate in US public opinion. I also look at it as a gesture consistent with President Carter's projected policy [of human rights]. . . . It is my opinion that this also creates a favorable climate for future negotiations on other topics."[10] An agreement between the two sides was concluded at the next meeting, in Atlanta, on August 8. The Americans agreed to receive the prisoners and their families after due screening, and Padrón handed over the documentation on forty-eight prisoners to start the process.[11]

Many other issues crowded the agenda. Washington sought the release of four Americans jailed in Cuba for espionage or counterrevolutionary activities; it wanted Havana to compensate the owners of U.S. property nationalized by the revolution and to mute its support for the independence of Puerto Rico. The Cubans said that the United States must eventually return the Guantánamo base. They agreed in principle to compensate owners of nationalized U.S. properties, but, Newsom reported, they "also had a bill to present to us for economic harm suffered as a result of acts of aggression and the blockade."[12] These acts of aggression included the U.S. failure to control the anti-Castro terrorists the CIA had trained in the 1960s. "As you recall," a senior aide told Brzezinski, "we have the leftovers of the CIA anti-Castro troops in Miami. Although the CIA has abandoned them, they have not abandoned terror throughout Latin America, targeting Cuban citizens, diplomats."[13]

There was one issue that trumped all the rest because the Americans were emphatic: no progress toward normalization was possible until the Cuban troops left Africa. Whatever argument Havana might bring forth to explain its presence—South Africa's threat against Angola, the Somali invasion of Ethiopia—was irrelevant. The Cuban soldiers must leave Africa.

This was the subject that dominated the talks after the two tracks—the NSC and State Department—merged. The Cubans did not budge. On October 19, 1978, Brzezinski and Deputy Secretary of State Christopher informed Carter that another meeting would take place in nine days in Cuernavaca. Newsom and Aaron would, once again, batter at the same wall: they would tell Padrón that if Castro "had been responsive to our concerns on Puerto Rico and Africa, we would have been prepared to take actions in the trade and economic area"— small steps toward the lifting of the embargo. They would offer the Cubans yet another chance. "We would specifically cite the following two examples of areas where we would take action if they were prepared to meet our concerns": the administration would grant a license to Neptune International (a nickel company based in Atlanta) to provide design technology, through its Belgian subsidiary, for new nickel plants in Cuba; and it would review the May 15, 1964, ban on the sale of U.S. medicine to Cuba. "We would be prepared to consider lifting this aspect of the embargo in the light of concrete and positive Cuban actions in Africa."[14]

The meeting at Cuernavaca had its light moments. Padrón recalls, "The day we arrived at Cuernavaca was the birthday of Stephanie van Reigersberg [the U.S. interpreter]. We wanted to buy her flowers, but it was late [in the evening] and we couldn't find any. So we went to a funeral home, and we gave some money to the employee there in exchange for some flowers. When they [the U.S. delegation] learned where the flowers had come from, you can't imagine how much they laughed. In our meetings with them, we always tried to create a relaxed atmosphere. We sought to break down their stereotypes." The Cubans succeeded, at least with the State Department. "The atmosphere of our meetings was quite friendly," Newsom agreed. "We shared an interest in baseball and often discussed individual stars and the fate of the Yankees. I vaguely remember the gesture on Stephanie's birthday."[15]

"He only vaguely remembers!" laughed Stephanie when I told her what Newsom had said.

> It wasn't just flowers! They tried to turn it into a bouquet of flowers, but it was very clear that it had originally been lying on a coffin. It was very funny!
>
> We had arrived [the two delegations] on the 27th—my birthday. The two delegations had dinner at separate tables, not together—the negotiations would only start the next day. At our table someone started singing "Happy Birthday" to me. The Cubans must have overheard us.
>
> I went to my room and prepared to go to bed. I was in my pajamas. Someone knocked at my door. I peeked—there were José Luis Padrón and Tony de la Guardia [another member of the Cuban delegation] with an armload of flowers. I had to tell them to come into my room—they were making too much noise. Padrón said, "We wanted to offer you a bouquet of flowers, but at this hour in this city. . . ! But at last we saw a funeral home . . ." They had bribed the guy and grabbed all the flowers from a coffin—or from several coffins. Or from the coffin of a very important person! There were a lot of flowers![16]

But baseball and flowers could not change the stark reality. The meeting "resulted in a complete impasse," Aaron told Carter. The Cubans said "their presence in Africa was not negotiable, and explicitly held open the option of increasing their forces in Angola and elsewhere in Southern Africa because of what they termed adverse developments in Namibia and Rhodesia."[17] (South

Africa was reneging on its acceptance of the Contact Group's plan for the independence of Namibia, and in Rhodesia Prime Minister Ian Smith had forged an agreement with tame black leaders that would leave power in white hands.)

At Cuernavaca, Padrón repeated an invitation he had made in the previous months: that U.S. officials go to Havana and meet with Castro. The NSC, however, had been opposed to any conversations in Cuba, and now it wanted to end the entire exercise. "The State Department said, 'the talks cannot conclude without talking to Castro,'" Newsom recalls. Carter hesitated. A note in the president's handwriting, a few days after Cuernavaca, said "Call David Newsom. . . . Do not plan on another meeting."[18]

Soon, however, Carter would relent. Again the principle prevailed: both State and the NSC would be represented, so that Brzezinski could keep an eye on State. Newsom and Aaron, however, stayed in Washington. "The reason given was that my position was at a higher level than they wanted to grace the talks with Castro," Newsom explains.[19] The real reason may have been that the relationship between Newsom and Aaron was strained. The two officials who flew to Havana were Peter Tarnoff, the executive secretary of the State Department and Vance's right-hand man; and Robert Pastor, who was the Latin America expert at the NSC. Tarnoff and Pastor enjoyed the confidence of their principals and had a very good personal and professional relationship with each other.[20] They arrived in Havana on December 2 and met immediately with Vice President Carlos Rafael Rodríguez.

The following day, at 10:00 P.M., Tarnoff and Pastor met with Fidel Castro. Throughout their five-hour meeting they focused on Africa. "Africa is certainly central to our concerns," Tarnoff told Castro. "As I look over the transcripts of our talks [the previous evening, with Rodríguez], I see that we have spent 70 percent of our time on Africa."[21]

## Two Visitors in Havana

The arrival of Tarnoff and Pastor had been preceded by U.S.-British air and naval maneuvers held in mid-November off the northern coast of Cuba, "the most important since 1962," Le Monde noted. The State Department's director of Cuban affairs, Wayne Smith, wrote, "We gave the Cubans no notification of these maneuvers. Their first warning came as Cuban radar screens showed a large fleet approaching. Also, in what the U.S. later insisted was a coincidence, on almost the same day we resumed SR-71 reconnaissance overflights."[22]

The Cubans did not believe in coincidences, and much less in Washington's right to invade their air space. "On the SR-71, the U.S. can adduce no argument to justify these flights," Castro told Tarnoff and Pastor. "All arguments are and will always be very weak, because there is no way to justify this flagrant violation of Cuban sovereignty and international law. I asked what the U.S. Government would think if we sent planes to photograph U.S. military installations. . . . We have never attacked you, sabotaged you, sent in arms and explosives, or carried out acts of piracy. The U.S. has done all this to us."[23]

The SR-71 overflights had been halted by the Carter administration in early 1977 as needlessly provocative. Satellites and peripheral reconnaissance made them unnecessary. When the Department of Defense asked in October 1978 that the overflights be resumed, the State Department objected, but the White House wanted to "get tough" with Cuba. As Professor Lars Schoultz points out, the overflights did more than collect intelligence. They also sought "to intimidate and humiliate." Predictably, Brzezinski supported their resumption. Cuba had kept its troops in Angola, was helping the Namibian and Rhodesian insurgents, and had intervened in the Horn. Carter, therefore, "sided with the hawks."[24] Resuming the overflights was a cheap way for the administration to vent its frustrations about Cuba, and a poor omen for the forthcoming talks.

The conversations in Havana were tense. Castro was deeply disappointed in Carter. "We felt that he was the first American president in all these years [since 1959] with different attitudes and a different style of treatment of Cuba," he told Pastor and Tarnoff. This perception had been shattered, however, by Carter's false allegations of Cuban involvement in Shaba, the resumption of the spy flights, the insistent demand that the Cuban troops leave Africa, and the continuation of the embargo. "We feel it is deeply immoral to see the blockade as a means of pressuring Cuba," Castro said.

> We are deeply irritated, offended and indignant that for nearly 20 years the blockade has been used as an element of pressure in making demands on us. . . . Perhaps I should add something more. There should be no mistake—we cannot be pressured, impressed, bribed or bought. . . . Perhaps because the U.S. is a great power, it feels it can do what it wants and what is good for it. It seems to be saying that there are two laws, two sets of rules and two kinds of logic, one for the U.S. and one for other countries. Perhaps it is idealistic of me, but I never accepted the universal prerogatives of the U.S.—I never accepted and never will accept the existence of a different law and different rules. . . . I hope history will bear witness to the shame of the United States which for twenty years has not allowed sales of medicine needed to save lives. . . . History will bear witness to your shame.[25]

In their report to Carter, Pastor and Tarnoff wrote, "As he [Castro] spoke, it seemed to us that we were viewing a man who had bottled up 20 years of rage and was releasing it in a controlled but extremely impassioned manner. . . . His principal message was that Cuba wants to be treated with respect, as an equal, by the same rules. He views the embargo as 'morally indefensible'—'a dagger at Cuba's throat'. . . he seeks legitimacy for Cuba; he believes his quest to be just, and our position isn't. . . . His words were precise and his arguments were well thought out."[26]

## The Crisis of the Mini Brigade

U.S.-Cuban relations deteriorated further in the two remaining years of the Carter presidency. Through late 1978 U.S. officials had regarded Cuba's policy in Africa as "the most intractable obstacle to significant improvement in bilateral relations,"[27] but following the Sandinista victory in Nicaragua in July 1979, Central America moved to the eye of the storm. U.S. officials knew that Cuba had assisted the Sandinistas and that it was helping the insurgents in El Salvador. They were upset by the close ties between Cuba and the left-wing government of Grenada which seized power in March 1979. "The Grenada coup has seriously set back US policy in the Caribbean," the CIA warned. "Havana now has firmly in place an extremely friendly legitimate government in the eastern Caribbean, where it has long sought to extend its influence. It has another ally in the UN and the OAS and another advocate in regional bodies formerly hostile to the Cuban revolution."[28]

Jimmy Carter was increasingly on the defensive. Buffeted by double-digit inflation at home, he could boast of important foreign policy successes. The Canal Treaties with Panama had solved a problem that had festered for more than a decade. The establishment of full diplomatic relations with China had successfully concluded what Nixon had begun and Ford had been unable to bring forward. The peace treaty between Egypt and Israel—Carter's handiwork—had anchored Egypt in the pro-American camp and greatly strengthened Israel's position in the Middle East, an important priority for U.S. policy makers. But for the American public, and even for many U.S. officials, these successes paled before the administration's reverses: the fiasco in the Horn, the fall of the shah of Iran in early 1979, the leftists' takeover in Grenada, the Sandinista victory in Nicaragua, and the continuing Cuban presence in Africa. In all but one of these crises—the Iranian revolution—Americans detected the hand of Castro.

Robert Pastor, Brzezinski's bright specialist on Latin America, wrote to his boss in 1979 that Cuba was a source of "unmitigated frustration.... The frustration is a function of three simple facts ... (1) Cuba causes us terrible problems; (2) Cuba is a little country, and we are a super power; and (3) we have almost no leverage or influence over the Cubans.... I view the Soviet-Cuban relationship," Pastor went on, "as somewhat analogous to the U.S.-Israeli relationship. Most of the world believes that we have over-powering influence over Israel ... but in reality, they are pulling us around a lot more than we are pushing them. Similarly, my guess is that the Cubans are pushing and pulling the Soviets into riskier areas than the elder Soviet leadership would normally choose to tread. The Cubans are nobody's puppet."[29]

In June 1979 Carter and Brezhnev signed the SALT II treaty in Vienna. It was, at best, an uneasy respite. Brzezinski fanned Carter's uneasiness: "On rereading the Vienna protocols," he wrote on July 6, "I was struck by how intransigent Brezhnev was on regional issues. In spite of your forceful statement, the Soviets simply gave us no reason to believe that they will desist from using the Cubans as their proxies." Later in the month, he told the president, "Cuba's foreign military and subversive activities have steadily intensified since the mid-seventies— and this might become a political issue here. Castro's successes abroad, and Soviet sponsorship of his activities, now confront us with an increasingly difficult foreign policy problem. Accordingly I have asked [CIA director] Stan Turner to intensify analysis and intelligence in three key areas: A. Soviet military deliveries to Cuba itself; B. Cuban activities in Central America and the Caribbean; C. Cuban activities in Africa. .... I think it is fair to assume," he warned, "that Cuba's military/subversive successes (and our actual or perceived responses) are almost certain to be an important foreign policy campaign issue in 1980."[30]

The intensified focus on Cuba led, on August 22, 1979, to a coordinated intelligence finding from the National Foreign Assessment Center confirming the presence on the island of a "Soviet combat brigade" of about 2,600 men, with forty tanks, armored personnel carriers, and artillery. The unit appeared to have been on the island since at least 1975 or 1976. Unlike the Soviet Advisory Mission, which had 2,000–3,000 military personnel who advised and trained the Cuban armed forces, the brigade had no observable connection with Cuban military forces. "The word 'combat,'" Raymond Garthoff notes in his careful dissection of the crisis, "was used to characterize its [the brigade's] weapons and equipment and to distinguish it from logistics or advisory units."[31]

The intelligence finding was right on the mark—except on one point: the brigade had not arrived in 1975. "Further investigation," Carter explained in his memoirs, "confirmed that the presence of these troops was not a new development; the brigade was only a remnant of a much larger force that had been there since the early 1960's." At the end of the 1962 Missile Crisis, the Soviets had intended to withdraw all their troops, but the Cubans had insisted that some remain. In Fidel Castro's words, "40,000 Soviet soldiers were in Cuba at the time of the Missile Crisis. There were several brigades, and one remained here at our request."[32] On May 29, 1963, Havana and Moscow had signed a secret agreement "about the permanence on the island of a symbolic contingent of Soviet troops: a motorized brigade."[33] U.S. intelligence had been aware of the brigade in the 1960s, but it had then lost track of it and of its own records. It was a stunning oversight. "The principal lesson out of all this," Under Secretary Newsom concluded, "was that the State Department and government has no institutional memory." It was, Vance noted, "a very costly lapse in memory." It led, DCI Turner observed, to "the most serious intelligence failure of my tenure."[34]

Had the finding about the brigade remained secret, an unnecessary crisis would have been avoided. But the report was leaked. The presence of the Soviet combat brigade in Cuba became public in late August 1979, against the backdrop of an administration—and a president—accused of being soft on Cuba and the Soviet Union. It provoked a political storm. Not only did conservatives assail this egregious Soviet violation of détente, but they were joined by liberal supporters of the administration who faced difficult reelection campaigns in 1980, foremost among them the most liberal of all, Frank Church (D-Idaho), chair of the Senate Foreign Relations Committee, who demanded at a hastily called press conference on August 30 "the immediate withdrawal of all Russian combat troops from Cuba."[35] Within the administration, Brzezinski led the charge. "Today much of the world is watching to see how we will behave on the Soviet/Cuban issue," he told Carter. "The country craves, and our national security needs, both a more assertive tone and a more assertive substance to our foreign policy. I believe that both for international reasons as well as for domestic political reasons you ought to deliberately toughen both the tone and the substance of our foreign policy." The Soviet brigade in Cuba provided an opportunity to demonstrate resolve—whereas "failure to cope with it firmly can have the effect of . . . conclusively stamp[ing] this Administration as weak." Brzezinski worried about the State Department's backbone—"I feel uneasy," he told the president, "about how and with what determination the brigade issue is now being negotiated."[36]

He had a point. Vance wanted to avoid posturing because he knew that the intelligence about when the brigade had first arrived in Cuba was shaky. Also, he did not want to jeopardize the ratification of the SALT treaty. "Cy has strong reservations about going public," Brzezinski told Carter on September 4. Carter was well aware that the intelligence was weak. The previous day he had jotted in his diary, "Chances are they'd had approximately this level of troops for the last 15 or 20 years."[37] But Brzezinski, not Vance, had the president's ear. And the presidential elections loomed. Carter sided with Brzezinski's muscular approach. Dutifully, Vance fell in step, as he had a year earlier during Shaba II, when he had toed the White House's line that the Cubans had lied to cover up their involvement in the Katangans' invasion. As Lars Schoultz writes, "On September 5, Vance became appropriately bellicose, telling reporters, 'We regard this as a very serious matter affecting our relations with the Soviet Union . . .' Then he drew what would become the administration's line in the sand: 'I will not be satisfied with maintenance of the status quo.' Two days later, Carter repeated: 'This status quo is not acceptable.'" The *Guardian* remarked that the "growing row about the discovery of a Soviet brigade in Cuba . . . tells you rather more about the threat to . . . Democratic seats in the Senate to be contested next year than it does about the state of American security."[38]

Through September, Vance writes, "I met half a dozen times with [Soviet ambassador] Dobrynin and twice with [Foreign Minister] Gromyko to discuss unilateral Soviet measures that would alter the status quo [about the brigade in Cuba] and resolve our concerns. I was unsuccessful." The Soviet reply, first delivered to Vance on September 5, and then expanded in *Pravda* on September 11, stated: "For 17 years there has been in Cuba a training center in which Soviet military personnel have helped Cuban servicemen master Soviet military equipment that is used by the Cuban armed forces. Neither the number nor the functions of the Soviet personnel have changed throughout all these years. All allegations about the arrival in Cuba of 'organized Soviet combat units' are totally groundless."[39] The statement combined truth and fiction: it was true that the brigade had been in Cuba since 1962. Since then, as the *Pravda* statement said, the size and the duties of the brigade had not changed. But it was not and had never been a "training center." It was a combat brigade.

The day after the *Pravda* statement, an aide told Brzezinski, "The Soviets have essentially made what they consider to be a concession and offered a way out of the impasse by reiterating both publicly and privately that the unit is attached to a 17-year old training center." It was, Garthoff explains, "a false claim by Moscow to make the unit seem less objectionable, in an effort to help the American administration get off the limb it had climbed out on."[40]

If this was the Soviet intention, it was spurned by the White House. "There are three possible outcomes for the Cuban problem," Brzezinski wrote Carter. "A political victory for the United States and for you. In its essence, this should involve the removal back to the Soviet Union of some of the equipment and

associated personnel (e.g. tanks and bridging equipment) and the disaggrega-
tion of the brigade. An alternative formula would be for us to concede that the
brigade is a training one, and for the Soviets to announce that they are pulling
out on the completion of their mission." The second possibility, which Brzezinski rejected, was to accept "a cosmetic solution. Some formula for the dis-
aggregation of the brigade and the enhancement of its training role."[41] Vance,
Brzezinski told Carter, "strongly prefers" the "cosmetic solution."[42]

The third outcome, Brzezinski argued, was "Steady toughening up in our
overall policy toward the Soviet Union but without a victory or a cosmetic
solution for the Cuban problem. This would mean a frank acceptance of the
fact that we cannot force the brigade out but that as a consequence we will
be imposing on the Soviet Union other costs for its disregard of our interests.
Clearly," Brzezinski concluded, "the first outcome is the best for you and for
the country." But if it proved impossible, "the third in my judgement is much
better than the second. A cosmetic solution will not wash. The country will see
through it. . . . A gradual but steady toughening in our policy is therefore the
preferable alternative. It will require telling the country quite frankly that we
cannot get the brigade out short of a head-on military confrontation. Instead
there are other things that you are prepared to do." Brzezinski's list included
an increase in the military budget, "explicitly related to this issue," the deployment of additional U.S. troops at Guantánamo, the sale of advanced technology to China, a six-week delay in the Senate SALT deliberations, "general denunciation of Soviet/Cuban activity in Africa, Yemen and Afghanistan—with
the implication that Soviet conduct negatively and directly affects US-Soviet
relations," and the enunciation of a Carter Doctrine for the Caribbean, "to the
effect that the U.S. will directly oppose the organized deployment of Soviet/
Cuban troops or revolutionaries across national borders."[43]

Brzezinski told Carter that this third course would show the nation "that
you are prepared to confront the Soviet Union with the fact that détente must
be a two-way street. . . . In brief we have to make the Soviets understand that
détente has to be comprehensive and reciprocal—a point which you have frequently made during the last two years but which I do not believe is now credible to Moscow."[44] Because the brigade had been in Cuba since 1962, and previous presidents had been aware of it and tolerated it, Brzezinski's definition of
the two-way street was as one-sided as had been his interpretation of the rules
of détente during the crisis in the Horn.

With that particular sensitivity that made him so valuable to Carter, Brzezinski stressed domestic considerations. "There is a direct political benefit in
the adoption of this third course," he wrote. "It will put [Senator Ted] Kennedy

[who was expected to challenge Carter for the Democratic presidential nomination] on the spot. By toughening up our posture vis-a-vis the Soviets, you will either force Kennedy to back you, or to oppose you. It will be difficult for him to remain silent. If he backs you, he is backing an assertive and tough President. If he opposes you, he can easily be stamped as a latter-day McGovernite."[45]

On September 20, 1979, Vance presented Ambassador Dobrynin with specific proposals that included dismantling the brigade, reassigning its personnel to advisory duty, and transferring its tanks and artillery to the Cubans.[46] The Soviets refused to oblige. Carter personally appealed to Brezhnev to make the unilateral concessions demanded by Vance. A refusal, he warned, would hurt the chances of the Senate ratifying the SALT II Treaty. "It would be a tragedy if this work for peace would be today put under threat as a result of the fact that both our governments could not resolve the problem which has caused on one side a feeling of deep concern." Brezhnev rebuffed Carter's appeal. He pointed out that the brigade was an "artificially created issue." It was not the brigade that threatened SALT, but "the artificially created campaign" about it.[47]

By then Carter knew that the whole fracas was based on a serious intelligence blunder. "Closer examination of records," Vance writes, "revealed that earlier American administrations had known of Soviet ground units in Cuba and had not regarded them as worth concentrated intelligence surveillance.... The more resources the intelligence community devoted to the brigade, the farther back in time information about it went—eventually all the way to 1962.... By late September it was evident that the unit in question had almost certainly been in Cuba continuously since 1962." Undeterred, Brzezinski told the press that the Soviet brigade in Cuba stemmed from a Soviet "pattern of disregard" for American interests, and Carter insisted once again, on September 25, that "the status quo is not acceptable to us."[48]

On October 1, Carter spoke to the nation. Over the previous month he had backed himself into a corner. He had decreed the Soviet combat brigade in Cuba "unacceptable," but Moscow had refused to budge. The brigade was, Carter now told the country, "a matter of serious concern to us." He outlined measures he would take in response—increased surveillance of Cuba, a promise to assist Western Hemisphere countries threatened by Cuban forces or Soviet forces in Cuba, increased economic aid to countries in the region, and the establishment of a permanent Caribbean Joint Task Force.[49] After so much bluster, it would have been embarrassing to tell the American people that his administration had blundered: that the brigade had been in Cuba since 1962 and previous administrations had known it, that therefore there had been no Soviet breach of the rules of détente, and that there was no reason for concern, "grave" or otherwise. Carter's handling of the crisis shows that for domestic reasons he was willing to worsen relations with the Soviet Union and endanger SALT, even though he had written in his diary, a week before his speech, "that I would rather be defeated [in the elections] than pull down or endanger SALT in any way, so my guiding premise will be what's best for ratification of SALT."[50] Obviously, this did not include telling Americans the truth.

The entire episode, in which Brzezinski had hoped to score political points for the administration, had backfired. If the brigade was unacceptable, as U.S. officials had declared throughout September, Carter's countermeasures were little more than pinpricks that reinforced the image of a weak president. "America's allies in Europe also found the episode disturbing," Under Secretary Newsom points out. "To them it was another manifestation of the curious and unpredictable nature of U.S. politics. . . . The incredulity was even greater in the Third World. The suspicion that the brigade was 'discovered' to embarrass the nonaligned conference that opened in Havana on September 3 was not confined to Cuba and the radicals." On one point friends and foes of the administration agreed: the squabble over the brigade dealt a heavy blow to the already tenuous chances that the senate would ratify SALT. In Brzezinski's words, "Our ratification difficulties . . . were greatly and almost fatally compounded" by the crisis. "As Marx said," Ambassador Dobrynin muses, "history repeats itself, first as tragedy and then as farce. But this farce cost the ratification of the [SALT] treaty. And our relations further deteriorated."[51]

Had U.S. officials been aware of it, they might have found solace in the fact that the Soviet handling of the crisis had offended the Cubans. As Castro told Petr Demichev, a nonvoting member of the Soviet Politburo,

> When this matter [the Soviet brigade] became public, the Soviets made what was, in our opinion, an unnecessary concession. They asked for our input, but before we could reply they announced publicly that they did not have a brigade in Cuba, but only soldiers staffing a Training Center. . . . I wonder, why did they have to make this concession to the imperialists? . . .
>
> This created therefore a difficult, delicate situation for us . . . I don't know why it was not possible to acknowledge that there was a Soviet brigade in Cuba. . . .
>
> For us, the brigade was an important symbol. That is why, when we heard that it had become a "training center," we felt that the symbol had been destroyed and that you had adopted a timid and hesitant stance.[52]

The Cubans could have accepted had the Soviets said that the brigade had a "training" function, but they wanted it to be called what it was, a "brigade," not the staff of a "Training Center." Castro explained to GDR leader Honecker a few months later, "There was a reason for our position. We cannot renounce the right to have Soviet brigades in our country." Risquet remarked that "a brigade, even if it is performing a training function, is a combat unit, and it can fight; the staff of a training center cannot fight." In his sensitive account of the crisis, Ambassador Vorotnikov writes, "Why did I support Cuba's position? I thought that for the Cuban government the presence on the island of a 'symbolic Soviet military unit' was something more than a detail. It had moral and psychological significance. . . . This is why, in my opinion, the Cuban government instinctively understood that the change in the designation of the brigade was not just a matter of words, and it wanted to maintain the status quo and thereby counter the arrogant pressure of the Americans and reassure the Cuban people that 'the Soviets are with us.'"[53]

## The End of Détente: Afghanistan

The Soviet brigade fiasco strained détente and delayed consideration of the SALT II treaty by the U.S. Senate. The Soviet invasion of Afghanistan, in late December 1979, killed both. Haunted by the prospect that the communist regime in Kabul might be overthrown, the Politburo sent troops into Afghanistan against the advice of its generals, reversing its own conclusion—reached the previous March—that "we can suppress a revolution in Afghanistan only with the aid of our bayonets, and that is for us entirely inadmissible. We cannot take such a risk."[54] Compounding the error, the Soviets killed the country's communist president, whom they suspected of being in secret contact with the Americans, and brought his replacement with them, eliminating even the feeble pretense that they had intervened at the request of the Afghan government.

Carter withdrew the SALT treaty from the Senate, announced a massive increase in military spending, and imposed economic sanctions on the Soviet Union. He also "dramatically expanded" the covert aid program for the Afghan mujahedin that he had approved in July 1979, from $500,000 to a grand total of $60 million that included "all manner of weapons and military support."[55]

Led by Carter, U.S. officials clamored that the Soviet Union was on the move, seeking world domination. The Soviets had the mirror image of U.S. policy. In February 1980, GDR intelligence minister Erich Mielke and one of his most senior aides, Markus Wolf, had a long conversation in Moscow with a man they knew well, Yury Andropov, the head of the KGB. "I had never seen Andropov so serious and worried," Wolf writes. "He outlined to us a grim scenario, in which nuclear war was a real possibility. His sober analysis led to the conclusion that the US government sought to achieve nuclear superiority over the USSR by every means. . . . GDR Foreign Minister [Oskar] Fischer returned from a visit to . . . Gromyko with the same impression that I had garnered from Andropov." In Havana, Fidel Castro told Tarnoff and Pastor when they met for a second time on January 16, 1980, "I think that in the last twenty-one years I have never seen such a serious confrontation as now, nor such movement toward war."[56]

Pastor remarks that the conversation with Castro in January 1980 was "Just absolutely fascinating." Brzezinski had opposed the trip—"he said it was a useless exercise. Carter decided that it was worth trying for a reason no one had thought: that we might be able to convince Fidel to break with the Soviet Union because of Afghanistan. What we [Pastor and Tarnoff] found was a totally different Fidel Castro. The most interesting part of the conversation was after the formal meeting had concluded. Fidel told us of his quarrel with the USSR during the Missile Crisis. He made clear that his silence at the UN [on Afghanistan] should not be taken as support for the Soviet invasion. From a substantive point, the meeting brought no progress, but it was the first time we had really connected with him, we shared a mutual respect. What Fidel is, he is not only anti-American, he is a nationalist."[57] For his part, Tarnoff noted, "Unlike our meeting last year [December 1978], Castro was extremely open, cordial, non-rhetorical and open to dialogue."[58]

Less cordial was Castro's conversation with Politburo member Demichev a few weeks later. Ambassador Vorotnikov writes, "Fidel . . . began to speak more rapidly. . . . It was evident that he wanted to unburden himself of all his pent-up complaints about the Soviet leadership. . . . Whenever Fidel paused, Petr Nilovich [Demichev] tried to speak, but Fidel . . . kept talking. I was silent. Demichev gave up trying to speak." The main item in Castro's indictment was the Soviet invasion of Afghanistan.[59]

"Afghanistan created a great strain in our relations," Risquet remarked.[60] The Cubans disapproved of the decision, of how it had been carried out, and of the fact that they were confronted with the fait accompli. "Afghanistan is an active member of the Non-Aligned Movement . . . and Cuba is now the president of the movement," Castro told Vorotnikov. "And all this occurs without even informing us beforehand!"[61] Arguably Castro did not have much ground to complain about this (but complain he did): Cuba, after all, had not informed the Soviets before sending troops to Angola in November 1975. The difference, however, was in the nature of the two actions: Cuba had acted to repel the South African invasion of Angola, while the Soviets had invaded Afghanistan, a member of the Non-Aligned Movement. To condemn Moscow openly, however, would have placed Cuba on the same side as the United States against its closest ally. When, on January 14, 1980, the General Assembly of the United Nations debated a resolution condemning the invasion, the Cuban delegate did not endorse the Soviet action but said that "we will not vote against socialism."[62] Cuba was one of 18 countries that voted against the resolution, while 104 voted in favor and 30 abstained. The vote hurt Cuba's international prestige and crippled its chance to win the UN Security Council seat reserved for Latin American countries. A few months later, Castro told Honecker, "The situation in Afghanistan has hurt us greatly, especially in the Third World. We were placed in an absolute minority. . . . At the time we were fighting for a seat in the Security Council . . . because of the events in Afghanistan we had . . . to abandon our quest. It would have been absurd [to have continued], we had lost many votes, and this has hurt the Non-Aligned Movement greatly."[63]

## Mariel

On February 2, 1980, two weeks after Castro had met with Pastor and Tarnoff, a U.S. SR-71 flew over Cuba, the first in several months. Wayne Smith, who had been the head of the U.S. Interests Section in Havana since July 1979, reported: "At his request, I called on Vice President Carlos Rafael Rodríguez at his office Feb. 19, the day after I returned to post. Highest levels of Cuban govt, including President Castro, he said, were highly irritated and mystified by recent hostile and provocative actions of USG." The SR-71 overflight, Rodríguez added, had been carried out "in a particularly blatant, offensive manner. It had broken windows all over Cuba. With satellites, peripheral photography and electronic methods now available, Cuban leadership could not believe overflights were necessary or were undertaken for any purpose other than to humiliate and intimidate Cuba, but Cuba had never been intimidated and never would be. It wanted to have better relations but it would not be coerced; reaction, in fact, would be just the opposite."[64]

On March 17, 1980, the day Angola's President dos Santos arrived in Havana on his first state visit to Cuba, another SR-71 flew over the island. Wayne Smith reported that "Cuban officials, convinced of causal relationship, expressed outrage that US had conducted overflight practically at moment dos Santos was arriving. Hard conviction was that we had done it simply to humiliate them."[65]

A memo to Brzezinski, the following month, noted that "Castro is reportedly extremely upset and concerned about U.S. military maneuvers scheduled to take place in Guantanamo in May."[66]

Castro was not, however, intimidated. The stage was set for the Mariel crisis—Cuba's decision, in April 1980, to invite the Cuban Americans to come with boats to the port of Mariel, fifty kilometers west of Havana, to pick up Cuban citizens who wanted to leave the island.[67]

The backdrop of the Mariel boatlift includes a serious economic slump in Cuba and unprecedented interaction between Cubans and Cuban Americans. As part of a new policy of improving relations with Cuban Americans, Havana had opened its doors to visits by the exiles. In 1979 more than 100,000 Cuban Americans traveled to their homeland to visit their families. "At a time when most Cubans were asked to tighten their belts," Wayne Smith remarks, "relatives from Miami and New Jersey were flooding back into the country with tales of the good life in the U.S. To hear them tell it, everyone had a mansion, three cars, an unlimited number of TV sets, and more food than anyone could eat."[68] The United States beckoned: the 1966 Cuban Adjustment Act allowed any Cuban who reached the United States (except those deemed inadmissible because of serious criminal records or severe mental problems) to apply for lawful permanent residency in the United States a year and a day after their entry with a visa or with humanitarian parole, whatever their motivations. This was a status only Cubans enjoyed.

In 1979 the number of Cubans who stole boats to get to Florida increased; others forced their way into foreign embassies. On October 20, 1979, "a new and more urgent problem arose," Wayne Smith writes.[69] Twenty-two Cubans hijacked a Cuban barge and forced the crew, at gunpoint, to take them to Florida. "They held guns to my head and kicked me in the neck," a crewman said. The State Department promptly announced that the hijackers would not be prosecuted. Instead, they were turned over to the Miami Cuban Refugee Center.[70] In a protest note, the Cuban Foreign Ministry pointed out that Cuba detained and prosecuted aerial hijackers coming from the United States. To no avail. Another boat hijacking occurred on January 31, 1980, as the crew of a Cuban ship was forced, at gunpoint, to sail to Miami. The crew appeared "stunned. They were kind of pathetic, just like you'd expect someone who was hijacked," a U.S. Coast Guard officer told the *Miami Herald*. The hijackers promptly received political asylum. Two additional boat hijackings followed on February 16 and 25. Again, U.S. authorities failed to act, despite Cuba's protests, while in Miami Cuban Americans welcomed the hijackers as heroes.[71] "In this latest case," Vance wrote Carter after the February 25 hijacking, "[the] Justice [Department] believes that there may be aggravating factors (i.e., attempted murder) which would warrant prosecution." The problem, he added, was that "Justice normally does not prosecute if there is not a 'substantial' chance of obtaining a conviction—and convictions of Cuban hijackers are questionable in the Miami environment." Carter jotted in the margin, "I suggest you and [Attorney General] Ben [Civiletti] discuss this and submit to me what you decide."[72] None of the hijackers was indicted.[73]

In a speech on March 8, 1980, Fidel Castro charged that the United States "was encouraging the illegal departures from the country and the hijacking of boats, by welcoming the hijackers as heroes." He warned that Cuba's patience was running thin.[74] On April 1, six Cubans rammed a bus through the gates of the Peruvian Embassy, where a Cuban guard was killed by a random bullet.[75] The Peruvians granted asylum to the six. The next day *Granma*, the Communist Party daily, announced that the Cuban guards at the embassy would be withdrawn and that anyone who wanted to leave the country should go to the Peruvian Embassy.[76] Within two days, 10,000 Cubans had congregated on the embassy grounds. An arrangement was worked out whereby the Cuban government allowed the asylum seekers to leave the country, and Costa Rica, gently prodded by the United States, agreed to serve as a staging area for moving the refugees to the United States and other countries willing to receive them. "From the U.S. standpoint the Costa Rican airlift was ideal," Wayne Smith writes. "The U.S. would not be inconvenienced by a wave of refugees; rather, at our own measured pace, we would be able to take them out of the Costa Rican [refugee] center. Meanwhile, by interviewing arriving refugees and playing up their reasons for leaving Cuba, we could embarrass Castro day after day at no cost to ourselves. The Costa Rican airlift was all to our advantage, none to Castro's. . . . If he had any doubts, they were certainly dispelled as he watched the way the first arrivals were handled in San José."[77] When the first plane landed, on April 16, "more than 40 journalists from different countries" were waiting, as well as Costa Rica's President Rodrigo Carrazo, "who proclaimed that the exodus was proof of the tragedy that the regime of Fidel Castro represented for Cuba."[78]

The celebrations, however, were short-lived. On April 18, the Cuban government suspended the airlift. On April 21 it opened the port of Mariel. "The United States will now reap the rewards of its policy," said *Granma*.[79]

By the time the Cuban government closed Mariel the following September, 125,000 Cubans had left the island: members of professional classes but also blue-collar workers; blacks as well as whites; practicing Catholics and members of the Communist Party. And also individuals with criminal records or mental problems. By September 1980, 1,774 Cubans known to have committed violent crimes in Cuba were being held in U.S. prisons, and another 400 were undergoing psychiatric evaluations.[80] Under U.S. law, even though they came from Cuba, these people were "excludable."

The Cubans should not have been surprised by the wave of departures. In a conversation with two U.S. congressmen, in December 1978, Fidel Castro had made a very valid point: "If Cuba opened the doors to immigration, many people would leave. If, for example, Mexican immigration to the U.S. were totally opened, many more people would leave there. Anyone seeking a higher income and standard of living would want to leave, and economic immigration would result. The U.S. has a much better standard of living, and Cuba is afraid of losing its professional class. . . . Between capitalism in a developed country and socialism in an underdeveloped country, . . . many people will leave and have left."[81]

The Mariel crisis had several consequences. The Cuban government had humiliated the Carter administration. Trapped by its own propaganda—every Cuban who left the island was a political refugee deserving asylum—and fearful of losing the Cuban American vote in the forthcoming presidential elections, the administration was unwilling to prevent the "freedom flotilla" from entering the United States, but the result was a wave of unwanted immigrants. It seemed that Jimmy Carter could not even control America's borders.

But Cuba lost, too. The spectacle of tens of thousands of Cubans bent on leaving the island, and the acts of violence perpetrated by pro-government mobs against those who wanted to leave, was humiliating and disturbing. "No thoughtful Cuban should be able to look back on what happened during those spring and summer months of 1980 without a deep sense of wrong," Wayne Smith writes.[82] The crisis dealt a further blow to U.S.-Cuban relations and provided Ronald Reagan with useful fodder for his campaign against Carter.

On November 4, 1980, Carter went down in defeat to Reagan. He left an uncertain record in foreign policy. His successes included the establishment of diplomatic relations with China, the Panama Canal treaties, and the peace treaty between Egypt and Israel. His failures included the inept handling of the crises in the Horn, Iran, and Central America. In southern Africa, his legacy was mixed.

CHAPTER 6

# Carter and Southern Africa
## *A Balance Sheet*

## The Birth of Zimbabwe

In April 1980 Carter scored a major foreign policy success: the birth of Zimba-bwe.[1] For three years, the administration had been trying to strong-arm Rhode-sia's Prime Minister Ian Smith into accepting free elections based on universal suffrage and with the participation of the country's two guerrilla movements, Joshua Nkomo's ZAPU and Robert Mugabe's ZANU. Smith tried to dodge this plan by striking a deal with those black leaders who agreed to preserve white privilege. In other words, he sought an internal settlement in Rhodesia similar to the one Pretoria wanted to impose in Namibia.

Policy toward Rhodesia provoked little controversy in the United States in 1977, but things changed in the spring of 1978, when Smith reached an agree-ment with Bishop Abel Muzorewa and two other black leaders that assured, the CIA said, "continued white domination of the military, police, judiciary and civil service." Many in the U.S. Congress and the American press demanded that Carter endorse this internal settlement and lift the mandatory sanctions that the UN Security Council had imposed on Rhodesia in the late 1960s. Their ranks swelled after Smith held elections in Rhodesia in April 1979 that supported his internal settlement. Black turnout was high, and international observers reported that the voting had been largely free and fair. (A few days before the elections, the CIA had predicted that "Government pressure and intimidation by the black parties [that had joined Smith] and their auxiliary forces should result in a fairly high turnout.")[2]

"Carter faced a choice," Nancy Mitchell writes: "bow to the will of the US congress by accepting the results of the first multiracial Rhodesian elections or defy congress by declaring the election invalid. Carter chose to defy congress, explaining that the election was not acceptable because the guerrillas fighting

139

against the white minority regime in Salisbury had not participated in them. The uproar was immediate."[3]

In their recollections, top Carter officials—from the president down—explain that their firm support for universal suffrage in Rhodesia stemmed from their concern for basic human rights.[4] But when one reads the available documents, it becomes evident that a specter haunted Washington—"the looming possibility of a Cuban factor in the Rhodesian/Southern African situation."[5] U.S. officials feared that if the guerrilla war against Smith continued, the Cubans might send troops to Mozambique, which was enduring devastating military raids from the Rhodesian regime, and to Zambia, at the request of Presidents Samora Machel and Kenneth Kaunda. Vance told a group of senators in May 1978: "My own view is that if we are going to support the internal settlement . . . it would result in the fighting continuing. As a result of the continuation of the fighting, the likelihood of the Cubans and the Russians coming in in a major way would be very substantially increased. That is why I feel so strongly that we must continue to try to find the way to somehow bring these people together. If we don't, I really believe there is a strong likelihood that the battle will continue. . . . What I can see happening in the situation is this: The fighting continues. You find attacks from Rhodesia into Zambia against the ZAPU troops. Kaunda then turns himself to the Cubans because he has nowhere else to turn." Assistant Secretary of State for Africa Dick Moose added, "He [Kaunda] would ask for antiaircraft units to begin with and then, there you go."[6]

This was not a scare tactic to prod a reluctant Congress to support the administration's policy. U.S. officials feared that the Cubans might intervene directly in Rhodesia, and their fears were shared by the British, who were the Americans' junior partners in southern Africa.[7] "I will say that the United States draws the line in Southern Africa," Deputy National Security Adviser Aaron told Brzezinski on April 13, 1978, as he prepared to meet Castro's envoy, José Luis Padrón. "The intervention of Cuban combat forces into the struggle in Rhodesia and Namibia will have the most serious adverse consequences for direct US/Cuban relations. Intervention in Southern Africa will directly affect the interests of the United States and its principal allies, and Cuba would have to be prepared to confront the consequences."[8] Castro's successful intervention in Ethiopia heightened these fears. "It will also make more likely increased Cuban involvement in the Rhodesian conflict," Brzezinski warned Carter in February 1978. "We do believe," the CIA wrote, "that if the frontline states agreed, Havana would deploy additional forces to help defend them [from Rhodesia's attacks] and that small numbers of Cuban cadres would be willing to accompany guerrilla units into Rhodesia from Zambia or Mozambique." Pastor told Brzezinski that the "Cuban factor" had given the liberation movements in Rhodesia and Namibia "a feeling that they have a trump card. . . . When the Cubans begin to send troops, we will find ourselves in the same position of awkwardness and ineffectiveness as we found ourselves in the Horn and Angola."[9]

In a thoughtful June 1978 report, the U.S. ambassador in Maputo noted, "The weight of evidence suggests that he [Mozambican president Machel] has resisted the temptation to seek large numbers of Cuban troops . . . to repel Rhodesian attacks and strengthen the efforts of the Patriotic Front [the fragile alliance between ZAPU and ZANU]. We expect this policy will prevail over the next years unless a combination of the following events occurs: A) Collapse of the Anglo American negotiations efforts; B) Progress on implementation of internal settlement with seeming western connivance; and C) Intensified Rhodesian attacks in Mozambique." The following October, Vance told the Chinese foreign minister, "Quite frankly, we are concerned by the prospects of the increasing Soviet and Cuban involvement in Rhodesia if it is not solved promptly. Indeed, in the last few days there are indications that some 400 additional Cubans have been introduced into Mozambique, and I am afraid there will be more if we do not find a solution to the problem." Cuban involvement in Rhodesia would place the United States in a most embarrassing position since, as Brzezinski lamented, opposition to it "will put us, de facto, on the side of apartheid."[10]

In December 1978, in Havana, Pastor and Tarnoff had probed the Cubans' intentions regarding Rhodesia and Namibia. Carlos Rafael Rodríguez's response was firm: "You must understand that we will be willing to help if peaceful solutions are not reached. And if Smith and all his forces combine to try to crush the liberation movements it would be a similar situation to the ones in which we helped Guinea Bissau and Angola." Cuba had sent to Guinea-Bissau military instructors, who had provided decisive assistance to the rebels who fought for independence from Portugal; and, as the Americans knew only too well, Cuba had sent troops to Angola. The next day, Castro hammered home the same message.[11]

Back in Washington, Pastor told Brzezinski, "The Cubans don't trust the negotiating process [in southern Africa]. They think their military presence is helpful in preventing mass killings by the whites; we believe that their presence undermines the possibility of negotiating a peaceful solution. There really is no way to bridge the gap between our positions. However I do think they will give us room to seize the initiative (if we can do it); I believe Castro when he says that Cuba will not be an obstacle to peace. They won't be helpful; we shouldn't have any illusions about that, but they won't be an obstacle, at least in their own terms, at this time. You can be sure, however, that if we trip, they will strike like vultures."[12]

Several months later, Under Secretary Newsom told the Africa subcommittee of the House Committee on Foreign Affairs, "It is hard to see the constructive hand of either the Soviets or the Cubans influencing the government of Angola, or any other government in which they have a presence, toward a constructive attitude toward the peace efforts [in southern Africa]." The subcommittee's chairman, Stephen Solarz (D-N.Y.), interjected, "I was under the impression, Mr. Secretary, that at least in the case of Angola, the government of that nation has played a very constructive role in the search for a settlement in Namibia. Whether that was in spite of the presence of Cuban troops or because of them, or whatever, the fact is that they have been as cooperative as I gather we have asked them to be and as we could have expected them to be." Newsom acknowledged that the Angolan government had "pursued a constructive policy," but argued that the Cubans were not a constructive presence, an assertion that was contradicted by the State Department's own conclusion that "Cuba encouraged Angola to improve relations with Zaire. It also encouraged and assisted Neto in disarming the Katanganese and moving them away from the frontier. Cuba did not play a spoiler role in the Namibian settlement; on the contrary, it supported SWAPO in accepting it."[13]

Indeed, the Cubans hoped that the negotiations for majority rule in Rhodesia and Namibia would succeed. They saw their role as strengthening the liberation movements and preventing an unjust settlement. They did not want to intervene militarily if they could avoid it. In December 1977 Raúl Castro said as much to President Machel, when the latter mused that he might have to ask for Cuban troops to help defend Mozambique against Rhodesian incursions. "I must tell you frankly," Raúl said, "that in addition to our country's normal limitations—its level of economic development, its lack of natural resources, its small size, its location ninety miles from the United States, etc., etc.—one must now add several other factors . . . including the military aid we are giving to ten friendly countries and the present concentration of our men and material resources in Angola and Ethiopia. . . . This represents not only an economic burden for us, because we bear all the costs of our military assistance, but also a significant reduction in our own ability to defend our homeland and in the availability of materiel and military cadres at home."[14]

In January 1979, one month after meeting with Pastor and Tarnoff, Fidel Castro told Agostinho Neto that the United States would like . . . to be reassured about Namibia and Zimbabwe. . . . I have always thought that it is not likely that we will intervene in this struggle, but we have categorically refused to give them any promise about this. . . . I think that if we reassured them . . . about [what we intend to do in] Zimbabwe and Namibia, we would free their hands to carry out their colonialist policy. . . . The Americans would have been happy if we had told them: don't worry, there is no possibility that we will provide any direct assistance to these movements. We have refused to give them this peace of mind. . . . They would like it, they have tried to get from us some sort of promise that we won't give any direct assistance. . . . There is a fundamental principle: we must give no solace to the enemy. This is the approach that we have followed. . . .

Rhodesia's acts of aggression against Mozambique have been increasing. . . . They [the Mozambicans] have asked us to help them, but they wanted military assistance, planes, artillery and all the rest. Comrade Neto, we are in a situation where it is very difficult for us to do more than we are doing.

Lately we have received many requests for military assistance. A year ago, when the war was raging in Ethiopia, Samora [Machel] asked us for help. . . . Not long ago, he asked us again because of all the attacks he was enduring from Rhodesia. I took advantage of [UN secretary-general Kurt] Waldheim's visit to Cuba approximately fifteen days ago, and I explained the situation to him . . . and said that the Mozambicans were very angry because of the Rhodesian campaign of attacks on their country. I told Waldheim that it was important to avoid a new complication and that the United Nations had to do something to stop Rhodesia's systematic aggression against Mozambique.

This worried Waldheim, and he promised that he would speak with the United States and with all the countries that . . . could help stop the aggression against Mozambique. Later he sent me a message saying that he had spoken with Vance and with the South Africans, that he had spoken with everybody, warning that the attacks had to end, because they threatened to ignite a serious conflict in the region. . . .

We thought that this was the best we could do, this kind of démarche, resorting to diplomacy and asking the United Nations, Neto, because there wasn't anything else we could do. Do you understand? Because we cannot intervene militarily by ourselves. What resources would we have to deal with a situation like this? The Soviets could do it, but right now . . . with all the international complications, in the midst of the SALT negotiations, it seemed to me very difficult, really very difficult, to imagine that Mozambique could receive the military assistance—the materiel, weapons and soldiers—that it needed. One thing is clear: we absolutely could not do it alone. . . . It would have to be a coordinated effort of the Socialist camp as a whole, and especially of the Soviet Union.[15]

Castro's words may suggest that U.S. officials overstated the likelihood of Cuban military intervention in southern Africa, but it is impossible to be sure. If the war in Rhodesia had gone on much longer, the Cubans might have finally agreed to send troops to help defend Mozambique, and Cuban military instructors might have eventually appeared in Rhodesia. After all, for many months in 1977, Castro had resisted Mengistu's demand for troops. The Americans knew it would be difficult for Castro to open another front, but they also knew that it would have been possible: "There remain substantial constraints on the size and scope of Cuban/Soviet involvement in Rhodesia," the CIA said in June 1979. "Nevertheless if the Patriotic Front and the Frontline Presidents should endorse either a limited or direct intervention in Rhodesia, we believe Cuba is prepared to provide the necessary troops and would receive logistic and materiel support from the Soviets."[16] This fear that the Cubans might "strike like vultures" helped keep Jimmy Carter on the straight and narrow path. Despite Congress's pressure, he refused to lift the sanctions after the April 1979 elections in Rhodesia. This prodded British prime minister Margaret Thatcher, who was sympathetic to the internal settlement, to follow his lead, reluctantly.

Unable to win U.S. and British support, and facing a growing guerrilla challenge, Ian Smith bowed to the inevitable. At Lancaster House, in late 1979, he and his black partners agreed to free elections under international supervision and with the participation of ZAPU and ZANU. Mugabe's ZANU won in a landslide, gaining fifty-seven out of eighty seats to ZAPU's twenty.

In 1976–78, Cuba had supported only ZAPU and distrusted ZANU, which it considered pro-Chinese. By 1979, however, Castro had come to appreciate ZANU. "I have the impression that ZANU has been fighting much harder [than ZAPU]," he told Neto when they met in January 1979. And he added: "We have decided to give ZANU . . . some economic aid; . . . but it is very difficult for us to increase our aid beyond this as long as there are tensions and divisions between them [ZANU and ZAPU]." ZANU's leader, Robert Mugabe, was sending signals that he wanted a closer relationship with Cuba—"he wants to get closer to the Socialist countries, he wants to develop his relations with the USSR." The problem, from Castro's perspective, was ZAPU, whose leader, Joshua Nkomo, "is very opposed to us developing our relations with ZANU."[17] Furthermore,

Cuba's two closest allies in the region, Angola and the Soviet Union, maintained a privileged relationship with Nkomo's ZAPU and did not intend to change. As Angolan foreign minister Jorge told Soviet deputy foreign minister Leonid Ilyichev in February 1979, Angola "is ready to help [Mugabe's] ZANU, if the latter normalizes its relations with [Nkomo's] ZAPU," but by "normalize" Jorge meant "take a subordinate role"—and this ZANU was not about to do. The Soviets' position was similar. They continued to distrust Mugabe as pro-Chinese.[18]

Castro feared that the fragile alliance between the two movements would collapse. "It is very hard for them to work together," he told Neto.

> There is a real risk of conflict between them. We will continue to help ZAPU, because we have a longstanding relationship and commitments that have deep roots. But we have an obligation to do everything we can to help them reach an understanding and work harmoniously with ZANU; we have the duty to make sure, as far as possible, that on the day the country becomes independent, it will not plunge into a civil war. I think that we can have a positive influence. . . . We will continue to help ZAPU. . . . But we also have the right to maintain some contacts, some relations with ZANU. We are not ZANU's enemies, and we cannot fail to acknowledge that . . . many ZANU guerrillas are fighting and dying to free Rhodesia from the fascists.[19]

Cuba gave ZANU some economic aid and urged the Soviets to do likewise. "'In Moscow they are taking care of this,'" Gromyko told the Soviet ambassador in Havana, Vorotnikov, "quite sharply" when the latter reminded him, in October 1979, that the Cubans "were waiting for an answer from Moscow." Gromyko's subtext was, "Don't push us," Vorotnikov explains in his memoirs. A month later, Venyamin Chirkin, a Soviet adviser to Nkomo, met Mugabe at a diplomatic reception. "The encounter was frosty," he writes. "Mugabe kept complaining that the Soviet government was ignoring him even though he was one of the leaders of the liberation movement." As the two foremost experts on ZANU note, Mugabe's "approach to Havana elicited some response, while the one to Moscow fell on deaf ears."[20]

Moscow paid a price. After ZANU won the February 1980 elections, Mugabe's government established diplomatic relations with Cuba immediately,[21] but the Soviet Union had to wait until February 1981 before Mugabe allowed it to open an embassy in Harare—as a Soviet official remarked bitterly, it had taken Moscow ten months of efforts.[22] Adding insult to injury, the United States was "the first country to open an embassy," on the very day Zimbabwe became independent.[23] For the Carter administration, Zimbabwe was a success story.

# Resolution 435

Rhodesia had been Carter's priority in southern Africa. For Agostinho Neto and his Cuban and Soviet allies, however, Namibia was a far more pressing problem. It was from Namibia that South Africa attacked Angola. While Rhodesia disappeared as a Cold War troublespot in 1980, the crisis in Namibia festered. It was, through the 1980s, a major reason that the Cuban troops remained in Angola, and it was an important battleground of the Cold War.

In 1977 the Carter administration had created the Contact Group, also known as the Five (the United States, Great Britain, France, Canada, and West Germany), to press Pretoria to accept free elections—and independence—in Namibia. On April 25, 1978, South Africa had accepted the Contact Group's plan for UN-supervised elections for the territory. The plan left the enclave of Walvis Bay, Namibia's only deep-water port, in South Africa's hands. The head of Policy Planning at the State Department told Vance: "On the status of Walvis Bay, we are not including it as part of a settlement package. Instead, we have been working with African representatives in the United Nations on a resolution calling for post-independence negotiations between South Africa and Namibia and urging that these negotiations result in Walvis Bay's being included as part of Namibia."[24]

The U.S. representative on the Contact Group, Ambassador McHenry, explains, "We knew there could be no agreement with South Africa if we insisted [on Walvis Bay]. Therefore we worked with the Frontline States on the idea of separating the issue of Walvis Bay. We told SWAPO: you got 99 percent—why hold up agreement for 1 percent?" McHenry conveniently sidesteps the importance of Walvis Bay, the poisoned fruit the Contact Group was leaving behind. More candidly, Assistant Secretary Moose remarks, "We sort of gave away the Walvis Bay issue—that cast a real shadow over the sovereignty of Namibia." SWAPO's president Nujoma told Risquet in July 1978, "This is the most delicate point and the one that's most difficult to solve." Confronted by the united will of the Contact Group, the Frontline States caved and, as the French chargé in Luanda reported, applied "strong pressure" on SWAPO.[25] Zambia's president told Nujoma that "on Walvis Bay he should follow the example of the Cubans, who tolerate the existence of Guantanamo on their territory"[26]—not a very encouraging comparison, as the Cubans could have pointed out.

Neto was in a difficult position. He knew the importance of Walvis Bay. Angolan foreign minister Jorge had told Vance in May 1978, "There is danger that if settlement of the Walvis Bay question is postponed until later, it will become an instrument of pressure or blackmail against Namibia. . . . [There is] no sure guarantee that South Africa would relinquish its control over Walvis Bay in a post-independence negotiation."[27] But Neto desperately wanted a settlement in Namibia and was willing to apply pressure on SWAPO as long as the central point—free elections under UN supervision—was upheld. In June 1978, at Neto's request, McHenry visited Luanda for bilateral talks. The Angolans were eager for U.S. recognition and U.S. help in restraining South Africa; McHenry insisted that Angola support the Contact Group's plan. Under pressure from the United States and his fellow Frontline presidents, Neto agreed to apply "strong pressure" on Nujoma.[28] "All of the Frontline States accepted the Five's [the Contact Group's] position on Walvis Bay," recalls Theo-Ben Gurirab, a key SWAPO negotiator. "It was accepted by Angola, by all of them. The talks between us and the Frontline States were not always happy!" SWAPO reluctantly gave in. "It took a lot of counseling from the representatives of the Frontline states," two Zambian officials remarked.[29] On July 12, 1978, SWAPO accepted the Contact Group's plan.

On July 27, following the script prepared by the Contact Group, the Security Council voted on two resolutions. The first, Resolution 431, endorsed the Five's plan. The Soviet Union and Czechoslovakia, the two Soviet bloc countries on the council, objected to the exclusion of Walvis Bay and cast the only abstentions. Non-aligned countries expressed concern about Walvis Bay but voted in favor, and the resolution was approved, with two abstentions. Next, the Security Council unanimously approved Resolution 432, which stated that Namibia's territorial integrity and unity "must be assured through the reintegration of Walvis Bay within its territory" and that South Africa must not use Walvis Bay in any manner "prejudicial" to Namibia's independence or its economy. After the vote, Vance addressed the council on behalf of the Five. While "we recognize that there are arguments of a geographic, political, cultural, and administrative nature which support the union of Walvis Bay with Namibia," he said, "this resolution [432] does not prejudice the legal position of any party."[30] The *New York Times* remarked, "In an obvious attempt to steer between the opposite sides, Mr. Vance said that the West supported the second resolution, recognizing that there were geographic, political, social, and administrative arguments favoring its being unified with Namibia. But he balanced this with an interpretation intended to mollify South Africa, saying that there was no prejudgement of the legal issues, no intention to 'coerce,' and that in calling for steps toward 'reintegration,' direct negotiations between the parties were being suggested." The South Africans, however, were not mollified. Foreign Minister

Pik Botha told the Security Council, "I want to make it absolutely clear that Walvis Bay is South African territory. . . . We categorically reject the resolution on Walvis Bay."[31]

On July 13, the day after SWAPO had accepted the Contact Group's plan, Carter wrote to Tanzania's President Nyerere: "Recent events in Namibia are particularly encouraging. . . . Although much remains to be done, prospects for a successful resolution of this problem have never been better."[32]

It was now time for the United Nations to enter the scene. As UN under-secretary Brian Urquhart writes, the Five's plan "contained a number of uncertainties and ambiguities"[33]—for example, it stipulated that there would be a UN peacekeeping force in Namibia, but it did not specify how many troops and from which countries. Resolution 431 had instructed Secretary-General Waldheim to fill in the blanks. On August 29, Waldheim presented his report. It proposed a UN force of 7,500 troops and a UN police component of 360 men to monitor the South African police; elections would take place seven months "from the date of approval of the present report by the Security Council."[34]

The report was greeted with rumbles of discontent in Pretoria. "A complete collapse looms over Southwest Africa [Namibia]," the Cape Town *Burger* wrote. "A dark cloud hangs over the plan for the Southwest." Echoing the government's line, it warned that Waldheim's report included "serious deviations" from the Contact Group's plan that South Africa had accepted the previous April.[35] Pik Botha lamented, "We always try to give the Western powers courage so that they will stand by their own proposals, which they told us were final and definitive." Condemning the West's "hypocrisy," he added, "Now, for the first time, I can understand what the black leaders of Africa must have suffered under the colonialists."[36]

The Contact Group went to work "to alleviate South African concerns," Deputy Secretary of State Christopher reported to Carter.[37] At Vance's urging, Waldheim explained to Pik Botha that the figure 7,500 "would be the authorized upper limit of the military component and it is obvious that the actual size [of the UN force] at any given time will depend upon the development of the general situation, which I shall keep under constant review."[38] To no avail. On September 20, 1978, Prime Minister Vorster delivered his country's response. In a televised press conference, he announced that he was going to resign as prime minister because he was in poor health. (He was also about to face a major political scandal.) Then he turned to Namibia: Waldheim's plans for 7,500 UN troops, 360 UN police, and a spring 1979 election were flagrant deviations from the Contact Group's proposal. "Efforts to resolve the differences over the Southwest had failed," he said. "We could not allow the impasse . . . to continue indefinitely." Therefore, he announced, South Africa would supervise elections in Namibia for a constituent assembly in late November 1978—without UN participation.[39] A few hours later, the administrator general of Namibia told a press conference in Windhoek that "the elected assembly would be given wide powers to pilot the territory to independence. . . . One of the prerogatives of the elected assembly would be to request the continued presence of the SADF [South African Defence Force] in the territory after independence. SA would consider such a request 'favorably.'"[40]

*Die Republikein*, mouthpiece of Pretoria's client in Namibia, the Democratic Turnhalle Alliance (DTA), celebrated. "Only sixty more days, and the Southwest will have its own government," it blared above the fold. The DTA leaders knew that they would win any election controlled by South Africa, and they could taste power. "One sensed this," the liberal *Rand Daily Mail* reported from Windhoek, "in the jubilant atmosphere at the DTA press conference shortly after the election announcement. Whisky and wine were served to pressmen after a short speech welcoming South Africa's decision."[41]

In a well-reasoned editorial, the *Rand Daily Mail* debunked Vorster's claim that Waldheim's report contained substantial deviations from the Contact Group's plan. It pointed out that the Five had asked the secretary-general to determine the size of the UN peacekeeping force and had stipulated that the elections would take place after a seven-month preparatory period. "But whatever the niceties of these arguments, the important question is: Do they really matter? What is so serious about a four-month postponement of independence? And what is wrong with a peacekeeping force of 7,500?"[42]

A few days later, on September 28, 1978, the parliamentary caucus of South Africa's ruling National Party chose Defense Minister PW Botha to succeed Vorster. In a perceptive analysis, the CIA wrote that the choice of PW Botha as prime minister "shows that South Africa intends in the future to rely more on self-sufficiency than on international cooperation to solve its problems. As minister of defense for the past 12 years, Botha built up the country's strong defense force. He has taken a hawkish military stand, ordering the 1975 South African incursion into Angola and the recent retaliatory attacks against SWAPO bases in Angola and Zambia. Botha also led the cabinet in its recent decision to break off negotiations with the UN on the Namibia settlement proposals. He can be expected to continue this policy of swift action against the threat of guerrilla raids. Botha . . . will continue his uncompromising position on international issues affecting South Africa, such as Namibia."[43]

On September 29, the UN Security Council adopted Resolution 435, which endorsed Waldheim's report on the implementation of the Contact Group's plan by a vote of twelve to zero. (The Soviet Union and Czechoslovakia abstained; China did not vote.)[44] PW Botha immediately rejected the resolution. "The probable reasons for South Africa's decision to walk away from their earlier agreement to the proposals are various," three senior aides wrote to Vance. First, Pretoria was convinced that its "security was not compatible with a Namibia dominated by SWAPO—the presumed winner in an internationally supervised election." Second, it "was persuaded that the West would never agree to sanctions against South Africa." Third, it may have "never intended to go along [with the proposals] but assumed that SWAPO would torpedo the negotiations at some stage."[45]

## Brzezinski versus Vance

On October 3, 1978, Vance told the Tanzanian foreign minister, "It is now up to the Contact Group to try to get South Africa to change its mind."[46] Two weeks later, a top-level delegation from the Five—Vance; the foreign ministers of England, Canada, and West Germany; and the French deputy foreign minister—flew to Pretoria to persuade Prime Minister Botha to cancel the Namibian elections and accept Resolution 435. "The talks will provide a major test for the credibility of Washington's Africa policies," the *Washington Post* wrote. "South Africa's intransigence could pose Washington and its allies with the necessity of demonstrating to black Africa that its threat to back sanctions is not empty."[47]

The South African Foreign Ministry feared sanctions. In 1979 it warned: "Whereas in the past South Africa has been able to avoid the imposition of sanctions, against expectations even at the time of [the SADF's attack on the SWAPO refugee camp at] Cassinga, a final break in the [Namibia] negotiations will represent a confrontation of a totally different magnitude. Easily institutable [sic], punitive and highly effective measures against South Africa, such as the denial of landing-rights and refusal to handle South African cargo, have in the meantime already been formulated. These can be instituted at short notice and with minimum effect on those instituting them."[48]

The Contact Group's negotiations with South Africa had begun, in April 1977, with the implicit threat of sanctions. "Whenever you make a threat like this," McHenry remarks, "you have to explore how to back it up. We created a very high-level group of experts from all the five members of the Contact Group to look at the question, what tools were available, and how effective they would be."[49] Following Vorster's rejection of Resolution 435 in September 1978, the experts presented the foreign ministers of the Five with a list of twelve possible sanctions that the UN Security Council could adopt against South Africa.

The experts, Foreign Secretary David Owen told the British cabinet, "had concluded that the two measures most likely to administer the short sharp knock which might bring the South Africans around [on Namibia], were a mandatory embargo on air transport to and from South Africa and an embargo on imports of agricultural and food products from South Africa."[50]

In his memoirs, Vance noted, "My advisers strongly urged that we seek a decision from the president that the United States be prepared to support and initiate sanctions if necessary."[51] An NSC meeting on Africa had been scheduled for October 6, 1978. In a forceful October 5 memo to Vance, Assistant Secretary Moose and Policy Planning Director Lake wrote: "The agenda prepared by the NSC staff . . . proposes the discussion of Rhodesia, Namibia, South Africa, Angola . . . within the context of confronting Soviet/Cuban military activities on the continent. Concentrating on the Soviet/Cuban angle is analogous to treating the symptoms, not the disease." The meeting, they argued, should focus instead on Namibia and the possible adoption of sanctions against South Africa, adding, "The South African regime doubts that the West will have the resolve to impose economic sanctions. Only this resolve offers hope of turning them around."[52] The following morning, at the October 6 NSC meeting, just days before he left for South Africa with his colleagues from the Contact Group, Vance said, "We will probably be unsuccessful and have to go on to sanctions." He proposed a cutoff of all air transportation to South Africa and a suspension of credits. "Both of these would be for three months." He believed that "the other Contact Group members are with us."[53]

Brzezinski thought that Vance was focusing on the wrong issue. The problem, he asserted, was not South Africa, but Cuba and the Soviet Union. "There is a larger issue," Brzezinski said at the NSC meeting:

This administration has been activist, morally motivated, and urged moderation. The President's prestige is involved. I do not believe we will be successful because the Soviets and the Cubans offer military radical solutions. There are two courses of action open to us. First, if the Soviet and Cuban problem is a long-term threat we should make it a major issue in our relations with them. We must demonstrate to the Africans that military solutions are not viable. Second, if we cannot do this we should slowly and subtly lower our level of involvement. We could maintain our moral position but admit that there is little we can do. We are not able to succeed unless we face up to the Soviet and Cuban problem. The African moderates in time might also realize the harm that the Cuban presence brings about.

It required a fevered imagination to make the Cubans and the Soviets responsible for the impasse in Namibia. Vance replied, "I believe that there is a third
way and that is bringing about peaceful solutions. We should continue along
that route. The next step is sanctions directed to the Namibia problem." He
was strongly supported by UN ambassador Andrew Young, who argued that
"Namibia is the key: a limited success there will undercut the military option." Addressing the possible sanctions, Young added that "the three-month
period banning air travel is fortunate. Congress will be out of session and it
will cover the Christmas season when many South Africans go abroad. It will
show the South Africans what it is like to retreat into the laager [circle the
wagons]."

Vice President Mondale, Treasury Secretary Michael Blumenthal, and Defense Secretary Harold Brown also spoke, briefly. They were on the fence. But
not Brzezinski: "We must also consider the impression here," he countered,
raising domestic considerations. "We would be setting up an air blockade
while Soviets and Cubans fly troops to Africa; we would be suspending credits while our allies give credits to Cuba. We should put pressure on them."
Powerful words that addressed the concerns of a president who was haunted
by the accusation that he was soft on Cuban and Soviet aggression in Africa.
Carter responded. "We are on shaky ground pressing South Africa too far."[54]
He did not reject the possibility of sanctions outright, but he deferred making a
decision.

## High Noon in Pretoria

Vance left for Pretoria without having the sanctions arrow in his quiver. Instead
he carried a letter from Carter "earnestly" urging PW Botha to support Resolution 435 and dangling a carrot: the possibility of an invitation to the White
House.[55] The South African prime minister was in a belligerent mood: "My advice is—stop shouting at us," he said in his welcoming remarks to Vance and his
colleagues on October 16. "Stop creating stumbling blocks in our way. . . . Our
different indigenous people, White, Brown and Black, have never been slaves.
We do not intend being slaves now or in the future." As two biographers of
Botha note, "Thereafter followed a couple of days of drama."[56] PW Botha "was
as tough as nails and a bully to boot," recalls British foreign secretary Owen.[57]

The bully, however, wanted to avoid a rupture that might force the Five to
support economic sanctions, and the Five were even more eager to find a way
to avoid them. And so, an agreement was reached. It was, as the *Washington*

*Post* noted, "a patchwork of deliberately ambiguous understandings."[58] South Africa insisted that the internal elections would take place in Namibia, and the Five reiterated that they would consider the vote "null and void." But PW Botha promised that the South African government would "use its best efforts to persuade" the leaders elected at the polls to work with the UN secretary-general to achieve a resolution "within the framework" of Resolution 435.[59]

"According to well informed sources," the *Washington Post* wrote, "staff members of the Five Western foreign ministers were uneasy over the accommodations the ministers displayed in meeting with the South Africans." None more than McHenry. "The normally ebullient diplomat who . . . is primarily responsible for the progress that has been made in the Namibian negotiations, was noticeably withdrawn and worried, refusing to talk to reporters and resembling Abraham being asked to put a child to sacrifice."[60]

The foreign ministers, however, chose to hope that Resolution 435 was still on track. "In public presentations the efforts of the Five were devoted to trying to make the agreement reached with the South Africans sound better than it really was," Foreign Secretary Owen told the British cabinet.[61] Accordingly, Vance said that the agreement represented "a step forward," Owen called it "a fresh commitment by South Africa to seek an internationally acceptable solution in the territory," and West German foreign minister Hans-Dietrich Genscher said that it represented decisive progress.[62] While Vance, Owen, and Genscher tried to dress up what had been achieved, and the French deputy foreign minister said nothing, the Canadian foreign minister was frank. He "made it plain that the real objective of the compromise formula was to avert U.N. sanctions against trade with South Africa."[63]

The Africans were not duped. They "suspect rightly that our actions were strongly influenced by the wish to avoid putting our economic links with South Africa at risk," Owen admitted. Nor was the London *Times* impressed: "The Western Powers will have difficulty in persuading the United Nations that the compromise reached in their foreign ministers' talks with the South African government is anything but eyewash."[64]

Eyewash was all that was needed. On November 13, 1978, when ten members of the UN Security Council voted in favor of Resolution 439, which threatened South Africa with economic sanctions if it did not cancel the elections in Namibia and cooperate with the United Nations on the implementation of Resolution 435, the Five abstained, arguing that threatening sanctions amounted to "prejudging" South Africa's response.[65] As Vance writes, "Western credibility with the African states was damaged by this vote."[66]

From December 4 to 8, elections took place in Namibia in an environment of massive intimidation. *Le Monde* reported, "Several churchmen have publicly denounced and given examples of the acts of torture carried out by the South African army as well as the irregularities that took place at the registration of the voters. Judge [M. T.] Steyn [the South African administrator general of Namibia] immediately ordered these clerics' deportation."[67] Only the DTA and four minuscule parties participated in the vote. Predictably, the DTA gained forty-one of fifty seats in the Constituent Assembly. In Windhoek *Die Republikein* applauded: "A giant victory for democracy." On December 21, the forty-one DTA deputies duly approved a motion proposing that the assembly cooperate with the United Nations on the speedy implementation of Resolution 435; this fulfilled the promise that PW Botha had made to the Contact Group the previous October. "The breakthrough decision," the *Rand Daily Mail* explained, "follows strong pressure" from the South African government. PW Botha and Foreign Minister Pik Botha (no relation to PW) "applied pressure during a two day visit to Windhoek."[68]

On December 4, 1978, the same day the fraudulent elections began in Namibia, Andrew Young told President Machel of Mozambique "that we were rapidly approaching a showdown in Namibia that would climax in not more than a month." If South Africa refused to move on the implementation of Resolution 435, it would mean, Young explained, "a move toward sanctions that were not too costly to anyone. . . . A complete ban on airline transportation, commercial and otherwise, had been contemplated by some of the Western Five." Machel was not impressed. He told Young that "the five powers had lost the battle with SA."[69] He was right.

The State Department continued to propose that serious consideration be given to sanctions, but with diminishing credibility. "The difficulty," Policy Planning Director Lake told the British ambassador, "was that Botha placed little credence on the Western position. It was not easy to see how we could convince him that we meant business."[70] In April 1979 a State Department cable said, "On the sanctions issue, we believe the Contact Group must stick with the basic position that we would support some form of Chapter VII [which authorizes mandatory sanctions] action against South Africa if the SAG [South African government] refuses to cooperate on Namibia." But all that happened was another letter from Carter to Prime Minister Botha, gently waving the stick ("Should the UN plan fail to receive South Africa's support, I believe that UN measures against your country would be inevitable") and dangling the carrot ("If there is agreement on the UN proposals, I believe it would be useful for us to get together at an early date").[71] Botha was neither intimidated nor tempted.

Penelope's Web

For Pretoria the two approaches—the internal settlement and Resolution 435—ran along parallel tracks. As Jay Taylor, who was the political officer in the U.S. Embassy in Pretoria tasked with Namibian affairs, remarks, "The South Africans were willing to go on with 435, but on the assumption that the DTA would win [the elections]. They had poured a lot of money into it." They hoped that, given more time and money—and an iron fist against dissenters—the DTA might eventually "win even under UN supervision."[72]

An "election under UN supervision (Resolution 435 with a few adjustments)," the SADF warned in December 1978, "can only be accepted if the risk of a SWAPO victory is kept within acceptable limits."[73] As the months passed, Pretoria became ever more convinced that SWAPO, not the DTA, would win a free election. Therefore, through Carter's last two years, the South Africans dodged and delayed. No sooner was one issue settled with the UN secretary-general or with the Five than Pretoria raised a new objection. As UN undersecretary Urquhart notes, South Africa's strategy "was to give the appearance of cooperation but to block actual progress."[74]

Pretoria's strategy of masking its "inflexibility" with a display of "outward reasonableness," as its Foreign Ministry explained,[75] made it easier for the Five to delude themselves. Time and again the South Africans promised, as Vance told Carter, that they were ready "to accept the 'original' Contact Group proposal"[76]—if only the Five could adjust the implementation modalities established by Waldheim. It was a transparent ploy, but it provided enough cover for the Western governments to delay sanctions they were eager to avoid. It made it possible to tell Africans with a straight face that sanctions were untimely, because the negotiations were ongoing. As Moose remarked, "They [the South Africans] kept stringing the negotiations out."[77] It was, simply, a sham.

In January 1980 PW Botha revealed how he would protect South Africa's security to his top aides, explaining that "if the coordinated use of the military, political, economic and social measures could not achieve the desired results, then one must achieve a solution not through conciliation and compromise, but through violence." Turning to Namibia, he concluded that "Resolution 435 will not be implemented, and there will be no UN-supervised elections in Southwest Africa."[78]

Washington, however, clung to hope. In February 1980 the CIA reported, "South Africa appears to be delaying a settlement in Namibia until it sees how things go in [the forthcoming elections in] Rhodesia and until it is confident that SWAPO will lose a UN-sponsored election."[79] As a senior aide of Pik

Botha writes, the South Africans made "every effort . . . in terms of money, organization and even weapons, to promote the cause of Bishop Muzorewa," Smith's partner in the internal settlement in Rhodesia.[80] They failed miserably. The results of the Rhodesian elections—the overwhelming victory of the most radical faction—were the worst possible outcome for Pretoria. "South Africa's attitude is bound to harden . . . if Mugabe's party comes to power," the Zambian ambassador in Gaborone had warned in an insightful report.[81] Mugabe's victory also shocked white Namibians. "The DTA is terrorized that what happened in Rhodesia could happen to them," PW Botha told the State Security Council.[82] The council concluded in April 1980 that "an election in Southwest Africa [Namibia], with or without UN supervision, would not be in South Africa's interest." It reiterated in October 1980 "that under no circumstances would the whites of Southwest Africa be 'sold out.' South Africa would rather break with the UN than deliver Southwest Africa to SWAPO. . . . If there must be war, South Africa would rather fight where its troops are now [in Namibia] than along the Orange River [the border between Namibia and South Africa]."[83]

The vigor and venom of the State Security Council's remarks reflected the importance of Namibia to South Africa's sense of security. Pretoria could tolerate an independent Namibia only if it was subservient. Under SWAPO, Namibia would be hostile to South Africa and friendly to the hated MPLA, Cuba, and the Soviet Union. The South African army would lose its powerful bases in northern Namibia, from which it could project its power well beyond South Africa's borders, destabilize the MPLA regime in Angola, and assist Savimbi. The whites of Namibia—60 percent of whom were Afrikaners, "kith and kin" to the voters of South Africa's ruling National Party—would be abandoned to hostile black rule. The betrayal of the Namibian whites and the contraction of South Africa's power would demoralize whites in South Africa and give hope to the country's restive black majority.

On January 20, 1981, the day a new administration came to power in Washington, McHenry sent a long cable to the secretary of state. "Following is my assessment of the current situation of the Namibia settlement effort," he wrote: "We have suspected for some time that the SAG's main concern . . . is the virtual certainty that SWAPO would win a UN supervised election in the territory. . . . The SAG has calculated that it faces no serious threat of international action in the foreseeable future. Certainly the experience of the last two years could only reinforce that conclusion. . . . If anything, the SAG would be justified in concluding that the Western Five have been more anxious to avoid a confrontation over Namibia than has the SAG itself. At each juncture when a confrontation could have developed . . . it has been the Five who have taken the initiative to avert such a confrontation and keep the negotiations alive."[84]

## The Blundering Giant

"From the beginning we understood," McHenry told me, "that the Contact Group had a chance to reach a settlement only if we made it clear to South Africa that we could not guarantee, in case of failure, that there would be no sanctions, that is, no guarantee of a veto in the Security Council."[85] It was with this threat that the Contact Group first approached Prime Minister Vorster in April 1977. "In fact, this was the strongest language we ever used in our negotiations," a West German official said. He explained that throughout the negotiations "South Africa displayed two hopes: (i) that SWAPO would be too radical and too suspicious to accept any proposal that the Contact Group would come up with . . . and (ii) that somehow they would manage, with our help . . . to keep the Turnhalle proposals alive and intact."[86]

Pretoria accepted the Contact Group's plan in April 1978 because it thought that SWAPO would reject it. The SADF's attack on the Cassinga refugee camp in May 1978 failed to derail the negotiations, but it tested the Five's mettle: the United States and its allies, "against expectations," as the South African Foreign Ministry wrote, failed to impose economic sanctions even after the massacre. The tepid Western response to Cassinga strengthened Pretoria's belief in the pusillanimity of the West.

When SWAPO accepted the Contact Group's plan in July 1978, South Africa wriggled out of its pledge with spurious objections to Waldheim's implementation report. The showdown came in October, when Vance and his cohorts—three foreign ministers and one deputy foreign minister—descended on Pretoria to face PW Botha. They left with an agreement that was, as the London *Times* suggested, "eyewash." The *Burger* celebrated. "The danger of sanctions is now diminished," it wrote, and it congratulated PW Botha: "For the Prime Minister this was an extremely successful test so soon after he had assumed his office. His conduct has completely inspired confidence and was impressive." The Five had come to Pretoria with "the firm intention" of making South Africa cancel the election it had scheduled for Namibia. They failed.[87]

The feeling of confidence evident among South African whites in the 1960s and early 1970s had been shattered by the Angolan debacle, the Soweto uprising, continuing black unrest, and the growing international outcry against apartheid. A sense of deep insecurity had gripped South African whites, and they feared sanctions.[88] The South African government, on the other hand, was divided. It had, as Pik Botha explained, "two cultures": the Foreign Ministry, which focused on South Africa's "image in the world" and feared the economic and psychological impact of sanctions, and the "securocrats" in the military and police establishments who focused on internal and external threats and downplayed both the likelihood and the impact of sanctions.[89] We will never know whether Pretoria would have defied sanctions. What we do know is that the credible threat of sanctions, followed by their imposition, if necessary, was the only hope the West had to make South Africa agree to free elections in Namibia.

Almost two decades later, McHenry directed blame at the other members of the Contact Group: "We began to have changes in the Contact Group," he argued. "The election of Margaret Thatcher in England [in May 1979]; change of government in Canada [from May 1978 to February 1979 the Liberals were replaced by the Conservatives]. There was a rightward movement in the Contact Group and the South Africans were eager to exploit any kind of opening of this kind."[90] There was indeed a rightward drift, but that is not what prevented the United States from demanding sanctions against South Africa. That decision had been made well before Thatcher came to power, and it did not hinge on U.S. perceptions of the possible reaction of the other members of the Contact Group. What had been decisive was Brzezinski's argument, clearly expressed at the October 6, 1978, NSC meeting, that the problem was not South Africa, but Cuba and the Soviet Union and that sanctions, therefore, would have struck at the wrong target. Brzezinski prevailed not because his argument was well grounded but because the president agreed with him.

Through four long years, Carter's conservative critics accused his administration of acting abroad like a bumbling, ineffectual giant, projecting an impression of weakness and ineptitude when resolve was needed. This accusation was often unjust, but not in the case of Namibia. There, the Carter administration allowed South Africa to run circles around the Contact Group.


## The Angolan Dead End

The administration's policy was also at an impasse in Angola. The positive approach of early 1977 had been placed on ice by Shaba I, and there was no movement in the months that followed, through the end of 1977. With hindsight, this was the window of opportunity, before the arrival of Cuban troops to defend Ethiopia infuriated the administration and spurred Brzezinski to seek revenge in Angola. Then came Shaba II. "Shaba," remarks McHenry, "was a godsend for the cold warriors. They seized on it to urge a more hardline foreign policy on Carter."[91] In late 1978, the Carter administration's inability to cope with the collapse of the shah's regime in Iran heightened Americans' sense that the president was inept. In April 1979, in one of his weekly reports, Brzezinski offered Carter advice on how foreign policy could help his reelection prospects in 1980. In the obsequious tone he used with the president, the national security adviser wrote: "It is important that in 1980 you be recognized as the President of both Peace and Resolve. Both dimensions are important to the American people. . . . The country wants its president to be a successful world leader and it will be influenced by that when it makes its choice in 1980." Brzezinski reassured the president that the administration's handling of foreign policy had been impressive: "As I think of the last two years, the only two issues on which perhaps we might have taken a different course involved the ERW question [Carter's decision to defer production of the Enhanced Radioaction Weapon, or neutron bomb] and the nature of our response to the Soviet/Cuban military intrusion in Africa. In both cases, I would have favored a different policy. . . . On all other matters, this Administration has been both responsible and, when necessary, decisive." Unfortunately, however, the mass media had "unfairly . . . stimulated the widespread perception of this administration as being indecisive in regard to foreign policy issues. It is very important for you to deliberately counter the impression that American leadership is not firm." Looking toward the 1980 elections, Brzezinski offered the president a list of "things you *must* do in order to maintain momentum in your foreign policy and to shore up your important tangible accomplishments . . . and things you *should not* do because they either detract from your foreign policy accomplishments or because they would complicate your domestic political situation." One of the six items in the "should not" category had to do with Angola: "Normalization without evidently tangible benefits to the U.S. with Cuba, Vietnam and Angola."[92]

Despite the lack of diplomatic ties, U.S. economic relations with Angola were good. As an Italian Communist Party leader perceptively observed after a visit to Angola in September 1977, "We see in Angola, as in Mozambique and other African countries, the familiar paradox: during the war for independence, the assistance of the socialist countries is decisive, but after independence it is the economic, financial and technical contribution of the capitalist West that is desirable and indispensable in the struggle against underdevelopment."[93] Western companies, foremost Gulf Oil, were Angola's key economic partners, and Western countries, foremost the United States, were Angola's major trading partners. Gulf Oil, an American Company, had operated the major Angolan oilfields off the coast of Cabinda when Angola was ruled by Portugal; after the country's independence, it had negotiated a new contract with Sonangol, the

Angolan state oil company, in which Sonangol took a 51 percent interest and Gulf continued as operator. "Gulf has encountered no ideological or discriminatory problems of any significance," a Gulf official told Congress in September 1980. "The government of Angola has proved to be a knowledgeable and understanding negotiator as well as a reliable partner. Moreover, Angola has not interfered, directly or indirectly, in the actual production and/or export of the crude oil produced in Cabinda. . . . In 1979 total production in Cabinda was . . . 98,000 barrels per day . . . Gulf itself has plans for an average annual investment in the region of $110 million over the next 5 years and expects to more than double the present production rate in Cabinda by 1985."[94]

Not only were U.S. economic relations with Angola good, but U.S. officials were also pleased with the constructive role Angola had played in the Namibian negotiations. "Angola was an important factor in securing SWAPO acceptance of our Namibia settlement proposals," Deputy Secretary Christopher told Carter in April 1979. Assistant Secretary Moose told a congressional committee in September 1980, "Angola has played a leading role among the frontline states in working with SWAPO and in developing initiatives to further the Namibia negotiations." The following month Secretary of State Edmund Muskie, who had replaced Vance, told the Angolan foreign minister that Luanda's role in Namibia "has been useful and valuable."[95]

The State Department argued that if the United States took one more step and recognized the MPLA government, it could reap even more benefits from the relationship. "Our Western allies have recognized Angola," Christopher told Carter. "Many have urged that the West, including the United States, should provide Angola with an alternative to extensive dependence on the USSR and Cuba. . . . A diplomatic presence in Angola would enable us to work more effectively for Cuban troop withdrawal. . . . It also would provide us with far better information on the situation there. . . . Normalization would enhance our relations with the Front Line African States." Furthermore, Moose said, "Angolans have indicated to us that trade with the United States would in all likelihood increase substantially if there were diplomatic relations. Similarly, there are American businesses which are reluctant to pursue existing opportunities in Angola absent an official U.S. presence there." And he added, "If it can be this good without a presence there, just think how much better it would be if we were there."[96]

The problem was that there were Cuban troops in Angola. A few Americans dared suggest that their presence was justified. In a 1980 congressional hearing on Angola, Professor Gerald Bender made a telling point: "The situation is analogous to events in other areas of the world where the United States provides troop protection to allies in order to discourage foreign incursions. How would Americans react, for example, if South Korea were to suffer the same level of external aggression as Angola and the Soviet Union, or others, called for the immediate withdrawal of all American troops? We would conclude immediately that such a call was nothing more nor less than a cynical plot to overthrow the South Korean government."[97] Moreover, Italy, West Germany, and Turkey had large numbers of U.S. troops on their territory, although they faced no immediate military threat from the Soviet Union.

No U.S. official dared to make this point publicly—it would have been heresy—but some did note that Angola was threatened by South Africa's aggression. Assistant Secretary Moose told Congress: "The South Africans have increased their attacks on the Angolan infrastructure, including targets such as bridges, key railroad links, trucks, factories, and other facilities. They have also bombed Angolan towns and villages. . . . While the South African attacks are highly damaging in themselves, they also support Angolan fears of another South African invasion on the order of that of late 1975."[98]

In late 1979 Vance and McHenry told Carter that the Cubans were in Angola in part because there was no resolution of the Namibian issue. They argued that "the Namibia problem remains despite far-reaching Angolan efforts to reach a solution," that the reason was "South Africa foot dragging," and that Angola had legitimate security concerns as long as South African troops remained in Namibia. They explained that the Angolan leaders—Neto as well as his successor—had assured them "that the Cubans would be withdrawn upon a Namibian settlement."[99]

Brzezinski was not impressed. He reminded the president that diplomatic relations with Angola would lead to "domestic difficulties . . . Savimbi," he added, "will be a guest of [AFL-CIO leader] Lane Kirkland next week, and the chances are that the AFL-CIO will rake you over the coals for 'betraying' a pro-Western African leader." Carter needed union support for his reelection. "Moreover," Brzezinski warned, "we should be careful not to eat our words too rapidly": the administration had consistently said that there could be no relations without a "reduction of the Cuban presence and its eventual elimination."[100] Brzezinski did not address Angola's security concerns or South Africa's responsibility for the Namibian stalemate. His position rested on one bedrock principle: the Cuban troops must leave Angola. In the words of two senior State Department officials, "the Administration's policy as articulated by Dr. Brzezinski [was] that we would not normalize relations with Angola until the Cubans were withdrawn."[101]

The president agreed with Brzezinski. Therefore, diplomatic relations with

Angola were out of the question. "Brzezinski stayed out of Africa—except when the Cubans popped up," Moose remarked.[102] This meant the Horn. And it meant Angola. On July 1, 1980, in one of his first speeches after resigning the previous April, Vance said, "It makes no sense not to recognize the Government of Angola, a government with which we have cooperated in the search for peace in southern Africa despite fundamental differences on other issues." And he wrote in his 1983 memoirs, "This was and remains a serious error."[103]

At no time was there a serious debate within the administration about establishing relations with Angola. "It is too easy to say 'Brzezinski,'" Assistant Secretary Moose candidly remarks. "While I rarely miss an opportunity to point my finger at Brzezinski, the truth is that the State Department chose not to challenge him on diplomatic relations with Angola." Some tried. "I remember writing so many memos urging normalization with Angola," muses Marianne Spiegel, who was the Africa specialist at Policy Planning. "I must have written a memo every week." But she was not sufficiently senior. "It would have been necessary to have one of the [State Department] principals to place Angola very high on the agenda," she adds. Within the State Department, four principals were involved with African issues: Andrew Young; McHenry, who by virtue of his role on Namibia was, by default, the administration's point man on Angola; Moose; and Policy Planning Director Lake. All favored normalization with Angola. Young could have tried to generate a debate on his own, without going through Vance. He had direct access to the president, and he was bold. He wrote a letter to Carter in March 1979 urging that the administration establish diplomatic relations with Angola. But he did not push the issue. Moose, McHenry, and Lake were very close to Vance, but they did not urge the secretary of state to start a debate on Angola within the administration. Moose remarks, "Angola looked too hard because of the Cubans. I was better disposed toward Angola than most people [within the administration] were. But we were running into opposition in Congress and the press on Rhodesia. Furthermore, Carter in Shaba had shown great sensitivity to the way Americans felt about the Cubans." Moose's close ally and friend, Tony Lake, agrees. "It was intractable," he recalls, because of the Cubans and because of domestic politics in the United States. McHenry focused on Namibia. And Vance, who favored normalization in principle, faced more pressing problems. He did not believe that Angola was important enough to try to change the policy, particularly when it went against the inclinations of the president. He had to pick his battles. As Lake observes, "He had so many."[104]

The administration would have faced the opposition of important and growing segments of the public and Congress if it had decided to recognize Angola.

Nonetheless, in January 1979 two influential members of Congress (Senator McGovern and Representative Solarz) assured Moose that they "would anticipate substantial support for outright normalization." The following month, Lake and Deputy Assistant Secretary of State for Africa William Harrop told Vance, "Dick Moose has completed his part of the consultations on the House side, meeting notably with [Congressmen Clement] Zablocki [D-Wis.], [William] Broomfield [R-Mich.], [John] Anderson [R-Ill.], [Charles] Diggs [D-Mich.], Solarz, [John] Buchanan [R-Ala.], [John] Brademas [D-In.], [David] Obey [D-Wis.], and [Dante] Fascell [D-Fla.]. Many of these members predicted flak but none recommend against going ahead, and the reaction was generally favorable." In April 1979, Christopher told Carter, "We would undoubtedly face opposition on the Hill, but we also would have some strong supporters. We would emphasize that we are moving in the context of the cooperation Angola has shown on Namibia and other issues. Opposition could, we believe, be diminished by arguments that we are offering Angola an alternative to dependence on the USSR. Angola's active interest in trade and investment ties, and its good relations with some major American companies, also would be helpful in gaining congressional support."[105]

But nothing happened. Egged on by Brzezinski, the president of the United States opposed establishing diplomatic relations with Angola. Behind the scenes Carter went further: the minutes of the February 23, 1978, NSC meeting and Brzezinski's March 3, 1978, memo to Carter indicate that the administration was funneling covert aid to Savimbi.

## A Failed Administration?

Jimmy Carter assumed the presidency at a time when U.S. prestige abroad was at low ebb: the Vietnam debacle, Watergate, Angola, stagflation, and the CIA scandals had taken their toll.

As a presidential candidate, Carter had criticized Kissinger for being so eager to improve relations with the Soviet Union that he had ignored the West Europeans. He had promised that if he were elected he would seek a new partnership with Western Europe and Japan. His presidency, however, was dominated by what Brzezinski would call the rising arc of crisis, which covered much of the Third World. The earliest hints of the arc were in southern Africa; by late 1977 it had stretched to the Horn of Africa; a year later it extended to Iran; and in December 1979 it ended in Afghanistan. This was the region that absorbed much of the Carter administration's focus. It was in the Third World that the administration scored its victories and suffered its defeats.

By the time Carter stepped down, an image was etched in the mind of most Americans, and it endures to this day: the United States stumbling, on the ropes, pressed by an aggressive Soviet Union. The reality was starkly different. "The striking feature of the widespread perception of American weakness in 1980," Nancy Mitchell writes, "is how wrong it was."[106] The Soviet Union had "won" in the Horn, but what did "victory" mean? It lost its useful military base at Berbera, in Somalia—and gained none in Ethiopia. Mengistu, stubborn, deeply nationalistic, and suspicious of the Soviet Union, granted Moscow only facilities on the Dahlak islands. The fall of the shah was a grievous loss for Washington but no gain for Moscow. Khomeini loathed the United States, but the Soviet Union was a close second. As Mitchell writes, "The Iranian Revolution cracked one of the pillars of the Cold War—that it was a zero-sum game. While the Kremlin did not lose an ally and its embassy was not besieged, the rise of an Islamist state on its border threatened Soviet security in much more immediate ways than it imperiled the United States."[107] And whatever schadenfreude Soviet officials might have enjoyed because of America's discomfiture in Grenada and Nicaragua, neither country offered significant advantages to the Kremlin.

The Soviets had little time to celebrate Carter's reverses because they had their own to mourn. The stagnation of the Soviet economy, already evident in 1976, deepened through the late 1970s, while the West's technological edge over the Soviet Union widened. This had serious military implications, of which the Soviet leaders were acutely aware. The peace treaty between Egypt and Israel consecrated Egypt's status as an American client and crippled Soviet influence in the Middle East. Furthermore, Carter made real the nightmare that had haunted Moscow since Kissinger's trip to Beijing in 1971: he forged a strategic relationship with China directed against the Soviet Union.[108] The Soviet invasion of Afghanistan—perceived by many in the United States as part of a master plan toward the warm waters of the Persian Gulf—was in fact an attempt to prevent the establishment of a deeply hostile regime on the Soviet Union's sensitive Central Asian border. It was an act of despair taken against the advice of the Soviet military leadership. Just months after the invasion, it was obvious that the Soviet army had marched into a quagmire, its own Vietnam. And then, just as the Kremlin was reeling from this right hook came the left jab: Poland.

Economic stagnation and rising dissent in Eastern Europe had deepened through the Carter years. In the summer of 1980, a wave of strikes engulfed Poland. Within a few weeks the Polish government capitulated. The Gdansk Accords granted the workers the right to strike; complete autonomy for the new trade unions; and freedom of expression. On November 10, 1980, Solidarity became the first officially registered independent trade union in a communist country, with an estimated 10 million members. The Soviet Union, desperate to bolster Poland's teetering economy and political stability, increased its economic aid to Poland, adding one more burden to the struggling Soviet economy. Eastern Europe was the heart of the Soviet bloc, far more important—strategically, economically, and psychologically—than Angola, Ethiopia, or Nicaragua. By the end of the Carter administration, it was Moscow, not Washington, that had lost ground in the competition between the two superpowers.

But this was not the view in the United States. Americans were obsessed by the image of an aggressive Soviet Union on the offensive, emboldened by its victories in the Third World and poised for new adventures. And in this headlong offensive, one country was envisioned rushing forward alongside its Soviet masters: Cuba, with its battle-hardened troops marauding southern Africa and Central America.

It was inevitable that Cuba loomed large in the public debate in the United States, given the presence of thousands of Cuban soldiers in Angola and the dispatch of thousands more to Ethiopia. The administration's rhetoric, however, exacerbated the problem, first, by proclaiming the Cuban intervention to prevent Ethiopia's dismemberment by Somalia a gross violation of détente, then by making false accusations against Cuba during Shaba II, and finally with its spurious claims over the Soviet "combat brigade" in Cuba. It puffed up the image of the Cuban threat and then failed to find a way to deal with the monster that was, to a large extent, of its own making. Cuba became a symbol of the administration's weakness.

## CHAPTER 7

# Enter Reagan

## The World of Ronald Reagan

As he ran for the presidency, in 1976 and in 1980, Ronald Reagan sounded a simple theme: America was in decline, but this decline had subjective rather than objective roots. "Do we lack the power?" a prominent Reagan supporter asked. "Certainly not if power is measured in the brute terms of economic, technological and military capacity.... The issue boils down, in the end, to the question of will."[1]

America's will had flickered during the Vietnam War, Reagan argued—not on the battlefield, but at home, when public opinion, misled by craven politicians and a misguided media, turned against a war that America's soldiers were winning. The world had witnessed America's humiliation with ill-concealed satisfaction.

For Reagan, Richard Nixon's détente had been naive—"a one-way street that simply gives the Soviets what they want with nothing in return."[2] No one bore more responsibility for this than Henry Kissinger, with his pessimistic outlook on America's future. Angola in 1975 had epitomized the poisoned fruits of détente. For the first time, the Soviets had dared to engage in a massive military intervention in Africa and had found the gamble painless and profitable. For the first time, the Cuban upstart had taken on a role that was rightfully reserved for great powers. Ford and Kissinger had flailed, unable to devise an effective response—"We blustered and made demands unbacked by action," Reagan said.[3] The debacle deepened the sense of malaise that haunted the American people. That Castro was behind it intensified Americans' outrage and confusion.

Carter's election in 1976 dealt the already faltering and insecure America another blow. For the next four years the United States would be saddled with feeble and hesitant leadership. Meanwhile, an emboldened Soviet Union continued its relentless arms buildup and resorted ever more blatantly to force and subversion. Terrorists were allowed to triumph in Rhodesia, South Africa was spurned as a pariah, and the Cubans—Moscow's proxies—humiliated the United States in the Horn of Africa and spread revolution in Central America.

But the Carter years, Reagan believed, had served as a catharsis. The national pain induced by those four years of humiliation helped the nation to purge its misplaced sense of guilt and to overcome the Vietnam syndrome. In the 1980 presidential campaign, Reagan promised that a resurgent America would regain the military superiority over the Soviet Union that Carter had squandered and would reverse the Soviet gains abroad. For the second time in the Cold War, the theme of liberation was proclaimed in a presidential campaign. In 1952 the Republicans had promised "liberation" of the captive peoples of Eastern Europe and China—but it had been an empty slogan to liberate the White House from the Democrats' clutches. Reagan, however, meant what he said: he would roll back Moscow's gains. His focus was not Eastern Europe, where rollback would have meant war with the Soviet Union, but the Third World where the U.S. defeats of the 1970s had occurred: Vietnam, Afghanistan, Angola, Ethiopia, Zimbabwe, Nicaragua, Grenada.

The Reagan presidency would be defined by two major themes—military superiority over the Soviet Union and rollback in the Third World. There would be a shift in U.S. relations with Moscow in Reagan's second term, roughly corresponding to the coming to power of Mikhail Gorbachev. But there would be no shift in policy toward the Third World.

Reagan rode into the White House at the head of a coalition that included mainstream Republicans (of the Nixon/Kissinger brand) and "Reaganites"— hard-line Republicans and neoconservatives. The latter were converted Democrats who had deserted a party that, they believed, had lost its faith in America's greatness. From the outset there were important differences between the two wings of the Reagan coalition, and they would be amplified and emerge openly in Reagan's second term—when there were fierce debates about how to deal with the Soviet Union as well as rollback in the Third World.

During Reagan's first term, the Soviet leaders believed that a surprise U.S. nuclear strike against the Soviet Union was a real possibility. As the careful study by a CIA analyst indicates, this perception was fueled by the aggressive rhetoric of the new administration and by a series of U.S. psychological warfare operations—air and naval probes near the Soviet borders—that began in February 1981. "It really got to them," recalled a senior U.S. official. "They didn't know what it all meant. A squadron would fly straight at Soviet airspace, and other radars would light up and units go on alert. Then, at the last moment, the squadron would peel off and return home." The sense of danger felt by the Soviet leaders was heightened by the searing memory of Hitler's surprise attack against the Soviet Union, when Stalin disregarded many warning signs, and by the haunting knowledge that the technological edge of the West was widening and that "the correlation of world forces" between the United States and the USSR was turning "inexorably" against the Soviet Union.[4] In late 1983, Reagan wrote in his diary, "I feel the Soviets are so defense minded, so paranoid about being attacked that without being in any way soft on them we ought to tell them no one here has any intention of doing anything like that."[5] The psychological warfare he had authorized was an odd way to convey that message.

## The Reagan Administration and Cuba

If the Soviet Union was, in Reagan's words, the "evil empire," Cuba was its malignant proxy. "I saw Amb. Dobrynin [the Soviet ambassador to the United States] last night," Secretary of State Alexander Haig told the NSC on February 6, 1981. He had told Dobrynin that "the first order of business" in East-West relations was not arms control, but "Soviet activity in Afghanistan and the use of Cuban proxies in troubled areas."[6]

During the presidential campaign, Reagan had proposed blockading Cuba as a way to force the Soviet Union out of Afghanistan "because, let's make no mistake, the Soviet Union owns Cuba lock, stock, and barrel. We blockade it, now it's a grave logistical problem for them [the Soviets]. I'm quite sure they would not come sailing over with a navy and start shooting. But we blockade Cuba, which could not afford that blockade, and we say to them: 'Get your troops out of Afghanistan and we give up the blockade.'"[7]

Soon after Reagan had moved into the White House, an interagency task force on Cuba recommended "a policy of steadily escalating tensions [against Cuba]. . . . Normalization was ruled out even as a distant possibility, no matter what Cuba did."[8] Reagan and his advisers had a burning desire to make Castro pay for his sins. They were also deeply worried about Central America. The backyard, so long an oasis of pro-American stability, was ablaze. The Sandinistas had won in Nicaragua, a strong insurgency threatened the survival of the Salvadoran government, and the guerrillas were gathering strength in Guatemala. In the Caribbean, leftist rebels had seized power in Grenada. At the core of the problem, the president and his aides believed, was Cuba. Cuba was "the source of Central American/Caribbean unrest," National Security Adviser Richard Allen warned in February 1981.[9] "This area is our third border," Haig said. The countries of the region were weak and troubled, but they "could manage if it were not for Cuba." Cuba was "the main issue," he stressed. Secretary of Defense Caspar Weinberger agreed, "The problem stems from Cuba."[10] Haig was relentless: "We must look to Cuba for a part of the solution. The American people won't support another Vietnam situation where U.S. troops are stationed in Central America. Therefore, we must go to the source of the problem and we are preparing a program of actions in regard to Cuba." Reagan concurred: Cuba was "the source of the problem."[11]

It is unclear—because the relevant documents are classified—whether the administration sought merely to intimidate Cuba or to actually use force against it, if the opportunity arose. On February 11, 1981, Reagan jotted in his diary, "Intelligence reports say he [Castro] is very worried about me. I'm very worried that we can't come up with something to justify his worrying." Two weeks later, Haig threatened that if the arms flow to the Central American insurgents continued, the United States would "deal with it at the source," that is, Cuba. Haig fervently argued, Weinberger writes, "that it was quite clear we would have to invade Cuba and, one way or another, put an end to the Castro regime." Robert "Bud" McFarlane, who in 1981 was the State Department's counselor, recalls, "At an early meeting, he [Haig] announced peremptorily: 'I want to go after Cuba, Bud. I want you to get everyone together and give me a plan for doing it.'. . . With the Soviet Union preoccupied with Poland and Afghanistan, he apparently believed that with boldness and sufficient resources we could close Castro down. Further, he believed that doing so was the key to preventing a tide of Soviet-supported subversion from sweeping through Central America and ultimately to South America. . . . By mid-March 1981, the possibility of Soviet intervention in Poland had become acute once more. Haig told me to look at the possibility of going after Cuba as a reaction to a Soviet move into Poland."[12]

McFarlane's account is corroborated by Jon Glassman, who in 1981 was a close aide of Paul Wolfowitz, the director of the State Department's Policy Planning Staff, and by Richard Burt, who was the director of political-military affairs in the State Department. According to Glassman, Haig named McFarlane "as a point man to do a paper, and the object of the paper was to build a case for military action against Cuba, probably invasion. . . . Other people in the [State] Department, Paul Wolfowitz, Richard Burt and others were contributing. The paper never was right, it was done in many, many versions. Finally the CIA took dead aim at the paper. The CIA wanted to make the case that any invasion of Cuba would involve massive American military casualties. They were not the only ones that did not want the invasion to occur." White House Chief of Staff James Baker was opposed, as was Assistant Secretary of State for Latin America

Thomas Enders. "So you had a kind of internal conflict within the Department with harder elements, meaning Wolfowitz, Burt, [UN ambassador] Jeane Kirkpatrick and Bud McFarlane" supporting the idea of military action against Cuba. The Joints Chiefs of Staff, who had been brought in on the planning, were also opposed. "The Chiefs didn't want to do it," Burt noted.[13]

The Soviet Union did not use force in Poland, and "in the end," McFarlane writes, "despite Haig's passionate attitude on the Cuba question, calmer heads prevailed. . . . Haig took his ideas about Cuba to the president himself, who shelved the proposal."[14] It is impossible to determine, however, how firmly Reagan shelved the idea of using force against the island.

The Cubans took the threat of an American attack seriously. Fidel Castro had told GDR leader Honecker in May 1980, "Some Yankees, some groups of intellectuals, argue that when a serious crisis breaks in Iran or Afghanistan . . . or anywhere else in the world, the United States should respond in Cuba. They have said this frequently. Whenever there is a confrontation with the Soviet Union in a place where the balance of forces is not favorable to the United States, then they argue that Washington should respond somewhere where the balance of forces favors the United States."[15] Reagan and his team were now in power in the United States, and their hatred for the Cuban revolution was palpable. A March 1981 Cuban memo noted: "Not since the so-called October Crisis of 1962 has the U.S. attitude toward Cuba been as fraught and aggressive as it has been since the Republicans' 1980 victory." The tension between Washington and Moscow over Poland increased Cuba's peril. "Right now the most important and dangerous problem is Poland," the memo continued. "The Communist Party of Cuba believes that if the members of the Warsaw Pact extend direct assistance to Poland [i.e., intervene militarily], the United States could escalate to a total blockade or an invasion of Cuba."[16]

The Cuban leaders knew that if worse came to worst, they would be on their own. They had faced this prospect during the missile crisis, when Khrushchev had negotiated over their heads with Kennedy. Castro told a high-level East German delegation in 1968, "The Soviet Union has given us weapons. We are and will be forever thankful . . . but if the imperialists attack Cuba, we can count only on ourselves."[17] This realization had not mattered so much in the 1970s, when the danger of U.S. military aggression had receded. But the election of Ronald Reagan changed everything. To appreciate Cuba's policy in Angola, one must keep in mind this double constraint: the threat from the United States and the fragility of the Soviet shield.

On November 23, 1981, at the initiative of Mexico's foreign minister, Haig met in Mexico City with Cuba's Vice President Carlos Rafael Rodríguez.

Throughout the lengthy conversation, Haig treated Rodríguez with respect. "I'm very grateful that you have come from a long distance to this unofficial, secret meeting," he began. His message was simple. The Reagan administration was willing to coexist with Cuba. "Our capability for coexistence, notwithstanding ideological conflicts, is manifested most graphically in relations with other Communist regimes: China, Yugoslavia and a growing number of countries in Eastern Europe." The United States, he hinted, might even lift the embargo: "I know that President Reagan considers trade with Cuba a possibility." But there was a price. Cuba must renounce its subversive activities in Latin America, end its support for the guerrillas in El Salvador, and terminate its military ties with Nicaragua. Even the presence of Cuban teachers in Nicaragua was unacceptable. "They are teaching your philosophy to Nicaraguan children. . . . We do not believe that you have the right to do that." (Rodríguez replied, "These are elementary school teachers who can hardly teach Marxism-Leninism. . . . We think that only the government of Nicaragua, no one else, can decide whether the country needs our teachers.")

Cuba must also withdraw its troops from Africa, Haig said. He was not interested in Rodríguez's explanation of Cuba's policy. "I do not doubt the facts you have marshaled regarding Shaba or the situation in Ethiopia. . . . However we regard this as a serious threat to our vital interests and to the interests of peace and stability." The United States and Cuba were at a crossroad, Haig warned, and there was little time left. He did not explicitly threaten that if Cuba refused to comply the United States would launch an attack on the island, but that was the implication. The urbane tone in which the message was delivered made it more chilling. "We are at a critical juncture in the history of these twenty-odd difficult years," Haig said. "We are faced with a choice. No matter what happens, we think it is essential to conduct negotiations between the two governments prior to proceeding further. . . . We have come to a crossroads which . . . could be described as dangerous. . . . America's national spirit has significantly strengthened lately, which has allowed us to attain unprecedented levels of military expenditures. . . . I can assure you that the mood of the people in the United States is definitely itching for a change in our relations with Cuba, a change that would not be positive for Cuba. . . . [President Reagan] is ready to go to the brink."

Haig and Rodríguez were like ships passing in the night. The Cuban stressed, "We have never refused to engage in dialogue. We have always considered that dialogue must take place in conditions of equality and mutual respect." Haig, however, was not interested in a dialogue and, clearly, the United States did not consider Cuba an equal, with equal rights. Haig demanded that Cuba bow to the will of the United States, and this, Rodríguez said, Cuba would not do. "We are giving and will continue to give Nicaragua our solidarity and support. We consider this our obligation and our right," he said. "You touched on our difficulties and our vulnerability. It is true. We are vulnerable, and our people have suffered a great deal from the American blockade. You call this an embargo. We consider ourselves to be blockaded by the United States. We have suffered physically. Our hospitals at times have been without medicine. We have suffered economically. . . . But I would like you to understand our point of view: we do not intend to sacrifice our fundamental principles for the purpose of achieving that [better relations with the United States]. . . . We are also prepared for a confrontation. We know that such a confrontation would be dramatic for our people. We have no doubt about this. But neither are we afraid of a confrontation." Cuba would honor its commitments to its friends—"There is no obligation that we have taken upon ourselves with any country, group or government that we have failed to honor. This should be clear to the United States."

The meeting ended. Haig returned to Washington and Rodríguez to Havana. Their encounter had served only to highlight their irreconcilable differences. They agreed to remain in contact. Haig said, "We could send our ambassador with special authority, General [Vernon] Walters, to Havana." He repeated that time was short. "We must commence a dialogue immediately." But Haig made clear that this "dialogue" would be the Americans reiterating their demands and the Cubans bowing to them: "Unfortunately, the time has come when the rhetorical debate cannot solve the problem. . . . Cuba is exporting revolution and bloodshed. . . . We believe that it constitutes a threat to peace and stability, and we cannot see it in any other light. . . . You complained about the embargo. So far, the embargo has been ineffective, but we could impose a real embargo." And he repeated, "We must find a solution, if we are interested in peace and stability. . . . Otherwise we will be forced to pursue a different course which, I believe . . . would not be good for you. The United States does not desire this, but after many years of not being in a position to act, we are now prepared to act very quickly. That is why I am saying that we need to find a solution immediately. . . . It would be much easier to achieve our goals by force, but that is not our intention. However, frankly speaking, time is slipping away." If Cuba proved obdurate, "then we move to confrontation, and fast."[18]

Four months later, in March 1982, General Walters flew to Havana to speak with Castro. In his diary Reagan draws an improbable picture. He writes that he had told an NSC meeting on January 15, "My own thought is that we should create a plan to urge Cuba and yes Castro to come back into the orbit of the Western Hemisphere. Castro is in trouble—his popularity is fading, the ec.

[economy] is sinking and [the] Soviets are in no position to help. We could start a campaign to persuade him and the disenchanted Cubans to send the Russians home and once again become a member of the Latin Am. community." Therefore, he sent Walters "to open talks with Castro. It's just possible we could talk him [Castro] into moving back in to this hemisphere."[19] If Reagan believed what he wrote, then he was living in a dreamland, something that should have been clear after the lengthy exchange between Haig and Carlos Rafael Rodríguez, in which the latter, on Castro's behalf, had not given an inch despite Haig's threats.

The talking points prepared for Walters's meeting with Castro make clear that he was expected to threaten, not discuss; demand, not negotiate. "The two countries are headed inexorably toward confrontation," the talking points began.

— We did not seek it, but Cuban activities in Central America challenges [*sic*] our security in a way we cannot and will not ignore;
— We do not propose—as we did in Vietnam—to engage U.S. forces in the terrain of our adversary's choosing. That is neither necessary nor desirable. But the use of force, if necessary, against the source is an option which we do not exclude. That way of dealing with the problem would be both more efficient and more acceptable to the U.S. public;
— Cuba has sent various signals that it is interested in negotiation. . . . We would be willing to try to find an alternative before facing up to that escalation.

That would require, however, that Cuba agree to four nonnegotiable U.S. demands: the end of Cuban "organizational, training and logistical support" for the guerrilla movements in Central America and Colombia; the end of Cuba's security and military assistance to Nicaragua; the withdrawal of the Cuban troops from Angola; and the return to Cuba of the "excludables"—those Cubans with a criminal record or mental problems who had arrived in the United States during the Mariel exodus.

"Time is short for us," the talking points warned. "We hope we do not have to address the solution to the Cuban problem by force. But if we must, it is better to do so early in the administration and when Cuba's protector is tied down in Poland and Afghanistan."[20]

Walters was in Cuba on March 4–5. Since neither the Cubans nor the Americans have declassified the minutes of his conversations in Havana, it is impossible to know what was said. José Luis Padrón, the Castro aide who was one of the few Cubans who participated in the talks with Walters, recalls: "It was a sham. He had no intention of negotiating. He spoke Spanish very well. He even had a South American accent. He was very relaxed. He ate a lot of fruit and lobster; this caught my attention. He came to reiterate the administration's predetermined position—and with his visit our direct contacts with Washington ended." Walters writes in his memoirs, "I thought that he [Castro] believed that we were preparing some sort of action against him and that as long as he could keep some sort of dialogue going, it might postpone this happening. Still he was not prepared to make any concession to ensure this." Reagan, however, appears to have imagined a different meeting. After hearing Walters's report, the president jotted in his diary: "heard Gen. Walters story of his meeting with Castro. Walters does one h-l of a job. He's going back again. . . . He says Castro really sounds like he'd like to make up. Walters let him know we have a price." Two days later he wrote: "Situation room for a hush hush on Cuba. They are uptight thinking we may be planning an invasion. We aren't but we'll let them sweat."[21]

The Cubans were uptight and they did fear an attack. Nevertheless, they were not willing to do what Washington demanded.

## The Cuban Response

Unfortunately, the Cuban government has kept under lock and key the documents that detail its response to the threat posed by the Reagan administration. A sense of what they might contain, however, can be gleaned from other Cuban documents that have been declassified.

The Cubans considered the possible threats to range from an invasion to a total blockade to a partial blockade and finally to surgical air strikes. "Our plans for the possibility of a total blockade," a senior Cuban official explained, were "to resist for a year, evacuating the entire population of Havana and other cities to the countryside. . . . We considered an invasion—which we deemed rather unlikely—and a total blockade the two worst possibilities. In the first case, we calculated that the Yankees would suffer more casualties than in the Second World War. . . . In the second case, the total blockade, a year of resistance would give us enough time to mobilize the world and force the Yankees to lift the blockade."[22]

While the Cubans believed that a full-fledged U.S. invasion was unlikely, they did not think it impossible, and they prepared for the worst as the safest way to deter it. The Revolutionary Armed Forces (Fuerzas Armadas Revolucionarias or FAR) were the first line of defense. The U.S. Defense Intelligence

Agency (DIA) reported that they were "a powerful, well-trained and united military force. Encouraged by what they perceive as successful encounters with the United States and, more recently, by their successful support of both the . . . MPLA and Ethiopian forces, the Cuban government and military exude pride and confidence. Looking to the past as a source of inspiration, MINFAR [Ministry of Defense] is continuing its modernization and development. . . . Thousands of troops have now had actual combat experience in Angola and Ethiopia." Including the "ready reserves" (those reservists who received frequent training and could be mobilized at short notice), the FAR were about 200,000 strong. "The well-trained ready reserves," DIA explained, "are included with the regular forces because they are combat ready and could be mobilized within 4 hours. . . . The Cuban soldiers are literate and well-trained in their specialty. They are politically indoctrinated, well disciplined and loyal. They are accustomed to simple living conditions. . . . Almost all Cubans would defend the homeland without hesitation, particularly against an attack either by the United States or by Cuban exiles. . . . Officers generally are highly motivated, heavily indoctrinated, well trained and accustomed to nonpretentious living conditions. . . . The Cuban Armed Forces," DIA concluded, "are capable of providing a tenacious defense of the island."[23]

Reagan "forced us to change our military concepts, our defense strategy," Fidel Castro told Soviet foreign minister Eduard Shevardnadze. The Cubans began developing this new military strategy in 1980. In Raúl Castro's words, "When we saw the possibility, during the U.S. presidential campaign, that Reagan . . . would win the elections, we began to develop a new military doctrine, based on our own experience and on the idea of the War of the Entire People. . . . It would be a war without fronts or rearguard, in every corner of our country."[24] It would be fought not only by the armed forces but by the entire population, organized into Territorial Militia Troops (MTT). "In the event of an invasion," DIA noted, "MTT men and women are expected to defend key installations in their municipalities, among them factories, bridges, roads and railways. . . . Irrespective of MTT shortcomings, the fact remains that large numbers of Cuban militia and reserves allow the military to defend many installations and areas and thus probably cause substantial losses to an invader." The Cubans were also preparing to resort to guerrilla warfare against the Americans. "We have, in addition to the Soviet advisers for the regular army, Vietnamese military advisers, the wise Vietnamese who know the Yankees' psychology and have defeated them," Risquet said.[25]

Within a few years, Cuba acquired 1.5 million weapons for the MTT. The major supplier was the Soviet Union. In Castro's words, "At the end of the Second Congress [of the Cuban Communist Party, in December 1980], when Reagan was president-elect, . . . we asked [Politburo member Konstantin] Chernenko, who had attended the Congress, for the first weapons for the MTT. We asked him for half a million weapons." The Soviets gave these weapons free of charge, and later they gave more, but not enough to satisfy Cuba's demand. Cuba turned to other countries: "We had to buy arms from everyone, from Poland, Bulgaria, Yugoslavia, [North] Korea. . . . Some gave us weapons for free, Bulgaria . . . also the GDR. . . . Poland sold them to us at a very low price . . . Yugoslavia, a little more expensive . . . and we are grateful, because we needed the weapons."[26] Cuba also bought 100,000 rifles from North Korea. "They gave them to us at cost and offered very good terms of payment."[27]

By the time Reagan took office, the Cubans believed that "the heart of the conflict" with the United States was "in Central America." They thought that the situation in El Salvador was stalemated and that the guerrillas should seek a negotiated solution. They were convinced that Nicaragua was facing an immediate threat from the United States and urged restraint on the Sandinistas: "There is a danger that in their revolutionary fervor the Nicaraguans might try too hard to help the Salvadoran guerrillas," Risquet told Soviet foreign minister Gromyko in December 1981. "We must constantly restrain them, reminding them this carries a high risk."[28]

But if Central America was the major source of tensions between Havana and Washington, Angola was next. The MPLA government faced two threats: Savimbi's UNITA, which enjoyed increasing levels of assistance from South Africa; and, above all, the South African Defence Force (SADF), which was increasingly aggressive and had carried out, in 1980, a raid 180 kilometers deep into southwestern Angola. Because of the SADF's air superiority, the Cubans had withdrawn their troops to a defensive line some 250–300 kilometers north of the border with Namibia. This line protected the heartland of Angola and, by extension, Luanda. The Cubans feared that South Africa, encouraged by Reagan, would launch a major strike against Angola to breach their defensive line. Therefore, they wanted to strengthen their forces, and they turned to the Soviet Union. In May 1981, Cuba's first deputy minister of defense, General Casas, went to Moscow for discussions with the Soviet military leaders. He asked Marshal Nikolai Ogarkov, the chief of the General Staff of the Soviet Armed Forces, for more modern weapons for the Cuban troops in Angola. Ogarkov replied, "It makes no sense to try to have super modern weapons when the enemy [UNITA] does not have them. . . . He stressed that the enemy has antiquated weapons." Casas pointed out that Angola is far away from Cuba. This heightens every threat. . . . South Africa . . . is becoming very dangerous. . . . Fidel thinks that our troops must have everything they need to resist a South African attack. . . . Our major concern is the distance, because if a dangerous situation develops, we don't know how we could reinforce our troops. . . . Marshal Ogarkov said that he understood all this, and that of course it is better to have the best weapons, but it is necessary to think of the cost. We do not send our most modern weapons to Afghanistan. The rebels there don't have modern weapons. . . . He said that in Angola the enemy might have 20,000 men, or 40,000 men . . . There is no need to run after every rebel. The armed forces must hold the key points. Let the insurgents do the running. This is why we don't understand your request for modern weapons. . . . We are delivering arms to the FAR even when it means taking them from our own troops. We have to take care of many needs. Our stocks are exhausted. . . . We urge you to take our problems into account.[29]

Casas and his hosts were talking past each other: the Cubans were thinking of arms to face the SADF, the Soviets only of UNITA. As Casas wrote, "Whenever I stated the need to replace the obsolete armament of our forces in Angola, Ogarkov focused on UNITA. . . . he said that he did not believe that the sophisticated armament should go to Angola, where the enemy has nothing of the kind."[30]

## The Reagan Administration and Southern Africa

Policy toward southern Africa had not entered the public debate in the Carter years. The one exception was Rhodesia, in 1978–79, when Carter rejected the internal settlement crafted by Ian Smith. There was no debate about U.S. policy toward Angola and Namibia for the simple reason that the Carter administration had done nothing to provoke American hard-liners: it refused to normalize relations with Angola, and it opposed sanctions against South Africa. Vis-à-vis apartheid, after an initial roar the administration retreated into morose passivity. There was no powerful constituency in the United States insisting on diplomatic relations with Angola, Namibian independence, or a more aggressive stance against apartheid—not even among African Americans, who were focused on economic problems at home. Southern Africa was not an important issue in the 1980 presidential campaign.

The region was important, however, for the incoming Reagan administration. The Cubans were still in Angola, and their military presence there had grown. They were using the country as a base to train South African and Namibian guerrillas, and the Soviet Union had an important military mission there.

As the CIA noted, southern Africa was "the priority policy concern" of the new administration in sub-Saharan Africa.[31] The omens were good, U.S. officials believed. "The climate for achieving the results which it [the United States] desired had never been better," Deputy Secretary of State William Clark told the South African foreign minister, noting that the Soviet Union was "bogged down in Poland and Afghanistan."[32]

Reagan's assistant secretary for Africa, Chester Crocker, was a conservative academic, highly intelligent and with a caustic sense of humor. But he was not conservative enough for hard-line Reaganites; many within the new administration looked on him with suspicion.

As did the South African government. In his first meeting with Crocker in April 1981, Foreign Minister Pik Botha "raised issue of trust. . . . He said he is suspicious of U.S. because of way U.S. dropped SAG [South African government] in Angola in 1975. He argued that SAG went into Angola with USG support, then U.S. voted to condemn it in UN." Crocker did not deny the charge, but pointed out that "the new Administration is tired of double think and double talk." Instead, in its approach to South Africa it would rely on "constructive engagement."[33]

Crocker was the intellectual father of constructive engagement. Constructive engagement, he wrote in a seminal article in *Foreign Affairs* in late 1980, was predicated on several premises: "the clear Western refusal to resort to trade or investment sanctions against Pretoria"; Western support for "change in the direction of real power sharing" (majority rule was not mentioned); empathy not only for blacks "but also for the awesome political dilemma in which Afrikaners and other whites find themselves." A more friendly U.S. policy, Crocker argued, would encourage Pretoria to make concessions to blacks at home and be less aggressive abroad.[34] "Some of us," UN under-secretary Urquhart writes, "pointed out at the time that 'constructive engagement' implied a very optimistic and innocent view of Afrikaner psychology and politics, but nobody wanted to listen."[35]

It was more than naiveté. Constructive engagement reflected the Reagan administration's empathy for South African whites. As a presidential hopeful, Reagan had endorsed South Africa's policy of separate development—the creation of nominally independent Bantustans. "The Black majority in S. Africa is made up of several different tribes with long histories of conflict and animosity between them," he had explained in a July 1977 radio broadcast. "If . . . the black majority came into power tomorrow, there could very easily be outright tribal war. . . . In coping with this problem, S. Africa has embarked on a plan of setting up separate republics for each tribe, with self rule & complete autonomy for each. . . . One such state has come into existence already, the Republic of Transkei. . . . The new little Republic is pro-Western and anti-communist. . . . The U.S. should recognize Transkei and stop acting foolish." As president, Reagan was more cautious, but his words betrayed his sympathies. In March 1981 he told Walter Cronkite, "Can we abandon a country that has stood beside us in every war we've ever fought, a country that strategically is essential to the free world in its production of minerals we all must have and so forth? . . . If we're going to sit down at a table and negotiate with the Russians, surely we can keep the door open and continue to negotiate with a friendly nation like South Africa." Reagan's words, Crocker wrote with hindsight, "epitomized the insensitivity that would be the sad hallmark of his sporadic personal involvement on South Africa in the years to come."[36] They also epitomized Reagan's ignorance: the National Party, in power in South Africa since 1948, had actively opposed the country's participation in the Second World War. Both Prime Minister PW Botha and his predecessor, John Vorster, had been members of the pro-Nazi Ossewa Brandwag, and Vorster had been interned from September 1942 to February 1944.[37]

In May 1981 Foreign Minister Pik Botha visited Washington to touch base with the new administration. After meeting Reagan, Haig, and other top officials, he reported to the South African cabinet, "I believe that in the entire period since the Second World War, there has never been a US government as well disposed towards us as the present government."[38]

Pretoria also appreciated the new administration's stance toward UNITA. During the presidential campaign, Reagan had publicly expressed his desire "to provide them [UNITA] with weapons."[39] Two months after his inauguration, he approved a memo on "Strategy in Southern Africa" submitted to him by Haig. "The situation in Southern Africa requires urgent action on two issues," the memo began: "(1) whether we should continue to support the UN-sponsored resolution for the independence of Namibia; (2) how to curtail Soviet influence in Angola, manifested by the Cuban troops there." The document included one key idea: "Strengthen Jonas Savimbi and his UNITA group through public support and indirect, covert help, so that he can harass the Cubans in Angola, as part of a broader strategy of pressing the MPLA into dealing with Savimbi and getting rid of the Cubans."[40]

On Namibia, the memo was less straightforward: it paid lip service to Resolution 435, but also proposed to circumscribe Namibia's independence to assure the country's neutrality. Whereas the Carter administration had maintained an ambiguous position on the future of Walvis Bay, Namibia's only deep-water port, Haig's "Strategy in Southern Africa" was categorical: the administration "would stand behind South African retention of Walvis Bay unless and until the SAG itself decides to divest itself of this position." Pretoria's control of Walvis Bay and the "extreme dependence" of any future Namibian government "on Western and South African assistance, investment and trade" would help guarantee that an independent Namibia would not embark on a pro-Soviet path.[41]

What is striking about this document is its lack of any serious consideration of how these goals would be achieved. Crocker addresses this very well in his memoirs. "Neither the detailed terms of an acceptable outcome nor the exact tactics for achieving it were spelled out," he writes. "Rather, the Haig proposal described best-case outcomes designed simply to overwhelm any conceivable resistance."[42] On March 24, 1981, Reagan jotted in his diary his understanding of the plan: "Nat. Security Council meeting . . . We adopted a plan to persuade African States of our desire to help settle the Namibian question—an election after a const. is adopted. At the same time we would urge Angola's govt. to oust the Cubans at the same time we helped Savimbi. Our hope being that with the Cubans out Neto & Savimbi could negotiate a peace."[43] A fuzzy plan, certainly—just as fuzzy as the president's knowledge of Angola (Neto had died in September 1979)—but the intention to help Savimbi was spelled out loud and clear. In fact, as early as February 6, 1981, at one of the administration's first NSC meetings, the president had told his advisers: "We don't throw out our friends just because they can't pass the 'saliva test' on human rights. . . . In Angola, for example, Savimbi holds a large chunk of Angolan territory. With some aid, he could reverse the situation."[44]

Congress rebuffed the administration's request that it repeal the Clark Amendment, which prohibited covert operations in Angola, but the evidence that exists (U.S. documents on aid to Savimbi during Reagan's first term remain classified) suggests that Reagan increased U.S. aid to UNITA. South African general Thirion claims that U.S. aid to Savimbi grew with the new administration, and in December 7, 1983, David Steward, a senior aide of Pik Botha who was deeply involved in Angolan matters, wrote that "the United States might possibly be persuaded to *increase* its support for UNITA."[45]

## Linkage

Whereas there was continuity between Carter and Reagan in terms of support for Savimbi, the new administration broke ground on Namibia by introducing the principle of linkage: South Africa should implement Resolution 435 if, and only if, the Cuban troops left Angola. U.S. officials argued that the key reason South African troops remained in Namibia was to guard against the danger posed by the Cuban troops in Angola. According to Crocker, linkage "would give us a far better chance to nail Pretoria down to a categorical commitment to implement Resolution 435. . . . It would offer a major visible, strategic quid pro quo for agreeing to implement the Namibia decolonization plan."[46]

The Americans first proposed linkage when Deputy Secretary of State Clark visited South Africa on June 10, 1981, for two days of talks, flanked by Crocker and Assistant Secretary for International Organizations Elliott Abrams, who was—not coincidentally—one of the most hard-line members of the administration. "Mr. Clark has requested," Pik Botha reported to the cabinet, "that our officials not conduct discussions with Dr. Crocker unless Mr. Abrams is also present. 'I brought Abrams with me in order to balance Crocker,' Mr. Clark said."[47]

On June 11, the talks began. The Americans' focus was Namibia. Clark urged the South Africans to accept Resolution 435. The South Africans gave their standard reply: they accepted the Contact Group's plan but not the implementation modalities that had been included in Resolution 435. But this was foreplay. The key issue was SWAPO. Pik Botha was more blunt than he had been when talking to officials from the Carter administration: SWAPO was a Marxist movement and a proxy of the Soviet Union. "South Africa's position was clear," he said: "SWAPO could not be allowed to win an election in Southwest Africa [Namibia]. We were not ready to exchange a war on the Cunene [River, marking the border between Namibia and Angola] for a war on the Orange [River, marking the border between Namibia and South Africa]. . . . If Southwest Africa was governed by SWAPO there would be a serious risk that the Russians would threaten South Africa from that territory. . . . Should SWAPO govern Southwest Africa, Botswana would be directly threatened, Dr. Savimbi [South African officials routinely inflated Savimbi's master's degree from the University of Lausanne into a doctorate] would be shut out, and South Africa would be entirely surrounded by powers inspired by Russia." Clark assured Botha that the United States had no sympathy for SWAPO and that "the US was ready to listen seriously to South Africa about South Africa's opinion of how to minimize the risk that SWAPO might win an election in the territory. Although the US believed that it could not guarantee that SWAPO would not win an election, it would take every reasonable step to prevent it." There would be no "internationally acceptable solution" in Namibia, however, unless Resolution 435 was implemented. Until Pretoria accepted the resolution, the war would continue, international pressure against South Africa would grow, and only the Russians would benefit.[48] This—the fear that the Soviets would profit—explained the Reagan administration's support for Resolution 435. "The U.S. believes," Pik Botha had reported after his conversations in Washington in May, "that Russia's interests will be furthered if a solution for the SWA [Namibia] question is not speedily found. The U.S. does not consider a SWAPO government to be in the interests of the U.S. but I am convinced that it would prefer a SWAPO government that had come to power as the result of a fair and free election over a situation in which the conflict would escalate and become so internationalized that Russia could intervene with African support."[49]

Through most of the day each side repeated the same points. Finally, in the late afternoon, Abrams asked "whether the situation would change if there were no longer Cuban troops in Angola." Pik Botha answered, "In this case there would be a completely new situation."[50]

At 7:15 the next morning, a select group met with Prime Minister PW Botha: Pik Botha and Brand Fourie, who was the director general of the Foreign Ministry; and Defense Minister Magnus Malan and General Pieter Van der Westhuizen, head of military intelligence. They decided to accept linkage: if the Cubans left Angola, South Africa would agree to implement Resolution 435. But they added conditions that they spelled out in a memorandum that Pik Botha handed Clark later that day: "1. The Cubans must and shall leave Southern Africa. . . . 2. Savimbi will be assisted appropriately, and South Africa will not be forced out of South West Africa in such a way that Savimbi cannot be assisted. 3. We cannot accept the establishment of a Marxist regime in South West Africa."[51] As Brand Fourie points out, it was on this basis that Pretoria accepted Resolution 435.[52]

The essence of Resolution 435 was that free elections would be held in Namibia. But South Africa's "acceptance" of the resolution specifically precluded the victory of SWAPO, which Pretoria deemed Marxist-Leninist. All experts—and the South African government—anticipated that SWAPO would win free elections. Therefore, in what sense did South Africa accept the resolution? The implicit demand that after the elections Namibia continue to serve as a conduit for South Africa's aid to Savimbi added an exquisite touch to Pretoria's vision of an "independent" Namibia.

There is no indication that Clark and his colleagues raised any objection to the memorandum. They had papered over a serious rift with Pretoria and gained time. Furthermore, many in the Reagan administration—and Clark was one of them—sympathized with the South African position on Namibia, SWAPO, and UNITA. Pik Botha reported that later that same day, June 12, "Mr. Clark was quite optimistic that the U.S. would get the Cubans out of Angola, that it would be possible to help Dr. Savimbi to achieve a victory or to attain a position of power in Angola, and thus to prepare the way to defeat SWAPO in Southwest Africa."[53]

After an exchange of letters between Pik Botha and Haig, and a further meeting in September in Zurich that Crocker called "frank, straight-forward and friendly," the deal was concluded. "Withdrawal [of the Cubans from Angola] and drawback [of the SADF from Namibia] . . . had to take place simultaneously," Crocker said, repeating a pledge that Haig had made to Pik Botha a few days earlier.[54] ("Withdrawal" meant that all the Cuban troops would leave Angola within three months of the beginning of the implementation of Resolution 435; "drawback" meant that 1,500 South African soldiers would remain in Namibia through the UN supervised elections.)

Henceforth the South Africans happily expressed their support for linkage. At the same time, however, they sent clear signals that it was a sham. They had few illusions about the outcome of a free election. The State Security Council noted that "SWAPO at the present time in all probability will win an election in Southwest Africa." And Pik Botha, who was the Americans' major interlocutor and represented the most liberal wing of the South African cabinet, bluntly told the U.S. chargé, Howard Walker, one month after Zurich, "that a SWAPO victory will mean a Soviet presence there [in Namibia] which could threaten South Africa and lead to war." In case the American missed the point, he stressed, "You cannot have [SWAPO President] Nujoma without a red flag."[55]

One may wonder how, in these circumstances, U.S. officials could assert that South Africa would accept free elections in Namibia. In Crocker's words, "The dominant trend of thinking within the Reagan camp [in 1981] looked at Angola—not Namibia—as the Southern African issue that demanded urgent attention."[56] Linkage had a great advantage. It shifted the focus from Namibia to the issue that obsessed the administration and on which all agreed: getting the Cubans out of Angola. It was a clever sleight of hand, shifting the blame for the failure of South Africa to end its illegal occupation of Namibia onto the Cubans, who were legally helping the Angolans defend their country from the South Africans. It is possible that the more moderate members of the administration, including Crocker, believed that the South Africans would eventually relent and accept free elections in Namibia if the Cubans left Angola. Other officials, however, did not care; they sympathized with the South African point of view because they agreed that SWAPO was a Soviet proxy. Secretary Haig told Urquhart and other top UN officials in February 1981 that "the United States had no intention of allowing 'the Hammer and Sickle to fly over Windhoek.'" Urquhart writes, "Like the South Africans, Haig evidently was not prepared to tolerate an internationally supervised election in Namibia which might result in a SWAPO victory."[57]

Nor was, apparently, President Reagan. No one has ever claimed that he knew much about Namibia, but his views were firm. South Africa had accepted the Western plan for Namibia in good faith, he told his listeners in a July 1979 broadcast, but "no sooner had South Africa given in than the U.N. began changing the plan to which S. Africa had consented." Nujoma was, Reagan announced, "a terrorist," and SWAPO was "a Marxist terrorist band." His assessment of the unilateral elections South Africa had held in Namibia in late 1978 would have warmed the heart of any supporter of apartheid: "As the U.N. sputtered around, unilaterally changing the contract it had signed and postponing an election in Namibia, Nujoma's SWAPO forces . . . were busily murdering and pillaging. The government of South Africa decided the only way to settle once and for all who spoke for the people of Namibia would be to hear from the people by way of a free and open election." The Democratic Turnhalle Alliance won, hands down, but the Carter administration had refused to recognize the legitimacy of these elections. Hence Reagan's cry of pain: "It boggles the mind to think that our government believes it is in our best interests to turn Namibia over to a pro-communist government when it is obvious that the people of that country prefer a government favorable to the West and certainly non-Communist."[58]

What then can one conclude from these early steps of the administration's policy toward southern Africa? There was one key idea: the Cubans had to leave Angola. This was the fulcrum on which all fervently agreed. There was also agreement about helping Savimbi and seeking national reconciliation, that is, power sharing, in Angola. What was less clear was whether the United States should help Savimbi overthrow the MPLA government. This led to another question: would Savimbi ever be strong enough, even with South African and U.S. help, to seize power by force? Finally, how hard should the administration press South Africa on Resolution 435? No one within the administration had any sympathy for SWAPO, but views about it varied—from those who damned the movement as Marxist and a Soviet proxy, to the more sophisticated analysis of the CIA, which stated, "While Moscow has considerable influence within SWAPO . . . there is a significant element within SWAPO that is not pro-Soviet. . . . Nujoma himself enjoys friendly relations with the Soviets and has leaned increasingly to the left in recent years, but he is probably more an opportunist than a committed Marxist. Nor is the USSR the only foreign influence on SWAPO. Most of SWAPO's financial and humanitarian support comes from international organizations like the UN, the World Council of Churches,

Lutheran World Federation, the OAU Liberation Committee, and a number of European countries, especially Sweden."[59]

As Crocker says, "In the loose-knit procedural setting of the early Reagan period, many things were not spelled out—partly for tactical reasons and partly because there might be no consensus. . . . It was better, in these dangerous early days, to leave awkward questions unasked so that they would remain unanswered." And he adds, wryly, "My job [in 1981] was to press SA toward realistic negotiations without losing the confidence of superiors in Washington who often empathized with Pretoria's view of the United Nations, SWAPO, Angola, and even [West German foreign minister] Hans-Dietrich Genscher."[60]

The other members of the Contact Group—England, France, West Germany, and Canada—were confronted with the fait accompli of linkage. Washington expected them to support it. Thatcher was happy to oblige. "The British," Crocker's senior deputy Frank Wisner says, "gave us, throughout, strong understanding and effective support." They were the exception. The Germans "were never very comfortable," Wisner recalls. The Canadians "also were not very comfortable."[61] France had since May 1981 a socialist president, François Mitterrand. "We can feel a change in France's posture toward Angola," a senior MPLA official remarked, "but even Mitterrand coming to power is not enough to change, by itself, that country's vocation to be the gendarme of Africa."[62] More to the point, Mitterrand was not ready to challenge the United States over Namibia. Acquiescence was made easier by the fact that the United States did not demand that the Contact Group formally adopt linkage. With a straight face, British foreign minister Geoffrey Howe told Zimbabwe's Prime Minister Mugabe in 1985, "We do not accept that Namibia's independence should be linked to an agreement on the withdrawal of the Cuban troops from Angola or to other issues." He added, "That said, we must take account of the political reality that unless there is an arrangement over the Cubans which South Africa is prepared to accept, there will be no agreement on the implementation of the UN plan."[63] Sanctions, of course, were out of the question.

Linkage was a boon for South Africa. As Pik Botha told the South African parliament in May 1988, after Reagan "had come into power the Americans came here to Cape Town and asked us what our attitude would be if they could get the Cubans out. We then said that if they could get the Cubans out it would be a 'new ball game.' That is how it happened that . . . we again became involved in negotiations based on Resolution 435, but with a Cuban withdrawal as a prerequisite. During the seven years in which Pres Reagan has governed, this standpoint has formed a shield against sanctions and no sanctions were imposed against this country because of the South West Africa issue."[64]

## Pretoria Strikes: From Protea through Meebos

In 1981, comforted by the sympathetic understanding of the Reagan administration, PW Botha ratcheted up the pressure on South Africa's neighbors to dissuade them from helping the ANC and SWAPO. The SADF increased the tempo of its cross-border raids, bombings, sabotage operations, and targeted murders in southern Africa. Zimbabwe, Zambia, Lesotho, Swaziland, and Botswana were hit, but Pretoria's two main targets were Angola and Mozambique.

The ANC had a strong presence in Mozambique, and it was from there that its guerrillas infiltrated into South Africa. Mozambique was, Pik Botha said, "the main channel for ANC terrorists."[65] South Africa's most lethal weapon against this errant neighbor was the Mozambique National Resistance (RENAMO). RENAMO had been created in 1976 by Rhodesian intelligence officers, who developed it into a military force to punish President Machel for his support of Zimbabwean rebels. It began around a nucleus of soldiers from elite black units of the Portuguese colonial forces. As Zimbabwe's independence drew close, the Rhodesians approached the South Africans. "The South African response was immediate and enthusiastic," the director of Rhodesia's secret service writes. "Within days, the final arrangements were completed and the MNR [RENAMO] was transferred lock, stock and barrel" to its new patrons. Pretoria moved RENAMO's rear bases from Rhodesia to South Africa and assumed responsibility for training and arming the insurgents. Under South African sponsorship, RENAMO became a larger, better-organized, and more effective military force.[66]

Angola was twice guilty. It harbored the main ANC guerrilla camps, and it was SWAPO's rearguard base. It was from Angola that the SWAPO guerrillas entered Namibia, and it was to Angola that they returned. Pretoria's aggressive policy against the MPLA government, manifested by its support for UNITA and its raids into Angola, had been obvious before Reagan came to power. But it became bolder with the arrival of a new, friendly administration in Washington. Pretoria increased its assistance to UNITA as well as its attacks on southern Angola. "The new strategy," a SADF document noted, "entailed a drastic escalation in the level of hostilities."[67]

The opening salvo came on August 23, 1981, when South African planes attacked the radar installations of the Angolan armed forces (FAPLA) south of the Cuban defensive line, "so that the SADF could provide unhampered air support to its ground forces."[68] The following day, August 24, the SADF launched Operation Protea. "Like a stinging gust of August wind, security forces swept across the Angolan border," the *Pretoria News* reported poetically.[69] The gust carried 4,000 to 5,000 soldiers with tanks and air support. They advanced into Angola's Fifth Military Region, which comprised the country's three southwestern provinces—Namibe (on the coast), Cunene (east of Namibe), and Huila (north of Cunene)—and which was intersected by the Cuban defensive line. Even though both Namibe and Cunene bordered Namibia, the troops invaded only through Cunene. "Namibe is desert and mountains, and it had no infrastructure. The mountains slow you down, and the desert creates problems with water," remarked a former SADF officer.[70] Therefore, Cunene was, consistently, the invasion route of the South Africans.

Protea was "the biggest mechanized operation by the SA Army since the end of World War II," writes General Jannie Geldenhuys, who was the chief of the army. PW Botha explained that the "so-called" invasion was merely hot pursuit against SWAPO, and that the FAPLA would not be attacked if it did not interfere. "Security forces have been at pains to avoid such skirmishes," the *Pretoria News* announced, "even dropping pamphlets at target areas telling the Angolans to stay away."[71] It is true that in Operation Protea the South Africans inflicted heavy blows on SWAPO. But they did much more, venting their fury against the FAPLA and the country's infrastructure.

When Protea began, there were three Angolan brigades in the Fifth Military Region, south of the Cuban line, in the towns of Ondjiva, Cahama, and Xangongo. Each brigade had approximately 2,000 men and 12 Soviet military personnel.[72] The Soviets enjoyed a sense of security; several even had their wives with them. Until then the SADF had moved back and forth across the border but had never attacked the towns where the three brigades were stationed.

In its official statements, Moscow said that no Soviets were fighting in Angola, and it meant it. "As a rule, our advisers in the Angolan brigades moved to the rear when there were military operations," a senior member of the Soviet military mission writes. "We were told time and again that we should 'only instruct, train and advise . . . but not fight," another officer who served in Angola explains, adding that Moscow feared "an international scandal if an adviser was captured or killed in combat." Soviet policy was to avoid fighting, a senior Angolan commander agrees, but when South Africa launched Protea, "they were taken by surprise."[73]

The SADF attacked Ondjiva, the capital of the province of Cunene, and Xangongo. The brigades that defended the two towns were badly mauled and fled northward. On August 27, 1981, South African military intelligence reported, "An enemy convoy from Ondjiva that included Russian advisers and their wives fell in an ambush by elements of Task Force Bravo." A Soviet colonel, a lieutenant colonel, and two Soviet women were killed, and a noncommissioned officer was captured.[74] The third FAPLA brigade stayed put in Cahama, while the SADF roamed unmolested south of the Cuban defensive line. In a post-mortem on the operation, the SADF noted, "Operation Protea has without doubt further destabilized the political, economic, social and military situation in southern Angola. This could fan discontentment among the LP [local population] against the MPLA government and SWAPO. Operation Protea has also demonstrated to the LP the FAPLA's inability to protect them from SA's 'aggression.'"[75]

The invasion was so brazen that it provoked widespread condemnation from Western governments—in Paris, in London, in Bonn, and in Ottawa, but not in Washington. The U.S. State Department immediately deplored any escalation of violence by either side in the conflict but added that the South African attack had to be understood "in its full context." SWAPO raids into Namibia from Angola were "part of that context. . . . The continued presence of Cuban combat forces in Angola six years after its independence and the provision of Soviet originated arms for SWAPO are also a part." It was, the liberal *Rand Daily Mail* said, "a carefully worded statement which avoided outright condemnation" and was crafted "in moderate terms." In plainer words, it placed South Africa, which illegally occupied Namibia, on the same plane as SWAPO, which fought to free the territory. The conservative *Burger* wrote, "The U.S. reaction to the incursion in southern Angola is encouraging. It is the reaction of a government that sees things in a broad perspective and stays focused on what is for it the main issue: to oppose everywhere the spread of communist power."[76]

Then came the UN Security Council debate. The headline in the *Rand Daily Mail* summed it up aptly: "UN fury—but US backs SA." As the article explained, "The United States emerged as South Africa's lone protector after all major Western allies joined countries of the other power blocs in a torrid Security Council onslaught over the Angola raid." When the vote came, thirteen of the council's fifteen members voted in favor of the resolution that harshly condemned the invasion but did not impose sanctions. The United States cast the lone veto, and Thatcher's Britain abstained. "South African diplomatic sources were jubilant about America's action," the Johannesburg *Star* reported, as was the white South African press. "It is refreshing," the *Burger* applauded, "to see that there is a Western power that has the courage to be guided . . . by the realities of a situation and refuses to take the popular approach and summarily condemn South Africa as the only offender. . . . That America has decided to proceed without the support of other Western countries, especially those that are her partners in the Contact Group, indicates how strongly the Reagan administration feels about the presence of the Cubans in Angola and Russian intrusion. . . . For South Africa this demonstration of America's new realism about Southern Africa and the Soviet Union has great significance."[77]

South Africa was emboldened. Like waves in the wake of Protea, Operation Daisy was launched in November 1981, and Operations Super and Meebos in March and July 1982 respectively. "South African strategy in Angola entailed more than hot pursuit against SWAPO guerrillas," an account sympathetic to Pretoria explains. "South Africa was trying to establish a neutral buffer zone along the Namibia/Angola border. In order to achieve this, the South African troops were killing livestock, poisoning wells, disrupting local communications, and preventing distribution of food. Such tactics would alienate the local population from Luanda and SWAPO. UNITA, on the other hand, was being supplied with arms, as well as food, to distribute in the border areas." The FAPLA was impotent. "The South Africans have absolute control of the skies," President dos Santos said, "in an area that stretches about 200 kilometers north from the Namibia border." The Cuban planes could not intervene. "The South Africans were much stronger," remarked Foguetão, the senior Angolan officer who was the commander of the Fifth Military Region in 1981. "To challenge them in the air would have been suicidal." Lacking mobile antiaircraft systems, the Cuban troops could not leave their defensive line to confront the invader. The SADF roamed freely in the southwest stopping short of the Cuban line, which barred access to the Angolan heartland.[78]

When the violence ebbed, the SADF remained in control of a part of the province of Cunene, including its capital, Ondjiva. "The world has become accustomed to *faits accomplis* like the illegal occupation of the base of Guantánamo in Cuba and of a part of Angola by the South African racists," Mozambique's President Machel observed in January 1982. "No one talks about Pretoria's occupation of Angolan territory because it is just par for the course."[79]

Even African governments stood by passively. During the June 1981 summit of the Organization of African Unity, President dos Santos had asked African countries to send troops to Angola as a gesture of solidarity against South African aggression, but "no one agreed, not even Nigeria, not even Algeria."[80] The only country willing to send troops to Angola was Cuba. Africa "is in debt to Cuba," Tanzania's President Nyerere told Risquet the following January. "When I say Africa I don't mean just Angola but Africa as a whole. Had it not been for Cuba's timely help in 1975, Angola would have been occupied by South Africa, and Savimbi would have come to power, and this would have changed the course of the liberation struggle in our continent." Zimbabwe would not have achieved its independence, and Namibia's prospects would appear hopeless. "Angola will survive because you [Cubans] are there. . . . I already told you that we have a debt to Cuba, and sometimes I feel ashamed because we ... have let you carry all the burden. .... Cuba is a small country but its actions make it a pillar of the liberation struggle, and what are bigger countries doing? You can see that here [in Africa] there are big countries and yet we have left you alone in Angola." A few months later President Kaunda of Zambia, who had bitterly criticized the dispatch of Cuban troops to Angola in 1975, told Reagan's special ambassador, Vernon Walters, that when Raúl Castro had informed him, in 1979, that "Cuba is prepared to withdraw its troops from Angola," he had replied "that this was a poor idea because as long as South Africa maintains an aggressive posture towards Angola the Cubans are Angola's only reasonable defense."[81]

## The FAPLA's Woes

From the moment they established a military mission in Angola, in 1976, the Soviets strove to create a strong FAPLA, and the Cubans thought that they were botching the job. "There was a problem of vision," remarks an Angolan general, Ita. "There were heated disagreements between the two military missions. It began with the question as to whether the FAPLA's main enemy was the SADF or UNITA."[82] The Soviets believed that it was the SADF and that Angola should build a conventional army with tanks and heavy weapons that would keep the South Africans at bay. The backbone of this army would be the regular brigades (Brigadas Regulares), which were the focus of the attention and assistance of the Soviet military mission. The Cubans agreed that the SADF was Angola's main enemy, but they sharply disagreed with the Soviets about how best to confront it. They argued that the FAPLA was not strong enough to confront the South Africans; the Cuban troops would bear this responsibility and the FAPLA should concentrate on the war against UNITA. This required not a conventional army, but counterinsurgency units (Brigadas Ligeras) with light equipment and training in irregular warfare.

Creating a modern Angolan army was a daunting task. In 1976 the FAPLA was a simple guerrilla force. "We had no idea whatsoever of conventional warfare," recalls a senior Angolan officer, Ngongo. The guerrillas had almost no formal education. Defense Minister Pedalé, who had replaced Iko Carreira in 1980, was an intelligent man who had been a good guerrilla commander, but he had a fourth-grade education. With rare exceptions, his officers fared no better. "Some had reached the second grade, others the fourth," remembers General Tozé Miranda. The rank and file were virtually illiterate—not the men to use sophisticated weapons. Undeterred, the Soviets continued to focus on the regular brigades that would fight against South Africa. "Guerrilla warfare was very complex for the Russian generals," another Angolan commander, Foguetão, remarks: "They knew about conventional warfare, tanks against tanks, planes against planes. The regular brigades had tanks, artillery, etc. None of this is necessary against guerrillas."[83]

The Angolans were seduced by the Soviet approach, which promised a strong army with heavy weapons, and they were deluded by the relative weakness of UNITA. Looking back, Ngongo recalls: "In the late 1970s we all [FAPLA commanders] were looking south, toward South Africa; we got a little sidetracked by this, and we didn't worry too much about UNITA. We wanted to create a strong conventional army. 'We have a rich country,' we said, 'We must be able to protect it!' We did not think that UNITA could grow so quickly. Our concern was to create an army that could fight against South Africa; we were thinking about South Africa, and this distracted us. The Cubans understood quickly that the main enemy was UNITA. They would tell us, 'We will stop a South African invasion, you must focus on the war against the bandits [UNITA]. We are here. You don't need a conventional army. You are wasting your time.' But we were mesmerized. 'Hell no,' we said, 'we want a strong army, a conventional army!'" It was "a strategic error," concludes another senior commander, Ndalu. The result was that when the Cubans withdrew from the war against UNITA in early 1979, the effectiveness of the counterguerrilla operations decreased considerably. The regular brigades that were the focus of the Soviet military mission and the FAPLA high command did not participate in operations against UNITA. "They remained idle or were undergoing training to repel the foreign enemy," a Cuban aide-mémoire said. "Worse, it soon became evident that this training had been woefully inadequate."[84]

Savimbi profited from the FAPLA's mistakes. In the words of one of his generals, Nunda, "The most difficult period for UNITA was in the late 1970s," when it was largely confined to the southeastern corner of Angola, in the province of Cuando Cubango. The years 1979 and 1980, after the Cubans withdrew from fighting against "the bandits," were for UNITA "a period of recovery and development," the Cuban aide-mémoire noted. "In 1979, they carried out ambushes, acts of sabotage and operations against villages."[85] In 1980 UNITA began expanding its activities toward the central region, and it captured and held several small towns. "Up until the end of 1979," Savimbi's biographer writes, "whenever UNITA had overrun small MPLA-held towns its policy had been to destroy their infrastructure before surrendering them again to the enemy. However . . . [it] intended eventually to defend and hold territory it had won from the MPLA. . . . The strategy effectively began with the capture on 14 April

1980 of Cuangar [a small town in Cuando Cubango on the border with Namibia], which had changed hands four times over the previous three years. . . . Cuangar became the first town (as opposed to small settlements) to fall under permanent UNITA control. . . . UNITA was now ready to clear out MPLA forces from a clutch of other small south-eastern towns." In September 1980, UNITA took Mavinga, "a beautiful little trading and administrative town," in eastern Cuando Cubango, 250 kilometers north of the Namibian border.[86] Mavinga would later gain fame as the forward defense of Savimbi's "capital," Jamba.

Unlike Delta—Savimbi's first headquarters, in northern Namibia—Jamba was in Angola, barely. General Nunda recalls that in mid-1979 Savimbi asked him to find a place in Cuando Cubango where UNITA could establish its base. "I found it in Jamba (in Ovimbundu Jamba means elephant). It was a region with many lagoons, many animals, many elephants, about 50 kilometers north of the border." By late 1979, Savimbi had moved his headquarters to Jamba.[87]

In May 1981 the FAPLA tried to retake Mavinga and was repulsed. It was UNITA's first successful defense of a town. For the FAPLA, it was a shock—"we realized that UNITA was very strong!" remarks Ngongo.[88] A few weeks later, the South Africans launched Protea. Staggering under the blows of the SADF and facing UNITA's growing strength, the Angolans turned to Cuba. In October, a top Angolan official, Lúcio Lara, approached Cuban general Abelardo Colomé, who was visiting the Cuban troops in Angola. In Raúl Castro's words, "Comrade Lara said that the working relationship between Angolans and Cubans was no longer characterized by the common search for solutions and by the active participation of the Cubans, as it had been in an earlier period. 'Now the Cubans limit themselves to making recommendations and observing,' Comrade Lara said."[89] Lara told Colomé that he would like to discuss these matters in Havana.

## Meeting in Moscow

In early December 1981, two weeks before Lara arrived in Havana, a Cuban delegation flew to Moscow at Soviet foreign minister Gromyko's invitation to discuss Angola. The delegation was led by Risquet, who was a member of the Communist Party's Political Bureau. He was accompanied by General Colomé. Both had Angolan experience: Risquet had headed the Cuban civilian mission from December 1975 to May 1979; Colomé, the military mission from December 1975 to July 1977.

Soviet policy toward Angola had evolved from the early days in 1975 when the Kremlin had not approved of the dispatch of Cuban troops. In early 1976, Brezhnev had embraced Cuba's decision but had demanded that its troops leave

Angola quickly. He soon dropped this demand, aware that the Cubans were Angola's only shield against South Africa. Moscow had embarked on a major program of military aid to the FAPLA and had been given access to naval and air facilities in Luanda.

Angola had become the Soviet Union's most important ally in sub-Saharan Africa. However, as the CIA pointed out in March 1981, "the new Soviet activeness in Africa does not signify that the region as a whole has any higher priority in Soviet eyes relative to other regions than it had previously. Sub-Saharan Africa still ranks lower than the United States, Eastern Europe, Western Europe, China, Southeast Asia, Southwest Asia, and the Middle East as an area of Soviet foreign policy concern."[90]

The Soviets were disappointed in the performance of the FAPLA, and they were overstretched. At home, the economy was deteriorating, and living conditions were worsening. Abroad, their friends' victories in the Third World—in Vietnam, Angola, Ethiopia—meant that there were more demands for Soviet economic and military aid. Afghanistan was turning into a disaster; in Poland, Solidarity was a deadly threat to communist rule; the Reagan administration was intent on achieving nuclear superiority, and U.S. planes and warships waged psychological warfare at the borders of the Soviet Union.

In December 1981 Gromyko hoped to lower the tensions with Washington in at least one domain: southern Africa. He was planning to meet Haig in Geneva in January 1982, and he wanted to tell him that the Cubans would be flexible about the withdrawal of their troops in Angola. With Risquet and Colomé, he hinted at a possible de facto acceptance of the principle of linkage, although he was not very precise. He was trying to get a sense of the Cubans' position. "Absolutely no decision has been made," he stressed. "This is why we have invited you to Moscow, in order to consult you in a sincere and comradely fashion, to weigh together all the arguments and consider all sides of the problem." The Cuban position, however, was that concessions would only encourage the aggressor, who would see them as weakness. Risquet rebuffed Gromyko's suggestions. The Cubans would make no promises about the withdrawal of their troops. "As long as South Africa is ruled by racists and fascists, Angola will be in danger," Risquet said. "The South African troops can reach its borders in a matter of hours, but it would take weeks for Cuba's help to reach Angola. To leave Angola before its independence and its revolution have been completely secured would be a grave error, unless the Angolans themselves ask us to leave, and we don't think that they will." Risquet concluded bluntly, "It is clear from our discussions that even though we agree on many points, we differ on some important issues. . . . I am confident that our governments will consider these issues with all the necessary urgency."[91] A few hours later, in a cable to Castro, Risquet wrote, "Our fundamental difference is that the Soviet comrades wanted our approval to tell the Americans in the conversations they will have with them in January, that if we were to reach a solution of the Namibian problem on the basis of UN Resolution 435 and there were guarantees for Angola's security, it would be possible to agree on a plan for the gradual withdrawal of the Cuban troops." He had rejected Gromyko's suggestions firmly, stressing that Cuba and Angola did not accept the principle of linkage, that no withdrawal was possible until Angola was safe from external aggression, and that "we must not appear impatient before the United States . . . while they deepen their commitment to Savimbi and tighten all kinds of ties with South Africa."[92]

## Angola Turns to Cuba

A few days after the Moscow talks, an Angolan delegation led by Lúcio Lara arrived in Havana for three days of conversations with the top Cuban leaders. Lara began, "If we compare our relations now with the time when we had constant brotherly contacts, when we worried together and searched together for solutions, it is evident that there has been a certain distancing."[93]

Lara was right, Raúl Castro said. "There is a key issue that emerges when we compare the degree of involvement of the Cuban advisers during the first period, more specifically until December 1978, and from then on. We here, our party leadership, reached the conclusion that the earlier behavior of our advisers, both civilian and military, led Angolans to think that we were impinging on the sovereignty of Angola and the authority . . . of its cadres." Therefore, he continued, "we told our advisers not to stray beyond the limits of their assigned functions, so that no Angolan official could complain that he was being sidelined, overlooked or manipulated." Raúl urged the Angolans to consider carefully whether they wanted to return to the relations of the earlier period— "We want to be sure that in making this request you have thought about what happened, and we need to know exactly what you mean when you say that we should go back to the spirit of the first period." He noted that since 1975, 683 Cubans had died in Angola, including 84 aid workers.[94]

Angola wanted to return to a closer relationship, Lara repeated, and it wanted increased Cuban participation in the war—on the battlefield and in the war councils. "The gap between us Angolans and the Soviets is great," he explained. "The Soviets, well, what they recommend is well beyond our capabilities and, frankly, not relevant to the real situation in Angola. Their officers have no experience of guerrilla warfare. They see everything through a conventional prism. . . . They don't understand that we cannot operate like this. . . . For instance, we don't have the necessary mobility. They say that something can be done in 24 hours, but we need six days, or a week. We don't have the airplanes, or we have the plane and we don't have the fuel. . . . The Cuban experience is far more relevant and therefore, for us, of decisive importance."[95]

The Cubans agreed to the Angolans' requests. Two things had changed since they had scaled down their participation in Angola in early 1979: South Africa had become even more aggressive, and UNITA had become much stronger. Following Lara's visit, the Cubans decided to assign military advisers to the war against UNITA "at the level of the Angolan general staff, the Military Regions, the brigades and the battalions, with a total participation of 2,238 men."[96]

As he presided over the third—and last—day of talks, Fidel Castro urged the Angolans to focus on the war against UNITA: "If the Cuban troops can guarantee that the South Africans will not advance into the Angolan heartland, then you can use all the power of the FAPLA . . . against the bandits." The FAPLA, he added, should not maintain regular units in the far south, below the Cuban defensive line. "Any attempt to engage the South Africans in a frontal battle where they enjoy absolute superiority in the air . . . would mean giving the enemy the upper hand. . . . If you want to engage them in battle, you must wait until they reach the line that is defended by the Cuban troops. . . . To send the brigades south of the line means to launch them in an irrational operation without the possibility of success."[97]

Lara had brought to Havana a new, more flexible policy on the withdrawal of the Cuban troops. The negotiations with the Americans for the implementation of Resolution 435 were about to resume, and Angola did not want to reject outright the principle of linkage. "The result," Risquet explains, "was a subtle modification in the position we had maintained in Moscow in December 1981. We abandoned the very harsh line for which we had almost quarreled with the Soviets."[98] The new policy was expressed in a Joint Declaration that Angola and Cuba made public on February 4, 1982. It stipulated that if Namibia became independent "on the basis of the strict implementation" of Resolution 435, and the SADF withdrew south of the Orange River (i.e., also from Walvis Bay), "which would considerably lessen the threat of aggression against Angola, the governments of Angola and Cuba would consider the resumption of the program of gradual withdrawal of the Cuban troops, to be carried out in a lapse of time decided by both governments."[99] As Castro said, "It was the first time that the withdrawal [of the Cuban troops] was linked with the solution of the Namibian question, with Resolution 435."[100]

It was a tenuous link—the tempo of the withdrawal would be decided by the two governments, and a strong Cuban force would remain in the country after the implementation of Resolution 435, because South Africa could continue its war against Angola even after Namibia was free. In Raúl Castro's words, "Angola will not be safe . . . even if South Africa withdraws completely from Namibia, whose territory . . . it can cross in a matter of hours in an airborne operation, or days by train. . . . Angola and the other countries will only be safe the day when apartheid no longer rules South Africa."[101]

The following January, Gromyko met Haig in Geneva. Reagan jotted in his diary: Gromyko "talked arms limitations. Al talked Poland and Cuba." In a lengthy and heated exchange, Haig lashed out at Havana's actions in southern Africa and Central America. He cabled Washington, "I hit hard [on Cuba] . . . [Gromyko] obviously nervous we may act soon and requested us not to do anything harsh."[102]

## CHAPTER 8

# The Wonders of Linkage

## PW Botha's Reforms

In South Africa, PW Botha was engaged in a daring experiment: when he be-came prime minister in 1978, he decided to strengthen apartheid by co-opting important segments of the nonwhite population. He would amend the con-stitution to grant limited political rights to Coloreds and Indians, transform-ing the all-white parliament into a tricameral institution in which real power would remain in the hands of the white chamber. Blacks would continue to be denied political rights, but many of them would, he hoped, be satisfied with improvements in their standard of living and their labor rights. In 1979 they were granted the right to unionize, and many jobs previously reserved to whites were opened to them.

But Botha's policy backfired. In June 1981, the CIA reported that "the in-creasing militancy of black workers is largely a result of the government's own actions." Pretoria had believed that concessions "would create a stable black labor force. Instead, black workers are flocking to more militant unions and are demanding even more concessions from the government and business community. Neither the government nor the business community can afford to renounce past reforms. The economy faces a growing shortage of skilled workers that realistically can only be met by employing more blacks. . . . South African insurgent groups, including the African National Congress, are intent on infiltrating the black labor movement. . . . The government is likely to intro-duce additional labor reforms, but such changes probably will heighten black expectations and increase their dissatisfaction with their continuing exclusion from the political system."[1]

Botha's reforms raised the hackles of many whites who thought that he was conceding too much. A group of disaffected National Party leaders created the

Conservative Party in March 1982. A few months later the CIA reported, "The government has instituted a tougher policy toward blacks partly to counter Conservative Party criticism of its limited racial reform proposals. Pretoria is enforcing apartheid laws more strictly and is focusing on reducing inflation, the main economic concern of white voters, while failing to take measures to alleviate the resulting black unemployment." The agency also noted that "South Africa's blacks are bearing the brunt of inflation and rising unemployment. They are being hurt most by austerity measures adopted in response to the economic slump that has gripped the country since 1981."[2]

## Trying Linkage

The turmoil in South Africa formed the backdrop to the international minuet over Namibia, which resumed in the fall of 1981. In Zurich, on September 21, 1981, Assistant Secretary Crocker explained to the South Africans that "the process will consist of three sets of negotiations." In the first, the Contact Group would negotiate with South Africa, the Frontline States, and SWAPO about Namibian independence. In the second, the United States would negotiate with South Africa about both aspects of linkage—Namibia's independence and the withdrawal of the Cuban troops from Angola. And in the third, the United States would negotiate with Angola about the withdrawal of the Cuban troops.[3]

Washington and Pretoria agreed that the U.S. conversations with Angola—and with South Africa on Angolan matters—"would be held . . . *outside* the framework of Security Council Resolution 435 and would not be part of the Contact Group's mandate."[4] As Secretary of State Haig explained to South African foreign minister Pik Botha, the other members of the Contact Group had to protect their virtue: they could not "accept the direct linkage of the Namibia and Angola questions as integral elements of a single plan. This would not be acceptable internationally." The British, Canadians, Germans, and French recognized, however, "the de facto relationship that exists on the ground between Namibia and Angola. Furthermore they recognize that whatever is said publicly, your readiness to proceed to a settlement in Namibia is dependent on coordinated movement of Cuban withdrawal from Angola. Our allies do not, however, consider Angola to be on the agenda of the Contact Group per se. . . . To address the concerns of our Contact Group partners, we are not asking them to join in our understanding with you on the Angolan track of our strategy, but this does not alter that understanding." The Contact Group would deal exclusively with South Africa's reservations about the implementation of Resolution

435. In particular, it would discuss the set of constitutional principles that Pretoria wanted included in any future constitution of Namibia, the guarantees it demanded about UN impartiality, and the concerns it expressed about the size and composition of the force that the United Nations would send to Namibia to oversee the elections (United Nations Transition Assistance Group). "Consequently," Haig had told Pik Botha in September 1981, "Angola will not be addressed in the forthcoming Contact Group message to you [proposing the reopening of negotiations on the implementation of Resolution 435], and I suggest it would be helpful if you did not raise it in your response or in other communications with the Contact Group."[5]

It was an arrangement that suited everyone. Pretoria would discuss linkage with its congenial partner in Washington; France, West Germany, Canada, and England would proclaim their innocence by never discussing linkage with the South Africans or the Africans. The United States would hold center stage, keeping the other members of the Contact Group as informed or uninformed as it wanted. The Europeans and Canadians would toe the line when the moment came, Crocker assured the South Africans. If they were to claim that "they were surprised or not part of the understanding" on linkage, he averred, "the United States would say that the Contact Group were liars."[6]

Once again, as in the Carter years, the United Nations was relegated to the margins. The UN secretary-general "will have to become involved later," Crocker explained, "but the Five [the Contact Group] will do the hard work." For Crocker, the "Five" was really "One": the United States.[7]

The entire process had a fundamental flaw: the South Africans continued to pepper their exchanges with the Americans with comments that indicated their repugnance for Resolution 435, with or without Cuban withdrawal from Angola. Pik Botha told the U.S. chargé, in January 1982, that "South Africa now thought that SWAPO would win an election." He asked Haig to "consider South Africa's dilemma if SWAPO were to win control [of Namibia]: whether it is achieved by electoral ploy or through violence and intimidation, the outcome would inevitably be the same—the Red flag in Windhoek," that is, "the imposition of a Soviet presence on South Africa's doorstep."[8] He kept hammering this point. "South Africa could not survive if it had to accept the red flag in Windhoek," he repeated to Crocker in November 1982. Furthermore, he added, Resolution 435 involved the United Nations, and "when the United Nations was involved the Soviet Union was involved too, because of its presence on the Security Council. . . . The United Nations supervisory process would no doubt lead to a Soviet presence in South West Africa [Namibia]." Therefore, Pik Botha insisted, the Americans and South Africans should try to devise an alternative approach—one that would exclude UN supervision and would be based on Namibia's "democratic forces" (i.e., Pretoria's clients).[9]

The other members of the Contact Group had a healthy skepticism about Pretoria's willingness to implement Resolution 435, with or without Cuban withdrawal from Angola. After a meeting of the Group on December 17, 1982, Crocker reported: "Several . . . including the British, noted their uneasiness with continued signals from Pretoria that there was no predilection for actually agreeing to implement 435—even if the last SAG demand (Cuban withdrawal) was successfully resolved. Squire (UK) said that UK was not convinced that the SAG would or could settle when it was a foregone conclusion that a Namibian government would be controlled by SWAPO. There was considerable discussion on this hardy perennial, and consensus that there are compelling counter-arguments as well. We agreed that there was little choice but to continue pressing the SAG to look beyond their misgivings. . . . The SAG, I added, was not a monolith, and there were those within it who did not support a diplomatic solution. It was our job, however, to strengthen the position of those like Pik Botha who did lean toward a successful Namibia negotiation."[10]

Meanwhile U.S. officials sought to convince the battered Angolans that they had no alternative but to agree to "the simultaneous withdrawal" of the Cuban troops from Angola and the SADF from Namibia. Crocker argued the case with Foreign Minister Jorge in Paris in January and March 1982 and again in early April in Luanda.[11] Reagan's special envoy, General Vernon Walters, descended on Luanda in June 1982. "I left dos Santos no illusion about the necessity for a commitment on Cuban withdrawal from Angola parallel with the SAG withdrawal from Namibia," Walters cabled Washington at the end of his visit, adding, "I tread carefully on the reconciliation [with Savimbi] issue, telling dos Santos in a nonthreatening way that we hoped as part of a regional settlement that all Angolans would be able to sit down at the same table. The message that reconciliation is a logical requirement of an overall regional settlement involving Cuban withdrawal was clear but not shouted." Walters left Luanda upbeat, but his optimism vanished after his second trip in late July, when dos Santos flatly rejected the principle of "simultaneous withdrawal" on which, Walters asserted, the South Africans "insisted absolutely."[12]

The Luanda talks were "difficult," Crocker told Secretary of State George Shultz, who had replaced Haig in July 1982. "The Angolan leadership is suspicious of us, our motives and what they perceive to be our association with South Africa. . . . They are convinced it is South Africa's intention to destroy their Marxist regime. . . . Angolan paranoia runs deep and explains their reluctance to enter into binding undertakings at this point."[13] Crocker was right about Angola's deep distrust of South Africa and of the United States. He failed to note, however, that Pretoria's acts of aggression, the West's failure to respond with anything more than toothless UN Security Council resolutions, and Reagan's publicly expressed desire to help Savimbi more than justified Angola's "paranoia."

## The SADF's View of Things

The South African generals had great plans for Angola. It would be the centerpiece of the Constellation of Southern African States that they sought to create. The concept had first emerged under Prime Minister Vorster, but it was PW Botha who had given it "a substance previously lacking." The constellation, the generals hoped, would stretch beyond South Africa, its Bantustans, Lesotho, Malawi, Botswana, and Swaziland, to embrace Angola, Mozambique, Zimbabwe, Zambia, Zaire, and a nominally independent Namibia. The black members of the constellation would be anticommunist, tolerant of apartheid, and eager to persecute the ANC and SWAPO.[14] With bitter irony, a Zambian official summed up Pretoria's grand design: "The focal point, or Big Brother, will of course be South Africa. All these states are expected to cooperate in the economic, political and social fields. On top of all this we would be expected to sign a mutual non-aggression treaty with Big Brother. This would mean that all our problems in these fields would be over, and we should live happily thereafter."[15]

The plan seemed delusional, but it had a rational core. Zaire showed the way: it was anticommunist, it had good though unofficial relations with South Africa, and it was hostile to the ANC and SWAPO. The toughest nuts to crack were Angola and Mozambique. Angola was the more important of the two, because the outcome there would determine the future of Namibia.

In the early 1980s the South African generals were optimistic about Angola. "South Africa is now in the situation where its military strategy toward SWAPO and Angola is within reach of success," General Niels van Tonder, the powerful chief of the Directorate of Special Tasks of Military Intelligence, wrote in December 1982. "The core of it [this strategy] consists of pro-active military actions against SWAPO and expanded support of UNITA." Van Tonder's words reflected the views of Pretoria's military establishment. In a February 1983 memo, General Constand Viljoen, chief of the SADF, wrote bluntly to the director general of foreign affairs: "We [SADF] are of the opinion that a very favorable situation for SA is developing in Angola" that would result in that country joining "in a constellation of states with South Africa." The first step would be power sharing in Luanda between the MPLA and UNITA with some form of "federal agreement. In this way we would be assured that Dr. Savimbi will control the south of Angola (which would have great military and political value for us)." If Savimbi "takes over Angola, or at least controls the southern part of Angola," General Viljoen told Defense Minister Malan a few days later, then South Africa could expect Savimbi's help "in support of its efforts in SWA [Namibia]."[16] Deprived of its rearguard, SWAPO would be annihilated, and a nominally independent Namibia could become a full-fledged member of the Constellation of States.

The Angolan precedent could be eventually repeated in Mozambique, "if RE-NAMO [the insurgent movement supported by South Africa] can apply enough military pressure on [President] Machel to force him to negotiate." Isolated, cowed by the fate of the governments in Luanda and Maputo, and lured by economic carrots, Zambia and Zimbabwe would have to fall in line, that is, join the Constellation of Southern African States.[17]

## The Cape Verde Talks

While the SADF generals were exchanging cheerful thoughts about the future, South Africans and Angolans were meeting at Sal Island, Cape Verde—first on December 7–8, 1982, and again on February 23, 1983. It was the Angolans, battered by Protea and the operations that had followed, who had requested a meeting.[18] "Since 1978 we have had periodic talks with officials from the MPLA government," General van Tonder noted before leaving for Sal with the South African delegation. "Except for the liberation or exchange of prisoners, the talks have led nowhere." Nonetheless, another meeting could be useful to give the United States and the other members of the Contact Group the impression of South African moderation and to sow suspicion between SWAPO and Angola.[19]

One wonders why the Angolans had sought a meeting. They had nothing to offer. Pik Botha, who chaired the South African delegation at Sal, was categorical: "Under no circumstances will South Africa tolerate that its neighbors harbor terrorist organizations that act against South Africa and SWA [Namibia]." There would be no peace as long as Angola continued to help SWAPO and the ANC, and Resolution 435 could be implemented only if the Cubans withdrew from Angola. This was a price that the Angolans were unwilling to pay. They demanded that Pretoria withdraw its troops from their country and implement Resolution 435, but they were not ready to abandon SWAPO and the ANC, and they would not discuss the departure of the Cuban troops.[20] "The talks were a dialogue of the deaf," van Tonder told the South African minister of defense.[21]

But even if the Angolan government had been willing to sacrifice the ANC and SWAPO and renounce the Cubans, the South African military and PW Botha would have wanted more: they wanted Savimbi to come to power in Angola.

As they would do on many other occasions, the Angolans—who were anything but puppets of Moscow or Havana—conducted the talks without consulting, or even informing, their allies. Risquet told Soviet officials in February 1983 that "we both [Cubans and Soviets] learned about the Cape Verde talks through the press." And he told a top aide of President dos Santos: "Only after the international press had broken the news about the meeting . . . did the head of the MPLA's department of foreign relations, M'Binda, brief our ambassador in Luanda. And it was a very cursory briefing. When our ambassador compared notes with the Soviet ambassador, it was clear that M'Binda had given them both the same talking points and had answered their questions either superficially or not at all."[22]

## The View from the South African Foreign Ministry

The South African generals did not believe in linkage. For them, getting the Cuban troops to leave Angola was a desirable goal, but it was not linked to whether they would agree to hold free elections in Namibia. That would happen only when they were sure that SWAPO would lose at the polls—which, they were well aware, was impossible in the present circumstances. They believed, however, that those circumstances could change: if they could bring Savimbi to power in Luanda, then he would help them crush SWAPO. Then—and only then—would they agree to hold "free" elections in Namibia.

The officials in the South African Foreign Ministry worried that the generals were overly optimistic about Savimbi's chances. They did not think he would be able to seize power in Angola. They were acutely aware, moreover, that openly rejecting Washington's idea of linkage would have dire consequences. The United States was South Africa's shield against international sanctions. The South African Foreign Ministry understood with a clarity that the military lacked that sanctions could grievously hurt the country. The problem for Foreign Minister Pik Botha and his aides, however, was that, like the generals, they abhorred the MPLA government and rejected the possibility of free elections in Namibia as long as there was a chance that SWAPO could win them. Therefore, they too rejected linkage—but they had no viable alternative to offer, only a healthy skepticism of the military's rose-tinted views. Knowing full well that the generals enjoyed the strong support of Prime Minister PW Botha, they did not voice their skepticism openly. Instead, they shared their misgivings among themselves. Thus in March 1983 a senior Foreign Ministry official, David Steward, wrote to Pik Botha,

> The message we have recently conveyed to the U.S.—that we expect UNITA to achieve a military victory in Angola—has undoubtedly changed the equation for the Americans because it clashes with their present policy toward the MPLA government. This has the following significant implications for the United States: Given that South Africa has decided that UNITA will win in Angola, it is most likely that South Africa will increase its aid to UNITA and will not accept any agreement with the Angolans that might place UNITA in a vulnerable situation. This means that
> — bilateral negotiations between South Africa and Angola, on which the U.S. places great value, will make no progress;
> — the war in Angola will definitely escalate, significantly diminishing the possibility of a Cuban withdrawal;
> — the Russians may decide that they cannot afford a UNITA victory and therefore send more Cubans or other reinforcements to Angola;
> — South African troops will not leave southern Angola in the near future—something that, according to Chet Crocker, may cause significant problems for the US "at the UN and elsewhere";
> — under these circumstances it is most likely that the South African military presence in Angola will increase.
> These complications, *as the Americans see them*, will be disastrous for their present policy toward southern Africa.

Noting that South Africans and Americans were going to meet the following week, Steward warned: "It is . . . important that we don't create the impression that we are necessarily seeking a military solution or that we won't implement Resolution 435 under any circumstances. It is very important that the Americans don't decide that there are basic differences between our approach to the problems of southern Africa and theirs, because this would make continued cooperation between us impossible."[23]

The meeting between the South Africans and the Americans on March 17–19 was an exercise in shadowboxing. The South Africans duly proclaimed their support for linkage, and the Americans did not openly question their sincerity. When the conversation turned to Angola, General van der Westhuizen, the head of South African Military Intelligence, stressed Savimbi's military strength, while the Americans insisted that Savimbi could not win and that Pretoria overestimated his strength. Crocker reported that "despite agreement between the U.S. and South Africa on the basic facts of the situation [in fact no such agreement existed] there appeared to be a fundamental difference in the conclusion which both sides had reached. South Africa thought that time was on our side. The Americans disagreed. Time was not on our side," Crocker warned, because "the Contact Group could not be held together forever. The Group included the United States' three major [European] allies, and . . . the U.S. attached the greatest importance to its relations with its West European allies."[24]

Secretary Shultz met with the French, British, German, and Canadian foreign ministers in Williamsburg on May 29, 1983. "The Ministers were outspoken in expressing their frustration over the slow pace of the Namibia effort and the need for new momentum," he told Reagan. "We face a tricky situation with the South Africans. Despite their commitment to the principle of a settlement, they are not eager to take the political risks involved. The South African leadership is of several minds and the military, in particular, is disinclined to take chances or to favor negotiated solutions."[25] Shultz failed to understand the depth of Pretoria's opposition to Resolution 435. The State Security Council had just affirmed, once again, "that a SWAPO government in Southwest Africa is unacceptable."[26] For the South Africans, linkage was a smokescreen that the Reagan administration had conveniently provided. They wanted the Cubans out of Angola (the Angolan end of linkage), but they were not willing to hold elections in Namibia (the Namibian end of linkage) unless they could be sure SWAPO would lose. Therefore, said the Secretariat of the State Security Council, "the implementation of Resolution 435 must be delayed until the international climate is favorable to its modification or until a victory for the democratic parties of SWA [Pretoria's clients] in an election conducted under 435 can be assured in advance."[27] The South African government was convinced that an election under Resolution 435 would have "catastrophic consequences."[28]

## Pérez de Cuéllar in Cape Town

By the time of the Williamsburg meeting, the South Africans had run out of pretexts. With only minor exceptions, the Contact Group had resolved all contentious points about the implementation of Resolution 435, often on the basis of concessions by SWAPO. Nujoma "was always cooperative," UN secretary-general Jávier Pérez de Cuéllar wrote in his memoirs, while Chester Crocker noted that "the United States had sweetened Resolution 435 through strenuous efforts" to satisfy the South Africans.[29]

The most important of these "sweeteners"—one that would have bloody consequences—concerned SWAPO bases in Namibia. In 1978 the Contact

Group's plan had stipulated that after a cease-fire the SWAPO guerrillas would be restricted "to base," without explaining where these bases would be. The UN secretary-general's report of February 26, 1979, had stated, "Any SWAPO armed forces in Namibia at the time of the cease-fire will . . . be restricted to base at designated locations inside Namibia to be specified by the Special Representative [of the UN secretary-general] after necessary consultations." Pretoria had objected, fiercely. In June 1982 the Five promised South Africa that SWAPO would not be granted any base in Namibia. This was implicitly confirmed in Pérez de Cuéllar's report of May 19, 1983, which stated that the United Nations would monitor SWAPO bases in Zambia and Angola, and failed to mention SWAPO bases in Namibia.[30] This resolved Pretoria's last major objection to the implementation modalities of Resolution 435.

It was time to bring in the United Nations, which, until that moment, had watched from the sidelines. On May 31, 1983, the Security Council asked the secretary-general "to undertake consultations with the parties . . . with a view to securing the speedy implementation of Resolution 435."[31] On August 22, the day Pérez de Cuéllar arrived in South Africa, the State Security Council decided that the government would demonstrate its goodwill by making "some small concessions" in order to settle the remaining issues—the participation of a Finnish battalion in the UN peacekeeping force in Namibia, the electoral system for the elections of the constituent assembly, and the liberation of political prisoners. Then—and only then—would Pik Botha make "it very clear to him [Pérez de Cuéllar] that there could be no progress toward a solution for Southwest Africa unless the Cubans withdrew from Angola."[32]

And so it was. At the end of two days of talks, Pik Botha graciously announced that all the outstanding issues had been settled, and then the 800-pound gorilla came roaring: "of course," he said, Resolution 435 could be implemented only if the Cubans withdrew from Angola.[33] "I hate the idea of linking the two things," Pérez de Cuéllar told the press. In his report to the Security Council he emphasized that "the question of Cuban troops" was not part of Resolution 435. "I do not accept this so-called linkage."[34]

On October 28, 1983, fourteen of the fifteen members of the UN Security Council voted in favor of Resolution 539, which stated that "South Africa's insistence on linking the independence of Namibia to irrelevant and extraneous issues" was "incompatible" with Resolution 435 and warned that "in the event of continued obstruction by South Africa," the Security Council would "consider the adoption of appropriate measures under the Charter of the United Nations." The United States abstained. "We are disturbed," U.S. ambassador

Charles Lichenstein explained, "by the resolution's implicit allusions to possible future actions under Chapter VII of the Charter of the United Nations. We regard such allusions as premature."[35]

The previous year Chester Crocker had assured South African generals Geldenhuys and van Tonder that the new socialist leaders of France, despite their Third World rhetoric, were opportunists and "only interested in trade."[36] But even French opportunism had a limit. On December 7, 1983, the French government announced that it had suspended its participation in the Contact Group. "Unable to fulfill its responsibilities honestly, the group has decided to go into hibernation," Foreign Minister Claude Cheysson told the French parliament. "For us, after the departure of France, the Contact Group has ceased to exist," the Angolan ambassador to Italy remarked. The London *Times* reported that British officials insisted that the group had not been disbanded, "but there is no frenzied desire on the part of anyone to meet at the moment."[37]

## Building a Puppet Government in Namibia

Parallel to the negotiations, South Africa had pursued its efforts to develop a client government in Namibia. After the December 1978 elections for a Constituent Assembly, in which its tame Democratic Turnhalle Alliance (DTA) had won forty-one out of fifty seats, Pretoria transformed the Constituent Assembly into a National Assembly and established a Council of Ministers in Windhoek supervised by the South African administrator general. The council was chaired by the white DTA leader Dirk Mudge and included eleven ministers, one for each of the eleven ethnic parties that formed the DTA. The DTA, one of Namibia's foremost scholars writes, was "the centre-piece of South Africa's efforts to consolidate a dependent anti-SWAPO power bloc," but the scheme was flawed. Dividing the country into eleven autonomous ethnic areas, each with separate services for its own ethnic group, wasted money and scarce resources; furthermore, "the representative authorities" were "racked by corruption and financial mismanagement."[38] In April 1982 the Secretariat of the State Security Council concluded that the DTA was "a house built on sand."[39] Relations between Pretoria and the DTA grew strained. The South Africans were frustrated by the DTA's failure to gain popular support. Mudge was upset by South Africa's growing contempt. He wanted more autonomy. The straw that broke the camel's back was the administrator general's decision, on January 10, 1983, to veto a bill approved by the DTA-controlled assembly that replaced South African national holidays with dates that would reflect the history of Namibia. "I refuse to be humiliated any further," Mudge declared, as he announced that he was re-signing as chairman of Namibia's Council of Ministers. After much hesitation, the ministers followed suit. ("The members of the Ministers' Council had been reluctant to resign because they feared they might not be able to meet financial commitments they had," the *Windhoek Advertiser* reported.) In response, the administrator general dissolved both the Council of Ministers and the National Assembly and reestablished direct rule. A defiant Mudge announced that the DTA would continue "to forge greater unity amongst the people. 'We are the opposition now, and we like that. Now it is our turn to criticise.'"[40]

The war continued. SWAPO's military strength had grown in the late 1970s, and the insurgents, using the friendly Angolan territory as a springboard, began penetrating deeper into Namibia. The South Africans designated the northern strip of the country, where more than half of the population lived, as an "Operational Area," where they imposed a dusk-to-dawn curfew and a reign of terror. They were determined to prevent the SWAPO guerrillas from infiltrating into the white farming area further south, separated from the northern strip by a wide semi-arid area. Thousands of South African soldiers (a reliable Namibian historian estimates 20,000)[41] were stationed in Namibia. In addition, in 1980 Pretoria had created the South West Africa Territory Force (SWATF), composed of Namibians. Recruits flocked to the SWATF. Some were motivated by political considerations—"I grew up in a house that was very anti-SWAPO," recalls Karel Nojoba, a black Namibian whose father was a senior official in the Ovamboland authority established by Pretoria. "When I was in high school I was ostracized by my classmates as a child of the puppets." Others were attracted by a military career. "I had no political or financial motivations," a colored, John Robinson, explains. "I loved the uniform. I wanted to shoot; I love shooting. When I was a kid I loved cowboy movies and war movies." But most joined because they feared punishment if they refused or because they were desperately poor. The *Windhoek Advertiser* reported in January 1985, "Unemployment has escalated tremendously in the past few years. . . . People from the rural areas are steadily pouring into . . . [the black townships adjoining the white cities] in search of jobs. Employers tell applicants they must have at least completed their military training before they can be offered a job."[42]

The SWATF was controlled by South Africa. SADF officers staffed its senior ranks. Eventually a few nonwhite Namibians became officers. John Robinson finished the war as a Second Lieutenant—"We struggled to become officers, to get more rights, privileges," he observes. Karel Nojoba became a senior captain—one of the highest-ranking nonwhite officers in the SWATF.[43]

## SWAPO

SWAPO was not a powerful guerrilla movement; it had only several thousand fighters arrayed against the South African army. But the SWAPO guerrillas fought with great courage. At times the Cubans had unrealistic expectations about what this small guerrilla army could achieve, and they vented their frustration with the Soviets, criticizing SWAPO's military performance.[44] Nevertheless, Cuba's support for the organization did not falter. The USSR and Angola were likewise at times critical of SWAPO, but steady in their support.

South Africa's incursions into Angola in 1981–82 had dealt very harsh blows to SWAPO. The guerrillas' infiltration routes ran from the province of Cunene in southwestern Angola into the Bantustan of Ovamboland, immediately south of the border, where almost half of the population of Namibia lived; it was there, among the Ovambos, that SWAPO enjoyed overwhelming support— more than anywhere else in the country. From the coast to Cunene, a river separated Angola and Namibia, making infiltration more difficult. To the east of Cunene was the province of Cuando Cubango, the lower half of which had become, by the early 1980s, UNITA territory; a river ran between it and Namibia, and SWAPO guerrillas entering their country at this point would have to traverse the Caprivi strip, which was rife with South African camps. It was from Cunene, therefore, that SWAPO entered Namibia.

But by 1982 the SADF had occupied large chunks of Cunene. "We were pushed back," said General Malakia Nakandungile, who was a senior SWAPO commander. "We had to travel long distances through territory controlled by the enemy before entering Namibia. We went on foot without food except for what we could carry on our own backs."[45] Yet they kept coming. "War in Owambo [Ovamboland] Reaches New Heights," the *Windhoek Advertiser* announced on February 21, 1983, as it reported a large SWAPO infiltration from Angola into northern Namibia. "The insurgents," a South African military analyst observed, "would sometimes really astound the pursuing troops with phenomenal feats of physical endurance and excellent bushcraft techniques."[46] Among the South African troops that hunted the guerrillas was the Buffalo Battalion, one of the two non-white units of the SADF—black soldiers with white officers. "When we lost black soldiers in action, they were mourned only within the battalion," wrote one of these white officers. "Sadly, those black soldiers who died in action with the battalion were not considered to be of any significance to the South African public, which seldom, if ever, was informed of those casualties. There were no announcements by Army Headquarters or notices in the press that they had been killed in action while fighting for South Africa—that honour was reserved solely for white soldiers."[47]

In two quadripartite meetings—the first they had ever held—high-level delegations from Angola, the Soviet Union, Cuba, and SWAPO met in Havana in April 1982 and in Luanda the following September.[48] Deputy Foreign Minister Ilyichev, who on both occasions led the Soviet delegation, had little useful to say, beyond stressing that Moscow would continue to help SWAPO, and showed surprisingly little understanding of the situation on the ground or of SWAPO. This was not the case for Lara and Risquet, who headed, respectively, the Angolan and the Cuban delegations.

SWAPO's President Nujoma acknowledged that the SADF's control of Angolan territory was a serious problem for his guerrillas. "This has affected us considerably," he said, "not just in terms of logistics, but also by impeding our efforts to bring recruits from Namibia to our camps in Angola to receive military training."[49] He also pointed out that Angola alone, among Namibia's neighbors, allowed SWAPO to use its territory as a springboard for military operations. Botswana had never permitted it. Zambia had allowed it "until early 1980," when, following a series of South African raids into Zambia, President Kaunda "asked us not to operate any longer from his country."[50]

Lara assured Nujoma that Angola would continue to allow SWAPO to use its territory. He also urged, gently, that SWAPO keep the FAPLA better informed of its military plans. "We have been guerrillas, the MPLA waged its guerrilla war from friendly countries, and we know that guerrilla movements are always wary of giving information to the host governments. . . . This is why we want to be very clear. We are absolutely not asking for SWAPO's operational plans. We are asking to be informed in broad strokes so that we can coordinate our strategy, our tactics with yours." He was supported strongly by Risquet:

> Given the present situation in Angola, thorough and precise coordination is absolutely necessary. You might decide to cross the border into Namibia at such and such place. But the South Africans may retaliate with an air strike, and there might be four schools there. . . . I remember when I went to Chibia, in southern Angola. We were looking for a good site for a SWAPO camp. . . . We found a very good place, but there was a little school nearby with forty children and we said: "Wait, first we must move the school from here, in case there is an air strike." . . . To be a guerrilla fighter and to be bombed by the planes—well, that's the lot of the guerrillas, but we have to move the school and protect the children. . . .

The leaders of the MPLA . . . have given their territory to organize and train the fighters of SWAPO and as the springboard to penetrate into Namibia. The South African racists are punishing Angola for this internationalist position, launching air strikes, invading, massacring the population in the villages. . . . The people are suffering, and they are not as politicized as the MPLA leaders. . . . Any friction, any misunderstanding, any tension in the relationship between a SWAPO unit and a FAPLA unit in any part of the country . . . could create hostility among the Angolan population. . . .

It is the same for the Cuban troops. We know that any friction between our troops and the FAPLA, or with the population, damages the excellent relations that must exist between us and Angola. We . . . make mistakes. Everyone makes mistakes. But we know that we must do everything possible to avoid any strain, any misunderstanding because we are the Angolans' brothers and because . . . we and the Namibians are guests in their country. . . . Therefore it is very important that we maintain strict coordination with the Angolan authorities at every level—not only in Luanda, but in the Military Regions, in the provinces, in each town, in every village.

. . . I believe that the most important outcome of these talks would be to heighten our awareness that it is essential to coordinate. . . . That if we fail to coordinate it has a negative impact on the revolutionary struggle.[51]

Risquet also raised the issue of Walvis Bay, Namibia's only deep-water port. In 1978 SWAPO had been forced to accept that the status of Walvis Bay would be discussed only after independence, between the new Namibian government and South Africa. Nujoma was not optimistic. "We know that the South Africans are very arrogant," he said. "They will never surrender Walvis Bay. They will maintain their troops there." They might let Namibia use the port, "but they will impose conditions," using Walvis Bay as a stick vis-à-vis the Namibian government. Risquet agreed: "The racists will remain in Walvis Bay for a long time, for as long as their ignoble system of apartheid endures. SWAPO made this concession [on Walvis Bay] because it was alleged that otherwise the negotiations [over Namibia] would not advance. But what did we gain in return? That was five years ago, and since then the negotiations have not progressed one inch, and the issue of Walvis Bay has been cast aside. It is considered a *fait accompli*, a lost cause." Risquet urged—and it would be Cuba's position over the following years—that in the negotiations about the implementation of Resolution 435 SWAPO and its friends must insist that the SADF evacuate Walvis Bay as soon as Namibia became independent. "We must demand that the racist troops withdraw south of the Orange River" (the border between Namibia and South Africa); that Namibia immediately have the right to use the port, even though it would still be administered by Pretoria; and that South Africa acknowledge that it has no rights over the rich waters of Walvis Bay. "We mustn't say in advance that this is unacceptable to the South Africans. The Contact Group constantly presents proposals that are unacceptable to SWAPO. Once the negotiations have begun seriously—and this will happen only when the armed struggle has forced the South Africans to negotiate—we will consider which of these demands should be abandoned and in return for what."

Risquet's words were met by silence. Lara said merely "We're facing a *fait accompli*, and all we can do is to say OK, we'll talk about Walvis Bay after Namibia's independence.'" He had been more loquacious a few months earlier, in Havana, when he told the Cubans, "There's nothing we can do about Walvis Bay. It has been tacitly accepted to leave negotiations about it until Kingdom come. In theory, it should be discussed between the government of an independent Namibia and South Africa, but we have told the comrades of SWAPO that they must give up hope of recovering Walvis Bay and prepare to coordinate with us for the use of the port of Namibe [in southern Angola]."[52]

## CHAPTER 9

# Angolan Travails

## The Cuban Military Mission in Angola

UNITA began to gather strength in 1980, and its growth continued unabated in 1981 and 1982. By 1983, a senior FAPLA officer writes, "the situation was critical. In the last four months of 1982, UNITA had stepped up the tempo of its operations." It was solidly entrenched in southeastern Angola, it was gaining strength in the central provinces of Huambo and Bie—densely populated and economically important—and it had gained the upper hand in the vast province of Moxico in the east. Moxico had a small population but it was the back door to the diamond-rich provinces of Lunda Sur and Lunda Norte in the northeast, and to the border with friendly Zaire. By early 1983, UNITA guerrillas had begun operating in the northeast of the country. They were "devastating the Angolan economy," the CIA remarked.[1] The glimmers of recovery that the country had experienced in 1977–78 were a fading memory, as production continued to decline owing to a myriad of factors: the blows of the SADF and UNITA, the mounting cost of the war, government incompetence and corruption, and the growing demoralization of the labor force. The only bright spot was the oil industry, located off the coast of Cabinda and run by Gulf Oil.[2]

Cuban participation in the war against UNITA was limited. As Risquet told Soviet officials in February 1983, "One thing is very clear: we're not going to wage a war against UNITA. That's a war that the Angolans must fight, but we are willing to help them."[3] A protocol signed between the two countries stipulated that 2,729 Cubans would serve in the FAPLA units (light brigades) that were carrying out counterguerrilla operations.[4] There were Cuban troops in Cabinda, near Luanda and the towns of Malanje, Quibala, and Luso. But the greatest concentration was in the southwest. Because of the SADF's air superiority, the Cuban forces had withdrawn from the far south of Angola.

They manned the key points of the defensive line that had been created in 1979 and stretched for 700 kilometers from Namibe on the Atlantic to Menongue in the east to bar the South Africans from the easiest and most direct access to the heartland of Angola and, by extension, to Luanda. The Cubans also kept a reserve force in Huambo. "Our idea," Castro explained, "is that the reserve . . . will counterattack if a critical situation develops along the line."[5]

Manning the defensive line did not mean, of course, occupying a continuous 700 kilometer stretch. "The war against South Africa in Angola has always been called the war of the roads," explains José Angel Gárciga Blanco, one of Cuba's foremost military historians. "The advance of the enemy's tanks would be more difficult through the bush or over sandy ground. The Cuban troops on the defensive line were stationed at key points where we thought the enemy would try to advance." These points were near the towns of Namibe, Lubango, Matala, Cubango, Jamba,[6] and Menongue, all of which were connected by a "good, paved" road that allowed the Cuban troops to move quickly along the line if the South Africans attacked.[7]

A Cuban military history notes, "From 1979 to 1981, our troops . . . carried out engineering projects along the line that enabled them to construct the best possible defenses against enemy air strikes." They constructed an elaborate system of tunnels. "We slept underground on beds made of grass," recalls Second Lieutenant Juan Moreno. "Whenever the alarm went off everyone ducked into the tunnels, except those on sentry duty," adds Private Carlos Manuel Serrano.[8]

Like many of the Cuban soldiers in Angola, Serrano and Moreno were reservists. After serving in the military, Serrano recalls, he had begun working as an electrician. "I was summoned to the military committee. They asked if I was willing to participate in an internationalist mission." He replied that he was willing. So, too, did Moreno, who was a reporter at *Juventud Rebelde*. "You have been selected for an internationalist mission," he was told. "Are you willing to go? Yes or no." Like all the other reservists, before leaving for Angola Moreno filled out a form specifying whether the government should pay the salary he had been earning as a reporter to his family, or deposit it in a bank in his name until his return. Service in military missions abroad was supposed to last no more than twenty-four months, and in the case of conscripts the three-year military service was cut to two, "because," a senior Cuban official points out, "we took into account that they were far away from Cuba, from their families."[9] At times, however, because of lack of transportation or because the replacement was not ready, the tour of duty could last up to thirty months—as was the case for Juan Moreno. When the reservists returned home, they had the right to go back to their old jobs.

All able-bodied Cuban men had the obligation to serve for three years in the military. However, no one was obliged to participate in an internationalist mission. The hundreds of Cubans who went to Zaire, Congo Brazzaville, and Guinea-Bissau in the 1960s had volunteered to serve abroad without being asked. When, in late 1975, Cuba began sending tens of thousands of soldiers to Africa, it began to ask reservists, conscripts, and professional military if they would be willing to go. Some refused. "Everyone who goes there [to Angola] . . . has said he is willing to go," Raúl Castro told Angolan officials in late 1981. "Those conscripts who don't want to go can do their military service in Cuba, but there are very few of them. . . . Only two or three officers refused to go to Angola in the [1975–76] war, and we sacked them from the armed forces."[10]

There was social pressure to go, and there might be costs to not going. If a leader or an activist in the Communist Youth refused to go, his career in the party was over. If a professional soldier refused to go, he would be dismissed from the armed forces. If a recruit resisted, he would do his military service in Cuba, but he was likely to be confined to a separate camp for several months. For most reservists, however, there were no sanctions.

The 1978 military agreement between Cuba and Angola stipulated that Cuba would pay the salaries of its soldiers in Angola, and Angola would provide the daily necessities—food, clothing, as well as equipment such as trucks. The Angolans, however, were unable to keep up their end of the bargain. Despite its oil resources, Angola was in dire economic straits that were getting worse. In February 1983, a Cuban aide-mémoire noted: "the fact that the FAPLA has failed to fulfill our agreements . . . affects the living conditions of our troops, and their fighting ability. In the first half of 1982 it supplied only 60 percent of the food for our troops that it had agreed to provide. There are also difficulties with the footwear, pillows, towels, mattresses, sheets and other personal necessities. Until October, when we finally received a shipment of boots, 17,000 of our soldiers had to wear sneakers."[11] This remained a problem throughout Cuba's time in Angola and, for Havana, an economic burden.

The number of Cuban soldiers in Angola fluctuated over time—from 36,000 in April 1976 to fewer than 24,000 one year later. Then, as the South African threat grew, the number moved upward, reaching 30,000 by early 1983.[12] The Cuban leaders were very aware that the entire South African army required only a few days to invade Angola from its bases in Namibia and South Africa, whereas reinforcements from distant Cuba would take weeks to arrive. They were also painfully aware of Pretoria's air superiority. "We were practically at the mercy of the air force of the racists," Risquet said.[13] Fearing that the Reagan administration might launch an attack on Cuba, Havana kept its best planes, its best pilots, and its most sophisticated antiaircraft weapons at home, all the while haunted by the prospect of a massive South African air strike against the Cuban positions along the defensive line in Angola. Requests for more planes and more sophisticated antiaircraft weapons for their forces in Angola were a constant refrain in Cuban-Soviet talks.

## Winter in Moscow

But if the Cubans worried about the South African threat in Angola, they were even more concerned about the threat the United States posed to their own country: they feared a U.S. attack. This led to a dramatic meeting between Raúl Castro and Yury Andropov, the new Soviet general secretary, in Moscow in December 1982.

Fidel Castro had spoken with Andropov the previous month when he had gone to Moscow for Brezhnev's funeral, but it had been a brief conversation. Risquet recalls, "We were expecting [Defense Minister] Ustinov, a man we knew better than Andropov, to come to Havana. Fidel intended to talk to him about our anxiety that there could be a U.S. attack," but Ustinov fell ill, and his visit was postponed. This made Raúl Castro's trip to the Soviet Union in late December all the more important, and when Andropov invited him to a meeting, "it was decided to take advantage of this opportunity." Raúl would ask Andropov if the Soviet Union would take some visible steps to indicate its support for Cuba: "more frequent visits of Soviet warships, visits of very senior officials, etc." Above all, he would ask "that the USSR tell Reagan that he could not touch Cuba, that doing so would be comparable to the USSR attacking West Berlin."[14]

On December 29, 1982, Raúl Castro was received by Andropov. Their conversation was blunt. Raúl briefly described the aggressive stance of the Reagan administration against Cuba and added, "The situation could become even more threatening depending on what happens in Central America. . . . Given Washington's aggressive foreign policy and the tensions that exist in our region, we are concerned about the frequent declarations of U.S. government and military leaders, and important newspapers . . . that the Soviet Union would not come to Cuba's aid if we were attacked by the United States." Raúl pointed out that Reagan administration officials, "first for one reason, then for another, whether because of Central America . . . or even Poland . . . have hinted that they might attack Cuba." He explained, "This is why Fidel told you last November that it was necessary to think about ways . . . to deter the enemy."

When Andropov asked, "Do you have any suggestions?" Raúl went straight to the point: "We know that first and foremost it is our responsibility to defend

Cuba through our own efforts; furthermore, we are very satisfied with the modern weapons that we have received from the USSR." But, he continued, "we also know that this is not enough. What else needs to be done? I think that Fidel already mentioned it when he spoke with you: it is absolutely critical that the Soviet Union tell the United States in a clear and categorical manner that it will not tolerate any military aggression against Cuba."

It was now Andropov's turn. He had said very little up to that point. "Comrade Raúl," he began, "I will start with the most unpleasant and important fact, one that both our countries must always bear in mind: we cannot fight in Cuba. For the very simple reason that you are 12,000 kilometers away from us . . . . It is not a question of being afraid. I spoke about this once with Che Guevara. . . . He wanted us to participate in the defense of Cuba. I replied that it wasn't a question of what we wanted or didn't want, or of whether we were afraid or not afraid—it was instead a sober military assessment. We would inevitably fail. To go all the way to Cuba only to be beaten to a bloody pulp? No! This would help neither you nor us."

Raúl interrupted. "We are very aware of this. . . . We understand it very well. It is as obvious as two plus two equals four." Cuba was not asking the Soviets to promise to intervene militarily on its behalf. Nor was it asking that the Soviet Union resort to nuclear weapons to defend Cuba. "For our Political Bureau, for Comrade Fidel, and even for the most immature Cuban communist it would be immoral to ask the Soviet Union to start a nuclear war on our behalf. This idea doesn't cross anybody's mind." What Cuba wanted, he repeated, was a Soviet warning to the United States. But Andropov poured cold water on the idea: "We can't agree to any declaration that would threaten the United States. Because what leverage could we bring to bear? Before the Chinese attacked Vietnam [in February 1979], we made the kind of declaration you're talking about: don't touch Vietnam, because otherwise . . . The Chinese laughed at us and got on with their business. If we're going to make threats we have to have some means to back them up."[15]

Andropov did not question the gravity of the U.S. threat against Cuba. He even believed that Reagan might launch a nuclear attack on the Soviet Union itself. But his message to Raúl was clear: if the United States attacks you, you are on your own; there's no point pretending otherwise. His demeanor intensified the chill. "Andropov's tone was very businesslike," remarks Risquet, who learned about the conversation from Raúl.[16] The minutes confirm this.

Andropov himself must have had second thoughts. Three days later, on January 1, 1983, he phoned Raúl, who was still in Moscow. "Let me explain right away why I'm calling," he said. "Well, first of all you're our guest, it is the New

Year, and therefore I want to show you the courtesy and consideration that is due to a friend, as I consider you to be. This is why I am calling. Furthermore, I have heard that after our conversation you have been a little glum. Therefore, I want to state our position once again. We will give Cuba all the assistance you need to strengthen your defenses, including the most modern weapons."

Andropov stressed his appreciation and friendship for Cuba and repeated that Soviet warships and high-level military delegations would visit the island more frequently to underline to the United States how close Soviet ties with Cuba were. He did not mention, however, what the Cubans most wanted, a declaration that the Soviet Union would not tolerate a U.S. attack against Cuba. Raúl said little. He corrected Andropov, "After our conversation I wasn't depressed. I was quiet because I needed time by myself to think." He thanked Andropov for the call and for the warm words.[17] But Andropov's central message was unchanged, as Raúl well understood.

Several months later, in a Politburo meeting, Andropov told his colleagues, "I told the Cubans that we won't fight for them and won't send any troops to Cuba. And it went over all right; the Cubans accepted it."[18] What else could they have done? They accepted it with dignity, as is obvious in Raúl's exchanges with Andropov. But the message was sobering. In Raúl's words, "Even though we had known for a long time that the Soviet Union would not go to war for Cuba and we could count only on ourselves for our own defense, it was precisely at this moment of greatest danger that the Soviet leaders told us unequivocally that if we were attacked by the United States we would be dramatically alone.... We kept this a carefully guarded secret in order not to encourage the enemy, and we redoubled our preparations to launch the War of the Entire People if the United States attacked us."[19]

## Searching for a Strategy

The conversation in Moscow did not change Cuba's foreign policy. In Central America, the Cuban military mission in Nicaragua grew from 200 members in July 1981 to 500 in early 1983, and to 1,100 the following June.[20] In Africa, there was no thought of withdrawing from Angola to soften Reagan's wrath. In February 1983, in Moscow, Risquet told Ustinov that the Cuban troops would remain in Angola as long as the MPLA faced a foreign threat.[21]

Two months later, Risquet flew to Luanda where he handed President dos Santos a forty-three-page aide-mémoire that bluntly expressed Cuba's deep concern about Angola's deteriorating economic and military situation, "which threatens all the sacrifices and efforts that have been made by the Angolan people and their loyal friends." The memo stressed that "in the struggle against the internal counter-revolution [UNITA], the Cuban troops cannot reprise the role they played . . . [in 1975–76] against the South African and Zairean invaders. . . . The struggle for national liberation and social revolution is a noble cause that deserves the aid of all revolutionary governments and people, but it is, above all, the duty and responsibility of the country's own people, of its combatants, of its political vanguard. . . . Therefore the leading and decisive role must always be taken by the MPLA, the Angolan government, the FAPLA and the Angolan people." In the aide-mémoire, the Cubans stressed, as they had time and time again, that "it is absolutely necessary" to treat the enemy wounded and prisoners of war with humanity and also to pay more attention to the needs of the population. And they once again urged the Angolans to rethink the military strategy the Soviets had persuaded them to adopt: "We think it is necessary for the Angolans, Soviets, and Cubans to decide how to focus the FAPLA's energies . . . on the war against UNITA, even though this could delay the creation of the conventional army that will protect the country from the South African danger." The document also reminded the Angolans that the Cuban soldiers would eventually leave: "We repeat that we will do everything in our power to save the Angolan revolution, but our means are limited, and . . . our military presence in Angola cannot continue forever, at least in its present size and role." Once Namibia was free, most of the Cuban troops would depart, and the remainder would follow "over a period of time."[22]

The Angolan leaders had been drawn to the Soviet approach because of the appeal of building a strong conventional army, but by 1983 reality had made them receptive to the Cuban point of view. This became evident when Angolans, Cubans, and Soviets met in Moscow in May 1983. The tripartite session was preceded by bilateral meetings between the delegations. In their bilateral, the Cubans and Russians talked past each other. Risquet reiterated his government's position: "The task of the Cuban troops in the south of Angola . . . is to protect the heartland of Angola from an invasion by the racist troops. I want to stress that . . . the fight against UNITA is the exclusive responsibility of the FAPLA. Nonetheless, even though this struggle is the Angolans' duty, their unavoidable, historic responsibility, we have been helping them within strict limits on the number of our men participating, the type of mission and the length of time they are engaged."

Then Ustinov spoke. He explained that he had told the Angolans that "they must fight against both the South African troops . . . and . . . UNITA. . . . The FAPLA must fight against the South Africans and against UNITA," he repeated. Risquet disagreed: "Comrade Ustinov, as I just said, the Cuban troops will repel an invasion by the South Africans, so the principal, fundamental, and if necessary the *only* task of the FAPLA is to liquidate UNITA. . . . That is, there is a real division of tasks, Comrade Ustinov, an international division of labor: the Cubans to prevent a South African invasion, and the FAPLA and the militia to liquidate UNITA."[23]

Later that day, Cubans, Angolans, and Russians met together. It was as though the conversation with Risquet had never taken place:

> *Ustinov*: As we said yesterday, the FAPLA, helped by the Cuban troops, will fight against the South Africans and against UNITA. . . . The FAPLA must fight against both.
>
> *President dos Santos*: As a result of our conversations with the Cubans we have reached the following conclusion. . . . Comrade Risquet has said that the FAPLA should concentrate on the fight against UNITA. . . . We agree. It is obvious that if the South Africans try to penetrate deeper into Angola, they can be stopped only with the help of the Cuban troops. I think that it would be best to divide the tasks in the struggle against South Africa and UNITA.
>
> *Ustinov*: . . . You must fight against both, against the South African troops and the bands of UNITA.
>
> *Dos Santos*: . . . But we have agreed that for now we will concentrate our efforts above all against UNITA.
>
> *Risquet*: I would like to add to what Comrade José Eduardo [dos Santos] has said. What is the military situation in Angola? There is a strip of Angolan territory in the far south along the Namibian border that is occupied by South African troops. There is a defensive line occupied by the Cuban troops that stretches from Namibe to Lubango and Menongue, with fortified positions, where the terrain favors us. This line is at a good distance from the South African airports in Namibia and is close to our airports, which would facilitate the intervention of our small air force. The South Africans enjoy complete superiority in the air, they have a great many planes and airports in Namibia close to the border. If we were to engage in combat with the South African troops near the border, we would be at a complete disadvantage. . . . However, if the South Africans who now occupy this strip in the south were to advance northward and attack our positions, we would then fight in favorable conditions. . . . Therefore, our troops will repel an in-depth attack by South Africa. We will also defend northern Angola and Cabinda from an attack by Zaire. The FAPLA and the militia will fight

against UNITA with some Cuban assistance. About 2,700 Cubans are participating in the war against UNITA as advisers and combatants, and their number will grow to 3,000. . . . Does Comrade José Eduardo agree?
*Dos Santos*: I agree.[24]

## Cangamba

Nevertheless, the impasse continued. The Cubans insisted that the FAPLA focus on UNITA, the Soviets disagreed, and the Angolans wavered. On July 29, 1983, Castro told Angolan defense minister Pedalé and Lúcio Lara, "The fundamental task of the MPLA, of the FAPLA, of you all, is the struggle against UNITA. . . . This is the key. . . . You must not worry about the South African army. . . . As long as we are there, they will not be able to breach our line, or, if they do, they will pay a very high price."[25]

Four days later, at dawn on August 2, UNITA attacked the small town of Cangamba, in southeastern Angola. The Cuban government celebrates the battle of Cangamba as a tale of heroism in which a handful of Cubans and a few hundred FAPLA withstood the assault of a much larger UNITA force for eight days. For Rafael del Pino, a Cuban general who defected to the United States in 1987, however, Cangamba is a tale of Cuban treachery. He told U.S. journalists after his defection: "Our troops will leave them [FAPLA] high and dry at the time they most need us, as happened at the battle of Cangamba. When the battle . . . began, our troops were alongside theirs, but there was a spell of quiet in the battle in which the UNITA troops fell back a bit. We then pulled the Cubans out of the siege by helicopter, leaving the Angolan troops to their fate, and they were wiped out later by UNITA."[26]

Del Pino is right on one point: the Cubans did withdraw, leaving the Angolans behind, but he fails to explain why this happened. The ongoing argument about strategy between the Cuban and Soviet military advisers in Angola had repercussions on the ground. Cangamba was one of the most tragic. It led to an escalation in SADF involvement in Angola, and a strong Cuban and Soviet riposte.

Cangamba, a town of about 8,000 inhabitants 250 kilometers northeast of Menongue, which was the eastern end of the Cuban line, was a lonely outpost in a region controlled largely by UNITA. It was garrisoned by a FAPLA brigade of 818 men and 92 Cuban advisers. The attackers numbered 6,000. They were well led—"The performance of the semi-regular units of UNITA during the fighting indicates that they have well-prepared officers and specialists," a Cuban military analysis noted.[27] Unbeknownst to the Cubans, the SADF "had supplied advisers and Special Forces elements to assist UNITA in . . . the capture of . . . Cangamba."[28]

The defenders held out, helped by the intervention of Cuban and Angolan military planes; Cuban helicopters dropped approximately 100 Cubans in Cangamba to stiffen the resistance. On August 10, UNITA withdrew after suffering heavy casualties. Sixty FAPLA soldiers were dead and 177 were wounded; 18 Cubans had died and 27 had been wounded.

That same day, after learning that UNITA had withdrawn, Castro sent an urgent message to dos Santos: "We have achieved a great victory. . . . Now we must be practical"—FAPLA and Cubans should leave Cangamba. Castro feared that Pretoria might seek to avenge UNITA's defeat with an air strike against the troops in Cangamba, which had "no antiaircraft defense in that isolated position 250 km from our lines."[29] But when, early the next morning, the head of the Cuban military mission, General Polo Cintra Frías, and the Cuban ambassador, Rodolfo Puente Ferro, met with President dos Santos and his senior military aides, they were in for a surprise: the head of the Soviet military mission, General Konstantin Kurochkin, was also there, and he had a plan—the opposite of what the Cubans proposed. "We must exploit this victory," he urged. He wanted to use Cangamba as the springboard for an offensive in the southeast, toward the province of Cuando Cubango, using additional FAPLA brigades and Cuban forces. He stressed "that this was the opinion of the Soviet General Staff and of the Soviet leaders." Not for the first or last time, Polo and Konstantin clashed in front of their Angolan hosts.[a] "At the end of the discussion," Polo reported, "since the Soviet held fast to his opinion and I to mine, President dos Santos decided to postpone a decision."[30]

For the Cubans, an offensive in the southeast made no sense. Cuando Cubango was a sparsely inhabited province with almost no roads or economic value, and it was largely controlled by UNITA. The deeper the troops advanced into Cuando Cubango, the closer they would get to the Namibian border and to the South African air bases. Cangamba, which was only tenuously linked to the territory controlled by the FAPLA, was a springboard to nowhere. It was a trap.

"On August 11, we sent four messages" to convince the Angolans to withdraw from Cangamba, Fidel Castro recalled.[31] Upon receiving Polo's report about his clash with Konstantin, Castro cabled back, "You must insist with the Angolans that it would be a grave error to keep a FAPLA unit in Cangamba. . . .

a. In the Cuban documents Generals Polo Cintra Frías and Konstantin Kurochkin are usually identified by their first name (more exactly, in the case of Leopoldo Cintra Frías, by his nickname Polo). Henceforth, I will refer to them as Polo and Konstantin.

That your orders are to withdraw the Cubans, all the Cubans, at once, even if they decide to keep a FAPLA unit there." He added, "We are shocked by the words of the head of the Soviet military mission. They reflect a complete lack of realism. . . . We cannot let more Cubans die, nor can we risk a grievous defeat because of absurd decisions. . . . We must not let our victory at Cangamba turn into a defeat." General Ulises Rosales, Cuba's first deputy minister of defense, called Polo, who said that Defense Minister Pedalé had come to see him and had "asked that we keep our advisers [in Cangamba] for 4–5 more days, until they [Angolans] had made a decision." When Ulises[b] urged Polo "to persuade the Angolans not to leave any of their troops there," Polo replied that, "since the comrade [Konstantin] has told them that this is the moment to strike, they don't understand why they should abandon Cangamba."[32] Shortly thereafter, Cuban ambassador Puente Ferro cabled Fidel and Raúl Castro that dos Santos had just told him: "I am examining the situation with the General Staff of the FAPLA and of the Ministry of Defense, and I am also consulting the Soviet military mission, and I hope that by early next week we and the Soviets will have reached a consensus about the Cuban proposal."[33]

Havana's response was immediate. "Once again I order you and Polo categorically," Raúl Castro cabled Puente Ferro, "to withdraw our troops from Cangamba. . . . This decision is irrevocable. Do not waste one more minute."[34] That same evening the chief of staff of the Cuban military mission informed Konstantin and the FAPLA chief of staff, Ndalu, "of the decision that had been taken. This decision will be carried out in the early hours of tomorrow, August 12."[35]

As ordered, the Cubans left Cangamba on August 12. Two days later, the South African air force struck. "Fortunately, there was no AAA [antiaircraft weapons] in the target area," a South African officer wrote.[36] The town was destroyed. The FAPLA withdrew in haste, and UNITA occupied the remains of Cangamba.

Cangamba was indeed a tale of heroism—a few hundred FAPLA and a handful of Cubans resisted a much larger force for eight long days, until the enemy fell back. General del Pino, the defector, is right when he says that the Cubans withdrew from Cangamba while the FAPLA stayed behind, but he conveniently overlooks how the Cubans pleaded with the FAPLA to leave with them, and the very sound military reasons they proffered. This is how history is manipulated—a little truth mixed with many lies.

---

b. In the Cuban documents General Ulises Rosales is usually identified by his first name. Accordingly, henceforth, I will refer to him as Ulises.

After the South African air strike, Savimbi boasted that he had defeated FAPLA and the Cubans without any outside aid, while the chief of the SADF, General Viljoen, asserted that Luanda's allegation that South African planes had attacked Cangamba was a lie.[37] But the Cubans knew the truth, and they wondered what would happen next. Risquet noted that "at Cangamba, the South Africans struck 500 km north of the Namibian border in an area where there was no SWAPO activity. Until that moment the South Africans had never attacked so far north. Nor had they ever attacked in such a brazen way, without even the pretext that they were striking SWAPO."[38] No Western government criticized South Africa's aggression.

Castro feared that Pretoria, emboldened by the success of the operation and by its impunity, would raise the stakes and launch a major offensive against the Cuban line. He met with his close aides. "Risquet is important," he said. "I think that we must send Risquet to Luanda" to inform the Angolans of Cuba's assessment of the new danger of this "serious escalation, serious," and to tell them that Cuba was willing to increase its military assistance. "We must reinforce our troops in Angola," Fidel stressed. "We have no choice but to reinforce." Raúl interjected, "Risquet must make a longer trip, because if he goes to Angola he must also go to Moscow. . . . What will we do if the Soviets don't support us in this situation?" Fidel continued:

> The question is, How do we involve the Soviets to the greatest extent possible in our Angolan strategy? . . . Risquet must take a memo [to Moscow] informing the Soviets that we have decided to reinforce our troops in Angola and that we are ready to fight a war against South Africa if necessary, but only if we can count on them. . . . If we have to weaken our defenses here [in Cuba] a little, we will do it. . . . We will inform the Soviets of the steps we have taken, of what we have already decided; we will not consult them. We will tell them what we have decided: . . . We are ready to wage this war if you help us; if you don't, we will reinforce our troops in order to avoid a collapse, but then we will have to withdraw. . . . If you support us, however, we are ready to fight because it is a war against South Africa.

Risquet asked, "Who will go with me, Raúl?" And Raúl Castro jokingly responded "Jorge [Risquet's first name] and Risquet." "No, a military man, a military officer," Risquet insisted—he wanted a senior military officer who would address the technical military matters. "Well," Raúl answered, "It will have to be [General] Colomé."[39]

Risquet had a long relationship with Angola. In 1965–66 he had led a Cuban column in Congo Brazzaville that had trained the MPLA. From December 1975 until May 1979, he had been the head of the Cuban civilian mission in Angola. In late 1981 he had resumed his role as Castro's point man for Angola. After Cangamba, his involvement deepened. Castro told him, "You'll go to Angola for a month. Speak with everyone. Then come back here for a month. Then go back to Angola for a month, and on and on." He said he would write to dos Santos explaining that Risquet was "his personal representative."[40]

## To Luanda, and Moscow

On August 18, 1983, Risquet and Colomé met with dos Santos and his closest aides in Luanda. Risquet explained that in view of the heightened threat Cuba was ready to send reinforcements and would urge the Soviets to increase their military aid. Colomé also returned to an issue that was clearly painful for the Cubans: their inability to push the SADF out of Angola. "Comrade President," he told dos Santos, "here (pointing at the map) is the province of Cunene. . . . As a military man it is truly a bitter pill to admit that the enemy occupies a territory that we should defend and we cannot expel him. . . . If we advance southward, and our air force is not able to assist us, we would suffer a costly defeat. Therefore, this is a problem that at this time Angola and Cuba cannot solve. If we had enough planes and enough antiaircraft weapons, the South Africans wouldn't be here [in Cunene]. But we don't have them." He concluded, "Right now, the fundamental danger is clear": a South African invasion that would breach the Cuban defensive line.[41]

The Angolans thanked the Cubans warmly for their willingness to help and complained about the Soviets. "The Soviet comrades still don't fully understand the situation that we are facing," dos Santos said, "and they have not taken the extraordinary measures that are necessary to help the Angolan revolution. . . . The Cubans' contribution is crucial, but the Soviets must do more."[42] What dos Santos did not mention—not for the first or the last time—was that Angola's problems were also due to the corruption and incompetence of his administration and to its indifference to the welfare of its people. Dos Santos failed to acknowledge that it was his responsibility to do whatever necessary, to bear any sacrifice to remedy the situation.

The next day, Risquet and Colomé flew to Moscow to tell the Soviets that Cangamba "represents an escalation by the enemy that forces us urgently to reexamine the situation and adopt new and extraordinary measures. . . . We are willing," Risquet said, "to make one more major effort, within the limits of our capabilities. We could even say that it is almost beyond our possibilities, because . . . our great confrontation with the imperialists is in Central America and in the Caribbean. We are willing to send more troops and weapons to Angola. . . . But this is not enough. . . . More weapons are necessary, and they can only come from the Soviet Union."[43]

From August 18 to 23, while Risquet and Colomé were in Luanda and Moscow, three merchant ships left Cuba for Angola. The authoritative historian of Cangamba, Martín Blandino, writes that "in the holds of these ships, hidden from the intelligence services of the enemy, were three tank battalions and a battalion of motorized infantry."[44] More reinforcements followed. In little more than a year after Cangamba, the number of Cuban soldiers in Angola rose from 30,000 to 39,000—that is, a 30 percent increase.[45]

This was despite the constant threat that Cuba faced from the Reagan administration and despite its acute awareness that it faced that threat by itself. The international scene was very tense. Contacts between the United States and the Soviet Union were at a minimum. In his memoirs, Assistant Secretary Crocker writes, "As he left for his August [1983] vacation, I recalled to Shultz our earlier agreement to consider developing a more substantive exchange with the Soviets. . . . We might propose that African questions be placed on the agenda when Shultz next saw his counterpart. A follow-up session at the expert level could follow. I also noted that there had been no contact with the Cubans since Dick [Vernon] Walter's tete-a-tete with Castro eighteen months earlier. The absence of such contact meant that we were flying partially blind and could not explore and compare the positions of the three Marxist allies [the USSR, Cuba, and Angola]."[46]

There were no new contacts. Instead, tensions rose. In September, the Soviets shot down a Korean civilian airliner that had strayed over their airspace; all 269 people on board were killed. The local Soviet air defense commander had mistaken the plane for a U.S. reconnaissance aircraft deliberately intruding into Soviet airspace. "The situation in the region was not normal," a CIA analyst explained. "His forces had been on high alert and in a state of anxiety following incursions by US aircraft during the spring 1983 [US] Pacific Fleet exercise," the largest exercise to date in the northwest Pacific. The Reagan administration chose to believe that the Soviets had known that the plane was a civilian airliner, accused the Kremlin of "deliberate mass murder," and unleashed a campaign of extreme abuse, to which Moscow responded in kind.[47]

In October, the U.S. invasion of Grenada jolted U.S.-Cuban relations to a new low. There were 784 Cubans on the island—construction workers building an airport and 44 soldiers. For the first time since April 1961, when U.S. pilots had dropped napalm and bombs on the Cuban soldiers at the Bay of Pigs,[48] American soldiers killed Cubans—24 soldiers and armed civilians.[49]

After Grenada, the Cubans feared that Reagan might escalate and strike their country. Nevertheless, their commitment to Angola and to Nicaragua did not weaken. Looking back at those dark days, Castro told dos Santos in September 1986 that Cuba had felt

> constantly under threat, but we hadn't retreated. We continued to help Nicaragua, we continued to help the Central American movement, and we kept helping Angola. . . . How beautiful [*bonito*] this is. . . . It is perhaps our most important accomplishment, Comrade José Eduardo, that we were threatened . . . yet we not only refused to withdraw, but we reinforced our troops in Angola. . . . I believe that in the history of our revolution, Comrade José Eduardo, our internationalist actions are our most important accomplishments, because any other country, seeing itself threatened, would have brought its troops and weapons back to defend the homeland, but we did the exact opposite—because we had confidence in our people's, in our country's ability to defend itself.[50]

Following the visit of Risquet and Colomé to Moscow, the Soviets delivered. They were very worried about developments in Angola. A document prepared by the Africa section of the Central Committee of the Soviet Communist Party in late August 1983 painted a somber picture. "The situation in Angola continues to worsen. The survival of the country's progressive government is at stake." The document was scathing about the shortcomings of the Angolan regime, the growing corruption and internecine fighting within the leadership, the deficiencies of the FAPLA, and the lack of attention to the basic needs of the soldiers ("the soldiers are poorly fed, poorly clothed and receive little medical attention"). Only the Cuban troops could protect the regime against the combined blows of Pretoria and UNITA; otherwise, it would crumble.[51] In their conversations with Risquet and Colomé, the Soviets were receptive to the Cubans' demands for more aid to Angola. Over the next year they sent more and better weapons to the FAPLA.[52]

This was the repercussion of the fundamental clash between Washington's and Pretoria's goals. The Reagan administration sought Cuban withdrawal from Angola, but South African policy—a concerted, deliberate, and bold attempt to destroy the MPLA—led directly to Castro's decision to dramatically increase the Cuban commitment to Angola.

## Castro's Letter

On September 20, 1983, Fidel Castro sent a long, thoughtful letter to President dos Santos. "Comrade José Eduardo, I must speak to you with the frankness of a brother," he wrote,

> who has remained at your side for more than eight long and difficult years . . .
>
> The growth and strengthening of UNITA cannot be explained simply by the aid it receives from the imperialists and the close military cooperation of the South African troops. There have been mistakes. Of course, every revolutionary process makes mistakes. In Cuba, we have made many.
>
> I am not going to talk about mistakes in your economic policy. . . . I want to focus on military matters. . . . For years, you have adopted the wrong strategy: you have concentrated your efforts on preparing the regular brigades of the FAPLA to repel a foreign attack, but these troops do not participate in the war against the bandits [UNITA]. This strategy completely overlooks the immense effort made by Cuba: our troops, stationed along the Namibe-Lubango-Matala-Cubango-Menongue line, are there to defend Angola from a large-scale South African invasion. For years, despite South Africa's logistical advantage and absolute superiority in the air, we have fulfilled this mission, even though, if the South Africans tried to breach our line, it could entail heavy casualties. During these years several tens of thousands of Cuban soldiers have guarded this line with exemplary stoicism, living underground in very difficult conditions. . . .
>
> Since 1975, . . . more than 700 Cubans have given their lives for Angola. . . . For us, a small, distant country that faces its own dire threats, these are heavy sacrifices. Have they been entirely useful? Has the MPLA used our internationalist aid correctly? . . .
>
> Eighty percent of your cadres, men, weapons and supplies have been dedicated to the regular brigades of the FAPLA which do not participate at all in the fight against UNITA. Only a bare minimum of your efforts and resources has gone to the war against the bandits. In general, the Angolan units that have waged this war [light brigades] have lacked men, equipment, supplies, and adequate leaders. . . . Yet these troops have born the brunt of the fighting, have endured the

greatest sacrifices, have garnered the most experience and, predictably, have suffered the most casualties. . . .

For a long time we have been insisting in vain that all the brigades of the FAPLA, regular brigades and light brigades, . . . must concentrate on the war against the bandits.

This was the heart of Castro's message, that the military strategy the Angolans had adopted following the Soviet advice was hurting the war effort, and that it was imperative to reconsider that strategy. But the letter also included another message: "We will continue to help you even though we know that at present you cannot afford to pay for our doctors, our professors, our teachers and other aid workers. . . . We have decided that from October 1, and until the Angolan economy has recovered, we will not charge for our technical assistance."[53]

On October 28, 1983, an agreement between Luanda and Havana stipulated that Angola would pay only for the airfare and the board and lodging of the aid workers. At the time there were 4,168 Cuban aid workers in Angola. The loss of compensation meant for Cuba a loss of approximately $20 million per year.[54]

## South Africa Prepares to Strike

Dos Santos replied to Castro's letter on October 28, saying that "we agree completely with your analysis of the military situation."[55] Unbeknownst to him, as he penned his letter, South Africa was preparing to strike, hard.

Pretoria applied military pressure on Angola in several ways, beyond its vast and growing aid to UNITA, which included by the mid-1980s eleven training camps in southern Cuando Cubango and Namibia staffed by South African military personnel.[56] The SADF launched major offensives in southwestern Angola—such as Protea, Daisy, Super, and Meebos. Special Forces and other select units carried out smaller operations inside Angola almost constantly; usually they operated, the chief of the SADF explained, "independently of Kassala [UNITA] forces" that supplied "guides, bearers, etc." The commander of the Special Forces explained that "Kassala is to take credit" for the operations and "Special Forces troops are to wear Kassala type clothing and equipment."[57] These operations included attacks on major economic and logistical targets, such as the sabotage of the oil refinery of Luanda in November 1981, and the destruction of the 350-meter-long railway bridge on the Giraul River, a few miles north of the port of Namibe, in November 1982.[58] The SADF also assigned "specialist advisers and Special Forces elements" to assist UNITA[59] and launched air strikes into Angola.

The Reagan administration welcomed Pretoria's aid to UNITA as well as the SADF's small-scale operations inside Angola as a means to put pressure on the Angolan government, but it was ambivalent about major SADF operations in Angola. At times U.S. officials expressed what the SADF called "tacit approval."[60] They welcomed Protea in August 1981 and the operations that followed in its wake because, Crocker explained, "they wanted to break some diplomatic china" and prod the Angolans to accept linkage.[61] By late 1982, however, the Americans believed that the negotiations with Luanda on Cuban withdrawal were progressing well, and they feared that a major South African military operation could derail them. "We could lose this opportunity . . . through a sharp military confrontation," Under Secretary of State Lawrence Eagleburger warned Pik Botha. There was a time for the stick, and a time for the carrot. "The application of military power has a role to play," Crocker lectured South African generals Geldenhuys and van Tonder in November 1982, "but all the elements that can influence a solution must be coordinated. . . . A cooling-off period that can lead to a troop-withdrawal is necessary." The following March, Eagleburger bluntly told a South African delegation, "It was no time for military action—the United States simply would not understand such action. The administration had invested a good deal of time and reputation in the peace process and would not react well to events bringing that in question."[62] If launched at the wrong time, a major military operation could be counterproductive because it would make the Angolan government more reluctant to send the Cubans home. In the spring of 1983, the Reagan administration believed that the negotiations with Luanda over linkage had reached a critical stage. Eagleburger summoned the South African ambassador: "We are convinced," he told him, "that SA military operations against targets in southern Angola will have a deleterious impact on our talks with the Angolan government." He urged restraint.[63]

The South Africans considered the Americans fair-weather friends and did not share with them either the extent of their involvement in Angola or their military plans. However, Foreign Minister Pik Botha and his aides knew that the United States was South Africa's shield against UN sanctions and therefore argued that, when planning military operations in Angola, South Africa must take the international situation into account and, above all, consider the reaction of the United States. There was a constant tug of war between the foreign ministry and the SADF on the relative importance of military and diplomatic considerations.

The SADF had been demanding another sustained assault on southwestern

Angola—like Protea—since early 1983, but it had been forced to wait because the Foreign Ministry had argued that it would be a slap to the United States. By late 1983, however, the situation had changed. The visit to South Africa of UN secretary-general Pérez de Cuéllar in August had ended in a fiasco, and after Cangamba the Angolans had suspended their intermittent negotiations with the United States. The stage was set for another major offensive in the southwest. Its goals, the Chief of Military Intelligence said, would be to inflict heavy blows on both FAPLA and SWAPO, wreak havoc on the Angolan economy, and make clear to the Angolan population "the incapacity of the USSR and its surrogates to assure genuine peace, security and prosperity."[64]

## Operation Askari

On December 9, 1983, South Africa launched Operation Askari into southwestern Angola. The chief of the SADF, General Viljoen, told the press that his troops were engaged merely in "limited operations against SWAPO in southern Angola" and would strike at the FAPLA only in self-defense, but his words fooled no one—and certainly not U.S. intelligence, which reported in late December that the South Africans were bombing Angolan towns and attacking FAPLA military installations, that they had advanced 140 kilometers into Angola, and that their "use of artillery more than 100 kilometers inside Angola . . . is a significant departure from past practices."[65]

There were four FAPLA brigades in the Fifth Military Region, which covered the southwest of Angola. They were stationed south of the Cuban line, in the small towns of Caiundo, Cuvelai, Mulondo, and Cahama, and they included 7,000 men, that is, one-seventh of the Angolan army. Three were regular brigades, each about 2,000 men strong; they were probably the best-equipped units of the Angolan army. The fourth, a light brigade at Caiundo, had slightly fewer than 1,000 men.[66] Each regular brigade had twelve to fourteen Soviet military advisers; the light brigade at Caiundo had none.[67] Soviet General Valentin Varennikov, who visited Angola at the time, writes in his memoirs that "our military advisers . . . had the duty to fight alongside the units they advised," but this is not true. The rules had not changed since Protea in 1981. The Soviet military advisers could help plan an operation, Konstantin explained, but their participation in combat was "categorically prohibited." When Askari began, the Angolan officer who was the commander of the Fifth Military Region recalls that "the Soviet military advisers didn't want to fight. They wanted to get out of harm's way, they wanted to leave."[68]

On December 29, 1983, three weeks after Askari began, Polo reported that he had met with Konstantin. "Konstantin said that it was essential to reinforce the region [south of the Cuban line] with infantry, tanks and artillery. . . . On the other hand, he also asked me to help evacuate the fourteen Soviet advisers of the 2nd regular brigade [at Cahama]. I told him that he had to leave the advisers with the brigade because their evacuation would lower the Angolans' morale."[69] Konstantin relented: the Soviet advisers remained with the brigades.[70]

On December 30, Risquet urged dos Santos to withdraw the four brigades because they were exposed to the South African attacks—by air and "even from the infantry and the artillery. . . . If one of these brigades were surrounded . . . it would be very difficult for the Cuban troops to go to its assistance . . . because they don't have [mobile] antiaircraft weapons that would protect them." He reminded dos Santos of Cassinga, when the Cuban soldiers who had rushed from Chamutete to defend the Namibian refugees had been decimated by the South African air force. "To advance without antiaircraft protection in an area where the South Africans have absolute air superiority is suicidal; it means sending our troops to the slaughter."[71]

Dos Santos was inclined to follow the Cubans' advice, but Konstantin and General Varennikov urged him otherwise. Later, the Angolan president told Risquet, "I met repeatedly with the Comrade Soviet General [Varennikov] on the . . . 29 or 30 [of December]. He . . . was categorical, he told me: 'Comrade president . . . given their numerical strength and their armament, the brigades in Cahama, Mulondo and Cuvelai will be able to repel any South African attack.' He had no doubts."[72] Caught between the two opposite recommendations, dos Santos hesitated, and the four brigades stayed where they were, while the enemy roamed around them. The SADF's strategy was to avoid a frontal attack against the entrenched brigades that could be costly in South African lives. Instead, it resorted to what it called "squeezing dry": through air strikes, long-distance bombardments with its heavy guns, and quick probes that sought "to isolate [the towns], and grind down and terrorize their defenders so that they would flee or desert en masse."[73] The air strikes inflicted few casualties—the brigades had strong antiaircraft defenses and the planes "dropped their bombs from an altitude of 6,000 to 8,000 meters"[74]—but they packed a psychological punch. On January 4, 1984, the morale of the FAPLA brigade at Cuvelai—a regular brigade of approximately 2,300 men—collapsed. The soldiers fled northward toward the Cuban line in small groups, leaving behind their heavy weapons and a few hundred casualties.[75]

The South Africans morphed their victory over the hapless brigade into a glorious three-day pitched battle in which they defeated two Cuban battalions that had joined the defenders of Cuvelai.[76] This was a tall tale. There had been no Cubans south of the line when the invasion began, and there were only a handful thereafter. "Because we needed as much information about the enemy as possible," the military mission reported, Polo sent sixty Cubans—soldiers and officers—to the four FAPLA brigades "to gather and transmit every available piece of information." Twenty went to Cuvelai. This was the full extent of the Cuban presence south of the line during Askari.[77]

On January 10, in Moscow, General Colomé reviewed the lesson of Cuvelai with Ustinov, Chief of the General Staff Marshal Ogarkov, and other top Soviet officers. He urged that the three remaining FAPLA brigades "withdraw to our Line of Defense, where we can help them and where they will be protected by our air force and our antiaircraft weapons." He failed to convince Ustinov, who argued "that the brigades must not be withdrawn, because this would leave a large part of the south in Pretoria's hands." Colomé pointed out that the three brigades controlled only the towns where they were stationed "and the remainder of the territory is controlled by the enemy," but "Marshals Ustinov and Ogarkov . . . kept insisting that the brigades must remain where they are."[78]

Dos Santos followed the Soviets' advice, and the three brigades stayed put. (The South Africans were impressed by the grit of the brigade at Cahama.) Meanwhile 5,000 South African soldiers, supported by the air force, roamed far and wide over the southwest, south of the Cuban line, proceeding "geographically beyond anything they have undertaken in the past," Crocker told Shultz. General Viljoen boasted, "We will fight SWAPO as far north as possible." The SADF, however, did not attack the Cuban line that blocked its way into the heart of Angola.[79]

On January 6, 1984, the UN Security Council considered a resolution condemning the invasion and demanding South Africa's withdrawal—mighty words, but with no sanctions, of course. The United States and England abstained in the thirteen to zero vote in favor.[80] The *Cape Times* remarked that the resolution "was a watered-down version of a text that had contained a threat of sanctions against South Africa if it did not stop attacking Angola. In its new form, it referred only to more effective measures in accordance with appropriate provisions of the charter of the United Nations, but this was still insufficient to win US and British support." From behind the shield provided by Reagan and Thatcher, Pik Botha showed his defiance to the international community. "The time has come that the world understand that South Africa will not let herself be intimidated," he thundered. "This may bring it [South Africa] into collision with the entire world. We will accept it with all the consequences that it may bring. The time has come that the world understand that South Africa will not be intimidated."[81]

## Cubans and Soviets Clash

Following the debacle at Cuvelai, Konstantin criticized the Cubans for failing to send troops to support the FAPLA. He condemned their decision to conduct an investigation of what had happened at Cuvelai, claiming that it would violate Angolan sovereignty.[82]

The Cuban response was swift and uncompromising, delivered by Risquet to General of the Army Varennikov, the third-highest-ranking officer of the Red Army. They met in Luanda at the headquarters of the Cuban military mission. "After the customary exchange of courtesies, we turned to the business at hand," Varennikov wrote in his memoirs. "Risquet spoke first, and I did not object, but when it was my turn, I remarked, as if in jest: 'And to think that I had naively believed that I would speak first because I am the guest.' Risquet countered: 'We do not consider a Soviet general to be a guest among us.'"[83]

The discussion that followed sheds light on Cuban-Soviet relations in Angola, and on how the Cubans dealt with their bigger brother.

Risquet began by recalling that in November 1982 Andropov had told Castro "that our relations must always be frank, honest and loyal. He said something that Comrade Fidel liked very much . . .: 'We must not fail to tell a truth or express an opinion just to avoid an unpleasant moment.' . . . With you, now," he told Varennikov, "I will follow this principle." He went on: "Regarding Comrade General . . . Konstantin's . . . statement that we do not have the right to investigate what happened [at Cuvelai], our minister of defense, Comrade Raúl Castro, wants you to know that it was he, personally, . . . who ordered . . . the investigation of the events surrounding the twenty Cubans assigned to the brigade, who at first had been deemed missing." This had led, inevitably, to an examination of what had occurred at Cuvelai. "Furthermore, Comrade Raúl Castro has instructed us to tell Comrade General Konstantin that he, Raúl Castro . . . believes that . . . Konstantin has absolutely no right to lecture us about how to respect the sovereignty of Angola, which in the eight years we have been here we have never violated in any way. Comrade Raúl Castro adds that although he would prefer not to get into this kind of argument, he is obliged to point out, since we are talking about respecting the sovereignty of Angola, that Comrade José Eduardo dos Santos . . . agrees that the FAPLA brigades should be withdrawn and that . . . Konstantin has been constantly opposing a sovereign decision of the Commander-in-Chief of the FAPLA."[84]

The Cubans expressed their gratitude for the aid they received from the USSR, but when necessary, they stood up to the Soviets. This is what happened in the conversation with Varennikov. "I told you, a few days ago, about the friendship and fraternity we feel for the Soviet Union," Risquet said, "how we see in the Soviet military our teachers, our brothers, and how much your military expertise has meant for Cuba. But I also told you that we have had disagreements [in Angola]. . . . We want to make it very clear, comrade General of the Army, that the Cuban military command will not be dragged into any adventure. . . . We are responsible for the lives of our soldiers and cannot allow them to be sacrificed without reason."[85]

It was foolhardy to keep Angolan brigades in the far southwest where it was impossible for the Cubans to go to their assistance, Risquet said. "If the Soviet comrades want to implement the ideas of Comrade General Konstantin, they can do it with Soviet troops, but not with Cuban troops. We absolutely disagree with those ideas." The Cuvelai disaster was the responsibility of those who, like Konstantin, had insisted that the FAPLA brigade remain there. "We cannot . . . but respond with indignation when someone has the effrontery to blame us for the defeat of the 11th Brigade."

Risquet concluded: "You can be absolutely certain, dear comrade General of the Army, that if the South Africans attack the line that we are defending, we will fight fiercely without any hesitation, but know with equal certainty that we will refuse to endanger even a single Cuban life in an operation we consider ill-advised, wrong-headed and unrealistic. . . . Believe me, comrade General of the Army, it is very unpleasant to have to speak in this way. We understand how uncomfortable this must be for you, who bear no responsibility for what has happened. . . . We see the Soviets as our brothers, but we consider it necessary to tell you all this so that you will return to the Soviet Union with a complete and full understanding of the views of our Minister of Defense."[86]

Varennikov was gracious. "I am sincerely grateful for your frankness," he began. Referring to Fidel Castro's advice that the FAPLA brigades should be pulled back to the Cuban line. Varennikov said: "I am in no position to judge what has been recommended by a man of the stature of Fidel Castro. I can only state, once again, what the Soviet people and I feel toward this great man. When one mentions Cuba, every Soviet citizen feels warmth, and when one mentions Fidel Castro, every Soviet citizen feels inspired." Varennikov asked many pertinent questions about the Cuban defensive line and the military situation in Angola, but carefully avoided expressing any opinion about the issues Risquet had raised, beyond saying, "in principle I agree with what has been said by Comrade Minister Raúl." He would report to Moscow. He had, however, one proposal: "I have urged Konstantin . . . to develop as close a relationship as possible with Comrade Polo, and I would like to ask that Polo reciprocate, so that from now on . . . they can come to a consensus between themselves." When they could not, "they should not go to the Angolan leaders but rather consult with their respective general staffs at home. I am certain that our general staffs will always be able to develop a common position."[87]

## The Lusaka Agreement and the Nkomati Pact

"By the beginning of January 1984," a South African military history noted, "it was clear that Angola was beginning to wilt under the sustained pressure of Operation Askari." The SADF now controlled a broad swath of territory south of the Cuban line. "The stage was set for a concerted diplomatic initiative by . . . Chester Crocker."[88] Talks between Angolans and Americans from January 20 to 22, 1984, in Cape Verde paved the way for a meeting between Angolans and South Africans in Lusaka from February 13 to 16 in the presence of U.S. officials. It was the first time that representatives of the three countries met together. On February 16, Angolans and South Africans signed the Lusaka agreement, which called for the staged withdrawal of South African forces from Angola. The withdrawal would be completed by March 31 in exchange for an Angolan commitment not to allow SWAPO or Cuban forces to operate in the area vacated by Pretoria. The two sides agreed to establish a Joint Monitoring Commission to police the disengagement area. The Lusaka agreement said nothing about Pretoria's aid to UNITA. South Africa, Angola, and the United States signed a "Tripartite Statement," which mentioned Resolution 435. It noted that "the Lusaka meeting constitutes an important and constructive step toward the peaceful resolution of the problems of the region, including the question of the implementation of the United Nations Security Council Resolution 435."[89]

Angola had duly told the Cubans and the Soviets that it had agreed to U.S. offers for talks, but once the talks began, it did not inform them about what was being discussed, much less consult with them. At 12:50 P.M. on February 21, the Angolan foreign minister met with the ambassadors of the communist countries represented in Luanda and "said that today, at 3 P.M., he will brief both the national and the foreign press on the Lusaka talks among Angola, the United States and South Africa. Because of Angola's preferential relations with the socialist countries, he wanted to inform their ambassadors beforehand so that they would not be taken by surprise by the press reports. He would give them a more detailed briefing than that he would give to the press." Among those present were Polo and Ambassador Puente Ferro. This was the first time Cuba was briefed about the Lusaka agreement.[90]

On February 9, 1984, a week before the agreement was signed, Andropov died in Moscow. On February 13, the aged and sick Konstantin Chernenko was

Angolan territory occupied by South Africa, February 1984 (adapted from CIA, Directorate of Intelligence, "Moscow's Response to the Diplomatic Challenge in Southern Africa," May 1984, FOIA)

anointed his successor. "There was no reason to believe," the senior Soviet specialist at the NSC writes, "that Chernenko had either the mental capacity or tactical skill to change entrenched Soviet policy. Given his reputed ill health, he was likely to be another transitional figure. . . . Soviet foreign policy was on the defensive everywhere, just as domestic problems were becoming more acute."[91]

The weakening of the Soviet position was evident in southern Africa. The Lusaka agreement was followed on March 16 by a formal nonaggression pact signed by Mozambique and South Africa on the banks of the Nkomati River, which marked the border between the two countries. In the Nkomati accord, PW Botha and President Samora Machel pledged that neither government would allow its territory to be used as a staging ground for acts of violence against the other. This meant, Crocker told Shultz, the end of "Mozambican assistance for Soviet-sponsored ANC terrorism against South Africa" in return for Pretoria's pledge to end its aid to RENAMO, the rebel movement fighting against Machel's government. The CIA opined, "We expect both sides to work hard to make their detente succeed. Mozambican security personnel have raided ANC facilities in Maputo—showing Pretoria that Machel is holding up his side of the bargain." Machel was indeed doing his best to prove his goodwill to Pretoria. An ANC official complained that the Mozambicans "applied the terms [of the Nkomati pact] with what may be called religious zeal. They raided our houses at gunpoint and with fixed bayonets!"[92]

Nkomati seemed to confirm the virtue of Pretoria's "big stick" policy: the ANC was forced to virtually abandon Mozambique. It was also a victory for the United States, which had been "heavily involved" in brokering the negotiations to their successful conclusion. The pact promised to reduce Soviet influence in Mozambique; better still, "coming in the wake of the Lusaka accords," it marked, Shultz announced, "a fundamental turning point in southern Africa political relationships."[93] It did not mark, however, a change in Pretoria's behavior. Within a month of the signing of the pact, the U.S. Embassy in Maputo reported that there were strong indications that "neither the letter nor the spirit of the Nkomati agreement . . . are being observed by the SAG." Aid to RENAMO was continuing.[94] As President Kaunda, the moderate leader of Zambia, said a few hours before Botha and Machel signed the pact, "The problem is not Mozambique, it is not Zambia, it is not Angola. . . . The problem is the philosophy of Apartheid."[95]

## The Cuban Response

On March 16, 1984, the day the Nkomati pact was signed, President dos Santos arrived in Havana for talks with Fidel Castro.

These were extraordinary conversations. Castro had legitimate grounds for complaint, but he spoke with restraint and generosity. He briefly summed up the history of the bilateral relationship since 1975. He reminded his guest that the Cubans' role was to protect Angola against external aggression. He reiterated Cuba's desire to bring its troops home: "The day there is peace in Angola we will be able to withdraw. We will then be able to significantly strengthen our own defense, and our men will no longer have to bear the heavy burden of living thousands of kilometers from their families for two years. More than 200,000 Cubans have already made this sacrifice." But Cuba, he declared, would leave only with Angola's agreement. "How many times have the Americans tried to negotiate with Cuba about our troops in Angola. . . . We have always refused to discuss . . . the problems of Angola with the United States. We have always asserted that we would discuss them only and exclusively with Angola. . . . This has been our position toward Angola; but we feel that the Angolans have not treated us in the same way." Castro pointed out that the September 1978 military agreement, "which is the agreement that is still in force," stipulated that Cuba and Angola "agree to maintain regular contact at the appropriate levels in order to develop detailed and multifaceted analyses of the political and military situation . . . and to consult with each other before making decisions or taking actions in the military arena." He then expressed irritation. "To speak frankly, since we signed that agreement you have never once consulted us about any decision that was going to affect us; you have almost never informed us beforehand, and only on a few occasions did you inform us after the fact that there had been talks with the United States. At times we learned through our intelligence service in Western Europe that there had been contacts between Angola and South Africa or between Angola and the United States; at other times we read about it in the press."[96]

The Lusaka agreement fit this pattern. "We were faced with a *fait accompli*, as were the Soviets. I don't think this is proper," Castro told dos Santos. He objected to the terms of the agreement, but that was not the issue: "The final decision was yours, not ours, but at least we could have talked beforehand, and we, as well as the Soviets, could have expressed our disagreement beforehand. Then we would have had no grounds whatsoever to complain. But both the Soviets and us, your two main allies, the two who support Angola, who have been making immense efforts on your behalf, we were faced with a *fait accompli*. . . . Who's going to question Angola's independence when Angola is so independent that it feels free to mistreat its best allies and even to violate its agreements? Of course, Angola must determine its own future, but to honor your agreement with us you should have consulted us beforehand. These agreements give us, too, some rights." And he concluded, wryly, "I wonder whether our Angolan comrades have reread these agreements lately."[97]

Dos Santos's reply was lame. He acknowledged that they should have consulted their allies; it had been a mistake, an oversight, they were a young state, they would be more careful in the future. Castro did not press the point, and the discussion shifted to the military and the economic situation of Angola. Eventually it came to health care. Here a remarkable exchange took place among Cubans, while the Angolans listened in silence.

It began when Rodolfo Puente Ferro, the able Cuban ambassador in Angola, said, "There are regions, provincial capitals, where really there is no medicine.

The sick are given prescriptions, but then they have to go to the witch doctor, to the traditional healer, because there is no medicine. The mortality rate is high because of this lack of medicine." The Cuban health authorities had tried to help, offering fifty-five types of medicine that were manufactured in Cuba, "that are really necessary and indispensable for the diseases that are found in Angola." They had offered them at cost—$700,000 for a six-month supply. After months of silence, the Angolans had finally asked for twenty-nine of these medicines, but they had not yet been shipped because Luanda had failed to release the requisite letters of credit.

Castro asked, "Can we manufacture this medicine for $700,000?" After Puente Ferro confirmed that this was possible, Fidel continued, "Well . . . then let's do it and send it to Angola, and let them pay later. . . . We don't want to make any profit with this medicine; we will sell it at cost. . . . If the situation is critical, we'll send it on the first available ship, and let them pay later." He insisted, "We cannot let a man die in a hospital, or a child, or an old person, or a wounded person, or a soldier, or whoever it may be, because someone forgot to write a letter of credit or because someone didn't sign it. Besides, we're not talking about large quantities. We won't go bankrupt if you can't pay. We won't be ruined. If we were talking about one hundred million dollars, I would have to say, 'Comrades, we cannot afford it.' But if we're only talking about $700,000 . . . We can handle it."

The Angolans expressed gratitude, briefly. "I would like to thank Comrade Fidel Castro for this very generous decision," dos Santos said. He had one concern, however: "We know that Cuba has made another very important, very generous decision. . . . It has suspended the payment in hard currency for its technical assistance to Angola. . . . We would like to have an idea, more or less, of how long Cuba can bear this burden." Castro replied, "I believe . . . taking into account the situation of Angola, that you must not worry about this. We can bear it for as long as necessary. Don't worry. We will make this sacrifice." He added, "The major sacrifice is the human cost, you see? It is asking our people to leave their families behind. . . . It's a sacrifice for those who go and for our national budget." There was little left for dos Santos to say except, "Thank you very much, comrade."[98]

Dos Santos's visit ended with a joint communiqué that stated the two countries' position on a possible withdrawal of the Cuban troops. The terms were similar to those of the joint declaration of February 4, 1982, but for one key point: the 1982 declaration had not mentioned UNITA; the March 19, 1984, communiqué stipulated that "the end of all aid" to UNITA by Pretoria and Washington was a precondition for the beginning of the withdrawal of the

Cuban troops. This was done at the Angolans' request. Three years later, Risquet reminded dos Santos, "As you know . . . when you were in Cuba, we drafted two versions. One followed the same line as the February 4 [1982] declaration, and the other included the end of the South African and U.S. aid to UNITA as a new condition. You will remember that Fidel asked you whether we should include this new condition (even though UNITA was an internal affair), which helped Angola. You chose the second draft, which included the condition that the racists' aid to UNITA must end."[99]

The Cubans believed that the prerequisite for the departure of their troops from Angola was the independence of Namibia through the implementation of Resolution 435. But Resolution 435 left South Africa in control of Walvis Bay, Namibia's only deep-water port. This grim reality reinforced Havana's belief that, even after the independence of Namibia, a residual Cuban force would have to remain in Angola to protect the country from a sudden strike by South Africa, or from an attack launched by Zaire, or through Zaire, against Cabinda. However, if the foreign aggression against Angola ended, the Cuban troops would no longer fight against UNITA. As Risquet said in February 1984, "If we can obtain . . . the withdrawal of the South Africans from the south of Angola and from Namibia, and the implementation of Resolution 435, the struggle against UNITA, being an internal affair, will have to be carried out exclusively by the FAPLA, without the participation of our troops."[100] The Cuban troops are in Angola, Castro told a GDR official a few months later, "to fight against the external enemy, not against the internal counter revolution."[101] This had been Cuba's position in 1976 and remained consistent through the New York peace agreements of December 1988.

CHAPTER 10

# The Failure of Lusaka

## U.S.–Angolan–South African Minuet

The Lusaka agreement did not lead to peace. For the following fifteen months Angolan, South African, and U.S. officials met to discuss the implementation of Resolution 435 and the withdrawal of the Cuban troops from Angola. On June 25, 1984, President dos Santos flew to Lusaka to speak with South African representatives (Cuba was informed *post facto*), and senior Angolan officials met on several occasions with Foreign Minister Pik Botha and other high-ranking South Africans in Lusaka and Maputo,[1] but in general Angolans and South Africans communicated through the Americans, the self-appointed mediators. Chester Crocker and his senior deputy, Frank Wisner, traveled back and forth from Washington to Africa, trying to hammer out a settlement based on linkage. "The Americans move quickly," Risquet told Soviet foreign minister Gromyko in September 1984. "Today they may appear in Lusaka and tomorrow they'll be in Cape Verde, the day after tomorrow they'll fly to Luanda, and then they'll pop up in Pretoria, inventing one thing, making up another."[2]

Where the Americans did not go was Havana. Washington's position was that the Cubans could not join any talks, even those dealing with the departure of the Cuban troops. Castro "had indicated, with face saving in mind, that he would like to become a direct party to the negotiations," Crocker told Savimbi's aide Jeremias Chitunda in October 1984. "We did not want to do business with him. . . . We simply wanted him to behave. Our approach was to let the Cubans work out their concerns with MPLA, rather than let them get their nose under the negotiating tent." The only thing the Cubans needed to do was sign the final agreements about the withdrawal of their troops.[3]

The Angolans kept the Cubans informed and consulted with them—loosely at first, much more closely after October 1984, when a "Joint Cuban-Angolan

Support Group" was created. (The Angolans' willingness to consult with the Cubans increased as their frustration with Pretoria's intransigence grew.) "If we review the year 1984 and these first weeks of 1985," Risquet told Angolans and Soviets in March 1985, "we can say that we have achieved an optimal degree of coordination in the negotiations. Even though there were moments of lack of coordination, what characterizes this last period is the close coordination between us and our Angolan comrades."[4]

The Soviets watched from the sidelines. The CIA reported in May 1984, "Despite Moscow's uneasiness [with the Lusaka agreement] we have seen no evidence of a Soviet effort to stop the Angolan–South African dialogue."[5] The available evidence—the lengthy minutes of conversations between Cubans and Soviets, as well as among Cubans, Soviets, and Angolans—indicates that Moscow continued to provide Angola with military assistance, while sharing its doubts about the behavior of the Angolans with the Cubans. Gromyko told Risquet in September 1984, "We're dissatisfied with the level of communication from our Angolan friends. Usually we're informed *ex post facto*, if at all." The Soviets feared that the Angolans, pressed by blows from the South Africans and blandishments from the Americans, might sacrifice SWAPO and the ANC by agreeing to expel them from the country. "The United States is trying to force the Angolans to sign an agreement with Pretoria similar to Nkomati," Soviet deputy foreign minister Ilyichev told Risquet in February 1985. (In the March 1984 Nkomati pact, Mozambique had pledged that the ANC would no longer be allowed to operate within its borders.) "I can tell you frankly that Luanda's position is not very clear to us. . . . Unfortunately, in the past the Angolans have confronted us—and you—with a *fait accompli* more than once." The Soviets hoped that the Cubans could enlighten them. "Cuba has its hand on the pulse of the conversations," Ilyichev said.[6]

Cuba could help prevent an Angolan Nkomati, Castro asserted, "because we have a very powerful weapon: not our tanks, not our guns, not our troops. It is simply our right to withdraw from the country."[7] Cuba would have used this threat—as the weapon of last resort—had Luanda been on the verge of signing an agreement with South Africa that did not include Resolution 435 and prevented SWAPO from operating in Angola.

But the Cubans did not have to go this far because Pretoria's intransigence made any agreement impossible. On all points, the gap between South Africans and Angolans was too wide. The Angolans proposed that the Cuban soldiers in the south of the country leave within three years of the beginning of the implementation of Resolution 435; the remaining Cubans would be stationed in the north for an unspecified length of time; Luanda also demanded that Pretoria cease aiding UNITA. The South Africans countered that the Cubans had to withdraw in parallel with the reduction of South African forces in Namibia. They insisted that within three months of the beginning of the implementation of Resolution 435, the number of Cuban soldiers in Angola "must be reduced to zero."[8]

The South Africans also demanded that Luanda end all aid to the ANC. Pik Botha told the Angolan interior minister in April 1984 that there were "up to 2,000 ANC terrorists undergoing training in Angola, and it was his duty to ask the Angolan government to get rid of these people. This was not a matter that could be negotiated and the SA government could not tolerate that they remain there. They must leave Angola." He told Crocker "that if the ANC did not leave, South Africa would enter Angola and remove them." There would be no reciprocity, he added: South Africa would continue to aid UNITA.[9] The South Africans professed that they wanted to help the MPLA and UNITA to reconcile.[10] "For example," U.S. deputy assistant secretary Wisner told the hapless Angolans, "they offer to mediate between you and UNITA; they propose the creation of a constituent assembly in the south of Angola; they suggest the formation of a government of national unity in Luanda, and the end of all foreign military aid." Wisner urged the Angolans "to be extremely careful" and avoid angering Pretoria by raising the issue of its aid to UNITA. There were divisions within South Africa's ruling circles, he explained, "some want to play the card of UNITA to the hilt; others favor a negotiated settlement." Over time, after Luanda had demonstrated its good faith by agreeing to the departure of all the Cubans, Pretoria might soften its attitude and accept the existence of the MPLA government. Wisner used the example of the Nkomati pact, in which Pretoria had agreed to stop helping RENAMO—an unfortunate example, since Pretoria had definitely not stopped helping the rebels even though Mozambique was assiduously respecting its end of the agreement.[11]

## South Africa and UNITA

In February 1985 the CIA concluded that "most key officials in the South African government are determined that Savimbi eventually will take power in Luanda. Savimbi's triumph would at the same time eliminate one of the regimes most hostile to Pretoria in the region and serve as part of a ring of 'moderate' buffer states surrounding Namibia." South Africa, the CIA noted, would scuttle any settlement that did not pave the way for Savimbi's takeover. This was a sound judgment. In 1976, after withdrawing from Angola, the South Africans had continued to aid Savimbi. "At the time," General Thirion remarked, "we [Military

Intelligence] didn't know how far our government would be willing to support Savimbi or how much the international community would tolerate."[12] Pretoria's aid to Savimbi increased over the years, and its determination to bring him to power strengthened. In September 1983 the Secretariat of the State Security Council stated that "UNITA's control over at least the southern half of Angola is of crucial importance for South Africa in order to achieve a peaceful solution of the SWA [Namibia] problem. . . . South Africa's assistance to UNITA is part of its struggle against Marxist expansionism in southern Africa. The continuation of this assistance at least until the establishment of a government in Luanda dominated by UNITA is consistent with South Africa's strategy for southern Africa."[13]

This belief that Savimbi could be enthroned in Luanda was evident in the deliberations of the "Angola Group," a high-powered committee that the South African government had created in May 1983 "with the task of analyzing anew the SWA/Angola situation."[14] The group was chaired by the administrator general of Namibia and included the chief of the South African Defence Force (SADF), the senior SADF officer in Namibia, head of the Directorate of Special Tasks of Military Intelligence General van Tonder, and senior Foreign Ministry official David Steward.[15] On December 6, 1983, the Angola Group decided to organize "a meeting between Mario [code for Savimbi] and his men with leading South African industrialists to lay the groundwork for economic cooperation between Angola and South Africa after Mario has taken over the government." At a meeting of the group the following day, the administrator general of Namibia "discussed his general strategy with regard to SWA. This rested on four factors: the development of the internal political process [in Namibia]; the campaign against SWAPO; the establishment of a UNITA government in Angola; and progress in South Africa's ability to persuade key Western countries to adopt a more pragmatic approach to the problems of the territory [Namibia]."[16]

This strategy was bolstered by faulty intelligence. Whereas the U.S. State Department asserted that Savimbi could not overthrow the Angolan government—and this was a key determinant of U.S. policy—South African Military Intelligence presented a rosier picture. Savimbi was "a manipulator extraordinaire," remarked Colonel Breytenbach, the renowned Special Forces leader who had extensive dealings with him but did not fall under his spell. "Savimbi had charisma. He was very clever. He was also a very nasty piece of work; he knocked off his own people; he was a law into himself. . . . As a charismatic political leader he was very good. I would place him in a category with Hitler." Savimbi cultivated a close relationship with Prime Minister PW Botha and senior SADF officers. "PW was taken in by Savimbi," Breytenbach said. "Savimbi knew how to seduce him. At the time South Africa was the skunk of the world, and here was a black leader telling them 'You're not so bad; I love you,' and that's what they wanted to hear."[17] Savimbi pledged, for example, "We are working with South Africa to shape a common destiny."[18] He embraced the South Africans' dream of a constellation of states, with words that warmed their lonely hearts. "Angola is the key to a peaceful southern African region," he told a high-ranking South African delegation. "With Angola a big bloc of states could come into being—a bloc of states that would exert political and economic influence over all of Africa. South Africa could play a decisive role in this, and UNITA could be very helpful to South Africa by opening doors to other black states. . . . The South Africans," Savimbi said, "were the first and oldest freedom fighters in Africa." He told the delegation that he considered himself and his UNITA fighters "to be the youngest freedom fighters in Africa," and he added that "it is significant that today the youngest and the descendants of the oldest sit at the same table."[19]

He told PW Botha at a gathering of UNITA troops in his headquarters in Jamba: "We feel very honored with this visit. We not only share a common interest in fighting the Russians; we have developed brotherhood, we understand each other and we know each other. . . . We want to convey our love [to you] . . . and also to tell you that here in Angola there will be no retreat. . . . We find it unjust what the world is saying and doing to you." As General Thirion remarked, "PW was very impressed with Savimbi. If you wanted to impress PW, you made sure you were a UNITA man, a Savimbi man."[20]

Savimbi met frequently with PW Botha and other top South African officials in South Africa, in Namibia, and in southeastern Angola. General Geldenhuys, who was chief of the army from 1980 to 1985 and chief of the SADF from 1985 to 1990, recalled, "I went very often to Jamba to receive military briefings from Savimbi," as did many other generals, but it was the military intelligence officers permanently attached to Savimbi who provided the constant link with him. "They were the day-to-day contact," Geldenhuys explained. Military Intelligence, Breytenbach observed, "constantly exaggerated Savimbi's strength. That's what they wanted to believe" and, as they well knew, this was also what PW Botha and the senior SADF officers wanted to hear. When I interviewed him, Geldenhuys conceded: "We all knew that Savimbi wanted to come to power. Was there any hope [that he could succeed]? If there hadn't been any hope, I don't think we would have supported him." General Thirion was more blunt: "There were a lot of people who truly believed that it was possible that Savimbi would become the ruler of Angola. Among them were Geldenhuys,

[Defense Minister] Malan, van Tonder. Pik Botha was not really a true believer, but he was tagging along, afraid of Malan and of PW Botha."[21]

Pik Botha hoped to become president of South Africa when PW stepped down, and for this he courted the president's goodwill and that of Malan, who, as General Geldenhuys noted, was "PW's blue-eyed boy."[22] Furthermore, when it came to UNITA the Foreign Ministry took a back seat to the SADF. The Foreign Ministry was represented on the "Angola Group," and Pik Botha and his senior aides met with Savimbi and his representatives in South Africa, in Namibia, and, on occasion, in Jamba. But it was the SADF that was in charge of the aid program to UNITA without any participation from the Foreign Ministry. And it was the SADF that was in permanent contact with UNITA and maintained a constant presence in Jamba.[23]

I asked Neil van Heerden, a senior aide of Pik Botha, whether the SADF believed that it could bring Savimbi to power in Angola. At first he answered diplomatically that "elements in the SADF were confident that through military involvement in Angola they could influence the situation there very significantly." Then, as our hour-long conversation continued, he became less cagey: "The military had chosen Savimbi as their protégé," he said, "and set up an extensive program of support. As it grew, so did their confidence. They believed that Savimbi had the capacity and charisma to take over Angola." For his part, Savimbi told the Angola Group in late 1983 "that he hoped that UNITA could achieve its objectives by 1986. If UNITA wins it would be the beginning of a great change in the whole of Southern Africa. Prime Minister Botha would be invited to visit Angola officially."[24]

Military developments in Angola fueled Pretoria's optimism. In late 1983 Savimbi had "spelt out the aims of his offensive" for the coming year, his biographer writes. "It was a dual assault"—in the northwest against the province of Bengo and in the northeast against the two Lunda provinces, where the diamond mines were. "Additionally, UNITA intended that its units should push so far northwards that by March–April 1984 they would have reached Angola's northern border with Zaire."[25] UNITA met these goals. In February 1985 the Cuban military mission reported that the guerrillas had extended their activities to the north and the east of the country—not only to Bengo and the Lundas but also to the provinces of Cuanza Norte and Uige. They were active even in the vicinity of the capital. The report added, however, that this expansion had taken place "at a very high price": in 1984 UNITA had suffered more casualties than the FAPLA. "[Over the last year] the FAPLA has become better organized and better able to fight," the head of the military mission added. But the South

African generals failed to notice this warning sign, so mesmerized were they by the impressive geographic expansion of UNITA and the optimistic reports of Savimbi and the SADF's Military Intelligence officers attached to him. "At present UNITA has 36,000 men with an increase of approximately 6,500 new soldiers each year," the Secretariat of the State Security Council reported. The FAPLA's effective force was at most 50,000. The balance, the South Africans believed, was turning inexorably in favor of Savimbi.[26]

But how could Savimbi come to power, with the Cubans in Angola? According to General Thirion, while the Foreign Ministry worried that increased South African support for Savimbi would lead to a larger Cuban presence, "Malan and Company would say, 'how long can the Cubans last?' The war was costly for the Cubans. Confronted with rising costs in blood and money they would leave Angola. Granted, the weapons were given by the Soviet Union. But the Soviets, too, might eventually tire and decide to cut their losses."[27]

Alternatively, a moderate faction within the MPLA might gain the upper hand, make a deal with Savimbi, and tell the Cubans to leave. In September 1983 the Secretariat of the State Security Council argued, "Parallel with UNITA's continuing military confrontation, we must soon consider cautiously opening a dialogue with Luanda that could result in a political solution leading to a Cuban withdrawal" and, after the Cubans had left, to "a UNITA takeover." To create the conditions needed for a successful dialogue, the document continued, "the dos Santos government must be destabilized." This meant more military aid to Savimbi. "We wanted to help him to come to power," General Witkop Badenhorst says. "We hoped that he could gain enough strength to force the MPLA to the negotiating table."[28]

The Lusaka agreement, imposed on a battered Angola at gunpoint, opened new vistas: used creatively, it could be a lever to force power sharing on Luanda and thereby help maintain South Africa's control over Namibia. On March 5, 1984, the State Security Council concluded that "we must make every effort . . . to bring about an agreement between UNITA and the MPLA and get the Cubans out of Angola, without alienating the United States. This will make the handling of the Southwest Africa [Namibia] problem so much easier." Even Foreign Ministry officials found the dream irresistible. Pik Botha told Crocker "that the MPLA must be prepared to govern Angola together with UNITA." David Steward, the senior Foreign Ministry official in the Angola Group, mused, "Perhaps the best way of encouraging the right developments in Angola would be to make it clear to the moderates within the MPLA that they would also receive a slice of the cake if they agree to deal with UNITA."[29]

Any power sharing between the MPLA and UNITA would of course be temporary. The South Africans believed that once in the government, the charismatic Savimbi would impose his personality on a demoralized MPLA and seize control; Savimbi, for his part, told the South Africans that his talk about a coalition government with the MPLA was strictly for "tactical purposes. . . . By the time the MPLA accepts that it must talk with UNITA it will be so weak that it will for all practical purposes be finished."[30]

It was a confused scenario. The South Africans wanted the Cubans to leave Angola, but not too soon. As long as the Cubans remained in Angola, the Reagan administration would not force Pretoria to implement Resolution 435 in Namibia and it would veto UN sanctions against South Africa. South Africa would have time to craft an internal settlement in Namibia and strengthen UNITA in Angola. Given enough time, the South Africans could clear the path to Savimbi's takeover when the Cubans did eventually leave Angola. This would make it much easier for Pretoria to crush SWAPO and then—the danger quelled—to hold "free" elections in Namibia. Presto! The international community would be satisfied, and the Constellation of States would have gained two new members. In a way it all made sense. "We never thought that we would give away Namibia," General Badenhorst remarked, conveying the SADF's view. "If Savimbi ruled Angola the entire region would be safeguarded." In an October 1984 memo to the Secretariat of the State Security Council, the Chief of the SADF, General Constand Viljoen, reiterated, "The SWA [Namibia] question cannot be resolved favorably for South Africa until the Angola question has been solved." Disagreement about the strategy was not taken kindly. At one meeting, recalls General Thirion, when he voiced his doubts, army chief Geldenhuys cut him short: "'OK, we've heard you, Mr Thirion.' When you're called 'Mr' you know it's time to shut up."[31]

In July 1984, the State Security Council concluded:

In order to solve the SWA problem, the policy of South Africa is to bring about the withdrawal of the Cubans [from Angola] before the implementation of Resolution 435 . . . through sustained aid to UNITA. . . . The Angolan government, because of intensified UNITA actions and pressure from the U.S. and the "Frontline States," may consider entering into negotiations with UNITA to establish a government of "national unity." . . .

Continuing UNITA successes will help create a climate in this region that will contribute to a satisfactory solution of the SWA question. . . . Taking into account South Africa's aim to bring about a community of southern African states with common interests, it is necessary that the

Cubans leave Angola and that a government come to power in Luanda that will be ready to cooperate in a regional context with South Africa.[32]

Savimbi's closeness to the apartheid regime was flaunted for all to see on September 14, 1984, the day of the inauguration of PW Botha as South Africa's first executive president. "It was one of the grandest State occasions in recent years," the Johannesburg *Star* wrote, but "the pomp and ceremony was marred by the conspicuous absence of high-ranking foreign guests. Not even Israel and [Pinochet's] Chile, traditionally two of South Africa's most demonstrative friends, sent delegations." There were only five blacks among the 1,000 VIPs who attended the inauguration: two representatives from neighboring Swaziland, the presidents of Transkei and Ciskei (two of South Africa's Bantustans), and "a jaunty" Jonas Savimbi, who had "jetted" into Cape Town's airport, where he had been received by Pik Botha and a crowd of journalists.[33] Savimbi told the press that PW Botha "had been his friend for more than nine years" and added that he had often visited South Africa, beginning in 1974 when he had come for talks with Prime Minister Vorster.[34] The difference was that this visit was in full public view while all his previous visits had been clandestine. "It was good that Dr Savimbi and President Botha should have met openly together," Pik Botha explained, "because both were Africans."[35]

## The Joint Monitoring Commission

The Lusaka agreement had stipulated that the South Africans would withdraw from the territory they occupied in southwestern Angola by March 31, 1984. During the withdrawal a joint SADF and FAPLA force would police the area to keep SWAPO out. In other words, the Angolans and South Africans would work together to prevent the guerrillas from infiltrating into Namibia. A Joint Monitoring Commission (JMC) would supervise their work.

The soldiers, 300 SADF and 300 FAPLA, moved into position on March 2. Three weeks later, Pik Botha announced that joint SADF-FAPLA patrols had clashed three times with SWAPO guerrillas, killing eight—"to Pretoria's delight and Luanda's deep embarrassment," Crocker noted.[36] Very soon, however, the South Africans began claiming that the FAPLA was not doing enough against SWAPO. According to a knowledgeable South African analyst, the Angolans' "enthusiasm for making the JMC work did not burn very brightly . . . and at no stage amounted to anything more than the bare minimum required of them, and sometimes not even that." This was probably a fair assessment since the FAPLA was being asked to serve as apartheid's handmaiden. As SWAPO leader

Sam Nujoma pointed out, "The Angolans were our allies, and the South Africans the enemies of both of us."[37]

The Lusaka agreement had stipulated that the JMC would exist only during the withdrawal period, but soon after the agreement was inked the South Africans demanded that the JMC become permanent. To pressure the Angolans to accept this change, they halted the withdrawal of their troops. "If some arrangement could not be made to ensure continuing security along the border . . . South Africa would have to resume cross border activities," General Pieter van der Westhuizen, head of South Africa's military intelligence, told President dos Santos on June 25, 1984. Dos Santos responded that Angola had honored its side of the bargain—it had cooperated with South Africa in preventing SWAPO infiltrations into the territory the SADF was evacuating, but South Africa had not reciprocated. The "Tripartite Statement" signed by South Africa, Angola, and the United States in Lusaka had stipulated that the parties would work for the implementation of Resolution 435, but so far nothing had happened. Dos Santos explained, "If Angola should continue to control SWAPO, South Africa should continue to find a solution to the Namibian problem. It would not be possible for Angola to maintain the present situation for long. Angola was an African country. It was a member of the Front Line States and the United Nations. It had other obligations as well."[38]

The message was clear. Angola's restraint of SWAPO would not last unless the South Africans began implementing Resolution 435. If they did, and only if they did, "the JMC could be prolonged indefinitely."[39]

In the months that followed, the argument continued: Pretoria wanted a permanent commission to control the border, and Luanda replied that the South Africans must first begin to implement Resolution 435. Angolan deputy foreign minister Venancio da Moura asked Crocker's deputy Wisner, who kept urging him to agree to the South African demand, "Is it we—the government of Angola—who bear the responsibility of preventing the armed struggle of SWAPO, a movement that has been recognized by the international community? Are we the only ones who bear this responsibility?"[40] The South African withdrawal stalled.

## The Cabinda Raid

The Lusaka agreement had not stilled the SADF's zeal to carry out sabotage operations in Angola. On July 12, 1984, Special Forces commandos destroyed 200 meters of oil pipeline in the enclave of Cabinda, Angola's northernmost province, resulting in the loss of 42,000 barrels of oil "and some hiccups in production," according to Peter Stiff, the foremost authority on South Africa's covert operations; a few days later, an Angolan and an East German ship were badly damaged by mines the South Africans had laid in Luanda harbor. UNITA claimed credit for both operations.[41] U.S. officials knew better. Crocker writes that, when Americans and South Africans met at Cape Verde in October 1984, "my special assistant Robert Cabelly probed SADF military intelligence boss Pieter van der Westhuizen about the signals being sent by his covert operations far north of the border. 'It tells the MPLA you want to kill them, not to deal,' Cabelly noted. 'I agree,' replied the man we had nicknamed 'the ratcatcher of Southern Africa.'" Meanwhile, the SADF was hatching more ambitious plans to hurt Angola's economy. "The best target for maximum damage," Stiff explains, "was a choke point to create havoc with production, like the crude oil storage facilities [of Gulf Oil] at Malongo [in Cabinda] which had a holding capacity of 1.6 million barrels." The facilities were described by a Gulf Oil official: "The Gulf operation in Angola is located on a stretch of the Cabinda coast some 12 miles north of the town of Cabinda. . . . The oilfields are actually located offshore, but treating and storage prior to exportation takes place onshore."[42]

On April 17, 1985, while the preparations for the operation against Malongo were under way, the last South African troops withdrew from Angola. Chester Crocker welcomed the news: this was "the announced completion" of the Lusaka agreement, "which had been delayed for a number of months."[43] But a month later—on May 22—a communiqué from Luanda bespoke a different truth: the FAPLA had intercepted a nine-man South African commando team near Gulf's oil storage tanks in Malongo. The team leader, Captain Wynand du Toit, had been captured, two of his men had been killed, and the others had escaped. The SADF immediately issued a flat denial: it was not involved "in any operation in the oil-rich enclave." A few hours later, it reversed itself: General Viljoen said that a SADF commando unit had indeed been sent to Cabinda—not on a sabotage mission, but on a mission to gather intelligence about ANC and SWAPO guerrillas in the enclave. Defense Minister Malan told the South African parliament on May 28, "Our target was not, and is not, the state of Angola; our target was and is the ANC and SWAPO." In Luanda, that same day, the prisoner, Captain du Toit, flatly contradicted him. "No, we were not looking for ANC or SWAPO guerrillas," he said at a press conference. "We were attacking Gulf Oil." Their mission was to blow up the oil storage tanks at Malongo to cause a "considerable economic setback to the Angolan government." Along with their weapons and explosives, they also carried UNITA propaganda material, "which would have been left behind to make the authorities believe the rebels had carried out the attack."[44] The London *Daily Telegraph*, which was, the Johannesburg *Star* noted, "traditionally a friend of South Africa," was blunt: "Setting aside all the shortcomings of that [Angolan] government, it has plainly been double-crossed yet again by the South Africans." The incident showed "what everyone should already have grasped: that South Africa is prepared to go to any length, break any promises, threaten any alliance in order to protect what she regards as her own legitimate interests." This was not the first time that the SADF had carried out sabotage missions in Angola, but it was the first time it had been caught red-handed.[45]

According to Savimbi's biographer, "Captain du Toit's admission that he had been carrying UNITA propaganda caused major political discomfort to Savimbi." The captain also admitted that he had participated in the destruction of the Giraul River bridge near Namibe, that is, that it had been a South African operation, not—as was claimed—a UNITA raid. "This raised questions about what other UNITA 'successes' had been carried out by, or in cooperation with, the SADF." UNITA put up a brave front, issuing a communiqué that stated, "Only the ingenuous can believe the South African government would attack, either on the spot or from afar, interests [such as Gulf Oil] belonging to the United States."[46]

Among the "ingenuous" was the Reagan administration. A State Department spokesperson said, "We have made known to the South African government our deep displeasure . . . and we are seeking a full explanation."[47] U.S. officials had good reason to be upset: first, by the timing of the attack, which was launched when they were trying to promote negotiations between South Africa and Angola against mounting pressure from the American public and members of Congress who were demanding a stronger stand against apartheid; and, second, by the SADF's target, which would have destroyed American property and killed U.S. citizens. (A Gulf spokesperson said that fifty-five U.S. citizens lived in the terminal area, and "it was unclear how many . . . might have been killed in the planned explosion.")[48] It was a sorry way to thank the Reagan team for constructive engagement.

When I asked Pik Botha whether he had known beforehand about the raid, he was emphatic. "Not in the least. I needed that less than the biggest hole in my head. I told [General] Viljoen, 'This is one time that I'm not going to talk to the press. You do it!'"[49] He had to talk to the Americans, however, and he did so with customary chutzpah. He informed U.S. ambassador Herman Nickel on May 27 that the failed raid had been merely a reconnaissance operation to confirm the presence of an ANC camp near Malongo. The South African patrol was simply passing near the Gulf installation when it was attacked. "These were the facts," Botha told Nickel. "Gulf Oil was not a South African target, never has been and never will be." He repeated the tale the following day and again on June 3, impervious to Nickel's remark that the U.S. government could not understand why the patrol had gone "so close" to the Gulf Oil installation and "still insisted on an explanation." Four days later, on June 7, Nickel was back in Pik Botha's office with a verbal note from Washington. He informed Botha, "The Americans had some difficulty to accept what the South African government had come up with," but "we should not belabour the difference which exist [sic] re the Cabinda incident. We should 'agree to disagree' on what actually transpired." This was an exceedingly generous response to an operation that would have destroyed American property and killed U.S. citizens. Not mild enough, however, for Pik Botha. "He had gone out of his way over the last days to provide the Americans with the full picture of what had happened," he exploded, and yet Washington refused to accept his explanation. This "showed an arrogant attitude on the part of the Americans." He could not accept it and "expected an apology."[50] The Americans dropped the subject. When he met Crocker and National Security Adviser McFarlane the following August in Vienna, Pik Botha repeated the tired lie "that South Africa never had the intention of attacking the oil installation in Cabinda." Crocker and McFarlane did not challenge him.[51] "I just completed a 5 hour meeting with F[oreign] M[inister] Botha," McFarlane wrote in a two-page report. "The exchange covered the entire gamut of internal and external issues on our agenda. . . . In my presentation I went over the record of the President's [Reagan's] strong support for them [South Africans] and the difficulties he faced because of it given the primitive understanding of the strategic stakes in our Congress and at large." McFarlane's report said not one word about the Cabinda raid.[52]

## The Minuet Ends

The Angolans responded to the raid with less equanimity than the Americans. They suspended the talks, which, in any case, were going nowhere. Both Luanda and Pretoria had by then rejected a "synthesis" paper that Crocker had presented the previous March. The document—its official name was "Basis for Negotiations"—gave the Cubans more time to withdraw from Angola. In 1981 South Africans and Americans had agreed that all the Cuban troops should leave Angola within three months of the beginning of the implementation of Resolution 435. The synthesis paper, however, proposed that 80 percent of the 30,000 Cuban troops that U.S. intelligence thought were in Angola (there were actually close to 40,000) would leave within a year of the beginning of the implementation of Resolution 435. The remaining 20 percent (6,000 soldiers) would leave within the second year. ("After the beginning of the implementation of UNSC 435," the document stipulated, "the Cuban forces stationed in Angola will be assigned to garrisons and their mission limited to perimeter security, supply and training operations.")[53] Chester Crocker handed the synthesis paper to the Angolans on March 18, 1985, and to the South Africans three days later. "The document," he told Pik Botha, "was not a United States proposal but was just a framework, a basis. . . . It provided a framework for negotiations. . . . If this initiative worked, it would provide the basis for a settlement which the United States could support."[54]

Pik Botha was indignant. "There had never been any doubt concerning parallel and simultaneous withdrawal," he thundered. Crocker had shuffled the deck. "This was a deviation. He asked whether Dr Crocker agreed that the document constituted a deviation from what had already been agreed. . . . What he wanted now was the United States' acknowledgment that their proposal constituted a deviation."[55]

He was being disingenuous. As early as February 18, 1984, two days after the Lusaka agreement, Crocker had told Savimbi in the presence of SADF military intelligence officers that the United States might be willing to allow some additional months for the departure of the Cuban troops beyond the twelve weeks stipulated by Washington and Pretoria in 1981.[56] Pik Botha had decided not to question it. "It would not serve any useful purpose to try to iron out the differences between South Africa and the United States," he told the South African cabinet. "Dr Crocker should first test the Angolans."[57]

Botha may have been surprised that instead of just a few months, Crocker proposed that 6,000 Cubans remain until the end of the second year. "The idea of a residual presence of 6,000 Cubans was indeed something new," Crocker conceded.[58]

This was not, however, the key difference between Washington and Pretoria. It was not the timetable of Cuban withdrawal that separated them. They had different, virtually incompatible priorities. The entire negotiation was built on quicksand. The Americans' priority was to push the Cubans out of Angola. For this, they were willing to accept Resolution 435 even if it meant a SWAPO victory at the polls. (Control of Walvis Bay, Namibia's only deep-water port, would hand Pretoria a stranglehold over its neighbor, even if led by SWAPO.) As for Savimbi, U.S. officials argued that the departure of the Cubans would force the MPLA to negotiate with him, but they also made it clear, throughout, that this was not a condition for the settlement they sought.[59]

The South Africans' position was different. Their acceptance of Resolution 435 was conditioned not on linkage but on the imperative that SWAPO not win the elections. Given SWAPO's popularity, this meant that Resolution 435 could not be implemented. Therefore, their acceptance of Resolution 435 was a sham. They barely hid this. In June 1981 they had accepted linkage, and in the same breath they had told Deputy Secretary of State Clark that they would not allow a SWAPO government in Windhoek. Over the next two and half years, before the Lusaka agreement, they had continued to say that they supported linkage while adding conditions that made linkage impossible. They continued to do so after Lusaka. On March 12, 1984, for example, Pik Botha told Ambassador Nickel that "Resolution 435 could not be successfully implemented without a solution in Angola." Nickel almost got the point: "The United States felt strongly that we should proceed sequentially," he replied. "There was a serious difference between South Africa and the United States on tactics."[60] It was much more than tactics. For the South Africans it was imperative that Savimbi take power in Angola because this would allow them to crush SWAPO. Once SWAPO had been destroyed, they might implement Resolution 435.

On May 6, 1985, the Angolans replied to the synthesis paper: they reiterated their profound distrust of South Africa, demanded the implementation of Resolution 435, and politely rejected the U.S. timetable while not closing the door on some form of linkage.[61] Pretoria followed on May 30. "The South African response was delivered in an especially demeaning fashion," an NSC official told National Security Adviser McFarlane. "Pik Botha called in our chargé, handed over the response saying it was self-explanatory, then walked out of the room."[62] The South African note sternly reprimanded the United States for "the clear deviations" of the synthesis paper from the earlier agreement between the two countries. It also noted, "Another central element in the South African understanding with the United States has been that nothing should be done to jeopardize UNITA's position. One of the six principles which Minister Botha conveyed to the [U.S.] Deputy Secretary of State [Clark] on 12 June 1981 stipulated that 'It is accepted that Savimbi will be assisted appropriately. Furthermore South Africa should not be forced out of South West Africa in such a way that Savimbi cannot be assisted.' However South Africa understands that Dr Savimbi is of the opinion that the ideas contained in the United States 'Basis for negotiations' [the synthesis paper] would seriously jeopardize Savimbi's position."[63]

The South Africans had a point. While the Americans had never formally accepted the note Pik Botha had handed to Clark on June 12, 1981, they had never rejected it either. Nor had they expressed any reservations about it. Moreover, throughout the conversations that had followed the Lusaka agreement, U.S.

officials had stressed—to Pretoria and to UNITA—that they would do nothing that would jeopardize Savimbi's interests.

## Crocker and Savimbi

Ever since the Lusaka agreement, Crocker and his aides had been in contact with Savimbi's representative in Washington, Jeremias Chitunda, trying to reassure him that "the US and President Reagan have no plan to sustain Marxist governments, but rather to arrive at a settlement which in itself serves UNITA's interests."[64] Crocker told Chitunda, "We needed to be in touch as often as necessary. UNITA should give us its concerns and fears and furnish the information we did not have. . . . We were neutral only in the sense that we thought no one could win an outright victory in Angola."[65] If Crocker and his aides treated Chitunda with a courtesy they did not extend to Angolan officials, it was because they were aware that Chitunda could roam around Washington and speak ill of them with hard-line Reaganites, who already thought that Crocker and his cohorts had no stomach for Reagan's anticommunist crusade. Crocker complained to Savimbi that "Chitunda was not being helpful as his representative in Washington. Jerry [Chitunda] had ample, ready access to Crocker and Co. in the Department but seemed to have more interest in sowing trouble on the far right." Deputy Assistant Secretary Wisner pleaded with Chitunda, making it clear that "if Chitunda's confidence were ever shaken on any question the door is open to him to come in and talk about it." If Chitunda had any "complaints or concerns about USG policy, Wisner would much rather hear about them behind closed doors than in newspapers."[66]

Crocker met Savimbi repeatedly in South Africa, often in the presence of South African military officers. Savimbi urged the United States "to apply pressure on the MPLA government to enter into conversations with UNITA." Crocker explained that, while the United States favored national reconciliation, it would not make it "a requirement for settlement because doing so would destroy the US initiative."[67] He told Savimbi that "one cannot realistically accept a modus vivendi between the MPLA and UNITA as a precondition of a Namibian independence package. But that time must come." Savimbi was not impressed. "We have the feeling we are being left out," he told Crocker.[68] How, he asked, did the United States propose to resolve UNITA's problems?[69]

It is not surprising that Savimbi did not trust Crocker. A settlement that would mean that the SADF left Angola and a SWAPO government was installed in Windhoek was Savimbi's nightmare. Chitunda told Crocker, "He understood that we had to cross one bridge at a time. His concern was whether we had enough time and whether the bridges were being crossed in the right sequence." He also noted, wistfully, that "there is a serious distinction between the Cuban forces in Angola, who have no justification in being there, and the SADF in Namibia, which has a 'traditional role' and 'cultural ties' in the region"—a bold statement that even some of his American supporters must have found preposterous. The March 1985 synthesis paper enraged Savimbi. No sooner had Crocker handed the document to Pik Botha than a high-powered South African delegation, led by General van der Westhuizen, left for Jamba. "Dr Savimbi greatly appreciated the South African gesture of briefing him so soon after the talks with Dr Crocker," van der Westhuizen reported. "This made it possible [for him] to prepare adequately for his meeting with the U.S. delegation [that would visit Jamba] the next day." What Savimbi did not appreciate, however, was the fact that "Dr Crocker had not decided to speak to him direct [sic], but was sending his assistants instead."[70] He made this clear to the three midlevel U.S. officials who the next day made the trek to Jamba. Upon descending from the South African helicopter that had brought them to Jamba, the three—Crocker's special assistant Cabelly, an official from the U.S. Embassy in London, and the political counselor at the U.S. Embassy in South Africa—found no one waiting for them. Eventually, "two very young members of UNITA" appeared and took the three Americans to a hut, where they were kept waiting for forty-five minutes. "It is clear that the delegation was being sent a message," they wrote. Finally, they were taken to Savimbi, only to be yelled at. "UNITA was aggressive," they reported. Savimbi did not want to be briefed by a bunch of midlevel officials. "'I want the next meeting to be with Secretary Crocker in South Africa,'" he shouted. "'Sending this delegation to Jamba was a bad thing.'" One of the Americans "exploited the opportunity created by Savimbi's attempts to catch his breath" to explain that "sending this delegation to Jamba was not an attempt . . . to insult you." Crocker was simply trying "to avoid insulting you by asking you to come to South Africa on short notice." Savimbi cut him off. "'Meeting in the RSA [Republic of South Africa] is not a problem.'" Savimbi "was shouting at his visitors at this point," the hapless Americans reported. He did not like the messengers, and he did not like the message. "'On the synthesis [paper] I have no questions,'" he yelled. "'It is unacceptable.'"[71]

Two months later, in May, Crocker met with Savimbi in Zaire to clear the air. Back in Washington, he wrote him a letter bemoaning that "disperception [sic] or misunderstanding had developed between us" and suggesting that "there may be elements who wish to poison good relations between UNITA and the USA government." (This was a "clear reference to the SADF," remarked Defense

Minister Malan, who received a copy of the letter from Savimbi.)[72] Savimbi was not mollified by Crocker's letter. He told Pik Botha that "it was difficult to conduct serious and important discussions with a worried man. Dr Crocker was clearly worried about his personal position in Washington. . . . He was under attack from both left and right in Washington."[73]

By then, the negotiations between Pretoria and Luanda about the implementation of Resolution 435 and the withdrawal of the Cuban troops from Angola had collapsed, and SADF's raids into Angola had resumed. "South Africa will not allow itself to be attacked with impunity," Pik Botha warned the Angolan government in July 1985. "It will take whatever action it deems appropriate to defend itself. The MPLA should not make the error of imagining that South Africa will be daunted by threats from organizations such as the United Nations."[74]

The best epitaph to the fifteen months of negotiations that followed the Lusaka agreement was offered by Marrack Goulding, Margaret Thatcher's ambassador to Angola in 1983–85. He was a privileged observer: the United States had no diplomatic relations with Angola and U.S. officials kept in touch with their Angolan counterparts through the British Embassy. "For nearly seven years, the British served as our principal channel of communication to the Angolans," Crocker writes. "No foreign power, and few people in Washington, knew more of the intimate details of our diplomacy." According to Ambassador Goulding, "Crocker and Wisner were trying to persuade the Angolan government that Angola need not fear linkage. Once Namibia was independent, they argued, South Africa would no longer have reason to attack Angola or provide military support to UNITA. . . . I was always uneasy about the UNITA limb of the argument. The South Africans would still want UNITA to replace the Angolan government, which they saw as a malevolent Marxist influence in the region. . . . My other difference with my American friends," Goulding writes, "related to the Cubans. As far as I was concerned they were a good thing. They had done wonders for Angola's education and health services and were preventing the South African army . . . from running wild all over southern Angola."[75]

## Namibia

The Lusaka agreement had not changed Pretoria's policy in Namibia: the South Africans' professions of support for linkage went hand in hand with their efforts to craft an internal settlement to forestall or derail Resolution 435. In January 1983 the Democratic Turnhalle Alliance (DTA) and the South African government had parted ways, but they still needed each other. The DTA could come to power only with Pretoria's support, and Pretoria could not forge a client government in Namibia without the DTA: whatever its faults, it remained the strongest among the forty-odd political parties that vied for South Africa's favor.

Prodded by the South African administrator general, in late 1983 the DTA and five other ethnically based political parties formed a loose alliance, the Multiparty Conference. The administrator general began nurturing them to become the country's new transitional government. The Americans grew uneasy. A senior CIA officer told his South African hosts in Cape Town in April 1984 "that he had gathered that South Africa thought that an option outside of Resolution 435 would be in its best interest and that South Africa would therefore prefer a situation where the Cubans did not withdraw from Angola."[76] The South African ambassador reported from Washington a week later that Crocker was "deeply worried, even depressed, over developments in Southwest Africa." Upon landing in Johannesburg on May 25, 1984, Crocker told Pik Botha that "he had come to be reassured that South Africa had not changed its mind [about Resolution 435]."[77] Botha dutifully made the right noises, but he also continued to give strong hints that Resolution 435 should be set aside. When Ambassador Nickel told him that "there was a suspicion that South Africa had another agenda," Botha replied, "This was not the case." However, he added, "the United States should not become too attached to form." And he warned Crocker that "if an agreement is reached about Cuban withdrawal, they [the Americans] must not be overly eager to implement Resolution 435. In this context we would have to take UNITA into account." If, however, the effort to obtain total Cuban withdrawal failed, then they should all think about alternatives to Resolution 435. The status quo could not continue indefinitely, he stressed. The people of Namibia deserved their independence.[78]

In March 1985, the administrator general of Namibia shepherded the leaders of the Multiparty Conference to Cape Town, where they presented their plan for a transitional government to President Botha. This caused "heartburn" in Washington, Ambassador Nickel told the director-general of the South African Foreign Ministry. On April 18 PW Botha informed the South African parliament that he had approved the establishment of an interim internal administration in Namibia that would include a legislative assembly, a council of ministers, and a constitutional council. "The people of South West Africa, including SWAPO, cannot wait indefinitely for a breakthrough regarding the withdrawal of the Cubans from Angola," he said. "Should it eventually become evident . . . that there is no realistic prospect of attaining these goals, all the parties most intimately affected by the present negotiations will obviously have to reconsider how internationally acceptable independence may best be obtained in the light of the prevailing circumstances."[79]

Asked at a press conference the following day whether the creation of a transitional government indicated that Pretoria was not interested in Resolution 435—"Don't the two things operate in opposite directions?"—Crocker put up a brave front. "We don't see it that way," he said. "South Africa has itself said that it will continue to pursue an internationally acceptable settlement." In private, an aide told National Security Adviser McFarlane, "Another question is whether we should continue to commit our diplomatic prestige where the key player—South Africa—appears to be immune to any U.S. influence or suggestions which rub against its policy aims."[80]

In the din of condemnations that rained on South Africa from abroad, one friend stood firm: Jonas Savimbi. From Jamba, he issued a statement welcoming the establishment of a transitional government in Namibia; UNITA's deputy foreign secretary told the *Windhoek Advertiser*: "Our position is very clear that the outside world should not dictate to Namibia who should form its government."[81] Apparently South Africa did not belong to the "outside world."

In any case, foreign criticism did not deter Pretoria. On June 17, 1985, the Transitional Government of National Unity (TGNU) was established in Windhoek. In his inaugural speech, the chairman of the TGNU set the tone: "The people of Namibia are tired of the ravages of war and of the involvement of the international community in the struggle for the liberation of Namibia." When the chairman spoke of "international" involvement, he meant the United Nations and Resolution 435, not South Africa. President Botha, who presided over the ceremonies, was blunt. "We . . . have a message for the world," he said; "for Soviet strategists, shifting their pieces on the international chessboard; for Western diplomats, anxious to remove at any cost this vexatious question [Namibia] from the international agenda; for SWAPO terrorists lurking in their lairs in Angola—we are not a people to shirk our responsibilities. . . . The people of Southwest Africa," Botha concluded, "cannot wait indefinitely for a breakthrough on the withdrawal of the Cubans from Angola."[82]

Responding to Botha's professed concern for the people of Namibia, Colin Eglin, a leader of South Africa's Progressive Federal Party, the small cohort of white liberals, unleashed a frontal attack on linkage. "Surely it should be the people of South West Africa who must decide whether the Cuban troops issue is critical," he argued. "This decision should not be taken by either the Government of the United States or the Government of South Africa. It is their independence. If that is the last obstacle, they must decide whether that should hold up the process or not. We appeal to the State President [PW Botha] therefore to test the opinion of the people of South West Africa on the specific point as to whether they want the Cuban troops issue to be the obstacle to their independence or not. . . . If the people of South West Africa . . . in spite of the presence of Cuban troops in Angola say that they want the independence process to start, I believe the Governments of both South Africa and of the United States of America should respect their wishes and should throw in their full weight behind an independence process in terms of Resolution 435." Botha's rejoinder was categorical: "The United States adopted the attitude that there could not be any implementation of Resolution 435" unless the Cuban troops left Angola. "The United States adopted that attitude and we are supporting them."[83] How could Botha allow the people of Namibia to hold a referendum, when yet another secret South African intelligence report had just confirmed that "SWAPO will win an election conducted under Resolution 435 with a considerable majority"?[84]

Very few governments supported linkage. China, which had given Savimbi covert military aid in the late 1970s, had changed its tune. In January 1983 it normalized relations with Angola. "Beijing scrupulously avoids criticizing Luanda," U.S. intelligence reported in August 1985. "[It] privately favors the withdrawal of Cuban troops from Angola, but opposes linking such a move to Namibian independence."[85] Within the Contact Group, only England and West Germany remained loyal to Washington. France had defected in 1983, and Canada openly broke ranks in 1985. The Canadian ambassador told the UN Security Council with unusual candor, "linkage . . . has no warrant in international law, . . . is incompatible with Resolution 435 and . . . has been rejected by this Council. Perhaps worst of all, . . . [it] is totally unnecessary, is a deliberate obstacle and is the cause of grievous delay. . . . To hold Namibia hostage to what this Council has previously described as 'irrelevant and extraneous issues' is palpably outrageous."[86]

## South Africa Explodes

The Canadian ambassador's outburst was triggered by Pretoria's flagrant contempt for Resolution 435 and by the growing repression in South Africa. On September 3, 1984, the new South African constitution, which gave limited national political participation to Coloreds and Indians but denied it to blacks, took effect. That same month several black townships in the industrial heartland south of Johannesburg exploded. Protests spread like wildfire. The CIA noted, "The 1984 Constitution . . . served as a catalyst for black resistance to apartheid and the government. Many blacks saw the constitutional changes as denying them any hope of increased political rights and gave up on Pretoria's intermittent and slow reform program. Violent resistance to government authority broke out in black townships, at first over economic grievances, but, within a year, largely motivated by a political agenda of total resistance to government authority."[87] Demonstrations, boycotts of schools and of white-owned stores, funerals for the victims of the repression that turned into political rallies roiled the nation. There were attacks against blacks accused of working for the regime and, occasionally, against whites. Seeking to appease Western critics without appearing weak, PW Botha told the South African parliament on January 31, 1985, that he would free ANC leader Nelson Mandela if he would "unconditionally reject violence as a political instrument." Ten days later, at a huge rally in Soweto held to celebrate the awarding of the Nobel Peace Prize to Bishop Desmond Tutu, Mandela's daughter Zinzi read her father's reply to the government's offer, addressed, she told the crowd, "to you, the people." Mandela had written, "I cherish my own freedom dearly but I care even more for your freedom. . . . I am no less life loving than you are. But I cannot sell my birthright, nor am I prepared to sell the birthright of the people to be free. I am in prison as the representative of the people and of your organization, the African National Congress, which was banned. What freedom am I being offered whilst the organization of the people remains banned? . . . Only free men can negotiate. Prisoners cannot enter into contracts." In the words of Allister Sparks, one of South Africa's foremost journalists, "As Mandela's daughter's voice rang out, the big crowd erupted in a wild display of cheering and chanting. They were the first words anyone had heard from Mandela since his final address to the court that imprisoned him twenty-one years before, and if ever the South African government had doubted the durability of his stature in the black community, it could do so no longer."[88]

Botha's ploy had backfired. The regime would face, Sparks writes, "the most prolonged and intensive black uprising in South Africa's history . . . despite Botha's attempts to clamp down on it with two states of emergency and a savage use of force." Life in the townships became, in the words of a priest, "A world made up of teargas, bullets, whippings, detention, and death on the streets. It is an experience of military operations and night raids, of roadblocks and body searches. It is a world where parents and friends get carried away in the night to be interrogated. It is a world where people simply disappear, where parents are assassinated and homes are petrol bombed."[89]

In January 1986 the CIA warned that "time for a peaceful solution in South Africa continues to run out." As it later noted, "The protests and violence that erupted in South Africa in 1984 catapulted the African National Congress (ANC) . . . into the forefront of the antiapartheid movement."[90] In mid-1985 the ANC had no more than 500 underground operatives inside South Africa,[91] but it was a powerful symbol, the only organization that for more than two decades had raised the flag of armed resistance against the oppressor and in the recent past had been able to carry out armed attacks against the regime inside South Africa. "The ANC armed struggle failed by almost every yardstick," the biographer of a leader of the ANC writes, "but it did succeed as 'armed propaganda': armed struggle achieved a mythical status among the masses, especially the youth, for whom it provided hope of directly overthrowing the Apartheid state." A new generation of recruits sneaked across South Africa's borders to join MK, the ANC's armed wing. "In the mid 1980s a new wave of recruits began arriving," recalls an MK operative in Botswana.[92]

The government intensified its sabotage, assassination attempts, and cross-border raids against the neighboring states to destroy the ANC and to weaken the neighboring regimes and keep them dependent on South Africa. It continued to support the RENAMO insurgents in Mozambique in violation of the Nkomati pact. The Reagan administration sought to moderate Pretoria's behavior, without success. The Cabinda raid, which had threatened the lives and properties of U.S. citizens, was followed on June 14, 1985, by a bloody raid by SADF commandos against alleged ANC safe houses in and around Gaborone, capital of Botswana. Botswana, an NSC official pointed out, was "a close U.S. friend."[93] Under attack even by Republicans for being too soft on South Africa, the Reagan administration responded to the raid on Gaborone by recalling Ambassador Nickel from Pretoria for consultations. (He returned to his post two months later.) In Washington, Nickel told the White House that "our present influence on Pretoria is very low. . . . There is no sign of SA gratitude or even acknowledgment of the Reagan administration's more friendly attitude toward the Pretoria regime."[94] Constructive engagement was a one-way street.

Angola's first president, Agostinho Neto—shown here with Fidel Castro—was a "distinguished intellectual," as U.S. intelligence reports noted. Throughout his life, Neto had three ambitions: to free his country from Portuguese rule, to improve the living conditions of the Angolan people, and to help liberate all Africans from the scourge of apartheid. (Central Committee of the Communist Party of Cuba)

During the final years of Angola's war of independence, Yugoslavia was the MPLA's closest friend. (Here, Yugoslav president Josip Broz Tito greets Agostinho Neto, the leader of the MPLA, in February 1973.) After Angola became independent, Neto remained close to Yugoslavia, but Belgrade's contribution to the new nation was dwarfed by Havana's. "The Cubans play an irreplaceable role protecting Angola's security," a Yugoslav report noted in April 1977, "and they are becoming increasingly important in the economic sphere as well." (Fundação Dr. António Agostinho Neto)

Smiles hid the strain between Angola's President Neto and Leonid Brezhnev as they shook hands in Moscow in September 1977. "Our relations with Neto were complicated," a KGB officer wrote. "We did not trust him. . . . He was not a pliant figure in the hands of our apparatchiks. He always had his own views, his own ideas about what to do, about how to carry out the struggle. His views did not always—to put it mildly—coincide with ours." Neto was obdurate. "We are not going to change," he said. (Fundação Dr. António Agostinho Neto)

Incorruptible and brilliant, Lúcio Lara was the aide closest to Angolan president Agostinho Neto. When Neto died in 1979, Lara—had he not been a light-skinned mulatto in a color-conscious country— might have become the next president of Angola. But his influence waned in the 1980s, symbolizing the decay of the culture of personal integrity and political commit- ment that Neto had inspired. (Lúcio Lara papers in the Associação Tchiweka de Documentação [ATD])

When President Neto died in 1979, the Angolan leaders chose José Eduardo dos Santos (right) as his successor. Angola continued to be assaulted by the South African army and by insurgents loyal to Jonas Savimbi. Nevertheless, President dos Santos maintained Neto's policy of extending aid to Nelson Mandela's African National Congress and to the Namibian guerrillas who sought to free their country from Pretoria's rule. Throughout, Castro was dos Santos's most loyal ally. Dos Santos is greeted here by Jorge Risquet, Castro's point man for Angola. (Central Committee of the Communist Party of Cuba)

Jorge Risquet (in the middle) was Castro's point man for Africa. The Chief of Staff of the Cuban Armed Forces told a Soviet general in 1984, "In my country, whenever we discuss strategy, even military strategy, about Angola, Risquet has to be present, because for many years he has been at the center of everything related to Angola." Risquet, a man of brilliance and wit, became the bête noire of the Americans during the 1988 negotiations about Angola and Namibia, in which he defended the Cuban position with skill and grit. (Central Committee of the Communist Party of Cuba)

Ndalu, the chief of staff of the Angolan army, is shown seated next to Jorge Risquet, the lead Cuban negotiator at the 1988 talks about the future of Angola and Namibia. In 1962, Ndalu had been one of the members of the MPLA who received a full Cuban scholarship to study in Havana, where he earned a degree in agricultural engineering. While at the University of Havana, Ndalu became one of the island's best soccer players, and he also underwent rigorous military training. He returned to Africa to join the MPLA guerrillas fighting against Portugal. After Angola won its independence, Ndalu became a leading military strategist and a skilled diplomat. He played an important role in the 1988 negotiations with the Americans and South Africans. (Central Committee of the Communist Party of Cuba)

Sam Nujoma, pictured here with Fidel Castro, was the leader of SWAPO, the Namibian movement fighting for independence from South Africa. Nujoma was, Ronald Reagan asserted, "a terrorist," and SWAPO was "a Marxist terrorist band." Castro disagreed, and Cuba steadfastly helped SWAPO. "Our link with Cuba is very solid, cemented in blood," Nujoma told me. In 1990, Nujoma became Namibia's first president. (Central Committee of the Communist Party of Cuba)

From their bases in Angola, SWAPO guerrillas infiltrated into Namibia, where the South African army "hunted them down mercilessly. . . . So the carnage went on," a South African military analyst noted. "That they [SWAPO guerrillas] kept coming, it must be said, is a tribute to their courage and steadfastness in the face of daunting odds." (Hedelberto López Blanch)

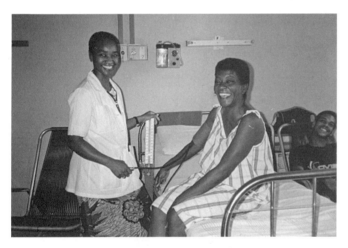

In May 1978, South African troops attacked the Namibian refugee camp of Cassinga in southern Angola. Cuban soldiers based nearby rushed to the camp, routing the South Africans, but not before 600 refugees had been slaughtered. "The first Cubans I ever saw were the soldiers who came to Cassinga," recalls Sophia Ndeitungo, a Cassinga survivor who was twelve years old at the time. "We thought they were South Africans" because some of them were white. "Later we understood that not all whites are bad." In late 1978, Sophia and 600 other Namibian children went to Cuba to grow up far from the bombs of the South Africans and to study. Sophia left Cuba in 1994, after earning a medical degree from the University of Havana. She is pictured here (on the left) in a Cuban hospital in 1991. (Sophia Ndeitungo)

In early 1988, joint patrols of SWAPO guerrillas and Cuban Special Forces spearheaded the advance of the Cuban army in southwestern Angola toward the Namibian border. The Cubans remember their Namibian comrades with respect and affection. "They had so much experience, and they were very brave and very intelligent," Pedro Ross Fonseca (second row, center) recollected while showing me a yellowing photograph of his Namibian friends that he keeps in his wallet. (Central Committee of the Communist Party of Cuba)

In July 1991, Nelson Mandela visited Cuba. "We come here with a sense of the great debt that is owed the people of Cuba," he declared. "What other country can point to a record of greater selflessness than Cuba has displayed in its relations with Africa?" (AP Photo)

In Pretoria's Freedom Park, which opened in 2007, the "Wall of Names" commemorates those who "paid the ultimate price" to free South Africa. Only one foreign country is represented—Cuba. The names of the more than 2,000 Cubans who died in Angola are inscribed on the wall. South African ambassador Thenjiwe Mtintso explained: "The blood of Cuban martyrs runs deep in the soil of Africa." (Freedom Park, Pretoria)

Raúl Castro (middle) led the Cuban delegation to the funeral of Soviet leader Konstantin Chernenko in March 1985. He met Mikhail Gorbachev (second from the right), Chernenko's successor. "We value greatly the good relations between our two countries," Gorbachev said. (Central Committee of the Communist Party of Cuba)

Fidel Castro embraces Soviet general secretary Mikhail Gorbachev, arriving in Havana in April 1989. The bonhomie, however, masked anxieties. "Castro was deeply worried and alarmed by what was happening in my country," noted the chief of the Soviet General Staff. Castro was increasingly uneasy about Gorbachev's domestic reforms and his foreign policy. The Soviet leader, Castro feared, was too eager to accommodate the United States. (AP Photo)

General Polo Cintra Frías (in profile) was appointed head of the Cuban military mission in Angola in 1983. Intelligent, sarcastic, and outspoken, he became the nemesis of his counterpart, General Konstantin Kurochkin, the head of the Soviet military mission. Soviet complaints about him notwithstanding, Polo remained in Angola until 1986, and in late 1987 he returned to lead the Cuban troops against the South African army. (Central Committee of the Communist Party of Cuba)

(opposite) The head of the Soviet military mission in Angola, General Konstantin Kurochkin (in sunglasses) was a formidable personality. "Konstantin! Even after he had left Angola, even when he was back in the Soviet Union, we could feel his presence," Ngongo, the impressive deputy chief of staff of the Angolan army, recollected. "He really wanted to impose his point of view; he didn't like to listen. He thought that since he was giving us the weapons, we had to do what he said." (Central Committee of the Communist Party of Cuba)

Doctors, teachers, and construction workers were the flag bearers of Cuba's humanitarian assistance program. More than 43,000 Cuban aid workers served in Angola. "I've offered my labor to these people who are in such need," Lourdes Franco Codinach (left), a pediatrician, wrote her mother as she prepared to return to Cuba after two years in Angola. "I will come home having fulfilled my duty. Despite the bad moments we've faced here, the difficulties and hardships, I am leaving with a feeling of pride." (Central Committee of the Communist Party of Cuba)

President Jimmy Carter (center) wanted to normalize relations with both Cuba and Angola, but he was troubled by the presence of more than 20,000 Cuban soldiers in Angola. Even though the CIA determined that the Cuban troops were "necessary to preserve Angolan independence" from South African aggression, National Security Adviser Zbigniew Brzezinski (left) insisted that the Cubans had to leave Angola before the United States could normalize relations with Havana or Luanda. Secretary of State Cyrus Vance (right) advocated a more flexible policy, but Carter sided with Brzezinski. (Jimmy Carter Presidential Library)

By late 1987, when Ronald Reagan and Mikhail Gorbachev, pictured here with their wives, Nancy and Raisa, met for the Washington Summit, relations between the two superpowers had warmed dramatically. Castro worried about what this would mean for Cuba. "We don't know how the United States will interpret peace and détente," he noted, "whether it will be a peace for all, détente for all, coexistence for all, or whether the North Americans will interpret 'coexistence' as peace with the USSR—peace among the powerful—and war against the small. . . . We are ready to improve relations with the United States if there is an opening." There was no opening: Washington urged Moscow to cut all aid to Cuba, and it tightened the embargo, hoping that hunger and despair would make the Cuban people turn against their government. (Ronald Reagan Presidential Library)

Chester Crocker (right) occupies center stage in any discussion of the Reagan administration's policy toward southern Africa. No assistant secretary of state for Africa had served as long as Crocker. None had been as influential. That he was a tireless and skillful negotiator was acknowledged by Cubans, Angolans, Soviets, and South Africans alike. (Ronald Reagan Presidential Library)

Jonas Savimbi, the Angolan guerrilla chieftain who fought against the Cuban-supported MPLA government, was intelligent and charismatic. He was also, wrote the British ambassador to Angola, "a monster whose lust for power had brought appalling misery to his people." (http://rubelluspetrinus.com.sapo.pt/savbimbi.htm)

"We don't throw out our friends just because they can't pass the 'saliva test' on human rights," President Reagan told the National Security Council in 1981. Jonas Savimbi (right) was one of those friends. The administration sent Savimbi increasing amounts of aid, despite the fact that U.S. officials acknowledged that he was "ruthless" and "extremely brutal." What mattered to the Reagan administration was that Savimbi's guerrillas were fighting against the Cuban troops in Angola. "We wanted to hurt Cuba," a senior congressional aide explained, "and we wanted to help people who wanted to hurt Cuba. Savimbi had one redeeming quality: he killed Cubans." (Ronald Reagan Presidential Library)

Pik Botha was South Africa's foreign minister. He was intelligent and relatively moderate on racial issues. He thought his government's foreign policy should be less provocative, but he wanted to be president of South Africa. Thus, instead of challenging Prime Minister (later President) PW Botha, he courted him, and he kowtowed to the military. As a senior U.S. intelligence officer wrote in 1987, "While some foreign ministry officials, including Foreign Minister Botha, would prefer a less confrontational regional policy, they have consistently been outmaneuvered by hard-liners in the defense and security establishments." (AP Photo)

In January 1980, South African prime minister PW Botha explained how he intended to preserve the status quo in his country: "If the combined pressure of military, political, economic, and social measures fails to achieve the desired result, then we must rely not on conciliation and compromise, but on violence." Relying on violence, PW Botha sought to make Jonas Savimbi the leader of Angola and to prevent free elections in Namibia. British Foreign Secretary David Owen noted that PW Botha was "as tough as nails and a bully to boot." (AP Photo)

CHAPTER 11

# The United States, South Africa, and Savimbi

## Reaganites on the Attack

In late 1984, for the first time in U.S. history, South Africa became the subject of widespread debate in the United States. In his memoirs Chester Crocker writes, "With hindsight it is astounding that apartheid had never before burst upon the American public consciousness as a topic of mainstream media interest and public debate. Other Western nations . . . had experienced their own apartheid debates over twenty years earlier. . . . Where was the American body politic during the 1950s, the era during which apartheid was built? . . . Where were the protests during the early 1960s, when the Rivonia trials resulted in Nelson Mandela's imprisonment and the banning of the ANC? . . . Americans discovered the existence of apartheid only in the mid-1980s."[1]

That Americans had discovered the evils of apartheid, albeit belatedly, complicated Reagan's policy of constructive engagement. A growing number of members of Congress began calling on the administration to impose sanctions on South Africa. "Dear Mr. President," Reagan wrote to PW Botha in January 1985, "the current debate in the United States concerning our bilateral relationship and your domestic policies has some internal and partisan reasons. Nevertheless, the debate does reflect genuine public feelings about sensitive issues deeply embedded in the political fabric of American society. I anticipate that in the months ahead, the Congress will propose a number of new legislative initiatives." The administration would oppose sanctions against South Africa, Reagan promised, "but I must ask that you recognize that we will need your help in conveying to the American people the determination of your government to pursue constructive change."[2]

Meanwhile, a battle raged among Reagan's supporters in the press, in Congress, and within the executive branch. Disagreement about policy toward southern Africa had existed since the beginning of the administration, but during Reagan's first term the public and Congress had paid scant attention to the region, and within the administration Crocker and the Africa Bureau had been given a relatively free hand. This changed, however, after Reagan's landslide victory in the 1984 presidential elections, which was seen as a broad mandate for bold actions in foreign policy. Developments in southern Africa, including the turmoil in South Africa, presented the administration with new challenges. The hard-liners in the Reagan camp were often called "true Reaganites" because they claimed to represent the president's instincts that the State Department sought to stifle. Their war cry was "Let Reagan be Reagan."

Southern Africa was one of their major battlegrounds. The *Wall Street Journal* argued: "A strategy that would help our real friends may not win applause from the U.N. but it would serve our interests and those of black Africa much better than anything we've heard from the left, or from a confused State Department." The true Reaganites demanded that the administration adopt an even more sympathetic attitude to the embattled Botha government in Pretoria. There was one villain in South Africa, Paul Johnson explained in a much praised article in *Commentary*: the ANC. "Its terror campaign" sought to kill "as many" nonwhite moderates as it could, "and to frighten the rest into non-cooperation [with the government]." The conservative weekly *Human Events* wrote, "While President Botha is moving at a fast and furious pace to end the apartheid system, Mandela remains as adamant a revolutionary as ever. He's still a Marxist, still a man of violence, still a supporter of the Communist-run ANC." The *National Review* warned, "All the reforms the Botha government has introduced . . . [would] vanish entirely on the coming to power of Nelson Mandela."[3]

The true Reaganites opposed Resolution 435. They abhorred the idea of a SWAPO government in Windhoek. "South Africa's withdrawal is not in America's interest," the *National Review* argued, "since Namibia would fall to the Communist SWAPO guerrillas if abandoned by South Africa." Like the South African government, they wanted the administration to help Savimbi come to power in Luanda. They poured scorn on the State Department's contention that Savimbi could not achieve a military victory. "UNITA is close to defeating the Communist regime," the *National Security Record*, organ of the Heritage Foundation, asserted. "A Savimbi victory," *Human Events* explained, "would deal both Gorbachev and Castro severe setbacks in southern Africa. . . . Angola itself would be transformed from a terrorist training ground—where SWAPO and the African National Congress operate—to a pro-Western bastion that could eventually tilt the whole of black Africa toward the center."[4]

Particularly outrageous for the true Reaganites was the administration's policy toward Mozambique, where the State Department sought to improve relations with the country's self-professed communist government and keep the RENAMO insurgents at arm's length. The Reaganites ignored the fact that the RENAMO rebels had a particularly unsavory reputation; the London *Times* noted that "RENAMO has long been one of Africa's least convincing liberation movements. Its military leadership in the bush has been brutal and inefficient. Its past habit of cutting off victims' lips and ears proved no help with fund-raising abroad." The U.S. Embassy in Maputo was categorical: "There can be no ambiguity as to the terrorist activities of RENAMO. . . . Its bush insurgents have engaged in increasingly cruel and senseless acts of armed terrorism." The true Reaganites, on the other hand, called RENAMO a "solid democratic movement."[5]

More than human rights was at stake. The debate over Mozambique exemplifies the clash between two interpretations of what became known as the Reagan doctrine. The true Reaganites believed that the United States should support any insurgent movement that fought against a communist regime—"failure to assist them would be not just a moral failure, but criminal negligence of our own interests and our own country."[6] These insurgents were "freedom fighters" who were rolling back communism. Two of these regimes were Angola and Mozambique. The Reaganites argued, correctly, that there were no ideological differences between their governments—both had adopted Marxism-Leninism in 1977. Deputy Assistant Secretary Wisner, who was Crocker's point man on Mozambique, told Secretary Shultz in late 1983 that the ruling party of Mozambique had "shared an ideological affinity with and received support from the USSR for a dozen years."[7]

The State Department, however, believed that the United States could tolerate a self-styled Marxist-Leninist regime in Africa. It advocated extending an olive branch to Mozambique to wean it away from the Soviet Union. The process had begun in late 1982 at the initiative of the Africa Bureau. In October 1983 Wisner wrote Shultz: "The policy has been successful as the Mozambicans have pledged not to permit Soviet bases and have quietly cooperated with us in a number of areas."[8] In March 1984 the administration achieved a major success when Mozambique signed the Nkomati pact with South Africa. Then, in early 1985, "to the dismay of the 'once a commie always a commie' conservatives," as Crocker wrote, the administration proposed sending $1 million in nonlethal military assistance and $15 million in economic aid to Mozambique. Congress defeated the proposal by a substantial margin.[9]

The State Department's proposal had incensed the hard-liners. "We've been suckered into backing an unholy alliance in which South Africa [because it had signed the Nkomati pact with Mozambique] and the Soviet Union jointly prop up bloody and sometimes deranged local tyrants with little popular support," the *Wall Street Journal* claimed. Arguing that "the increasingly successful RENAMO" was on the verge of victory, Howard Phillips, chairman of the Conservative Caucus, wrote that in Mozambique "we're imposing another Soviet tyranny on others who were about to rid themselves of its shackles." He demanded action: "It's past time for grass roots conservatives who contributed and worked for Ronald Reagan's re-election to insist that he overruled [*sic*] the State Department's pro-Soviet Africa policy, and fire the people responsible for it, beginning with Assistant Secretary of State Chester Crocker." The *National Review* aimed higher: "Cautious careerists at State are resisting Administration policy, a serious charge indeed when foreign affairs are at issue. That picture is complicated, however, by a Secretary of State who appears to have been captured by the careerist mentality, but as the President's representative cannot be charged as insubordinate as long as the President doesn't think he is. If the President is serious about supporting freedom-fighters he must get his own people in line."[10]

In a December 1984 open letter to Reagan, titled "Mr President: Why Is Chester Crocker Trying to Sell 20 Million Black Africans into Communist Slavery?" the leaders of thirteen of the country's most important conservative organizations drew their bill of indictment:

> When you accepted the Republican Party's nomination for a second term in Dallas on August 23, you proudly declared that "since January 20, 1981, not one inch of soil has fallen to the Communists."
> Indeed, your courageous liberation of Grenada from Marxist tyranny was the finest hour of your administration.
> Unfortunately not all of your appointees comprehend the evil threat of Communism as you do.
> Your Assistant Secretary of State for African Affairs, Chester Crocker, is actively pursuing a policy the consequences of which are likely to include:
> — The consolidation of a Marxist-Leninist dictatorship in Mozambique, where the courageous "Renamo" Freedom Fighters have been moving ever closer to toppling the pro-Soviet regime of Samora Machel and replacing it with a pro-Western democracy.
> — Undercutting Jonas Savimbi and his anti-Communist UNITA Freedom Fighters, who are just months away from defeating the Soviet-Cuban supported tyranny of the Marxist-Leninist MPLA in Angola.

MR. PRESIDENT:

WHY IS CHESTER CROCKER
TRYING TO SELL
20 MILLION BLACK AFRICANS
INTO COMMUNIST SLAVERY?

Conservative Americans harshly castigated the State Department during the Reagan years for pursuing a "liberal" policy in southern Africa. They thought Washington was betraying America's true friends—apartheid South Africa and its allies in Namibia, Angola, and Mozambique. They blamed, above all, Reagan's gifted assistant secretary of state for Africa, Chester Crocker.

— Installing the pro-Soviet terrorist organization SWAPO through a Soviet-manipulated United Nations "one man, one vote, one time" election in mineral rich Namibia. Instead, we should encourage independence under the leadership of one of the indigenous political movements which participate in the democratic pro-American Multi-Party Conference.[11]

In their struggle against "the invertebrates at Foggy Bottom,"[12] the hard-liners had several assets: the support of close friends of Reagan, of influential Republicans in Congress, and of the conservative wing of the Republican Party; as well as the president's own instinct to sympathize with the plight of the white South Africans and with anyone fighting communists. Within the administration, the NSC under McFarlane and Vice Admiral John Poindexter, who replaced him in December 1985, was hostile territory for the Africa bureau, even though, Crocker notes, McFarlane "was at times sympathetic." (Crocker was scathing about Poindexter.) The hard-line group also included Secretary of Defense Caspar Weinberger, a friend of the president and a tenacious infighter, but he did not focus on Africa; Jeane Kirkpatrick, who by 1985 had left the administration but remained influential; Bill Clark, also out of government after February 1985 but still very close to Reagan; White House communications director Pat Buchanan and White House chief of staff Don Regan. The pack was led by Bill Casey, the ruthless Director of Central Intelligence. In his memoirs, Shultz writes, "Within the administration, Bill Casey viscerally and unswervingly opposed all that Crocker and I were doing; his CIA officers ran channels to the South Africans from CIA headquarters at Langley and used CIA representatives in the field to undermine Crocker with Savimbi and other black African leaders. . . . My problems with Bill Casey and those he used in the CIA were not confined to Southern Africa but were represented in our cross-purposes there. He worked with South African intelligence, gave the benefit of the doubt to South Africa, and distrusted any negotiation or potential agreement with a Communist government." Chas Freeman, who became Crocker's senior deputy in April 1986, adds: "I have some reason to believe that Mr. Casey, who was prone to follow his own foreign policy . . . did become, to some extent, involved with RENAMO, against the declared policy, and indeed the strongly held internal policy of the administration. . . . I don't know how far Mr. Casey actually went. I know of this only because of a chance remark by a senior official in Saudi Arabia, who told me that Mr. Casey had tried to involve Saudi Arabia with RENAMO."[13]

The opposition to the true Reaganites was led by Shultz, a formidable figure because of his close relationship to Reagan. It included the mainstream, pragmatic wing of the Republican Party. On some issues, like arms negotiations with the Soviet Union during Reagan's second term and relations with the Kremlin under Gorbachev, the president was closer to Shultz's instincts than to those of the true Reaganites; on others—such as policy toward Nicaragua and, to a lesser degree, southern Africa—the reverse was true. That the Africa bureau could, most of the time, hold the line against the true Reaganites was due to the persistence and skill of Crocker, to Shultz's strong support of him, and—in the case of Mozambique—also to the support of Margaret Thatcher. "Periodically someone would tell Reagan 'We must help RENAMO,'" Crocker's deputy Freeman recalls, "and we would have to call London and have Margaret Thatcher straighten him out, which she did." To the frustration of British and U.S. hard-liners, Thatcher was an "improbable admirer" of the president of Mozambique, as one of them lamented.[14] She believed, as did Crocker, that the West could work with the Mozambican government and wean it away from the Soviet Union, and she had nothing but contempt for RENAMO. Prodded by Shultz and Thatcher, Reagan withstood the hard-liners' efforts to sway him toward supporting RENAMO. Instead, the administration developed increasingly cordial relations with the government of Mozambique.

In September 1985, the Reagan administration incurred the wrath of the hard-liners by imposing sanctions on South Africa. It was a rearguard action. Public outrage over South Africa's crackdown had galvanized Congress, which was preparing to approve broad sanctions against the apartheid regime. To preempt congressional action, Reagan imposed limited sanctions by executive order. They banned most loans to the South African government, most exports of nuclear technology, and "all computer exports" to the South African military, police, security forces, and agencies "involved in the enforcement of apartheid." As the *New York Times* noted, "By themselves, the sanctions . . . will have a negligible effect on the economy of South Africa and on the American companies doing business with the country." They were, however, the first economic sanctions adopted by the United States against South Africa. The *National Review* was scathing: "Mr. Reagan . . . has hurt his credibility and signed on with the forces promoting revolution in South Africa. . . . Mr. Reagan has made the wrong move."[15]

## Pretoria's May 1986 Raids

As the crackdown in South Africa continued, pressure grew in the United States for additional sanctions. On January 31, 1986, the *Washington Times* noted, "When President Reagan, last September, imposed limited sanctions against South Africa . . . pragmatists . . . celebrated what they saw as an inspired bit of football strategy. The president would get everybody running in his direction and before you knew it, South Africa would be off the front pages. . . . Clearly, South Africa did not depart from the front pages . . . Congressional staffs . . . are drafting tough new sanctions legislation. They're in clover, for Ronald Reagan, fumbling for a workable strategy last September, conceded philosophical defeat."[16] The administration, however, remained adamant in its opposition to new sanctions and sought to enlist Pretoria's help to avoid them. On May 2, 1986, Crocker met with the South African ambassador, Herbert Beukes. "He . . . raised with me," Beukes told Pik Botha, "the question of increasing reports of police brutality emanating from South Africa. . . . What he finds of particular concern is the fact that this is being used to create a new issue."[17] A few days later Beukes received a personal letter from Crocker. "In July 1984, we passed to Ambassador Fourie an informal paper on abuses of human rights in Namibia," Crocker wrote. "The paper noted that charges of torture, harassment of civilians in the operational area, and murder by members of the security forces . . . had regularly surfaced. We are convinced, after looking into a number of detailed reports in 1985, that such abuses have continued. These reports have included instances of murder, torture and assaults on children. . . . Abuses of human rights such as torture are, of course, abhorrent. They also damage the image and position of the South African government in the United States and can undercut mutual efforts to resolve the Namibia problem." Beukes warned that Crocker's words reflected "the growing American perception that brutal actions by the members of the South African security forces can provide fodder for the sanctions campaign in the US."[18]

At this critical moment, when the campaign for sanctions in the United States was gathering strength, Pretoria struck. On May 19, 1986, the SADF announced that earlier that day it had destroyed ANC targets in Zambia, Botswana, and Zimbabwe: fighter jets had "successfully attacked the ANC operational centre . . . 15 km southwest of Lusaka," and "small elements of the army" had attacked "terrorist transit facilities" five kilometers west of Gaborone, a "terrorist transit facility" in downtown Harare, and the ANC "operational center" in the city's outskirts.[19] "To date, such raids have been limited to one country at the time," the *Wall Street Journal* pointed out. It was the first time, the Johannesburg *Star* noted, that "South Africa had admitted sending its forces into Zimbabwe and Zambia."[20]

Ronnie Kasrils, a senior ANC official, remarked, "insofar as they reflected on South Africa's military intelligence, the raids were pathetic."[21] Only one of the targets, an office in downtown Harare, belonged to the ANC. In Zambia, the South Africans struck the UN High Commission for Refugees' transit camp near Lusaka. In Botswana they hit a refugee settlement and a house that the ANC no longer used. The London *Times* wrote, "The raids appear to have achieved very little in military terms." Johannesburg's *Business Day* quoted President Quett Masire of Botswana: "My reaction is that of horror. We don't know what we have done to deserve this, especially since we have been engaged in discussions with South Africa. If they had any people who [sic] they suspected were here, they could have told us and we could have found out all about it." (The raid, the *Botswana Guardian* explained, "came just days before Botswana and South Africa were meant to hold security talks.") The *Star* noted that "all three [countries], knowing how vulnerable they are to retaliation, have been at pains to draw a line between giving the ANC political as distinct from military sanctuary."[22] Even the Secretariat of the State Security Council had concluded that "[Zambian president] Kaunda is always an outspoken champion of peaceful solutions to the problems in southern Africa and tolerates violence only as a last resort." In March 1986 Pik Botha had told the West German foreign minister that "Botswana had removed the ANC from its country. South Africa's relations with Zimbabwe were also not bad."[23]

What were the South Africans doing? Why did they attack their neighbors, at a moment when the Reagan administration had asked them to moderate their behavior? The answers might lie in other international pressures on Pretoria. At the Commonwealth summit held the previous October in Nassau, Prime Minister Thatcher had faced down an attempt by almost all Commonwealth members to impose sanctions on South Africa. In order to paper over the rift, the summit had created the Eminent Persons Group (EPG): its seven members (the co-chairs were Australia's former prime minister Malcolm Fraser and Nigeria's former president Olusugun Obasanjo) would engage in a six-month effort to help achieve a negotiated solution between the South African government and its opponents. They would then present a report to the Commonwealth. "If in their opinion adequate progress has not been made within this period," the accord that created the EPG stated, "we [the Commonwealth] agree to consider the adoption of further measures."[24] Under strong pressure from Thatcher, President Botha agreed to let the EPG consult with members of his government and representatives of all sectors of South African society.[25] In mid-February 1986, the members of the EPG made their first visit to South Africa and then flew to Lusaka to speak with the ANC.

The leaders of the ANC did not believe that PW Botha would be willing to dismantle apartheid—the essential condition for meaningful negotiations—but they did not want to be the ones who would scuttle the EPG. "It wouldn't have been smart for us to tell them not to take it seriously because these people [the South African rulers] are fascists," ANC official Kasrils explained to the Cubans. Therefore, ANC president Oliver Tambo and other ANC leaders met with the EPG on February 29, April 3, and again on May 17, 1986, when the EPG presented the "Possible Negotiating Concept" it had developed. The South African government would enter into negotiations with the ANC and other groups with the aim of dismantling apartheid. It would free Mandela and other political prisoners, lift the ban on the ANC, remove the SADF from the townships, allow freedom of assembly and discussion, and suspend detentions without trial. The ANC, on the other hand, would suspend violence. The EPG explained to Tambo and his colleagues that the South African government, "while indicating that it was considering it [the proposal] seriously, had not yet said either 'yes' or 'no.'" Although the ANC leaders were sure that Pretoria would reject the proposal, they promised to study the documents and reply in ten days. "On this encouraging basis," the EPG wrote, "we returned to South Africa." They were ready for a new round of discussions to pin down the government's response.[26]

The government's response was the May 19 raids on Zambia, Botswana, and Zimbabwe. In Johannesburg, *Business Day* lamented, "The hopes which have been tentatively pinned to the Eminent Persons' Group ... have been shattered by the sound of gunfire." In London, "Raid against Reason" was the somber title of the *Times'* editorial. "The action against the three front-line states ... is hard to explain."[27]

Perhaps not. Foreign Minister Pik Botha, who claims that he had not been informed about the impending raids, told me, "I cannot say to what extent the military might have had in mind the scuttling of the [EPG] negotiations. PW

[Botha] knew of the negotiating concept and he knew of the impending attack and he allowed it. I cannot believe that he was unaware of the possible consequences." Relying on sources close to PW Botha, Peter Stiff—a conservative South African author who was well connected to the armed forces and intelligence services—was blunt: "The moment the ANC agreed to the negotiation process . . . PW Botha pulled the plug and launched the cross-border raids. . . . Botha wanted the EPG out of South Africa and their objectives spoiled. Expelling them arbitrarily . . . would have brought an international storm down on his head. . . . So he was faced with the EPG remaining in South Africa . . . or getting them to pack their bags and leave voluntarily. He apparently decided the only way left to achieve that was for South Africa to commit an outrageous act that would nullify their efforts." He succeeded. As *Business Day* reported, a few hours after the raids, "on order from the Commonwealth Secretariat in London, the EPG mission packed their bags and flew out of SA."[28]

I listened to Pik Botha talk about the 1980s for six hours one Saturday in December 2007 at his house near Pretoria. Most of what he said was in sharp contrast with the evidence, including that from the South African archives. But not everything. As Ambassador Nickel pointed out, "inside the South African government, even though P. W. Botha had a very oppressive effect on other members of his Cabinet—because he was a bully-boy and they were all scared of him—there were considerable differences among various ministers."[29] There is no question that Pik Botha represented the most moderate element within the cabinet, both on racial issues and on foreign policy. He was the cabinet member who said publicly in early 1986 that he could imagine a black president of South Africa.[30] He may not have known in advance of the Cabinda raid; he is probably telling the truth when he claims that he did not know that South Africa continued to help RENAMO in violation of the Nkomati accord; and he almost certainly had not been informed in advance of the raids of May 1986. Pik Botha and his close aides had real differences with the SADF. They did not want to violate the Nkomati pact. They favored aid to UNITA, but they did not believe that South Africa could bring Savimbi to power in Luanda. They opposed free elections in Namibia, but were far more worried about sanctions than the military. It was, however, the military that was in the saddle, basking in the president's favor, while Pik Botha and his cohorts in the Foreign Ministry tagged along.

Pik Botha was a dynamic minister of foreign affairs, a womanizer, and a very hard drinker. ("How he could put away so much without actually dying from it, I'll never know," U.S. ambassador Nickel remarked.) He was a bully, but he did not dare stand up to PW Botha. "PW was a disciplinarian," Pik Botha recalls.

When the president rebuked him in parliament for having told a journalist that he would be willing to serve under a black president, Pik Botha said nothing. "It is not a pleasant experience to sit in parliament in front of the gallery, the press and be reprimanded by the president," he noted.[31] His ambition to become president led him to court PW and cultivate the military. He tried to moderate the government's policy, but without challenging Defense Minister Malan. As a senior U.S. intelligence officer wrote in 1987, "While some foreign ministry officials, including Foreign Minister Botha, would prefer a less confrontational regional policy, they have consistently been outmaneuvered by hard-liners in the defense and security establishments."[32]

## The U.S. Congress Votes Sanctions

In deciding to launch the May raids, PW Botha and the military had been encouraged by the U.S. air strikes against Libya the previous month. The Reagan administration had bombed several targets in Tripoli and Benghazi in retaliation for a terrorist bombing in Berlin that it blamed on Libya. "The recent US military operation against Libya can have implications for South Africa," an April 22 SADF analysis had stressed. "The reasons that were given for the operation resemble the justifications that South Africa proffers when it launches attacks on foreign terrorist bases." PW Botha had hastened to congratulate Reagan: "Dear Mr President," he wrote, "Your action is a defence not only of American interests but also of the interests of the free world, which cannot allow the perpetrators of terror and protectors of internationally controlled terrorism to go unpunished. Decency is on your side and I am glad that you have acted to uphold it."[33]

South Africa's May raids did not shake Reagan's opposition to sanctions, but they fanned the rage of the antiapartheid movement in the United States. As Secretary Shultz writes, they "revived congressional interest, and new economic sanctions were proposed as violence inside South Africa worsened. Republicans in Congress urged President Reagan to speak out in unequivocal terms that would dramatize our opposition to apartheid and to South African behavior."[34] The forthcoming midterm elections added a special urgency to their demand.

Hard-liners were appalled by "the anti–South Africa wolves [who] were gathering" on Capitol Hill. *Human Events* thundered, "What never seems to be said in this country by U.S. officials or vote-hungry lawmakers is that the major purveyors of violence in South Africa, the major producers of the horror show now being staged are the members, supporters and allies of the outlawed, pro-Soviet terrorist organization, the African National Congress." Nathan Perlmutter, National Director of the Anti-Defamation League of B'nai B'rith, argued, "The fall of South Africa to such a Soviet-oriented and Communist-influenced force [the ANC] would be a severe setback to the United States."[35]

On June 12, the EPG released its report. "With studied starkness, the Eminent Persons Group draw their grim conclusions," wrote the London *Times*. The report called, unequivocally, for sanctions. It warned: "There can be no negotiated settlement in South Africa without the ANC; the breadth of its support is incontestable; and this support is growing. . . . The open identification with the ANC through banners and songs, in funerals and in churches throughout the country, despite the risks involved, supports the widely-held belief that if an election were held today on the basis of universal franchise the ANC would win it. . . . The strength of black convictions is now matched by a readiness to die for those convictions." The CIA agreed: "Popular support among South African blacks for the ANC as a symbol of black resistance has skyrocketed."[36]

Reagan was scheduled to deliver a much-anticipated speech on South Africa on July 22. The State Department hoped that by expressing outrage at Pretoria's behavior and repugnance of apartheid the president could mollify the critics of constructive engagement and rally the wavering Republican cohorts in opposition to sanctions. The preparation of the speech led to a bitter clash within the administration. On one side stood the State Department, led by Shultz and Crocker, who urged the president to criticize a "government from which," as Crocker noted, "he was so reluctant to distance himself." Arrayed against them were those who wanted to "let Reagan be Reagan," with White House Communications Director Pat Buchanan leading the pack. "I actually wrote a draft," Crocker's senior deputy, Chas Freeman, recalls. "I wrote a hell of a good draft. . . . That speech went to the White House pretty much the way I had written it. And exactly two lines of it survived the pen of one Pat Buchanan, who was the speechwriter for Reagan, and who, himself, has very definite views on racial issues and on Africa, about which he knows nothing."[37]

There was a vast difference in rank and influence between Shultz and Buchanan, and normally the president would have followed the advice of his secretary of state. But Reagan was ready to defy political calculus on an issue where his core values were at stake. He discarded the State Department's draft, with its harsh criticism of the South African government, and followed Buchanan's.

With dire results. While Reagan dutifully condemned apartheid, he lavished praise on the enterprising South African whites, whose country was Africa's success story. No other country on the continent had attained its level of economic development, and none offered blacks so much economic opportunity:

black incomes in South Africa had risen "very substantially," and tens of thousands of blacks flocked to South Africa from neighboring countries in search of a better life. Before the recent wave of violence, apartheid South Africa had enjoyed "a broad measure of freedom of speech, of the press, and of religion." The villain in Reagan's speech was not the South African government, but "the Soviet-armed guerrillas of the African National Congress" who were fomenting "racial war." Therefore, negotiations with the ANC were pointless. "The South African government is under no obligation to negotiate the future of the country with any organization that proclaims a goal of creating a Communist state—and uses terrorist tactics to achieve it." Finally, the president asserted that imposing economic sanctions on South Africa would impede PW Botha's reforms, hurt South African blacks, and help communist terrorists destroy the country. Sanctions were, Reagan said, repeating Prime Minister Margaret Thatcher's words, "immoral" and "utterly repugnant."[38]

Shultz delicately summarized the speech in his memoirs, "The president did not say much about the desperation and fear of blacks, but spoke eloquently about the security of the whites 'in this country they love and have sacrificed so much to build.'" In his memoirs, Crocker was blunt: "With this speech, the 'great communicator' became the great polarizer. [PW] Botha must have been delighted. . . . The abuse of logic reminded one of other times and places; South Africa's state of emergency was not the fault of the ANC."[39]

Hard-liners celebrated. "President Courageously Proclaims His 'No Sanctions' Policy," *Human Events* applauded, its confidence in the president restored. Reagan had "followed his finely-honed instincts" and taken "the brave, wise and honorable course," in his "extremely effective speech." Paying homage where homage was due, it singled out Pat Buchanan for praise. "Buchanan was not only the principal drafter of the speech, but he peppered the President with material that countered what State had to offer." The magazine suggested that in the looming battle over sanctions "the White House might begin by unleashing Pat Buchanan."[40]

It was a prescription for disaster, given the uproar the speech provoked even among mainstream Republicans. Wisely, the administration kept Buchanan under wraps and sent Shultz out on damage control. The day after Reagan's speech Shultz sat in front of the Senate Foreign Relations Committee. He assured the senators that he and the president shared their "sense of outrage at the situation in South Africa." While his distaste for the ANC was evident— "Soviet armed ANC guerrillas have embarked upon expanded terrorist violence inside South Africa"—and he worried about the ANC's "ultimate objectives" and communist influence within the organization, he told the senators, "We intend to raise the level and frequency of our contacts with the South African Government's black opposition, including, among others, the African National Congress."[41] A week later, on July 30, 1986, the U.S. ambassador to Zambia met for ninety minutes with senior ANC officials in Lusaka. He explained that "he had been sent by the Secretary of State." The conversation was superficial, but it was significant that for the first time there was a contact between a senior Reagan administration official and the ANC. Until then, occasional contacts had been engineered in Lusaka by Crocker's special assistant Cabelly, who always made it clear, an ANC official wrote, that the meetings had "no formal status."[42]

As Crocker points out, Reagan's "strident pro-Pretoria tilt . . . disarmed those in Congress who preferred to let the executive branch conduct policy toward this complex region. The speech triggered a bi-partisan storm. It literally forced a split in his party in the Senate—a mere three months before a mid-term election—and obliged legislators to make the best of a bad situation."[43] On August 15, thirty-seven Republican senators joined all forty-seven Democrats voting in favor of a sanctions bill. On September 12, the House approved the same bill by an equally lopsided margin: 308 to 77. Ninety Republicans, nearly half of those in the House, supported the bill which included a ban on new U.S. public and private loans and investments in South Africa as well as on imports of steel, iron, coal, uranium, textiles, and agricultural products. The *Wall Street Journal* waxed indignant: "It can be argued, of course, that the sanctions Congress has voted won't do any harm because they won't work. Most of the commercial clauses have escape hatches. . . . But the symbolism of sanctions says to the world that the American left has succeeded in aligning U.S. foreign policy with the destructive aims of the African National Congress's militant wing, and with the communist states that support it. . . . Congress has indulged itself in moral intoxication and only the president can head off the morning after. This is why the founding fathers gave him the veto."[44] Reagan did veto the bill, but on October 2 Congress overrode his veto, and the "Comprehensive Anti-Apartheid Act" became law. "The president's veto of sanctions was admirable, a breath of fresh air," wrote the *National Review*. More soberly, Shultz noted that it was the first time since Nixon's veto of the War Powers Resolution in 1973 had been overridden "that a president had experienced such a loss on a foreign policy issue."[45]

Constructive engagement was in shambles. It had been crushed not by the congressional sanctions, but by Pretoria's violence. PW Botha, facing an unprecedented popular uprising, responded with more violence at home and abroad against South Africa's neighbors. Pretoria was determined to eradicate the ANC throughout southern Africa. As the CIA pointed out in July 1986,

Pretoria's suspicions about its black neighbors reflect its severe anxieties about its black majority. No independent black state, except possibly Swaziland,[46] can ever do enough to satisfy Pretoria's demands on the ANC issue. Even Botswana's determined, albeit unsuccessful, efforts to eliminate ANC activity within its borders has won it little relief from South African saber rattling, assassination teams, and cross-border raids. . . .

Pretoria's profound skepticism about the longer term possibility of peaceful coexistence with neighboring black states, in our judgement, has led it to adopt a second major regional policy: keeping its neighbors—particularly those it regards as most hostile—weak and dependent. Pretoria has maintained its status as the region's superpower by creating instability and dependency throughout southern Africa: by backing insurgencies and dissidents in Angola, Mozambique, Zimbabwe and Lesotho; by its ready use of economic and transportation leverage to undercut regional efforts to reduce the dependence of black-ruled states on South Africa; and by conducting covert operations, such as the 1982 attack on Zimbabwe's Thornhill Airbase, that preempt challenges to South African power. Pretoria's realpolitik regional policy is reinforced, in our judgement, by a deeply rooted belief that, in order to maintain power over an increasingly restive black majority, Pretoria must demand respectful behavior from its black neighbors. . . . We suspect that the ruling Afrikaner's traditional need to show who is "baas" [boss] will increasingly be acted out on its black-ruled neighbors as Pretoria's frustration with its inability to suppress domestic unrest grows.[47]

This sober analysis exposed the folly of believing that constructive engagement would ever moderate Pretoria's behavior. PW Botha and his cohorts were defending apartheid against a mounting black threat. They responded like wounded beasts. The only way foreign governments could moderate the behavior of the South African leaders was by helping them to crush the threat, as the Reagan administration did when it urged "southern African states not to tolerate the presence of ANC or SWAPO guerrillas."[48] The alternative was to help eradicate the cancer by imposing punishing sanctions and extending aid to those fighting against apartheid.

The decision of the U.S. Congress to impose sanctions was part of a global wave of revulsion against South Africa. In September 1986, two weeks before Congress overrode Reagan's veto, the European Community approved slightly less stringent sanctions on South Africa. In October, the first mandatory trade sanctions adopted by a Canadian government became effective. As always when it came to fighting against apartheid, the Scandinavian countries led the West: Denmark banned trade with South Africa in 1986, and Norway, Sweden, and Finland followed suit in 1987.[49]

## The U.S. Congress, Israel, and South Africa

Even Israel, which conservative columnist Smith Hempstone aptly called "Pretoria's Defense Buddy," had to distance itself from South Africa—a heavy blow to the apartheid state. A CIA report noted, "South African leaders identify with Israel's position as a Western [state] surrounded by 'backward' and hostile neighbors; they were greatly impressed with Israel's military performance in the 1967 Arab-Israeli war and shortly afterward sought and received Israeli military advice and training." A close relationship developed between Israel's Defense Minister Moshe Dayan and PW Botha, then South Africa's defense minister. "Botha and Dayan built a special friendship," two biographers of PW Botha wrote, "and met each other often, at times openly; at times secretly; at times in South Africa, at times overseas."[50]

The relationship blossomed. The CIA explained, "During the 1980s, as South Africa faced increasing difficulty in trading with the West, Israel assumed a role of middleman; South African goods were shipped to Israel where minimal work was done on them to allow firms to affix a 'made in Israel' label; the goods were then sold more easily to Western Europe and the U.S." The two countries established close security links, including exchange of information on nuclear matters, intelligence sharing, and the sale of arms and weapons systems. "The intimacy of the intelligence relationship," the CIA reported in 1981, "is symbolized by Tel Aviv's appointment in 1979 of the former head of the Israeli intelligence service as Ambassador to Pretoria." Columnist Hempstone wrote in a well-researched article, "South Africa's new Cheetah jet attack aircraft bears a remarkable resemblance both to France's Mirage II . . . and Israel's Kfir fighter. South Africa produces under licence, and with Israel's technical assistance, versions of Israel's Uzi submachine guns, Galil assault rifles, Saar patrol boats, and Gabriel sea-to-sea missiles."[51]

This cozy relationship was disrupted in October 1986, when the U.S. Congress overrode Reagan's veto and the Comprehensive Anti-Apartheid Act became law. The act required that within 179 days of its enactment the president submit a report to Congress identifying the violators of the 1977 UN Security Council mandatory arms embargo on South Africa, "with a view to terminating United States military assistance to those countries."[52] The first report was due on April 1, 1987. Israel was, by many accounts, the worst offender and the only country with formal government-to-government arms contracts with South Africa. This is why the previous September, when rallying support for Reagan's forthcoming veto of the sanctions bill, the White House chief of staff and Buchanan had invited a select group to the White House to discuss "the implications of the South Africa sanctions bill on U.S.-Israel security relations."[53] But the veto had been overridden, and the bill had become law. Warned by its U.S. friends that its military ties to South Africa would jeopardize the more than $1.5 billion it received from the United States in military aid, Israel had to make some changes. On March 18, 1987, it announced that it would neither sign new defense contracts with South Africa nor renew existing ones when they expired. This was Israel's "first public admission," the CIA noted, "that military contracts existed with South Africa at all." It was "an effort," the *Jerusalem Post* reported on March 19, "to head off possible anti-Israeli criticism and actions by the U.S. Congress. . . . Sources in Jerusalem yesterday said that had there not been the 'threat of the presidential report, the Israeli government would have done nothing.'"

The announcement satisfied the U.S. Congress, "while not totally upsetting the apple cart," Hempstone noted, because several of the agreements had many years to run, and others had automatic renewal clauses unless they were specifically rescinded.[54] The South African government lamented the decision and blamed the U.S. Congress. "One sad aspect of this development," the state-controlled South African Broadcasting Corporation said, "is the international blackmail role—the bully boy tactics—that the United States Congress has now resorted to in its vendetta against South Africa." President Botha was blunt: "Israel had been bullied into cutting military ties with South Africa. 'I think Israel has been victimized.'"[55]

The State Department's report was issued on May 12, 1987. It duly noted the Israeli government's March 18 statement, and it graciously failed to note that the Israeli government, by its own admission, would continue to violate the Security Council's mandatory arms embargo against South Africa.[56] But because a new round of U.S. congressional hearings on countries trading with South Africa would begin in October 1987, Israel announced new measures on September 17; in particular, it would no longer serve as a transit station for South African goods—that is, as the *Jerusalem Post* explained, "as middleman for sanctions-busting by third countries." The director-general of the Israeli Foreign Ministry was blunt: "Israel had decided to reduce its ties to avoid endangering relations with the U.S. Congress." Bitterly, the *Burger* wrote, "The Afrikaners have, with the exception of a short period [when they were pro-Nazi], traditionally felt much sympathy for the Jews. Must this belief now be called into question?" In public, Israel distanced itself from its South African friends. In private, top Israeli officials promised Pretoria that the new sanctions would merely amount to "'window dressing.'"[57]

## Helping Savimbi

In the United States, the same Congress that was imposing sanctions on South Africa against Reagan's wishes had embraced UNITA, Pretoria's protégé. On June 11, 1985, the Senate had repealed the Clark Amendment, which had prohibited covert operations in Angola for almost a decade, by a sixty-three to thirty-four vote, and the House had followed suit on July 10. The repeal would become effective on October 1, 1985, with the beginning of the new fiscal year.

In seeking repeal, the administration and its supporters had argued, disingenuously, that they were not necessarily thinking of helping Savimbi, but wanted to eliminate a cumbersome restraint on the president's ability to conduct foreign policy.

After repeal, the stage was set for the next act. On October 24, 1985, Reagan set the tone. In his half-hour address to the General Assembly of the United Nations he singled out five countries where, he said, anticommunist movements were fighting against Soviet oppression—Afghanistan, Cambodia, Ethiopia, Angola, and Nicaragua—and he demanded that the leaders of these countries agree to "democratic reconciliation with their own people." He pledged that as long as they refused, "America's support for struggling democratic resistance forces must not and shall not cease."[58]

The Reagan doctrine was born. "Finally, our game plan," the *Washington Times* applauded. "The president has launched an impressive offensive, and the people of the world, slave and free, must pray that America has the nerve to follow through."[59] In fact, the seeds of the doctrine had already been sown. Aid to the Afghan rebels had begun in 1979 and was sharply increased in 1980 and again in 1984 and 1985; aid to the Nicaraguan Contras had been going on, fitfully, since 1981, and aid to Cambodian rebels since 1982.[60] In the U.S. Congress and in the press, a debate began in late 1985 about whether to provide aid to UNITA.

There were, during the Reagan presidency, two major public debates about whether the United States should support insurgent movements: the first, about aid to the Nicaraguan Contras, raged through most of the Reagan years; the other, about aid to UNITA, flared in late 1985 and was over, for all practical purposes, by early 1986.

The intensity of the debate on aid to the Contras was due to Nicaragua's location in the American backyard and to the fear that Reagan might send U.S. troops to overthrow the Sandinistas. Furthermore, thousands of Americans traveled to Nicaragua and acquired a firsthand impression about the country: it was easy to obtain a visa (and after July 1985 none was needed),[61] Nicaragua was not too distant, travel was not too expensive, and U.S. churches and grass-roots organizations developed a keen interest in the country. Sandinista and Contra spokesmen appeared often on American television.

Nevertheless, as Reagan wrote in his diary in April 1983, "it was astonishing how few people even knew where El Salvador & Nicaragua are."[62] Their knowledge of Angola was even worse. The quality of the debate about aid to Savimbi was aptly characterized by Howard Wolpe (D-Mich.), who chaired the subcommittee on Africa of the House Foreign Affairs Committee. "Most Americans and members of Congress didn't know what Angola was or much less care about it," he said. "Most of my colleagues in Congress didn't have a clue."[63] There was little incentive to learn. No one thought that giving aid to Savimbi would lead to U.S. military intervention. Very few Americans visited Angola. It was far away, it was expensive to get to, and the Angolan government rarely granted visas to Americans, including journalists. Whereas there was a steady flow of members of Congress and their staffs to Nicaragua, hardly any went to Luanda. However, a trickle of journalists and congressional staff journeyed to Jamba, Savimbi's headquarters, via South Africa and South African military bases in Namibia; the reception in Jamba was friendly and increasingly well organized. The head of an Angolan government delegation that visited the United States in the fall of 1985 noted: "UNITA, in cahoots with the South African government, often invites the major newspapers of the United States to visit alleged 'liberated regions.' While journalists told us that they would prefer 'to enter [Angola] through Luanda,' they had a great deal of difficulty getting entry visas. . . . Therefore, their view of Angola has been shaped by UNITA and its supporters."[64]

It was not only the U.S. press and Congress that were in the dark about Angola. So too was U.S. intelligence. Its reports in the 1980s about the domestic situation in South Africa were of high quality, and even those on Namibia were reasonably good, but those on Angola were poor. And for good reason. "We had few, if any, sources on Angola," recalls Daniel Fenton, who was the principal CIA analyst covering Angola through the 1980s. "We didn't have human sources [in Angola], we didn't have the kind of thing you have when you have an embassy and consulates. We relied on foreign embassies—on the British, but they knew very little." Fenton explains that the Portuguese also were ill-informed; the Brazilians were sympathetic to the MPLA; and the French, although they may have been knowledgeable, did not share. "Our major sources of information were South Africa, Savimbi and Zaire, but they all had their own agenda. The Gulf Oil people were very cooperative with us [CIA]," Fenton muses, "but they didn't know anything. Their only interest was to get the oil shipped from the fields. We talked with Gulf. All I got out of them was atmospherics, what it was like to work in Angola. They were happy in their separate world [Cabinda]." They also had no interest in doing anything that might threaten their company's profitable relationship with the MPLA government. "We had overhead photographs," Fenton adds, "that could give a rough idea of troop movements"—very approximate, when it came to small units. Sometimes Crocker and his team were the best available source of information. For an intelligence officer, it was a desolate picture. CIA, DIA, INR—their analyses might differ, but all were milking the same spare and skewed data. "We really had so little information," Fenton concludes, "We didn't know!" Doug Smith, who was the CIA station chief in Kinshasa from 1983 to 1986, emphatically agrees. "The intelligence on Angola was very poor. We didn't have anyone there!" The picture did not significantly improve when it came to UNITA. "You had to take what the South Africans said with a huge grain of salt," Fenton remarks, "and you were not going to get anything from Savimbi's people. He controlled the contacts of his people with us very closely." As for the Zaireans, Smith adds, "they knew very little. Their intelligence service was focused on keeping Mobutu in power, not on what happened elsewhere."[65]

Savimbi's champions—in the press and in Congress—did not care. They knew what mattered to them: there were thousands of Cuban soldiers in Angola, and Savimbi had promised to defeat them. In Representative Wolpe's words, Savimbi "had succeeded in posturing himself as a strong anti-communist: 'I am your friend, anti-communist, fighting the Cubans.' In those days this was the frame."[66] It crossed party lines, stretching to include people who were considered moderate and liberal. Many were motivated by deep hostility to Cuba and by the blandishments of powerful Cuban American groups.

The pro-Savimbi forces seized the high ground: they argued in terms of both U.S. interests and morality. For them, Savimbi was a heroic freedom fighter who sought national reconciliation and democracy in Angola. His nationalist credentials were, in their view, impeccable. "For years he fought for independence against Portugal," William Buckley explained in the National Review, "pursuing democratic government and civil liberties. And then, at the moment of victory in 1975, the coup d'etat happened. This was a Marxist-Leninist operation made possible by Cuban soldiers." Since then, Buckley asserted, Savimbi had been fighting against Cuban-Soviet colonialism. Senator Orrin Hatch (R-Utah) eloquently summed up the case for the UNITA chieftain. "I have had the privilege of meeting Mr. Savimbi and have been extremely impressed by his honesty, integrity, religious commitment," he wrote in the *Washington Times*. Savimbi had been fighting for twenty years "to liberate Angola, first from Portuguese control and later from the MPLA. . . . Mr. Savimbi's goal is to pressure the MPLA into negotiations with UNITA, leading to free elections with a guarantee that the winner of the elections will govern Angola. . . . The battle for Angola is not a 'civil war.' It is a battle over ideologies: Soviet totalitarianism vs. freedom, self-determination and democracy. U.S. aid to UNITA will send a strong signal to the world that the Reagan doctrine is not mere words, that we are determined to help freedom fighters resist Communist hegemony." Peter Worthington, a journalist who had visited Jamba, added a stirring detail: "Savimbi has 'political officers' throughout his army," he wrote in the *National Review*. "I found this disquieting until I sat in on lectures. . . . Lectures concentrated on the virtues of democracy, of multiple political choice, of free movement, of self-reliance, individual initiative, private property, free enterprise, fiscal accountability, balanced budgets, democracy, human rights, a humane and just judicial system, democratic institutions, rule by law and constitution, and other motherhood issues."[67]

U.S. officials understood that the myth these men were praising bore little relation to the real Jonas Savimbi. "Everybody knew that Savimbi had a dark side!" remarks Larry Napper, the deputy director of the office of Southern African Affairs at the State Department from 1986 to 1988. Savimbi had "a solid reputation for brutality and deceit," writes Brandon Grove, the U.S. ambassador in Zaire from 1984 to 1987. "Nobody on the U.S. side was duped about it," he adds. "Chester Crocker and his aides were under no illusion about the true nature of Savimbi as a ruthless man." Crocker's special assistant, Robert Cabelly, was the member of the Africa bureau who had the most frequent contact with Savimbi. "He was one of the most impressive men I have ever met," Cabelly recalls. "Ruthless. When you first met him he came across as very reasonable and a capitalist. But he was neither. He was very smooth, really a good speaker to any audience. But he was an extremely ruthless guy." Jeff Davidow, the director of the Office of Southern African Affairs from 1984 to 1986, is emphatic: "We all saw Savimbi as a charismatic figure who was extremely brutal."[68]

Charisma and ruthlessness were the attributes U.S. officials most often used to describe Savimbi. They captured the essence of the man. Anthony Hodges, arguably the foremost authority on independent Angola, painted a rounded portrait of the rebel leader: "A messianic sense of destiny drove him on in a quest for absolute power for more than three decades, whatever the setbacks or hurdles. Within UNITA he wielded absolute power, holding sway over his lieutenants in the manner of a cult leader. This was a product partly of his personal charisma and genuine leadership qualities, but it was reinforced by a fearsome security apparatus, a culture of zero tolerance of dissent and a personality cult that had parallels with those of Mao Tse-Tung and Kim Il-Sung."[69] Savimbi's biographer and erstwhile admirer wrote in 1995,

> in 1979–80, Savimbi began to execute those within UNITA who dared to question him, whatever the subject: politics, economics, or his unacceptable sexual behavior, or his right to tell his close aides whether they should get married or divorced. The leaders of the Chingunji clan . . . and the courteous foreign affairs secretary of UNITA . . . were among the first people in the leadership of the movement to challenge Savimbi in the late 1970s. They paid with their lives. As others dared say that the emperor had no clothes, the executions, tortures, and imprisonment in underground cells multiplied. The wives and children of the dissidents were burned alive in public displays to teach the others.[70]

## Savimbi's Critics

Whereas Savimbi's champions waxed eloquent about morality, those who opposed aid to UNITA argued in terms of U.S. narrow interests. This was true in the press and in Congress. I have examined seven newspapers that opposed aid to Savimbi: *New York Times*, *Washington Post*, *Christian Science Monitor*, *Los Angeles Times*, *Baltimore Sun*, *Atlanta Constitution*, and *Cleveland Plain Dealer*. Their opposition was based on two propositions. They feared, as the *Washington Post* explained, that "An aid connection with him would make the United States a working partner of South Africa, his leading sponsor, and would torpedo the administration's attempt to convey the idea that it is serious about wanting to end apartheid." And they also believed, as the *Los Angeles Times* said, that aid to Savimbi would make the Luanda government more dependent on Cuban-Soviet assistance and provide Angola "with justification for the prolongation of the Cuban expeditionary forces."[71]

These newspapers did not, however, challenge the heroic portrait of Savimbi drawn by his admirers, or they did so only fleetingly. They did not question his human rights record even though, in the words of Marrack Goulding, who was the British ambassador in Luanda in 1983–85, "UNITA's atrocities provided sufficient cause to oppose Savimbi's ambitions."[72] Granted, the Angolan government's policy of allowing very few Western journalists to enter the country was partly to blame for the U.S. press's ignorance, but UNITA's acts of terrorism were no secret. Indeed, UNITA itself often boasted of them. As the London *Times* noted, in July 1980 UNITA had taken credit for the bombing campaign in Angola's main cities. "Bombs were planted in the capital," Savimbi's biographer explains, "in the East German embassy, in the offices of Aeroflot, the Labor Ministry and the Luanda terminal of the Luanda-Malanje Railway." Amnesty International reminded its readers in 1983 and again in 1984: "In 1978 [UNITA] started an urban guerrilla campaign in Luanda, Huambo and other cities. Bombs exploded in public places, such as markets, and targets such as embassies or the commercial offices of East European countries were also bombed." And when Michael Hornsby, the London *Times*' southern Africa correspondent, visited Jamba in May 1984, Colonel Isidro Wambu Kasitu, one of Savimbi's senior intelligence officers, "had no hesitation in claiming responsibility for a bomb explosion in the central town of Huambo last month, which may have killed between 100 and 200 people. He also justified the blowing up of a Boeing 737 earlier this year on the grounds that 'we had good intelligence that MPLA . . . representatives were aboard.'"[73] In April 1984 the *New York Times* reported in passing that UNITA had claimed responsibility for the explosion in Huambo and had said that "the bombing killed 200 people, including 3 Soviet and 37 Cuban officers." And the *Washington Times* wrote, "Recently UNITA claimed responsibility for a car bombing outside Cuban airline offices in Luanda."[74]

The *New York Times* overlooked Savimbi's human rights violations until December 1984, when James Brooke, its correspondent covering Angola, reported from Huambo that "interviews here and in Luanda with health workers, religious leaders, military officials and international aid workers indicate that Mr. Savimbi's guerrilla campaign has wrecked the economy of the central highlands and is causing enormous hardship for the people of Mr. Savimbi's tribe, the Ovimbundu. These sources also assert that Savimbi has little control over units operating hundreds of miles from headquarters and that they often turn into freelance banditry."[75] During that same trip to Angola, Brooke wrote two more articles that referred to acts of terror perpetrated by UNITA: in one, datelined Luanda, he wrote that UNITA had "targeted Cuban workers for kidnapping and assassination" and that "UNITA's terror campaign has left the Cubans edgy," leaving readers the impression that the terror campaign was aimed only at Cubans. Brooke's only other reference to UNITA human right violations, in an article datelined Huambo, noted that the local MPLA military commander "charged that . . . [UNITA] burned crops, terrorized peasants and were trying to strangle the city." The fact that Brooke's only source was an MPLA official robbed the report of impact.[76]

The *New York Times* offered the most in-depth coverage of Angola of any American newspaper. (Its closest competitor was the *Washington Times*, a fervent champion of Savimbi.) It devoted the most ink to the debate that began in late 1985 about aid to Savimbi, but with the exception of a handful of columns by Anthony Lewis and the occasional op-ed, its reportage was shallow. It mentioned UNITA's human rights violations only twice, in passing.[77] The other newspapers that opposed aid said even less.

Just as they failed to convey UNITA's human rights violations, those U.S. newspapers that opposed aid to Savimbi did not probe his commitment to national reconciliation. Nor did they investigate his nationalist credentials, even though his collusion with the Portuguese during the Angolan war of independence had been extensively and publicly documented in Portugal. The mainstream Lisbon weekly *Expresso* had written in 1979: "The fact that Savimbi collaborated with the Portuguese colonial authorities has been so amply proved that no one can question it in good faith."[78] It was as if an iron curtain separated the West European press from the United States. The *Washington Post* wrote, "Mr. Savimbi has personal and *nationalist* credentials no less worthy, and by some lights perhaps more so than those of the Marxist-oriented president now sitting in Luanda." Alan Cowell, the *New York Times* South African correspondent, never referred to Savimbi's cooperation with the Portuguese colonial authority beyond one pithy statement: in April 1984, he noted that "Luanda propaganda" claimed that Savimbi had been "a sellout to the former Portuguese colonialists." Cowell did not elaborate.[79]

This is as far as the investigative drive of the U.S. press went—with one lone exception: in December 1985 Christopher Hitchens (a Briton) noted in the *Nation* that "we have it on the evidence" of General Costa Gomes, a former commander of the Portuguese troops in Angola, "that UNITA was a wholly owned subsidiary of the settler government [the Portuguese] in Angola and Jonas Savimbi was on the payroll."[80] The evidence that Savimbi had cooperated with the colonial authorities went well beyond Costa Gomes's words. Nevertheless, compared to everything else in the U.S. press, Hitchens had a scoop.

It may have been simple ignorance. Or perhaps journalists and editors did not think Savimbi's past cooperation with the Portuguese colonial authorities was important, not as important, for example, as the constantly repeated (and wrong) claim that he had received a Ph.D. from the University of Lausanne.[81] (In fact, the highest degree that Savimbi had received was a *licence* [Master of Arts] in political and legal sciences at the University of Lausanne in July 1965.)[82] Apparently the idea of a black African guerrilla leader holding a Ph.D. from a respected European university was more newsworthy than the fact that he had cooperated with the white colonial authorities or that his organization perpetrated atrocities against the population.

It was not only the press that was blinkered. A 1985 CIA analysis of the MPLA and UNITA noted, "Each side has accused the other of selling out its rival to the Portuguese during the anticolonial struggle (we suspect both charges may be accurate)." The State Department saw even less clearly. A 1987 study asserted that "UNITA has longstanding nationalist credentials . . . [and] is a credible nationalist force, with charismatic leadership and a heritage of anti-colonial struggle over decades."[83] These reports reflected the poor intelligence with which U.S. officials were saddled. Daniel Fenton, the only CIA analyst who worked full-time on Angola, had been a Soviet expert until 1981, when he joined the Southern Africa Branch. He received no detailed briefing, and he could neither read nor speak Portuguese. Perhaps, somewhere in the CIA archives there was a memo about Savimbi's connivance with the Portuguese colonial authorities, but if so, Fenton never saw it.[84]

Arguably, knowledge of Savimbi's collusion with the Portuguese would not have changed a single vote in the U.S. Congress, but it might have helped some Americans understand why the MPLA loathed him. A few years earlier, the diplomatic adviser of Portuguese president António Ramalho Eanes had bluntly explained to Crocker's senior deputy that "reconciliation with Savimbi was impossible. The MPLA reluctance to accept him was not just political, but psychological and related to what Savimbi represents in Angola. He had been linked to the colonial regime, including its secret police, . . . and had been ready to deal with the South Africans even before independence to 'cut his piece of the cake.'" These words seem not to have registered with U.S. officials. When I mentioned Savimbi's collusion with the Portuguese to Crocker—a former professor of African Studies—he replied, "It was not very high on my radar. I had heard rumors, reports about it in the *far left* Portuguese press."[85]

The poverty of the debate in the U.S. press was matched by the poverty of the debate in the U.S. Congress. With few exceptions, those members of Congress who opposed aid to Savimbi failed to question his human rights record, his nationalist credentials, or his commitment to political democracy.[86] When I asked Representative Wolpe whether he knew about Savimbi's collaboration with the Portuguese during Angola's war of independence, he replied, "I was more familiar with the fact that he had worked with the Chinese." (UNITA had received some military aid from Beijing in the late 1960s, and Savimbi had spouted pro-Chinese rhetoric.) "I was less familiar with the fact that he had worked with the Portuguese."[87] This was a disappointing reply from someone who had been an associate professor of African affairs at Western Michigan

University and, in 1985, the chair of the House Foreign Affairs Subcommittee on Africa. Steve Weissman, a respected scholar who was a staff member of the House Foreign Affairs Committee's Subcommittee on Africa, knew about Savimbi's collaboration with the Portuguese "but," he said, "I don't think that the anti-colonial issue was considered important by the members of Congress. And when you are briefing people you are constrained by what they want to know." Weissman and his colleagues sought to check Savimbi's human rights record. "We tried. We asked the CIA, the State Department [about human rights violations by UNITA]. They said there were none."[88] Perhaps Weissman and his colleagues failed to dig deeper because they knew that Savimbi's nationalist credentials and human rights record were not relevant for most members of Congress. The letter that Wolpe and 100 other members of Congress sent Reagan on November 25, 1985, opposing aid to Savimbi did not mention either.[89]

Probably few members of Congress read Savimbi's bombastic statement in *Policy Review*: "Do not underestimate the importance of your decision [on aid to UNITA]. For Angola is the Munich of Africa. Hesitation, the refusal to aid UNITA in its fight against the Cubans and the Soviets, will be taken as a signal by all the countries in the region that the United States has abandoned them to the Soviets as the West abandoned Czechoslovakia and Eastern Europe to Hitler in 1938."[90] But in a way, Savimbi hit the nail on the head: the vote in Congress about aid to UNITA was all about the U.S. fight against Cuba. This was why the truth—the sordid facts—about Savimbi was of no interest. "For Congress, Angola was of very minor importance, except as a way to hurt the Cubans," Weissman remarked as he explained why Congress approved aid to Savimbi. "We wanted to hurt Cuba, and we wanted to help people who wanted to hurt Cuba. When Savimbi said that he was 'fighting for freedom against Cuba'—this was his trump card. It was impossible to counter it. Savimbi had one redeeming quality: he killed Cubans."[91]

## What Kind of Aid?

A few hours after the repeal of the Clark Amendment had become effective on October 1, 1985, Representative Claude Pepper (D-Fla.) introduced a bill providing $27 million in humanitarian aid for UNITA. Pepper was a respected liberal. He also represented a Miami district that included a large number of Cuban Americans. He frankly told Congress that "a few months ago I was not any more aware of what was going on in Angola except in a general way that one is aware of other parts of the world that pass in a kaleidoscopic review from time to time before our mental and hindsight vision. But I was approached about

Hard-liners in the United States distrusted Secretary of State George Shultz. Their bill of indictment was long and included his policy toward Angola. This cartoon expresses their contempt for his advocacy of extending "moral support" to Jonas Savimbi, the chieftain waging guerrilla war against the pro-Cuban Angolan government, while withholding the military assistance they considered essential. In fact, Shultz did not oppose military aid for Savimbi, but he thought it should be kept quiet. (Copyright © 1986 The Washington Times LLC. This reprint does not constitute or imply any endorsement or sponsorship of any product, service, company, or organization.)

this matter by the Cuban-American [National] Foundation, which is in Miami, basically, although they have an office here. . . . They told me something about conditions in Angola. . . . I said I don't know anything about Savimbi . . . but I am for helping anybody that is fighting communism in Angola."[92]

Pepper's bill, which was cosponsored by presidential hopeful Jack Kemp (R-N.Y.), provoked a sharp reply from Secretary Shultz, who wrote to House Minority Leader Robert Michel (R-Ill.) urging him to "use his influence to discourage the proposed legislation." The bill was "ill-timed" and "will not contribute to the settlement we seek." Michel replied that aid to UNITA was "not only a geo-strategic, but a moral necessity."[93] Not to be outdone, Kemp vowed to complain directly to Reagan about Shultz's outrageous behavior. "I plan to take it to the Oval Office," he said.[94]

Hard-liners, who distrusted Shultz and the State Department, raised their war hatchets. "The State Department wrinkles a patrician nose at the disgusting idea of relying on force rather than negotiations to achieve a foreign-policy objective," wrote the associate editor of the *Dallas Morning News*, while Howard

Phillips, chair of the Conservative Caucus, mused, "Crocker has stalled for five years. I think he sympathizes with the communist government." This ridiculous statement reflected the views of an important segment of the Republican establishment.[95]

Contrary to what his critics claimed, Shultz was not trying to block aid to Savimbi. In his memoirs, he notes that in his letter to Michel he had asserted, "I feel strongly about Savimbi's courageous stand against Soviet aggression, but there are better ways to help." He explains,

> The last phrase was a way of reminding Michel of the far greater importance of covert and lethal assistance. The point was that the aid had to be delivered, and to obtain the cooperation of an acceptable neighboring state, delivery had to be deniable. . . .
>
> Conservatives in Congress, always suspicious of me and the State Department, went on a virtual rampage. Congressman Jack Kemp called for my resignation because I opposed open assistance to Savimbi. . . . The conservatives wanted an open vote as a matter of thumping their collective chests.
>
> On November 8, 1985, I had a stinging set-to with Jack Kemp in the Cabinet Room. The president turned pale at our harsh exchange, as Kemp harangued for an open vote for an open program and I tore into him, stating all the reasons why an open program would be a disaster. "Why don't you try thinking, Jack," I snapped. "How are we going to get aid delivered? Zaire and Zambia cannot openly support insurgents in another African state. And the aid has to go through there! If the aid isn't delivered, it's worthless to Savimbi."[96]

Zambia would not serve as a conduit for U.S. covert aid to what it called "the puppet UNITA movement,"[97] but Zaire would, as long as it was covert. The alternative would have been to provide aid through Namibia, but this would have increased Pretoria's leverage over the United States, and it would have exposed the administration to more charges of collusion with the apartheid regime. Crocker told the South African ambassador that this would not be done.[98]

Reagan's diary confirms Shultz's account of his November 8 clash with Kemp: "A meeting with our Repub. Cong. leadership," the president jotted on November 8. "Geo. S. [George Shultz] and Bud [McFarlane] reported on their Moscow trip. . . . Jack Kemp kicked up a fuss when he challenged the St. Dept about not supporting $27 mil. aid to Savimbi in Angola. Geo. replied that our objection was to Cong. making the aid overt. We want a covert operation for real help. Our problem is Cong. interference in what should be exec. office management of international diplomacy. Things got hot for awhile."[99] On November 12, 1985, four days after Shultz's clash with Kemp, Reagan signed a presidential finding authorizing a program of covert and lethal assistance to UNITA.[100] In early 1986 he approved $18 million in covert military aid to UNITA.[101]

The administration was not united on the purpose of the covert aid. Crocker and his aides did not believe that Savimbi would be able to seize power by force; they saw covert aid as a way "to give us leverage," as a Crocker aide says, in order to force President dos Santos to send the Cubans home. For many in the administration, however, the goal was "to help Savimbi win the war." This was the view of most within the intelligence services. Daniel Fenton, the senior analyst on Angola, remembers that he believed that "Savimbi had a chance, and people in the clandestine services and DIA were even more sanguine." Doug Smith, who was the CIA station chief in Kinshasa in 1983–86, agrees. He believed that Savimbi had a chance of winning despite the presence of the Cuban troops in Angola; he thought that "his army would grow big enough and strong enough to push the Cubans out."[102]

On February 19, 1986, the *Washington Times* announced the good news: "For the first time yesterday, the Reagan administration openly admitted that it is providing, or will soon provide, 'covert aid' to the rebel forces of Jonas Savimbi." The admission had been made by Crocker at an open hearing of the Senate Foreign Relations Committee. "Certain decisions have been made to provide both moral and material assistance [to Savimbi] . . . and to do so in ways that are effective and appropriate." Ronald Reagan had squared the circle: this "covert" assistance was overt. Former assistant secretary for Africa Richard Moose bluntly told the same committee, "It is certainly the most widely advertised and announced in advance program of clandestine, covert assistance that I think we have ever known. . . . I think what 'covert' now means is that everybody knows about it but it is deniable. I think this is one of the ways they talk about it in the Executive Branch." What remained unspoken was the route through which the weapons reached the rebels, but it too was an open secret. The administration had turned to Mobutu. "Events in Angola are unfolding rapidly," Reagan wrote the Zairean dictator on February 18, 1986. "We . . . will give Jonas Savimbi effective support. . . . I . . . am determined that the United States make a difference in Angola."[103]

## Enter Mobutu

Mobutu's regime was repressive and inept. "The level of professionalism and preparedness of even the best trained Zairean units . . . [was] abysmal," the CIA stated in 1982; corruption and mismanagement of the economy were rampant. "Mobutu and his cronies had been plundering the country for two decades and found it hard to stop," wrote Brandon Grove, who was the U.S. ambassador in Kinshasa in 1984–87. The result was "destitution, absence of human rights, disintegrating infrastructure, one-man rule."[104] Mobutu, however, had a redeeming quality: he was an enemy of the Soviet Union and Cuba, and he loathed the MPLA. In September 1984 Reagan jotted in his diary that Mobutu was "a darn good leader & friend of the U.S."[105]

Many times, during his long association with the United States, Mobutu had fretted that the Americans did not treat him with the respect he deserved. But once the Reagan administration geared up to help Savimbi, Mobutu would be courted. In late 1985, Ambassador Grove writes, Mobutu "was delighted by a 'black' clandestine visit from CIA Director William Casey, who arrived in his windowless C-130." Casey explained that the United States wanted "covert . . . access to Kamina airfield, near the Angolan border but in deplorable conditions, to supply Savimbi's forces with sophisticated antiaircraft and antitank weapons. We would restore the airport and its control tower and repair a gaping crater in the runway."[106]

Then, on May 22, 1986, General Vernon Walters, Reagan's peripatetic special emissary, left Washington for Kinshasa, hand-carrying a letter from Reagan to Mobutu. "Dear Mr. President," the letter read: "The last few weeks have prompted renewed reflection on the relations between the United States and Zaire. I take comfort in the realization that, throughout the period you have served at the helm of Zaire, our two countries have been steady, constructive and even courageous partners in Africa and beyond. . . . Secretary Weinberger informs me . . . that his staff has given intensive attention to the kind offer you made last fall [when the U.S. Congress was debating aid to Savimbi] concerning the possible utilization of Zairian facilities at Kitona and Kamina. . . . As you know I value your friendship greatly and am confident that working together we may preserve and expand the ties and interests our countries share in common."[107] Mobutu "loved getting messages from U.S. presidents," Ambassador Grove recalls. "It fed his ego. And he thought that Walters walked on water."[108]

On May 23, Walters cabled Shultz that he had spoken with Mobutu for four hours. The Zairean dictator was wary, or pretended to be, that his offer to help the United States assist Savimbi might expose him to retaliation from Angola and its friends. ("In fact he was eager to help," remarks Doug Smith, the CIA station chief in Kinshasa—he just wanted to be courted.) "I assured him categorically," Walters told Shultz, "that a country that had responded as it had in

Grenada [the October 1983 invasion] and in Libya [the April 1986 air strikes] and which had responded to previous attacks on Zaire as it had, would not stand by idly if a friend and ally like Zaire were attacked." When Mobutu "spoke warmly of his meetings with American leaders over the years, including former president Nixon [and] DCI Casey . . . I stressed throughout that I would bring all of his concerns to the attention of our president, who cared deeply about Zaire and about him personally. . . . We recognized him as a friend and ally willing to take a lot of African heat for being of assistance."[109]

Mobutu became, in the words of a U.S. official, "our indispensable partner," offering his country as the conduit for U.S. aid to UNITA.[110] Robert Gates, who was the CIA's Deputy Director of Intelligence until April 1986 (when he was promoted to Deputy Director of the agency), wrote that "weapons and other military equipment were soon flowing to Savimbi. . . . Our airlift was a masterpiece of logistical planning as we often used a single C-130 to ferry goods from our staging base to Jamba." The staging base was Kamina airfield in Zaire. From there, the cargo was flown "to Luyana, approximately 50 kilometers from Jamba," recalled UNITA general Nunda. "Everything that came from Kamina went to Luyana. Savimbi wanted to control the aid. After receiving it, he distributed it to the fronts."[111]

The Americans sent communication equipment ("radios that were much better than what the South Africans had given us," remarked Nunda), TOW anti-tank missiles, and Stingers, highly accurate shoulder-fired ground-to-air missiles with an effective range of about three miles. With the weapons came the instructors. "We trained UNITA on how to use these weapons; the CIA had people in Jamba," explained Herman Cohen, the NSC director for Africa. The training took place "approximately three miles from Jamba," Nunda added. "There were small teams of instructors who rotated frequently," recalled Kinshasa station chief Smith, who oversaw the beginning of the program, "as well as a liaison officer who maintained a permanent contact with Savimbi." It was the first time that CIA officers were stationed in Jamba. But they did not improve U.S. understanding of the situation. "They were isolated and under constant surveillance," laments Daniel Fenton, the senior CIA analyst on Angola. "They talked only to Savimbi and his chosen few. They lived in a compound, and they had no real freedom of movement."[112]

The SADF also had people in Jamba "to train us," said General Nunda.[113] As in 1975, South African military instructors and CIA paramilitary officers worked almost side by side, separated by just a few miles, helping UNITA. "There was good cooperation with the CIA," mused South African general Thirion, and he added, "The CIA supported UNITA already before 1986." The aid, he stressed, had begun under Carter and increased under Reagan.[114]

## Savimbi in Washington

The debate on whether to send aid to UNITA was almost over by the time Savimbi arrived in the United States on January 28, 1986. His ten-day visit included a brief meeting with Reagan followed by four hours with DCI Casey. Savimbi also met other senior officials, including Weinberger and Shultz—who assured him that Reagan was "'turned on' on this."[115] It was Savimbi's first visit since 1981. As the *Wall Street Journal* pointed out, he had become "the favorite anti-Communist hero of American conservatives."[116] It made sense. The Nicaraguan Contras had no charismatic leader; nor did the Cambodian rebels or RENAMO. The mujahedin leaders in Afghanistan were shadowy, foreign characters with none of the spit and polish of Savimbi, who did not hide their Islamist beliefs and made little attempt to praise the United States, capitalism, or Western values. Savimbi stood out. He spoke English fluently, he exuded confidence, and he told Americans what they wanted to hear. The debate of the previous months in Washington, in which his supporters had been far more eloquent than those who opposed aid, had burnished his luster. "Savimbi began to emerge as something of a folk hero," a senior Crocker aide mused. While in the United States, the chieftain was feted like a conquering hero and freedom's champion. He did not disappoint. He was charismatic and eloquent. The well-connected lobbying firm of Black, Manafort, Stone and Kelly had been counseling him since the previous summer—for a $600,000-a-year contract. "He was meticulously coached on everything from how to answer his critics to how to compliment his patrons," the *Washington Post* reported.[117]

The enthusiasm generated by Savimbi's visit intensified the pressure on U.S. companies doing business with the MPLA government. Until that point, the Reagan administration had not discouraged business ties with Angola. As President dos Santos told Castro in August 1985, the Reagan administration "could have hindered the economic and financial relations [between the United States and Angola], but it didn't. The United States is the foremost trading partner of Angola, and Angola is perhaps the fourth trading partner of the United States in Africa."[118] There were "probably close to 100 U.S. firms" doing business with Angola, a U.S. official told the *Washington Post* in early 1986. Gulf Oil, a subsidiary of Chevron, led the pack. With $600 million in Angolan assets, it was the country's largest foreign investor and had paid the Angolan government $580 million in taxes and royalties in 1985. In the first quarter of 1986, its 49 percent share of production in the Cabinda offshore fields reached 100,000 barrels a day. Since 1976, the U.S. Export-Import Bank had extended $214 million to U.S. firms doing business in Angola and was considering making additional loan guarantees and credits to help U.S. oil companies expand the country's oil production.[119]

Hard-liners in the United States had been grumbling about this. The *National Security Record* scoffed, for example, that "some Western bankers and businessmen not only will sell communists the rope that might hang them, they will do it on credit," while Representative Phil Crane (R-Ill.) fumed: "It is ludicrous for the bank to aid in the financing of a project for a communist nation, while President Reagan publicly embraces that country's rebel leader, Jonas Savimbi."[120] Chevron and the other American companies that did business with Angola opposed U.S. aid to Savimbi, but not loudly. "They would come to my office to plead with me to oppose it," recalls Congressman Wolpe, "but they weren't willing to say it publicly for fear of antagonizing the [Reagan] administration" and stoking the wrath of the Republican right.[121]

Savimbi's visit raised the heat. The major target of the conservatives' ire was Chevron. "Chevron's Cabinda operation should be recognized for what it is, a source of Communist funds, and shut down," the *Washington Times* wrote. On January 28, Chair of the Conservative Caucus Phillips announced the formation of a coalition of more than twenty-five groups pledged to force Chevron out of Angola. The campaign against Chevron included, *Human Events* reported, "the distribution of materials calling attention to the company's role in Angola. A 'wanted' poster features George Keller, chairman of the board of Chevron, who is charged with 'supplying $2-billion-plus of aid and comfort annually to America's Soviet enemy in Cuban-occupied Angola.'. . . Phillips, when asked if the Gulf installation in Angola should be considered a legitimate military target for Savimbi's forces, said, 'Absolutely.'" The head of the Freedom Research Center, Jack Wheeler, went further, urging that "conservatives and other supporters of Savimbi request of him," as a quid pro quo for their support, that he pledge "to inflict substantial damage to the facilities of Gulf Oil."[122]

Even the State Department distanced itself from companies doing business in Angola. On January 28, Crocker said, "'They should be thinking about U.S. national interest as well as their own corporate interests as they make their decisions.'. . . Crocker stopped short of asking American firms to leave Angola," the *Washington Post* noted, "but it was the first time a high-ranking State Department officer had suggested that they might be acting against the national interest by helping to finance the Marxist government."[123]

In the United States conservative groups were appalled that American companies did business with the government of Angola. Their major target was Chevron.

## The Minuet Resumes

Despite the hardening of its position toward Angola, the Reagan administration continued to endorse linkage. That meant not only forcing Luanda to ask the Cuban troops to leave, but also convincing Pretoria to implement Resolution 435—UN supervised elections in Namibia—once the Cubans left Angola.

Pik Botha, Bud McFarlane, and Chet Crocker had met in Vienna in August 1985 to clear the air after the SADF's attempt to blow up Gulf Oil's storage tanks in Cabinda and Pik Botha's rude rejection of the synthesis paper (which proposed that 80 percent of the Cubans leave Angola in the first year and 20 percent in the second). The following month, a South African delegation had flown to Washington to assure the Americans that Pretoria remained committed "100%" to linkage and would "seriously consider the 80/20 percent formula" but first needed to clear up some "reasonable concerns." After the meeting, David Steward, the senior Foreign Ministry official who headed the delegation, reported: "We were given a courteous hearing by the Americans but at times they did little to hide their exasperation. . . . We were struck in general by the degree to which U.S. confidence in South Africa had been poisoned by recent developments." These "recent developments" included Pretoria's attempted raid on Cabinda, its creation of the transitional government in Namibia, its attack on Botswana, and the revelation that it had continued to help RENAMO in violation of the Nkomati pact.[124]

On October 4, 1985, PW Botha wrote to Reagan. He could not resist a gentle dig: "As you know, my Government was dismayed when it learned that the United States had abandoned what we had always understood to be our common position that the withdrawal of Cuban forces would take place on a parallel and simultaneous basis with the reduction of our own forces in terms of United Nations Security Council Resolution [UNSCR] 435." The tone of the letter, however, was positive: South Africa was willing to let bygones be bygones. "My government will soon be considering the feasibility of 80% of the Cubans being withdrawn during the first year of the implementation of UNSCR 435 and 20% during the second." On November 22, Pik Botha wrote Shultz that South Africa would accept the U.S. 80/20 proposal if six conditions were fulfilled, the most important being the protection of UNITA's interests: the United States must confirm that it "would, in cooperation with the RSA [Republic of South Africa], compensate UNITA for any possible detrimental effect" caused by a settlement based on linkage, "in such way that UNITA's overall capability would not be impaired."[125]

The Americans chose to read Pik Botha's response as a green light to resume the negotiations, but Pretoria's policy had not changed. It still had no intention of honoring its pledges about linkage to the United States. Nor did it intend to grant Namibia independence unless and until Savimbi was in charge in Luanda. Pretoria saw UNITA's "final takeover of the government" as a precondition "for a solution of the SWA [Namibia] question." With Savimbi in Luanda SWAPO would be crushed, the docile Democratic Turnhalle Alliance would govern a nominally independent Namibia, and Angola would join "the community of southern African states" with Pretoria at its core.[126] This was South Africa's policy when the delegation led by Steward flew to Washington in September 1985 to resume talks with the Americans, and it remained South Africa's policy when Pik Botha told Shultz the following November that Pretoria accepted the synthesis paper: the South Africans were just stringing the Americans along. On November 1, 1985, Defense Minister Malan said that "our task is to bring a friendly government to power in Angola that will join in the establishing a group of states in southern Africa that will cooperate with each other in every sphere." Pik Botha could not have been more clear when he addressed the Namibian transitional government: "There can only be Cuban withdrawal if there is reconciliation in Angola. If there is reconciliation in Angola, then it's all over for dos Santos . . . and then it is definitely over for SWAPO."[127]

Talks between Luanda and Washington had resumed, haltingly, in October 1985, and the Americans were hard at work convincing the Angolans to accept the 80/20 percent formula,[128] when Reagan decided to extend military aid to UNITA and Savimbi arrived in Washington. Angola broke off the talks.

## CHAPTER 12

# The View from Cuba, 1984–1986

## The U.S. Threat

Reagan's landslide in November 1984 deepened Cuba's anxieties of a U.S. attack. Reagan's rhetoric fanned these fears. He told the American Bar Association that five countries—"a confederation of terrorist states . . . a new, international version of Murder Incorporated"—were responsible for "the growth of terrorism in recent years." They were Iran, Libya, North Korea, Nicaragua, and Cuba. The president warned: "These terrorist states are now engaged in acts of war against the government and people of the United States. And under international law, any state which is the victim of acts of war has the right to defend itself." His words were echoed by Secretary of State Shultz, who told the *New York Times*: "It is proper for the United States to strike at military targets in countries supporting terrorism, even if the target has no direct connection with a particular terrorist act."[1] This was no bluster: the United States launched air strikes against Libya in April 1986. Closer to Cuba, it was waging undeclared war on Nicaragua.

Administration officials urged Congress to continue funding the Nicaraguan Contras because otherwise, Secretary Shultz warned in May 1985, the United States would "be faced with an agonizing choice about the use of American combat troops" in Nicaragua. The *New York Times* wrote, "The administration contends that the 'contra' war is insurance against direct U.S. intervention. It could well have the opposite effect, provoking events that would eventually impel the use of American forces."[2]

Perhaps the administration's rhetoric was part of a psychological campaign to spur congressional aid to the Contras and to intimidate the Sandinistas. But Reagan did believe that the Sandinistas were Marxist-Leninists and that the United States could not tolerate a Marxist-Leninist regime in Central America.

He also believed that there could be no negotiated agreement with the Sandinistas. He told a group of close aides that it was "so far-fetched to imagine that a communist government like that [the Sandinistas] would make any reasonable deal with us" that there was only one reason to hold talks with Nicaragua: "to get Congress to support the anti-Sandinistas."[3] If Reagan was determined to rid Nicaragua of the Sandinistas, and if the Contras failed—and they were bound to fail—the only alternative was a U.S. invasion.

The Cubans took the threat seriously. "The Reagan administration has decided to liquidate the Nicaraguan revolution," Raúl Castro told GDR leader Honecker in April 1985.[4] There were several hundred Cuban military personnel in Nicaragua, and they were under orders from Havana to fight if the Americans attacked. This would cause Washington to retaliate, the Cuban government feared, with surgical air strikes against Cuba or a blockade. In a January 1985 interview, Cuban deputy foreign minister Ricardo Alarcón told James Nelson Goodsell, the well-known correspondent of the *Christian Science Monitor*: "We have to take seriously the threatening statements that various North American officials have made, including President Reagan himself. And we cannot play around with the reality that a very powerful neighbor maintains a hostile attitude that does not exclude an armed attack against our country."

Goodsell was not convinced. The Cubans' warnings of a possible U.S. attack were "a lot of rhetoric," he told his readers. They were "probably designed to stir public support for the Castro government" in the midst of an economic crisis. Goodsell thought it much more likely that Reagan would extend an olive branch to Cuba. "Cuban officials . . . are asking . . . whether in his second term Ronald Reagan might want to move to tidy up relations with the island," he reported.[5]

Alarcón dismisses that notion categorically. "Many journalists rely a lot on preconceived ideas. Goodsell came to Havana with a theory: Reagan had been reelected, and the best moment for any president, when he is the most free, is after he has been reelected. When Reagan's second term began, U.S. journalists said he would seize the opportunity to improve relations with Cuba. There was a whole series of dunces who repeated this ridiculous refrain. Whenever we mentioned the possibility of a U.S. attack, they dismissed it as propaganda. Perhaps Goodsell talked to some Cubans who voiced the hope that Reagan would improve relations, but this was not the view of the Cuban government. For us, Reagan's reelection meant that the danger increased!"[6]

The Cubans knew that if the United States attacked, they were on their own. This had been Andropov's message to Raúl Castro in December 1982. In January 1984 Fidel Castro told Demichev, a member of the Soviet Politburo:

I don't think we need to discuss the problems of Cuban security now. Comrades Raúl and Andropov touched on it, but there is more to say. . . . Someday Comrade Andropov and I should sit together and analyze all the problems related with the security of Cuba, beginning with the Missile Crisis and proceeding all the way to the present. . . . There may be many measures that can enhance our security without resorting to a nuclear war. . . . Some things are being done, concrete steps to strengthen our military capabilities. . . .

In short, I want to restate our position: the defense of our country is the fundamental task of our people, it is our duty. . . . But we didn't like the way this was addressed [in the meeting between Raúl and Andropov]. . . . This is something I have to discuss with Comrade Andropov, when he is in good health.[7]

Castro never had this conversation—not with Andropov, who died one month later, and not with his successors. Until late 1986, when the Iran-Contra scandal weakened Reagan, Cuba believed it faced a constant threat from the United States. Looking back, in November 1987, Castro told a group of top aides, "If the Americans launch an air strike . . . what can we do? . . . Ah! Well, [we can attack] their base [Guantánamo] and then we have a major war. . . . We don't have the means to respond to an air strike. . . . We can shoot down a plane, two planes, even three, but look at what they did in Libya: they jammed all the radars and all the antiaircraft weapons and waged a technological war. And in technological warfare they have the advantage. . . . While we are prepared [to fight], we have also done our best to avoid [an armed conflict with the United States] . . ., with dignity, and we will try to avoid it for as long as possible. In the final analysis, the greatest success of our military preparations has been to arrive to the end of the Reagan presidency intact . . . without a war, because the Americans . . . can wage a war against Cuba without taking any casualties: they would move their aircraft carriers into position and start bombarding our coasts in twenty different places and we wouldn't be able to do anything about it."[8]

## Bilateral Relations

"You must keep in mind that the United States is an important adversary," José Luis Padrón, a close aide of Fidel Castro, told me. "We had to be ready for any kind of emergency that might arise, in order to address it efficiently and avert a crisis. Therefore, we wanted a direct channel. Fidel has always been a person, since the days of the Sierra [Maestra], who has sought a direct channel to discuss important issues." The Reagan administration was not interested. "During the Reagan years my contacts with the U.S. government were very rare, practically nothing," recalled Ramón Sánchez-Parodi, who was the head of the Cuban Interests Section in Washington. This increased the importance of the U.S. diplomats in Havana, at least in Castro's eyes. The Cubans "understood that we didn't want to talk with them through their Interests Section in Washington," explained John Ferch, who headed the U.S. Interests Section in Havana in 1982–85. "If they wanted to talk to us it had to be in Havana. I was in contact with Padrón, [Deputy Foreign Minister] Alarcón, [Antonio] Arbesú [a senior intelligence officer], and [Carlos Martínez] Salsamendi [the foreign policy adviser of Vice President Carlos Rafael Rodríguez]. Salsamendi didn't like us. He couldn't get over his personal anger and deal with me in a relaxed way. The others could. They didn't want slip-ups; they wanted effective relations, effective communication. I took them to lunch, they took me to lunch. It was all very friendly, very professional."[9]

Ferch scrupulously informed the State Department of his conversations with his Cuban counterparts, but, he told me, he received no feedback. "Nonetheless, I was talking with the Cubans all the time." He also busied himself writing reports, particularly on the Cuban economy. But even so, he concedes, "It wasn't the busiest job in the world."[10]

Reagan was willing to negotiate with Cuba on only one issue, immigration, and this only after he had been persuaded that there was no other way to get rid of "the excludables," those Cubans who had arrived in the United States during Mariel and were not admissible under U.S. law because they were mentally ill or had committed serious crimes. "That's the only thing he would authorize us to talk about," remarked Kenneth Skoug, who was the director of the State Department's Office of Cuban Affairs.[11] The talks began in July 1984 in New York. "Cuba uses every possible opportunity to negotiate with the United States," Castro told a senior East German official. "We want to show the Americans that negotiations that are based on equality and are about specific issues are advantageous for both sides."[12] On December 14, 1984, the two countries concluded an immigration agreement. Cuba would allow the return of 2,746 excludables in groups of 100 per month. The United States agreed to resume normal visa processing in Havana, which had been suspended in 1980 at the height of the Mariel crisis; this meant the issuance of preference immigrant visas to up to 20,000 Cubans each year.[13] But when Castro suggested in a *Washington Post* interview that the two governments build on this first step and engage in conversations on other areas of mutual interest—such as coast guard activities, radio signal interference, and air hijacking—Washington's response was a stinging rebuff: first Cuba must prove its good faith by ending its subversive activities abroad and its human rights violations at home.[14]

There was nothing to discuss. The Reagan administration wanted the Cubans out of Angola. It even opposed Cuban technical assistance abroad. "They engage in all sorts of activity that we don't welcome," Skoug explained. "Sometimes they go into a country and teach people to read. Yet at the same time the things people are learning to read contain political indoctrination. Their engineers build roads, but at the same time the roads are militarily significant."[15] (Skoug did not mention doctors, but they too might have been subversive: by saving lives, they gained friends for Cuba.) As for Central America, Reagan's position was straightforward: the United States had the right, even the duty, to help the rebels who sought to overthrow the Nicaraguan government, and it could mine the Nicaraguan ports (as the CIA did in early 1984), but Cuban support for the Salvadoran and Guatemalan rebels, which was a fraction of the aid the United States was giving the Contras, was, like the Cuban presence in Nicaragua, intolerable.

In late April 1985, Elliott Abrams became the assistant secretary of state for Latin America. "'Tough' Guy for Latin Job," the *New York Times* declared.[16] In a State Department that the true Reaganites considered hopelessly effete, Abrams was the exception. A political appointee, he was a charter member of the neoconservative movement, and he was also very close to the furiously anti-Castro Cuban American National Foundation (CANF). "It was a little like having the CANF sitting on the Sixth Floor [which housed the offices of senior State Department officials]," Skoug remarked.[17] "As far as Cuba was concerned," he added, "Abrams's concern at first was that we hadn't been tough enough . . . so he was looking for ways to get tougher on Cuba. But we'd been over all that . . . I understood the Reagan administration to want a tough line on Cuba without getting involved in shooting, and that's essentially what we did. . . . While Abrams's basic element was that he wanted to be as tough on Cuba as possible, he very soon came to see that we were already being very tough on Cuba."[18]

On May 20, 1985, Radio Martí began broadcasting to Cuba from Miami. Officially placed under the Voice of America, it was run and largely staffed by Cuban Americans, "many of whom were recruited by Jorge Mas [Canosa]," the director of the Cuban American National Foundation.[19] The Cuban government considered the radio station "a calculated insult," the Canadian Embassy in Havana noted.[20] It responded that same day by suspending the immigration agreement. In a perceptive article, Arthur Schlesinger Jr. wrote,

The Cubans . . . especially resent the cynical exploitation of the revered national hero by politicians who had never previously heard of Jose Marti and still have not read a line he has written. (According to the useful publication Times of the Americas, the first White House press release announced the intention of establishing a "Radio Joe Marti.") Jose Marti, who lived for many years in Brooklyn, had great affection for the U.S. But he was also eloquently fearful of the impact of North American power on Latin America. "Once the United States is in Cuba," he asked in 1889, "who will drive them out?" "The further they draw away from the United States," he wrote in 1894, "the freer and more prosperous the [Latin] American people will be."

Schlesinger was also right on another point. He explained: "The Reagan administration, Mr. Castro concludes, interprets every Cuban gesture of goodwill as proof of Cuban weakness. . . . Lest a soft response to Radio Marti be taken as further proof of weakness, Mr. Castro struck back by suspending the immigration agreement."[21] The Cubans "overreacted to Radio Martí," Skoug adds. "They thought it would have a lot of impact on Cuba." They were, however, wrong, as the Canadian Embassy reported two years later: Radio Martí had "not lived up to American expectations."[22]

Ferch left Havana in the summer of 1985. He was replaced by the urbane Curtis Kamman, who had been the deputy chief of mission in the U.S. Embassy in Moscow. When I told Kamman about Ferch's lunches with Alarcón and company, he laughed. "I did see Alarcón, in his office—no lunch! Alarcón was the designated senior person in the Foreign Ministry to see me. I met Arbesú a few times. He and Alarcón were very smart. I don't think I ever met Padrón; I might have met Salsamendi once or twice." The meetings were formal. "The Cubans were not expecting very much from me [i.e., from the United States]," Kamman mused. "They were very polite to me, they didn't treat me badly, but there were no expectations." The Reagan administration had made it clear that it did not want to talk with the Cubans, and much less negotiate with them, except about immigration.[23]

When I asked Kamman what the State Department expected him to do in Havana, he replied, "What was I expected to do? I had to ask myself that question. I managed the Interests Section; there was a fair amount of consular work; I would talk to my colleagues from other embassies to find out what was going on in Cuba; I would learn what I could and report on what was going on; and I would deliver the occasional note on the Coast Guard, drug problems, etc." He concluded, "I was doing everything I could, but I didn't have very much to do. There was a sort of freeze in the relations."[24]

Neither Ferch nor Kamman communicated with Crocker and his aides at the Africa bureau of the State Department. "I don't think I had any meaningful discussion with them while I was in Havana. My channel was Elliott Abrams," Kamman recalls. There was a sharp division of responsibilities in the State Department concerning Cuba: the Africa bureau negotiated with the Angolans about the departure of the Cuban troops, but it had no contacts with the Cubans; the Bureau of Inter-American Affairs dealt with them.[25] This divide, which had existed from the outset of the Reagan administration, deepened in 1985 when Elliott Abrams took over Inter-American Affairs. The Africa bureau remained under the control of mainstream Republicans but Latin America passed to the ideologues. "The Africa bureau did not share our views on Cuba," Skoug said. "There was a distance, a coolness, you might say, between us."[26]

## Cuba and Central America

Havana's aid to the Salvadoran and Guatemalan rebels was heartfelt but limited to military training and medical assistance in Cuba, political advice, and diplomatic support. It is unlikely that many weapons reached the Salvadoran rebels in the 1980s from Cuba or Nicaragua. "The Salvadoran revolution . . . remains strong, even though they have received very little outside aid because it is very difficult to get it to them," Castro told Soviet foreign minister Eduard Shevardnadze in October 1985.[27] (As for the Guatemalans, they received very few weapons from abroad, whether from Cuba or other sources.)

Cuba's major commitment in Central America was its assistance to Nicaragua. In his October 24, 1985, address to the General Assembly of the United Nations, Reagan flatly stated that there were "in Nicaragua some 8,000 Soviet bloc and Cuban personnel, including about 3,500 military and secret police personnel." Nicaragua's president Daniel Ortega, who was present in the Great Hall of the General Assembly when Reagan spoke, told the journalists who surrounded him that either Reagan had been poorly briefed or he was lying, because there were only 700 military advisers, "all Cubans," in Nicaragua.[28] Four days later, Castro told Shevardnadze: "Daniel [Ortega] said . . . that there are approximately 700 Cuban military personnel in Nicaragua and this is true. . . . A few are military advisers. The others teach in military schools; they serve as instructors for the officers and for the troops because the Nicaraguans need to form many cadres." At one moment there had been more than 1,000 Cuban military personnel there, Castro added, but "we cut this down to the bone" at the request of the Sandinistas "in order to minimize grist for the U.S. propaganda mill."[29] The first group of Cuban military instructors had left Nicaragua in May 1985.[30]

There were also Cuban aid workers in Nicaragua. Their number had peaked to 4,000 in 1984. "We pay their salaries," Castro said, "and the Nicaraguans give them board and lodging. It does not cost us anything in hard currency. Therefore, it does not create a problem for us."[31] Initially, the largest group of aid workers—approximately 2,000 per year—were primary school teachers. The Sandinista government had decided to bring education to rural areas that had no schools and no teachers and had turned to Cuba for help.[32]

After the U.S. invasion of Grenada, Havana's fears of an attack on Nicaragua increased, and it withdrew the female teachers. By late 1985 all the teachers had returned to Cuba. They left for two reasons: in their isolated outposts in the countryside they were an easy target for the spreading Contra war, and they were also a convenient target for U.S. officials decrying Castro's efforts to subvert the country's rural population. No one replaced them.

By the time Castro met Soviet foreign minister Shevardnadze, in October 1985, the number of Cubans in Nicaragua—military and civilian—was down to 1,500. Only aid workers with extensive military training were sent to Nicaragua. Castro told Shevardnadze: "Our people have to be able to fight if there's an invasion like in Grenada. They have to have military training and be the right age." He added, "We've cut the number of Cubans there to the minimum. If we have to send more we will, . . . but we've tried to limit our cooperation to only the really indispensable areas, like medicine, military affairs and security. We've helped prepare thousands of cadres, and we also help them to form cadres here in Cuba."[33] While the number of Cubans in Nicaragua had been reduced, one principle remained, unshakeable: if the United States invaded Nicaragua, the Cubans who were there would fight, shoulder to shoulder with the Sandinistas.

## The Debt Crisis

Facing the implacable hostility of the Reagan administration, Cuba sought to strengthen its ties with Latin America, which was buffeted by an unprecedented liquidity crisis. By 1985 the external debt of the Latin American countries was almost $370 billion. They were unable to pay the interest, much less the principal when it came due. Their creditors—Western banks and Western governments—would renegotiate payment schedules only with those governments that agreed to follow the strictures of the International Monetary Fund. "Until now," an economist observed in August 1985, "the debtors have been obliged to shoulder most of the burden, through austerity and reduced living standards prescribed by the International Monetary Fund. Few if any concessions have been forthcoming from either banks or creditor countries. . . . In effect domestic [Latin American] development has been postponed indefinitely for the sake of preserving credit-worthiness in international financial markets."[34] As poverty deepened throughout the region, Latin American governments sought ways out.

Havana seized the opportunity. In Castro's words, "Cuba raised the banner and led the struggle to find a solution to this problem."[35] It became the dominant topic in its talks with other Latin Americans; it was the bridge that could span the chasm that separated them. Raúl Castro explained to Honecker in April 1985, "In Latin America a new situation has arisen that could have unforeseeable consequences. The cause is the immense debt burden that is crushing the Latin American countries. . . . Never before in the brief history of independent Latin America has there been a chance to unite all the people, regardless of class differences, under a common banner . . . . We have decided to begin a process of rapprochement with the other Latin American states in the hope of bringing us all together despite our different forms of government. We have embarked on this process without illusions and fully aware of its difficulties."[36]

In February 1986, Fidel Castro told the Third Congress of the Cuban Communist Party, "The formula proposed by Cuba is uncomplicated, easy to understand, and easily implemented . . .: Third World countries are in debt to First World banks; the governments of the developed countries must assume the debts owed to their banks."[37] There was no chance that Castro's solution would be adopted: the creditors rejected it out of hand. And yet, the *New York Times* wrote, "the leaders of many [Latin American] countries are privately delighted by the Castro campaign. 'He is improving our bargaining position with the banks,' said one diplomat. 'He is pushing them to the wall with the idea that we won't pay. We will pay; we have to pay. But we can only pay if the rules of the game are changed. We have to have better terms. Castro is pushing for all of us. He is saying things we don't dare say. He may help us find some middle ground, and we appreciate this.'"[38] A few months later Tad Szulc, one of the most perceptive U.S. journalists covering Latin America, concluded:

> Unquestionably Castro has rendered extraordinary service to all sides—including the U.S. banks and government—by calling attention, with his special flair for drama, to the immensely explosive political dimensions of the debt problem. He raised the consciousness of workers in Brazil and bankers in New York about the catastrophic potential of the debt, doing away

with the comfortable misconception that the issue was purely financial—not political. Sounding his alarm, Castro instantly commanded attention among fellow Latin Americans. Many governments were pleased that the Cuban president had brutally spelled out truths they dared not express in public, and the debt question became a shared concern around which a brand new relationship with Havana began to develop this year. Cuba's political and diplomatic isolation . . . was clearly coming to an end.[39]

The debt crisis also affected the Cuban economy. Most of its trade was with the Soviet bloc, but a precious 14 percent was in hard currency with Western countries. Drought, a poor sugar harvest, and lower prices for its major exports meant that by 1986 the value of Cuba's hard currency receipts had sharply decreased, and it was unable to meet its obligations to its Western creditors. In December 1986, Castro told the Third Congress of the Cuban Communist Party that Cuba would "have only half the amount that we have usually spent on imports in hard currency. Whereas in the past we had at least $1,200 million for imports, now that has been cut down to $600 million."[40] This would affect economic growth and living standards, which had steadily improved in the early 1980s.

Meanwhile, in Moscow a new leader, Mikhail Gorbachev, sought to restructure his country's economic relations with the other members of the Soviet bloc to relieve the burden on the ailing Soviet economy. In late October 1986, he told the Politburo: "We are going to have a meeting with the leaders of the countries of the COMECON [Council of Mutual Economic Assistance: the Soviet Union, the six East European countries, Vietnam, Mongolia, and Cuba] that will be unlike any we have ever had. It is a critical moment."[41] At Gorbachev's initiative the leaders of the ten COMECON member states congregated in Moscow for a two-day session on November 10, 1986. Castro led the Cuban delegation. The talks were tense. In his memoirs Gorbachev writes:

> We discussed restructuring our mutual economic relations on the basis of principles that are generally accepted in the world. The Cubans, like the Mongolians and the Vietnamese, were alarmed that this question was even discussed. Therefore, we decided to develop a special program of cooperation within the framework of the COMECON for Cuba, Vietnam, and Mongolia.
>
> It was clear that the old forms of direct assistance were no longer viable and not only because of our domestic constraints. The international situation demanded that we transition to mutually beneficial economic relations. This required that every country be considered an independent

actor in the international economy and that we build our relations [with each member of the COMECON] on the basis of mutual benefits. It was about this, these principles, that I spoke with Fidel and, shortly thereafter, with Vice President Carlos Rafael Rodríguez and [Leonel] Soto, Central Committee secretary for economic affairs, who came to Moscow. The Cuban government understood that the gradual transition to an economic relationship based on the principle of mutual advantage was inevitable, but it tried to delay it for as long as possible. A few articles in our press . . . arguing that we should pay world prices for [Cuban] sugar added fuel to the fire. Cuban officials reacted stormily, with protests and counterdemands. We had to explain that the era when our press reflected the official view was gone. We proposed to our [Cuban] friends that they explain their viewpoint in our press. . . .

We began to receive information that the Cuban government was wondering whether we had begun to reassess our entire relationship with Cuba. We declared that we intended neither to end our aid to Cuba, nor to decrease our cooperation; we stressed, however, that we had no choice but to search for new approaches. Several high level delegations traveled to Havana to discuss these new approaches with the Cuban authorities.[42]

In practical terms, this meant, the *Economist* noted, that Moscow took a "more hardheaded approach" to its economic relations with Cuba. There was more Soviet pressure on Havana to meet its export commitments to the USSR. Soviet economic aid decreased slightly, but it remained very generous, averaging $4.3 billion a year in 1986–90.[43]

## Cuba and Africa

Cuba's economic straits did not change its policy in Africa. There were small Cuban military missions in several African countries, but Cuba's only significant military presence other than in Angola was in Ethiopia, where 12,000 Cubans had helped defeat the Somali invasion in early 1978. The number of Cuban soldiers in Ethiopia had been cut to 8,500 by early 1981 and to 3,700 by early 1986.[44] They were based at the northern outskirts of the Ogaden region. They did not participate in the fighting against the low-level insurgency that continued there, with Somali support, through most of the 1980s, but they served as a deterrent to an increasingly unlikely Somali invasion. According to a Reuters report, they lived on friendly terms with the neighboring population. "Civilian inhabitants of the area [near Diredawa and Harar] said in interviews that they

liked the Cubans, praising them as good humored and willing to help on civilian community projects. . . . The people of the region also appeared to find the
occasional heavy drinking and brawling among the troops endearing."[45] Mengistu, however, was not happy with the Cubans. "Our relations with Mengistu
were good but no longer very close," recalls Tony Pérez, who became Cuba's
ambassador in Addis Ababa in March 1986. "The Ethiopians kept asking us to
join the fight against the Eritreans, who were waging a war for independence
from Addis Ababa, and we always refused."[46]

In the early 1970s, Cuba had provided some assistance and training to the
Eritrean rebels, but in 1975, after revolutionaries had come to power in Addis
Ababa, Castro had discontinued the aid. He thereafter trod a fine line: while
he consistently rebuffed Mengistu's entreaties that Cuban troops help quell the
rebellion in Eritrea, the thousands of troops he sent to Ethiopia in early 1978
to defend Mengistu's revolution from the Somali invasion freed up Ethiopian
soldiers to fight the Eritreans. Castro urged Mengistu to grant significant autonomy to Eritrea, but Mengistu sought, instead, to crush the rebellion.

This impasse—Mengistu doggedly pressing the Cubans to fight in Eritrea
and Castro just as doggedly refusing—persisted through the 1980s. Jorge Risquet, Castro's point man for Africa, told East German leader Honecker in 1989,
"At no moment did Cuban troops participate in operations against the rebels
in Eritrea. . . . Nor were Cuban military officers involved in the planning of
military operations."[47] The last Cuban troops left Ethiopia in early 1990, and
two decades later their contribution was acknowledged. In December 2007
the government of Ethiopia, led by men who overthrew Mengistu in 1991, unveiled the Ethiopian and Cuban Friendship Monument in Addis Ababa, "which
was constructed," the *Ethiopian Herald* explained, "to commemorate the 163
Cuban soldiers who lost their lives" during the 1977–78 war with Somalia.[48]
"The Cuban heroes" had died, President Girma Wolde-Giorgis said, to safe-
guard the sovereignty of Ethiopia, and they "would be remembered in Ethiopia
for posterity."[49]

The Cuban presence in Ethiopia was not merely military. Technical assistance began in May 1977, when Cuba agreed to send a medical mission of 313
members, including 140 doctors, to Ethiopia. (At the time there were only 347
doctors in all of Ethiopia, of whom 208 were foreigners.) Cuba would pay the
airfare and the salaries of the members of its medical mission, and Ethiopia
would provide board and lodging, as well as 60 bir ($30) monthly as pocket
money. "The terms offered by our Minister of Public Health were received with
surprise and appreciation by the Ethiopians," a Cuban official reported from
Addis Ababa. "They told us . . . that the Soviet and Bulgarian doctors who work

here receive a salary of 2,000 bir ($1,000) and also 300 bir ($150) for housing. The Ethiopians also pay for the airfare."[50] Cuba's aid continued through the 1980s, with the presence of several hundred aid workers, of whom more than half were health personnel. The Cubans created a faculty of medicine in the city of Jimma and a veterinarian school in Debre Zeit.[51]

About 3,000 Ethiopians studied in Cuba between 1978 and 1994. "Among us there are neurologists, gynecologists, internists, psychologists, dentists, veterinarians, biologists," Berhanu Dibaba, who studied medicine at the University of Havana, recalled, smiling. "It was a good harvest."[52] They were part of a larger community of more than 50,000 Africans, Latin Americans, and Asians who studied in Cuba during the Cold War on full scholarships funded by the Cuban government. Many arrived as primary school students and left as university graduates. Among them was Sophia Ndeitungo, a twelve-year-old survivor of the Cassinga massacre who had arrived in the Island of Youth in late 1978 and entered fifth grade. After finishing high school she studied medicine in Havana, graduating in 1994. Only then did she return to Namibia. When I met her, in November 2007, in Windhoek, she was a general, head of medical services of the Namibian armed forces, married to another Cassinga survivor whom she had met in the Island of Youth. She spoke to me in excellent Spanish, tinged with a slight Cuban accent.[53]

While thousands of foreigners studied in Cuba (22,543 in the academic year 1986–87),[54] thousands of Cuban aid workers went abroad. By the mid-1980s they were in Nicaragua, Iraq, South Yemen, Vietnam, Laos, Cambodia, and North Korea. Above all, they were in Africa: in 1985 the largest aid mission was in Angola (3,635); followed by Ethiopia (476), Mozambique (237), Libya (188), Algeria (70), Guinea-Bissau (59), and São Tomé and Príncipe (53). There were aid teams of fewer than 30 members each in thirteen additional African countries; they were mainly medical missions.[55] Cuban doctors went to Tindhouf, in southwestern Algeria, to care for tens of thousands of refugees who had fled the Western Sahara, occupied by Moroccan troops.

"They told me that the mission was in a very difficult place, that it was completely voluntary, and that if I didn't want to go it wouldn't hurt my career. But they didn't tell me where the mission would be," recalls Dr. González Polanco, who went to Tindhouf in 1979 with the second Cuban medical brigade which had fourteen members. "I said I'd go as long as it was a place where I could drink coffee, where there weren't flies and where it wasn't too hot. But when I got there I found out that there were lots of flies and heat, and no coffee. It was a sea of sand." The brigade's task was to give medical care to the thousands of Saharouis who lived in camps 30–40 kilometers from Tindhouf. There was a hospital in Tindhouf with three Algerian doctors, González Polanco recalls, "but they didn't go to the camps." By 1985 the Cuban medical brigade there had grown to fifty-five members.[56]

The conditions of Cuba's technical assistance had varied over time. It had been free of charge through 1977. In 1978 four countries began to pay: Angola (until October 1983), Algeria, Libya, and Iraq. Mozambique paid, between December 1982 and July 1985, for Cuban technical assistance in the productive sectors of the economy. The level of compensation varied according to the country—Algeria, Libya, and Iraq paid more than Angola and Mozambique. For the other countries the aid was free. For the poorest countries and the national liberation movements, Cuba assumed all the expenses. In all other cases board, lodging, and transportation were the responsibility of the host government. As Noemí Benítez, Cuba's foremost expert on the subject, explained, no countries other than Algeria, Libya, Iraq, and, for a time, Angola and Mozambique, were "charged a single penny for the services of the Cuban aid workers."[57]

## Technical Assistance to Angola

"The Cubans have achieved much in Angola, providing large numbers of doctors and putting up the few buildings constructed in the last few years," a Western journalist wrote in the London *Times* after visiting the country in 1985.[58] They faced formidable obstacles, which were caused in large part by the deterioration of the Angolan economy. The Cuban teachers taught children who lacked pens, books, and paper. The Cuban construction workers, who had played a key role in the first years, were hit hard. For example, Feliberto Arteaga, head of the Cuban civilian mission in the provincial capital of Sumbe, noted in May 1984 in his diary that the construction workers' brigade was "virtually paralyzed because of the lack of material. This is really worrisome. One hundred men are idle."[59]

Above all, security deteriorated. The aid workers had never been safe, but they became even less so in the 1980s. The two most serious incidents occurred in the provincial capitals of Sumbe and Huambo.

At 5:00 A.M. on Sunday March 25, 1,500 UNITA guerrillas suddenly attacked Sumbe, about 270 kilometers south of Luanda. "I woke up thinking that the carnival had begun," recalls Dr. Norberto García Mesa, a member of the Cuban medical brigade there.[60] It was, however, the roar of UNITA's guns as its guerrillas stormed the town. They wanted to seize Sumbe, free the prisoners from the local jail, capture Angolan officials and foreign aid workers, and then withdraw. Sumbe had many foreign workers from Western countries (Italians and Portuguese), 38 from the Soviet Union, 4 from Bulgaria, and 230 from Cuba (construction workers, teachers, and health personnel, including 43 women). There were no Cuban soldiers and only 300 Angolan militia in the town, because it was in an area that was considered safe. A later Cuban military analysis noted that "the military preparation of the small Angolan [militia] units was very poor, and the military preparation of the Cuban aid workers was also poor." This made their performance all the more impressive. For more than three hours, until the Cuban air force intervened, they resisted alone. After six hours of fighting, UNITA withdrew, before Cuban troops could reach the town.[61]

"Western intelligence concluded that Sumbe was not an unqualified UNITA success," Savimbi's biographer writes.[62] The attackers were able to overrun only part of the city, they freed the prisoners from the local jail but captured only a handful of foreigners (a few Portuguese and three Bulgarians). Seven Cubans (three teachers and four construction workers) died in the fighting. The Cuban postmortem noted that UNITA had demonstrated that "its troops are able to cover large distances quickly and stealthily, moving at night, so that it is able to assemble a large force made up of groups from many provinces, in a place from which they can then launch a sudden strike." It soberly concluded, "The attack against Sumbe demonstrates that there is no security in Angola for our aid workers if they are not in an area protected by Cuban troops."[63]

Following Sumbe, the Cuban military mission warned that "we must expect that in the future the enemy will make a sustained effort to capture foreign hostages, especially Cubans and Soviets. . . . Therefore, . . . we have taken measures to improve the training and armament of our aid workers and we have withdrawn those who are in isolated locations where we cannot protect them."[64]

These measures could not protect the aid workers from UNITA's terrorism. On April 19, 1984, three weeks after the attack on Sumbe, UNITA blew up a car loaded with explosives near an eleven-story apartment building that housed Cuban aid workers in Huambo, Angola's second city. The blast killed 15 Cubans and wounded 63, including 34 women. There were no soldiers among them; all were construction workers, teachers, or medical personnel. The explosion also killed or wounded more than 40 Angolans—men, women and children—who happened to be in the vicinity.[65]

The story of Dr. Lourdes Franco Codinach, who went to Angola in October 1986 when she was a thirty-two-year-old pediatrician working in one of Havana's major hospitals, conveys the experience of an aid worker. Lourdes was a practicing Catholic and therefore not a member of the Communist Party. "I was invited to apply to the UJC [the youth organization of the Communist party] when I was at the university," she recalls, "but at the time the party did not accept practicing Catholics, and so I could not join."[66]

I spoke with Lourdes several times. She is articulate and frank (as were many of the aid workers I interviewed, but not all: a few seemed to follow a script). And she happened to have an extra boon for a historian. When I asked whether she had kept a diary in Angola, she smiled: "My letters to my mother are my diary." When later I asked whether I could read her letters, she laughed. "My archives are open," she said, referring to my constant battles to claw my way in Cuba's closed archives. She allowed me to photocopy fifty-one letters—225 handwritten pages—that covered her second year in Angola. (She could not find the letters she had written to her mother during her first year.)

In September 1986 Lourdes had been asked by the administration of the hospital in which she worked if she would be willing to go to Angola. "I had to think about it. I was divorced and living with my mother, and I had a four-year old son. There was some social pressure to go." In a society in which tens of thousands went on aid missions abroad, to refuse without a compelling reason was difficult. "If you didn't go, it looked bad. You'd be looked down on. But I wanted to go, to see a new world, to help where I was needed most." On October 10, 1986, she filled out the required form, designating that her salary would be paid to her mother. Then she said her goodbyes. "All of us [the aid workers going to Angola with her] were gathered in a camp where we learned about the economic, political and social situation of Angola. There were good lectures, given by people who had been there." After a week, she boarded the plane to Luanda. "There were 162 of us, all health care workers." When they arrived in Luanda they were first housed in a high-rise reserved for health workers. She recalls, "The anxiety! I wanted to know where I'd be assigned, what it would be like, the anxiety to know." But her first destination was boot camp: "We were given fifteen days of intensive military training by military personnel. It was hard. It lasted for eight or ten hours a day or even longer, men and women. We'd say to each other, 'I can't take it any more.' Each of us got a rifle and a military uniform. All the time we were in uniform." The training was far more rigorous than that given to the aid workers in the late 1970s, reflecting the changed circumstances. It was only after the training had been completed that they received their assignments. Lourdes was assigned to the Cuban medical brigade in Benguela, a coastal city of 350,000.

In 1987–88 the brigade had, on average, twenty-eight members, including sixteen doctors; approximately half of the brigade was women, including seven of the doctors. They were the only health personnel in Benguela, except for a

Soviet team of five doctors and one nurse, two Angolan doctors (one of them the hospital's director), and several Angolan nurses. They received their salary in Cuba and a monthly stipend of 6,000 kwanzas, with which they had to buy their food.

They were housed in a five-story building reserved for the Cuban medical brigade (there were two other Cuban brigades in Benguela, one of teachers and the other of construction workers; each brigade had its own building). Lourdes shared a two-bedroom apartment with a colleague. "It was a big building," she recalls. "We didn't have to share bedrooms." There was no communal dining room; they bought their groceries in a commissary in the building at prices subsidized by the Cuban government, and they prepared their own meals. "We had plenty to eat. I spent 2,500–3,000 kwanzas a month on food." They could spend their extra kwanzas in the Candonga, the sprawling open-air market found in every Angolan town. "The stores of Benguela were empty, the only place where one could find something was the Candonga. You could buy a pair of sandals for 1,500–2,000 kwanzas, a T-shirt for 2,500–3,000, a pair of pants for 5,000. For security reasons we weren't meant to go to the Candonga, but we'd go anyway on Saturdays, without telling the head of the brigade. (On Sunday it was more dangerous because there were fewer people in the street.) We'd go in a group; we were our own protection. If the head of the brigade had seen us—well, I think nothing would have happened; I think he knew about it and turned a blind eye." Dr. Goliath Gómez, also a member of the Benguela medical brigade, laughed: "Any Cuban who says he didn't go to the Candonga in Angola is a liar. Everyone went to the Candonga!"[67]

If they had any money left (which was not easy, given the prices in the Candonga), they could spend it in Luanda at the Cuban store before boarding the plane that would take them home for their one month vacation at the end of their first year or when they left Angola for good.

In Benguela, Lourdes worked in the hospital, taught classes about pediatric medicine to a group of Angolan nurses, and once a week she was driven to a rural clinic to treat people who could not travel to the town. After a few months she was elected deputy head of the brigade. ("There was a vote. There were two or three candidates," she recalls, and the choice had to be approved by the head of the brigade.) Later, during her last three months, she was acting head of the brigade. "The fact that I was not a member of the Communist Party did not affect me in the least during my stay in Angola, nor has affected me in my career," she explains. (Still not a party member, she is now the head of general medicine at the Hospital Pediatrico de Centro Habana.)

UNITA was not strong in the area around Benguela, but the possibility of a terrorist attack was nonetheless omnipresent. "There are no problems here," Lourdes wrote to her mother. "Therefore don't worry. We are fine, although," she added, "this is a country at war. The possibility of dying is present everywhere, and we are all very aware of this, but here in the city there are no difficulties. . . . Our families never believe it when we tell you these things, you always think that we're in the middle of flying bullets, but this is not so."[68] For security reasons the members of the brigade were not allowed to leave their building after 7:00 P.M. or to receive visitors without the permission of the head of the brigade. "These rules were broken a little bit," she recalls. Her letters indicate that she was often invited to dinner by Angolan friends, people who were known to the brigade and lived nearby. Sometimes she went alone, sometimes with one or two other members of the brigade. They would usually stay until 9:00 or 9:30 P.M.; this seemed to be the hour of the real curfew. She and her friends also returned the invitations in their own apartments. There was also a fair amount of social life within her own building: members of the brigade invited each other to dinner and often pooled their food supplies and whiled away the evenings in small groups. There were also more formal activities that involved the entire brigade: infrequent trips to the beach or other nearby places; occasional social gatherings with representatives of Angolan organizations or the members of the Soviet medical brigade. (Unlike the Cubans, the latter led a lonely life—"[the Soviets] don't make friends with Angolans. They don't socialize with them etc. like we do," Lourdes wrote her mother.)[69] There was also the Saturday night party. "On Saturday evening we all—the entire brigade—gathered together. We'd invite the Cubans from the other brigades and some Angolan friends. . . . Everyone prepared snacks." All the members of the brigade were expected to attend unless they were on duty at the hospital. To be absent was considered poor taste, indicating a lack of group spirit. "Sometimes I don't feel like going," Lourdes wrote her mother, "It is the same thing every Saturday, the same people, the same music, four beers each, but then I get into the spirit of things, dance a little, and pass the night away."[70]

It was a regimented life, a group life. "Two years when we were together the whole day, sharing everything, laughing together. If we got sick, if we laughed, if we were in a bad mood—we had to put up with each other; if we were in a good mood—we had to put up with each other. Two years of living together, all the time." And yet, there was also room for private activities: Lourdes, the practicing Catholic, went regularly to mass on Sunday morning, as did a few other Cubans. And she sometimes had lunch or dinner at the local priest's house, sometimes alone, sometimes with other Cubans. "Last Saturday Roberto and I went to Fr. Bernabe's house, because there was a party," she wrote her mother.

"We had a very good time. We stayed until midnight, but then we had to leave because no one's allowed to drive after midnight. That was when the party really got going and it lasted until five in the morning."[71]

Lourdes's letters reflect a poignant nostalgia for her family, a deep longing to see her mother and her young son. Fortunately, she recalls, "the mail was good. Each week the suitcase with the letters arrived in Benguela. This was almost a religious experience. The day when the suitcase arrived was the day of rejoicing and tears."

Her letters also reflect something else, a feeling that was usually understated, an undercurrent amid the difficulties of daily life in a strange, dangerous country and the daily frustrations at work. This feeling, this undercurrent, burst through in a letter to her mother on June 27, 1988. Two days earlier she and four other members from her medical brigade had received the Medal of the Internationalist Worker that was given to aid workers in good standing when their two-year stint drew to a close. It had been a simple ceremony, attended by the staff of the hospital, Cubans and Angolans. She wrote her mother:

> There aren't words to express everything I felt when they pinned the medal on me. It has been a great day, full of emotions and of a truth I will never forget. This medal belongs also to you because you have helped me to accomplish my duty and you have supported me through it all. This medal represents the happy culmination of this time, when I've offered my labor to these people who are in such need. I will come home having fulfilled my duty. Despite the bad moments we've faced here, the difficulties and hardships, I am leaving with a feeling of pride.[72]

This is a snapshot. By the time Lourdes arrived in Angola in late 1986, the Cuban aid workers were concentrated in the country's provincial capitals (in addition to a small medical brigade in the port of Lobito, near Benguela). In some, living conditions were more difficult than in Benguela, but Lourdes's story is typical. All had two weeks of intensive military training in a military camp outside Luanda. "We called it 'The Hole,'" recalls another aid worker, Gilberto García. "They would put you there and you wouldn't come out until the training was over." All lived in buildings reserved for the Cubans. All prepared their own meals. By 1985 the communal dining halls had been replaced by commissaries in each building. "It was the famous 'Plan Shopping Bag,' which had been a demand of the aid workers," recalls one of them, Salvador Mateo. The aid workers received 6,000 kwanzas per month, irrespective of their salary in Cuba. Almost all stayed two years and returned to Cuba for a one-month vacation after the first eleven months. After they had concluded their mission, they had the right to return to the job they had held before leaving for Angola.[73]

James Brooke, who covered Angola for several years for the *New York Times*, wrote in February 1987, "For a society still trying to recover from the departure of 90 percent of its white population at independence, the contingent of Cuban teachers, construction workers and doctors . . . provides desperately needed technical assistance," adding that "Cuban civilians working in Angola seem drawn by an amalgam of political zeal, a desire to help others and, undoubtedly, the knowledge that Angolan service looks good in a resume in Havana."[74] In January 1987 there were 3,337 Cuban aid workers in Angola (including 554 women).[75] Cuba also continued to supply Angola with medicine, as Castro had promised in March 1984, and it dispatched a Cuban nurse, Serena Torres, to establish a distribution system to ensure that the medicines were not stolen. With an iron fist and the firm backing of the Angolan minister of health and the Cuban Embassy, Torres led a team of seven Cuban men who cleaned up the morass that existed. By the time Torres left Angola in May 1986, the system worked. In her words, "There was a central warehouse in Luanda, and each province had its warehouse. In each warehouse there was one Cuban in charge and one Angolan, so that they wouldn't say that we were colonialists! But the Cuban knew that he was the responsible one." Theft was minimized, and the medicines were efficiently distributed. Ambassador Puente Ferro told Risquet, "Serena has accomplished, in short order, something I consider nothing less than miraculous."[76]

The Cubans urged the Soviets to increase their aid to Angola. "A significant increase in the technical assistance of the socialist camp, given free of charge or with soft credits, would have a major impact," Risquet stressed in Moscow in February 1985. "This would not continue indefinitely, but only until the Angolan economy can afford to pay for it. . . . We're suggesting that you do what we have done. . . . We send our aid workers, the Angolans pay their airfare and their board and lodging and we pay their salaries in Cuba. . . . Therefore, we don't have to disburse hard currency, we just forego revenue in hard currency." The Soviets were not impressed. Deputy Foreign Minister Ilyichev replied that "Angola has great natural resources that aren't controlled by us—Soviets and Cubans—but by the Angolan government." He added, "At the beginning of 1984, 94.4 percent of Angola's exports went to the capitalist countries and 72.9 percent of its imports came from them; whereas the share of the socialist countries was 3 percent of Angola's exports and 23 percent of its imports."[77] The following year, meeting with Cubans and Angolans in Moscow, Soviet foreign minister Shevardnadze said: "We are not against Angola's economic ties . . . to capitalist countries, but, as a friend, I must warn my Angolan comrades, once again, how dangerous it would be if they became dependent on the West. One can see how dangerous is the dependence of several developing countries and, I must add, of some socialist countries, on the credits of capitalist countries."[78]

## Fighting Apartheid

The young South Africans who had left their country after the 1976 Soweto uprising had joined the ANC "with the single wish: 'To learn how to shoot, to get a gun and get back home to . . . finish the Boers,'" writes Ronnie Kasrils, a leader of MK, the ANC's military wing. MK had sent them to its camps in Angola, where, from 1977 to 1979, Cuban instructors had trained more than 1,000 fighters. By 1980, however, the training had virtually ceased, for the simple reason that very few recruits were arriving from South Africa. "There came a moment when we weren't doing anything," says Angel Dalmau, a Cuban official who worked with the ANC.[79]

For the young people who had joined MK in the heady days that followed Soweto, the early 1980s were a time of despair. They had imagined they would return to South Africa in a year or two to fight, Kasrils recalls, but the ANC had to face reality: the strength of the South African armed forces was overwhelming. In the late 1970s, "small [MK] units would infiltrate the country, carry out operations, and withdraw back to the neighboring states."[80] There was no room, in this strategy, for the battalions the Cubans had trained in Angola. Only a handful of chosen men was needed; the rest were stuck in the camps, under very difficult living conditions made worse by a justified fear of spies and the very heavy hand of Mbokodo, the ANC's Department of Security and Intelligence.[81] A "mood of depression and hopelessness" spread in the MK camps in Angola, an ANC commission of inquiry reported in 1984, as many fighters concluded "that the masses are ready for the armed struggle and question why MK is not intensifying the armed struggle. . . . A common theme in the camps is that 'Fighting in the home front should not be a privilege but a right.'" Bongani Cyril Mabaso, an MK member who was in Angola, remembers those dark days. "The frustration of being in the camps was very strong and the living conditions were very bad."[82]

The ANC refined its strategy: it decided to build an underground infrastructure in South Africa that would provide the safe houses and assistance to the cadres it infiltrated into the country; eventually this infrastructure would be able to carry out military operations on its own. Meanwhile, MK continued to send in small units—"at times just one or two people," ANC president Tambo told Castro. "South Africa's security was very strong, tight and effective," recalls an MK operative.[83] There were few infiltration routes into South Africa. To try to reach South Africa from Angola through Namibia would have been senseless. The governments of Zimbabwe and Botswana did not allow the ANC to use their territory as a launching pad for military operations against South Africa. In May 1983 Tambo remarked: "Last year the Frontline States decided that the ANC and SWAPO should intensify the war. SWAPO could do it because Angola allowed it. We went to Botswana . . . but they didn't give us the green light [to operate from their territory]." Nor did Zimbabwe.[84] Access was possible only from landlocked Lesotho (but getting there was a logistical nightmare), and, above all, from Mozambique through Swaziland. Conditions for infiltration became even more difficult when, in March 1984, battered Mozambique concluded the Nkomati pact with South Africa and prevented the ANC from operating on its territory. A few weeks before Nkomati, a mutiny had wracked the MK camps in Angola. It was put down, with bloodshed.[85] The ANC was mired in a deep crisis.

Suddenly, in late 1984 the people's struggle in South Africa acquired new and unprecedented strength, as a massive wave of demonstrations, strikes, and boycotts of schools and white-owned stores spread through the country. Castro told Angolan president dos Santos, in October 1985, "The South African people are showing courage and heroism that is truly astonishing."[86] Cuba was eager to help. In March 1986, when Tambo visited Havana, Castro told him, "We . . . are ready to help the ANC in every way possible." The next day, Tambo discussed the ANC's military needs with Risquet, who said that Cuba was willing to receive large groups of MK cadres for specialized military training. Reflecting Cuba's perception that the days of the apartheid regime were numbered, Risquet stressed that it was important to begin immediate training of the military cadres of the ANC who would lead the South African army in the future. Risquet added, "We need to know as much as possible about the internal situation in South Africa. . . . We don't know enough about it, and we need to learn."[87] The following June a high-level delegation from the South African Communist Party (SACP) visited Havana; it was led by Joe Slovo, general secretary of the SACP and chief of staff of MK. The SACP was the key ally of the ANC, and the ANC allowed dual membership. Slovo briefed the Cubans at length on the situation in South Africa. As he explained,

One of the obstacles that has made it difficult for us to wage an effective war has been the feeling of hopelessness among the population, the feeling that it was impossible to challenge this powerful fascist state that has ruled us for 350 years. We have begun to overcome this barrier. We have reached a point where the population has begun to feel that the regime can be defeated. . . .

Furthermore, another psychological barrier of immense importance has been breached: whites . . . have begun to lose confidence. Ten years ago . . . they had no doubts about the continuation of white rule. But beginning with the events of 1976 [Soweto] and especially since August 1984 [when the people's revolt began], this confidence has been shaken. . . .

I think it would be an exaggeration to say that the ANC has the monopoly of the internal resistance, . . . but it is no exaggeration to say that the overwhelming majority of the population sees the ANC as a decisive factor. . . .

The most important change is that our young people are no longer afraid to die, and the regime is impotent against this.[88]

Two days after Slovo's delegation left Cuba, Raúl Castro met with a group of top aides to brainstorm about the future, "taking as starting point," he said, "the fact that, unless the Angolans kick us out, we will stay in Angola for as long as apartheid exists." This was the new idea that had been taking shape among Cuba's top leaders: if President dos Santos agreed, the Cuban troops would remain in Angola until the end of apartheid, in order to hasten its demise. "Of course," Raúl added, "it is not we who will defeat apartheid, but the South African people. . . . Our help is the presence of our 40,000 soldiers. As a first step, when the time is right we will strike the South African forces in southern Angola, without crossing the border into Namibia. Whether we cross the border will depend on many factors." Risquet explained that Havana would increase aid to the ANC, "above all in the military preparation of its cadres," organizing courses in Cuba in different specialties "for as many fighters as the ANC wishes." This training had already begun "on a small scale, and sixteen recruits graduated a month ago," after attending a sixteen-month course in urban guerrilla warfare. This would be expanded: the ANC had asked Cuba to train 100 to 150 MK guerrillas in the next year, and the request would be honored—"as Comrade Raúl told Slovo, we will give them as much help as we can; we will welcome everyone they send us." Raúl concluded the meeting saying, "This [the struggle in South Africa] is moving quickly. I don't mean that the regime will collapse tomorrow, but the situation is changing."[89]

The following month a senior staffer of the Central Committee of the Cuban Communist Party, Angel Dalmau, traveled to the German Democratic Republic to brief Tambo, who was there to treat a serious heart condition. "I told him that we were pleased that the ANC had replied quickly to our offer to increase the number of cadres trained in our country, because, like the leaders of the ANC, we believe that now is the time to put more pressure than ever on the racist regime in every way, but especially militarily." Cuba was offering more than military aid. The previous March Castro had told Tambo that he would open a school for South African students on the Island of Youth. Dalmau repeated the offer. He explained Tambo's reply in his report to Havana:

> Tambo said that he has been thinking about it, but that there was a problem: "The hundreds of youths who have left South Africa in these last months, approximately 2,000 from 14 to 15 years old, don't understand the need to study. They want military training and then they want to return quickly to South Africa to fight against the racist army. Almost all of them are in our camps in Angola."
>
> Tambo explained that many of these young people have boycotted classes in South Africa for a long time and that, even though it was essential that they be concerned with the struggle, it was also necessary that they receive a certain amount of education. Furthermore, he added, the ANC can't infiltrate large groups into South Africa and therefore many will have to wait in the camps, where they will begin to protest vehemently and to criticize the leaders of the ANC.
>
> He said . . . that if we could offer these youths . . . the possibility of studying part of the time and receiving military training at the same time, it might be possible to convince them to go to the Island of Youth. He insisted that these young people should not neglect their studies completely, because if they did they would feel frustrated in the future, when there will be a new South Africa and they will realize that they have been left completely behind. This would be terrible because these are the youths who have sacrificed everything now, at the crucial moment. It was obvious that Tambo was very worried about this problem and wondered how to solve it.[90]

The conversation ended with Dalmau telling Tambo that the Cuban government was working to ensure that the eighth summit of the Non-Aligned Movement, which would begin in Zimbabwe on September 1, would focus on the struggle against apartheid. "We see this Summit . . . as an event of particular importance for the ANC." Cuba would do everything it could to help.[91]

The Cubans had been instrumental in the selection of Harare for the next summit. The choice was pregnant with meaning. Until 1980, Zimbabwe had been ruled by a white minority regime, and in September 1986, when the summit opened, Harare still carried the scars of the SADF's raid of the previous May. As the Manchester *Guardian* reported. "The shattered shell of the ANC's house and office in the heart of Harare, blown up by infiltrating South African soldiers in May, has been left in ruins to show all visitors here the every day price of South African action in the region. For many of the non-aligned, faraway from Africa and preoccupied with their own worsening economic problems, South Africa's civil war, its illegal occupation of Namibia, and its myriad attacks on the Frontline States, had previously been the stuff of a ritualised annual denunciation at the UN." This would now change, the Cubans hoped. *Le Monde* noted that "the question of southern Africa . . . is the 'plat de resistance' of this eighth summit."[92]

## Cuba's Linkage

On September 2, 1986, in Harare, Castro told the assembled leaders: "As long as apartheid rules South Africa . . . Angola will not be safe, no other country in southern Africa will be safe, and the independence of Namibia will be only a sham. . . . When apartheid has ended, when South Africa's fascist regime has disappeared . . . Namibia will be immediately independent, there will be no need for any Cuban soldier, and we will withdraw all our soldiers from Angola at once. Of course, Angola's leaders . . . can decide they don't need our troops at any time. I have simply said that we are willing to keep our soldiers in Angola as long as apartheid exists."[93]

This was Cuba's response to the quickening of the popular struggle in South Africa. Castro had first broached the idea to President dos Santos in an October 17, 1985, letter. "In these last months the struggle against apartheid has reached an unprecedented level within South Africa and this has provoked a worldwide wave of condemnation [of South Africa] that is also unprecedented," he wrote. "It is clear that a new situation has emerged and that the question of the final eradication of apartheid has moved to center stage. . . . Apartheid can be eliminated if the heroic revolt of the black people of South Africa is bolstered by the effective solidarity, moral and material, of all peoples, and especially of the Frontline States."[94]

Castro hammered this theme when dos Santos arrived in Havana ten days later. "In my opinion South Africa will not recover from this crisis. . . . Apartheid is in its death throes. . . . Two years ago [before the popular uprising in South Africa began], Resolution 435 seemed to us a great step forward; now, I think that the great step forward would be the end of apartheid." Dos Santos listened in silence, and when he replied, he was noncommittal: "We need time to think about this," he said. Three days later, Castro broached the idea to another visitor, Soviet foreign minister Shevardnadze. "In South Africa," he said, "an irreversible crisis has erupted. . . . I am in favor of saying publicly that as long as apartheid exists, the Cuban troops will remain in Angola." Shevardnadze made no comment.[95]

Three months later, in January 1986, Risquet returned to the same subject in Moscow. The continuing presence of the Cuban troops in Angola would serve as a beacon of hope for the black people of South Africa, strengthening their resolve. Again, the Soviets remained silent.[96] They offered no response for almost a year, but eventually they expressed their skepticism. In a December 1986 meeting in Moscow between high-ranking Cubans and Soviets, a senior Foreign Ministry official, Vladillen Vasev, said simply, "We believe that the elimination of apartheid will take a long time."[97] In March 1987, in Moscow, Defense Minister Sergey Sokolov and the new head of the International Relations Department of the Central Committee, Anatoly Dobrynin, raised the subject with Risquet:

> *Dobrynin*: According to your calculations, because your withdrawal
>     [from Angola] is linked to the end of apartheid in South Africa,
>     when will this happen?
> *Risquet*: Comrade, the fact that I have a beard does not make me a
>     prophet. . . .
> *Sokolov*: Well, do you really propose to stay [in Angola] all the way to the
>     victorious finale; or is there some tactical flexibility in your position?
> *Risquet*: We mean all the way, but we are not the only ones involved.
>     There are also the Angolans, and we don't know how long they can
>     accompany us in this kind of struggle.[98]

The Angolans did not need to weigh in on the Cuban proposal because, as long as Pretoria refused to implement Resolution 435 and continued to support Savimbi, the departure of the Cuban troops was out of the question.

Cuba continued to increase its aid to the ANC. "At the request of the ANC," a Cuban aide-mémoire stated in September 1987, "over the last twelve months we have trained about 250 cadres in various aspects of guerrilla warfare. By the end of 1988 we will have prepared more than 600 guerrillas."[99]

From September 16 to 17, 1987, Soviets, Cubans, and ANC representatives met in Moscow. The high point of the plenary session was a report by ANC official—and South Africa's future president—Thabo Mbeki on the situation in his country. "He was absolutely brilliant," recalls Risquet.[100] During the meeting, Risquet expressed Cuba's vision of what could happen in South Africa: "We believe that the resistance of the South African people coupled with all the international pressure that can be mustered could force the racists to enter into negotiations for the elimination of apartheid, as was the case in Zimbabwe. The ANC will have to make concessions ... but in order to get to a negotiated solution the ANC must intensify the popular struggle. ... Make South Africa ungovernable and obstruct economic activity until the country's leading capitalists will conclude that it is better to dismantle apartheid than to let the war go on."[101]

The Cubans also continued to offer to open a school for South Africans on the Island of Youth. They explained to Tambo when he visited Havana in late June 1987 that "all the measures had been taken to prepare the school." Two months later, Risquet told Castro: "Oliver Tambo has informed us that the ANC will send approximately one hundred students to the Island of Youth. ... We had assured Tambo that we would find a way to offer military training to the young South Africans who came to Cuba to study, whether during their vacations or over the weekends or at the end of the day of classes. ... With this pledge from us, the ANC was able to convince one hundred teenagers to come to the Island of Youth to study."[102]

Tambo had been overly optimistic. By September 1988 the ANC representative in Cuba reported that there were only fifty-seven South African students in the Island of Youth. Twenty-one other South Africans were enrolled in Cuban universities.[103]


## Reflections

The 1970s had been good years for Cuba, a time of economic growth free from the threat of American military aggression. Relations with the Soviet Union, severely strained in the late 1960s, had also been good. Cuba achieved impressive successes in Angola in 1976 and Ethiopia in 1978. The Sandinista victory in Nicaragua in 1979 breached the wall that had isolated Cuba in Latin America.

By the mid-1980s the situation had changed, for the worse. At home, the economy was in the doldrums. In a January 1985 report, the Canadian Embassy in Havana conveyed a snapshot: "Inadequacies in housing, unemployment, and the lack of consumer goods have caused general discontent. ... On the other hand, rather dramatic improvements are apparent in health care, nutrition, social welfare and education. ... It is also clear that charismatic President Castro remains extremely popular with the majority of the Cuban people."[104] In the second half of the decade, Cuba's economic difficulties worsened as the debt crisis deepened.

Abroad, Reagan's triumphant reelection in 1984 heightened anxiety in Havana. The United States and its allies were ascendant, and the Soviet bloc was on the defensive. The first years of the decade had not been good for the Kremlin: upheaval in Poland, quagmire in Afghanistan, economic crisis, and senescent leaders. If the arrival of Gorbachev brought the promise of more vigorous leadership, it also heralded, by 1986, cuts in Soviet economic aid to Cuba at a time when the Cuban economy was in dire straits. The Sandinistas, Cuba's only friends among the Latin American governments, were facing mounting threats. In Ethiopia, Mengistu's rule, cruel, inept, was a bitter disappointment for Havana.

In southern Africa Pretoria's aggression against its neighbors continued unabated. Namibia's independence seemed more remote than ever. South African support for Savimbi appeared unshakeable, and in early 1986 the Reagan administration had announced that it would extend "covert" military aid—including Stinger anti-aircraft missiles—to UNITA. The measure was popular in the U.S. Congress because it was seen as a way to hurt Cuba.

Forty thousand Cuban soldiers were mired in Angola, unable to prevent the South Africans from invading the southern reaches of the country. The days of Agostinho Neto, whose government had tried to improve the lot of the population, were gone; corruption and incompetence were rampant, and the MPLA had lost the support of large segments of the population.

In this grim scenario there was one exception: the struggle of the South African people. The ANC was spearheading a widespread, sustained uprising against the apartheid regime. The impact of this struggle was felt even in the halls of the U.S. Congress, which voted to impose sanctions on South Africa, overriding Reagan's veto. Castro dared to hope. For the first time he began to imagine that the end of apartheid was in sight. He wanted to help what he called "the most beautiful cause."[105] This led to his decision to keep the Cuban troops in Angola, if Luanda agreed, until the death of apartheid.

What difference could these troops make? After all, the Cubans had always planned to keep some of their troops in Angola to guard against South African aggression. Castro's "revolutionary linkage," however, went a large step further: *all* the Cuban troops would remain in Angola after the independence of Namibia. Whether this would have had a significant psychological impact on the people of South Africa is unknowable, but it was, for Havana, a resounding statement of support for the blacks in South Africa, a cri de coeur.

More quietly, in Cuba, parallel to "revolutionary linkage," another idea was taking shape: that the Cuban troops in Angola would take the offensive, surge forward from their defensive line and strike at the South Africans in the southwest of the country. Raúl Castro referred to this when he told his top aides after Slovo's visit, "As a first step, at the right moment we will strike a blow against the South African forces in southern Angola, without crossing the border into Namibia. Whether we cross the border will depend on many factors."[106] Pushing the SADF out of Angola would undermine white morale in South Africa and embolden the nonwhite masses, as it had in 1976.

This would require Moscow's assistance, however, and the Soviets disagreed with the Cubans' military strategy in Angola.

CHAPTER 13

# Havana and Moscow
*Conflicting Strategies*

## The Soviet Military Mission in Angola

By the mid-1980s, the Soviet military mission in Angola had grown to approximately 1,500 people (plus 500 family members).[1] As in the late 1970s, most of the Soviet military personnel served as instructors in the use of the weapons sent from the Soviet Union, and they helped maintain the equipment. Others were military instructors in a variety of academies, ranging from the Academy for Senior Officers in Huambo to the many schools for noncommissioned officers. "We had only Soviet professors," remembers General Tonta, who attended the Academy for Senior Officers in 1985, "but they weren't very knowledgeable about guerrilla warfare, and they hadn't adjusted to life in Africa."[2] Some 200–300 Soviets served as advisers to regular Angolan brigades; there were twelve to fourteen Soviets, including interpreters, in each of the brigades they advised. Soviets trained Angolan pilots and helped maintain the planes. The number of Soviet transport planes in Angola had sharply increased in 1984; "last year we had two AN-12 planes," the head of the Soviet military mission, General Konstantin Kurochkin, told Castro in February 1984, "and now we have twelve AN-12, with 200 Soviet pilots and technicians."[3]

Whereas the Cuban advisers always participated in the fighting, the Soviet approach in sub-Saharan Africa was the opposite. The CIA noted in a 1988 study that "Soviet advisers are, as a rule, not permitted to participate directly in combat. . . . Moscow apparently wants to avoid casualties and the political consequences of direct nondeniable involvement in what are essentially civil wars."[4]

Angolan officers are categorical: the Soviets did not participate in the fighting. When the South Africans launched Operation Askari in December 1983, General Konstantin first wanted to withdraw the Soviet advisers, but then he relented, a decision that the Angolan officers remember with appreciation. "Konstantin ordered his advisers to stay at the front," said a senior FAPLA commander, Ita, when I asked him for his assessment of Konstantin.[5] It had been a bold decision. "The Soviets are under strict orders not to join in the fighting," Konstantin reminded the head of the Cuban military mission in March 1984.[6]

## Cuban-Soviet Differences

From the outset Cubans and Soviets had disagreed on a key issue: against which enemy should the FAPLA focus its efforts? The answer to this question determined the kind of army the Angolans should create. The Cubans argued that they would protect Angola from the South Africans and that the FAPLA should therefore concentrate on the war against UNITA. The Soviets disagreed. A Cuban aide-mémoire bluntly told the Soviet General Staff in August 1984,

> The Soviet military advisers believed that the South Africans were the principal enemy of the FAPLA; they overlooked the struggle against UNITA. The Cuban advisers, on the contrary, argued that . . . the FAPLA and the Angolan government should focus on defeating UNITA. . . . The Soviet military mission in Angola believed that the regular units of the FAPLA should not participate in the war against UNITA and constantly urged that these units should receive the best [human and material] resources. The Soviets were oblivious of the needs of the light brigades, which were fighting against UNITA. . . .
>
> The fact that the Soviet and the Cuban military missions were unable to resolve their disagreements in a timely fashion created an extremely complex situation, because it meant that the leaders of the FAPLA were confronted with opposite proposals, plans, and opinions. They were forced to take decisions for which they were unprepared, and this led to backbiting and frustration toward the Soviets and Cubans.[7]

Fidel Castro told Soviet deputy foreign minister Anatoly Adamishin in March 1988, "From a military perspective, there were several differences between our ideas and those of the Soviet military. What was the first? . . . You underestimated the bandits [UNITA] and concentrated on creating a big army with many tanks, guns, artillery . . ., troops who knew how to parade. It was a great army for parades. . . . From the first year we were the only ones who remembered that there were bandits. . . . We were mired in these contradictions for almost ten years. . . . When finally, after the crisis in 1983 [the battle of

Cangamba], you accepted our stance that the FAPLA had to focus on the war against the bandits, . . . then we clashed on how to fight against the bandits."[8]

The three-year saga of Mavinga exemplifies this new clash between the Cubans and Soviets. Mavinga, a small town in the southeastern province of Cuando Cubango, roughly 250 kilometers north of the Namibian border, had been occupied by UNITA in September 1980. It was considered the gateway to Jamba, Savimbi's headquarters. "Jamba," said South African colonel Breytenbach, was "a bush base, quite big, with only bush-type structures, mud walls, and thatched roofs," about 200 kilometers southeast of Mavinga, and very close to the Namibian border. "It had a hospital staffed by South African doctors. We installed a printing press," recalled another South African, General Thirion, who was a frequent guest.[9] It had also "a big conference room," where Savimbi received his visitors.[10] "The landing strip," UNITA General Nunda explained, "was 25 kilometers from Jamba."[11]

For Soviets and Angolans, an offensive against Mavinga was synonymous with an advance on Jamba. In the words of a senior FAPLA officer, Andres Mendes de Carvalho, "When we spoke of an operation against Mavinga, what we were really talking about was the destruction of Savimbi's headquarters. Mavinga was a town that you could find on a map, unlike Jamba, and it was from there that we would launch our offensive against Jamba." Mavinga, another senior FAPLA officer said, "would be the springboard from which we would reach Jamba."[12]

## Konstantin

By the late spring of 1984, the attack on Mavinga had become the idée fixe of Colonel General Konstantin Kurochkin, the head of the Soviet military mission from May 1982 to June 1985. For the previous decade he had been first deputy commander of the elite Soviet Paratrooper Forces; he had gone to Angola straight from Afghanistan.[13]

Konstantin "arrived in Luanda with the prestige of his service in Afghanistan and in the Paratrooper Forces," recalls Polo, who headed the Cuban military mission. "In Angola he replaced an officer [Lieutenant General Georgi Petrovski] who did not wield much influence in Moscow. Initially, Konstantin played a very positive role. He got more and better weapons from Moscow for the FAPLA than had his predecessors. This gave him a lot of clout with the Angolans: he had succeeded where the others had failed." Furthermore, he spoke every day with the Soviet minister of defense and with the chief of the general staff. "At least that's what he claimed. Konstantin was really helpful at first:

he got the supplies that Moscow had long promised and he made the procedure less cumbersome." But time went by, and Konstantin's downside, that "he wanted to call the shots," became evident.[14]

Konstantin was a formidable personality who exerted strong influence on Soviet military strategy in Angola well beyond his tenure as head of the military mission. After his return to Moscow in 1985, where he was appointed first deputy head of the Main Directorate of Personnel of the Soviet General Staff, he became Moscow's resident expert on Angola, the link between the Ministry of Defense and the new head of the military mission, Lieutenant General Leonid Kuzmenko and Kuzmenko's successor, Lieutenant General Petr Gusev. "Konstantin would arrive in Luanda and tell Pedro [Gusev] what to do—he represented the Soviet high command, so he was in the driver's seat," recalled General Gustavo Fleitas, who replaced Polo as head of the Cuban military mission in September 1986. Fleitas's deputy, General Samuel Rodiles, observed, "Gusev was never overbearing with me; our relations were correct, he was always respectful. But it was Konstantin who was in charge." In terms of Soviet military strategy, the 1982–88 period is, for the Cubans, the Konstantin period.[15] This was also the Angolans' view. "No other head of the Soviet military mission was as influential as Konstantin, not before him and not after him," said Ngongo, who was the deputy chief of staff of the FAPLA. "Konstantin! Even after he had left Angola, even when he was back in the Soviet Union, we could feel his presence. He really wanted to impose his point of view; he didn't like to listen. He thought that since he was giving us the weapons, we had to do what he said."[16]

Each of the six Cuban and ten Angolan senior officers I asked about Konstantin paid homage to his achievements. He was the most effective advocate with Moscow for the FAPLA, and he was able to get more scholarships for Angolan officers to study and train in the Soviet Union. But he refused to adapt to the demands of guerrilla warfare. Ndalu, who was the FAPLA chief of staff in 1982–91, expressed the general consensus: "Konstantin was the head of the Soviet military mission who most helped us to get weapons, send people for military training to the USSR, and open centers of military instruction here. But as a military adviser he had an academic approach. His frame of reference was the Second World War. He created many problems for us. And he wanted to be the boss."[17]

Polo became Konstantin's bête noire. "Konstantin complained about me with the Soviet military leaders, and they then complained about me with Havana," he recalled.[18] Soviet complaints notwithstanding, Polo remained in Angola as head of the Cuban military mission until September 1986, and when the military situation became particularly difficult in late 1987, he was sent back to Angola.

Konstantin and Polo had clashed during the battle of Cangamba and during Askari, but the most bitter source of contention between them was the Mavinga operation.

## Seven Days in Havana

Konstantin first raised the idea of an operation against Mavinga when he visited Cuba from February 7 to 14, 1984. He had been invited by Fidel Castro, who was eager to improve relations with the powerful head of the Soviet military mission in Angola. He was received with all the honors due his rank and his position, and he was in turn gracious and, when he met Castro, on February 11, deferential. Castro had to leave the next day for Moscow to attend Andropov's funeral. "Because of this," he told Konstantin, "I will have to cut short my time with you."[19]

Konstantin's visit was taking place at a critical moment: President dos Santos was negotiating with the Americans and the South Africans, and Cubans and Soviets were neither consulted nor informed about the course of the talks. (Castro knew so little that on February 11 he surmised that "these negotiations will last at least one or two months"; in fact they were concluded five days later.) The Cuban leader was bitter. "José Eduardo [dos Santos] is a serious man," he told Konstantin, "but there are others. . . . What's most important, in my opinion . . . is that we—Cubans and Soviets—always come to a consensus, present a common front, and stand shoulder to shoulder in Angola."[20] Their shared frustration with the Angolans made Cubans and Soviets feel closer to one another in that complicated triangle that was Cuban-Soviet-Angolan relations. Konstantin was right when he told a Russian scholar, Vladimir Shubin, that there was no sense of friction during his visit.[21]

But behind the friendly facade—the politeness, the shared concern about the Angolans' behavior—disagreement remained about the major issue: the best military strategy for Angola. This was not addressed in Konstantin's conversation with Castro, which focused mainly on the weapons that the Soviet Union would send to Angola in 1984 and on Castro's analysis of the repercussions of dos Santos's negotiations with Washington and Pretoria. "I believe," Castro began, "that right now Angola is more a political than a military problem. . . . I'm not sure how necessary it is, given the situation, to discuss a lot of military details."[22]

Konstantin also met with the two top Cuban generals who dealt with Angola—Abelardo Colomé and Ulises Rosales, who was the first deputy minister of defense and chief of the general staff. With them he broached the idea of "a great operation on a large scale . . . in the provinces of Moxico [in the east] and Cuando Cubango [in the southeast]." He was tentative. "He said they were just ideas," the minutes of the conversation reported, "that he has not yet presented them to the Soviet General Staff. He explained that, although he had mentioned them to Polo, he would like to get the reaction of the Cuban General Staff." Ulises was wary. He believed "that we must pay special attention to Moxico, but that Cuando Cubango [the Mavinga operation] requires an in depth analysis to assess whether it is necessary to launch an operation there." Colomé was even less encouraging. "General Colomé," the minutes noted, "stressed how dangerous it was to operate in Cuando Cubango because of the South African air force, which is based in airports immediately south of the Namibian border. . . . A major operation there would be not only dangerous but unnecessary, because it is a sparsely populated region of no economic significance." Konstantin did not insist. After Colomé had spoken, the Soviet replied "that he agreed and that he had presented the idea only as something to consider and analyze."[23]

## The Battle over Mavinga

Vladimir Shubin writes that after Konstantin's visit to Cuba, Polo "lent a more attentive ear to his words. However, apart from goodwill, as 'General Konstantin' admitted, he had particular leverage in dealing with the Cubans (and Angolans for that matter): most of the transport planes in Angola and their crews were Soviets. . . . They were directly subordinate to him, and the supplies of both Cuban and Angolan troops depended on them to a large extent."[24]

Konstantin's "leverage" and Polo's "goodwill" were not sufficient to make the Cubans agree to the idea of a Mavinga offensive. In the months that followed his visit to Havana, Konstantin became more and more enamored of the plan. But Polo was opposed, and Havana supported Polo.

Clearly, the idea had some merit. As South Africa's Defense Minister Malan noted, the fall of Jamba would create "military, political and psychological" difficulties for UNITA.[25] But trying to take Jamba would create even greater problems for the FAPLA. Cuando Cubango, in the far southeast of Angola, had been called by the Portuguese "the land at the end of the world." It had virtually no roads, almost no population, and no economic importance. An offensive against Mavinga would have to start from the small town of Cuito Cuanavale, the FAPLA's southernmost base in Cuando Cubango, and then cut through 200 kilometers of very dense bush that was largely controlled by UNITA in order to get to Mavinga. Only dirt tracks linked the two towns. To the north and the east of Cuito, the dense bush of Cuando Cubango. To the west, connected by 180 kilometers of paved roads, was the town of Menongue, the eastern end of the Cuban defensive line. Menongue was Cuito's lifeline, its only link to the outside world, except for Cuito's small and poorly maintained airport. If the FAPLA reached Mavinga, and Jamba, it would be dependent on a very vulnerable supply line, while UNITA would enjoy a safe haven below the Namibian border, from whence it could attack at will. Furthermore, the fall of Jamba would disrupt only temporarily the SADF's ability to supply UNITA. As a South African officer points out, the SADF sent supplies to Jamba by road (a dirt track) and by air to a rudimentary airfield nearby. There was no way the FAPLA could control the 700-kilometer border between Cuando Cubango and Namibia, and in the immense wilderness of Cuando Cubango UNITA could have quickly created a new bush capital, and the SADF could have swiftly resumed supplying it.[26]

Whatever the theoretical merits of the operation, one fact should have settled the debate: it was not feasible as long as South Africa had air superiority.

After months of skirmishing with Polo, Konstantin exploded. "In the military arts one must choose the direction of the main blow," he lectured Risquet and Polo in June 1984, after reminding them that he had fought in four wars, including the Second World War (when Risquet had been an adolescent and Polo an infant). He wanted to capture Jamba, the enemy's lair. This was more important, he argued, than Polo's idea of striking at the bands of UNITA guerrillas that had spread to the central regions of Angola. They could be disposed of later. "Comrades," he told Risquet and Polo, "remember the lessons of history. For example, years after the civil war had ended in the Soviet Union we were still fighting the bandits in Central Asia." The two Cubans were not persuaded. "But that was Central Asia," Risquet objected. "If the bandits had been between Moscow and Leningrad you could not have waited so long. The problem for us is that the bandits are in the region that is most important for Angola's economy." Undeterred, Konstantin pressed on. He had broached his plan in Moscow, he had spoken with the chief of the general staff, Marshal Nikolai Ogarkov, and together they had briefed Defense Minister Ustinov for "two hours and seventeen minutes." Ustinov had approved the plan. But upon his return to Angola, Konstantin had faced Polo's resistance. There was an impasse, "and Moscow wants to know what's happening." He turned to Risquet: "Comrade Risquet, I don't agree with Comrade Polo. . . . Comrade Risquet, let's discuss and let's analyze everything in order to reach a common position." But Risquet agreed with Polo.[27]

And there matters stood until the following August, when Army General Varennikov, first deputy chief of the Soviet General Staff, arrived in Angola. He met with Risquet and Colomé in Luanda. It was not a happy encounter. Risquet began by telling Varennikov that "he and Colomé were under instruction to convey the following message from the Minister [of Defense], Raúl Castro." He proceeded to explain at some length why the strategy that the Soviet military mission had urged the FAPLA to follow when the SADF had invaded south-western Angola in December 1983 had led to disaster for the Angolan brigade in Cuvelai. Colomé stressed "that South Africa enjoyed air superiority . . . and that we [Cubans] lacked planes and effective antiaircraft weapons." Varennikov, who had listened in silence, thanked Risquet and Colomé for their frankness, "which is demanded of us by the closeness of our relations," and insisted on the impor-tance of Polo and Konstantin cooperating. Then he dropped the bombshell: "It was time to locate and destroy the headquarters of the enemy."[28] Varennikov thought that the FAPLA should "launch a major operation to annihilate UNITA in the provinces of Moxico and Cuando Cubango." In other words, he endorsed Konstantin's plan. Risquet and Colomé disagreed. The priority, they argued, should be to defeat UNITA in the central provinces of the country, which were economically and demographically far more important than Cuando Cubango. Furthermore, they warned, it would be "extremely dangerous" to launch an offensive against Mavinga because the South African air force could "inflict a physical and psychological debacle on the FAPLA."[29]

Throughout September 1984, Angolans, Cubans, and Soviets debated the issue. For example, on September 12, Konstantin and Polo met with Angolan minister of defense Pedalé, FAPLA chief of staff Ndalu, and his deputy, Ngongo. Konstantin insisted on the operation against Mavinga. Polo disagreed: "Com-rade minister," he told Pedalé, "I want you to know that almost always Comrade Konstantin and I meet together beforehand to work out, as far as possible, a common strategy to present to you, instead of confronting you with contrast-ing opinions, but in this particular case my view is the opposite of Comrade Konstantin's." Polo argued that the FAPLA must not attack Mavinga; instead, it should focus on the central provinces. Ndalu and Ngongo supported Polo.[30]

Two weeks later, Konstantin brought out the heavy artillery: "Comrade President," he told dos Santos at a meeting in Luanda that Polo attended, "yesterday I spoke with the minister of defense, Marshal of the Soviet Union Ustinov, and with the Chief of the General Staff [Marshal Sergei] Akhromeyev [who had just replaced Ogarkov]. This morning I spoke again with the chief of the General Staff, and he asked me to inform our Angolan comrades that to strike the decisive blow against UNITA it is necessary to defeat the enemy forces in the Mavinga region." Once again, Polo expressed his disagreement and warned that they would be attacking a region where South Africa enjoyed air superiority. After a lengthy discussion dos Santos concluded, "I agree that we must destroy UNITA, but not in Mavinga."[31] Polo knew that he had won only the first round. After leaving the meeting, he and Konstantin continued their discussion while being driven to the headquarters of the Cuban military mission. "Comrade Konstantin," Polo said, "today I want to speak with you as a communist, as a revolutionary, as your son if I may. Comrade Konstantin, the political and military situation is such that the Angolans cannot afford to make any mistakes, particularly ones instigated by us, by you or by me."[32]

## The Cuban Approach

The clash over Mavinga illuminates the difference between the Cuban and the Soviet approach to the war in Angola. The Cubans favored almost continuous small-scale operations that would involve all the FAPLA brigades. As Risquet urged, "One brigade in one small operation; another brigade in another. That is, we need to draw a grid in an area, assigning to each brigade a zone for which it will be responsible. . . . Each brigade should engage in a month-long operation, then rest for ten days and receive new supplies. It should carry out intelligence work to locate the enemy, and based on that information it should launch a new operation."[33]

The Soviets frowned on this. "These small operations don't produce results," Konstantin objected in one of his many clashes with Polo. He favored large sweeps, many brigades acting together in a major operation. "Only if we carry out 'classic operations' we will get results," he argued. This would not work against guerrillas, Polo countered. The enemy would just melt away and reappear when the operation had concluded. And he added, tongue in cheek, "I'm not against executing the kind of operations that Konstantin wants, but they won't achieve anything. . . . It isn't that we're against conventional warfare. If UNITA had been operating according to the rules of conventional warfare we would already have defeated it, but up to now it hasn't." Konstantin complained about Polo's criticism—"You keep saying that we . . . plan conventional operations without taking the terrain into account. . . . You always criticize us saying that we draw too many arrows [referring to the arrows on the Soviet diagrams of battle plans in Angola]."[34] Konstantin was right: the Cubans—Polo foremost—were forthright in their criticism, and they were unimpressed by the Soviets' tendency to plan complicated operations with a lot of arrows. In September 1983, looking at the Soviet plans of a major sweep to retake the town of Mussende in eastern Angola, Castro had said, "This looks like the operation against Berlin [at the end of World War II]." The Cubans dubbed the operation "Operation Berlin."[35]

The result of these clashes was that the Angolans were given opposite counsels. "We should have a consensus opinion," Konstantin exhorted Polo during a heated exchange on October 7, 1984, "because otherwise it will be again the same story: you will present your opinion and I mine. This looks bad. . . . I wanted to coordinate first with you in order to avoid disagreements." But Polo did not budge. "Konstantin, you have to listen to what I'm saying to you," he countered. Because he did not agree with Konstantin, he was obliged to tell the Angolans his advice, "and they will decide whether they prefer my strategy or yours." When Konstantin asked, "What should we do?" Polo cut him short: "You will present your views and we will present ours, and the Angolans will present theirs, and then they will decide." Konstantin lamented, "This is not good. It doesn't make us look good."[36]

The disagreements between the Cubans and Soviets "created problems for us," remarks a senior FAPLA officer. "We treated the issue with some diplomacy, some finesse. The Soviet military mission wanted us to pursue conventional warfare. The Cuban military mission advocated counter-insurgency tactics. They knew a lot about this, and it was more relevant for the situation we faced. There were things that the Soviets didn't understand well. We were closer to the Cuban position, but it was the USSR that gave us the weapons. This was the reality, and we had to find a compromise so we wouldn't quarrel with the Soviets."[37]

Konstantin was an intelligent man and a well-prepared military officer, but he was a product of Soviet military thinking. As the CIA noted in a 1988 analysis, "The Soviets have trained and equipped their allies' forces according to the Soviet model to meet a conventional, not an insurgent threat. . . . The continued emphasis on military campaigns better suited for engaging enemy forces in setpiece battles on the European plains perpetuates a tactical rigidity that is not well suited to the fluid nature of guerrilla wars. . . . Soviet advisers have consistently advocated large combined-arms sweep operations—reminiscent of battle plans for Europe—instead of small-unit tactics recommended by Western theory."[38]

Despite their experience since 1979 in Afghanistan, the Soviets had not adapted to fighting wars in the Third World. Their frame of reference was the Second World War, the great advance on Berlin, the battles that might be fought against NATO in the plains of Germany with large mechanized units. The Cubans, on the other hand, "were the product of their experience of the guerrilla war against Batista," Cuban General Antonio Lussón explained. "I was a guerrilla. . . . During the war against Batista I headed small guerrilla units and by the end I headed a column. Then we had the war against the bandits in Cuba [insurgents supported by the CIA from 1960 to 1965]."[39] These were two different worlds. It was not surprising, therefore, that Moscow and Havana disagreed about strategy in Angola.

A striking example of the chasm between these two worlds occurred in 1980 when the Soviet Union sent tanks and armored vehicles via Angola to SWAPO. The Cubans thought it made no sense, and neither did the Angolans. "We didn't understand why they sent tanks and armored vehicles to SWAPO because it seems to us that SWAPO has to wage a guerrilla war," President dos Santos told Castro. Therefore, the Angolans decided not to give the equipment to SWAPO but to keep it for themselves. "I must admit that . . . we worried that our decision might be misunderstood," dos Santos confided to Castro. Indeed, it was an irritant in Soviet-Angolan relations. In 1982 Ustinov complained to Colomé: "SWAPO has still not received the tanks we sent them. If they had them they would be able to fight better against the South Africans."[40]

## Akhromeyev's Gentle Touch

In late September 1984, while Polo and Konstantin clashed in Luanda, a Cuban military delegation led by Ulises met in Moscow with a group of Soviet generals including the chief of the general staff, Marshal Akhromeyev, and Varennikov. Varennikov was almost lyrical about the importance of the Mavinga operation. Pointing to the province of Cuando Cubango on a map of Angola, he claimed, "Everything grows from here. That is, this entire tree [UNITA] grows from here; it is from here that Savimbi receives everything; it is here that he has his key bases and his training centers." (He was less florid in his memoirs, but the point was the same: the operation would be "a turning point in the armed struggle against the counterrevolution.") Ulises forcefully repeated Cuba's objections.[41]

The issue that most concerned Akhromeyev—even more than the merits of the Mavinga operation—was the tension between Polo and Konstantin. "I think that we need to resolve the disagreements between us," he urged Ulises, "without bumping them up to a higher level. That is, we shouldn't take them to our political leaders." The Cuban minutes of the meeting make interesting reading:

Marshal Akhromeyev said that he wouldn't enumerate all the times that our military mission in Angola had failed to coordinate with the Soviet mission because we would be able to list an equal number of examples when . . . Konstantin had failed to coordinate with us. . . . He said that each side bore 50 percent of the responsibility for the situation. The problem, he stressed, is that since we're carrying out a joint internationalist mission in Angola, we need to do whatever is necessary to coordinate our positions. . . . He said that if Polo informed Ulises that there was a problem, Ulises should call him (Akhromeyev) and he would answer at once, without any red tape. And that in similar circumstances [i.e., if Konstantin informed him of a problem with Polo] he would call Ulises.

Akhromeyev said that both Konstantin and Polo were soldiers' soldiers and that at times they lacked the necessary diplomacy to deal with problems and that in these cases the intervention of our General Staffs was necessary.[42]

## Operation Second Congress

Four months later, in January 1985, a tense exchange between Polo and Konstantin signaled the beginning of a new round of debate about the Mavinga operation. Konstantin said he still wanted to launch it. Polo disagreed. "You haven't let me talk," Polo insisted.

> *Polo*: "Before we launch this operation, Konstantin, we have to consider the South Africans. We can't forget them. . . . We have to think about whether they will intervene."
> *Konstantin*: "Of course, but this is what happens in war."
> *Polo*: "But we can't begin an operation that is sure to be defeated. Because the South African air bases are very close to Mavinga, just south of the border, and ours are far away."[43]

This time Konstantin convinced the Angolans to attack Mavinga, over Havana's objections. No doubt, Moscow's position as Angola's arms supplier gave Konstantin leverage. But the Angolans were also seduced by the Soviet argument that by conquering Savimbi's headquarters and reaching the border, they would inflict a crippling blow on UNITA. "We thought," Lieutenant Colonel Foguetão, chief of operations of the general staff of the FAPLA, said, "that it would have a huge psychological impact throughout Angola. UNITA was based in Mavinga and Jamba, and from there it attacked the rest of the country. Savimbi was there, and his radio, which could be heard very well in Luanda, broadcast from there." Furthermore, Ngongo explained, "For us the operation against Mavinga was a question of national honor. How could we allow this man [Savimbi] to remain there? Looking at it dispassionately, with hindsight, we didn't have the means to carry it out, but it was a question of national honor. We had to occupy this territory!"[44]

The Cubans refused to participate in the operation. In his memoirs Varennikov explains the Cuban decision by rewriting history. "Unfortunately," he states, "our Cuban comrades tended to act unilaterally in the field and to change the plans that we had developed jointly and presented to the Angolans."[45] Varennikov fails to mention that the Cubans had opposed the plan throughout, consistently and loudly.

The operation was based on one key assumption: facing turmoil at home and growing international condemnation, Pretoria would not intervene. "We believed that the political and military situation of South Africa meant that they couldn't launch an offensive against our country," Foguetão explained in a postmortem of the operation. Defense Minister Pedalé added, "We did not expect a major intervention by the South African air force."[46]

The FAPLA launched Operation Second Congress (Operação Segundo Congresso) on August 18, 1985: four heavily armed regular brigades—about 6,000 men—began the advance from Cuito Cuanavale toward Mavinga, and beyond Mavinga to Jamba, the much-desired prize. They were accompanied by approximately sixty Soviet military advisers (including interpreters).[47]

At first the offensive progressed well. "UNITA tried to stop them," South African colonel Breytenbach writes, "but . . . they could not disrupt FAPLA's momentum." SADF Special Forces were flown to Mavinga to harass the advancing FAPLA—while the SADF carried out one of its periodic raids in Cunene Province in southwestern Angola. The FAPLA continued its advance, "harassed by somewhat feeble UNITA attacks and more effective South African artillery fire."[48] Then it paused on the southern shore of the Lomba River, about twenty kilometers northwest of Mavinga, to regroup and wait for much needed supplies. Suddenly, the South Africans struck. "Today, at 5:35 P.M., the South African enemy launched a massive air strike [on the brigades] with ten Mirages and eight Camberras," Polo cabled Havana on September 17.[49] (There were no Cubans with the brigades. However, as the military mission explained, "The brigades are in radio contact . . [and] we have a team of officers in Cuito.")[50] The SADF's long-range artillery joined the battle. U.S. intelligence remarked, "The progress of the offensive has forced the South Africans to become significantly and directly involved."[51]

The Washington Post reported that it was "an open secret" in Pretoria that the South African air force had attacked the advancing FAPLA brigades, but the South Africans denied any involvement. General Viljoen explained that the SADF was merely engaged in a "hot pursuit" operation against SWAPO in Cunene (i.e., hundreds of miles west of Mavinga) and that the FAPLA had been "asked not to interfere."[52] A few days later the tune changed. "Revealing what he described as an 'open secret,'" the Johannesburg *Star* reported, Defense Minister Malan stated on September 20, 1985, that the SADF had been helping Savimbi with material and humanitarian aid. "Now it is on record that South Africa supports Savimbi," he said. By helping Savimbi, "We serve South Africa and Southern Africa and the West's interests." Malan's statement reversed years of denials by Pretoria that it was assisting UNITA, but it was couched in general terms. He did not indicate what kind of material aid South Africa was giving UNITA, nor did he say whether the SADF had been helping Savimbi in the Mavinga campaign. The next day, at a news conference in Jamba, Savimbi asserted: "No South African soldier is involved in Mavinga."[53]

On October 7, 1985, the United States joined the other members of the UN Security Council in approving a resolution that condemned South Africa for its "premeditated and unprovoked" invasion of Cunene—a routine raid in the southwest—and demanded that it withdraw all its military forces from Angola forthwith. The resolution included no sanctions. The United States abstained on a separate vote on one article of the resolution that called on member countries to help Angola strengthen its armed forces in the face of South Africa's "escalating acts of aggression."[54] By then, the South Africans had left Cunene. The Security Council did not mention the SADF's ongoing and far more significant intervention in the southeast on behalf of Savimbi.

While the Security Council voted its high-sounding resolution, a batch of foreign journalists was flying to Cuando Cubango from South Africa to tour the battlefield near the Lomba River. "What journalists saw," Michael Sullivan of the *Washington Times* reported, "was an area of utter destruction where MPLA vehicles—caught grouped closely together—lay twisted and blackened in the scorching sun, the stench of dead and decaying bodies thick in the air as swarms of flies buzzed about a battlefield littered with scraps of uniforms and documents." Savimbi repeated: "'I want to deny reports of South African involvement. . . . We did not need it, we did not request it, and South Africa was not prepared to give it.'"[55] Savimbi paraded a captured Angolan pilot who swore that "he had never seen a South African plane." UNITA had defeated, alone, what he claimed to have been an MPLA-Soviet-Cuban offensive, killing more than 2,000 FAPLA soldiers, as well as 9 Russians and 38 Cubans.[56]

Not every South African officer appreciated Savimbi's bluster. Colonel Breytenbach wrote, "FAPLA abandoned the battlefield and left it strewn with hundreds of burnt-out vehicles, heaps of discarded equipment and hundreds of dead. . . . The carnage was horrible to see. It was, however, an excellent propaganda coup for Savimbi who quickly arranged for the press corps to be flown in. Numerous photographs of UNITA troops in heroic poses . . . appeared in the media. . . . Probably because they were so busy with the press, UNITA failed to follow up the thoroughly routed enemy in the demoralised retreat and annihilate the remnants."[57]

Staggering under the blows of the South African planes and heavy guns, the FAPLA brigades had hastily scrambled a few kilometers northward, beyond the northern shore of the Lomba River. "The air force continued to attack," Angolan lieutenant colonel Foguetão explained, "damaging the materiel; our troops had no ammunition, food or water."[58] The South African planes struck from a high altitude. "They did not inflict many casualties, but they caused great material losses," a Cuban military report noted. The brigades waited for supplies and for orders from the FAPLA high command. The high command sent a column from Cuito Cuanavale with supplies and fuel for the four stranded brigades, escorted by one of the FAPLA's best units, the 16th Brigade. While the column slowly advanced southward, Angolan helicopters tried to fly in supplies and evacuate the wounded, and Cuban planes sought to protect them from South African air attacks, but the distance they had to cover meant that they had only enough fuel to fly for a few minutes over the area of operations. More and more helicopters were being shot down by the South Africans.[59]

The Soviet military mission did not allow its pilots to fly in combat zones, but during the night of September 21, 1985, Soviet helicopters with Soviet crews reached the brigades near the Lomba River. The military mission had sent them, Soviet military adviser Danial Gukov explains, "to evacuate our advisers from the combat zone." In a concession to the Angolans, "the mission decided not to evacuate the advisers of the commanders of the brigades, the interpreters, and the technicians who repaired the materiel, but all the others were evacuated." A few days later the Soviets reconsidered: in his diary entry for September 30, Gukov writes, "From above came the order to evacuate all the advisers, but how to do it? The Angolan helicopter pilots refused to fly to the combat zone. Again a Soviet crew went to the rescue." During the night of October 5–6, "this crew extracted the advisers who had been left in the combat zone. They landed and departed under enemy fire. They were brave youths!"[60] Gukov does not mention how the Angolans may have felt, as the Soviet advisers fled the sinking ship.

On September 30, Angolan defense minister Pedalé told Polo that on the previous day he and President dos Santos had met with the new head of the Soviet military mission, General Kuzmenko. Kuzmenko had argued that the four FAPLA brigades must "remain on the defensive until, within a week, the supply column accompanied by the 16th Brigade has reached them. Then they will re-sume the offensive against Mavinga." Polo disagreed. The brigades must return to Cuito Cuanavale, he insisted. He reminded Pedalé that "due to the distance, our planes can't protect the brigades."[61] The Angolans hesitated and failed to reach a decision. Kuzmenko repeated to Pedalé on October 8 that the FAPLA must resupply the four brigades in order to "re-establish their fighting strength by October 25, . . . restoring their reserves of materiel, creating the necessary stocks of supplies, and reinforcing the antiaircraft defenses. . . . The brigades would thus be able to resume the operation."[62]

For the Cubans, however, the question was not whether the wrongheaded offensive should resume, but whether the four brigades could be saved from annihilation. The Cuban military mission was impressed with their endurance. It told Havana on October 4, "Never before has the FAPLA fought so well and in such difficult conditions. The brigades have resisted despite the enemy's air strikes, with a great many wounded who could not be evacuated, with little am-munition and little food, with the enemy attacking on land with armored ve-hicles and bombarding them with its artillery. They have resisted and according to the information that we received this afternoon, they maintain their fight-ing morale."[63] But how long could they last? Polo warned, "We have received reports from the troops of the first deaths by starvation."[64]

Two days later, October 16, Polo told Raúl Castro: "Today the situation is getting even more critical." The FAPLA high command had lost radio contact with the 16th Brigade, which was escorting the column bringing the supplies. "Furthermore, between yesterday and today forty soldiers [of the four stranded brigades] have died of hunger. If you have no objection, if we cannot find out where the 16th Brigade is, I will propose that the personnel of the other four brigades set fire to their equipment and decamp. I am suggesting this, comrade minister, because the men cannot endure the lack of food much longer and in this way we could save perhaps half of them." Raúl approved.[65]

The next day, radio contact with the 16th Brigade was reestablished. That evening the Cuban military mission told Havana that "the 16th Brigade had decided not to move during the night and to reach the four brigades at first daylight." It was not possible. On October 18 the mission reported, "The pilots that fly over the area . . . report that between the 16th Brigade and the other four there is only a narrow strip of land."[66] Finally, on October 19, the 16th Bri-gade reached the four devastated brigades. Resupplied and assisted by the 16th Brigade, the brigades began their trek back to Cuito Cuanavale, leaving most of their materiel behind. Two weeks later, on November 2, the Soviet defense minister, Marshal Sokolov, bowed to the harsh reality in a cable to Raúl Castro:

"We are taking steps to accelerate the supply to Angola of additional arms, including antiaircraft weapons. . . . But, as you can understand, this will require time. Therefore, we think that it is not opportune to resume the operation in the province of Cuando Cubango in the near future."[67] By then the survivors of the foolhardy offensive were straggling into the safety of Cuito Cuanavale.

A Cuban postmortem of the operation expressed surprise at UNITA's passivity: "Given the appalling vulnerability of the brigades . . . this lassitude suggests that UNITA lacked the strength to annihilate the brigades, or was unaware of their plight, or was too cautious and decided not to risk its forces in a frontal assault." It concluded with praise for the FAPLA soldiers who had "mounted a gritty resistance" under harrowing conditions, enduring their suffering "with stoicism." The CIA joined in the praise. A Special National Intelligence Estimate noted the "improved performance of the Angolan army against UNITA . . . this year." The offensive against Mavinga had been halted by "unprecedented South African air strikes," but the FAPLA had demonstrated that it could "meet and overcome UNITA forces in battle."[68]

Almost 2,000 Angolan soldiers did not make it back to Cuito Cuanavale. As the deputy chief of staff of the FAPLA, Ngongo, reported in his postmortem of the operation, 1,550 had died, and 300 were missing; 1,300 had been wounded, and great quantities of war materiel lost. Soberly, Ngongo pointed out: "We were unable to protect the brigades . . . from the South African air force, because of their almost complete lack of antiaircraft weapons and the weakness of the air cover, due to the distance from our airports. . . . We must significantly improve this if we want to operate in areas where the South African air force may intervene."[69]

I read these pages about Operation Second Congress to three senior Angolan officers who were involved in the operation: Ngongo, Foguetão, and Colonel Manuel Correia de Barros. I interviewed them separately. Ngongo agreed, emphatically, with the account. Foguetão said, "It is true. Everything you said is true." Only Correia de Barros hedged somewhat. He said, "That is more or less what happened." When I asked on what points he disagreed, he said, "That's exactly how it was." I also read these pages to the FAPLA chief of staff, Ndalu, who disagreed on one point: he believed that the reports overstated the number of helicopters shot down. Everything else, he said, was true.[70]

## Havana: A New Strategy?

For the Cubans, the defeat of the offensive was painful confirmation that Pretoria's air superiority had to be broken. It deepened their desire to adopt a new strategy, one that would force the SADF out of Angola, permanently.

In October 1985, when Foreign Minister Shevardnadze visited Havana, Castro had his first meeting with a senior member of the new Soviet leadership—Shevardnadze had been handpicked by Gorbachev. Their long conversation centered on two issues: Angola and Nicaragua. Castro criticized the Soviets' military strategy in Angola, especially their focus on creating a conventional army, which starved the counterinsurgency brigades of men and materiel. "There were two [Angolan] armies," he said, "one poor and without resources that fought against the bandits; and the Grand Army which did not participate in the war against the bandits and did not acquire combat experience." In the wake of the attack against Cangamba in August 1983, the Soviets had finally agreed that the regular brigades should fight in the war against UNITA. But then, another mistake had intervened: egged on by the Soviet military mission, the FAPLA had carried out military operations "as if South Africa did not exist. When South Africa intervened, surprise!" Castro was referring, of course, to the operation against Mavinga: less than two weeks earlier, near the Lomba River, four FAPLA brigades had faced annihilation.

Castro sought to impress on Shevardnadze that it was the SADF, not UNITA, that had defeated the offensive. This was the necessary backdrop for what he intended to propose.

"South Africa has absolute air superiority," he began. This had forced Cuba to create its defensive line about 250–300 kilometers north of the border, abandoning the far south of Angola to the SADF. It was time, Castro urged, to change this. "South Africa has its hands in Angola. It is time to cut them off." Then he revealed his inner thoughts: "I think that if we hit them hard we will help deepen the crisis of apartheid."

The Soviets, he told Shevardnadze, had to help Cuba gain air superiority in southern Angola. He wanted more and better planes—including MIGs 25 and 29 that the Cubans did not yet know how to fly. This might require Soviet pilots to participate in the fighting in Angola, he noted. He did not yet have a firm plan. He was thinking out loud: "Taking into account the international situation, we must analyze whether the Soviets should get involved. I do believe, however, that we, Angolans and Cubans, with Soviet technical cooperation, with Soviet weapons, we could strike a hard blow against apartheid. Because the problem is that the South Africans act with impunity, they attack where they please, they perpetrate their crimes, and we don't respond. Really, the weapons we have in Angola are insufficient."

Shevardnadze, who had listened in silence, interrupted: "I want to be sure I understand you: do you mean a blow in Angolan territory?" Castro replied: "I am thinking in Angolan territory, but we must not exclude completely the idea of counterattacking with our air force against their bases [in Namibia]. . . . My idea is to fight within Angola, without crossing the border with our troops. Then we will have to decide whether our planes will cross the border. . . . They could, in certain circumstances, attack the South African air bases. But right now I am not proposing this. What I am proposing is that we acquire the superiority in the air and defeat them there, in Angola. This is my idea. This is what I propose. . . . South Africa's only advantage has been its air force. If we neutralize it, we gain the upper hand."[71]

Three months later, in January 1986, Cubans and Soviets met in Moscow, first alone and then with the Angolans. Throughout the sessions, the Cubans' constant refrain was the need to end the SADF's air superiority in southern Angola. "This is our great weakness," Risquet argued. "We must eliminate it."[72] He insisted, "Cutting off the claws of the racists in southern Angola" would not only make it possible for the FAPLA to attack UNITA there; "it would also make it easier for SWAPO guerrillas to infiltrate into Namibia and it . . . would give great encouragement to all the people of southern Africa."[73]

This was discussed in more technical terms in meetings between senior Soviet and Cuban officers. Ulises was persistent, well prepared, and, when necessary, would lace his arguments with a subtle sarcasm. The Soviets, led by Marshal Akhromeyev, promised improvements in antiaircraft weapons and in airplanes, but Ulises pointed out, in detail, that what the Soviets were offering would not be sufficient to establish air superiority over southern Angola. "We can't continue to let the South Africans operate with impunity." Returning to the Cubans' favorite metaphor for the operation, he said, "We must chop off their hands inside Angola." He also reminded the Soviets that Cuba was facing challenges not only in Angola; it also had to deal with the ever present danger posed by the Reagan administration. "We have two problems—the defense of Angola and the defense of Cuba—and we must remain strong at home." The Soviets' reply was evasive: "We could coordinate with SWAPO. If the South Africans intensify their air strikes [in southern Angola], SWAPO could attack their airports [in northern Namibia]. The Vietnamese did this [against the Americans]; it can work." This was a wild overestimation of SWAPO's capabilities. All Ulises could do was repeat what he had already said to the Soviets, who were always polite, at times even deferential, but gave little ground. "We believe that the Soviet response is inadequate," Ulises concluded on behalf of his country's leaders.[74]

In late February 1986 Castro traveled to Moscow to attend the Twenty-Seventh Congress of the Communist Party of the Soviet Union. There, for the first time, he would meet Gorbachev.

## Fidel Castro and Gorbachev

The initial Cuban reaction to Gorbachev had been positive—he was a new, young, and dynamic leader. His desire to reform the Soviet economy was welcome. "We have great confidence in the new phase that has begun, with great dynamism, in the domestic and foreign policy of the Soviet Union," Fidel Castro told Gorbachev during a telephone conversation in November 1985. They had not yet met. Raúl had led the Cuban delegation at Chernenko's funeral in March 1985. "We had a lengthy conversation," Gorbachev writes in his memoirs about his encounter with Raúl. "At the time, there were a lot of problems in Soviet-Cuban relations. I thought it was important to stress our commitment to our mutual cooperation, and I think this is what the Cubans wanted to hear."[75]

Judging by the Cuban minutes, it had been a friendly encounter in which neither side had mentioned any problem in the relationship. Gorbachev had stressed the importance of Cuba to the Soviet Union. "We value greatly the good relations between our two countries.... Our policy, which includes every aspect of our relationship, ... remains unchanged.... We will continue to give you our aid, although I must tell you, as our friends, that its scope will be determined by our capabilities. But we will do everything that is possible, everything." He touched briefly on Angola—Cubans and Soviets must continue their common efforts to help the Angolan government—and on Central America. ("We think that the role of Cuba in the region ... will constantly grow stronger.") He gave Raúl a thumbnail sketch of his conversation with the U.S. delegation to Chernenko's funeral, which was led by Vice President George Bush:

> This U.S. "brigade" came to Moscow empty-handed. My conversations with the other Western delegations had more substance than that with the Americans. The only thing they brought was a letter from Reagan, but it was just empty words. All it said was that he is willing to meet . . . but in the United States. [In his letter, Reagan had invited Gorbachev "to visit me in Washington at the earliest convenient opportunity."][76] Apparently his idea is: "Let Gorbachev come see what a powerful country the United States is." . . . Furthermore, they think that the mere fact that the General Secretary of the Soviet Communist Party would travel to Washington "to bow before Reagan" would show to all the world how great the United States is. . . . We have no illusions. We will continue to assess every development in a realistic manner. Nevertheless, we believe that we must develop the political dialogue [with the United States].[77]

In November 1985 Gorbachev phoned Castro to brief him on his first summit with Reagan in Geneva. "It took us a long time to establish a dialogue," he said. "The first session, in particular, was deeply disappointing. He [Reagan] seemed to want to improve the atmospherics between our two countries. . . . But the minute he moved to concrete matters, he presented us with a list of accusations and demands. It all boiled down to the demand that . . . the Soviet Union change its policies and its behavior. . . . We argued a lot. But I think that the fact that we met is useful." They had agreed to meet again, and this was positive. "Time will tell what will happen. There haven't been any big changes yet, but the atmosphere has improved."[78]

In his speech to the Third Congress of the Cuban Communist Party in February 1986, Castro welcomed these signs of thaw in U.S.-Soviet relations: "Geneva brought no solutions, but it did offer hope that there will be better communication, and this might in turn lead to serious steps toward détente and peace." But, he warned, "We must not forget that even if Reagan were to change his behavior toward the Soviet Union, this would not necessarily mean that he would change his policy on regional issues. In some cases—in Central America, Angola, southern Africa and other countries—U.S. policy after Geneva has become even more aggressive."[79]

A few days later, on February 23, 1986, Castro arrived in Moscow to attend the Twenty-Seventh Congress of the Soviet Communist Party. "He was given the honor of being the first of the guests to speak," a Soviet official remarked. In his memoirs, Gorbachev wrote, "Fidel Castro . . . was received with great warmth. . . . His speech at the Congress was at once emotional and profound. . . . The delegates applauded Castro enthusiastically. It seemed to me, however, that while Fidel enjoyed the acclaim of the delegates, he did not fully understand the meaning of the change that was taking place in our country."[80] Gorbachev himself, who was intent on reforming, not destroying, the Soviet Union, did not fully understand "the meaning of the change."

Anatoly Chernyaev, who had just become Gorbachev's foreign policy adviser, writes that on March 2, 1986, Gorbachev and Castro had a wide-ranging conversation. Gorbachev spoke of how the arms race endangered humanity and must be stopped. He also "asserted the necessity of maintaining control in Angola, Ethiopia, Mozambique and other African countries that were 'taking the anti-imperialist path.'"[81] The Cuban and Soviet minutes of the conversation confirm that Gorbachev told Castro: "We must do everything we can, through our joint efforts, to help those movements that have already achieved successes and it is important to defend these achievements. Comrade Fidel, I greatly value the policy that we are following, our joint struggle to help Nicaragua, to help Angola. I also think that we must do everything we can to defend Ethiopia and also South Yemen. There is also now a very difficult situation in Mozambique. . . . I want to stress especially this: we greatly value our collaboration [with you]."

Castro spoke of Cuba's willingness to remain in Angola until the end of apartheid: "We've been there for twelve years, and we're willing to stay. Our people are ready; more than 200,000 Cubans have been there and some military officers have been twice. . . . We have suffered casualties; approximately 1,000 Cubans have died in these twelve years, one-third in combat and the others from sickness and accidents. For us, it is an effort, a sacrifice, but we have been careful to avoid unnecessary casualties, and politically and morally we are ready to stay." He then turned to the issue he had raised with Shevardnadze the previous October: the need to change from a defensive to an offensive strategy against South Africa:

> The crises of Angola and Namibia have not been solved because the South Africans have been able to commit crimes in Angola with impunity for nine years. . . . In 1976 they were defeated; they took fright when we assembled a lot of soldiers and tanks and began advancing [toward the Namibian border]. We were ready to fight, but we gave them the opportunity to withdraw. . . .
>
> Two and half years later they started again, attacking Cassinga. . . . Why were they able to do this? Because they had complete air superiority in southern Angola.
>
> We defend a line approximately 250 or 300 kilometers north of the Namibian border, where the terrain favors us. The South Africans have never advanced beyond our line; they operate in the strip further south, where they enjoy complete air superiority. . . .
>
> I told Shevardnadze that we must neutralize South Africa's air superiority. When I spoke with him, I thought that we wouldn't be able to do it without the participation of Soviet pilots. But now, having carefully analyzed the matter, we have concluded that this would not be necessary. We will provide all the pilots.

What Castro proposed was that the Soviet Union supply the planes—he wanted MIG 29s—and train Cuban pilots to fly them. With MIG 29s, Cuba would be able to gain air superiority in the far south of Angola. "If we have the planes, we won't need any Soviet pilots. This is a change from what I told Shevardnadze. All we need are two or three squadrons of MIG 29s. . . . It's possible that we won't even need to use them. I know the South Africans; we need to demonstrate to them that we have the means to end their attacks in Angola." He sought to reassure Gorbachev: "I am not talking about crossing the border [into Namibia], but of fighting within Angola, of attacking any South African planes or troops that enter Angola. That, in essence, is what we propose."

Gorbachev replied sympathetically, without committing himself: "We need to analyze this problem carefully and find a solution. We will ask our comrades to study your proposal both from the military and the political angle, and we'll find out what it is that our military are fussing about [Laughter]."

Castro: "They're afraid that we will cross the border, and I say that we will do what we both agree on."

Gorbachev: "Of course."

Castro: "I told Shevardnadze that there could be an occasion when, in response to an attack, we might strike South Africa's bases in Namibia. From a military point of view this might be the best thing to do, but we will do whatever it is that we have agreed with you, and if we have agreed that our troops will not cross the border, we won't cross it. Our Soviet comrades can trust us. We won't lie, and we won't seek pretexts to do something else."

Gorbachev: "We trust you completely. . . ."

Castro: "I want you to keep in mind that the most discredited regime in the world is the South African; it is hated in Africa, the entire Third World hates it, even public opinion in the Western countries repudiates it. Southern Africa is not Nicaragua."

Gorbachev: "We share your analysis."

Castro: "Nicaragua is a problem because it is close to the United States. . . . [But for] the Americans South Africa is an ally that is rotten, repulsive. It creates problems for them. I think that if we put an end to South Africa's adventures in southern Angola, not only will it be possible to implement Resolution 435, but apartheid will collapse. . . . Within South Africa itself there is a real popular revolt. If we neutralize the South African air force, Zimbabwe will feel safer and Mozambique will feel safer. All the Frontline States . . . will gain heart."

He concluded, "Stopping Pretoria's aggression in southern Angola would be a turning point for the liberation of South Africa. . . . All we are asking is that we do what is necessary to end their air superiority." Gorbachev promised, "We will study all this carefully."[82]

Castro's pitch was not successful. Arguably the Soviets were, as they said, overextended. The war in Afghanistan was placing extraordinary demands on a Soviet military budget that had not grown accordingly. "It is necessary to take into account," Marshal Akhromeyev points out in his memoirs, "that in the 1980s Soviet industry, including the defense industry, worked according to peacetime plans."[83] There was another, powerful reason that Gorbachev refused to agree to Castro's request. Moscow feared that if the Cubans achieved air superiority or even parity in southern Angola, they might plunge forward, eject the SADF from Angola, and advance into Namibia. Ulises remarks, "The Soviets wanted to curtail our ability to threaten the border [with Namibia] because they feared that we would cross it. They had antiaircraft weapons that could have neutralized the South African air force, but they didn't give them to us."[84] He told the head of the KGB in Havana: "Boris, personally I think that our Soviet brothers . . . have always worried that if they give them [the mobile antiaircraft systems Cuba wanted] to us, we will launch an offensive [into Namibia]."[85] The fervor of Castro's hatred of apartheid heightened the Kremlin's fear that if he obtained the weapons he sought, he might cross the border to free Namibia and inflict a crippling blow on the South African regime. In his memoirs Gorbachev refers to the Cubans' propensity "to encourage revolutions in the countries of Latin America, Asia and Africa." Then he adds:

> At the end of the 1970s the Soviet Union and Cuba developed a special relationship. The Soviet government used the Cubans for its own foreign policy objectives, but to be frank I must stress that Castro always maintained his independence. Our relations were between allies, not between patron and client. It is also true that the Cuban government got us involved in, to put it mildly, difficult situations, such as Angola. Our military was interested in establishing a reliable bridgehead in Africa, and so it supported Cuba's involvement in Angola and Ethiopia with enthusiasm. At the same time, Cuba's excessive engagement, which dragged in the Soviet Union, provoked serious objections in our political circles. In our "corridors of power" many said openly that the Cubans "were saddling us with a second Afghanistan."[86]

## Mavinga Again?

In Moscow, in January 1986, Ulises had stressed to the Soviets and the Angolans that the FAPLA must not launch another operation against Mavinga as long as the South Africans controlled the skies. His frank assessment led to an exchange with Iko Carreira, the head of the air-defense forces of the FAPLA. "We have listened carefully to our Cuban comrade," Carreira said. "His words are somewhat pessimistic. He does not take into account the abilities of our military. . . . We . . . must liberate our territory." Ulises replied, "With respect, when we analyze the situation we do not ignore the need to liberate the territory. But one must choose the correct moment to achieve this, and one must calculate the odds of success."[87]

A few months later, in April, Konstantin arrived in Luanda to urge the Angolans to launch yet another offensive against Mavinga. His conversation with Polo was almost cordial until he said, "The question now is how to attack . . . Mavinga."[88] The tug of war began anew. The Angolans wavered, torn between the bitter lesson of the previous year and the lure of the great victory, but they were increasingly receptive to the Cubans' admonitions. In July, Konstantin descended again on Luanda. Havana responded by sending General Arnaldo Ochoa, the deputy minister of defense in charge of Cuban military missions abroad. Because Ochoa had never served in Angola, he had not developed any animus toward Konstantin. The conversation between the two Cubans and the Soviet general was almost amiable; even Polo was at his sweetest, telling Konstantin that he was "the dear guest of our [military] mission," while Konstantin replied graciously that "ever since . . . my trip to Cuba I feel as if I were a Cuban." The bottom line remained the same, however: the Cubans opposed the operation. The Angolans sided with them.[89] Instead of attacking Mavinga, the FAPLA centered its efforts against UNITA in the central and northern provinces of the country.

In the south, the situation remained static. The Cubans continued to man their defensive line in the southwest; south of the line, the SADF came and went as it pleased. In the southeast the FAPLA continued to hold Cuito Cuanavale; south of Cuito, Savimbi ruled under the protective mantle of the South African air force. The Cubans grew increasingly frustrated. And their frustration deepened when, on June 5, 1986, South African Special Forces carried out a bold assault from the sea on Namibe, the major port of southern Angola, damaging two Soviet cargo ships, sinking a Cuban cargo ship, and destroying two fuel storage tanks.[90] The Soviet government issued a statement condemning Pretoria's "terrorist action"[91] and supported a draft resolution at the UN Security Council imposing sanctions on South Africa for the raid. On June 18, 1986, twelve countries voted in favor of the resolution, France abstained, and the United States and England cast their vetoes. Once again, South Africa went unpunished.[92]

## Dinner with Konstantin

The desire, ever more pressing, to take the offensive against the SADF dominated Castro's thoughts when he met Konstantin on September 8, 1986, in Luanda. Castro was in the Angolan capital for a short visit following the Harare Summit of the Non-Aligned Movement, and Konstantin had been sent by Soviet defense minister Sokolov to review the military situation. He told Castro, "Our main task in 1987 . . . will be to wipe out UNITA in the southeast of Angola, destroying its bases at Mavinga and Jamba." He promised that the Angolan troops engaged in the offensive would receive enough antiaircraft weapons and enough planes to withstand attacks by the South African air force.[93]

Like Konstantin, Castro favored a major offensive, but in a different direction and against a different enemy. Konstantin wanted to fight in the southeast against UNITA, whereas Castro proposed an offensive in the southwest, south of the Cuban line. There FAPLA and Cubans would meet not UNITA but the real foe, the South Africans.

The southeast lacked roads and its topography was less suited for the use of tanks and armored vehicles than the southwest. A Cuban offensive in the southeast, if successful, would lead only to the narrow band of Caprivi, in Namibia, south of which lay Botswana. In the southeast, UNITA ruled a vast territory under the protection of the South African air force. In the southwest, however, UNITA's presence was minor. It was the South Africans who dominated the area south of the Cuban defensive line and occupied Angolan towns.

"I ask, wouldn't it be better to concentrate our effort here [in the southwest] and throw the South Africans out?" Castro inquired of Konstantin. "What's the point of fighting against UNITA if the South Africans remain [in the southwest]? Why don't we fight against the South Africans? . . . Why do we want to get to Jamba when we'll still have the South Africans near Cahama, Mulongo, Tchamutete [in the southwest]? Isn't it more important to strike the South Africans and cut off their hands?"[94]

The Soviets had consistently opposed an offensive against the South Africans. This, Castro argued, was a mistake that had lasted too long:

> Listen, it's a problem of strategy. We've been implementing a defensive strategy in Angola, and that's why the enemy does whatever he wants . . . striking here, bombarding there, while we watch with our arms crossed. Our strategy is defensive, Comrade Konstantin, that's our problem. . . . They can bomb us but we can't bomb them. . . . Why don't we consider bombing all their bases and attacking them on the other side of the border

[in Namibia] to give them a taste of their own medicine? . . . If we don't want to cross the border, why don't we at least destroy their bases? . . . If we occupy all these places [in the southwest] and we then say, "No South African can come here," we will intimidate them, and if they attack us, we will counterattack. . . . We have spent ten years in this defensive posture. This is our tragedy. This defensive strategy enables the enemy to hit us here and there . . . to humiliate us, to create problems between Angola and Cuba, between Angola and the USSR. . . . Blows upon blows, and we never respond. . . . We must prepare to counterattack, but we have not yet been able to convince the Soviets of this. . . . We are losing patience. . . . For ten years we have let the South Africans attack us with impunity, Comrade—massacre in Cassinga, slaughter in Cuvelai, slaughter everywhere . . . blowing up trains, laying mines. They blew up a Cuban ship and two Soviet ships. The South Africans don't respect us, Comrade Konstantin. They don't respect us because the Soviets hardly complained when they blew up two of their ships. If someone had done this to the Yankees there would be an outcry and an international crisis, but the Soviets didn't even protest. And maybe it was for the best because the South Africans would have just laughed. The enemy laughs at our declarations. If we had responded by bombing the South African positions, then the enemy would no longer be laughing at us.[95]

Cuba was willing to send more men, more pilots, and more weapons for an offensive against the SADF. In the back of Castro's mind was the "revolutionary linkage" he had proposed at Harare: "Our objective is not Namibia, our objective must be apartheid." But Cuba could not do it alone. The Soviet Union had to help, sending more planes, better planes, more sophisticated antiaircraft weapons, more modern tanks. "Look," he told Konstantin, the Cuban troops in Angola had old T-34 tanks that were of World War II vintage, "and we should have T-55 tanks, more modern tanks in our defensive line. . . . We have more than one hundred T-34 tanks. Do you think that our army should confront South Africa with T-34s? Comrade Konstantin, does this make sense?"[96]

This was the message, Castro concluded, "that I would like you to convey to Defense Minister Sokolov and the General Staff; tell them that we have been pursuing a defensive strategy for ten years and this has made it impossible to win the war."[97]

The next day, Castro sat across the table from Konstantin at an extraordinary dinner. Castro was the host, and the guest of honor was President dos Santos, accompanied by his minister of defense, the FAPLA chief of staff, and another senior aide. Castro directed his remarks, however, at Konstantin. Castro was charming—"Comrade Konstantin is a great military leader . . . the kind of military man I like." He gently referred to past differences—"We haven't always agreed with Comrade Konstantin. . . . He is more the academic type, we are a little more, let's say, guerrillas." But what really interested Castro, the message he wanted to etch in Konstantin's mind, was what needed to be done next in Angola. He flattered Konstantin by talking about how the general "carries great weight in the Soviet Union." Castro went on: "Comrade Konstantin can achieve much. . . . I speak with the [Soviet] General Staff and they listen to me, but I have far less influence than Comrade Konstantin." Time and again, Castro returned to what he had told Konstantin the previous day: "The moment must come when we stop the South Africans from crossing the border; therefore, we should move our troops forward; Cuban troops and Angolan troops must advance step by step toward the border." This would require better weapons, above all antiaircraft systems and planes. Castro recalled that in 1976, when the Cubans had pushed the SADF out of Angola, "we had 26,000 men, 400 tanks that advanced toward the south . . . and the South Africans withdrew because we were strong. . . . If we become strong again, perhaps the South Africans will obey us. They are an obedient people when we are strong. . . . We might be able to solve the problem without fighting, but only if we are prepared to fight. We must be willing and ready to fight." The South Africans had been crossing the Angolan border at will,

> and we have had to tolerate this. Our border! Our territory! Our country! The South Africans do whatever they want! We've had to take it because we haven't been able to do anything else, but we have an obligation to create conditions that will allow us to put a stop to it. . . . If we are strong enough, we might not have to fire a single shot, but if we have to fire a bullet then we must be ready to fire one million bullets. Not one single white South African should remain in the area. . . . I am sure that deep down Konstantin agrees with me. There won't be any adventures. We won't be foolhardy. We have been patient for many years, but we must assemble a force that can eject the South Africans from Angola. . . . Then we will be in a position to give them orders: Go back to Pretoria. Don't step even half an inch over the border because if you do we will destroy you. . . . If we are strong we will find that there are no people more compliant than the South Africans.[98]

The plan could not succeed, however, unless the Soviet Union provided the weapons. Hence Castro's plea: "We have to explain this to the Soviets. I will talk with them, but it is very important that Konstantin does it too; if Konstantin agrees, then it will be easier to persuade the Soviets. We are not proposing adventures. . . . It is essential that the Soviets understand our strategy. It is essential that they help us."[99]

Castro's plan was straightforward: the Cuban-Angolan advance would be in the southwest, gradually pushing south from the Cuban line to force the SADF out of Angola. If the advance was successful, and this depended on Moscow's willingness to provide the weapons, then, and only then, the FAPLA could move in the southeast against Mavinga and Jamba. If the SADF dared to intervene, "then we can counterattack, and if they launch an attack there, they would lose everything here and in the principal direction." Castro was vague. His words ("in the principal direction") seemed to imply that Cubans would respond to a South African attack in the southeast by entering Namibia from the southwest. Or perhaps he meant that the Cubans would respond by striking at the SADF in the southeast: "If they attack an Angolan unit, we will throw all our forces at them to crush the attack, whether it is by air or land. . . . We will force them to behave. If they attack we will respond. We will counterattack."[100]

Pointing at the precedent of 1975–76, Castro argued that the SADF might withdraw without fighting if confronted with a superior force. If not, the Cubans would fight their way to the border. And beyond this border, beyond even the independence of Namibia, loomed the great prize: the defeat of apartheid. Castro told dos Santos, "When we are strong enough to prevent them [the South Africans] from entering Angola, Comrade José Eduardo, then I think that the end of apartheid will be close."[101]

He addressed a passionate plea to Konstantin: "Tell Moscow that . . . South Africa is isolated and in a very critical situation. . . . We must encircle South Africa with Angola, Zimbabwe, Mozambique, the ANC, SWAPO. We must be able to respond [to the South African attacks] and not allow them to act with absolute impunity. . . . Our policy of passivity is harmful. . . . When we are able to respond blow by blow to South Africa its aggression will end, apartheid will end."[102]

Fidel Castro was motivated by the struggle against apartheid, what he called "the most beautiful cause,"[103] but the Kremlin was increasingly focused on improving relations with the United States. Konstantin said very little during the dinner, just a few polite noises that promised nothing. A few days later he returned to Moscow. Dos Santos also said very little during the dinner, but in a separate conversation with Castro he embraced the idea of an offensive in the southwest: "We are in perfect agreement, but we must convince our Soviet comrades in order to avoid new mistakes."[104]

## UNITA on the Defensive

One month later, in October 1986, Assistant Secretary Crocker and Savimbi met in Paris. Crocker was upbeat. "The program of US assistance to UNITA is on a firm footing," he said. He asked Savimbi, "Give us a capsule view of this season's fighting. The President and the Secretary [of State] would be interested." Savimbi acknowledged that UNITA had suffered some setbacks. "We intend to concentrate our forces and recover key areas. When we tried to act more effectively in the North, our position in the center of the country weakened somewhat." He too was upbeat, however, or so he claimed. "The military situation is good at key points," he said, and would continue to improve.[105] Savimbi was spinning the truth. To be sure, UNITA was still very strong, but it had lost ground in the central and northern regions. "Despite the improved military hardware available to UNITA, its forces have not been able to prevent MPLA gains," Crocker's senior deputy told Secretary Shultz.[106]

Nor was Savimbi's pet plan—a surprise attack against Cuito Cuanavale—successful. In the summer of 1986 the UNITA insurgents under cover of the thick bush approached Cuito undetected, and South African artillery was sent to assist them. "Savimbi had decided that he was going to take Cuito," explained Colonel Breytenbach, who headed a team of South African military officers who helped UNITA plan the attack. In his memoirs, General Geldenhuys said, "On 9 and 10 August, 1986, an attack against Cuito Cuanavale was launched by 4,000 UNITA troops with very limited South African help. South African long-distance artillery caused considerable damage." Breytenbach concurred, "the guns did a hell of a lot of damage." But when UNITA infantry attacked Cuito, the FAPLA soldiers stationed there held their ground. When the FAPLA counterattacked with a few tanks, "the UNITA infantry just took to their heels," reported South African Colonel Fred Oelschig, who participated in the operation. "I have never seen people run so fast," Breytenbach remembered. "The entire operation was a total failure."[107]

Savimbi's reverses in 1986 meant that Pretoria began to lose confidence that he could come to power in Luanda. "The [South African] National Intelligence Service [NIS] believes that several changes have occurred in Angola," the NIS representative argued at a February 1987 meeting of the Angola Task Force of the Secretariat of the State Security Council. "The enemy has increased its pressure and UNITA has lost strength." The army's representative objected: "According to the SADF, UNITA's position has in fact improved." Four months later, however, the Secretariat of the State Security Council noted, "Although UNITA is able to tie down the MPLA forces, a large number of proxy [Cuban] troops and a significant number of SWAPO terrorists by means of revolution-ary warfare, the movement has not been able so far to threaten the MPLA outside the territory it controls in the southeast of Angola. . . . In light of the above, and given UNITA's alliance with South Africa, it is now unlikely that UNITA will be able to make the MPLA accept its participation in a government of national unity."[108]

But while the Angolan government's military situation had improved, its economic straits had worsened. The steep fall in oil prices in 1986 meant a loss of more than $200 million for Angola.[109] The economy was in shambles. The reasons were many. There was the open wound caused by the departure of the Portuguese in 1975, a loss that a few thousand foreign experts could not make up. There was also the incompetence of the government and the growing cor-ruption—what President dos Santos himself called "the excessive centraliza-tion in the methods of socialist planning, the excessive bureaucratization in the conduct of the economy . . . the disorganization and poor administration of [state] companies, the galloping indiscipline, and the rampant corruption."[110] The MPLA's Second Congress, in December 1985, saw one of the party's great leaders, Lúcio Lara, dropped from the Political Bureau. Incorruptible, brilliant, Lara had been Neto's closest companion. He could have been Neto's successor as president of the republic had he not been a light-skinned mulatto in a color-conscious country. His influence had been declining since the early 1980s. His political demise signaled the decay of a culture of personal integrity and politi-cal commitment that Neto had inspired. The Cubans watched his departure with deep sorrow. At the end of the Congress, when dos Santos brought up the subject, Risquet expressed his great appreciation for Lara—"as a historic leader, austere, hardworking."[111]

The country's ills were multiplied by the war. Not only did the war force the government to divert a large share of its resources to the military budget—"46 to 47 percent" in 1987, according to an authoritative Polish report—but Pretoria and Savimbi systematically attacked economic targets. "What the government tried to build by day, UNITA destroyed by night," Savimbi's biographer writes.[112] U.S. newspapers, which had long overlooked UNITA's sins, broke their silence. In the spring and summer of 1987, the *Washington Post* reported that Western diplomats, businessmen, and relief workers in Angola believed that "UNITA has been responsible for a number of atrocities against the civilian population."[113] A Western development specialist who had worked for several years in south-ern Angola told the *Post*'s Blaine Harden, "'There is no doubt that UNITA's policy is to terrorize civilians.'. . . This view," Harden added, "is widely shared by many Western diplomats here [in Luanda] and senior officials at UN relief agencies operating in Angola." UNITA sought to paralyze food production in areas controlled by the government by burying "antipersonnel mines in fields, roads and on footpaths near rivers." The deputy resident representative of the UN Development Program in Angola told Harden, "Many cases have been reported to us of women and children sitting in their huts, starving, while their maize ripens in front of them. They have seen too many people mutilated by mines." From Luanda, the special envoy of the *Christian Science Monitor* wrote, "Each side blames the other for the mines. Western diplomats and aid workers here, however, believe that Savimbi's men are the main culprits. . . . UNITA has in recent years focused much of its activity on 'economic' targets. . . . The main, and most successful, UNITA 'economic' offensive, diplomats here maintain, has involved the indiscriminate planting of land mines in grain fields."[114]

These reports did not seem to perturb the Reagan administration. The available record shows that U.S. officials never discussed UNITA's human rights violations with Savimbi or his aides. However, they did frequently admonish UNITA not to attack American citizens working in Angola or the property of American companies. This, Crocker warned a UNITA official, "would . . . be most unfortunate." The Americans stressed that "there need be no basic conflict between the conduct of UNITA's military operations and the good reputation of the movement." Savimbi understood the rules. After meeting with him in Cape Town in February 1985, Crocker reported, "On Western multinationals, Savimbi gave me categorical assurances that US personnel and US firms are not the target of UNITA's military planners." A year later, Deputy Assistant Secretary Wisner told a UNITA representative, "Keep yourself on the high road. The administration would see your attacking Americans as unfortunate."[115]

Despite its policy of terrorizing the civilian population, and the blows it had received from the FAPLA, UNITA remained in 1987, as the Polish Embassy noted, "an important . . . socio-political and military force that enjoys relatively broad support." This support was due, in part, to Savimbi's charisma and his ethnic ties (he hailed from Angola's largest ethnic group). But it was also due to the country's economic chaos, exacerbated by the MPLA's failings. The Polish Embassy wrote, "The Angolan authorities are aware that the people's patience is near the breaking point."[116] Corruption and mismanagement, however, continued unabated.

## Tripartite in Moscow, March 1987

Cubans and Soviets continued to disagree about military strategy. In September 1986, in Luanda, Castro had tried to enlist Konstantin's support for an offensive against the SADF in the southwest. When Castro visited Moscow two months later to attend the COMECON summit, he "complained about the poor quality of the armament of the Cuban troops in Angola," Gorbachev told the Politburo.[117] The following December, at a meeting in Moscow between top Cuban and Soviet military officers, the Cubans again urged a change in strategy. Pretoria was facing growing resistance at home and deepening isolation abroad, they said. It was time to help accelerate "the process of disintegration of apartheid. . . . The present situation in southern Africa and especially in Angola requires that we . . . adopt an offensive strategy." The moment had arrived "to eject the South Africans from Angola and impose our will on them: we won't allow them to cross the border and we'll respond with overwhelming force to any blow they try to inflict on us. . . . In this way . . . we will help undermine apartheid; and we will also create the conditions to destroy UNITA, which would lose its vital South African assistance. . . . But in order to achieve these objectives we must create in southern Angola . . . a highly mobile and maneuverable Cuban army with great firepower that will be able to carry out decisive offensive operations."[118]

Once again, the Angolans favored the Cuban approach. Dos Santos wrote to Castro, "As we discussed . . . we agree that the Cuban troops should advance [from the Cuban defensive line] all the way to the border."[119] However, once again, the Soviets were not persuaded. They feared that Castro's plan could lead to a major clash with Pretoria's army that would provoke a U.S. reaction, "both political and military."[120]

In March 1987 Angolans, Cubans, and Russians met in Moscow for one of their periodic tripartite meetings. The Cubans said that the FAPLA should continue to focus on fighting UNITA in the center-north of Angola, while stressing that domestic reforms must accompany the military actions, a point with which the Soviets agreed. "To be frank," Defense Minister Sokolov told the Angolans, "the war cannot be won by only military means."[121]

But Soviets and Cubans continued to differ about military strategy. The Soviets still favored an offensive in the southeast. Risquet reminded Angolans and Soviets of Mavinga—"Everyone has admitted that it was a mistake. . . . We almost suffered a disaster because we had not foreseen something that was very predictable—that is, the intervention of the South Africans." Sokolov acknowledged that another campaign in the southeast against UNITA risked the danger "of a clash with the South Africans," but he argued that the Soviet Union had provided Angola with SAM missiles and better aircraft, so that "the possibility of inflicting blows on the South African forces . . . is quite high."[122] The Soviets had indeed strengthened the Angolans' air force and antiaircraft defenses, but, as events would prove, the Cuban assessment was correct: the FAPLA was not strong enough to take on the South Africans. As the Cubans well understood, the South African air force was still stronger than the Angolan and Cuban air forces combined. An offensive against Mavinga, they argued, made as little sense in 1987 as it had in 1985. Vadim Medvedev, a senior Gorbachev aide who participated in the meeting, notes that "among the Soviet military chiefs" the Cubans' opposition to the operation "provoked irritation."[123]

## Raúl Castro Meets Sam Nujoma

A few weeks later SWAPO leader Sam Nujoma arrived in Havana. SWAPO was continuing its guerrilla war in northern Namibia despite overwhelming obstacles. In order to enter Namibia, a South African military analyst noted, the rebels first "had to walk hundreds of kilometers to the border, burdened with all the necessities for guerrilla warfare," through Angolan territory controlled by the SADF. Across the border, in Namibia, he added, the South Africans "were . . . waiting for the guerrillas and hunted them down mercilessly. . . . So the carnage went on. . . . That they kept coming, it must be said, is a tribute to their courage and steadfastness in the face of daunting odds."[124] In a lengthy conversation with Raúl Castro and other Cuban officials in April 1987, Nujoma repeatedly urged the Cubans to move their troops nearer to the Namibian border. "Comrades," he pleaded, "this would make it easier for us to increase our military actions within Namibia. . . . We are not asking the Cuban troops to enter Namibia," he insisted, "only that they be in Cunene [south of the Cuban defensive line]. The Namibian people want to be free. If the Cubans were in Cunene, it is certain that our ability to inflict casualties on the South Africans would increase tenfold or more." He was exaggerating, but his point was correct: the closer the Cuban troops got to the border, the easier—or, rather, less harrowing—it would be for the SWAPO guerrillas to get into Namibia. But Raúl Castro had to deny Nujoma's request time and again through the long conversation. Finally, he burst out, "This insistence of our friend Sam that our troops advance toward the border is called in Spanish 'being as stubborn as a mule.' But I am the son of a Spaniard, of a Galician, from the north of Spain, and I am more stubborn than Sam. . . . Sam, don't you see that we would love not only to get to the border, but to strike hard at the oppressors of Namibia? But there are things you wish for, and things you can have. Before we can advance to the border, we must strip the South Africans of their control of the skies and we must reinforce our troops. . . . When [the South African attacked] Cassinga, you paid a very high price and so did we, who came to your assistance, because the enemy dominated the sky." Raúl did not tell Nujoma that the Cubans had told the Soviets that they wanted to do exactly what he was suggesting but Moscow had not agreed to supply the necessary weapons.[125]

## Determination

In his September 1986 speech to the Harare Non-Aligned summit, Castro had announced his willingness to keep his troops in Angola until the demise of apartheid. And yet, the Cubans were deeply ambivalent about maintaining their soldiers in Angola. On the one hand, they had a great desire to leave. "We had a dream," recalls Puente Ferro, Havana's ambassador in Luanda in 1983–87, "the dream of a socialist Angola."[126] But Angola had evolved in a very different way. By 1986 it had a government that was, as dos Santos acknowledged, mired in corruption and failing to meet the basic needs of the population. The Cubans vented their frustrations, at times with harsh words, in conversations among themselves—from Fidel Castro down—and also when talking with the Soviets. But they were assiduous, when dealing with the Angolan government, to be respectful and courteous, as the many letters from Fidel Castro to President dos Santos, and memos of conversations between Cuban and Angolan officials, demonstrate.

In 1976, Havana had planned to withdraw its troops within three years. In 1986, they were still there, in the Angolan quagmire, manning a defensive line that barred Pretoria's advance to the north but failed to prevent its incursions to the south. Castro considered this status quo unacceptable, but he could not convince the Kremlin to provide the weapons necessary to change it.

For Cuba, its commitment to Angola was a heavy burden. In addition to the cost of maintaining 40,000 soldiers and several thousand aid workers in Angola, there was the human toll: the deaths, and also the hardship for tens of thousands of Cubans of spending two years on a distant continent under difficult living conditions far from their loved ones. "We are giving [Angola] as much aid as we can afford," Risquet told Gromyko in 1984, "and our people bear the sacrifice. Every time that we have to knock on a door and say 'Your son is dead.'. . . It is a responsibility we have, a responsibility for the lives of these men. And every day they die."[127] These young people could have been working instead at home, helping to bolster their country's economy and its defenses. As Castro told Ndalu and Angolan foreign minister M'Binda in October 1987, "The more we have shown solidarity with Angola, the more the threats of aggression against Cuba have multiplied. In this conflict we have been endangering the security of our country, we have been endangering our Revolution, and we have been endangering the life of tens of thousands of men . . . men who would have been involved in fierce battles if South Africa had unleashed a large scale invasion of Angola."[128]

Therefore, the Cuban leaders were eager to leave Angola. But how? A premature departure of the Cuban troops would give South Africa the opportunity to bring down the Angolan government. This would be more than an embarrassment for Cuba: it would be a victory of apartheid. "Of course we must, in the first place, protect the security of Angola," Castro told M'Binda and Ndalu. "But we also have the moral duty to think about Namibia, SWAPO . . . and the South African people . . . about Mozambique and about the Frontline States." In Risquet's words, "We believe that the presence of our troops in Angola encourages the struggle of the South African people; that the blows that we inflict on the racist troops in Angola, in the south of Angola . . . will encourage the struggle of the South African people, that the blows that SWAPO inflicts on the South African racists will encourage the struggle of the South African people. . . . This is how we see the situation in the region. We are ready to do our share. . . . We believe we have a duty in this part of the world: to defend the independence and territorial integrity of Angola . . . to contribute as much as possible to the independence of Namibia and to eradicate the cancer of the region, apartheid."[129]

The Cubans, therefore, were determined to stay in Angola until the apartheid regime collapsed, if the Angolans agreed: "Our troops will remain in Angola, if the Angolan government approves, until the abolition of apartheid," Risquet said at a tripartite meeting in Moscow in March 1987. Foreign Minister M'Binda, who headed the Angolan delegation, replied simply, "We agree completely with Comrade Risquet."[130] In fact, however, the Angolans had already decided otherwise.[131]

CHAPTER 14

# Negotiations in the Offing?

## The Backdrop

In March 1986, the Angolans had broken off the talks with Washington about linkage—Cuban withdrawal and Namibian independence—to protest the Reagan administration's announcement that it was extending military aid to UNITA. But in late 1986 they informed Washington that they were interested in resuming the talks. The Reagan administration responded favorably. In Moscow, in March 1987, Angolan foreign minister M'Binda informed Soviets and Cubans that a new round of negotiations was about to begin. No one objected. Risquet repeated that Cuba was willing to remain in Angola until the abolition of apartheid. "Pretoria's arms are long and aggressive," he warned. "Even if Namibia were independent and South Africa had withdrawn its troops south of the Orange River [the border between Namibia and South Africa], it could easily attack Angola by traversing Namibia or by sea or by air. Angola will not be safe as long as the apartheid regime exists, just as Mozambique will not be safe, Botswana will not be safe, Zambia will not be safe—none of the Frontline States will be safe."[1]

No better proof of the correctness of Risquet's words can be found than in Pretoria's betrayal of the 1984 Nkomati pact with Mozambique, which stipulated that neither government would allow its territory to be used as a staging ground for acts of violence against the other. This meant that Maputo would stop helping the ANC and Pretoria would stop helping RENAMO, the insurgent movement at war against the Mozambican government. Applauding the agreement, Secretary Shultz had said that it would help convince the South Africans that "it was possible to deal profitably and reasonably with their formerly antagonistic neighbors." A year later Raúl Castro told Gorbachev, "I remember that our friend [Mozambican president] Samora Machel told me in Cuba, before signing the Nkomati agreement: 'Raúl, if I have to make a pact with the devil in order to save the revolution, I will do it.' I replied: 'Well, if the devil is small, you can control him. But watch out! If the devil is big, he will control you.' And that's what happened."[2] Raúl Castro was right. In January 1987, a U.S. State Department memo noted, "Although the volume of South African assistance to RENAMO declined temporarily after signature of the Nkomati Accord . . ., Pretoria has maintained a key role in providing assistance to RENAMO. This flow of South African assistance to RENAMO has increased substantially in the past six months." The South Africans were using RENAMO "to destroy infrastructure, such as transportation lines crucial to FLS [Frontline States] economic survival or to Mozambique's independence, and to bring the GPRM [Government of Mozambique] to heel."[3]

President PW Botha had told Crocker with a straight face in January 1986 that "regarding the persistent stories that there were RENAMO training camps in South Africa . . . [he] wished to say that South Africa did not harbour, train or finance terrorist operations against its neighbors."[4] He may have been technically correct about the training: RENAMO was being trained not in South Africa but in Namibia, in West Caprivi, where Colonel Breytenbach ran a "Guerrilla Warfare School" for insurgent movements supported by Pretoria. "We took anybody who wanted to use our facilities," Breytenbach said. The different groups were housed in separate camps so that no group would be aware of the identity of the others. His charges included guerrillas from UNITA, the Lesotho Liberation Army, and RENAMO. Breytenbach was categorical: "We trained RENAMO for as long as I was there; that is, at least from 1983 through 1987, when I retired—in other words, before Nkomati and after Nkomati."[5] South Africa violated the Nkomati pact even though Maputo honored it. In the wake of Nkomati, Mozambique had expelled hundreds of ANC members, the U.S. State Department noted in January 1987, "and has since incurred further Soviet and black African displeasure for its tight control of ANC activities."[6]

## The United States Flexes Its Muscles

On April 5, 1987, Angolans and Americans met in Brazzaville for an exploratory meeting which, Crocker writes, "turned out to be a dry hole."[7] They decided to meet again, in Luanda, in the near future.

In early June, the White House informed the intelligence oversight committees of Congress that it had decided to continue military aid to Savimbi. (It increased the amount from $18 million in 1986 to $40 million.)[8] A few days earlier, a brief article in the *New York Times* had noted that Savimbi had recently gone to Johannesburg "with a message of support for President P. W. Botha and a rebuke for the South African black leaders who refused to negotiate with him." Addressing a crowd of 400 businessmen, Savimbi had praised Botha. "I am criticizing black leaders in South Africa. Why don't they talk? Someone who is running away from talking has something to hide. . . . President Botha needs support now." Savimbi, the Johannesburg *Star* wrote, had also "urged South Africa not to withdraw from the responsibilities it exercised as a regional power in southern Africa."[9]

Savimbi had good reason to pay obeisance to the apartheid regime. The previous May, General van Tonder, one of his most fervent supporters within the SADF, had told PW Botha, "There are definite indications that elements in the international community are trying to drive a wedge between UNITA and SA [South Africa]. Proof of this are articles in newspapers and magazines in which Dr. Savimbi is quoted allegedly making derogatory remarks about SA. These reports might be untrue, but they have an impact on South Africans and create doubts about the friendship between UNITA and SA. The fact that UNITA avoids contact with SA in international circles, for example that UNITA's representative in Paris will not make contact with the SADF staff there, even secretly, reinforces the doubts. Given the significant help that SA gives UNITA, Dr. Savimbi must realize that he cannot afford to have the South Africans doubting his friendship."[10] Savimbi needed to show his loyalty to his main benefactor.

Chester Crocker, who was eager to cleanse Savimbi of the Pretoria connection, must have flinched at the rebel leader's praise of PW Botha, but for true Reaganites Savimbi's words were one more proof of how reasonable their protégé was. What was unreasonable in their view was the attitude of American companies that continued to invest in Angola; Chevron, which had the largest investment, topped the list. In the United States hard-line conservatives continued their campaign to force Chevron out of Angola, appealing directly—and unsuccessfully—to the company's stockholders to be "patriotic citizens."[11] According to Peter Rodman, a senior NSC official,

> The formal U.S. position toward investment in Angola was to discourage it, but without penalties. Periodic efforts by Congress to impose formal economic sanctions on Angola were resisted by the administration. At one point in May 1987, as a review of southern Africa policy was proceeding in the interagency system, I managed to include in the options paper a consideration of a stronger warning to U.S. companies that investment

in Angola was inconsistent with U.S. foreign policy. . . . But Carla Hills, outside counsel to Gulf/Chevron, made a strong pitch in June to Frank Carlucci, then national security adviser, that the company's presence served American interests: It reduced our dependence on the Persian Gulf; forcing the company out would do nothing to get the Cubans out; European or Japanese firms would quickly step in. On Carlucci's recommendation, Reagan decided to oppose new restrictions.[12]

True believers in Congress sought to pick up the ball the administration had dropped. On July 9, 1987, the Senate debated an amendment to the trade bill that would have imposed a trade embargo on Angola. "For the life of me," Senator Lawton Chiles (D-Fla.) said, "I cannot understand a policy that says, on the one hand, 'This country gives aid [to UNITA]'—it is not covert anymore, it has been in every paper, everybody knows exactly what we are doing, it is sort of an announced policy that we are supporting the UNITA forces. . . . We talk loud and strong about how we feel about freedom fighters and the kind of support that we give. And then we turn around and, in effect, we help to finance the other side." Senator Steve Symms (R-Idaho) demanded boldly that the United States "break diplomatic relations with the Luanda government," unaware that no such relations existed. Those senators who opposed an embargo on Angola stressed that importing Angolan oil was in the U.S. interest, that if Chevron left Angola thousands of American jobs would be lost, and that Europeans and Japanese oil companies would eagerly replace Chevron. As Nancy Kassebaum (R-Kans.) said, "the administration opposes this amendment, and strongly opposes it. It is not just someone in the basement of the State Department. It is the president and the administration. I think that is a very telling point." Not telling enough, however, for thirty-one senators. After a sharp debate, the amendment was defeated by a vote of sixty-eight to thirty-one.[13]

## The Road to the Washington Summit

Meanwhile the United States and the Soviet Union were advancing toward détente. The November 1985 Geneva summit had led to an improvement in the atmosphere but no concrete results. A second summit at Reykjavik in October 1986 ended in disarray.[14] The two countries remained poles apart on regional conflicts—in Central America, southern Africa, Cambodia, and Afghanistan. However, the Soviet position on Afghanistan had shifted. At a Politburo meeting on November 13, 1986, the Soviet leaders had acknowledged defeat. With customary bluntness, the chief of the general staff, Marshal Akhromeyev, said: "After seven years in Afghanistan there is not one square kilometer where a Soviet soldier has not set foot. But as soon as he leaves, the enemy returns and everything goes back to the way it was. We have lost the struggle. In Afghanistan now the majority of the people support the counterrevolution." Gorbachev announced the decision: "We have agreed on our objective: to help accelerate the process that will lead to a friendly, neutral country, and to get out of there. . . . We will leave in the next two years, withdrawing fifty percent of our forces each year."[15] However, as one of his aides noted, the question was not "whether to leave or not to leave. . . . The real question was how to leave—when and under what conditions."[16] Gorbachev wanted a friendly, neutral Afghanistan with a government of national reconciliation that would include both Communists and rebels. The rebels, however, fiercely rejected this dream, and the United States continued to support them. The bloody impasse continued.

Just as the Vietnam War had not prevented détente between the United States and the Soviet Union in the Nixon years, so the war in Afghanistan did not prevent a thaw in relations between Washington and Moscow in the Reagan years. Gorbachev was bent on arms negotiations. "Thanks almost entirely to continuing concessions from Gorbachev," writes Robert Gates, then CIA deputy director, by the summer of 1987 the two countries were getting close to agreement on intermediate-range nuclear forces (INF), the first treaty that would eliminate an entire class of nuclear weapons.[17] In the United States, the debate over the treaty was splitting the Reaganite camp. Hard-liners either opposed it outright or were extremely skeptical. They demanded Soviet concessions on regional conflicts in return for Washington's signature on the treaty. Noting that Shultz and Shevardnadze had just announced "the virtual completion" of the treaty, the *Washington Times* lashed out in a September 21, 1987, editorial:

> Also shameful is the apparent willingness of the administration to forego any serious pressure on the Soviets to come to terms with regional conflicts in Afghanistan, Nicaragua or southern Africa, or to address human right issues in the vast penitentiary that calls itself the Soviet Union. . . . What emerged last week was not, of course, the final treaty, but it is now clear that a treaty will be concluded and sent to the Senate. . . . This may fulfill the Reagan family's desire to make history, but one should always remember that in securing peace [at Munich], Neville Chamberlain also made history—and propelled Europe into the Second World War.[18]

## The View from Havana

While Americans and Soviets were negotiating the final points of the INF treaty, the Angolans were preparing for talks with Washington. This time, they consulted closely with the Cubans. President dos Santos visited Havana at the end of July 1987. He and Castro concurred that the Angolans should not agree to any deal that did not include the end of outside aid to UNITA and the implementation of Resolution 435, which guaranteed UN-supervised elections in Namibia.

Dos Santos and Castro also knew, however, that there would be no Namibian settlement without some form of linkage. Obviously, they would reject the linkage that Pretoria and Washington had proposed in 1981, which stipulated that all the Cuban troops would have to leave Angola within three months of the beginning of the implementation of Resolution 435. The Americans themselves had adopted a more flexible form of linkage with their "synthesis paper" of March 1985, which proposed that 80 percent of the Cuban troops in Angola would leave within the first year after the beginning of the implementation of Resolution 435 and the remaining 20 percent within the second year. Dos Santos and Castro wanted a much weaker form of linkage: the implementation of Resolution 435 would be accompanied by a partial withdrawal of the Cuban troops; the remainder would stay in Angola until the end of apartheid.

Since 1982, the Cuban troops had been divided into two groups. The Agrupación de Tropas del Sur (Southern Troops or ATS) included all the Cubans defending the Namibe-Menongue line against a possible South African attack; these troops were south of the 13th parallel. The smaller Agrupación de Tropas del Norte (Northern Troops or ATN) included the Cubans stationed mainly in Cabinda and in camps near Luanda and near the towns of Malanje, Quibala, and Luso; they guarded against a possible attack from Zaire (or through Zaire) and were positioned north of the 13th parallel.[19]

Pretoria and Washington insisted that the Cuban troops in southern Angola were a serious threat to free elections in Namibia and to that country's future independence. This meant that in the forthcoming negotiations Washington's first priority would be the departure of the ATS. Therefore, Castro told dos Santos that if the ATS had to withdraw, it was important for Angola's security that a strong ATN remain. "The true reason for the continuing presence of the ATN," he explained, "would be that there is no guarantee that South Africa will end its policy of subversion and destabilization." But Castro stressed that the final decision on the withdrawal of the Cuban troops was Angola's to make. "Look, Comrade José Eduardo," he said, "the only right that we have in Angola is the right to leave. We have always understood that we have no right to remain one second longer than the Angolan government wishes. Our only right, Comrade José Eduardo, is our sovereign right to leave."

Castro stressed that Angola should decide how to deal with its internal problems, such as whether to negotiate with UNITA. "If you ask for our opinion, I can answer, 'We think this or that,' but we will support whatever position you take."[20]

Risquet summed up the tone of this encounter well in a conversation with a senior Soviet official, Anatoly Dobrynin, a few weeks later: "In Havana we told them: 'Tell us what your position is and we will support it.' We have given them enough advice. If they want to make this or that concession, we will support them. We have also told them that we think this is a good moment to negotiate, that it is possible to reach an agreement, but that they must try to get the best possible agreement, even though every negotiation requires concessions from both sides."[21]

The Cubans' conclusion that "it is possible to reach an agreement" was based on a straightforward assessment: "The South African regime is now weaker than in the past," Risquet said. "Three or four years ago the South African people were not waging a powerful struggle against apartheid. Today they are, and its intensity is growing. As a result, the world's mobilization against apartheid is much stronger than a few years ago." The FAPLA and the Cuban troops in Angola were also stronger than they had been in 1984, at the time of the desultory negotiations that had followed the Lusaka agreement. "I think that the circumstances are favorable [for negotiations]," Castro told dos Santos in their July 1987 talks. "We wanted a settlement before but it was not possible, the circumstances were not ripe; but I agree with you, Comrade José Eduardo, now they have ripened."[22]

## The View from Pretoria

Castro was wrong: the South Africans were not ready to negotiate seriously. They still dreamed of bringing Savimbi to power, and they were not interested in free elections in Namibia. They knew that their Namibian clients were incompetent and self-serving, and they upbraided them for their failure to gain popular support.[23] U.S. ambassador Nickel remarked in May 1986 that the Transitional Government of National Unity that Pretoria had installed in 1985 in Windhoek was "unloved by both the SAG [South African Government] and the greater Namibian public." The antipathy was mutual, he reported. "Interim Government officials . . . are bitter at what they consider high-handed treatment from the South African government. . . . They contend that [Foreign Minister] Pik [Botha] was rude to cabinet ministers [Andreas] Shipanga and [Jariretundu] Kozonguezi when the two were in Cape Town. According to the story, Shipanga and Kozonguezi were kept waiting for several hours in Pik's outer office, then told that Pik would only see them at the airport. There, they were kept waiting again, then shown into the VIP room where Pik and Defense Minister Magnus Malan treated them brusquely, not even offering them a seat. . . . Pik and Malan's dismissive treatment of the two interim government cabinet ministers," Nickel explained, "reflects Pik's known disdain for Namibian leaders . . . [and the] disappointment, if not disgust [of the South African Foreign Ministry] with the interim government's performance so far."[24]

The weakness of the interim government made free elections inconceivable to officials in Pretoria. A joint task force of the South African departments of foreign affairs and defense concluded in April 1986 that "the implementation of Resolution 435 would not be in the interest of South Africa."[25] The Secretariat of the State Security Council hammered home the same point.[26] Pretoria still hoped that someday, somehow, it would be able to impose its own Namibian solution—without Resolution 435 and without SWAPO. It continued to place its hopes on Savimbi, even though by early 1987 confidence in his chances had dimmed. The Secretariat of the State Security Council asserted that "a UNITA takeover, or at least active participation in the [Angolan] government, is a possibility within the medium term and will be of great benefit for SWA [Namibia]."[27]

Meanwhile Pretoria reined in its Namibian clients, who were eager to jettison Resolution 435 and proclaim Namibia's independence—with themselves as the government. Pik Botha told the chairman of the Transitional Government that "it was extremely important that nothing be done which would turn the United States against South Africa." The Transitional Government must first garner enough support from African states friendly to the West and gain strength at home. Botha recommended that "the Transitional Government should say that they accepted UNSC [Resolution] 435 as a possibility but should at the same time point out that if UNSC 435 did not work, why could another arrangement with African states not be worked out? It was his view that the moment the Transitional Government reached an agreement with African States, UNSC 435 could be thrown out of the window." Botha added that "he saw no reason why the Government of an independent Southwest Africa could not call its friends [South Africa] to assist in the security field. After all Luanda had been given the right to call in its so-called friends."[28]

And so Pretoria continued to chat with the Americans about linkage, while it was in fact proceeding along two very different tracks. The first was to help UNITA and hope that it would eventually take power in Luanda. This would spell disaster for SWAPO. The second track was to win the war in Namibia by destroying SWAPO. The Secretariat of the State Security Council explained, "If SWAPO can be neutralized militarily, it will be easier to achieve an internationally acceptable internal settlement. The strategic situations in SWA and Angola are linked; therefore our policies toward them must be co-ordinated as carefully as possible."[29]

In this misty future—full of alluring possibilities—dangers lurked: UNITA might be unable to come to power, international pressure for the implementation of Resolution 435 might grow, the security forces might fail to destroy SWAPO, and the puppet government in Windhoek might remain as unpopular and irresponsible as ever. The alternative, however, was even more perilous: free elections—Resolution 435—meant a SWAPO victory, and this remained as unacceptable as ever. Pretoria was comforted by the belief it still had time. It saw Namibia "as still on a backburner," U.S. ambassador Nickel pointed out in March 1986. Linkage—which meant that Washington would oppose the implementation of Resolution 435 until the Cubans left Angola—gave South Africa breathing room during which it could turn the situation in Namibia to its advantage. "International pressure on South Africa to implement Resolution 435," the Secretariat of the State Security Council said in 1987, "will not be effective without the cooperation of the USA."[30] Meanwhile, the South African security forces continued to inflict heavy casualties on the SWAPO guerrillas; the military situation in the war against the insurgency, the South Africans believed, was slowly turning in their favor.

As always, the South Africans were blunt about their attitude toward elections in Namibia, while at the same time professing allegiance to Resolution 435. President Botha publicly declared on March 25, 1987: "We cannot allow the Communist flag to fly over Windhoek because if we allow the Communist flag over Windhoek, South Africa's enemies will stand with their rifles on the banks of the Orange River."[31] The next month, Nickel's successor, Ambassador Edward Perkins, reported from Cape Town that the South African government "is more implacably negative on the SWA/Namibia issue than perhaps at any time over the past ten years." The hard-liners, who "are increasingly in the driver's seat here," sincerely believed that a SWAPO victory would mean "'the takeover of Namibia'" by the communists, "'which is the prerequisite for the takeover of South Africa.'" They also believed that the iron fist was working—in South Africa and in Namibia. "Admittedly, the SAG has been unable to create a political solution [in Namibia]," Perkins wrote, "but that is seen to be less pressing, given the improved military context." (In fact the war against SWAPO was stalemated.) He concluded his cable with a chilling warning: "We see almost no prospect that the SAG can be cajoled or persuaded into accepting a 435 settlement regardless of what paper agreement on CTW [Cuban troop withdrawal] the MPLA might be prepared to sign. . . . We suspect . . . that the SAG might only be willing to contemplate a 435 settlement if faced with the prospect of severely punitive measures, e.g. closely coordinated and rigorously applied international censure and/or sanctions. If we ourselves are not prepared to think about that prospect—or to accede to demands of it from others if a milder approach is tried and fails—then we would recommend a hard look at whether it is advisable to move toward a revived Namibia negotiation at this time."[32] Perkins's advice fell on deaf ears. Washington was not interested in punitive measures against Pretoria—they ran against constructive engagement and, more importantly, against the personal sympathies of Ronald Reagan.

## Luanda-Brussels: The Negotiations

After the false start in Brazzaville in April 1987, the talks between the Angolans, led by Foreign Minister M'Binda, and the Americans, led by Crocker, resumed on July 14–15 in Luanda, continued in Luanda on September 8–9, and ended in Brussels on September 24. The Angolans were unwilling to discuss the withdrawal of the Cuban troops in the north (the ATN); they would remain, M'Binda asserted, until apartheid was defeated. The Angolans also demanded the implementation of Resolution 435 in Namibia and the cessation of South African and U.S. aid to UNITA. In exchange, they offered to be flexible about the tempo of the withdrawal of the Cuban troops in the south (the ATS). Their opening offer, in July, had been three years; by September they had gone down to two and were hinting that they might go down a bit more.[33]

Crocker flatly refused to discuss U.S. aid to UNITA—"I will be blunt. I don't think that it is useful that you ask about it." He warned that Angola must not raise the issue of Pretoria's aid to UNITA—"If you ask the South Africans if they will end their aid to UNITA, they will ask whether you will end your aid to the ANC, because Angola is the country that most helps the ANC in southern Africa. I don't think it is useful to get into this kind of polemics."[34] Crocker categorically rejected "the new linkage introduced by Cuba that you [M'Binda] now repeat, that is, the linkage of the ATN with apartheid."[35] He asked, instead, for concessions that he could take to Pretoria. And he insisted on symmetry between the withdrawal of the South African troops from Namibia and the withdrawal of the ATS, while conceding that the ATN might remain a few additional months. He brandished the stick: there was pressure in the U.S. Congress for sanctions against Angola. And he dangled the carrot: if an agreement was reached, he would recommend to President Reagan that the United States establish diplomatic relations with Angola and not oppose Luanda's entry in the International Monetary Fund and the World Bank. However, U.S. aid to UNITA would continue as long as the Soviet bloc gave military aid to the Angolan government, or until there was national reconciliation with Savimbi.[36]

M'Binda told Crocker, when the talks began in July, that he needed to know the position of the South Africans. "Until now, all we've gotten from South Africa is aggression and death, but not one concrete proposal to solve the problems of our region and implement Resolution 435." He wanted to know what parts of the Angolan proposals Pretoria accepted or rejected. "Without knowing this, we cannot move further." When the two delegations met again in September, M'Binda insisted, "I would like to know what South Africa's position is." But Crocker replied, "Even though it may seem incredible to you, we have not yet informed the South Africans of your proposals. We want to make as much progress as possible before we present anything to them." He stressed that Angola must make significant concessions before he would even approach Pretoria: "It would be useless to go to South Africa without anything big to offer."[37] He reminded M'Binda of what Washington's—self-styled—role was: "My task is to convey to you what South Africa will not accept and to work with you to devise a proposal that would be acceptable to the South African government and solve the problems of the region."[38]

The noises coming from South Africa were not encouraging. Referring specifically to the conversations between Crocker and M'Binda, President Botha told the South African Parliament in August 1987 that his government wanted national reconciliation in Angola. Defense Minister Malan told the same assembly, "I want to caution hon. members, and all South Africans, that we cannot permit the Reds to hoist their flag in Windhoek."[39]

Under the circumstances, one can appreciate M'Binda's lament: "Mr. Crocker has said that he cannot go to South Africa unless we are more flexible. But South Africa will certainly demand that we make even more concessions. Then what? What else can Angola do? Commit suicide?"[40]

## Cuban Participation

It was during the talks between M'Binda and Crocker that, for the first time, the Angolans insisted that Cuba should participate in the negotiations. Until then, through all the years of intermittent conversations, the Angolans had bowed to the Americans' desire to exclude the Cubans—even though the focus of the talks was the withdrawal of the Cuban troops from Angola. For the Cubans, this brought back searing memories. "The Americans have always wanted to exclude us from any negotiation," Risquet told Dobrynin, a senior Soviet official. "Last century we won our war of independence against Spain [in 1898], and then the United States and Spain negotiated in Paris, and the victorious Cuban Army of Liberation was excluded. During the Missile Crisis [in 1962] the Americans negotiated with the Soviets, who were the owners of the missiles, but they didn't speak with us, the owners of the land on which the missiles sat. . . . Now they want to speak with the owners of the land [the Angolans] but not with us, the owners of the troops." The Cubans did not want to participate in every phase of the negotiations, but, Risquet told Dobrynin, "We must be present when they talk about our troops. If the Angolans are talking with the Americans about the establishment of diplomatic relations, this is a problem between them. If they are talking about Gulf Oil, about their commercial relations, it is none of our business."[41] The Cubans continued to insist that it was up to the Angolans to determine when they would leave, but given their history it was a matter of honor that the negotiations were not carried on behind their back. On this, the Cubans were categorical: "We will not allow history to be repeated for a third time."[42]

On July 15, 1987—the second day of the first round of the negotiations—M'Binda presented Crocker a document that stated, "Yesterday you proposed that we reduce the period for the withdrawal of the ATS to one year, so that you could take an impressive proposal to the South Africans. You also said that we had to include a timetable for the withdrawal of the ATN in the agenda. As we said yesterday, the withdrawal of the Cuban troops cannot be discussed without the participation of the sovereign state that sent these troops. . . . The moment has arrived to include Cuba in our discussions. Your fear that Cuba may inject its bilateral problems with the United States into our negotiations is groundless. The Cubans have assured us . . . that they will not do it."[43]

Two weeks later, in Havana, Castro told dos Santos that Cuba insisted on participating in the negotiations about the withdrawal of its troops from Angola. Dos Santos admitted, "We have always been worried about the reaction of the U.S. government to Cuba's participation in the negotiations." But he now thought that the U.S. attitude had changed. At the next round of talks, he believed, Crocker would agree to include Cuba.[44]

He was wrong. The Angolan request triggered a debate in Washington. "Nobody liked the Cubans. Nobody trusted the Cubans. Nobody wanted to negotiate with them," recalls a senior Crocker aide, Larry Napper, "but we—the people in the Africa Bureau involved with the negotiations—believed it was essential that the Cubans participate, because the Angolans were completely dependent on them. Everyone on the team [in the Africa bureau] agreed about this." Charles Freeman, Crocker's senior deputy, is emphatic: "I wanted the Cubans to join the talks. It made no sense to exclude them."[45] Crocker and his aides wanted—badly—to get the Cubans out of Angola, but they were not interested in humiliating them.

U.S. policy toward Cuba, however, was in the hands of the State Department's Bureau of Inter-American Affairs, which had been controlled by the true Reaganites ever since the appointment of Elliott Abrams. These ideologues stood well to the right of Shultz and Crocker. Their hostility to Cuba was visceral. "They hated the prospect of negotiating with Castro," Napper said. They wanted to force the Cubans out of Angola, and they also wanted, with equal if not more passion, to humiliate Castro. "To let the Cubans into the negotiations would significantly enhance their reputation," a senior Abrams aide, Kenneth Skoug, remarked.[46] Therefore, the Cubans must play no role in the talks.

Robert Cabelly, Crocker's special assistant, smiled as he recalled those distant days. "Those meetings with Elliott Abrams!" he exclaimed. Abrams and his aides "were furious. They had a knee-jerk reaction. They didn't want to give the Cubans the time of day. 'Those Godless Communists! Those horrible people in Cuba!' Our meetings with them were awful. The Cuba thing was really tough!"[47]

Jay Taylor, the new chief of the U.S. Interests Section, arrived in Havana in September 1987 and unwittingly fell into the midst of this debate. Taylor believed that the Reagan administration should talk with the Cubans to determine whether Havana was willing to make concessions on Angola and Central America in exchange for improved relations with the United States. He expounded on this in a lengthy cable to Washington one month after his arrival, but he was "slapped down" by Elliott Abrams. "He said I didn't know what I was talking about," Taylor recalls. "I had never gotten a cable like this, abrasive, hostile." It would be the first of many. "It was very unusual for a Chief of Mission to get the kind of hostile, aggressive cables I was receiving." Taylor, Skoug said, drily, "was not on our wavelength."[48]

Elliott Abrams was embraced by the ideologues, who relentlessly lambasted the State Department and the secretary of state for fecklessness. His passionate support of the Contra war against Nicaragua echoed Reagan's views, rather than Shultz's less extreme stance. Shultz tread carefully with Abrams. He chose his battles. On Cuban participation in the negotiations with Angola, he sided with Abrams. "That was a mystery," Freeman muses. "I can't say why Shultz did it. The bottom line was that Abrams was influential."⁴⁹ The fact that Reagan shared Abrams's views on Cuba was probably decisive.

When Crocker returned to Luanda in early September 1987 for the second round of talks, he told M'Binda that the United States might let the Cubans sign the final agreements: "We have never excluded the possibility that the Cuban government could endorse the results of our mediation." Havana could not, however, participate in the negotiations. Crocker raised the South African boogeyman: "It is impossible to predict how the South Africans would respond to the participation of other parties." Furthermore, he said—raising the old argument to which the Angolans had already responded—"the Cuban government will want to introduce extraneous issues about U.S.-Cuban relations into an agenda that is already delicate. . . . You are in constant contact with the Cubans. . . . We think we can continue as we have done until now." M'Binda repeated what he had already said: "The Cubans will not raise their bilateral problems with the United States."⁵⁰ Two weeks later, in Brussels, Crocker repeated that if Angola was reasonable—if it accepted the American demands about the withdrawal of the Cuban troops—he would return to Washington and "recommend that the United States receive formally your response in the presence of a Cuban representative." Crocker put this "Brussels formula" in writing in a memo to M'Binda: if Angola accepted the U.S. timetable on Cuban withdrawal, he would recommend to his government that "a Cuban representative could be present when Angola so informed the United States." Risquet remarked bitterly. "That is, Cuba can be the mute witness of the Angolan concessions about the withdrawal of our own troops, mute but not deaf, because we would have to hear from the mouths of Angolan officials, and in the presence of the representatives of the Empire, when our internationalist troops will have to withdraw. This would be even more humiliating than being excluded."⁵¹

CHAPTER 15

# Cuito Cuanavale

## Salute to October

While Crocker and M'Binda skirmished at the negotiating table, the war continued in Angola. On July 12, 1987, the FAPLA launched a major offensive, Salute to October. Its purpose was "to capture UNITA's headquarters [Jamba] and reach the border with Namibia," explained the head of the Soviet military mission, General Petr Gusev. The plan of the operation, a Cuban military report noted, was "a carbon copy" of Operation Second Congress, the disastrous operation carried out by the FAPLA in 1985, and its moving spirit was, again, Konstantin.[1]

Even though the preparations for Salute to October had been under way for several weeks, the decision to launch it had hung in balance until the last moment. As in 1985, the Cubans were opposed to an offensive against Mavinga, and President dos Santos and the FAPLA high command wavered.[2] Konstantin landed in Luanda on June 23, 1987, to make sure that the operation took place, and General Arnaldo Ochoa, Cuba's deputy minister of defense in charge of military missions abroad, arrived six days later to scuttle it. Ochoa met immediately with the FAPLA chief of staff, Ndalu, and cabled Havana that "they [the Angolans] agreed with us that they could not, they should not, run the same risks they did before." Then, on June 30, Ochoa met with Konstantin. He reported: "I presented to Konstantin all the reasons why . . . we should not carry out the operation. . . . Konstantin said that he agreed with us and that the FAPLA needed more equipment and weapons."[3]

After speaking with Konstantin, Ochoa informed Havana that Salute to October had been "definitively abandoned." Instead, some of the forces that had been assembled at the small town of Cuito Cuanavale, the staging point for the advance on Mavinga, would be used for a limited sweep—some eighty kilometers in depth—east of Cuito.[4]

The Cubans were in for a bitter disappointment. Konstantin had lied to Ochoa. He continued to press President dos Santos and the FAPLA high command to launch Salute to October. "There was a lot of hesitation," remembers Ngongo, the FAPLA deputy chief of staff, who was in favor of the operation. Ndalu was against it, but at the critical moment he was hospitalized with appendicitis. Konstantin seized the opportunity. He persuaded Defense Minister Pedalé to support Salute to October. Ngongo and Pedalé then convinced dos Santos.[5]

As in 1985, the Angolans were dazzled by Konstantin's prestige and the power of the Soviet Union. "It was the Soviets who gave the weapons," Ndalu points out. "Therefore, they had much more clout than the Cubans." As in 1985, however, this was only one reason they backed the plan and perhaps not the main one: after all, the Angolans showed scant respect for Moscow's views when it came to negotiating with Pretoria and Washington. They were lured by the Soviets' vision of a smashing victory that would break the back of UNITA. "If we went to the heart of the enemy, if we destroyed its headquarters at Jamba, then we would have practically won the war. This was a very seductive idea," mused Mendes de Carvalho, who headed the Political Directorate of the Angolan Ministry of Interior. "For dos Santos," Ngongo added, "it was important to be in a strong position in the negotiations [with the United States that were about to begin,] and this influenced the decision to launch Salute to October. Furthermore, our sovereignty was at stake!" The relative improvement of the military situation vis-à-vis UNITA over the previous eighteen months "meant that we thought that we could move on to something bigger," Mendes de Carvalho recalled. The Cubans kept saying that in the fall of 1985 the South African intervention had doomed Operation Second Congress, but "we told ourselves, and Konstantin told us, that now we had more powerful antiaircraft weapons."[6]

On July 9, 1987, the Cuban military mission informed Havana that Salute to October was on.[7] Three days later, the offensive began.[8]

According to reports in the Western press, the offensive was led by General Konstantin Shaganovitch, "the highest-ranking Soviet officer to have been posted to a command outside Europe or Afghanistan."[9] In fact, the operation was led by Angolan officers, and no Soviet general participated in it. Furthermore, as Vladimir Shubin explains, Konstantin Shaganovitch did not exist: the name was the fusion of "someone dead with someone alive." General Vassily Shakhnovich had headed the Soviet military mission in Angola in 1977–80. He died in Moscow soon after returning from Angola. "The obituary was duly

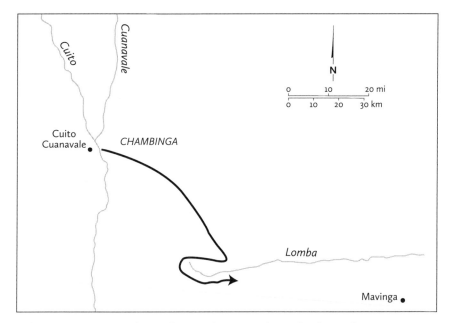

Military operations near the Lomba River, late September and early October 1987 (adapted from South African Defence Force, "A Concise History of Operation Moduler [Phase One] May–October 1987," JFH, gr. VERS, box 30, Department of Defence Documentation Centre, Pretoria)

published in the Soviet official military newspaper . . . *Red Star*."[10] Konstantin Kurochkin did exist. He was the mastermind of the operation, but he did not participate in the offensive: he was in Moscow.

The elite force of the FAPLA—four reinforced brigades of 11,400 men—participated in the attack with sixty-two Soviet military advisers. It confronted about 8,000 UNITA insurgents. SA-8 and SA-13 surface-to-air missile batteries, the Soviets believed, would protect it from South African air attacks.[11]

Pretoria was aware of the Angolans' plans and stood ready to assist Savimbi. On June 22, 1987, the South African Army's Directorate of Operations had issued the instructions for Op Moduler. Several hundred Special Forces and a battery of heavy guns with their crews would help UNITA "in a clandestine covert way" repel the FAPLA offensive. If this proved inadequate, additional means would be committed.[12]

The FAPLA met little resistance in its slow, deliberate advance. Morale was high. The SADF history of Op Moduler noted that "the UNITA forces in the area appeared totally incapable of halting the offensive on their own." Therefore, more Special Forces were sent in, but by late August two of the four FAPLA brigades—the 47th and 59th—had reached the Lomba River, the last significant barrier before Mavinga, and the remaining two were approaching the river. Mavinga was to the southeast, about twenty-five kilometers from the nearest FAPLA unit. The SADF reported on August 29 that the 47th Brigade had begun to move westward along the Lomba River. "Two days later, on August 31, the brigade had reached the source of the Lomba and had began to swing around . . . in a southerly and then easterly direction." The South Africans concluded that the brigade intended "to create a bridgehead" that would make it easier for the three other brigades to cross the river. The situation had become "extremely serious."[13]

## Saving UNITA

By then, a South African Task Force of 1,568 men had been assembled near Mavinga to help defend the town.[14] However, the SADF history of Op Moduler said, with 47th Brigade already south of the Lomba, a second FAPLA brigade poised to cross the river, and two more "manoeuvering ominously farther to the north, it had become clear that a further increase of the SADF levels assigned to Op Moduler was necessary."[15] The chief of the SADF, General Geldenhuys, ordered a mechanized infantry battalion to join the task force; furthermore, he called on the air force, which had been used only to ferry troops and materiel to Mavinga, to join the fight against the FAPLA brigades. Pretoria still hoped to hide its role as much as possible, however. "Where feasible, operations are to be undertaken as UNITA operations, and any clues of South Africa's role must be kept to a minimum," Geldenhuys ordered on September 7.[16]

Beginning in early September, the four FAPLA brigades were pummeled by South African air strikes and artillery bombardments. The brigades dug in and assumed defensive positions. "The vegetation was typical of the greater part of southern and south-eastern Angola—sandy grey soil sparsely covered by tufts of coarse grass, with a profusion of tall, leafy sub-tropical trees to provide overhead cover," wrote South African major W. Dorning. The SAM-8 and SAM-13 batteries offered the Angolans some protection against air strikes: a spotter plane (a Bosbok) was shot down by a SAM-8 on September 4. "This . . . meant," the SADF history of the operation said, "that . . . air strikes on the enemy brigades would have to be planned and executed very carefully to avoid losing further precious aircraft." A senior South African air force officer noted in late September, "We have been inhibited . . . by the SAM deployment. . . . We can't get too close to the brigades."[17] But the South Africans had another trump card: "With their extreme range," their heavy guns were "able to bombard the enemy brigades at will without fear of counter-bombardment."[18]

The Cubans urged the Angolans to pull back the four brigades before it was too late. The FAPLA high command refused. Instead, it ordered the troops to remain in position near the shores of the Lomba and await fresh supplies. "The situation is becoming dangerous for the FAPLA, and they may end up . . . suffering a major defeat," a Cuban intelligence officer warned on September 16.[19]

For the following two weeks, Major Dorning reported, the situation was "almost completely static, with the enemy brigades dug in along the line of the Lomba River," enduring occasional air strikes and more constant artillery bombardments.[20] On September 30, the Johannesburg *Star* wrote: "Deep in the Angolan jungle something is stirring—something big and bloody."[21] The South Africans were preparing to crush the 47th Brigade, the only FAPLA unit south of the Lomba. On October 1 and 2, "as part of the softening up process prior to the planned attack," they subjected the brigade to intense air strikes and artillery bombardments. Then, on the morning of October 3, two South African combat groups, Alpha and Charlie, "moved into position. . . . As luck would have it," the SADF history of Op Moduler said, they "caught the whole 47th Brigade on the move" as it prepared to cross to the northern shore. "The ensuing engagement was dramatic. The 47th Brigade had been caught completely unprepared and in the open." Only three FAPLA vehicles made it across the pontoon bridge the Angolans had constructed before it was destroyed by South African fire. The brigade's tanks, SAM-missile carrying vehicles, and trucks were trapped south of the river. The brigade was doomed, but it went down fighting. The South Africans noted that "a number of the enemy tanks made a determined last stand against . . . Alpha and Charlie mechanized forces." The battle lasted seven hours. Finally, it was over as the surviving Angolans swam across the river, leaving their armament behind. "The 47th Brigade has been annihilated," the SADF reported.[22]

By then "it was an open secret that South Africa was up to something with UNITA in southeastern Angola," General Geldenhuys writes.[23] Pretoria, however, admitted only that its troops were launching raids against SWAPO in Cunene Province, hundreds of miles west of Mavinga. Meanwhile, Savimbi was thumping his chest. The SADF flew forty journalists from South Africa to Mavinga, where they were treated to a "highly sophisticated press conference." *Business Day* reported, "In his well equipped bunker headquarters at Mavinga, the rebel leader—wearing camouflage fatigues and a pearl handled revolver on his hip and surrounded by his high-ranking officers—gave a high-tech display of his recent victory. Overhead projectors, tape recorders and video cameras were used to highlight the war effort while captured FAPLA soldiers . . . were paraded for the press." Savimbi's message was stark: his forces, alone, had driven off the

FAPLA troops, who were backed by Cubans, in a ten-hour battle.[24] Sotto voce, the SADF generals grumbled that it was they, virtually unaided by UNITA, who had stopped the FAPLA. ("We need to make UNITA realize that this is their war," the chief of the Army wrote.)[25] As for the Cubans, they had been nowhere near the battlefield. "The fighting on the Lomba River," Castro told Gorbachev, had taken place "350 kilometers from the nearest Cuban military unit."[26]

In Luanda, tempers flared. President dos Santos met with the FAPLA general staff and representatives of the Cuban and Soviet military missions. The head of the Cuban military mission, General Fleitas, was exasperated: "We Cubans were always against the [Mavinga] operation," Ndalu, the FAPLA chief of staff who had recovered from his bout of appendicitis, recalls. The head of the Soviet mission, Gusev, "acted as if he were blameless: 'I'm just an adviser. It was the minister [Pedalé] who gave the order.'"[27] In his memoirs, however, Gusev struck a different tone. "I informed [the chief of the Soviet General Staff, Marshal] Akhromeyev about the result of the operation, but the most difficult task, in moral terms, was to inform the president of Angola, whom I had assured that the operation would succeed and that Savimbi would be crushed."[28]

On October 7, the FAPLA high command gave the order to retreat, and the four brigades began their trek back to Cuito Cuanavale, from which they had departed in high spirits the previous July.[29] The South Africans decided not to repeat the mistake they had made in 1985, when they had failed to pursue the FAPLA as it fell back. "We started with essentially the same battle plan we used in 1985—simply to stop the offensive," General Thirion explained, "but our plans changed when everything went so well. It was decided, halfway through the battle, 'Let's take Cuito!'"[30]

The decision had been made by President Botha in a most unusual setting: the forward headquarters of the SADF task force, near Mavinga. On September 28, 1987, the task force "was graced," the SADF history of Op Moduler reported, "by the visit of a powerful cabinet delegation." The president, flanked by the minister and deputy minister of defense, the chief of the SADF general Geldenhuys, the chief of the army, and a covey of lesser generals descended on the headquarters. For two days, PW Botha was briefed about the task force's exploits. He departed "impressed enough by what he had seen and heard to give his personal approval to plans for a more offensive phase of Op Moduler."[31] That is, Major Dorning explained, the president approved "the total destruction of the enemy forces north of the Lomba and the advance to and possible capture of Cuito Cuanavale itself."[32] Botha assured General Geldenhuys "that he would authorize the deployment of whatever additional forces . . . [the general] might deem necessary to achieve Op Moduler's new objectives."[33] Botha made this decision even before battle groups Alpha and Charlie had annihilated the FAPLA's 47th Brigade.

Reinforcements—men and materiel—would be flown to the SADF in Mavinga. "The significance of Op Moduler . . . can scarcely be exaggerated," the SADF history of the operation stated. It was "the biggest single operation" of the SADF ground and air forces since the Second World War. In it the SADF deployed the "most sophisticated" weaponry it had ever fielded, "with several state of the art weapons being introduced . . . for the first time." The South African generals believed that Op Moduler could provide "the decisive breakthrough" in Angola and in Namibia.[34]

## A Missed Opportunity

The South African generals squandered their great opportunity. Contrary to their expectations, the FAPLA brigades did not flee in panic; instead, Geldenhuys writes, their withdrawal was "generally orderly." They were, nonetheless, vulnerable. They could have been annihilated in the long trek back to Cuito Cuanavale. The generals decided, however, to wait for the arrival of reinforcements from South Africa. "A powerful new attack force crossed the Kavango River from Namibia . . . on 20 October," Savimbi's biographer explains. From there, "the big convoy began to arrive on 30 October at Mavinga." A few days later, the South African Task Force began to advance toward Cuito Cuanavale.[35] Precious weeks had been lost, but the South African generals remained confident. Even if the FAPLA brigades made it to Cuito Cuanavale, they would be destroyed when the town fell. Cuito Cuanavale was a trap, and the FAPLA brigades were doomed.

Throughout October, while the South Africans dallied, UNITA followed suit. "UNITA was not pulling its weight," Major Dorning wrote. "Its attitude seemed to be very much one of 'Well, the Boers are here so we don't have to do any of the fighting.'"[36]

Instead of pursuing the retreating brigades, Savimbi bragged about the "magnificent victory" his troops had achieved, forcing the FAPLA, and their Cuban and Soviet backers, into full retreat. He said, the Johannesburg *Beeld* remarked, "not one word about South African support."[37] This rankled. "UNITA's fiction, backed by Pretoria, that it alone was winning 'great' victories in southeast Angola was deeply resented by the SADF's fighting men. 'Hell, our guys were dying there and no one back home was being told how or why,'" an officer of one of the SADF units at the front said.[38] The South Africans "were doing the work and UNITA got the kudos," Colonel Breytenbach groused.[39]

## Pretoria Raises the Stakes

Then something unprecedented happened. On November 11, 1987, General Geldenhuys announced publicly that the SADF was fighting in Cuando Cubango alongside UNITA against the FAPLA and its Cuban and Soviet allies, who were "using tanks, sophisticated ground-to-air missiles, fighter aircraft . . . and attack helicopters . . . to capture the Cuando Cubango province. . . . The SADF will continue to act," Geldenhuys said, "as long as Russian and Cuban forces intervene." *Beeld* blared above the fold: "Cubans on the run!" and it explained that the South African soldiers "had fought with passion and perseverance . . . [and] the Cubans had quickly turned tail"—a creative statement, since no Cubans were involved in the operation. The Johannesburg *Star* remarked. "This is the first time the SADF has confirmed direct involvement in support of UNITA."[40]

The day after Geldenhuys's statement, Savimbi addressed a group of foreign journalists who had been ferried to Jamba on a South African plane. UNITA had decisively defeated the Russian-led offensive, he declared. "No SADF 'troops or aircraft [had been] involved.'" When the journalists pressed him on the contradiction between his and Geldenhuys's words, Savimbi repeated his assertion that UNITA had fought alone and said that he was "'surprised'" by Geldenhuys's statement. "Clearly exasperated . . . he suggested that the journalists return to South Africa and 'ask General Geldenhuys'" what he had meant.[41] That same day South African defense minister Malan made a public statement that supported Geldenhuys's version of reality: "The Russian and Cuban-controlled offensive against UNITA . . . forced South Africa to make a decision: accept the defeat of Dr. Jonas Savimbi or halt Russian aggression." A few days later, Malan added that UNITA's defeat "would have opened the way for the Soviets and the Cubans . . . to Botswana, Zimbabwe, Zambia, Namibia and eventually South Africa itself, . . . 'the cherry on the top' for the Communist forces." He revealed that President Botha had "very recently" visited the war zone in southeastern Angola where he had made "a dramatic midnight address to South African troops waiting to go into battle."[42] Botha's visit, Malan said, was "proof of his empathy, commitment and sense of personal responsibility."[43]

It was strong stuff. General Geldenhuys told me that the government had decided to make public the SADF's participation in the fighting because "it was impossible to hide it. It would have been a lie that would never stick; it was just impossible." Given the scope of the SADF's participation, it is a reasonable explanation. When I asked Geldenhuys why the government had also made public PW Botha's visit to the South African troops inside Angola, he countered: "They all do it. Was it wrong for the U.S. president to visit the troops in Vietnam?

This South African cartoon depicts an Angolan, a Cuban, and a Soviet fleeing because—as the notice on the tree announces—the South African president, PW Botha, was in Angola to praise his troops for winning a major battle. The Cuban urges the others to run and reminds them of how harshly Botha had treated a former friend, Koedoe Eksteen. The two words in Cyrillic are gibberish. In fact, however, there had been no Cuban troops within 200 miles of the battle. (Copyright *Beeld*)

Kings, presidents have always visited their troops on the battlefield." After a pause, he added, "The president wanted to score points with the public."[44]

The progovernment press in South Africa approved the government's actions in Angola and its sudden candor. "It is good," the *Burger* wrote, "that information about the actions of the SADF . . . in Angola has been made public so quickly." It praised Botha for visiting the troops. His presence, and his speech, "had inspired the soldiers." *Beeld* congratulated the president for traveling hundreds of kilometers inside Angola to visit the troops "who are still involved in bloody combat with Russian and Cuban troops. Exactly how deep into Angola President Botha ventured cannot at present be revealed. But there is no doubt that he endangered his life in order to be there."[45]

Pretoria's behavior was so brazen that in a unanimous vote on November 25, 1987, the UN Security Council condemned Botha's "illegal entry" into Angola and demanded that South Africa "unconditionally withdraw all its forces occupying Angolan territory."[46] South African officials were unfazed. In Washington, Ambassador Piet Koornhof told Crocker that Pretoria viewed the U.S. vote in support of the resolution "as a necessary sop to the MPLA to keep the negotiation process in play." Crocker agreed—it was just a sop: "the resolution did not contain a call for comprehensive sanctions, and did not provide for any assistance to Angola. That was no accident, but a consequence of our own efforts to keep the resolution within bounds."[47] Within bounds—while the SADF destroyed the best units of the FAPLA.

## Cuito Cuanavale

On October 27, 1987, the chief of the South African army, General "Kat" Liebenberg, had issued a new set of instructions for Op Moduler. The first two phases—"stopping the [FAPLA] offensive and taking the initiative"—had been successfully concluded. Phase 3—the destruction of the FAPLA units as they retreated to Cuito Cuanavale—"is now underway." Phase 4 "is the capture of Cuito Cuanavale."[48] The mood was optimistic. As Pik Botha told the members of the Namibian Transitional Government on November 6, "Events in Angola in the next couple weeks could have a decisive influence on the course of history in the whole of southern Africa." Geldenhuys believed that Cuito might fall without a serious fight. On November 18, he told army chief Liebenberg: "The enemy's morale is now very low. We should exploit this to the utmost . . . in order to capture Cuito Cuanavale without having to fight—using leaflets and harassing fire, and *grondskree* [operations in which vehicles with powerful loudspeakers would drive close to the enemy positions at night and broadcast propaganda intended both to frighten the Angolans and deprive them of sleep]." Two weeks later, Geldenhuys told the State Security Council, "Our goal is for UNITA to win the military and political struggle." Looking back at those dark days, the deputy chief of staff of the FAPLA, Ngongo, said, "The loss of Cuito Cuanavale would have been a disaster for our sovereignty and our territorial integrity."[49]

If the South Africans had launched a major attack on Cuito Cuanavale in November or early December, the town would have fallen. But they wanted to keep their own casualties low and, above all, to minimize the political cost abroad. "You don't want to do it too openly with an assault that shows South Africa's role," says General Thirion. "There was the international aspect. We were so thick into the thing."[50] Pretoria had been taken aback by the ferocity of the international indignation at its revelation that the SADF was engaged in a major operation deep inside Angola and that PW Botha had visited the troops at the front. Geldenhuys warned the commanders in the field that "the South African forces must maintain a low profile because of the international climate."[51]

On November 25 Pretoria had to face the fact that the FAPLA's morale had not been crushed. The South Africans sought to seize the Chambinga plateau, approximately fifty kilometers east of Cuito, and the FAPLA managed to fight them off. "Our failed attempt was a shot in the arm for the Angolan troops' morale which had been very low," the SADF noted.[52] Chambinga did not dent the South African generals' optimism about the final outcome, but it did indicate that the fall of Cuito could take longer than they had anticipated and require more than psychological warfare. The generals decided that they would overcome the FAPLA resistance through air strikes, bombardment with heavy guns, and cutting the supply lifeline from Menongue. They would also exploit the geographic separation of the defenders of Cuito: the town and the bulk of the troops were on the western shore of the Cuito River, which ran in a north-south direction through Cuando Cubango; but the FAPLA had also established a bridgehead, defended by some 1,500 soldiers, on the eastern shore across from the town. The South African generals decided that they would launch tank attacks supported by UNITA infantry against the bridgehead. The fall of the bridgehead would demoralize the defenders in Cuito and lead to the fall of the town. It would take a few more weeks. The South Africans would have to be patient. But Cuito was doomed. Geldenhuys's instructions were that after the town had fallen it should be left "in the hands of UNITA."[53] The SADF would give Savimbi the credit for the victory, hoping to boost his international prestige and hide its own role.

The SADF leaders "were lulled by intelligence and situation reports that indicated that the FAPLA units were increasingly demoralized," General Thirion remarks. "The collection of information from the battlefield and gathering intelligence were difficult tasks," the SADF later noted. "The main source of information was UNITA and . . . it turned out to be unreliable." UNITA's claims were readily accepted at the time, however, because they reinforced the illusions of the South African military. Lieutenant Colonel Les Hutchinson, who was at the Directorate of Operations at Army Headquarters in Pretoria, recalls that "the situation reports from the front said over and over again that the FAPLA were badly demoralized." The South Africans, therefore, believed that time was on their side. "So the idea," Thirion explains, "was to wait and let Cuito fall on its own."[54]

## Fidel Castro in Moscow

Cuito did not fall. The Cubans saved the town and blunted the South African offensive. To understand what happened it is necessary to examine Cuba's policy as it unfolded after the advance of the FAPLA brigades stalled at the Lomba River and they began their retreat toward Cuito Cuanavale. Throughout October Castro had followed the situation in Angola with concern mixed with hope—the FAPLA troops were withdrawing in good order, and the South Africans were not pursuing them.

Meanwhile in Moscow preparations were under way for two grand events: the celebrations of the seventieth anniversary of the Bolshevik revolution and the third summit between Gorbachev and Reagan, which would be held in Washington on December 7–10. At this summit there would be a breakthrough: the two leaders would sign the intermediate-range nuclear forces (INF) treaty.

The improvement in Washington's relations with Moscow did not lessen tensions between the United States and Cuba. "We are . . . trying to join this international détente," Castro explained to a group of top aides in November 1987, immediately before renewing the immigration agreement with Washington that had been suspended in May 1985. "We are trying because we, too, want to enjoy peace. This is why we are . . . negotiating with the Americans [about immigration]. . . . All our friends among the [U.S.] Democrats, all the people who are our friends, progressive people, think that this agreement enhances the possibility of better relations in the future."[55] Immigration, however, was the only issue the Reagan administration was willing to discuss with the Cubans.

While U.S.-Soviet relations had improved since Gorbachev had become general secretary, relations between Moscow and Havana had cooled. The Cubans resented the Soviets' failure to give them the weapons they needed to push the SADF out of Angola, and they were wary of the Kremlin's growing propensity to strike deals with Washington while Reagan maintained his vendetta against Cuba and hard line toward Central America and Angola. They were also increasingly uneasy about perestroika. Gorbachev was stressing market mechanisms in the economy, while Castro was stressing "rectification," a process that moved away from the market mechanisms that had been introduced in Cuba in the early 1980s. In other words, Cubans and Soviets were moving in opposite directions. In July 1987 the CIA suggested, "While he seems to respect Gorbachev for his audacity, vitality and decisiveness, Castro is also convinced that the Soviet leader has embarked on a disastrous course."[56] Articles in the Soviet press began to criticize Cuba. On August 24, 1987, the prominent Moscow weekly *New Times* ran a column belittling Cuba's economic performance. The *Washington Times* noted, "Although the criticism was expressed in moderate terms, several US officials . . . voiced surprise that such an article could appear in a publication such as the *New Times*, which is described as 'fairly authoritative' and very influential."[57] The Cubans were even more surprised—and not happy.

The strain in Cuba's relationship with the Soviet Union was reflected in Castro's decision not to attend the celebrations of the seventieth anniversary of the Bolshevik revolution in Moscow. These celebrations were divided in two parts: first, a solemn joint session of the Central Committee of the Soviet Communist Party and the Supreme Soviet, attended by Communist Party delegations from foreign countries; then, a conference to which representatives from a broad array of movements had been invited, including social-democrats, liberation movements, the Green Party of West Germany, the Congress Party of India, and the Baath Party of Syria. Vice President Carlos Rafael Rodríguez and Risquet had arrived in Moscow on November 1 to represent Cuba. Over the next two days, the joint session took place in the Kremlin. Gorbachev delivered the keynote address; the heads of the delegations of foreign communist parties also spoke, among them Carlos Rafael Rodríguez. "The Soviets expected that Fidel would participate at least in the second event," Risquet recalled. "But Fidel did not want to go, and he had told me to speak on behalf of the Cuban delegation. Oleg Darushenko [the head of the Cuban section of the Soviet Central Committee] came to see me and when I told him that I would be speaking for Cuba he grimaced. I don't know if the Soviets spoke to Carlos Rafael [Rodríguez], but he told me, 'I'm going to cable Fidel urging him to come.'"[58]

Castro relented, but he did not arrive in Moscow until the afternoon of November 4. He gave a brief speech the next day.[59] On November 6, he met with Gorbachev. "Welcome, Comrade Fidel. Your presence in Moscow is very important," Gorbachev began. "If you had not showed up, clearly we both—Soviets and Cubans—would have been wondering how we would be able to explain it." Castro replied, "I could not fail to come, for three reasons: first, because I wanted to share in these celebrations; second, because I myself suggested to you that we have a conference with a broad participation . . . ; and, third, because we have to avoid giving rise to rumors."[60]

The Russians have not declassified the minutes of the meeting between the two leaders. In his memoirs, Gorbachev says merely, "During our conversation Fidel was holding a copy of my speech about the 70th anniversary of the October Revolution, and I noticed that it was heavily annotated. We talked about many theoretical and political questions. Castro said that our discussion confirmed 'our total agreement of viewpoint, perception, and understanding of the events taking place in our countries.'"[61]

The Cuban minutes of the meeting reveal a surprisingly superficial conversation. Castro was effusive in his praise of Gorbachev and his policies. And Gorbachev was equally effusive in his praise of Castro and Castro's policies. Referring to the "rectification" process under way in Cuba, Gorbachev said:

"I have seen how you have involved yourself fully, profoundly in these matters, and how the [Cuban Communist] party and its leaders . . . are leading the country to a new stage and developing the potential of socialism in Cuba, and that it is the party . . . that is at the head of this process, is generating it, and is guaranteeing it ideologically." When Castro stated, "We have placed the party at the center . . . of this entire process of rectification. . . . That's something that I feel very strongly about . . . that the party is at the center," Gorbachev heartily agreed. "I, too, am convinced that it's the right approach. On more than one occasion, I have said that our party cannot abandon any sphere [of activity], and least of all the economy." It was a mutual admiration society.

At the center of the conversation—which also included Gorbachev's description of the arms negotiations with the United States and his forthcoming summit in Washington—was a discussion of the impact of neocolonialism on the underdeveloped world. On this point, the two men were in total agreement. "Neocolonialism is worse than colonialism; it is more subtle but its ravages are worse," Castro said. Gorbachev replied, "Contemporary capitalism, and to a large degree the metropole, sustain themselves . . . by plundering thousands of million of people. . . . Can one say that a regime is just or efficient if it guarantees the standard of living of the metropole by robbing all the other countries?"

Angola was mentioned only briefly, toward the end. Castro said that if Reagan asked about Angola at the summit, Gorbachev should reply that if South Africa agreed to implement Resolution 435 and the United States ended its support of UNITA, "it would be possible to find a solution acceptable to everyone that would include the departure of the Cuban troops." Gorbachev said merely, "The issue might arise." Not one word was said about the profound military crisis in the southeast of Angola.[62] Gorbachev was focused on his meeting with Reagan, and among the regional conflicts, it was Afghanistan that drew his attention.

## Decision in Havana

By the time Castro returned to Havana on November 7, 1987, the SADF had received its reinforcements and was pursuing the FAPLA brigades that were falling back to Cuito Cuanavale. This was soon reflected in the reports of the Cuban military mission. On November 12, the mission reported "a worsening of the situation" in the area of Cuito Cuanavale and a weakening of the morale of the FAPLA troops as they faced "the mounting activity of the enemy."[63] Two days later, the head of the Cuban military mission, General Arnaldo Ochoa, cabled Raúl Castro: "The situation in the area of Cuito Cuanavale has continued to deteriorate. . . . If the morale and the fighting capacity of the units are not reestablished, a catastrophe is inevitable." Angolan military leaders were complaining that Cuba was not sending troops to save Cuito, and the head of the Soviet military mission, General Gusev, was egging them on. "Today Ndalu told me," Ochoa reported, "that Gusev had urged him to speak with me because I had the authority to send Cuban troops to Cuito Cuanavale. . . . I will continue to resist these pressures so that our troops are not directly involved in Cuito Cuanavale, but we cannot lose sight of the fact that we should do everything we can to prevent the town from falling into enemy hands."[64]

Geldenhuys's and Malan's unprecedented candor on November 12–13 about South Africa's aid to UNITA fueled the Cubans' apprehension that Pretoria might be preparing to escalate and might even attack the Cuban defensive line. The Cuban military mission reported the arrival of South African troops in northern Namibia and noted that the SADF—ground units and air force—was increasingly active in southern Angola."[65]

Castro later told Gorbachev that when they had met in Moscow he had not been fully aware of the gravity of the situation in Angola; it was only after his return to Havana that it had become obvious.[66] The situation had indeed deteriorated by then, but this was not the only reason Castro did not focus on Angola in his conversation with Gorbachev. He had not yet decided what should be done, and he thought it was a decision that Cuba should reach alone, without Soviet input. It might be best to confront the Soviets with a fait accompli, because they might not approve of Cuba's decision. In Risquet's words, Reagan and Gorbachev were going to hold a summit in Washington at which they would sign the INF treaty, "an important step towards détente. Angola, however, required a decision that went in the opposite direction."[67]

On November 15, at 5:25 P.M., Castro met with his brother Raúl, seven other generals, one colonel, and one civilian—Risquet. The meeting lasted more than ten hours and the transcript runs to 182 pages.[68] They met to discuss the military situation in Angola and decide what to do. They faced the possibility that Cuito would fall and the FAPLA units that had retreated there would be annihilated by the SADF. They had to decide, as Castro later told Gorbachev, how to respond to "the desperate requests of the Angolan government and the Soviet military mission that we send our troops to that remote place, to wage a battle on terrain chosen by the enemy."[69]

Several key decisions emerged from the meeting. The Cubans would send more troops to Angola, and, above all, they would send more arms—the best planes with the best pilots, the most sophisticated antiaircraft weapons, and the most modern tanks. They would send all the fuel needed for the planes.

("Otherwise . . . we'd have an air force for one day," General Polo Cintra Frías warned.) They would send a small group of approximately thirty military advisers to Cuito Cuanavale; it would not be necessary to send ground troops, they believed, because the Cuban planes would deprive the South Africans of their greatest advantage—air superiority. They would not let Cuito Cuanavale fall to the enemy, but neither would they use the town as a springboard for a new offensive in the southeast. "We have to avoid this," Castro said, "because it would mean fighting where the enemy has the advantage. . . . The South Africans have chosen the worst place for us to fight; it is at the end of the world." Cuito Cuanavale and Cuando Cubango were not the theater where the Cubans would seize the offensive.[70]

That theater would be the southwest. There too, Cuban planes would gain control of the skies. "Raúl, we have to be the masters of the air," Fidel said. Cuban troops would advance from their defensive line toward the Namibian border. "Listen," Fidel insisted, "we are going to create the conditions to strike a very heavy blow. . . . Finally, we will wage war down there [in the southwest]."[71]

For more than two years Castro had longed to expel the South Africans from southwestern Angola, but he had been stymied by the refusal of the Soviets to supply the necessary weapons. By November 1987, the situation had changed. A year earlier the Iran-Contra scandal had exploded in the United States: U.S. officials had sold weapons to Iran—a breach of U.S. law and policy—in the hope of securing the release of Americans held hostage in Lebanon. They had siphoned part of the profits of that illegal sale to the Nicaraguan Contras—another illegal act. The scandal weakened President Reagan and forced him to purge some of the hard-liners in the upper reaches of his administration. "The aftermath of Iran-Contra," a top CIA official writes, "produced a dramatic change of senior officials and the constellation of power in the administration, with significant consequences for foreign policy." National Security Adviser Poindexter was replaced by the pragmatic Frank Carlucci, with General Colin Powell as his deputy. White House chief of staff Donald Regan was replaced by Senator Howard Baker, a moderate Republican. Furthermore, DCI Casey was incapacitated by a brain tumor in December 1986 and was replaced by a far more moderate man, FBI director William Webster. Defense Secretary Weinberger, "now the lone hardliner left at the top of the national security team, would not be stilled, but his influence with Reagan on US-Soviet issues was fading fast," and he resigned in November 1987.[72]

For the Cubans, the impact was dramatic: Reagan had been defanged, and the danger of a U.S. military attack against their country receded at the same moment that the South Africans had become even more aggressive in Angola. "I think the possibility of war there [in Angola] is twenty times greater than here in Cuba," Castro said in November 1987. "For us the greater danger is . . . in Angola. . . . The war is there, not here."[73]

In making his decisions on November 15, 1987, Castro did not consult the Soviets. General Ulises Rosales would go to Moscow to inform them, but only after the first reinforcements had left Cuba. He would confront the Soviets with a fait accompli. He would explain Cuba's decision, and he would ask for weapons. Castro said, "We must tell them, 'Look, we've taken this decision, and it will weaken our defenses at home. . . . All we are asking is that you replace the arms we are sending to Angola.'" But Cuba would send the reinforcement in any case. Its decision did not depend on the Kremlin's approval. Risquet would go to Luanda to inform the Angolans, but not before Ulises had left for Moscow, in order to avoid untimely leaks to the Soviets.[74]

The Cuban decision had been triggered by the South African escalation in Angola. It had been made possible by Iran-Contra. And it reflected the desire Cuba had held for a long time: to seize control of the air and push the SADF out of Angola, once and for all. Until 1987, the Cubans had been unwilling to deplete their own stocks of weapons. Therefore, escalation in Angola had hinged on Soviet support—the dispatch of the necessary weapons. But after the Iran-Contra scandal, the Cubans felt able to go it alone. They hoped Moscow would supply the arms they needed, but they would seize the initiative in Angola in any case, with the weapons they would send from their own arsenals at home. They hoped that, as in 1976, Pretoria would choose to withdraw from Angola rather than fight a well-equipped Cuban army, but they were ready to fight their way to the Namibian border if necessary.

As Chester Crocker points out, "It was a risky strategy. . . . [Castro] would be stripping some of his best units and equipment for a deployment 7,000 miles from home, adding significantly to his Angolan 'commitment.' . . . The SADF had world-class artillery, superior knowledge of the terrain, the home-turf advantage as the Cubans moved south, a large cadre of seasoned and high-spirited military leaders, and substantial manpower reserves that could be mobilized if necessary."[75]

The Cuban operation—code-named Maniobra XXXI Aniversario del Desembarco del Granma (Maneuver 31st Anniversary of the Landing of the Granma)— began in utmost secrecy. "The first step," a Cuban military report notes, "was the dispatch of our most experienced combat pilots to Angola. They immediately began to support the FAPLA in Cuito Cuanavale." The first troops left Havana by plane on November 23, the heavy weapons followed by ship, beginning on November 25. On December 11 and 12, the first two ships loaded with tanks and antiaircraft weapons reached the Angolan port of Lobito.[76]

As had been true for every other mission abroad, the soldiers and reservists could refuse to go to Angola. "We don't send any recruit unless he is willing," Raúl Castro assured Fidel. "And if some recruits don't want to go . . . we transfer them to another unit." The armed forces' postmortem of Maniobra XXXI Aniversario noted that the soldiers were sent "only if they agreed to go. . . . Therefore, during the selection process we interviewed more soldiers than was needed."[77]

The South Africans learned very soon that something was afoot. In Luanda, on December 4, 1987, the Angolan chief of staff, Ndalu, told the Mozambican and Yugoslav news agencies that strong Cuban reinforcements were on their way to Angola and that the famed 50th Division—one of the elite units of the Cuban army—had already arrived and was en route to southern Angola. The South African media relayed the information. The news was proof, the *Burger* wrote, of the "diabolical onslaught" that South Africa faced. The Johannesburg *Star* noted, "The report . . . caused some concern." General Malan reassured the public. "To move an army's division was 'no child's play,'" he explained. The Cubans "couldn't do it in six months." Furthermore, "Even if it were true, there was no great cause for concern, as the Cubans were not 'real fighters.'"[78]

The Cubans took charge. Castro wrote dos Santos: "Comrade José Eduardo, it is essential to have the closest cooperation and understanding between the FAPLA high command, our military mission in Angola, and our general staff in Cuba. When Soviets, Angolans and Cubans disagree, everything becomes paralyzed, and then wrongheaded decisions are made. The majority of our troops are in the south, we are responsible for these men, and we will not allow anyone to dictate a strategy that is wrong or foolhardy." This warning was directed— above all—at the Soviet Union. "When we sent the reinforcements . . . we said, if we want to save the situation we have to do A, B, and C, and this is what we did," Fidel Castro later told the general secretary of the South African Communist Party, Joe Slovo. "We and the Angolans were in agreement, and the Soviets had nothing to do with it—nothing, not even to offer an opinion."[79]

## Unhappiness in Moscow

On November 19, 1987, Ulises had informed the head of the Soviet Military Advisory Group in Cuba, General Alexei Zaitsev, that the Cuban government had decided to reinforce its troops in Angola and that he would leave for Moscow on November 23 to inform the minister of defense of the USSR of this decision.[80]

On November 23, the day that Ulises left for Moscow, Risquet arrived in Luanda with a letter from Castro to dos Santos. "Unfortunately, what we had predicted has occurred," Castro wrote, "because of an ill-prepared offensive [against Mavinga] on the terrain most favorable to the South Africans, near their bases. . . . Twice in two years [1985, 1987] the same grave error has been made, and errors always entail a high military and political cost. However, this is not the moment for recriminations. We must now deal with the situation." Cuba would send more men and weapons. "The enemy is now emboldened," Castro concluded. "We must show them that we are strong and ready to fight." Dos Santos replied, "After reading your letter and receiving a detailed briefing from Risquet about your analysis of the situation and your proposals, I told him that I agreed with you." Risquet told Castro, "My impression is that José Eduardo was pleasantly surprised by Cuba's decision."[81]

The Soviets were less pleased. When Ulises arrived in Moscow on November 24, General Dmitry Yazov, who had replaced Marshal Sokolov as defense minister the previous May, was in Romania, and so Ulises met with the chief of the Soviet General Staff, Marshal Akhromeyev. He began by reading an aide-mémoire that explained the Cuban decision and included a long list of weapons that Cuba wanted from the Soviet Union for its troops in Angola and to reinforce its defenses at home, which were being stripped to the bone for the Angolan operation. As Ulises read, for forty-five minutes, Akhromeyev interrupted him only once to ask, "When do you plan to send the first ships from Cuba?" Ulises replied: "The first group is now on the high seas heading toward Angola; the others are loading at the docks as we speak." (The Cuban note taker wrote, "At this moment we noticed a slight gesture of annoyance on the part of Marshal Akhromeyev.")[82] Recalling the conversation, Ulises remarked, "When I met with Akhromeyev, he thought I was going to present a proposal to him, but then he realized that we were not consulting him, we were informing him. He was taking notes with a pencil, and when I told him that the first group had already left, he pressed down hard on the pencil and broke the point."[83]

Akhromeyev was "a soldier's soldier who had risen from the ranks," the U.S. ambassador to the Soviet Union wrote. "Personable and with a keen sense of humor, he never left you in doubt where he stood, but he was also willing to listen, and he could negotiate vigorously without personal acrimony."[84] He had worked for years on Angolan matters, and he had worked for years with the Cubans. He was, judging by the transcripts of his many conversations with the Cubans, always well informed and polite, even when disagreeing. On this occasion too, he was courteous and fair. He frankly admitted that the Soviet military had erred in urging the FAPLA to launch the offensive against Mavinga. "We did not force them, we did not pressure them, but we—the Soviets—strongly expressed our opinion that this operation was necessary to definitively defeat UNITA in the southeast. . . . Obviously, this was a mistake." Stressing that he was offering only his personal opinion, he said, "It seems to me that your decision to send the reinforcements to Angola . . . is absolutely correct in a purely military sense." Politically, however, it would provide fodder to those powerful forces in the United States who opposed the INF treaty that Gorbachev was planning to sign during his visit to the United States, from December 7 to 10—a fortnight away. "Of course, there is no connection between the treaty and your decision—no connection for those who look at it objectively—but, well, those who are eager to grasp any pretext to oppose the treaty will make hay with it." Akhromeyev reminded Ulises about what had happened in 1979: "After the SALT II treaty had been signed and brought to the U.S. Senate to be ratified, what riled American public opinion? The presence of the Soviet troops in Cuba, the so-called Brigade. Do you remember it?" Akhromeyev was a realist. "Well, what's on its way is already on its way," he admitted, but he added a request: "send the bulk of the reinforcements to Angola after December 10. I repeat, this is my personal opinion. Don't convey it to your government, because, well, first my government must decide."

Ulises did not give an inch. "We understand that our decision has complex ramifications, but it is not Cuba that has complicated the situation; it is South Africa."[85]

Two days later, on November 27, Ulises met with Soviet defense minister Yazov, who had returned to Moscow the previous evening. "In a word, their conversation was far from diplomatic," remarks Alexandr Kapto, the Soviet ambassador to Cuba.[86] Unlike Akhromeyev, Yazov knew very little about Angola. (In the course of the discussion he asked "Where is Cuito Cuanavale?") Nor was he accustomed to working with the Cubans. He launched into a bitter, intemperate attack about the failure of the Cuban troops to assist the FAPLA during Salute to October, using language I have not seen in the thousands of pages of transcripts of Soviet-Cuban conversations I have read. "How can you be in another country and do nothing?" Yazov demanded.

When I was in Cuba in 1962, I couldn't have imagined sitting there and crossing my arms if the Americans had invaded. I would have immediately joined the fighting.[87] It is from this perspective that I judge the actions of the Cuban troops in Angola. I've been Minister of Defense for only a short time, but every week I have listened to reports about the situation in Angola, and in these six or seven months the Cuban troops haven't done anything. Well, when the Angolans were on the offensive and scoring some successes, this was understandable, but now, when the Angolan troops are in a difficult situation, you have to do something. . . . If the Cubans had not been permanently stuck in some garrison but had somehow maneuvered, if they had advanced behind the Angolan troops, then, of course, it would have been possible to achieve something. . . . This is why things are such a mess: the Cuban troops are in the country, but they're not doing anything.

Ulises offered no apologies. "I would like to clarify one matter to the minister: we have not been sitting on our hands; rather we have said very clearly where and how we must fight, where the principal enemy is, where we should strike the main blow," he replied. "I must remind the minister that we repeatedly expressed our opposition to this operation." Salute to October had been launched at the insistence of the Soviets. They had been wrong in 1987, just as they had been wrong in 1985. Akhromeyev intervened: "Comrade Ulises is right in the sense that the Cuban comrades have never been in favor of these offensives in the southeast."

Yazov's anger was due in part to his ignorance of the background—he was apparently unaware that Havana had opposed the offensive—but, above all, it was due to Castro's decision of November 15. The Soviets would have welcomed a Cuban defensive operation to save Cuito Cuanavale, but they were alarmed that Havana intended to do much more. "The point is not to defend just one city," Ulises stressed, "but to demonstrate that we can counter the [South African] aggression." It was the Cuban decision to force the SADF out of Angola that worried the Soviets. They feared, as Akhromeyev explained, "a massive response from South Africa . . . South Africa is not going to abandon this territory without a fight." Akhromeyev predicted that the Cuban decision would lead to major clashes with the South Africans at a particularly inopportune moment. Yazov insisted, "You know that our General Secretary will soon go [to Washington] to sign the INF treaty." Cuba's actions were "undesirable from the political point of view. . . . The United States is the United States, and the Americans will use whatever pretext they can to accuse the Soviet Union, and Cuba, of pursuing an aggressive policy, etc. In any case," he concluded, "we don't want to do anything that the Americans can use against the Soviet Union and Cuba."[88]

Before boarding the plane that would take him back to Havana, Ulises had one last conversation with Akhromeyev. In the Cuban military archives, two sets of handwritten notes (a draft with corrections and a final draft) indicate that Ulises prepared what he would say with great care. For good reason. He was going to complain, strongly, to Akhromeyev about Defense Minister Yazov, his immediate superior.[89] The minutes of the meeting make clear that Ulises repeated verbatim what he had written in his notes. "We came prepared to explain everything about the reinforcement of our troops," he told Akhromeyev. "But I must tell you, sincerely, that we were not prepared to listen to accusations that we Cubans are doing nothing in Angola and that the offensive had been defeated because we were sitting on our hands." With characteristic grace, Akhromeyev admitted immediately that Yazov had been wrong, and he took the blame for it: "It is my fault because I failed to give the minister a detailed briefing about the fact that the Cuban troops . . . had made no commitment regarding Cuito Cuanavale, and it was not expected that they would act in support of the FAPLA." He told Ulises that "we have informed the Central Committee of our party about your request [for weapons]. . . . Within three weeks . . . the Ministries of Industry and of Defense will determine what we can do." The answer would be sent directly to Castro.[90]

## Gorbachev and Castro Cross Swords

Three days later, on November 30, the Soviet chargé in Havana, Vladimir Kisilev, delivered a brief note to Raúl Castro. It said nothing about the Cuban request for weapons:

> The Soviet government agrees with the assessment presented by Comrade Ulises of the military situation in Angola. However, to be blunt, we were surprised by the news that Cuba had dispatched an additional contingent to Angola because it is more than the military situation in Angola requires.
>
> Given that the troops are already on their way, it may be best if we say that it is a planned troop rotation. Later, if the South Africans escalate their offensive in Angola, we can return to the issue.[91]

Raúl Castro, after reading the note, "felt compelled" to respond immediately. Saying that he "was speaking only for myself," he told the chargé that "we were not going to waver." The decision to launch Salute to October had been wrongheaded, "and now we must deal with the consequences. . . . We told you ad nauseam that the operation would be a mistake." Raúl added that he doubted that Fidel would agree "to say it is a troop rotation because this is a lie, and we don't tell lies. Within 24 or 48 hours we will give you our official reply."[92]

Less than twenty-four hours later, Gorbachev received a letter from Fidel

Castro. After pointing out that the situation in Angola had become critical, Castro wrote:

> We do not bear any responsibility for the military situation that has been created there. The responsibility belongs entirely to the Soviet advisers who insisted on urging the Angolans to launch an offensive in the southeast. . . . We have always been against foolhardy operations like this which cannot solve the problem, squander resources, and divert attention from operations against the UNITA guerrillas in those regions of the country that are truly strategic in military, economic, social, and political terms. . . .
>
> The behavior of the Minister of Defense of the USSR toward the Chief of the General Staff of our armed forces [Ulises] was offensive. Minister Yazov made accusations against our troops that, in our opinion, were unjust, hurtful and humiliating.
>
> The Soviet note criticizes our decision to send reinforcements because— I quote—"it is more than the military situation in Angola requires." . . . The military situation has continued to worsen. The facts prove that our decision to send reinforcements without delay was absolutely correct. We cannot exclude the possibility of armed clashes with the South Africans. Anyone can understand how dangerous it is to be weak in such circumstances. . . .
>
> The Soviet note proposes that we say we are conducting a normal troop rotation. To do so would be a mistake. There is no reason to invent an excuse or resort to lies. It would undermine morale and weaken the correctness of our stance. If, during your talks, the Americans ask about these reinforcements, they should simply be told the truth: the flagrant and shameless intervention by South Africa [in Angola] has created a dangerous military situation that has obliged Cuba to reinforce its troops in an absolutely defensive and legitimate action. The Americans can be assured that Cuba sincerely wishes to cooperate in the search for a political solution to the problems of southern Africa. At the same time, they must be warned that South Africa's actions have gone too far, and the result may be serious conflict with the Cuban troops. . . .
>
> In closing, I want to assure Comrade Gorbachev that Cuba will do everything in its power to help Angola overcome this difficult situation.[93]

In his memoirs, Gorbachev briefly refers to the Cuban-Soviet tensions of late 1987: "It was precisely at this moment that there were sharp disagreements between the Cuban military leaders in Angola and our Soviet military advisers there. Our military leaders reproached the Cubans for not being sufficiently active and engaged; they asserted that the Cubans had everything they needed to defeat UNITA. The Cubans responded in a similar tone, saying that if the Soviets were conducting the war in Afghanistan in the same way [as in Angola], it was no wonder that victory eluded them. At this juncture I received a letter from Fidel. It was on the whole friendly, but it included strong criticism of our military in Angola."[94]

On December 5, virtually on the eve of his departure for Washington, Gorbachev replied to Castro's letter. It was a short missive, written in a tone that sought to avoid an escalation, but it offered no concessions: it said nothing about the Cubans' request for weapons, and it complained, gently, about the Cubans' decision to send the reinforcements to Angola and their failure to consult Moscow. "Dear Comrade," Gorbachev began,

> I tell you sincerely and as a friend that your letter . . . worried me. . . .
> First, I want to tell you that we do not consider this episode in any way indicative of a crisis of confidence in our relations. Both you and I know well that Soviet-Cuban relations are based on a long-standing fraternal friendship and are characterized by special sincerity and trust.
>
> During your visit to Moscow for the celebrations of the 70th anniversary of the Great October Revolution we exchanged views about a broad range of subjects, including Angola. I got the impression that the situation in that country was complicated but did not require extraordinary measures. Therefore, the news of Cuba's decision to send additional troops to Angola was for us, frankly, a complete surprise.
>
> Maybe you coordinated with dos Santos but, in any case, I find it hard to understand how you could have taken such a decision without consulting us, when we have relied for a long time on tripartite consultations to develop a coordinated policy in Angola.

Castro had confronted Gorbachev with a fait accompli, and Gorbachev sought to establish guidelines that would prevent it from happening again:

> Regarding the conduct of the military operations in Angola, we assume that they will be coordinated among the Angolan high command, the Cuban high command and the Soviet military advisers. It is a fact of life that military operations are not always successful. In war anything can happen. I think that we must now proceed calmly and deliberately in order to cool the passions.
>
> At the same time we must significantly improve the coordination between our military representatives when planning future military operations in Angola. I think that you share this desire. For our part, we have

ordered our military representatives in Angola to maintain the strictest collaboration on the ground with their [Cuban] comrades in the elaboration and implementation of military operations.[95]

Castro later defended his decision, telling Gorbachev, "Really, we did what we had to do: to inform. Not to consult. There are matters about which one cannot consult, but only inform, because they have to do, as in this case, with the life and the security of tens of thousands of our sons. At issue was not just the fate of Angola, but also of the Cuban internationalist fighters who are in Angola." Castro explained that an Angolan military collapse would have threatened the security of the Cuban troops; furthermore, the South Africans might have attacked the Cuban defensive line.[96] It is highly unlikely, however, that the Cubans would have consulted the Soviets, even without any danger to their troops, given that they believed that Angola's survival was at stake. This is what had happened in November 1975, when Castro sent his troops to save the country from the South African invasion.

## Turning the Page

As in 1975, the Soviets' irritation in 1987 gave way to acceptance of the fait accompli. The first signs of this appeared just days after Gorbachev wrote to Castro. On December 8, during the Congress of the French Communist Party in Paris, Risquet met with Yegor Ligachev, second only to Gorbachev in the Kremlin hierarchy. "I had a half-hour conversation with Ligachev; the main subject was Angola, at his initiative," Risquet cabled Castro. "I explained the military situation to him and why the reinforcements had been necessary. . . . To this he said, 'You act first and inform us later.' He was laughing, and he gave me a playful nudge, but he said it . . . and it was clear that he was concerned. . . . He asked me what the USSR should do, and I said that they should replace as much of the war materiel that we are sending to Angola as they could, so that we would be able to rebuild our defenses in Cuba. I added that Fidel had written to Gorbachev about this, and he said he knew." Risquet concluded the cable, "The conversation was very cordial even though it took place in a boxing ring—the only spot that was available in the sports arena where the Congress is being held."[97]

That same day, in Washington, Reagan and Gorbachev signed the INF treaty. For Gorbachev, the summit was a great success. "America seemed in the grip of Gorbymania," historian David Reynolds writes. Back in Moscow, in the Politburo session about the results of the summit, Gorbachev was upbeat. "This was not Geneva, or Reykjavik, as important as they were," he said. "This was an even more significant proof that our policy is succeeding." The key moment of the visit had been the signing of the INF treaty. "Everything depended on this—the future of Soviet-American relations and the stability of the international situation as a whole. . . . The world was waiting for it; the world demanded it. Trust in our foreign policy demanded it. . . . The INF treaty was the turning point." It opened the door, Gorbachev concluded, to progress on other disarmament agreements, and it created the groundwork for a similar pragmatic approach that could be used to resolve regional problems.[98]

The fact that the Washington summit went well, and Angola did not become a major obstacle in U.S.-Soviet relations, was a relief to the Soviet leadership. Moreover, the Cubans were trying to reassure the Kremlin that they were not seeking military victory in Angola. "As I explained to your ambassador," Castro told Gorbachev, "we are not doing this in order to win a war but to guarantee a just and reasonable political negotiation that will allow Angola to preserve its sovereignty, its integrity and its peaceful development, as well as assure the independence of Namibia."[99]

After Ulises's showdown in Moscow with Yazov and the tense exchange of letters between Gorbachev and Castro in early December, there was no open clash between the two governments. On at least one occasion, a ship that carried advanced antiaircraft weapons from the Soviet Union to Cuba was diverted to Angola at Havana's request.[100] But the Soviets said not one word about the weapons that Ulises had requested in his November visit to Moscow. The Cuban leaders grew increasingly irritated. The Soviets' response had been "very bad," Castro grumbled. "They have told us nothing."[101] The Kremlin was aware of the Cubans' growing frustration. Fidel Castro's sharp letter to Gorbachev had been followed by Raúl Castro's announcement that he would not go to Moscow to attend the February 1988 celebration of the seventieth anniversary of the Soviet Army—an invitation he had already accepted. For the Kremlin, "this was a serious signal," remarks Ambassador Kapto. "Such a rebuff could not help but provoke anxiety," Gorbachev's aide Medvedev adds. "Our long delay in answering the Cubans' request to replace the weapons they had sent to Angola added fuel to the fire."[102]

Castro kept steady pressure on the Soviet leadership. "We are urging the Soviets to speed up the delivery of the Pechoras and the spare parts for the Cuadrados [two very sophisticated antiaircraft systems]," he wrote the head of the Cuban military mission in Angola on January 14. "I am insisting on the need to complete our fourth squadron of MIG-23s with the eight planes that we don't have. And I have also told them that we are running out of bombs and ammunition for the planes."[103] He urged General Polo Cintra Frías, who was leaving for Angola, to be nice to Konstantin, who was due to visit Angola shortly: "Your tactic with Konstantin," Castro said, "is to tell him, 'Look Konstantin, you have to understand that . . . we're not children anymore; we are old enough to know what to do. Don't tell us what we should do, because we won't do what we don't think is right. . . . Instead help us in another way. . . . You might even want to make up for the mistakes that have been made here. Damn! Send us parachutes! Send us spare parts!'"[104]

Moscow's silence did not stop the Cuban leaders from sending weapons to Angola from Cuba's own arsenals. "We must keep thinking about planes and more troops for Angola," Castro said. "Our troops are necessary there, not here [in Cuba]. It is there that we need the air force, not here." In Raúl's more graphic words, "Today I told the Soviet [General Zaitsev] that we'll go without underpants if we have to. We will send everything to Angola."[105]

Castro's fait accompli had left the Soviets few options. As Risquet points out, refusing to supply the weapons "would not have prevented the operation, because we were sending the weapons from Cuba, but it would have left Cuba very vulnerable because we were depleting our own stockpiles." The Cubans, Soviet ambassador Kapto writes, "made it clear that if we refused to send the weapons they had requested for their troops in Angola, they would do whatever they had to do to equip them, at whatever cost."[106] A Soviet refusal to help would have threatened the security of the Cuban troops in Angola and the survival of the Angolan government, should the South Africans escalate further. And it would have led to a confrontation with Castro. Yuri Pavlov, who headed the Latin American department of the Soviet Foreign Ministry, noted that "the Soviets believed that it was dangerous 'to drive Fidel into a corner' because he could react unpredictably, and unwanted surprises had to be avoided, given Moscow's interests in Cuba."[107] For the Kremlin, Castro was a valuable, if difficult, ally.

Finally, the Soviets replied. On January 23, 1988, they informed Havana that they would send most of the weapons Ulises had requested when he went to Moscow the previous November. Their silence had lasted fifty-nine days "in which they told us nothing," Castro noted.[108] The next day, surveying the military situation in Angola, he told Risquet, "Things have gone well during this period . . . when we have acted on our own, while quarreling with the Soviets. . . . Now that we can count on some Soviet cooperation we will proceed with much more pleasure. This is good."[109] Castro kept up the pressure, urging Gorbachev "not to delay even for a minute. . . . [In Angola] there is a war and men are dying."[110]

Ulises returned to Moscow on February 21, 1988. He briefed Akhromeyev on the campaign that was unfolding in southern Angola. He pointed out that in the ninety days since the beginning of the operation Cuban planes and Cuban ships had ferried 7,500 soldiers to Angola, as well as 218 tanks, 122 armored cars, 112 artillery pieces, and other heavy weapons. "But there are still difficulties." He unfolded his shopping list—weapons and materiel Cuba still needed from the Soviet Union. Most prominent on the list were the eight MIG-23s and the range-extending fuel tanks for the MIGs that Cuba had already requested, and antiaircraft weapons.[111]

Akhromeyev wanted to help. One thing bothered him, however. The Cubans were conducting the campaign without consulting Moscow or the Soviet military mission in Angola. Akhromeyev "expressed concern" that the once-close coordination between the Cuban and Soviet military missions in Angola had been lost. Ulises replied, "I agree with you that the coordination has ended . . . It ended in 1985 with the offensive against Mavinga." Akhromeyev conceded the point: "True, Comrade Ulises, you are right. Let's not mention it again."[112] The page was turned. The Soviets accepted the facts: it was a Cuban campaign, the Cubans alone would direct it, the Soviets would be informed, but they would not be consulted.

CHAPTER 16

# Maniobra XXXI Aniversario

## The Cubans Arrive

For the first eight months of 1988, Cuban ships and Cuban planes continued to ferry troops and war materiel to Angola. Before Castro decided to launch Maniobra XXXI Aniversario in November 1987, there were 38,000 Cuban soldiers in Angola. By August 1988, when the last reinforcements arrived, the number had increased to 55,000.[1]

Even more than the additional soldiers, the most dramatic aspect of the operation was the quality of the weapons sent to Angola: Cuba's most modern tanks, virtually all its mobile antiaircraft systems, and its best planes. It was—in numbers and armament—by far the most important operation ever launched by the Cuban armed forces.

Castro's strategy was to break the South African offensive against Cuito Cuanavale and then to attack in the southwest. "By going there [to Cuito] we placed ourselves in the lion's jaws," he explained. "We accepted that challenge, and from the very first moment we planned to gather our forces to attack in another direction, like a boxer who with his left hand blocks the blow and with his right—strikes. Cuito Cuanavale was the left hand, and the right hand was the forces that we assembled [in the southwest]."[2] The preparations for the offensive were conducted in the greatest secrecy, lulling the South Africans into a false sense of security, making them believe that the Cubans' focus was the defense of Cuito Cuanavale. "Rubén," Raúl Castro had told the head of the military mission in Angola on December 1, 1987, "do not make any movement that might signal our future intentions to the enemy. South Africa must continue to believe that our attitude is passive."[3]

Rubén was the nom de guerre of General Arnaldo Ochoa, one of Cuba's most respected military officers. He had been one of the nine Cubans who had joined the Venezuelan guerrillas in 1966–67; he had headed the Cuban military mission in Ethiopia at the most critical time, in 1977–78, and the Cuban military mission in Nicaragua in 1983–86. In March 1986 he had been appointed deputy minister of defense in charge of military missions abroad. Contrary to the oft-repeated story, however, he had not participated in the 1975–76 Angola operation; at the time he was studying at the Voroshilov Military Academy in Moscow. In fact, he had not served in Angola until he was appointed head of the military mission there in early November 1987.[4] On November 15, a few days after his arrival in Luanda, Havana decided to launch Maniobra XXXI Aniversario.

Fidel Castro supervised Maniobra XXXI Aniversario very closely. The documents in the Cuban archives make it incontrovertible that he directed every aspect of the campaign, from grand strategy to tactics. He expected prompt feedback from the field. "I asked if you had replied to my instructions of the 30th [of November]," he cabled Ochoa on December 2, "and they tell me that nothing has arrived, and that you don't send many reports. I expect this to change."[5]

Throughout Maniobra XXXI Aniversario, Ochoa remained in Luanda, heading the military mission and in constant contact with President dos Santos. Castro appointed another prestigious general, Polo Cintra Frías, to lead the Cuban forces in the south—the main war theater. Unlike Ochoa, Polo had long experience in Angola: he had been one of Cuba's senior commanders there in 1975–76, he had returned in November 1982 to command the Cuban troops in southern Angola, and he had headed the military mission from July 1983 to September 1986. On December 5, 1987, he returned to Angola. At the beginning Castro sent instructions to Ochoa and, through him, to Polo; but soon Castro's cables were addressed to both men.

## Cuito Cuanavale

The immediate task was to save Cuito Cuanavale. The FAPLA brigades that had retreated there lacked supplies because SADF air superiority made it impossible to resupply them by air. Supplies had to be moved overland from Menongue in large convoys that were exposed to strikes from the South African Air Force along a 180-kilometer road through woods. On November 30, the Cuban military mission reported that Ochoa had returned from Menongue, "and he thinks that the 8th FAPLA brigade [which was escorting a convoy of supplies] will not reach Cuito Cuanavale because its discipline is poor, it has other problems, and furthermore today it was attacked by the South African Air

Force near Menongue. If the 8th brigade does not arrive, Cuito Cuanavale will not be able to hold out much longer, mainly because it will run out of ammunition."[6] The convoy made it to Cuito, but only after suffering "heavy losses" from South African air strikes. The SADF was confident that it could virtually cut off the Menongue-Cuito lifeline.[7] "In Cuito there was an atmosphere of profound panic," recalls a Soviet military officer who was attached to one of the Angolan brigades there. The Soviet military mission "had already prepared the plans for the evacuation of our advisers from Cuito to Menongue.... The senior Angolan officers were utterly demoralized, until the Cubans arrived."[8]

On December 5, 1987, the first Cubans arrived in Cuito Cuanavale: 106 Special Forces and 15 officers "who immediately began to organize the command structure, to reorganize the defense, and to prepare the artillery." Havana had initially intended to send only a few military advisers, but had soon realized that Cuban troops were necessary to save the town. By late January there were 1,500 Cubans in Cuito. They were, Castro told Gorbachev, "in part organized in Cuban tank, artillery and infantry units, and in part serving as advisers in all the Angolan brigades."[9] They were only men, until early January, when a woman—a certified nursing assistant "whose husband, a doctor, is in Cuito"—joined them. "She asked [Polo] for permission to go, and he consulted, of course, her husband. She said that she wanted to show . . . what a woman could do, and Polo gave his permission."[10]

The South Africans had believed that time was on their side, but they were wrong. After Castro's November 15 decision to launch Maniobra XXXI Aniversario everything changed. Taking off from Menongue, Cuban MIG-23s flown by Cuba's best pilots gained control of the skies over Cuito Cuanavale. (UNITA's vaunted Stingers proved of little use against the Cubans; "apparently at this stage the Stingers were no longer so dangerous," the SADF reported.) The Cubans also secured the vital road from Menongue to Cuito. Because the MIGs provided "virtually uninterrupted air cover," the SADF remarked in late December, it had become "extremely difficult" for the South African air force to attack the convoys along the road. Supplies therefore resumed from Menongue to Cuito. Cuban crews manned the tanks and artillery that defended Cuito. "Even if the Cubans did nothing else, this alone would have considerable influence on the fighting," the SADF had warned in December.[11]

The South Africans had counted not only on their control of the skies but also on their superiority in artillery. "The FAPLA was powerless against our long-range bombardments, because its artillery had nowhere near the same reach as our G-5 guns," a SADF analysis had noted before the Cubans arrived. By late December 1987, however, Cuban air superiority over the battlefield meant that every shot fired by a G-5 offered the Cubans an opportunity "to locate the G-5 guns so that the MIGs . . . could destroy them."[12]

The FAPLA brigades fought with renewed determination. "They . . . have really behaved very well and they have been very brave," Castro told Soviet deputy foreign minister Adamishin in March 1988. "They have endured the bombardments and the hunger; they have resisted with great courage."[13]

The exact number of South African soldiers deployed against Cuito in the first months of 1988 will be known only when the South African archives are fully opened. General Geldenhuys told *Le Figaro* in April 1988 that they were "a little more than 5,000."[14] This figure is consistent with that given by Lieutenant Colonel Les Hutchinson, who was at the Directorate of Operations at Army Headquarters in Pretoria. "The entire force arrayed against Cuito Cuanavale was about 5,000–6,000 men, not including UNITA," he says. "It was the largest conventional force we ever had in Angola."[15] After the failure of the campaign, Pretoria claimed that there had been no more than 3,000 SADF soldiers in southeastern Angola, a deliberately deflated figure.[16] Geldenhuys's statement to *Le Figaro* is the most authoritative, since he was in a position to know and had no interest in inflating the numbers.

As the weeks passed, the South Africans were unable to crack the defenses of Cuito. They concentrated their efforts on the bridgehead east of the town. "The capture of this key position of the FAPLA has become the all dominating question," the SADF noted in mid-February 1988. But their attacks on the bridgehead failed. "This has had a negative impact on the morale of many of the South African troops," the SADF admitted.[17] Instead of a great South African victory, Cuito was sapping the SADF's credibility. On February 25, 1988, the *Sowetan*, South Africa's most important black paper, wrote, "We have been keenly watching developments in Angola, and are now convinced that anybody who still believes what the South African Defence Force says on the situation there will believe anything." South African whites were anxious. On February 26, Colonel Fred Rindle, the South African army attaché in Washington, told a U.S. official that "'white' casualties are clearly becoming a problem, there is increasing questioning [in South Africa] of the value of losing 'boys' inside Angola."[18]

The morale of the FAPLA soldiers rose. In late February, the Angolan government escorted a group of Western journalists to the town. "The [Angolan] troops and officers we spoke to were assertive and confident," the correspondent of the London *Times*, Jan Raath, wrote in an article datelined Cuito Cuanavale. Raath also talked with Cuban soldiers, youths like Ernesto García Ramírez, who had been in Angola for sixteen months, "and is counting days until he can be back in Santiago de Cuba with his wife and two-year-old raton (little rat). But he adds, 'We will be here for as long as necessary. We are fighting for a just cause.'" Cuito, "a row of wrecked stores and mud huts amid miles of trackless wilderness, doesn't look like much," a South African newspaper, the *Weekly Mail*, noted a week later. But it had an airport, the best units of the Angolan army, and immense symbolic value. "Until the battle of Cuito Cuanavale," the *Weekly Mail* commented, "South Africa was able to control perceived threats to its security by selective and (mostly) unilateral application of its regional power. . . . But Cuito Cuanavale's dusty streets and battered airfield may well prove the bridge too far."[19]

Cuito was no longer an isolated outpost of beleaguered FAPLA fighters. In an April 1988 analysis, the U.S. Joint Chiefs of Staff noted that the Cubans had secured the road from Menongue to Cuito, and "any SADF/UNITA attempt" to cut it off would be met "with very heavy resistance." The Cubans had also gained air superiority over Cuito Cuanavale, and the absence of the SADF air force in the area had become "notable." The South Africans could no longer supply their troops by air, and supplying them by land from Mavinga was far more hazardous and cumbersome. Morale suffered. The U.S. Defense Intelligence Agency reported that the South African forces on the ground "complained of a lack of air support." The Americans' sober assessments were confirmed by the SADF, which conceded that the enemy had "complete air superiority."[20] The commander of the South African force arrayed against Cuito wrote in his war diary on March 1, 1988, "The enemy is strong and clever."[21]

And yet President Botha and his military chiefs refused to accept reality. General Geldenhuys told the president on February 15, 1988, that Cuito's fall was only "a matter of time." On March 14, Botha told the State Security Council: "The enemies of South Africa are losing the war in Angola."[22] Nine days later, on March 23, the South Africans launched their last major attack against the bridgehead east of the Cuito River. It was "brought to a grinding and definite halt," Colonel Breytenbach writes. In Washington, the Joint Chiefs noted, "The war in Angola has taken a dramatic and, as far as the SADF is concerned, an undesirable turn."[23]

No climatic battle was fought at Cuito Cuanavale. The South Africans did not launch a major assault on the town; nor did the Cubans and the FAPLA surge from the town to push them back to Mavinga. The "battle of Cuito Cuanavale"—the defeat of the South Africans—consisted of two key elements. First, the Cuban victory in the air. Second, the Cuban and Angolan defensive victory on the ground repelling the South African attacks on the bridgehead east of

Cuito. This saved key FAPLA brigades, and it had great psychological importance. South Africa's onslaught had been broken, for all to see, and its troops were demoralized.

Cuito Cuanavale became a symbol. In the words of Nelson Mandela, it "destroyed the myth of the invincibility of the white oppressor . . . [and] inspired the fighting masses of South Africa . . . Cuito Cuanavale was the turning point for the liberation of our continent—and of my people—from the scourge of apartheid."[24]

It was, however, a defensive victory. As Castro said, Cuito Cuanavale was the fist that stopped the blow. But what decided the campaign and forced the South Africans out of Angola was the Cuban advance in the southwest.

## Adamishin in Havana

While the guns roared at Cuito Cuanavale, Soviet foreign minister Shevardnadze visited Washington, on March 21–23, 1988, for talks with President Reagan and Secretary of State Shultz. He confirmed that the Soviet Union had decided to withdraw from Afghanistan: "By the end of the year, the withdrawal would be complete—and this would happen under the Reagan administration." The Soviet Union no longer demanded that in return the United States end its military aid to the Afghan rebels. Soviets and Americans also discussed the Iraq-Iran War and other regional conflicts in the Middle East, Central America, Cambodia, Korea, and southern Africa. Deputy Foreign Minister Adamishin—who was in charge of African affairs—discussed Angola and Namibia at length with Assistant Secretary Crocker. "When we met at the State Department for three hours on March 21, Anatoly Adamishin fell short of our expectations," Crocker writes in his memoirs. "The Soviet Deputy Foreign Minister offered no specific ideas for advancing the process [of negotiations] and no concrete support for our efforts. . . . Adamishin declined to discuss the Cuban withdrawal timetable [from Angola], claiming that this was not a Soviet issue." Adamishin's own reading of the meeting was "that the U.S. was seeking the maximum number of concessions . . . without offering anything in return." He told Shultz and Shevardnadze "that the discussions were useful, and should continue," but the Americans must understand "that the Soviet Union strongly supported the positions Angola had taken in the discussions thus far."[25]

On March 26, Adamishin was in Havana to brief the Cubans. First, he met Risquet. Then, on March 28, he had "one of the most interesting meetings of my diplomatic life—with Fidel." In his memoirs he recalls that Castro listened in silence to his briefing about the Washington talks. "Suddenly, when I ended my report, he began to speak about Angola. And this—virtually a mono-logue—went on for four hours. . . . He spoke in a surprisingly animated man-ner, gesticulating, drawing diagrams on pieces of paper and on the map. While speaking he often jumped up and paced around the room. (The first time he stood up, out of respect I started to stand up too, but he told me 'sit down.')" Adamishin, whose entire career had been in the Soviet foreign service and who had no military experience, could not resist—in his memoirs—some boasting. He gave Castro military advice: "When I could, I tried to correct him: don't leave northern and central Angola without troops; don't let the enemy choose where to fight, etc. etc."[26]

The Cuban minutes of the conversation, 102 pages, confirm Adamishin's recollections—up to a point. Castro was mainly silent as Adamishin briefed him. Then he spoke at length about Angola: he reviewed the differences be-tween Cuban and Soviet military strategies there, detailed the Soviet mistakes, and stressed how wrongheaded the two offensives against Mavinga had been. Adamishin said very little. When he spoke, it was not to offer advice but to earnestly agree with Castro, even when the latter lambasted Soviet strategy.[27]

The previous evening, Adamishin had told Risquet that Crocker had warned him that "[South Africa] will not withdraw from Angola until the Cuban troops have left the country" and that the South African military "feel every day more comfortable in Angola, where they are able to try out new weapons and inflict severe blows on the Angolan army." Crocker's message was clear: if Havana and Luanda wanted Pretoria to withdraw from Angola, they would have to make significant concessions.[28]

Castro was not impressed. "Ask the Americans," he told Adamishin: "If the South Africans are so powerful, . . . why haven't they been able to take Cuito? They've been banging on the doors of Cuito Cuanavale for four months. Why has the army of the superior race been unable to take Cuito, which is defended by blacks and mulattoes from Angola and the Caribbean? The powerful South Africans . . . have smashed their teeth against Cuito Cuanavale . . . and they are demoralized."[29]

## The Cuban Offensive in the Southwest

As Castro spoke, thousands of Cuban soldiers were advancing hundreds of miles southwest of Cuito through Cunene Province toward the Namibian bor-der.[30] It was a region, Crocker notes, "of sand and scrub through which SWAPO infiltrated to reach Namibia. It was also the place where an intermittent SADF/SWATF [South West Africa Territory Force] presence moved in and out to break up and preempt SWAPO actions. Token FAPLA units stayed as far out of sight as possible, hunkered down in bush camps and a few towns populated largely by wild dogs and helia monsters. Much of the southwest could be considered a no-man's land. The South African forces looked upon it as a free-fire zone for their lightly armed special forces . . . and they traditionally controlled its airspace." UN undersecretary Margaret Anstee, who visited the capital of Cunene, Ondjiva, writes that "the town . . . was virtually no more, gone, obliterated by one of the savage South African air bombardments and never rebuilt. Eyeless and gaping, the shattered walls and empty rooms of what had once been attractive little houses with tiled roofs lay open to the sky. . . . There was only one intact building that I remember."[31]

The Cubans were convinced that South Africa had a few nuclear bombs. (In fact, it had six.)[32] They believed that Pretoria would not dare to use them, at least as long as the Cuban army did not enter Namibia. Nevertheless, they took whatever precautions they could. As Castro explained, "Our troops advanced at night, with a formidable array of antiaircraft weapons, . . . in groups of no more than 1,000 men, strongly armed, at a prescribed distance from one another, always keeping in mind the possibility that the enemy might use nuclear weapons."[33]

When the advance through the southwest began, on March 9, 1988, the Cubans' southernmost airfields were Lubango and Matala, at more than 250 kilometers from the Namibian border. The Soviets had not sent the range-extending fuel tanks Havana had requested for its MIGs, claiming that they had none available. In early January, the Cubans sought to buy the fuel tanks from Poland, East Germany, and Czechoslovakia. Prague and Berlin immediately replied that they had none available. Only the Poles gave a positive reply. They sent thirty, and they did not arrive until late May. "It was very little," remarks Ulises. "It had only symbolic value."[34]

Moscow's and its East European clients' inability to send Cuba range-extending fuel tanks can be explained only by the Kremlin's desire to restrain Castro and make sure that he would not push his offensive too far south, risking major clashes with the SADF and attempting to assert control over the skies of northern Namibia.

The Cubans, however, were not so easy to restrain. There was an old airport in Cunene, near the ghost town of Cahama, which had been destroyed by South African air strikes, 125 kilometers north of the border. On March 22, Castro cabled Generals Ochoa and Polo, asking, "How long would it take to construct an operational airfield for fighter planes at Cahama, if we work at full speed?" It would take "at least ten months," they replied, if they had all the necessary equipment.[35]

While Cuban teams worked night and day to build a new airport near Cahama, the Cuban troops advanced toward the border, relying above all on the protection of their mobile antiaircraft systems, which had been sent from Cuba and the Soviet Union since the beginning of Maniobra XXXI Aniversario. The Cubans were accompanied by several thousand FAPLA troops and about 2,000 SWAPO insurgents. As General Charles Namoloh, who was SWAPO's chief of staff, notes, "It was the first time that SWAPO participated in a major operation with the Cubans."[36]

"These SWAPO guerrillas walk sixty kilometers a night in a normal march and 100 kilometers in a forced march," Ochoa remarked. And they knew Cunene like the back of their hand.[37] Throughout the advance, joint patrols of SWAPO guerrillas and Cuban Special Forces served as scouts. Some twenty years later, the Cubans remember their Namibian comrades with respect and affection. "They had so much experience, and they were very brave and very intelligent," Pedro Ross Fonseca, who was then a young Special Forces lieutenant, recollected in Havana, while showing me a yellowing photograph of his Namibian friends that he keeps in his wallet. "Without them we could not have accomplished our mission as successfully as we did." Felix Johannes, one of the Namibians in the photo, smiled as I repeated Pedro Ross's words to him in Windhoek: "The Cubans depended on us because we knew the terrain, but they moved excellently," he said in his halting English. "I was happy. I had a good feeling. I felt that victory was near."[38]

Describing the military situation to Adamishin in late March 1988, Castro said, "The further we advance, the greater the distance from our airfields. We are reaching the limits of the range of our planes. We must think very carefully before we take any step forward. . . . Until now, the South Africans have offered no resistance to our advance. It is possible that they will withdraw without fighting, but we cannot be sure, and we cannot bank on this assumption. We must analyze the situation very carefully. . . . Look, my beef with my comrades [generals] is that they tend to underestimate the South Africans. Every step we take, we have to assume that they are going to react, that they are going to fight." Castro urged Ochoa: "We must always take precautions as though the enemy will attack. We cannot assume that the South Africans will withdraw without fighting. . . . We are now entering a phase in which we must avoid even the smallest mistake. We must evaluate as carefully and dispassionately as possible the enemy's resources and likely reactions. We have time; we don't need to rush things."[39]

Colonel Rindle, the South African army attaché in Washington, belittled the Cuban advance. He told a U.S. official in early April that "the SADF is going to give the Cubans a 'bloody nose' now that they are down 'in our operational area.'. . . . It's territory we're familiar with and they are not. . . . [They have] one very vulnerable supply line." U.S. intelligence was not so sure: "Pretoria appears to be taken aback by the Cuban reaction to its own involvement and may now realize that it cannot unilaterally force concessions from Luanda, renewing its interest in negotiations."[40] By April the South African generals were aware that the Cubans were building an airport at Cahama and that the situation in the air had become "favorable" for the Cubans; they knew that powerful Cuban columns were moving toward the Namibian border.[41] In happier times, these Cuban troops would have been tempting targets for the South African air force, but now the SADF leaders were paralyzed by the Cuban antiaircraft defenses. "The implications of this," the SADF noted, "are that no airplane can be flown within the range of the enemy's antiaircraft defenses. . . . Reconnaissance flights between 10,000 and 59,000 feet are impossible. Helicopter flights are severely limited . . . Our ability to surprise is curtailed, and the interception of our planes by enemy planes is likely."[42]

Colonel Breytenbach looked back at the situation twenty years later. "Bloody Fidel Castro outwitted South Africa's generals. It became dangerous."[43]

The Cubans did not know whether the SADF would withdraw from Angola without a major battle. "We cannot predict what the South Africans will do," Risquet told President dos Santos in late March. When a Cuban general, who had just returned from southwestern Angola, told Risquet that it seemed as though the South Africans "aren't doing anything to stop us or to attack us. It appeared that they were withdrawing," Risquet replied, "If this is true . . . we will achieve the implementation of Resolution 602 [which demanded the SADF's unconditional withdrawal from Angola] without great battles. This would be best. It would be like what happened in 1976."[44] But if the South Africans chose to resist, the Cubans would fight their way to the Namibian border. In Havana, a few days later, Fidel Castro told his close aides: "The strategic objective of this war is to free Angola from the South African occupation and to achieve the implementation of Resolution 435 [granting independence to Namibia]. . . . It is not to wage a decisive battle with the South Africans in which many precious lives will be lost." He wrote dos Santos on March 31: "The enemy cannot ignore the magnitude and the seriousness of our immense military effort and the consequent change in the correlation of forces. I hope that this will contribute to fruitful negotiations. But if we have to fight, we will be stronger than ever."[45]

CHAPTER 17

# Chester Crocker Meets Jorge Risquet
## *Talks about Talks*

## Cuba Joins the Negotiations

Angolans and Americans had begun a new round of negotiations in July 1987. The talks were based on Luanda's implicit acceptance of linkage—Namibian independence was linked to the withdrawal of the Cuban troops from Angola. Americans and Angolans differed, however, on the timetable and scope of this withdrawal: Washington demanded that all the Cuban soldiers leave Angola; Luanda insisted that only those based in the south of the country would leave.

In Havana, Castro urged President dos Santos in July to resist the Americans' demand that all the Cuban troops depart, but he also stressed that the decision was Angola's to make. On one point, however, he was adamant: Cuba had the right to participate in the negotiations that dealt with the withdrawal of its troops. This demand put the Cubans in direct opposition to the Americans, who had insisted that Havana had no place at the talks.

Americans and Angolans were still far apart on the tempo and scope of the Cuban withdrawal, and on Cuban participation, after their third round of talks in Brussels, in late September 1987. They agreed to meet again in November, but then the South Africans struck, hard, at the FAPLA brigades that were advancing toward Mavinga.

The Angolans were torn. Anger and indignation made them want to suspend the talks with the Americans, who were Pretoria's friends. But fear and insecurity prodded them back to the negotiating table as quickly as possible in order to find a solution that would forestall a military disaster.

Castro urged dos Santos to wait. "We can't rush. We can't be impatient, even though we have difficulties," he argued. "We wanted the Angolans to wait until the military situation improved," Risquet explains. "To negotiate in the middle of a military crisis meant playing with a much weaker hand."[1] Castro was per-

431

suasive—in part because the Angolans, ever more dependent on Cuba's military assistance, were reluctant to spurn his advice. And so they kept postponing their next meeting with the Americans, while wondering whether this was the right decision. Would the military situation improve, as Castro promised? Or would they have to negotiate later with an even weaker hand?

Reeling from the South Africans' blows, unsure of whether Cuito could hold, afraid of what Pretoria might be planning next, dos Santos sent Foreign Minister M'Binda and FAPLA chief of staff Ndalu to Havana in mid-October 1987 to inform Castro that the Angolan government had decided to accept the American demand that in return for the implementation of Resolution 435 all the Cuban troops would leave Angola. Since this was what dos Santos wanted, Castro agreed, but he urged, "If the Angolans want to . . . talk about the withdrawal of all the Cuban troops, well, they must demand, in exchange, complete guarantees for the security of Angola. . . . The key is not whether our troops leave in four or five years, but whether there is a solid, serious agreement about all the problems that concern Angola." In other words, "a comprehensive solution" would include the withdrawal of the SADF from Angola, the end of foreign aid to UNITA, international guarantees for Angola, and the implementation of Resolution 435 about Namibian independence.[2]

One month later, on November 15, 1987, Cuba launched Maniobra XXXI Aniversario. Additional Cuban troops and weapons began arriving in Angola.

On Christmas Day, the head of the U.S. Interests Section in Havana, John Taylor, went to Risquet's office to hand him an aide-mémoire from his government. "The state of the negotiations and prospects for a political settlement [in Angola] had been thoroughly discussed with the Soviets in the period leading up to the [December 7–10, 1987] Washington summit. We were therefore encouraged by General Secretary Gorbachev's statement to President Reagan that he saw 'good opportunities' for a political settlement." This was either wishful thinking or an attempt to intimidate the Cubans by letting them know that Americans and Soviets might reach an agreement without them. The aide-mémoire continued, "There is also growing African interest in achieving a negotiated settlement. . . . In view of this growing international support for the diplomacy now underway, we find it strange that Cuba has thus far done nothing to help achieve a settlement. We note, for instance, reports of an augmentation of Cuban military strength in Angola. . . . In view of these developments, what are Cuba's intentions in Angola? What is your view of prospects of a negotiated settlement? Do you share Gorbachev's view that there are now 'good opportunities' for a political solution? Is it Cuba's intention to facilitate or obstruct Angola's announced intention to table a concrete and comprehensive schedule for withdrawal of all Cuban forces that would represent a major step forward in the negotiations?"[3]

Risquet reminded Taylor that Havana's actions in Angola were in response to Pretoria's escalation there. He emphasized that both the Angolan and the Cuban governments had asked that Cuba be allowed to join the negotiations. He added, "I want to stress that in these negotiations we would discuss only Angola and southern Africa and no other subject. The U.S. government fears that we would use these negotiations to raise issues about our bilateral differences. We assure you that we will not. . . . We are still waiting for an answer from the U.S. government."

Taylor had a reply, of sorts. "We are waiting for the Angolan proposal about the withdrawal of the Cuban troops. . . . Right now that is the key." If the proposal was satisfactory—that is, if Luanda accepted the U.S. timetable—then Cuba might be allowed in the negotiating tent. The U.S. position remained that enunciated in the "Brussels formula": Crocker would recommend to his government that if Angola accepted the U.S. timetable on Cuban withdrawal, "then Angola could inform us of that with a Cuban presence in the room."[4]

Risquet sent the minutes of the conversation to dos Santos and noted in an accompanying letter, "I explained to Mr. Taylor that we support a comprehensive solution, but the U.S. idea of a comprehensive solution may not be the same as that of Angola and Cuba. . . . For the United States a comprehensive solution means primarily the timetable of the withdrawal of all the Cuban troops. . . . For Cuba it means, first of all, the cessation of South African and U.S. aid to UNITA. Only after this has been agreed upon and only after other guarantees for Angolan security have been accepted, should we begin to discuss the withdrawal of all the Cuban troops."[5]

On January 3, 1988, dos Santos told the Cuban ambassador, Martín Mora, that he had read Risquet's letter "in which he describes his conversation with Mr. Taylor." Dos Santos was grim. He feared that Cuito Cuanavale would fall to the South Africans. The previous day he had written to Castro, "The difficult situation we're in because of South Africa's aggression is getting worse every day." He told Mora: "The Americans are holding very good cards because our situation has deteriorated." He explained that he was over a barrel: he would have to negotiate with South Africa and the United States, and his priority would have to be getting the SADF to withdraw from Angola. "Everything else is secondary." The independence of Namibia would have to take a back seat. "Namibia is not an immediate interest. Why should Angola bear all the burden, when the burden belongs to the entire international community?" Dos Santos's frame of reference, as he anxiously wondered whether Cuito would fall, were the difficult days of early 1984, when, reeling from another successful SADF offensive, Angola had negotiated alone with Americans and South Africans—and obtained nothing. This time, Cuba must join the negotiations, at Angola's side. Reading the minutes of dos Santos's conversation with Mora, comparing it with the exchanges between Angolans and Cubans on this same issue the previous summer—that is, before the SADF offensive—it is evident that in the summer of 1987 the Angolans had asked that Cuba join the negotiations primarily because the Cubans had insisted, but by early 1988, frightened by the SADF's blows, dos Santos desperately wanted Cuba to be present at the talks. The Cubans, dos Santos hoped, would be Angola's best shield against a South African diktat supported by the United States.[6]

In early January 1988, Angolan foreign minister M'Binda proposed to Crocker that the negotiations resume in Luanda on January 28, but only on the condition that the Cubans be invited. "Their participation is, for us, a *sine qua non*," he asserted.[7] Castro decided to send Risquet to Luanda to participate in the talks, if they took place. On January 24, a few hours before Risquet departed, Castro reviewed the Cuban position on the negotiations with him. Cuba was willing to be part of a joint delegation with Angola; Angola could lead the delegation, but "our representatives would have the same rights as those of Angola and the United States. Cuba and Angola will coordinate their positions fully. It is one position, but at the negotiating table both Angolans and Cubans will speak, clarify, respond." Cuba would not raise any issues about its relationship with the United States. But it would insist that the agenda include the immediate withdrawal of the SADF from Angola, the end of foreign aid to UNITA, the implementation of Resolution 435, and guarantees to secure the territorial integrity of Angola. If the Americans accepted this agenda as well as Cuba's participation in the talks, Angola and Cuba would be ready to start negotiating at once. If not, "Crocker would have to return to the United States to consult with his government. Once the Americans give a positive reply, then we would like the negotiations to begin as soon as possible."[8]

The next day, January 25, Risquet arrived in Luanda carrying a letter from Castro to dos Santos. It was a stern retort to a letter dos Santos had written Castro two weeks earlier. "Unfortunately," the Angolan president had said, "our military situation has worsened considerably since December. . . . The disagreements about military strategy among Angolans, Soviets and Cubans have allowed South Africa and UNITA to deploy their forces more effectively. . . . At times it seems to me that we are standing still, waiting for a miracle."[9]

Castro sharply disagreed. He reminded dos Santos of what Cuba had done since November 15, 1987: "From here, at a distance of 10,000 kilometers, we have accomplished true miracles to save Angola from an almost insoluble crisis, a crisis which was not of our making. In less than six weeks entire units of our army—our best—have arrived in Angola with all their armament, including hundreds of tanks, armored vehicles and artillery pieces." Castro's assessment of the military situation was upbeat. "The military balance of forces has changed considerably," he wrote. With Cuban help, the South African onslaught against Cuito Cuanavale had been halted, and the Cuban troops were preparing to challenge the SADF in southern Angola. "Therefore, I cannot agree with you that the situation in January was worse than in . . . December. I also do not agree that South Africa and UNITA are maneuvering their forces more effectively because of the differences among Angolans, Soviets and Cubans. It would be more correct to say that the enemy has benefitted from the wrong military decisions of the Soviets and the Angolans, decisions with which we very rightly disagreed." Castro ended his letter: "Please do not be offended by the frankness with which I have discussed some issues. I believe that our close and loyal friendship must always be based on the confidence, sincerity and respect with which we are able to express our opinions."[10]

On January 26, after reading Castro's letter, dos Santos received Risquet. Because of the improving military situation, he was far less anxious than he had been in early January. He admitted, "I think that I may have exaggerated the problems because I was tense about the situation in Cuito Cuanavale." Significant Cuban reinforcements—1,500 soldiers—had joined the Angolan defenders of Cuito; Cuban planes controlled the skies over the town and had secured the vital road from Menongue to Cuito. Dos Santos's growing confidence was reflected in his decisions: the Angolans would meet with Crocker to ask whether he agreed that the Cubans should participate in the negotiations; if Crocker refused, the talks would end then and there. Dos Santos also agreed with the agenda proposed by Castro, and he agreed that the timetable of Cuban withdrawal would be discussed only after the other points had been satisfactorily settled. When dos Santos asked, "What do the Soviets think?" Risquet replied: "We haven't spoken with them about this lately. . . . The Soviets are in favor of negotiated solutions everywhere but in this specific case they accept that we are the ones making the decisions. They have already replaced some of the arms we are sending to Angola. This is a positive gesture, and we have let them know that we appreciate it." Before leaving dos Santos's office, Risquet reminded him of Cuba's position on UNITA—the constant refrain that "if UNITA is receiving foreign assistance it is an intervention. . . . But UNITA with no foreign aid is an Angolan problem."[11]

## Round One: Crocker in Luanda, January 1988

The next day, January 27, Crocker arrived in Luanda. He was flanked by NSC Africa director Herman Cohen, who had been at his side since the negotiations with the Angolans had resumed in March 1987. A career foreign service officer, Cohen had become NSC director for Africa as a result of Iran-Contra. "For the first six years of Reagan's presidency," he writes, "a series of CIA officers had served as senior director for African Affairs on the NSC staff. When I took the position in January 1987, I was the first non-CIA person to handle Africa for the president and the national security advisor. In December 1986, in the aftermath of the Iran-Contra affair, Frank Carlucci was appointed the new national security advisor and General Colin Powell the new deputy. To demonstrate that a real change was taking place, Carlucci and Powell fired virtually all the NSC staff, including the unimplicated CIA officer in charge of Africa [Philip Ringdahl]."[12] An unintended benefit for Crocker, Cohen adds, was the departure of "my predecessor who was hostile to Crocker."[13]

Before January 1987, when he had accompanied Shultz and Crocker on an African trip, Cohen had not had a close relationship with Crocker. But "during that trip we had a lot of opportunities to talk. Crocker was so worried about the conservatives' animosity toward him and their fear that the State Department was going beyond the limits of Reagan's policy that he wanted me to give him cover. And he also wanted, for the same reason, a representative of the Department of Defense—[Deputy Assistant Secretary James] Woods. I believed in what he was trying to do, as did Woods. Crocker, Woods and I worked very well together. [Senators Jesse] Helms [(R-N.C.)], Hatch, de Concini and others were very mistrustful of Crocker. My job, Carlucci told me, was to keep them happy, keep them briefed, reassure them that Savimbi was not being undermined. I went to see them many times. I gave Crocker the cover he badly needed."[14] This became particularly important as the negotiations moved into high gear in January 1988.

When I told Crocker what Cohen had said, he agreed: Cohen and Woods gave him cover with Congress—"but more importantly with the executive branch." I expressed my surprise: by early 1988 Shultz's nemesis, DCI Casey, was dead, Secretary of Defense Weinberger had resigned, and National Security Adviser Poindexter had been fired. Crocker paused, and then explained, "Shultz himself wanted reassurance that we weren't going to get him in trouble with Reagan, who was very committed to Savimbi." Crocker's senior deputy, Freeman, was blunt: "Savimbi's visit in 1986 had a strong impact on Shultz. He became quite infatuated with Savimbi. We [Africa bureau] had to assure him we were giving Savimbi a fair chance."[15]

On the evening of January 27, 1988, while Crocker and Cohen settled into Luanda's Hotel Presidente and prepared for their customary dinner at the British ambassador's residence ("it was all so depressing," recalls Cohen), M'Binda and his negotiating team met with Risquet. "Our conversation occurred in an atmosphere of mutual understanding; they are going to coordinate everything with us," Risquet cabled Castro. "The impact of the improved military situation is obvious, as is the fact that once again Fidel and our people have saved Angola from the catastrophe."[16]

The next morning, January 28, Crocker informed M'Binda that the Angolans had to present a timetable for total Cuban withdrawal before the Cubans would be allowed to participate in the negotiations. M'Binda showed Crocker the agenda for the talks, which included the discussion of the timetable as the fifth, and last point. This was not what the Americans had demanded. They had said that the timetable was the precondition to Cuban participation. The military situation in southern Angola had changed, however: Cuito Cuanavale was not going to fall and Cuban reinforcements were pouring into Angola. On the morning of January 28, 1988, as the Americans and Angolans met around the conference table, Crocker backtracked. Without fanfare, he agreed that when they convened the next day, the Cuban delegation should join them. He demanded, however, that Angolans and Americans first meet alone to discuss "some things that I have to tell you about UNITA and that we cannot discuss with the Cubans present." He told M'Binda: "Mr. Secretary, . . . it would not be helpful to include the question of U.S. relations with UNITA in the negotiations. It would overload our agenda."[17]

On January 29, Angolans and Americans met again. On behalf of the Angolan delegation, the FAPLA chief of staff, Ndalu, told Crocker that while "we want the United States to end its aid to UNITA . . . we are not asking you to make a decision about it now. We ask only that you inform the government of the United States of our request. We don't expect an immediate response, . . . but we think that the least your government can do is to analyze this question, think about it. . . . If you agree, then I propose that we leave this matter aside, and . . . move to the plenary session with the participation of the Cubans." This signaled that U.S. aid to UNITA would not be discussed in the plenary sessions, and the agenda item that referred to the end of foreign aid to UNITA would henceforth mean only the end of South African aid.[18]

This settled, Crocker writes, M'Binda and Ndalu "adjourned the meeting to fetch Risquet. . . . The negotiation was about to change for good. Risquet's presence changed the ambiance in our modest conference room at Futungo do Belas. We could hardly believe the man's body language as he strutted in my direction, eyes twinkling, and proudly introduced his colleagues to us. . . . He lit up a long, aromatic Cohiba. Suddenly, the table seemed small as four Cubans squeezed alongside the Angolans."[19]

The first order of business was Crocker's demand that the Angolan government respond "to the proposals we presented in Brussels stipulating that all the Cuban troops would leave Angola in little more than a year." The response of Ndalu and Risquet set the tone of the meeting. They were categorical: Luanda and Havana would discuss total Cuban withdrawal only as part of a comprehensive solution, and only after the other points on the agenda had been satisfactorily settled. In Ndalu's words, "if we reach an agreement on the preceding four points, then we will discuss the timetable." The tension mounted. Crocker warned that agreeing on the implementation of Resolution 435 would be "extremely complex." He added: "We have brought working drafts of the agreements that would be signed by Angola and South Africa, with the United States and perhaps Cuba as observers." But when M'Binda asked for a copy of the documents "to study them before our next meeting," Crocker sternly replied: "Your Excellency . . . the documents are for serious working sessions." He would keep the documents, and he admonished M'Binda, "It is obvious that . . . your side needs to do more work before we see the need to come to other meetings." He would inform his government that the inclusion of the Cubans in the negotiations "didn't solve anything and didn't lead to any progress on the fifth point of our agenda," that is, the timetable of the withdrawal of the Cuban troops, which was what most interested the United States.[20] Crocker left with a parting shot: "I have just one thing to add before I leave for the airport. . . . I am not optimistic about reaching a quick solution."[21] Risquet cabled Castro, "Thus the meeting ended with the U.S. delegation departing in a huff."[22]

Risquet was not intimidated. "We made progress," he told dos Santos. The Angolan-Cuban proposal for a comprehensive solution was on the table, and Cuban participation in the negotiations was a fact. The military situation in southern Angola was improving: soon Cuban troops would be advancing toward the Namibian border. Crocker would return to the table.[23]

From Havana, Castro sent dos Santos encouraging messages, stressing that the military situation was improving. Whereas the Americans argued that South Africa's willingness to negotiate was contingent on the Cubans and Angolans making concessions, Castro argued the opposite. "The South Africans listen only to strength. We have to neutralize them militarily. Then and only then will they negotiate," he wrote on February 19, 1988. "Otherwise the negotiations will be fruitless. We are reinforcing our troops in southern Angola with arms and men."[24] On March 6, as the Cuban columns were poised to begin their advance in the southwest, Castro told dos Santos,

> Our objective is to make the South Africans end their attacks against Cuito Cuanavale . . . and withdraw their troops from Cunene and Huila [the southwest]. If they resist we will force them out. We must achieve this step by step, acting with intelligence, decisiveness, and caution.
>
> South Africa will then not be able to reject or sabotage the negotiations. The balance of power has changed in our favor. . . . We will face our enemies across the negotiating table in a very favorable situation. But we cannot afford the smallest mistake. . . . Our cooperation must be seamless and absolute. I beg you, Comrade José Eduardo, to trust us. We think that we might be able to achieve our objectives without bloodshed—and if we have to fight, our military superiority will be so overwhelming that our casualties will be minimal. Our display of force will accelerate the tempo of the negotiations, and it may lead to success without a major battle. This would be the best outcome because our goal is not to achieve a military victory, but to guarantee that the negotiations be conducted in a fair and honorable manner.[25]

## Round Two: Luanda, March 1988

Crocker had left Luanda in late January muttering warnings that the Cubans' and Angolans' stubbornness would paralyze the negotiations. In February, as the talks were on hold, the military situation in Angola continued to turn against the South Africans. On March 9, as the first Cuban units began advancing south of the Cuban defensive line, a small team of U.S. diplomats, led by Deputy Director of Southern African Affairs Larry Napper, arrived in Luanda for talks at "working-level" with Angolans and Cubans. The Angolans were led by Minister of Justice Fernando Van-Dúnem, the Cubans by Puente Ferro, one of Cuba's most able diplomats. Risquet did not participate in the talks, but he was on hand in Luanda supervising the Cuban team and handling communications between Castro and dos Santos. Castro cabled Risquet, "I expect that you will work like true geniuses of diplomacy. Don't scrimp paper or time to keep us informed." The Americans later paid their counterparts a handsome compliment: "The Angolans and Cubans took the working sessions seriously, fielding teams of high rank and quality."[26]

For Napper, this was the first time he had faced Cubans across a negotiating table. Looking back on the series of talks that occurred in 1988, he remarked, "Those guys [the Cubans] were really rock solid. They were professionals. They were very tough, hard as nails, and they were kept on a short leash—they could not make a decision without consulting Fidel. But when they made a commitment they would keep it." This is a telling comment given that, before the negotiations began, Napper had considered Cuban officials untrustworthy. The Angolans, Napper added, "were very different. Their demeanor was like a deer in headlights. They were frightened. They didn't want the Cuban troops to leave. The Cubans were clearly the senior partner throughout the negotiations. But they treated the Angolans with respect."[27]

Unlike Crocker, who often seemed to believe that arrogance was a useful attribute for a U.S. diplomat, at least when dealing with Angolan officials, Napper was invariably urbane and often pleasant. "The Yankees were cordial and treated the Angolans and Cubans like friends," Risquet cabled Castro on March 9, 1988, after the first day of talks.[28] But behind the smiles, the U.S. message had not changed: for the negotiations to move forward, Luanda and Havana must make concessions. Napper explained that Crocker was going to meet South African foreign minister Pik Botha in Geneva on March 14 and that he, Napper, would fly to Geneva to report to Crocker about the talks. "When I meet with my boss, Dr. Crocker, on Friday, I don't want to have to tell him, 'We haven't made any progress.' Dr. Crocker is already wondering whether it's worth his while to return to Angola to continue the negotiations. . . . I would like to give him a positive report." He returned to the point the next day: "The only way to convince Dr. Crocker to return to the talks in Angola is to show that we have made concrete progress."[29]

The Cubans and Angolans did not budge. They told Napper that the withdrawal of the Cuban troops would be carried out over a period of forty-eight months after the beginning of the implementation of Resolution 435 (an unacceptable length of time for Pretoria and Washington), and they refused to discuss the timetable until the other four points of the agenda had been satisfactorily settled, "as we said at our last meeting," Van-Dúnem stressed.[30] This was the message that Napper should take Crocker in Geneva.

Angolans and Americans met without the Cubans to discuss U.S. aid to Savimbi. "We are very worried about the aid given by the U.S. government to UNITA," Van-Dúnem told Napper, who replied courteously: "I understand . . . your concerns." But Napper was obdurate: U.S. aid to UNITA would end only when the Cubans and Soviets ended their aid to the Angolan government.[31]

On March 16, Napper returned to Luanda from Geneva with a letter from

Crocker to M'Binda. He was flanked by Crocker's special assistant, the tough-talking Robert Cabelly. In his letter, Crocker said that Pik Botha had expressed interest in the negotiations but that his reaction to the forty-eight-month schedule had been "extremely negative."[32]

Then, as in a well-rehearsed play, Napper and Cabelly proceeded to explain the facts of life to Cubans and Angolans. Napper said that Cabelly, "who has several years of experience in dealing with the South Africans . . . understands how they think. Therefore, I have asked him to give you a general idea of the South African mentality." Cabelly was happy to oblige. He asserted that in Pretoria those who wanted a negotiated settlement were a minority consisting of Pik Botha and his Foreign Ministry officials, and they were opposed by the military. "The South African military leaders . . . think that the war is going well for them." They therefore had no desire to withdraw from Angola. When Puente Ferro asked whether the U.S. government "will demand the immediate and unconditional withdrawal of the South African troops from the south of Angola?" Napper replied that the United States had shown its goodwill by voting the previous November for UNSC Resolution 602, which demanded the SADF's unconditional withdrawal from Angola, "but our Cuban friends will certainly understand that one thing is that we demand, and another is that they comply with our demands." (U.S. officials liked to point to their vote on Resolution 602 as proof of their good faith but failed to mention that the United States had made sure that the resolution was toothless.) Then it was Cabelly's turn: "If you want to negotiate with South Africa about the withdrawal of its troops," he warned, "you have to offer something in return, and so far you haven't offered anything." Napper concluded, "As soon as you give us a realistic offer about the departure of the Cuban troops, our government will use all its political influence to pressure the South African government." The Cubans and Angolans, however, stood their ground. They would discuss the timetable of Cuban withdrawal only after all the other items on the agenda had been settled.[33]

The talks ended inconclusively, but Risquet was confident that they would continue because the military situation continued to improve for the Cubans and the FAPLA. On March 19, 1988, before returning to Havana, he met with dos Santos for a final exchange of views. He told the president "that it was important that at the next meeting . . . South Africa be present. . . . It would be better to have South Africa at the negotiating table than having the Yankees relay proposals back and forth. . . . Dos Santos agreed: 'The Americans claim to be mediators, but they are also a party to the conflict. . . . It is better for us to have a quadripartite meeting.'"[34]

Nothing happened on the diplomatic front for almost two months, while on the ground the military situation continued to turn against the South Africans. Tens of thousands of Cuban soldiers were advancing toward the Namibian border. On April 15, 1988, the U.S. Joint Chiefs concluded, "The war in Angola has taken a dramatic and, as far as the SADF is concerned, an undesirable turn."[35]

The day before, April 14, Crocker had cabled M'Binda that Pretoria was ready to meet with "an Angolan delegation that would include Cuban representatives, with the participation and mediation of the United States, in late April or early May."[36] The parties had finally reached the starting line. Quadripartite negotiations could begin.

## The Balance Sheet

The United States had obtained an important concession: in October 1987, President dos Santos, eager to reach an agreement with the Americans at a time when the military situation appeared particularly grim, had accepted that a timetable for the withdrawal of all Cuban troops from Angola would be determined in the negotiations. Crocker writes in his memoirs, "We managed to extract a significant price for agreeing to Cuban participation: the Angolan-Cuban commitment in January 1988 to the principle of total Cuban withdrawal."[37] He overlooks, however, the important fact that dos Santos endorsed Castro's demand that the timetable for withdrawal be discussed only *after* agreement had been reached on the other points of the agenda.

On Christmas Day, 1987, Jay Taylor, the head of the U.S. Interests Section in Havana, had appeared at Risquet's office to inquire about Cuba's intentions in Angola. This was the first time the Reagan administration had asked the Cubans about their views and plans. Then, on January 28, 1988, the administration had finally agreed to let the Cubans participate in the negotiations. The Cubans' demands had not changed: they still refused to discuss the timetable for the withdrawal of their troops until the other issues on the agenda had been settled. What had changed—and was changing—was the situation on the ground in southern Angola. Cuba's growing military strength, the successful defense of Cuito Cuanavale, and the Cubans' advance in the southwest gave Cuba and Angola leverage at the bargaining table.

## Can Moscow Be Trusted?

As soon as M'Binda received Crocker's cable proposing quadripartite talks, the Cubans and Angolans began hammering out a joint position for the first meeting that would begin in London on May 4, 1988. In 1986 Castro had pledged that the Cuban troops would remain in Angola until apartheid had been defeated in South Africa, but he had consistently added the caveat, "if the Angolans so wished." When the Angolans decided that all the Cuban troops should leave sooner, Havana did not question it. Castro told Soviet deputy foreign minister Adamishin, "If you asked: 'Are you willing to remain there ten more years?' we would reply, yes . . . we can stay ten more years, until the end of apartheid. . . . Because as long as it exists there can be no peace, no security for Namibia, Botswana, Mozambique, Tanzania, Zambia, Angola—not even for Mobutu! . . . I doubt that apartheid will last ten more years. . . . I would be surprised if it still existed five years from now, because of the struggle of the South African people and the pressure of world opinion." He added, "If someone asked us 'if you were willing to remain ten more years, why are you willing to leave now?' The answer is very simple: we must consider what the Angolans want. . . . We must be willing to subordinate any other objective to the interests of Angola."[38]

The Angolans were alarmed by indications that Moscow was growing soft. They worried about Gorbachev's propensity to strike deals with the Americans and were unnerved by the suggestions of Soviet officials—including the ambassador, Vladimir Kasimirov—that they try to reconcile with UNITA. Gorbachev wrote Castro on February 25, 1988, "I think that we have finally found the right way to move toward the resolution of the regional conflicts that have long aggravated the international situation. . . . Their causes are diverse, but they have much in common, and this has made it possible to find a 'common key' for their resolution. What I mean is the policy of national reconciliation that has already begun in Afghanistan." It was a chilling model, because the keynote of Moscow's new policy in Afghanistan was the Soviets' willingness to unilaterally withdraw all their troops without receiving anything, including "national reconciliation," in return. This was why the policy was applauded by the West. After noting that progress toward national reconciliation was also being achieved in Cambodia and Nicaragua, Gorbachev cut to the chase: "We must ask, is it not time to elaborate a strategy for a political solution of the problems of southern Africa, and particularly in Angola, which is the conflict that most worries us?" He offered no concrete suggestion, but returned to the example of Afghanistan: "The situation in Afghanistan is much more complex [than that in Angola] and if even there we are beginning to see rays of hope, God himself, as the saying goes, demands that we find a solution for Angola. Indeed, the Angolans themselves are leaning more and more in that direction. In sum," Gorbachev concluded, "it is time for us to develop a joint approach and begin to take concrete steps, of course with our Angolan comrades." He added that two of his close aides, Dobrynin and Medvedev, would soon arrive in Havana for the annual meeting of foreign secretaries of the ruling parties of the Soviet bloc. "They could discuss this problem with you."[39]

Castro was underwhelmed. "We Cubans are not in the least opposed to any internal peace settlement in Angola," he told Gorbachev, "whether it is an agreement with UNITA without Savimbi, as the Angolans have hinted on occasion, or even with Savimbi. This decision . . . is the sovereign right of the MPLA and the Angolan people." The Cubans believed, however, that the forthcoming quadripartite negotiations should deal only with the international aspects of the crisis, by which they meant South African and U.S. support for Savimbi's insurgency as well as the independence of Namibia. "We must now strive for an agreement that will end the external factors that have inspired and fueled this internal struggle [between the government and UNITA]," Castro told Gorbachev. It was up to the Angolans to solve their own problems once the foreign meddling had been stopped. This was Cuba's position and, more importantly, this was Angola's position. Castro set the record straight: "I must inform you," he told Gorbachev, "that the Angolans, especially José Eduardo and the leadership of the MPLA, . . . have complained bitterly about being pressured by Soviet officials." Castro concluded, "Regarding the 'common key' that you mentioned in your letter to me—that is present in every regional conflict and would allow them all to be resolved through national reconciliation—I must tell you, Comrade Gorbachev, that in my opinion these regional conflicts are as diverse . . . as the political, military, economic and social problems of today's world." Angola was not Afghanistan.[40]

Castro made the same points on March 3, 1988, during a long conversation with Dobrynin and Medvedev, and again the following day, as he took them on a tour of Havana. Medvedev writes: "During our conversation, Fidel's irritation and bitterness toward the actions of the Soviet military advisers in Angola erupted from time to time."[41] As soon as Gorbachev's aides departed, Castro wrote a reassuring letter to an anxious dos Santos. "I spoke at length with Dobrynin and Medvedev, and I wrote to Gorbachev, telling him that in my opinion the negotiations should be focused on solving the external factors that are affecting the situation in Angola. . . . [I stressed that] the problem of internal peace in Angola must not be addressed at this stage. Once the external factors have been solved, it will be the sovereign right of the MPLA to adopt the measures it considers necessary to achieve peace as quickly as possible."[42]

The Angolan president was not reassured. On March 10, Risquet cabled Castro: "[Dos Santos] gave me two documents to read, one reporting the statements of two Soviet delegations, and the other of an East German delegation, all urging reconciliation with UNITA. After reading both documents I told him what had happened during the foreign secretaries' meeting . . . that had taken place in Havana." At that meeting, Risquet had warned the participants, among them Medvedev and Dobrynin, that "just as there cannot be . . . a single model for the construction of socialism, so there cannot be a single model for the resolution of regional conflicts." In other words, what worked in Afghanistan might not work in Angola. This was also, Risquet reminded dos Santos, what Castro had told Gorbachev.[43]

A week later dos Santos repeated to Risquet "that he was worried that the conversations between the Americans and the Soviets would wreck everything." Angola would be sacrificed for détente. "The Americans hope to convince Moscow to pressure us." Again Risquet reminded dos Santos of "the exchange of letters between Gorbachev and Fidel . . . and Fidel's categorical statement about the differences among regional conflicts. . . . As I was leaving," Risquet cabled Castro, "I told the president that I was confident that the differences with our Soviet brothers will be resolved. I reminded him that when we sent our reinforcements [to Angola]—without informing them—they had worried that it could have a negative impact on the INF Treaty [with the United States]. But nothing had happened, and now the Soviets accept that sending the reinforcement was the right thing to do. . . . The same will happen with the negotiations. In the end they will agree that we are right."[44]

## The View from Pretoria

The big question—not only in Havana and Luanda but also in Washington—was what position would the South Africans take at the negotiating table? The omens were not auspicious. In February 1988, Foreign Minister Pik Botha expressed skepticism that any progress could be made unless Resolution 435 was modified. The following March Defense Minister Malan and President Botha said that South Africa would withdraw from Angola only "if Russia and its proxies did the same," and they did not even mention withdrawing from Namibia. "South Africa speaks from a position of strength," Malan asserted, "as proven by the successes it has achieved at UNITA's side in southeastern Angola."[45] In a secret memo, the chief of the SADF, General Geldenhuys, restated the military's objective: an independent Namibia under a government "that is well disposed toward South Africa." In order to achieve this it was necessary that a specific sequence be followed: first, UNITA had to come to power in Angola. This would gut SWAPO's strength, enabling a pro–South African government to come to power in a nominally independent Namibia. The military's view about the interconnectedness of the two crises was endorsed by President Botha, who told the State Security Council that he was "convinced" that if the SADF withdrew from Namibia "UNITA would collapse and the present Transitional Government [in Windhoek] would not survive."[46]

The long-standing disagreements between the South African Foreign Ministry and the defense establishment were manifested on the ground in southern Angola. The SADF remained in control of South Africa's relations with UNITA. It was only in early 1988 that the Foreign Ministry was allowed to have a permanent representative, John Sunde, at the SADF's base in Rundu, in northeastern Namibia. Rundu was the last stop on the way to Jamba, Savimbi's headquarters, and it was from Rundu that the SADF ran the aid program to UNITA. Colonel Oelschig, who was in charge of the aid program in Rundu, informed Sunde that he was "under my direct command." The hapless diplomat would be allowed to travel to Jamba and help UNITA edit its newspaper, *Kwatcha*, and radio program, but he could meet Savimbi only with Oelschig's authorization. "Any liaison with President Savimbi must be done through me," the colonel announced. Sunde reported to his superiors in the Foreign Ministry that he and Colonel Oelschig could get "along together" as long as he respected Oelschig's "total overall control." The deputy director general of the Foreign Ministry lamented, "I am disturbed by the prescriptive style which Colonel Oelschig adopts . . . [with] Mr Sunde." But there was nothing that he, or his superiors, could do.[47]

In South Africa, meanwhile, unrest continued, and the government intensified its repression. On February 24, 1988, it banned seventeen leading antiapartheid organizations from "carrying on or performing any activities or acts whatsoever," and it imposed draconian restrictions on the country's largest black trade union.[48] The CIA reported the next day, "Pretoria's action yesterday effectively banning the black opposition will reassure whites of the government's commitment to security but will probably convince many blacks that nonviolent opposition is no longer an option. . . . Unrest is likely to increase . . . as angry blacks protest the new measures."[49] The government was unable to quell the unrest. The minister of internal affairs told the State Security Council on March 14 that "the revolutionary temperature remains . . . high. The organizations that were recently banned have reappeared in new forms and with new names." All the while, the ANC was gaining influence and prestige, in South Africa and abroad. An insightful CIA report, appropriately titled "South Africa's African National Congress: Weathering Challenges," stressed that the ANC had successfully met "the challenges posed by turbulent events in South Africa over the last few years by maintaining its organizational cohesion, retaining its dominant position in the antiapartheid movement and broadening its contacts with the West," while enjoying the full support and cooperation of the Soviet bloc.[50]

President Reagan stood firm in his opposition to imposing economic sanctions on South Africa, stressing that the problem in South Africa was more "tribal" than "racial."[51] His remark was applauded on South Africa's state-run television.[52] At home, however, he faced rising congressional pressure—and on May 3 the battle was joined as the House Foreign Affairs committee approved a bill barring all American investment in South Africa and imposing a near-total trade embargo on that country. In Johannesburg the usually steady *Business Day*—which had a healthy fear of economic sanctions, despite much bluster that they would be ineffectual—lashed out: the hearings the House committee had held "were the legislative equivalent of a Stalinist show trial, a nauseating little charade intended to cloak a predetermined outcome with the trappings of due, democratic process."[53]

Amid the growing din of international condemnations, several of South Africa's few remaining friends drew back. When the UN Security Council voted on March 8 on a draft resolution imposing mandatory sanctions on Pretoria, the United States and Great Britain cast the lone negative votes. For the first time, West Germany abstained, with France and Japan. West German president Richard von Weizsäcker said that Bonn was reappraising its firm opposition to economic sanctions.[54]

## Preparations in Havana

On April 22, 1988, and again on the 23rd, Castro met with Risquet, who would lead the Cuban delegation, to hammer out the Cuban strategy at the forthcoming London talks. "We cannot make mistakes," he urged. "We need to show firmness and some flexibility. . . . Risquet, we cannot make the smallest error, not even the smallest. . . . The fact that they have agreed to this meeting in London . . . indicates that they want a solution because they have seen that we have gained the upper hand [on the battlefield]. . . . This worries the Americans. . . . They are worried because of our advance [toward the Namibian border]. . . . Anyone who looks at a map and sees that we are building the airport [Cahama] at full speed and that more troops, tanks, and materiel are arriving [in Angola], will understand that we are serious." Addressing the meeting that the Cuban delegation would have with the Americans in London the day before the conference began, Castro said, "Our message for the Americans must be: 'We will not accept bluffs and lies from the South Africans. . . . We want to negotiate seriously, but we won't accept haggling, blackmail, and things of this kind. If the negotiations are serious, we won't present any obstacles to the search for a solution.' Because we really want a settlement, that is our goal."[55]

Cuba would go to London with two nonnegotiable demands. The first was the full acceptance by the South Africans of Resolution 435, without any change whatsoever. The other demand was that South Africa stop aiding UNITA. There could be no agreement if these two conditions were not satisfied. . . . The military situation had turned against South Africa—"our position is extremely strong." The South Africans could no longer use promises of withdrawing from southern Angola as a bargaining chip, as they had done over the years with the Angolans; the Cubans were chasing them out. "And you must tell them," Castro added, "that we cannot give them any guarantee that we won't move into Namibia."[56]

On all other matters, Castro told Risquet, "you must coordinate with the Angolans, and there are two risks: that they will want to be too soft or too intransigent."[57] Cuba should offer them advice and support during the negotiations. "We must stand by them." One major issue would be the timetable for the withdrawal of the Cuban troops. In terms of Cuba's own narrow interests, Castro said, the faster the soldiers left Angola the better. But Angola would benefit from a slower tempo. "We must consider more than what's best for us," Castro urged, "we must consider what's best for them. . . . Our withdrawal does not have to take 36 months; it could be 30 or even 26 months, but not one minute less than 26 months." As for U.S. aid to UNITA, the Cubans would follow the Angolans' lead. "If they demand an end to U.S. aid to UNITA, we will support them. If they want to accept that U.S. aid to UNITA will continue, we will encourage them not to make this concession. But if they insist that they are willing to pay this price to bring the negotiations to a close, we must accept it." Cuba would defer to the Angolans on all points, except its two nonnegotiable demands: the implementation of Resolution 435 and the cessation of Pretoria's aid to UNITA. If Angola decided to sign in any case, Cuba would claim its sovereign right to withdraw its troops, and it would get out fast: "If there is an agreement that for us is unacceptable, we will leave in six months. This is our weapon, our great weapon."[58] He added, "If we sign an agreement, we will carry it out scrupulously."[59]

When I asked Risquet why Cuba was willing to compromise on U.S. but not South African aid to UNITA, he replied, "We were fighting against South Africa, our troops were advancing in the southwest, and therefore we had the means to force the South Africans to make concessions." Cuba, however, had no way to force the United States to abandon Savimbi. Therefore, demanding that it end its aid to UNITA would condemn the talks to failure. Castro believed that this had to be Luanda's—not Havana's—decision.[60]

In late April, Risquet arrived in Luanda for one last consultation with the Angolans before the London meeting. On April 30 he cabled Castro, "I spoke with José Eduardo for one hour and forty minutes. . . . I presented in detail during fifty minutes our assessment of the situation, and the strategy that we propose [for the negotiations]. I argued that the correlation of forces has changed in our favor. José Eduardo was in complete agreement." Therefore the two delegations would go to London with a common program that included the end of Pretoria's aid to UNITA and the implementation of Resolution 435.[61]

The previous March the Cubans had asked that SWAPO be included in the negotiations because Namibia would be a key issue and SWAPO was, according to the General Assembly of the United Nations, the sole legitimate representative of the Namibian people. Pretoria and Washington had categorically refused, arguing that only representatives of states could participate, and the Angolans had remained silent. The Cubans were forced to concede, but they tried to keep SWAPO informed. "We must make a special effort to protect the rights of SWAPO in the negotiations," Risquet told Castro. "The Cubans gave us detailed briefings," Nujoma wrote in his memoirs.[62] Theo-Ben Gurirab, a top SWAPO official tasked by Nujoma to follow the negotiations, recalled, "After each meeting the leader of the Cuban delegation would come and give us a full account of what had happened, and of who said what."[63]

## CHAPTER 18

# The Negotiations

## The World in 1988

Nineteen eighty-eight was the year that Mikhail Gorbachev ceased being a Communist. Through his first three years as general secretary of the Communist Party of the Soviet Union he had sought to reform the economy and the party to make the Soviet system more efficient and more humane. He was, as a scholar writes, "a within system reformer." But "from the spring of 1988 onwards," as perestroika foundered, he became "a systemic transformer."[1]

Nineteen eighty-eight was also the year in which a conservative opposition to Gorbachev's policies surfaced in the Politburo. For the first time, his authority was challenged. Gorbachev was able to defeat his critics—for the time being—but he was not able to fix the country's economy. While he gave the Soviet people growing freedom of expression and the hope of other political freedoms unprecedented in Soviet history, he was unable to offer them better living conditions. To the contrary, living standards deteriorated. The Soviet economy was in worse shape in 1988 than it had been when Gorbachev had become general secretary.

For Gorbachev, 1987 had ended with a great success: the Washington summit and the signing of the INF treaty. But this success was not repeated. Gorbachev was a man in a hurry—he wanted to achieve a strategic arms treaty (START) with the United States by the next summit, in Moscow in late May 1988. He told the Politburo that "without a significant reduction in military spending we will not be able to solve the problems of perestroika."[2]

Washington, however, was not in a hurry. While Secretary Shultz was sympathetic to the idea of moving fast on START, many in the top echelons of the administration and in Congress preferred to take it more slowly because they wondered how much they could trust Gorbachev. They won the argument. To

Gorbachev's deep disappointment, the Moscow summit, while rich in symbolism, was short on real achievements.[3]

By late 1987, as the last U.S. ambassador to the Soviet Union noted, lower-level meetings between Soviet and U.S. officials about regional conflicts had become "regular occurrences."[4] The most important of these conflicts was Afghanistan, because it was the only one that engaged troops of either superpower. In Geneva on April 14, 1988, the Kremlin announced that it would withdraw all its troops from Afghanistan by February 15, 1989; the decision had been delayed by Gorbachev's vain attempts to obtain some concessions from the Americans in return: a cessation of U.S. arms supplies to the rebels and help in creating a nonaligned government in Kabul that would include both communists and mujahedin, thereby avoiding a fundamentalist takeover. He got nothing. On May 15, the Soviet withdrawal began. The CIA believed that the Afghan regime would fall within months of the departure of the Soviet troops; in fact it endured until April 1992, outlasting the life of the Soviet Union.

Elsewhere, the Soviets were eager to find common ground with the Americans, but they were not ready to turn against their friends. Thus, Gorbachev urged the beleaguered Sandinista government in Nicaragua to reach an agreement with the United States, but he continued to send it weapons. As the end of Reagan's term approached, the Sandinistas were still in power, despite Reagan's efforts to bring them down, but how long could the Soviet Union continue to give them the economic aid that had become their lifeline? The bankruptcy of the Soviet economy cast a pall over Nicaragua.

And over Vietnam as well. In 1978 Hanoi had overthrown the genocidal Khmer Rouge regime in Cambodia. As 1988 began, 100,000 Vietnamese troops helped defend the weak Cambodian government that Hanoi had installed, which was being attacked by insurgents led by the Khmer Rouge and assisted by China, the United States, and Thailand. In May 1988 Vietnam announced that it would withdraw 50,000 soldiers from Cambodia by the end of the year. The Soviets, eager to strengthen détente with the United States and improve relations with China, had encouraged the decision. Later in 1988 there was another breakthrough in a regional conflict when a cease-fire was declared in the war between Iraq and Iran.

Gorbachev's reforms at home were encouraging dissenters in Eastern Europe. In May 1988 a National Intelligence Estimate noted, "These new winds blowing from Moscow, as well as serious economic and political dilemmas, have ushered in an era of considerable uncertainty—and potentially of significant change—in Eastern Europe."[5] In Poland, the people's discontent erupted in strikes and demonstrations; the government replied not with repression but with the offer of political dialogue with the protesters; in Hungary, reformist communists seized the reins of the government. In Czechoslovakia, Bulgaria, and Romania, the regimes appeared to be in control, and smaller demonstrations in the German Democratic Republic were easily repressed. No one foresaw that communism in Eastern Europe would collapse in 1989—not the CIA, not Gorbachev, not the East European officials, and not the dissidents—but the foundations were crumbling.

Fidel Castro and the Angolan government were very fortunate that the negotiations about southern Africa with Washington and Pretoria were successfully concluded in late 1988. Castro believed that time was in his and Luanda's favor because the Cuban troops were gaining the upper hand on the battlefield, while popular resistance in South Africa and international opprobrium were weakening the apartheid regime. Like everyone else, he missed the more important truth: the Soviet Union was rushing toward disaster. As historian John Lewis Gaddis writes, by the beginning of 1989, "the Soviet Union, its empire, its ideology . . . was a sandpile ready to slide. All it took to make that happen were a few more grains of sand."[6] Cuba could not have maintained his army in Angola without the Kremlin's support.

## The London Talks

In London, on May 3, 1988, the quadripartite negotiations about southern Africa began. "It was a new experience," Neil van Heerden, the senior Foreign Ministry official heading the South African delegation, said. "Until that moment we had never spoken face to face with the Cubans." Jorge Risquet, leading the Cuban delegation, began with a blunt demand. He informed the South Africans that, before anything else be discussed, they must accept "in its entirety" UNSC Resolution 435 on the independence of Namibia. "There can be no progress," he stated, "without your full acceptance, in letter and spirit, of Resolution 435. Only its full implementation would cut the Gordian knot of the conflict in southwestern Africa." Van Heerden replied that South Africa had already accepted Resolution 435 and "stood by its acceptance."[7]

Pretoria was not yet ready to negotiate. As van Heerden had explained to Savimbi a few days earlier, when he had flown to Jamba, "The purpose of the SAG [South African government] attending the London talks was aimed at gathering information directly from the MPLA as to how they viewed the situation. To see if they were serious about seeking a settlement. The SAG delegation had no mandate to negotiate or to accept anything." In fact, as Crocker writes, "South Africa's decision to come to the London meeting . . . did not signify that a basic national choice had been made in favor of a settlement." The South Africans listened to what Cubans and Angolans had to say and vowed that they would present their own proposals before the next meeting, to take place in late May or early June. "The London meeting was not bad," Risquet noted. "The South Africans were respectful. . . . [We can be] cautiously optimistic . . . but we must be vigilant. . . . The next meeting . . . will reveal whether the South Africans really want to negotiate."[8]

After the London meeting, Crocker flew to Kinshasa to reassure Savimbi: "The U.S. and UNITA must remain in close consultation to ensure that UNI-TA's interests are met in the ongoing contacts. The next major step would appear to be the four party meeting in June, and the U.S. welcomes any thoughts or requests which UNITA might have before it takes place."[9] True Reaganites, who had always distrusted Crocker, were breathing down his neck. On May 4, the day the London talks ended, an editorial of the *Washington Times* blasted,

> This week . . . Crocker is huddling with Cuban, Angolan and South
> African officials in London. . . . As the Reagan era draws to a close, the
> danger is that US diplomats will be tempted to compromise American
> military support for . . . Savimbi's UNITA. . . . Without the 45,000 Cubans,
> the MPLA would quickly crumble before UNITA guerrillas; free elections
> could be held, and the resulting pro-western and anti-Communist govern-
> ment would kick out the terrorist bases of the African National Congress
> and the South-West Africa Peoples [*sic*] Organization. . . . Mr. Savimbi's
> UNITA has been one of the most successful anti-communist resistance
> movements and now controls perhaps a third of Angola. If we abandon
> it now, as it moves toward real victory, we will not merely have destroyed
> the Reagan doctrine, we will have betrayed millions of people around the
> world fighting to escape the grip of communist imperialism.[10]

## The Cuban Advance in the Southwest

When the London meeting opened, the Cuban army was advancing toward the Namibian border. Bloody skirmishes between Cuban and South African patrols had occurred on April 18 and 23, on May 4, when the London conference was in session, and again on May 21. The director of Intelligence and Research of the State Department, Morton Abramowitz, wrote in mid-May, "Over 10,000 Cuban troops are at key locations in an area ranging from 50 to 125 miles from the Namibian border. . . . The deployment includes several mechanized and elite infantry units and over 200 tanks, as well as a number of SAM batteries, anti-aircraft sites and early warning radars. The Cubans are also upgrading several airfields which, when operational, will extend their air coverage into Namibia." Abramowitz added that the Cubans were accompanied by some 7,000 FAPLA. He failed to note the presence of 2,000 SWAPO insurgents, and he gave an inaccurate impression of the number of Cuban troops: by May there were close to 40,000 Cubans in the southwest, spread from the defensive line southward, with thousands spearheading the advance toward the Namibian border in small units of 1,000 men each.

South Africa, Abramowitz said, had some 2,000 troops immediately south of the Cubans, in Cunene province, and it had 7,000–10,000 troops and four military airports in northern Namibia. "At any other time," Abramowitz continued, "Pretoria would have regarded the Cuban move as a provocation, requiring a swift and strong response. But the Cubans moved with such dispatch and on such a scale that an immediate South African military response would have involved serious risks. Pretoria's failure so far to implement even a matching augmentation, which would be within its capabilities, suggests the government may be divided on how to proceed. South African military operations in southeastern Angola in support of UNITA were costly in money, men and materiel and many civilian officials in particular want to avoid a similar struggle in the southwest. . . . Cuba's recent decision to commit massive resources," Abramowitz asserted, "underlines Castro's determination to see Angola negotiate from a position of strength." The Cubans and Angolans "[are convinced of] South African unwillingness to relinquish Namibia, or to cut off [aid to] Savimbi, and US inability to force it to do so. If this assessment of Pretoria's intentions is accurate—*and we believe it is*—immediate progress on the 'hard' issues of CTW [Cuban Troop Withdrawal] and [Resolution] 435 seems unlikely and another test of strength is possible."[11] On May 23, 1988, the SADF reported that the Cubans were "approximately 30 kilometers north of the [Namibian] border."[12]

Would the Cubans continue their advance into Namibia? As early as December 3, 1987, Castro had told his generals: "We do not intend to cross the border with troops. . . . We may cross it with special forces, with scouts and so on, but an invasion of Namibia with ground units would be something else. . . . In this war . . . we will cross the border more than once, but by air."[13] The Cubans feared that an invasion of Namibia might lead to a desperate riposte from South Africa, a country which, they believed, had several nuclear bombs. Furthermore, Castro told his generals, "An invasion of Namibia by our army would have very serious political repercussions. . . . We cross the border, and there would be an international scandal." The Soviets were acutely aware of this. "This is why Boris is worried," General Ulises Rosales interjected, referring to the KGB representative in Havana. "This is what the Soviets fear, coman-dante," that the Cuban troops invade Namibia.[14]

Castro wanted to keep the South Africans and Americans guessing. "We must not reassure them," he said. "Our intentions are one thing, and their fears are another. We want them to worry that we will occupy one of the South African bases there [in northern Namibia]."[15] From the Angolan capital, a South African newspaper reported, "Cuban diplomats in Luanda, taking a cue from South African diplomacy, take immense pleasure in joking about 'hot pursuit raids into Namibia.'" South Africans and Americans were less pleased. Defense Minister Malan warned that the Cuban advance could trigger "a terrible bat-tle," and General Geldenhuys said that it posed a "serious" military threat to Namibia.[16] In Lisbon Crocker complained to Soviet deputy foreign minister Adamishin about "the Cuban advance in the south" and urged Moscow to re-strain Castro.[17]

In late May Crocker joined the U.S. delegation to the Moscow Summit "to continue his detailed discussions" with Adamishin.[18] He "chided" Adamishin "for sitting on his hands." Why hadn't the Russian found out what Havana's in-tentions were? Adamishin knew Cuba's plans, and he knew that Castro wanted to keep the Americans guessing. "Of course we don't intend to cross the Namib-ian border," Havana had assured the Kremlin a few days before the summit, "but we must not give assurances to the South Africans or the Americans. . . . Any such guarantee can only be given as part of a negotiated settlement." Ac-cordingly, Adamishin told Crocker that "the Cubans had sent the message that the sooner the South Africans left Angola, the lesser the chances for a renewal of serious hostilities." In his memoirs Adamishin writes, "When we [he and Crocker] reported the results of our talks to our ministers, Chester Crocker complained forcefully that the Soviet Union either didn't want a solution or was helpless to achieve one. He stated that Moscow was refusing to restrain its allies. He reproached us for backing whatever Havana and Luanda proposed, and he said that he had expected more from us. The 'logic' of the Americans was simple: you proclaim from every roof that you embrace the policy of the 'new thinking,' but you must prove it in practice. How? Very simple: support the American position."[19]

Meanwhile, in Angola, 250 Cuban construction workers were rushing to build the airport at Cahama, 125 kilometers north of the border. "We were working against the clock," recalls Lieutenant Colonel Roger Reyes Carrasco, who headed the team. "There was nothing there; we had to start from scratch." On June 3, 1988, the first runway was operational. Castro wrote to dos Santos, "The completion of the air base at Cahama . . . will . . . considerably strengthen our troops. We have never been so strong. . . . We have strengthened our antiaircraft defenses. . . . If necessary, we will send more antiaircraft weapons. Now the side with the strongest nerves will prevail in the negotiations, and I am certain that it will be us, Angolans and Cubans."[20]

The South Africans were alarmed. Cuban planes had already begun to fly over northern Namibia, and in late May General Geldenhuys acknowledged, "During the last six weeks the air space above Ovamboland has also been violated four times in rapid succession by, among others, MIG 23 jet fighters."[21] From Cahama, Cuban planes could now easily attack the South African airports in northern Namibia.

Through most of the spring the South African press had been confident that the SADF had the upper hand in Angola. On May 5, Johannesburg's *Business Day* had written, "In Angola the SADF has created a new reality which makes obsolete the past assumptions about that region. . . . Today, thanks to an aggressive military strategy, President Botha is in a position to say bluntly the SADF will not withdraw from Angola—much less from Namibia!—so long as the Cubans remain. . . . Willingness to use force as an instrument of foreign policy is terribly, terribly risky, but it does give a resolute state an advantage in the face of irresolution." One month later, however, on June 7, *Business Day* lamented, "Not long ago we observed that the SADF had, by forcing its way to Cuito Cuanavale, established a new bargaining position for South Africa. It enabled President Botha to offer withdrawal from Angola—rather than withdrawal from Namibia—in return for withdrawal of the Cubans. This military-driven strategy, we also observed, carried very high risks if the Soviet Union and its surrogates decided to play the same game. Today it would appear that those fears were justified. . . . There was a time when South African aircraft ranged with impunity across Angola, and no hostile aircraft dared to come south. That situation would appear . . . to have been reversed."[22] The MIGs flew within twenty kilometers of SADF airbases in northern Namibia. "They never attacked but people were asking why the SADF was not reacting," a South African officer told Savimbi's biographer. *Business Day* proclaimed, "Cuban MIGs Taunt SA Forces." The London *Times* warned: "South African bases in northern Namibia are facing the real possibility of air attack for the first time." Even the conservative *Washington Times* conceded that the Cubans had "the edge . . . in the air."[23]

Castro believed that the South Africans might retaliate with a sudden air strike against Cuban positions. "They have suffered setbacks, and they feel humiliated," he cabled the head of the military mission, General Ochoa, on June 7. "Therefore, they may be tempted to do something that in their view will not endanger too many white lives and could inflict serious damage on us. . . . Of course, we have always taken into account the possibility that the enemy might launch a sudden, massive air strike, but now this is more possible than ever before." He authorized the military mission to respond "to a sudden air strike against our troops at once and without consulting us." The mission must act "with great intelligence and responsibility. . . . It is very important not to overreact to a minor enemy air strike. . . . You must calibrate your response to the lethality of the enemy attack." If necessary, the Cuban planes should strike the South African airbases in northern Namibia, including "a very heavy attack against Oshakati," the most important of them.[24] Havana also informed General Zaitsev, the head of the Soviet Military Advisory Group in Cuba, that the South Africans might soon launch "a sudden massive air strike against our troops in southern Angola. . . . If this happens we will respond with immediate air strikes against the South Africans. If necessary, our air force will cross the border."[25] The Soviets were informed; they were not consulted.

On June 8, 1988, the SADF announced that it was calling up army reserves. "Cubans Getting Closer; Situation Deteriorating," said the banner headline of the *Burger*. Below, the words of General Geldenhuys: "A broad front about 450 kilometers long has now advanced to scarcely 20 kilometers north of the [Namibian] border, while [Cuban] reconnaissance patrols have moved even further south. A South African reconnaissance patrol recently made contact with a Cuban reconnaissance patrol only 12 kilometers from the border. . . . The buildup and southward advance of the Cuban forces has changed the status quo, with serious military and political consequences."[26]

For the SWAPO fighters who joined the Cuban and Angolan advance, the moment was exhilarating. They were part of a large, powerful army. For the first time, they were advancing openly toward the Namibian border, without having to hide from the South African planes and helicopters that hunted them. The sky now belonged to the Cubans, and "the enemy's planes weren't flying anymore," recalls Major Vilho Nghilalulwa. "We were so happy; we were already savoring our independence," says Major Alfeus Shiweda Kalistu. "We felt that with the Cubans we could go anywhere," adds General Malakia Nakandungile, who was SWAPO's chief of reconnaissance and plans.[27]

## Namibia Simmers

South of the border, in Namibia, unrest was mounting. Students, miners, and religious leaders were in the forefront. Resistance to the forced conscription of Namibians into the South West Africa Territory Force was growing. On May 4, the SADF held a military parade in the northern Namibian town of Oshakati to celebrate the tenth anniversary of its attack on the Namibian refugee camp of Cassinga. General Ian Gleeson, chief of staff of the South African army, boasted that the raid had been "the most successful paratroop operation of its kind anywhere in the world since World War Two." The parade was "an impressive show of strength," the Johannesburg *Star* noted. However, the Namibian people commemorated the massacre with an unprecedented show of defiance. Holding black banners emblazoned with the words, "Cassinga, 1978–88—We Remember," demonstrators congregated in massive rallies and marched through the streets of Katatura, the black township adjoining white Windhoek, and other Namibian towns, defying rubber bullets and tear gas. "Only when Namibia is independent will there be no more Cassingas," the general secretary of the Council of Churches in Namibia declared. "It makes us weep more bitterly when we know that the Western countries which like to speak so loudly of democracy and human rights (Britain, the United States and Germany) actually collaborate with South Africa to perpetuate our suffering and delay our independence. We refuse to accept their hypocritical excuses that we, the Africans, would suffer most if mandatory sanctions are imposed on South Africa. . . . We cry and refuse to be comforted because we value and respect life, liberty, freedom and independence of all our people. We are children of God who are entitled to take our rightful place as a free people amongst the nations."[28]

Over the following weeks, a school boycott spread through the country, accompanied by a solidarity strike by miners. On June 20, a two-day general strike began. The *Washington Times* reported soberly: "It is the first time in recent years that large-scale anti-government action by students and the increasingly active trade unions has been planned." The Johannesburg *Star* lamented that "the unrest [in Namibia] is now breaking into the open."[29] SWAPO, which enjoyed strong support among workers and students, played an important role in this upsurge of popular resistance.[30] So too did the military developments in southern Angola. In Pretoria, the Secretariat of the State Security Council reported that the Cuban advance "has given rise to the perception that the independence of Southwest Africa [Namibia] is close at hand, and this has led to greater political consciousness among the colored population." John Pandeni, a SWAPO member who was the secretary general of the country's largest trade union, recalls, "We saw the dawn of our independence coming; it encouraged us to strengthen and sharpen our pressure." SWAPO's vice president Hendrick Witbooi agrees: "Absolutely."[31]

In the opening months of 1988, reports in the Namibian press about the battle of Cuito Cuanavale had been contradictory, but by March one thing was

clear: Cuito had not fallen, despite all the predictions of South African officials that it would. In mid-April the SADF felt compelled to put out an "information kit" to correct "distorted perceptions" of military developments in Angola: it had never intended to seize Cuito Cuanavale, it asserted. The *Namibian*, the newspaper most read by the territory's black population, responded with a cartoon that showed Defense Minister Malan saying "2 + 2 = 10. . . . You ain't seen nothing yet." Then, on May 27, the paper's banner headline declared, "Build-Up on the Border." For the first time since 1976 the build-up was not the SADF massing to invade Angola. This time, in the words of General Geldenhuys, "heavily armed Cuban and SWAPO forces, integrated for the first time, have moved south within sixty kilometers of the Namibian border." The South African administrator general of Namibia warned that the Cubans were "encamped" thirty kilometers north of the border, together with their SWAPO allies, and publicly acknowledged that Cuban MIG-23s were flying over Namibia, a dramatic reversal from happier times in which the skies had belonged to the SADF. He added that "the presence of the Cubans had caused a flutter of anxiety throughout the RSA [Republic of South Africa]."[32] Among whites, that is. For the blacks of Namibia and of South Africa, the advance of the Cuban columns toward the border, pushing back the troops of apartheid, was a clarion of hope.

## Tête-à-tête in Brazzaville

One element seemed to play in South Africa's—and Washington's—favor: the Soviet Union was rushing toward implosion. No one—West or East—foresaw the speed of the Soviet demise or even the possibility of a Soviet collapse, but everyone understood that Gorbachev was eager to withdraw from regional conflicts. This perception was fueled by the Kremlin's decision to withdraw all its troops from Afghanistan. The withdrawal began on May 15, 1988. "The Soviet Union can no longer afford its expansionism and is returning home," Defense Minister Malan told the South African Parliament on May 16.[33] Significantly, the Soviets did not participate in the quadripartite negotiations on Angola that were beginning—the Americans were the only "mediators." This led to a telling exchange between Pik Botha and Angolan minister of justice Fernando Van-Dúnem when South Africans and Angolans met in Brazzaville on May 13, 1988. "My question is the following," Botha asked: "How do you think the Kremlin will react to negotiations in which the United States plays a prominent role and the Soviet Union is excluded?" Van-Dúnem naively replied: "We haven't detected any desire on the part of the USSR to play a role in these negotiations."[34]

This tête-à-tête in Brazzaville had been held at Pretoria's initiative. "This will be seen everywhere as a significant success for South Africa's diplomatic initiative in Africa," the *Burger* wrote. As on so many previous occasions, the Angolans did not inform the Cubans about the meeting. "We were surprised by the news of the Brazzaville meeting which we learned about from news agency reports," a senior Cuban official told the head of the U.S. Interests Section in Havana.[35] The South Africans had descended on Brazzaville with a delegation of heavyweights that included both Foreign Minister Pik Botha and Defense Minister Malan bearing manifold demands: the Cuban advance toward the Namibian border must stop; Angola's aid to the ANC and SWAPO must end; the negotiations that had begun in London could succeed only if there was reconciliation in Angola between the MPLA and UNITA; Resolution 435 must be modified to take into account the new realities in Namibia. When Angolan justice minister Van-Dúnem inquired, "We would like to know if there will be another quadripartite meeting, as was agreed in London," Botha replied, "That will depend on our conversation today."[36]

Having sought to impose what Castro aptly called "the rules of the colonizer and the colonized,"[37] the South Africans declared that they were leaving Brazzaville with "cautious hope,"[38] presumably because they believed that they had intimidated the Angolans. In fact, the encounter only soured the atmosphere.

U.S. officials reported, "The Angolans . . . noted a marked difference in the SAG 'tone' in Brazzaville which they didn't like."[39] President dos Santos immediately sent the minutes of the conversations to Havana. In his reply, Castro wrote:

> We must not give the South Africans the slightest guarantee that we will halt our advance at the Namibian border. Even though we have never intended to have the Cuban troops cross the border, we must not give this assurance to South Africa, a country that occupies Namibia illegally and has violated the Angolan border hundreds of times. . . . If South Africa had this assurance, the negotiations would not move forward. . . . We have taken all the precautions necessary to counter a major South African assault against our troops. Whenever Cuban and South African patrols have clashed near the border, the South Africans have fared very badly. . . . Our units are being reinforced, and our positions are being strengthened. We have no reason whatsoever to be anxious or impatient. It is the enemy who is getting anxious and desperate—with good reason. We must let him stew in his own juices.[40]

Doves in London, hawks in Brazzaville—the South Africans' intentions were a mystery. A few days after Brazzaville, in the South African parliament, Pik Botha announced: "The Government's standpoint on South West Africa/ Namibia and Resolution 435 is very clear. The Cubans must get out of Angola— then attention can be given to this question." In early June, however, a U.S. intelligence analysis noted, "The SAG appears to be divided over how to proceed in Namibia and with the talks; it still is not yet ready to accept the possibility of a SWAPO-led Namibia but is unable to devise any internationally acceptable alternative." Robin Renwick, who was the British ambassador to South Africa, remarked, "The South Africans hitherto had never really been prepared to contemplate giving up Namibia," but by mid-1988 a moderate group centered in the Foreign Ministry was seeking a peaceful solution, even if it meant accepting a SWAPO victory. Among the hard-liners were the military leaders, led by Defense Minister Malan. "Giving up Angola is one thing," a prominent South African analyst wrote, "but abandoning the hugely developed (and expensive) bases in Namibia from where the SADF can exercise a long reach over the entire sub-continent is quite another," particularly if SWAPO were to replace Pretoria in Windhoek. It would be necessary "to upend the worldview so beloved of General Magnus Malan." And of President Botha himself, who, as Renwick said, "had long since ceased to listen to the advice of anyone except his security chiefs."[41]

## Pretoria's Demands

In London the four delegations had agreed to reconvene in late May or early June, but seven weeks elapsed before they met again, in Cairo, on June 24, 1988. The delay was due to bitter sparring over the choice of venue for the meeting. Moreover, none of the parties was in a hurry. Cubans and Angolans needed time to strengthen their position on the ground. The South Africans were developing the "comprehensive set of proposals and a detailed implementation plan" that they had promised in London.[42] Not an easy task. The military leaders, who had been complacent before the London meeting because they believed that the talks would, as senior Foreign Ministry official van Heerden explains, "come to nothing," sprang into action when London did not end in a disaster. "Suddenly they were concerned that the negotiations might indeed take off," and they went to work to impose their views on what a settlement should be.[43]

Stolidly, their position had not changed despite the military reverses of the past few months: Namibia must become independent under a government friendly to South Africa, and in order to achieve this "the Angolan problem must be solved first." That is, the Cuban troops must leave Angola, Savimbi must come to power in Luanda, and then Namibia could become independent "in a manner acceptable to South Africa."[44] If Foreign Minister Pik Botha and his aides presented more realistic proposals, they have not been declassified. Perhaps Pik Botha was intimidated, as so often in the past, by the fact that the president shared the military's views. What is clear is that the proposals that South Africa brought to the Cairo meeting reflected the military's wishes.

On June 17, upon learning from Sánchez-Parodi, the head of the Cuban Interests Section in Washington, that Pretoria would deliver its proposals to the U.S. State Department the next day, Castro summoned his brother Raúl, Risquet, and other close aides for a brainstorming session. What would Pretoria propose? Would it be reasonable, in line with its behavior at London—or unreasonable, as at Brazzaville? When an aide said that the South Africans might ask "for some guarantee" that the Cuban troops would halt their advance, Castro cut him short: "How can a country that invades Angola dozens of times . . . dare to ask that we set a limit to the advance of our troops in Angolan territory? . . . How can a country that is occupying Namibia illegally dare to ask us to guarantee that we won't cross the border? We are willing to give guarantees, but only as part of a settlement. We must be categorical about this." If a settlement were to prove impossible, the Cuban troops would advance to the border and wait. "We must be willing to accept the risk that there won't be a settlement. . . . To have made all this effort only to accept a half-baked deal—this is impossible!" He told Risquet, who would lead the Cuban delegation to Cairo, to call Sánchez-Parodi in Washington. "Tell Parodi to send us the South African proposals by open telex, even by telephone [since neither Cuba nor Angola had diplomatic relations with South Africa, the Americans acted as go between forwarding proposals between the parties] . . . because we need them here by tomorrow. . . . On Sunday [two days later] you must pack your suitcases. [The delegation would fly to Luanda to consult with the Angolans and from there to Cairo.] . . . We must try to get the South African proposals by 3 P.M. tomorrow, so that we can . . . go over them in detail." He mused, "I bet that they'll be arrogant and unacceptable."[45]

Pretoria's proposals arrived the next day. They were the demands of a victorious power. South Africa stated that its acceptance of Resolution 435 was qualified: there had been "important changes" in Namibia since 1978 that would have to be taken into account. In any case Pretoria placed Namibia's decolonization on the backburner. First came Angola. Pretoria introduced its own brand of linkage: it called not for the simultaneous withdrawal of the SADF from Namibia and the Cubans from Angola, but for the "synchronized departure" of the South African and Cuban troops from Angola. This withdrawal would be accompanied by the establishment of a zone in southern Angola that would be placed under the supervision of an international authority, where the FAPLA could move only after notifying Pretoria. Only after the Cuban troops had left Angola (or the bulk of these troops—the proposals were ambiguous on this point) and after Angola had engaged in "a process of national reconciliation" with UNITA could the implementation of (a revised) Resolution 435 begin. There was more. Before continuing with the negotiations, Pretoria expected Luanda to agree in principle to its demands. And it also wanted replies to several specific questions, such as "the exact number of the Cuban troops in Angola; . . . where they were stationed," and "the number of Cuban soldiers that would want to remain in Angola because they have married Angolans."[46]

Castro and his aides studied the document. "This is a proposal written by idiots!" Castro exclaimed. "They are not intelligent." He had expected something egregious, "but what we got is even more outrageous." The South Africans had gone to the London meeting "disguised as grandmothers, and now they have reappeared disguised as lions, but if you scratch the surface, what you find is a vulture." Raúl Castro was cautiously optimistic: "I think this is their opening position, and then they will soften it. . . . I think that they want an agreement." The South Africans must realize, Raúl argued, that their situation was worsening. "We've flipped the tortilla, and things are getting rough for them. Never before has there been such a strong popular movement in Namibia. And our troops are at the border." Perhaps, he mused, Pretoria hoped that the Soviets would cave in to American pressure and "cut off the supplies they are sending us."[47]

The South Africans may have hoped that the Kremlin would fold, but Fidel and Raúl were not worried. The Cuban documents cast an interesting light on Havana's perceptions of the Soviet Union. On the one hand, the Cuban leaders were increasingly wary of Gorbachev: of his domestic reforms, and of his foreign policy. Marshal Akhromeyev, the chief of the Soviet General Staff, who visited Cuba in July 1988 and spoke at length with Castro, noted that "it was evident that Castro was deeply worried and alarmed by what was happening in my country."[48] Moreover, Castro believed that Gorbachev was too eager to reach agreements with the United States. He did not regret that Moscow was not participating in the quadripartite talks, and when the Soviets hinted in June that they might look "very attentively" at an invitation to join ("we are ready for it," Gorbachev said), the Cubans did not encourage them. Jokingly, but behind the smile was utter seriousness, Raúl Castro told a group of high-ranking Soviet officers that Cuba was not opposed to Soviet participation in the negotiations, but he reminded them of the Missile Crisis when Soviets and Americans had spoken to each other and Cuba had been left out. "We will sink our island in the Caribbean Sea before we let that happen again," he said. "We are in charge in these negotiations. Everyone laughed. . . . But my message was clear." Fidel told his aides that the Soviets were welcome to join the negotiations, but "at the meetings they would have to wait in silence until the Angolans had spoken, and until we have spoken. We let the Angolans speak first out of politeness, as a delicate, elegant gesture. The Soviets will have to wait until we have spoken because they won't have any choice."[49]

On the other hand, the Cuban leaders believed that despite his eagerness to reach agreements with the United States, Gorbachev would not go so far as to blackmail them; he would not withdraw military or economic aid to force them to make concessions they opposed. Any anxieties were laid to rest by the fact that Soviet military and economic aid continued to flow, and Moscow did not try to interfere in the negotiations.

This confidence informed the discussions of Castro and his aides on June 17–19, 1988, as they considered what Cuba would do if Pretoria refused to negotiate seriously. "We have created the best possible conditions to face any challenge," Fidel said. The Cuban troops would not enter Namibia, but after pushing the SADF out of Angola they would wait at the border. Time was on their side. In Fidel's words, "The situation of South Africa is grim: revolt at home and a serious threat on the border. They have had to mobilize the whites and ask them to serve for months at a time, in dangerous conditions. . . . Our situation, on the other hand, is improving every day." If no agreement was reached in 1988, Cuba would use the time constructively: "We will build better fortifications, better hangars for our planes, everything better. . . . And if necessary we will ask the Soviets for more planes and spare parts, and more OSAKA [sophisticated antiaircraft systems], and if we have to send more tanks we will send more tanks, and if we need more spare parts, we will send them." At no moment did Fidel express any doubt that the Soviet Union would help. Rather, his concern was for the welfare of his troops who would have to remain in Angola, after peace had seemed within reach, as an armed wall to prevent South African incursions and as an ever present threat that the Cuban army might cross the border into Namibia. "We will pay special attention to the living conditions of our troops there," Castro said. "If they want Copelia ice cream [a famous Cuban treat] we will build an ice cream factory in Cahama. We will do whatever we need to do."[50]

Castro's instructions to Risquet were straightforward. Cuba would not break off the negotiations but simply state that Pretoria's demands were "absurd and unacceptable." The ball would be in Pretoria's court. "My sense is that even though the South Africans try to conceal it, they want to negotiate," he said. "We must probe this and see how far they are willing to go." But Cuba had two clear demands: Pretoria's aid to UNITA must end and it must accept Resolution 435. Again and again Castro repeated, "Even though we will coordinate our positions with the Angolans, Risquet, we must speak up. . . . Our voice must be heard."[51]

## Showdown in Cairo

The South Africans may have arrived in Cairo making the demands of a victorious power, but they knew the truth: the Cubans were poised for victory on the battlefield. President Botha, who three months earlier had asserted that his troops had won the war in Angola, told the State Security Council on June 20, 1988, that "the situation in SWA [Namibia] and southern Angola is one of the most serious that has ever confronted South Africa."[52] When South Africans and Americans met in the U.S. Embassy in Cairo in the morning of June 24, Foreign Minister Pik Botha did not indulge in his usual bluster. He was worried about the Cuban advance, and he wanted the Americans' assessment of the military situation in southern Angola. U.S. deputy assistant secretary of defense James Woods replied that the Cuban "southward thrust . . . has been the subject of much attention by the intelligence agencies in the United States. . . . A primary fact was that Fidel Castro was personally deeply involved. He was making all the major decisions and it was therefore necessary to read Castro's mind, which at the best of times was a difficult thing to do. The US had been surprised by the size and nature of the Cuban deployment." U.S. intelligence estimated that between 8,000 and 10,000 Cubans were advancing toward the border, and that FAPLA and SWAPO units brought this number to between 15,000 and 20,000. (Woods must have been referring to the Cuban troops closest to the border; from the defensive line south there were approximately 40,000 Cubans.) Woods noted that the Cubans had 800 pieces of heavy armor, 300 artillery and rocket launchers, and 250 air defense weapons. The burning question was: What did the Cubans intend to do with all this firepower? Woods explained: "Initially the US had estimated that this was a political build up so as to improve the negotiation posture at the talks. However the force had become too big for that to be the only reason and now it appeared to be an offensive force looking for a fight." The Cubans might advance to the border and stop. But they might also cross the border, "take and occupy South African bases in SWA [Namibia] and drive South African forces further south."[53]

It was against this backdrop that the Cairo conference opened. Angola's Foreign Minister M'Binda spoke first. "The South African proposal . . . reveals an absolute lack of seriousness." M'Binda was not a powerful speaker, but for once he was direct and assertive. As Castro later said, M'Binda "rose to the occasion."[54] But it was Risquet, eloquent, passionate, a master in the art of sarcasm, who dominated the session. "A document devoid of both seriousness and realism such as that presented by the South African government is a tasteless joke. . . . The era of your military adventures, of your despoliations carried out with impunity, of your massacres of refugees—as in Cassinga in 1978—and of similar crimes against the people of Angola, this era has ended. . . . The South Africans must understand that they will not win at this table what they have failed to win on the battlefield. . . . They cannot act like victors when they are in fact an army of aggressors that is battered and in retreat. The South Africans want to know the exact number of Cuban troops in Angola and where they are stationed. This is not information one gives to the enemy. Let them try to get it on the battlefield."[55]

It seemed for a moment that the South Africans might leave the room in protest. But they stayed. And when the negotiations resumed the following morning, June 25, the South Africans were in a more reasonable frame of mind. Pik Botha declared that his delegation had studied the ten-point document that the Angolans and Cubans had presented the previous day. "It contained important elements with which the South African government could associate itself." He said not one word about his government's June 18 proposals—it was as if they had never existed.[56] "Everything had changed," a Cuban report said; "the atmosphere became less tense." By the time the conference ended, that afternoon, no agreement had been reached on any specific point, but it was agreed that the delegations would meet again in two weeks in the United States at a lower level.[57]

Asked at a press conference the following day whether Pretoria sincerely wanted a peaceful solution, Risquet replied, "It is always difficult to assess the sincerity of states, particularly if the state is South Africa, which is certainly not known for its respect of international law. . . . However, in this case it is not a matter of sincerity but of facts, and these facts will force Pretoria to abandon the Angolan territory that it still occupies and which is steadily shrinking due to the advance of the Angolan and Cuban troops. These same facts will compel the South Africans to implement Resolution 435. . . . Therefore, whether the South Africans are sincere or not, we believe that the facts on the ground will assure the security of Angola and the independence of Namibia." He added, "We think that the negotiating round that just ended has been useful."[58]

A headline in the *Burger* stated, wildly, "Cairo—the conference was a triumph for South Africa," but the text noted more soberly, "It was quickly evident that the Cubans were the big fly in the ointment."[59] This was true, for the South Africans and for the Americans. Had the Cubans not saved Cuito Cuanavale, Pretoria would have been in a position to dictate terms to a dejected Angolan government. Had the Cubans not launched an offensive in the southwest toward the Namibian border, their voice at Cairo would have been stripped of its ability to threaten.

On the eve of the Cairo talks, PW Botha had told the State Security Council: "Regarding South Africa's negotiating strategy in Cairo . . . it must be made absolutely clear during the negotiations that we insist that the Cubans withdraw from their present positions before the talks can progress."[60] But there had been no discussion about the Cuban soldiers in Angola at the conference except for Risquet's proud references to the continuing advance of the troops toward the border.

On June 26, Crocker cabled Secretary Shultz, "The Cairo round took place against the backdrop of increasing military tension surrounding the large build-up of heavily armed Cuban troops in southwest Angola in close proximity to the Namibian border. . . . The Cuban build-up in southwest Angola has created an unpredictable military dynamic."[61] Would the Cubans stop at the border? It was to answer this question that Crocker sought out Risquet. "My question is the following," he told him: "Does Cuba intend to halt the advance of its troops at the border between Namibia and Angola?" Risquet replied, "I can't answer you. I can't give you or the South Africans a Meprobamato [a well-known Cuban tranquillizer]. . . . I am not saying whether or not our troops will stop. . . . Listen to me, I am not threatening. If I told you that they will not stop, it would be a threat. If I told you that they will stop, I would be giving you a Meprobamato. . . . I want neither to threaten you nor to reassure you. . . . What I have said is that the only way to guarantee [that our troops stop at the border] is to reach an agreement [on the independence of Namibia]."[62]

## The Ground Shifts

On June 26, 1988, the South Africans struck: their tanks attacked a Cuban patrol near the Namibian border and their artillery unleashed a merciless bombardment of the Cuban positions along the front. "This happened," Fidel Castro noted, "just as the Cairo meeting ended." The timing suggests that the South African generals were responding to their setbacks at the Cairo round. Ten Cubans were killed.[63]

"We cannot allow the enemy to carry out these actions with impunity," Castro cabled Ochoa and General Polo Cintra Frías, who led the Cuban troops in southern Angola. "Respond by attacking the South African positions near Calueque [a dam twelve kilometers north of the border]. . . . Do everything possible to avoid the loss of civilian lives."[64] A few hours later, in the early morning of June 27, ten Cuban MIG 23s carried out the attack, killing eleven South African soldiers—fifty according to Cuban sources—and damaging their installations.[65] "It was a very deliberate, well-planned attack," a SADF colonel recalled. The CIA reported: "Cuba's successful use of air power and the apparent weakness of Pretoria's air defenses . . . illustrate the dilemma Pretoria faces in confronting the Cuban challenge. South African forces can inflict serious damage on selected Cuban-Angolan units, but Cuba retains advantages, particularly in air defenses and the number of aircraft and troops."[66]

On June 27, a few hours after the Cubans' successful strike against Calueque, the South Africans destroyed a nearby bridge over the Cunene River. They did so, the CIA surmised, "to deny Cuban and Angolan ground forces easy passage to the Namibia border and to reduce the number of positions they must defend."[67] Never had the danger of a Cuban advance into Namibia seemed more real. "Cuba Takes the Lead," blared the *Namibian* on July 1. The Cubans had launched "an unprecedented drive" and had "rolled forward with reinforcements to within a few kilometers of the border. . . . Angolan troops and Namibian nationalist guerrillas are taking part in the advance." An editorial in the same issue noted that "following Monday's clash . . . at Calueque, all eyes are on Pretoria to see if it will be foolish enough to launch attacks on Cuban and FAPLA strongholds in the southern provinces of Angola. It is unlikely, however, that South African troops will be ordered to advance, as Pretoria is fully aware that the balance of power in the region has shifted since Cuban contingents moved south two or three months ago."[68]

The Cubans waited for Pretoria's reaction. "We have delivered the first blow," Castro cabled Ochoa and Polo. "Now it's up to them to decide whether to fold or raise the ante." He warned, "Remain at the highest alert. . . . You must be ready to strike hard at the enemy's bases in northern Namibia."[69]

The South Africans responded with extreme violence—verbally. Defense Minister Malan minced no words. "The aggressive and uncalled for Cuban conduct is in direct conflict with the spirit of the talks between South Africa, Cuba, and Angola," he asserted. "Enormous psychological pressures were being placed on South Africa," he explained, "and the country was being subjected to aggressive provocations. South Africans are not week-kneed, they are people who meet challenges with courage and strength."[70]

Malan's words failed to reassure his countrymen. A few days later, an editorial in *Die Kerkbode*, the official organ of South Africa's Dutch Reformed Church and a strong supporter of the government, expressed disquiet "on Christian-ethical grounds" over the "more or less permanent" presence of the SADF in Angola. "Doubts about the wisdom of the Government's military strategy are not new," the Johannesburg *Star* noted in an editorial. "But what is especially significant about *Die Kerkbode*'s querying the ethics of the Angola operations is that the doubts are now being expressed from within the National Party's own constituency. Hardly a revolt, but this subterranean questioning from the guardians of the Afrikaner conscience cannot be easily ignored by government."[71] *Die Kerkbode*'s uneasiness was widely shared. "Public disenchantment is at unprecedented levels," *Business Day* noted. Crocker wrote, "In Afrikaner churches and Afrikaans-language theaters and night clubs, one could detect popular misgivings about Angola. Such mainstream white sentiment did not constitute a full-blown anti-war movement. But it unquestionably weighed on decisionmakers who had no desire to see one develop." Crocker went on to note, astutely, that "these harbingers of Angola ennui did not represent a shift to the left in white attitudes."[72] Indeed, the country's most recent parliamentary elections, on May 6, 1987, had witnessed a decisive conservative wave. "There is no doubt that the election in its totality represents a lurch to the right," admitted Colin Eglin, leader of the moderate Progressive Federal Party, while Archbishop Desmond Tutu lamented that the elections had ushered in "the darkest age" in South African history. The CIA remarked that "white resolve—the determination of South African whites to retain control of the levers of power and privilege despite increasing costs—remains strong."[73] In March 1988 white voters again went to the polls in three by-elections in rural Transvaal, and the Conservative Party sorely trounced the National Party. "Big Swing to the Right," the *Pretoria News* titled above the fold. Afrikaners "are migrating in large numbers" from the National Party to the Conservative Party, *Business Day* wrote. "It is another Great Trek."[74]

Therefore, for white South Africans the "ripening agent" in the Angolan matter—to use a term dear to Crocker—was not a deepening sense of justice, but Cuban military power. Pretoria, the *New York Times* noted, "has been badly bloodied in recent engagements, and as casualties have mounted, so has the war's unpopularity." Among South African whites, the SADF's aura of invincibility was tarnished. *Business Day* warned, "The Cuban advance to Calueque and the deficiencies in South African military resources which it exposed, have put the future of Namibia firmly on the bargaining table. . . . For SA whites, it is . . . a moment of choice. At Calueque they face Cuban forces which are equipped to do great damage—perhaps irreparable damage—to South African military resources; at Cuito Cuanavale, they face stiffened FAPLA forces which they, and their UNITA allies, have not been able to dislodge."[75]

The South African government worried about white casualties, and with good reason: the loss of even a handful of white soldiers eroded white popular support for the war. This influenced military strategy. Black deaths were, of course, less important because blacks did not have the right to vote. (Recruitment of black South Africans into the SADF had begun in the mid-1980s. Black units under white officers were involved in combat in Angola, as was the South West Africa Territory Force, whose rank and file was overwhelmingly black.)[76] The South African government announced the names of the white soldiers who had been killed, and white newspapers published obituaries of each of them and often interviewed their families. Black fatalities were not even reported. When the SADF said that four South Africans had been killed in a clash, it meant four whites. Black soldiers were invisible. "It was also a way of keeping casualties down," a South African officer remarks. "If we had a clash in which the FAPLA lost one hundred men and we lost an officer (white), one NCO (white) and twenty soldiers (black), the Defense Force would only announce that FAPLA had lost one hundred men and we had lost two."[77]

South African blacks took note. It is instructive to read the *Sowetan*, which had the second largest circulation among South African dailies (surpassed only by the Johannesburg *Star*) and the largest black readership. The *Sowetan* walked a very cautious, moderate line. Perhaps it did so in order not to offend its owners. (While the editor, staff, and readership of the *Sowetan* were black, the paper belonged to the white-owned Argus Group.) Perhaps its moderation reflected the outlook of its senior staffers; as its editor later said, "We had no choice but to oppose apartheid. But we were not leftists in any way."[78] Perhaps it reflected their desire to avoid jail and having the paper banned. The *Sowetan* lamented the SADF's presence in Angola and called Savimbi "an arm of South Africa," but through the spring of 1988 it avoided anything that might sound like approval of the Cuban presence in Angola. Its comments on Havana's role were oblique. It mused—"We cannot, for instance, understand—though there is room for speculation—why Cuban troops are massing along the Namibian border." After reporting, on June 10, General Geldenhuys's statement that the SADF "is calling up Citizen Force members [reservists] in response to the Cuban presence on the border," the editor remarked—with irony?—"I don't know about other people, but I would not be able to recognize a Cuban if one faced me with a loaded gun. I don't know what these guys look like. I don't know why I should be fighting them. But there you are. The call to arms is for the protection of the motherland and it does not matter who the perceived enemy is supposed to be." Finally, on July 12, the cautious *Sowetan* did something unexpected and very bold: it published an interview with Jorge Risquet by one of its correspondents, datelined Havana. It was the first time, ever, that a South African newspaper had printed an interview with a Cuban official. At length—the interview filled two pages—Risquet explained why the Cuban troops were in Angola and why they were advancing to the Namibian border. The *Sowetan* offered no editorial comment, it just let Risquet speak: "Cuba was not seeking a military victory," he said, "but wanted an honourable agreement which 'has to be on the basis of independence in Namibia and the halting of foreign intervention in Angola." A few days later, the *Sowetan* published another article datelined Havana that explained that Cuba "has established two schools for Namibian children and has 56 South African pupils in schools on its second largest island—The Isle of Youth." The 931 Namibian pupils had been sent by SWAPO, it wrote, the South Africans by the ANC. In addition to the standard school subjects, the children received special lessons in the language, history, and geography of their home countries. The article was titled: "Education: Cuba to the Rescue."[79]

## New York

On July 4—eight days after Calueque—Castro met with a group of senior aides in Havana to hammer out the Cuban position at the next negotiating round that would begin in New York the following week. The first, indispensable demand was the unconditional withdrawal of the SADF from Angola. Furthermore, Castro stressed, "We won't accept any modification of Resolution 435, and we won't agree that the withdrawal of our troops from Angola and the South Africans from Namibia should be simultaneous. We can't accept that."[80]

When the negotiations resumed in New York on July 11, 1988, Risquet, M'Binda, and Pik Botha were absent. At the Cairo round the parties had decided that at the next meeting the delegations would be led by officials of lower rank. Henceforth, the South African delegation was led by Neil van Heerden, the director general of the Foreign Ministry; the Angolan, by Ndalu, the FAPLA chief of staff; and the Cuban by Carlos Aldana, a member of the Secretariat of the Cuban Communist Party. Crocker continued to lead the U.S. delegation.

In New York the South Africans no longer spoke of the simultaneous withdrawal of the SADF and the Cuban troops from Angola; they no longer demanded national reconciliation between Savimbi and the MPLA government. The Cubans stressed that the withdrawal of the SADF from Angola was "the essential prerequisite to the implementation of Resolution 435 and the withdrawal of the Cuban troops."[81] While no agreements were initialed, the tone was polite and constructive. "It was clear from the outset that all the parties had come . . . ready to work," Crocker reported as the round ended.[82] Before departing, Angolans, Cubans, and South Africans agreed ad referendum on a statement of basic principles that included a pledge to establish a date for the implementation of Resolution 435 and reaffirmed the principle of "a staged and total" withdrawal of the Cuban troops from Angola—but no dates were set for either. The statement also stipulated that the parties supported "noninterference in the internal affairs of states"; the subtext was that if a final agreement was reached South Africa would stop helping UNITA and Angola would stop assisting the ANC.[83]

On July 13, 1988, as the delegations prepared to leave, a small incident hinted at the possibility of better times. General Geldenhuys approached a member of the Cuban delegation, Colonel Eduardo Morejón, who spoke English perfectly. "Geldenhuys asked me if at our next meeting I could bring him a cassette with Cuban music," a surprised Morejón reported.[84]

It had been agreed in New York that the governments in Luanda, Havana, and Pretoria had until July 20 to decide whether they approved the statement of principles. All did, and the statement was published in the press on July 21.[85]

## Havana and Moscow

The negotiations continued through the summer and fall with meetings in Sal Island (Cape Verde), Brazzaville, Geneva, and New York. Throughout, the Soviets remained on the sidelines. U.S. officials demanded that they apply pressure on the Angolans and, if possible, on the less malleable Cubans. "As a responsible power, the Soviet Union should be providing Angola with ideas," Crocker admonished Adamishin, but Moscow declined the honor. "If anyone gives advice to the Angolans, it will be you Cubans," Adamishin told Risquet. In June, U.S. intelligence concluded, "The Soviets seem to want an early resolution, but have so far only offered vague and tentative ideas regarding the forms it might take. They are still unprepared to press their allies. . . . But they want to be seen, particularly by the US, as playing a constructive role." President Botha, who for years had delighted in belittling the Cubans as Soviet proxies, told the South African parliament in August that Gorbachev wanted peace. "However, it is not clear to what extent the Russians can influence President Castro."[86]

Risquet claimed that "the Soviets put no pressure [on Cuba]; they were very respectful,"[87] and the evidence supports him. Throughout the negotiations, the Cubans did not seek Moscow's advice before making decisions. At times, they briefed the Soviets about what they intended to do. At times, such as during the July negotiating round in New York, they were more reserved. The Soviet government had sent Leonid Safonov, a first secretary at the Soviet Embassy in Washington, to New York to observe the negotiations. On July 10, the eve of the first plenary session, the Cubans and Angolans had met with the Americans. The next morning a senior member of the Cuban delegation cabled Castro that, "after repeated requests" from Safonov, "we decided that Puente Ferro [of the Cuban delegation] would meet with him. . . . Puente Ferro informed Safonov briefly about our meeting with the Americans, and he explained our proposals for a settlement. . . . He did not give Safonov a copy of these documents; he simply explained them briefly. . . . I do not think that I should meet with Safonov until these talks are over, just as we did in Cairo. However, we can keep him more or less informed through Puente Ferro."[88]

At each stage of the negotiations a Soviet official, usually Adamishin's senior aide Vladillen Vasev, flew to the city where the next round would be held and met separately with the Americans and the Cubans. "Vasev was very circumspect," a member of the Crocker team, Larry Napper, remarks. "I can't remember him ever criticizing the Cubans or the Angolans. Sometimes he would explain their position." Throughout, the Soviet government deferred to the Cubans. "You have the leading role in these negotiations," Anatoly Dobrynin, head of the Central Committee's International Department, told Risquet in May 1988. Crocker understood this: "Castro was driving the Communist train in Angola," he wrote.[89]

## Pretoria Blinks

There had been no military clashes between South Africans and Cubans after the bloody encounters on June 26–27, but the situation on the ground in southern Angola remained tense. In New York, on July 12–13, in separate sessions among military officers, General Geldenhuys had suggested that there be an immediate cease-fire without waiting for the SADF to withdraw from Angola. He had explained that "it was very difficult for his government to order the withdrawal" because the South African public would ask, "Why have we fought so many years in Angola?" He added that a withdrawal would be easier if the Cubans would offer to return to their defensive line. "That is," he said, "if they conceded something to palliate South African public opinion."[90] Cuban general Ulises Rosales cabled Castro, "I replied categorically that there will be no cease-fire as long as there are South African troops in Angola. It would be best for them to withdraw as quickly as possible." Geldenhuys retorted that if he agreed to the Cuban demand, "I won't have a job when I return to Pretoria."[91]

In South Africa, a debate raged among top officials, civilians and military. Should they accept the Cuban demands—in particular, should they accept free elections in Namibia that would certainly lead to a SWAPO government in Windhoek? The South African dilemma was summed up by a close aide of Pik Botha: "If we are not prepared to grant independence to SWA [Namibia]—even at the cost of a SWAPO takeover of the country—we must face up to the consequences." These included "the very real risk of becoming involved in a full-scale conventional war with the Cubans. The results of which are potentially disastrous." He opined that the Cuban troops in Angola were better trained and better led than the South African forces and had "apparently unlimited access to sophisticated Soviet weapons." At best, "we must be prepared to accept white casualties running into the thousands."[92]

Two days later, on July 22, senior Cuban and Angolan military officers met with their South African counterparts and U.S. Department of Defense officials in Sal Island, Cape Verde, to discuss a possible cease-fire in southern Angola.

The Cubans were led by Ulises, the Angolans by Ndalu, the South Africans by Geldenhuys, and the Americans by Deputy Assistant Secretary Woods. The curtain opened at 11:00 A.M. on a meeting among Angolans, Cubans, and Americans. The South African team was not present. The Americans no longer talked of South Africa's military superiority. Woods "characterized the South Africans as cornered." He told Ulises that the Cubans had to "understand a cornered beast," and he urged them to offer some concessions to ease Pretoria's humiliation.[93] The Cubans were willing—up to a point. Fidel Castro had instructed the delegation to say that if the SADF withdrew from Angola within three weeks, the Cuban troops would halt their advance, and only the FAPLA would go all the way to the Namibian border.[94] This was the only concession Ulises offered. But Geldenhuys insisted that his government "had approved only the cease-fire, not the withdrawal from Angola." He argued that in early August the full delegations would meet in Geneva, and there they could discuss the SADF's withdrawal from Angola, provided progress had been made on a timetable for the departure of the Cuban troops. He was roundly rebuffed by Ndalu and Ulises. There would be no cease-fire, they insisted, without the SADF's withdrawal.[95] Thus ended the first day of talks.

"It is a total failure; the South Africans are playing for time," Ulises cabled Castro that evening. "Stay calm," Castro replied. "Maintain a diplomatic tone. Show the mediators that the South Africans are not behaving seriously. Do not make any concessions." Later he added. "Tell Ndalu to stay patient and level-headed. Tell him that I am confident that we hold all the cards and that we have the means to respond to any South African attack. We have virtually won this battle. We are stronger [than the South Africans] and will get stronger every day. Therefore, we must be tactically flexible but fundamentally rigid."[96]

The next day, Geldenhuys capitulated. After an attempt to extract a concession—that the Cuban troops withdraw to the positions they occupied in March ("as if we were the defeated ones," Ulises fumed)[97]—he accepted the Cuban demands ad referendum. In exchange for a cease-fire, the SADF would withdraw from Angola by September 1, 1988, at the latest. A timetable for the withdrawal of the Cuban troops from Angola was barely mentioned.

Upon returning to South Africa, Geldenhuys explained to the State Security Council: "At Sal Island the South African delegation could not achieve much. We had hoped that the Cubans and the Angolans would reciprocate our 'concession' [the SADF withdrawal from Angola] with the withdrawal of the Cuban troops . . . and by exerting control over SWAPO's activities. However, all we got was a Cuban commitment to a cessation of hostilities—in other words, an informal cease-fire—and an undertaking that their troops will not advance further southward. . . . As for restricting the activities of SWAPO, the Cubans were inflexible and stated bluntly that SWAPO is their 'ally.'"[98]

There was desultory talk in the State Security Council that Pretoria should announce that the SADF would remain in Namibia as long as the Cubans remained in Angola. President Botha declared that "if Cuba takes three or four years to withdraw, then we will take three or four years to implement Resolution 435."[99] But it was bluster. The military situation in southern Angola had turned against South Africa, and South Africans, Cubans, and Americans knew it. On July 28, the U.S. Joint Chiefs of Staff stated: "The South African Defense Force (SADF) is extremely concerned about the tactical advantage that the Cuban forces have in southern Angola. The SADF sees the Cubans . . . moving into the southern part of Angola to the extent that they 'can't go any further south' without entering Namibia. The SADF grudgingly concedes that the Cuban forces are in an excellent field position. The Cubans have organized themselves tactically into defensive positions which would be very hard for the SADF to attack." If the negotiations deadlocked, the JCS continued, "Cuban forces will be in position to launch a well-supported offensive into Namibia, possibly within the first two weeks of October." For the South African government, "the battlefield turmoil is reflected in the political turmoil back home. . . . If it comes to major battles with the Cubans, there will be significant losses in the SADF. This will have a disastrous effect on internal South African politics. . . . Once the casualties really begin to mount, the public will call for a halt, and no amount of skillful oration will convince the typical citizen that the SADF needs to fight a pitched battle with great losses against the Cubans in order to save Namibia." The JCS succinctly concluded: "Cuban air superiority and excellent anti-air capability pose a real problem to the South African Air Force."[100]

The SADF was also worried about what the Cubans might be planning to do in the southeast of Angola. In July, South African Military Intelligence reported, "We have information that the FAPLA will be ready to launch an offensive from Cuito Cuanavale against Mavinga in September 1988" with more than 7,000 men. Military Intelligence believed that UNITA would not be able to handle the attack, and, as in 1987, the SADF would have to intervene. This would trigger a Cuban riposte. "The Cuban reaction to a SA military intervention in favor of UNITA will be determined above all by the nature and magnitude of the SADF's involvement. . . . The use of our air force . . . will trigger powerful retaliatory attacks against our air bases and troop deployments in the north of SWA [Namibia]." The Cuban air force was stronger than the South African, Geldenhuys said. "We must therefore do our utmost to prevent a confrontation. If this is not possible, and a confrontation is inevitable, then we should take the offensive knowing that our air force will be neutralized in a short time." Geldenhuys warned that a SADF intervention in southeastern Angola in defense of UNITA would also "increase the possibility of a Cuban offensive from southwestern Angola into northern Namibia."[101]

Until late 1987 the South Africans had been waging the war in Angola on the cheap, with just a few thousand soldiers. They had suffered minimal casualties. But if they decided to counter the Cuban challenge, the stakes would rise, dramatically. On paper, it was possible: the South African armed forces had a professional core of 17,400 men, plus 50,000 conscripts performing their two-year national service, and an active reserve of about 130,000 men.[102] The government, however, faced significant unrest at home, and thousands of white soldiers were helping the police maintain order in South Africa's townships. Furthermore, thousands of South African soldiers were in Namibia, hunting SWAPO. The South African generals were painfully aware that the Cubans had gained superiority in the air, that the Cuban antiaircraft defenses were formidable, and that the Cuban units advancing to the Namibian border were powerful and battle-ready. They knew that a major confrontation with the Cubans would entail heavy white casualties. And they also knew, as General Geldenhuys warned, that if they deployed enough forces to take on the Cubans in Angola it would mean that "no conventional forces would be available for action in South Africa"[103] where they were needed to quell the rising unrest.

For many months, General Geldenhuys had shared the delusions of his colleagues and refused to face the fact that the military situation in Angola was shifting against South Africa. In February 1988, when the Cubans were already in control of the skies over Cuito Cuanavale, he had assured the State Security Council that Cuito's fall was just "a matter of time."[104] But by the early summer he faced reality.

Therefore, he played an important and positive role in the negotiations. On August 2, 1988, the U.S. Defense Intelligence Agency wrote that Geldenhuys "has his hawks to contend with, however he is committed to the peace talks and seeing them through to a negotiated settlement for the war in Angola." When I interviewed Geldenhuys, he was modest, claiming that all the generals had worked together for a fair, negotiated solution.[105] But, in fact, he had been in the awkward position of telling his minister of defense and his president what they refused to see: that the military balance had tipped in favor of Cuba, and they must abandon their long-held dreams about the future of Angola and Namibia; it was time to bow to reality. Van Heerden, who led the Foreign Ministry team at the negotiations, told me, "I never strayed more than five steps from Geldenhuys because I knew I needed his support when we came back [to South Africa]. . . . Geldenhuys led his people to a more realistic view of the strategic aspects of that conflict." Crocker, who led the U.S. team throughout the talks, adds, "There was a marked lack of candor and realism at the top of the South African leadership about what it could obtain at the negotiating table. . . . Whereas van Heerden and Geldenhuys were in touch with reality, at home they often faced the 'wish-list' approach to foreign policy-making."[106]

## The SADF Leaves Angola

When Angolans, Cubans, South Africans, and Americans convened in Geneva on August 2 for another negotiating round, Pretoria had not yet approved the Cape Verde agreement on the withdrawal of its troops. The day before the talks began, Soviet deputy foreign minister Adamishin and his deputy Vasev briefed Aldana and Ndalu, the leaders of the Cuban and Angolan delegations, on their recent conversations with Crocker. "The attitude of the Soviets was very friendly and open," Aldana concluded at the end of a long cable to Castro. "They stressed throughout that they supported our views and recognized our right to conduct the negotiations however we thought best. They gave us useful information about the aims of the Americans for this negotiating round."[107]

At the first plenary meeting, on August 2, the South Africans tried to re-shuffle the deck. After declaring that "the recent meeting at Sal Island . . . did not in all respects produce the kind of concrete results that we hoped it would," van Heerden said nothing about the SADF withdrawing from Angola. Instead he proposed a new plan: the implementation of Resolution 435 would begin on November 1, 1988; seven months later, on June 1, 1989, elections would take place in Namibia. "The phased and total withdrawal of the Cuban troops from Angola . . . will be completed by June 1, 1989, the date of the elections in Namibia."[108]

As van Heerden unveiled the proposal in the closed meeting in Geneva, Pik Botha made it public at a press conference in Pretoria. The loyal *Burger* enthused over the brilliance of its country's leaders. "Consternation, astonishment and even shock reigned yesterday at the peace conference in Geneva when South Africa unexpectedly unveiled its dramatic peace plan for the Southwest [Namibia] and Angola. . . . In diplomatic circles the South African initiative was labeled yesterday evening as a masterstroke." In an editorial it explained where the genius lay: "With this plan South Africa has dramatically seized the initiative. This country, which has often been accused of destabilizing its neighbors, came forth with a detailed timetable to bring about peace swiftly! This explains the consternation. It doesn't suit them [Cubans and Angolans] that South Africa is seen in the role of peacemaker." The *Burger* told its readers that the Cuban and Angolan delegations had responded to this "splash of cold water" by turning to their governments for guidance: "Yesterday evening both the Angolan and the Cuban delegations conferred urgently with their governments." It predicted that the next day they would offer a counterproposal.[109]

Not quite. The Cuban team at the talks did not need to consult its government. "We will reject this unacceptable offer," Aldana cabled Castro.[110] And so they did. Having gained the upper hand on the battlefield, the Cubans imposed their will at the negotiating table. The South Africans folded quickly, their weak hand exposed. The "masterstroke" lay in shambles.

The talks then focused on the withdrawal of the SADF from Angola. The delegations drafted the Geneva Protocol, which stipulated that the parties would propose to the secretary-general of the United Nations that the implementation of Resolution 435 begin on November 1, 1988. It also reaffirmed the Cape Verde agreement: "The complete withdrawal of South African forces from Angola shall begin not later than 10 August 1988 and be completed not later than 1 September 1988." Meanwhile the parties would maintain "the existing de facto cessation of hostilities," and the Cuban troops would halt their advance toward the Namibian border. Havana and Luanda agreed to establish "a schedule acceptable to all parties" for the withdrawal of the Cuban troops from Angola, but there was no indication as to what that schedule would be.[111] On August 5, when the final plenary session began, van Heerden informed the delegates that "he had been authorized by his Government to approve the Protocol of Geneva. . . . The South African government would ratify the Protocol after it had informed the internal leaders in Namibia of its decision. He regretted that this procedure would entail a delay of a few days," but the decision to approve the protocol was irrevocable.[112]

On August 9, 1988, a banner headline in the *Burger* announced: "Guns Silent in Angola."[113] The Geneva Protocol was not published, but its key provisions were widely reported, and the joint statement approved by South Africa, Angola, and Cuba stressed that the talks had been "detailed, positive and productive."[114]

The headline in the *Sowetan*, reflecting black perceptions, was "SA Troops Rescued by Ceasefire." The Johannesburg *Star* remarked, "There have been 'breakthroughs' and bright promises of peace before now in the long Namibia/ Angola saga. Each time the hopes have faded like desert mirages, and the fighting, the wrangling and the stalling have gone on." This time, however, peace might come. "South Africa, challenged militarily, cornered diplomatically and squeezed financially, has real reasons for wanting peace."[115]

While the SADF prepared to leave Angola, South Africans, Americans, Cubans, and Angolans met in Brazzaville on August 24 to begin discussing the other items on the agenda. Crocker cabled Secretary Shultz: "Many questions can still be raised about the bona fides of both sides. We sense some stormy moments within the SAG delegation. . . . Behind such behavior may be continuing divisions over this whole exercise." About the Cubans he wrote, "Reading the Cubans is yet another art form. They are prepared for both war and peace. . . . We witness considerable tactical finesse and genuinely creative moves at the table. This occurs against the backdrop of Castro's grandiose bluster and his army's unprecedented projection of power on the ground."[116]

Five days later, on August 30, the last South African soldiers left Angola. The *Burger* tried to put up a brave front: "The South African withdrawal did not take place under coercion. It was in fact at South Africa's own suggestion," conveniently forgetting that until the Cuban advance toward the Namibian border Pretoria had demanded the simultaneous withdrawal of the South African and Cuban troops from Angola. More accurately, U.S. officials told the *Washington Times* that "the South Africans decided to withdraw from Angola after recognizing that the Cuban buildup had changed the power balance in the southern part of the country, leaving South African troops vulnerable."[117]

Just as had been the case twelve years earlier, when the SADF had been forced to withdraw from Angola by the Cubans, the retreating army tried to create the illusion of a victory. The South African army trucks and armored cars that arrived at Rundu, the Namibian border town that was their point of entry from Angola, were daubed with signs that said "No Retreat, No Surrender," and they drove under a banner that proclaimed "Welcome Winners." Pretoria had flown journalists to the spot to broadcast their arrival. The plan backfired. The *Namibian* noted, "Perhaps the 'Welcome Home Winners' banner erected in Rundu was an attempt to boost the morale of the returning SADF troops, but in reality they did not come back as winners." Nor did the boastful signs restore the morale of the soldiers. The *Washington Post* reported, "The young white soldiers streaming across the border seemed relatively subdued considering the event. Some had to be coaxed by photographers to smile and give the thumbs-up signal." The conservative *Windhoek Advertiser* agreed: "Some of the soldiers waved victory signs or cheered, but most looked weary and did not react to the barrage of reporters and television cameras that awaited them."[118] The army of apartheid had been defeated.

In South Africa Defense Minister Malan shared with his generals "his grave misgivings . . . about the erroneous impressions prevalent . . . among large sectors of South Africa's population, who thought that, for example, 'The SADF got a bloody nose at Cuito Cuanavale,' 'The SADF no longer has air superiority and therefore cannot win the war,' and 'The SADF is no longer the strongest armed force in Africa.'"[119]

The Cuban victory in southern Africa occurred at a time when the situation in the Soviet bloc was sharply deteriorating. Bad news continued to reach Havana from Eastern Europe and Afghanistan. From Prague, the Cuban ambassador reported on May 18, 1988, that a top Czechoslovak official, Vasil Bilak, had warned him, "We have reached a juncture when almost no one in the socialist camp can predict what is going to happen next." The economic dependence of the Eastern European countries on the West was increasing. "Bilak said, 'The Western countries are overwhelming us economically so as to weaken us and then overwhelm us politically. And we aren't countering this in any way.'" When he expressed his concerns to the Soviet leaders, "he got only smiles: 'Don't worry. Don't worry.'" Risquet forwarded the report to Castro. "Commander-in-Chief," he wrote on the margin, "this conversation of Bilak with our ambassador in Prague is a little long, but it is very important that you read it." Risquet wrote on the margin of a September 2, 1988, cable from the Cuban ambassador in Warsaw that the anticommunist opposition in Poland would soon join a power-sharing arrangement with the communist government. Six days later the Cuban ambassador in Afghanistan, where the withdrawal of the Soviet troops was under way, cabled: "The worsening of the situation makes me think . . . that some Afghans who are our friends might eventually ask us for political asylum. . . . Because of our material circumstances it would be very difficult for this embassy to accept political refugees. . . . On the other hand Cuba has never rejected friends who sought asylum and I don't think that this would be the best place to start rejecting them. . . . We seek instructions." Forwarding this cable to Castro, Risquet wrote on the margin: "Commander-in-Chief, judging by this request our ambassador foresees the fall of Kabul."[120]

CHAPTER 19

# The New York Agreements

## The State of Play

By August 30, the South African army had left Angola. What was there to ne-gotiate? South Africa no longer demanded national reconciliation between the MPLA government and Savimbi, it no longer claimed that Resolution 435 should be placed on the backburner, and it agreed to end its aid to UNITA. Only one major issue remained, therefore: the timetable for the withdrawal of the Cuban troops from Angola.

A civil war was still raging in Angola. The withdrawal of the SADF was a heavy blow for Savimbi, but UNITA remained active through most of the coun-try. The quadripartite negotiations ended Pretoria's aid to Savimbi, but they would not cut off his lifeline from the United States.

The Cubans had agreed that they would not fight against UNITA once the negotiations had been successfully concluded. Therefore, how significant was the length of time it took them to withdraw? Would whether they left in six months or three years affect the course of the civil war? The answer to this question depended on one's assessment of Pretoria's intentions. Would the South Africans honor the agreements they had signed? While it was true that an independent Namibia would create a buffer between South Africa and An-gola, the SADF could still attack Angola by air or by sea, and it had an eager ally in Savimbi; furthermore, Pretoria might refuse to implement Resolution 435 and remain in Namibia.

This seemed unlikely by late 1988. The apartheid regime was on the ropes, weakened by the struggle at home, increasingly threatened by economic sanc-tions from the international community, and humiliated by the Cubans in An-gola. But could one depend on Pretoria's sanity? Or was it, in Bertolt Brecht's words, "The still fertile womb from which the foul beast sprang."[1]

## Searching for a Timetable

In Geneva, on August 2, 1988, the South Africans had demanded that all the Cubans leave Angola seven months after the beginning of the implementa-

In September 1988, as the negotiations among the South Africans, Americans, Angolans, and Cubans stalled, the South African defense minister threatened that if the Cubans did not agree to his demands, "they would learn the same lesson they learnt at Cuito Cuanavale." An odd threat, given that the Cubans had won the battle of Cuito Cuanavale. The *Namibian* scoffed, "Some people just don't know when to Quitto . . ." (Copyright *The Namibian*)

tion of Resolution 435. Cubans and Angolans had rejected the demand out of hand and repeated that they would not even discuss a timetable until all the South African troops were out of Angola. By the end of September, Pretoria had stretched the time frame to twenty-four months, whereas Havana and Luanda offered thirty months. The two sides differed, however, not only about the length of the withdrawal but also about the tempo: the South Africans demanded that 94 percent of the Cuban soldiers leave Angola within the first year, Cubans and Angolans offered 50 percent. ("They wanted to take out the elephant in the first year, and the tail of the elephant in the second," Risquet observed.)[2] South African defense minister Malan warned that if the Cubans did not want peace—that is, if they did not accept Pretoria's demands—"they would learn the same lesson they learnt at Cuito Cuanavale." Not a very apt threat, considering what had happened at Cuito Cuanavale. The *Namibian* scoffed. "Some people just don't know when to Quitto . . .," read the caption above a cartoon that showed a heavily bandaged and beaten up Malan uttering his empty threat.[3]

When the delegations met again, in New York on October 6, Crocker suggested that the Cuban troops leave within twenty-four months, as Pretoria demanded, with 73 percent of the Cubans leaving within the first year.[4] The South Africans agreed, while Cubans and Angolans flatly rejected the proposal. Tempers flared, as the American delegation assailed the Cubans and the Angolans. In a separate session without the South Africans, Crocker's special assistant Robert Cabelly warned that if the Cubans squandered this opportunity, "the South Africans, who had a strong army, would make their life hell." Then, at a plenary session—the last session of the round—Crocker exploded. After listening to General Ulises Rosales reject his proposal, Crocker announced that his patience had come to an end: Angola and Namibia were "unknown quantities for the people of the United States, who thought 'Angola' was an exotic cloth and 'Namibia' a disease that afflicted old people. The U.S. government had no interest in wasting time in expensive negotiations that were going nowhere. They should look for another mediator."[5]

The head of the Angolan delegation, Ndalu, asked for a recess. During the recess, Ndalu and the head of the Cuban delegation, Aldana, conferred hurriedly. Aldana advised Ndalu to respond sharply to Crocker's outburst, but Ndalu demurred, arguing that if he responded as the Cubans suggested "his president 'would make him disappear.'" Aldana told him that he could answer according to his instructions and that the Cubans would answer according to theirs. When the meeting resumed, the South Africans listened in silence (they were virtually silent throughout the entire session), while Ndalu briefly expressed distaste for Crocker's words and said that the Americans were not behaving like mediators. Then Aldana spoke. Since the beginning of the negotiations, Castro's instructions had been to be polite as long as the other side was polite, but not to allow insults: "Be very calm, laugh, and smile," but if the others became offensive, then "put them in their place." Aldana behaved accordingly. "Cuba would have no problem . . . announcing publicly that the negotiations had deadlocked," he began. He then went where Ndalu had not dared to go, stressing "the ignorance, the racism and the contradictions" that characterized American society. He said that it was not surprising that in a country whose president mistook Brazil for Bolivia (as Reagan had done) and placed Jamaica in the Mediterranean (another Reagan lapse), the population would not know "what Angola is and what Namibia is." This was not the kind of language that Crocker was used to hearing. Wisely he took it. When he responded, he referred neither to Aldana's tirade nor to his own, which had provoked the storm. Changing the subject altogether—the meeting was coming to an end—he urged the delegates to be cautious in their comments to the press and above all not to give "the impression of a breakdown."[6]

The next day, Aldana told the press that the negotiations had reached an impasse, and he stressed, "The withdrawal [of the Cuban troops] must be carried out in an orderly fashion and with honor, while safeguarding Angolan security. Ours are not defeated troops, unlike the U.S. troops in Vietnam." From Havana, Castro cabled Generals Ochoa and Polo Cintra Frías, "The South African demands are unacceptable. . . . Though I don't think that the South Africans want to resume fighting, we must be on guard, especially against the risk of an air strike. . . . We must be prepared for all contingencies." Across the ocean, at a briefing in northern Namibia attended by the top brass of the SADF, the South African commander of the South West Africa Territory Force warned that "an entire Cuban division . . . consisting of formidable armor, artillery and missile forces," was deployed immediately north of the border.[7]

## Shift in Moscow?

The Soviets had remained on the sidelines during the stormy New York round. Adamishin's deputy, Vasev, had met in New York with the Cubans on the evening of October 6, the first day of the meeting, and again on October 10, the day after the conference ended. Vasev "agreed with our position on all points," Aldana reported.[8]

In late October 1988, for the first time since the negotiations had begun, there was a discordant note in conversations between Cubans and Soviets. In Moscow four weeks earlier—on September 30—a hastily called Central Committee Plenum had led to "the biggest leadership shakeup in many years," strengthening the position of Gorbachev and his supporters.[9] Gorbachev's ally, Alexander Yakovlev, became the secretary of the Central Committee overseeing international affairs.

On October 27 Risquet met with Yakovlev in Moscow. In a November 2 memo to Castro he wrote, "I am sending you the transcript of my conversation with Yakovlev about the negotiations. . . . What is interesting are the nuances. . . . We are both in favor of a negotiated solution. But we Cubans are not in favor of just any solution, at any price; nor are we anxious to reach an agreement, even though we want one. I can't swear that this is precisely the Soviet position, even though, at the end of the day, they support our position."[10]

The minutes of the conversation reveal that Yakovlev said very little. After praising Cuba's and Angola's role in the negotiations and asserting that the agreement—which was almost within reach—represented "a defeat" for the United States, he stressed that it was important that the negotiations not stall over details, such as whether 50 or 55 percent of the Cubans withdrew. "We don't want the negotiations to grind to a halt, unless it is over a matter of principle. We must defend our principles but be willing to compromise over the details." This earned him a sharp reply from Risquet. Cuba and Angola were not inflexible; they were willing to make reasonable compromises. The question was how to proceed. "It is the change in the balance of power on the battleground that has forced the South Africans to seek an agreement," he explained. "We must not act as if we are anxious to seek an agreement at any price. If we do, the enemy will immediately grab us by the neck and demand more and more concessions. . . . I expect that we'll end up agreeing on a 24 to 30 month timetable, but to get there we have to put on our poker face and not give the impression that we are desperate to reach an agreement. . . . I think that this is going to end well. Victory will go to those with stronger nerves and stronger forces on the battlefield." Yakovlev responded without hesitation: "I agree completely with you." And there the conversation ended.[11] The nuance that Risquet had grasped was just the hint of a shift in the Soviet position.

The Soviets put no pressure on Cuba, but President dos Santos did, tentatively. When dos Santos met with Risquet in Moscow on October 27, he objected to the Cuban draft of a joint note to Crocker and asked Risquet to soften it. He complained that calling the United States "a party to the conflict" was "too aggressive." Risquet "eliminated a few paragraphs," and dos Santos approved the revised draft.[12] In the days that followed, the Angolans urged the Cubans to be flexible. They wanted to conclude the negotiations quickly.

This was also what the Soviets wanted. The U.S. Embassy in Moscow had predicted that "the Soviets will apply moderate—but by no means heavy-handed—pressure on Angola to move toward the U.S. mediated proposal."[13] It was an accurate assessment. The pressure was gentle, but unmistakable. Dos Santos told Castro that when he met with Gorbachev in Moscow to ask for more weapons, the Soviet leader had promised that the Kremlin would continue to help Angola, but he had also insisted on a speedy conclusion of the negotiations, which were a potential complication in Soviet relations with the United States. "It was necessary to speed up the negotiating process. It was important not to miss the right moment," Gorbachev had said.[14]

This created a thin wedge between Angolans and Cubans, but its significance should not be overstated. It emerged only late in the negotiations, when the most important decisions had already been made; furthermore, despite the Soviet calls for speed, the Angolans continued to reject the timetable that Crocker had proposed at the New York meeting in early October. Like the Cubans, they sought a compromise. They were, however, inclined to be more forthcoming than were the Cubans.

When the delegations met again in Geneva from November 11 to 15, 1988, both sides made concessions. They split the difference between the two timeta-bles: rejecting both the twenty-four-month schedule Washington and Pretoria advocated and the thirty months Havana and Luanda proposed, they settled on twenty-seven months. (Castro's bottom line, which he had set the previous spring, had been twenty-six months.)[15] Likewise on the percentage of Cuban soldiers leaving Angola in the first year both sides gave ground: between the 73 percent Washington and Pretoria wanted and the 50 percent Havana and Lu-anda preferred, the final agreement stipulated 66 percent. (The Cubans wanted a slightly lower figure, but dos Santos cabled Castro "We can accept it.")[16]

## Savimbi Joins the Party

Savimbi had followed the negotiations closely and with growing concern. In late June 1988 he visited Washington to seek reassurance from top Reagan ad-ministration officials that their support was unfaltering and to conduct a public relations campaign. In a White House meeting, President Reagan assured the rebel chieftain that the United States "will not stop its support of UNITA until the goal of national reconciliation is met."[17]

But as the summer turned to fall, the news from the negotiating table had been disquieting for Savimbi: "Because . . . of UNITA's fear of being 'sold out,' tension and dissension have increased within UNITA," the secretariat of the South African State Security Council reported, "as well as between UNITA and South Africa."[18]

At a well-attended press conference in Jamba, UNITA's headquarters, on September 3, 1988, Savimbi blasted the negotiations and Crocker. "Is he trying to dig graves for his friends?" Savimbi asked. Didn't he realize that the Cubans had no intention of leaving Angola? They wanted to annihilate UNITA! While the diplomats chatted, Cuban troops were pouring into Angola.[19]

Savimbi could afford to lash out publicly at Crocker, venting his frustration and rallying the true Reaganites, who also disliked and mistrusted the assis-tant secretary. He was careful, however, not to attack the U.S. government. Crocker, who had many enemies in Washington, was a safe target, unlike, for example, the irascible PW Botha, his generals, or even Foreign Minister Pik Botha—Savimbi said not one word, publicly, against the South Africans.

Beyond tantrums and media blitzes, there was little Savimbi could do. South Africa, his main patron, had decided to fold. In Washington, Secretary Shultz, who had become Reagan's closest adviser, stood firmly behind the negotiations, which offered the only realistic possibility of getting the Cubans out of Angola before Reagan left the White House. Furthermore, the proposed agreement did not require the administration to abandon Savimbi. "We have your interests very much in mind," Shultz assured the UNITA leader. "The United States remains with you and will support you in the future as we have in the past."[20]

The true Reaganites, who had been Savimbi's fiercest supporters, were torn. "Savimbi's survival was very high up in the conservatives' agenda," Cohen muses, "but even more important for them was the withdrawal of the Cuban troops. That was the red flag! Holding that up was really what Shultz and Crocker knew would protect them. My role, and [Deputy Assistant Secretary of Defense] Woods' role, was to convince the conservatives that even with South Africa's help Savimbi could not win, and that he could not be defeated even without South Africa's help, as long as we provided the right equipment—the Stingers and the Milan anti-tanks weapons. James Woods was the chief persuader because he was from the Department of Defense. The CIA supported our assessment."[21] It was a much more sober CIA by then: Casey, the firebrand, was dead, and the new DCI was the pragmatic Webster; moreover, the display of Cuban military power in Angola had laid many illusions about Savimbi's chances to rest.

Savimbi accepted the fait accompli and salvaged what he could from the negotiations. His goals were to make sure that American aid increased and that Pretoria's largesse continued as long as possible. On November 29, 1988, he met with Crocker in Kinshasa. "It was a very good meeting, the most productive meeting we have had in several years," Crocker reported. "Our chat was especially useful in setting the stage for cooperation through the remainder of the Reagan administration and into the Bush presidency. . . . I also stressed that, in relation to the eventual decrease in SAG aid to UNITA, we need to cooperate more closely and effectively regarding our support for UNITA. I was pleased that he agreed to meet with members of my team to discuss the specifics of ensuring that our support is most effective."[22]

## Brazzaville

After meeting Savimbi, Crocker crossed the Congo River to Brazzaville for what was supposed to be the last quadripartite negotiating round to iron out the last kinks and initial the final drafts of the agreements. For the occasion, Foreign Minister Pik Botha led the South African delegation. He might as well have stayed home. On the evening of December 3, 1988, the meeting screeched to a halt. Deputy Foreign Minister Alarcón, who led the Cuban delegation, cabled Castro: "At 8:45 P.M. Brazzaville time Crocker met with the Angolan and Cuban delegations. He told us . . . that the South African delegation would have to depart to consult with its government." Two hours later Pik Botha's aide van Heerden went to see Alarcón. "He said that sudden developments in his country force them to go home. He regretted that he could not give a fuller explanation." The entire South African delegation abruptly left the hotel. The Johannesburg *Star* lamented, "Instead of breaking out the champagne to celebrate the end of nearly forty years of international dispute over the future of Namibia, the South African delegation and the large contingent of journalists who had accompanied them found themselves climbing wearily back on to their aircraft in the dead of the night to return home."[23]

In Pretoria, South African officials explained that this last-minute hitch was due to Havana's refusal to allow South Africa to participate in the verification of the departure of the Cuban troops. The *Burger* asserted: "To leave the verification in the hands of the United Nations—given the UN's notorious prejudice against South Africa—is clearly unacceptable."[24] This made no sense. The Cuban position had been consistent throughout: the verification would be carried out by a group of UN observers that would include no South Africans, Americans, Angolans, or Cubans. On December 1, 1988, General Geldenhuys, who was participating in negotiations about verification, had pronounced the draft agreement "satisfactory, although some points still need to be ironed out."[25]

In an insightful article, the *New York Times* suggested that the real reason for the abrupt departure was last-minute qualms in Pretoria about agreeing to Resolution 435. Free elections in Namibia "would likely lead" to a SWAPO government, the *Times* wrote, and the implications of this would reverberate beyond Namibia. "A victory by the insurgents [SWAPO] could have heavy political symbolism for whites and blacks in South Africa, who might interpret it as a foreshadowing of the unfolding of the struggle there." Looking back, van Heerden confirmed the *Times*' analysis: "We had come within sight of an agreement," he recalled. "We could see it and taste it—and then Pretoria pulled on the emergency brake. That was precipitated by the hawks in the military establishment who had a lot of influence on President Botha."[26]

Even the SADF knew, however, that the military balance had shifted in favor of Cuba. On December 13, the South Africans returned to Brazzaville, and that same day they, with the Angolans and Cubans, initialed the "Brazzaville Protocol." It stated that "the parties agreed to recommend" to the UN secretary-general that April 1, 1989, be established "as the date for implementation of Resolution 435." It confirmed the agreement reached in Geneva on November

15 about the timetable for the withdrawal of the Cuban troops. There would be a signing ceremony in New York on December 22, 1988, at the United Nations. Angola, Cuba, and South Africa would sign the agreement requesting the Security Council "to commence implementation" of Resolution 435 on April 1, 1989. Furthermore, Angola and Cuba would sign a bilateral agreement confirming the calendar for the withdrawal of the Cuban troops.[27] The withdrawal would be verified by a small UN mission of approximately seventy unarmed military personnel and twenty civilian support personnel provided by member states and selected "in consultation with Angola and Cuba and with the Security Council." The commander of the force would be a Brazilian, with a Norwegian deputy. There would be no personnel from the United States or South Africa.[28]

The Brazzaville Protocol did not mention UNITA or the ANC, but it confirmed the principle of "non-interference in the internal affairs of states" that had been established at New York the previous July. This meant, the State Department noted, that South Africa "has agreed to withdraw from the conflict and to end its support to UNITA (in return for the withdrawal of ANC bases from Angola)."[29] It was understood that this stipulation did not affect Cuba's aid to the ANC or U.S. aid to UNITA. It came down to leverage. The United States and South Africa wanted Cuba to stop aiding the ANC. Cuba and Angola wanted the United States to stop aiding Savimbi. But none of them had the leverage to demand it. Therefore, to get an agreement, they scaled back their desires.

The disbanding of the ANC camps in Angola—moving the fighters farther away from South Africa to Uganda and Tanzania—did not affect the ANC's strategy or resources. The ANC's military strategy—"A People's War"—was to create a network within South Africa able to carry out military actions. As ANC president Tambo said in July 1987, "At present we are infiltrating men [into South Africa] with the objective, in many cases, that they will not only hit targets, but will also train others inside the country who want to join the armed struggle."[30] What the ANC needed, at this stage, was specialized training for a handpicked group of guerrillas who would infiltrate into South Africa, and this could be done much better in Cuba and the Soviet Union than in Angola, Uganda, or Tanzania. Therefore the Angolan pledge to cease aiding the ANC was of little consequence. The South African pledge to cease aiding UNITA, on the other hand, had enormous significance. The SADF had supported UNITA on the battlefield and had sent UNITA massive amounts of military supplies across a border that was virtually open. "We're getting . . . a ton and giving a kilogram," Castro commented.[31]

## A Rough Ceremony

"Before the signing of the New York agreements," recalls NSC Africa director Cohen, "Shultz went to brief Reagan and took Crocker and me with him. Reagan needed to be reassured. He had such trust in Shultz. He was pleased. It was something that would make his administration look good: the Cubans were leaving! I don't think he knew enough about the issue to think about SWAPO." Speaking at the University of Virginia on December 16, Reagan said, "In Brazzaville, just this Tuesday, an American-mediated accord was signed that will send 50,000 Cuban soldiers home from Angola—the second reversal of Cuban military imperialism after our rescue of Grenada in 1983."[32]

On December 21, Aldana told Crocker that "the Cubans were becoming increasingly irritated by the way U.S. officials were presenting the agreements." He complained specifically about Reagan's speech at the University of Virginia. He warned that "the official Cuban comments at the signing ceremony would address our interpretation of these statements by the U.S. government. We will avoid insulting language, but since you are the hosts, we want to forewarn you of this."[33]

At the signing ceremony, Cuban foreign minister Isidoro Malmierca was stern. "History will establish . . . the true meaning and the scope of the agreements that have just been signed, irrespective of all the lies and spin that we can expect," he began.

> We are here because, after thirteen years of aggression by the South
> African army, of violations of the sovereignty and territorial integrity
> of the People's Republic of Angola, and of a cruel war that was supported
> primarily by South Africa and, for the last several years, by the United
> States . . . the South African army has been forced to withdraw from
> Angola. . . .
>   We have thus created some of the conditions necessary to guarantee
> the security of the People's Republic of Angola and to make it possible for
> the Angolan people to resolve the fissures that have fueled a fratricidal
> war. This highest aspiration of the Angolan nation however . . . is blocked
> by the policy of the government of the United States, which [through
> its aid to UNITA] assumes the interventionist role that South Africa is
> renouncing with this agreement.[34]

Ten years later Jorge Risquet, who had led the Cuban delegation to the New York ceremony, wrote about the emotions that surged through him as he watched Malmierca, with Cuban general Colomé at his side, sign the agreements. He found himself thinking about another ceremony, the one that had concluded the 1898 War, when the United Sates had excluded Cuba from the peace negotiations in Paris with Spain even though the Cubans had borne the brunt of the fighting and the talks would determine the future of their island.

> I thought of . . . Calixto García [a leader of the Cuban war against Spain]. . . . about how—if there had been any justice—he should have been in Paris in December 1898 representing the Liberation Army, to sign the peace treaty that officially ended the Spanish-Cuban-American war and that should have acknowledged the birth of an independent nation, our heroic Cuba, which had fought with unequaled bravery [against the Spanish] for thirty years. . . . As we all know, however, history turned out differently.[35]

## Aftermath in Cuba: The Ochoa Trial

The Cuban soldiers who returned home after the New York agreements found a country facing an unprecedented crisis. Cuba's East European allies were teetering on the brink of collapse, and the Soviet Union was stumbling, torn by centrifugal forces. In June 1988 Castro had told his senior aides that the war in Angola might have to continue one more year, and he had expressed complete confidence in continuing Soviet support. A year later, his tone had changed. Speaking to the Cuban people on July 26, 1989, he said, "The Soviet Union is in dire straits. This is no secret, and the imperialists' dream is that it will disintegrate." He thanked the Soviets for what they had done for Cuba: "Our appreciation is immense . . . as is our infinite gratitude." He then addressed the crisis at hand, defiantly: "The imperialists should not fool themselves. . . . If tomorrow . . . we wake up to the news that a great internal strife has broken out in the Soviet Union, or even that it has disintegrated—something we hope will never happen—even then Cuba and the Cuban revolution will continue to struggle and to resist."[36]

The sense of crisis was deepened by an extraordinary event: the detention, on June 12, 1989, of General Arnaldo Ochoa, who had headed the Cuban military mission in Angola from November 1987 to January 1989. A drama in two acts followed, under the glare of Cuban television. In the first act, on June 25 and 26, Ochoa appeared before an honor tribunal of forty-five generals and two admirals, accused of corruption and drug trafficking. In his opening statement, he confessed to all the charges against him: "It is all true." The tribunal stripped him of his honors and expelled him from the armed forces.[37] In the second act, on June 30, Ochoa and thirteen other officers were tried by a military tribunal. They all confessed to charges of drug trafficking and corruption. At the end of the eight-day trial Ochoa and three other defendants were sentenced to death. They were executed on July 13, 1989. As a knowledgeable American journalist reported, Ochoa "was not well known outside the armed forces" before his trial began. He was however, as the prosecutor said, "one of the most prestigious and important Cuban military leaders."[38]

His trial and conviction raise questions about Cuban behavior in Angola because most of his illegal activities occurred while he headed the Cuban military mission there. The relevant questions are, How much did his illegal activities affect Angola, and Were they anomalous?

In 1988, while in Luanda, Ochoa had tried to strike a deal with the Medellín drug cartel that would have involved smuggling Columbian drugs to the United States via Cuba. This was the reason he was sentenced to death, and it did not concern Angola.[39] But the lesser charge, corruption, did.

In his testimony to the honor tribunal on June 25, 1989, Raúl Castro accused Ochoa of defrauding the Angolan government. Three days later the *New York Times* reported, "In scenes broadcast from the tribunal's Monday [June 26] session, a series of former aides to General Ochoa gave detailed testimony portraying an extensive network of black marketing and corruption in the Cuban military mission in Angola when it was under General Ochoa's command."[40] More detailed evidence was offered by Ochoa and other defendants during the court-martial that began on June 30.

They all told a similar story. The Angolan government had given Ochoa $508,000 to buy 100 field wireless sets. An aide of Ochoa bought them in Panama for $435,000, and Ochoa diverted the difference to a bank account in Panama. Furthermore, on Ochoa's instructions, another aide sold Angolan kwanzas on the black market to buy dollars. That aide told the court, "We got $61,190 for all these kwanzas." Ochoa had also ordered his aides to sell food belonging to the military mission on the black market. "We sold a little sugar, a little fish," he admitted. "We sold two or three things." Ochoa explained that with the money received from these black market operations his aides had bought "a few diamonds; I don't know how many," which they eventually sold in Panama. The evidence at the trial indicated that the diamonds were of low quality, and the scheme brought in only paltry rewards.[41]

It is difficult to assess how much Ochoa collected from his illegal operations in Angola. The sale of Cuban food on the black market does not seem to have been lucrative; the prosecutor himself, in his summation, spoke of "ridiculous crumbs of money."[42] Ochoa pocketed $73,000 that belonged to the Angolan government from the purchase of the field wireless sets, and he sold kwanzas on the black market for $61,000. The sum total of the money gained through these illegal operations may have approached $200,000.

The amount of money Ochoa stole was modest, and the damage to the Angolan state was minimal. But if Ochoa did this, might not other heads of the Cuban military mission have done likewise, perhaps on a much larger scale?

It is a fair question. To my knowledge, no one has made a credible accusation against any of Ochoa's predecessors or his successor, or any of their aides, but this does not necessarily prove much, because no one has studied the inner workings of the Cuban military mission in Angola. I have sifted through thousands of pages of Cuban documents about the Cuban military presence in Angola, but it would be naive to expect that I would find evidence of corruption, even if corruption had occurred. After all, I found no indication of Ochoa's corruption.

What then can I say? I have spent two months in Angola in two separate visits, and I have interviewed more than twenty Angolan officials on the record, and I have spoken informally with many more; some were pro-Cuban, others were not.[43] No one claimed, or hinted, that the Cuban military mission defrauded the Angolan state—beyond the Ochoa episode. This, of course, is not conclusive proof. But it is very difficult to prove a negative, and in the absence of any indication to the contrary I must conclude that Ochoa's behavior was anomalous.

## The Cubans Come Home

Cuba's deepening economic woes did not affect the withdrawal of its troops from Angola. "The operation . . . went extremely well," UN secretary-general Pérez de Cuéllar writes. The Cubans "moved out of Angola on schedule and in a disciplined manner."[44] On May 25, 1991, the last troops boarded the planes in Luanda that would take them home.

Castro had told Risquet in early 1988: "What I regret is that when we withdraw the troops, we'll also have to withdraw the aid workers." They could not be left behind, because UNITA would target them. When President dos Santos asked Castro to reconsider, he replied, "It pains me deeply to have to tell you that we will not continue our technical assistance, but it is not a question of what I want."[45] On the eve of the New York agreements, 2,195 Cuban aid workers were in Angola.[46] In June 1991, a few days after the last Cuban soldiers had departed, Cuba's technical assistance to Angola ended.

The Cubans were leaving Africa. The small military missions that Havana had maintained in several African countries were closing. I remember walking in Bissau in May 1996 with a local official and with Víctor Dreke, who in 1967–68 had led the Cuban military instructors who helped the Guinean guerrillas fighting for independence against Portugal. After the country had become independent in 1974, a Cuban military mission had trained its army—until 1991, when it was replaced by the Portuguese. Tongue in cheek, Dreke asked the Guinean official, "Why the change?" He knew the answer: "Because the Soviet Union lost the Cold War," was the predictable reply. African countries did not want to offend the world's only superpower.

The aid missions were also closed down. Buffeted by a terrible economic crisis, the Cuban government could no longer afford them. Nor could it afford scholarships for new foreign students. It pledged, however, that those who were already in Cuba—23,845 in 1988 (including 18,075 from sub-Saharan Africa)[47]—could remain and complete their education. It also allowed the 1,500 Namibian students who had left Cuba in July 1989 to participate in their country's first elections to return to finish their studies.

They had left at Castro's suggestion. "I told [SWAPO President] Nujoma," Castro explained, "that the best election workers he could have would be the Namibians who are studying abroad—1,500 students of voting age in Cuba and 1,500 in other socialist countries."[48] In January 1989, Castro spoke to the Namibian students in the Island of Youth. "It is very important," he said,

> that every Namibian student who is in Cuba and who is of voting age should go back to Namibia. . . . They will participate in the electoral process and then they will return to Cuba. . . . We will try to be sure that you all return, so that you will be able to complete your studies, because . . . the better prepared you are, the better you will be able to serve your country . . .
>
> Therefore, my Namibian comrades, a new chapter is beginning in your lives and in the life of your country. You must be more conscientious than ever, more disciplined than ever, more studious than ever and more responsible than ever, because the responsibilities that fall on the shoulders of those of you who are at least eighteen years old are very important.
>
> Today I rejoice because I know that the independence [of Namibia] is a reality that no one or nothing will be able to prevent. . . . But I also feel sadness . . . because I think that some among you will not return after the elections.[49]

## The Clash over UNTAG

As Castro spoke, Cubans and Soviets were arguing in public, for the first time in two decades. The subject was Namibia. On the eve of the signing of New York agreements the five permanent members of the UN Security Council had agreed to deep cuts in the size of the United Nations force that would be sent to Namibia (UNTAG) in order to reduce the cost of the operation. This led, in the words of a West German representative to the United Nations, "to an unprecedented confrontation between the Permanent Members and the Non Aligned."[50] For the first time, the United States and the Soviet Union squared off against the African states, which feared that the cutback would affect UN-TAG's ability to accomplish its mission. On December 21, 1988, in New York, Risquet confronted Soviet deputy foreign minister Adamishin, who had just arrived, complaining that Cuba had not been consulted. Risquet added that the Cuban delegation had spoken with the nonaligned members of the Security Council, with SWAPO, and with the UN secretary-general, and "they are all against the proposed cutbacks. This will lead to a confrontation between the permanent members and other countries, among them Cuba."[51]

At the United Nations, Cuban officials lobbied against the decision, while in Havana the government publicly criticized it.[52] When he met Gorbachev's aide Yakovlev the following January, Risquet was bitter: "There is . . . a bloc of the five Big Powers, imperialists and socialists united versus a bloc of the Non Aligned who are defending the interests of the people of Namibia." Yakovlev apologized for the procedure—"Our representative at the UN should have consulted your representative"; he would instruct him "to stay in permanent contact with the Cuban representative." But, Yakovlev said, the Soviet Union would not modify its position.[53]

Finally, on February 16, 1989, the Security Council approved a compromise resolution proposed by Secretary-General Pérez de Cuéllar. The UN force in Namibia would initially comprise 4,500 troops, but if it became evident that this was insufficient, the Security Council could deploy more troops up to 7,500, the number stipulated in Resolution 435.[54]

## The Namibian Elections

The New York agreements had stated that the implementation of Resolution 435 would begin on Saturday April 1, 1989. A seven-month transition period would lead to elections for a Constituent Assembly the following November. The assembly would adopt a constitution and set the date for independence.[55]

"A new era opens for the Southwest [Namibia]," was the *Burger's* headline on April 1, only to announce the following Monday in an even larger font, "SWA [Namibia]—the fighting is ever more violent." During the night of March 31, and through the next day, approximately 1,300 heavily armed SWAPO guerrillas had crossed from Angola into Namibia. "The only possible conclusion that can be drawn from this," the *Burger* explained, "is that SWAPO never deviated from its stated aim to seize power in the Southwest by force of arms."[56]

But this was no power grab. It was SWAPO's clumsy, poorly conceived attempt to force the United Nations to return to the promise made by UN secretary-general Waldheim in 1979.

The April 10, 1978, plan of the five Western members of the Security Council—which was the basis of Resolution 435—had stipulated that the SWAPO combatants would be confined to base during the transition period. But where would these bases be? Only in Angola and Zambia, as Pretoria demanded, or also in Namibia, as SWAPO wanted? The Five had left this to be resolved at a later stage. In his February 26, 1979 report, Waldheim had proposed that "any SWAPO armed forces in Namibia at the time of the cease-fire will . . . be restricted to base at designated locations inside Namibia to be specified by the Special Representative [of the UN secretary-general] after necessary consultations."[57] Pretoria had categorically rejected the prospect of a SWAPO base within the country, and in 1982 the Five had agreed that there would be no SWAPO bases in Namibia.

This remained an academic question until the New York agreements were signed. On March 23, 1989, the UN under-secretary-general for special political affairs, Marrack Goulding, informed SWAPO president Nujoma that there would be no SWAPO bases in Namibia. It was, Goulding writes, a stormy conversation.[58] Nujoma's reply came on the night of March 31, when the SWAPO guerrillas began infiltrating into Namibia.[59] They were not looking for a fight. "They had been instructed not to engage the security forces," UN secretary-general Pérez de Cuéllar later wrote. Instead, they wanted to establish bases in Namibia "where UN personnel would take care of them."[60]

The UNTAG troops, however, had not yet arrived in Namibia. They had been delayed, Pérez de Cuéllar explains, "because of the serious financial crisis with which the United Nations was afflicted, owing primarily to the withholding of a substantial portion of the U.S. budgetary contribution."[61]

South Africa demanded that the SADF be allowed to repel the SWAPO "invasion." Under pressure from the United States and Britain, and from the UN representative in Windhoek, Martti Ahtisaari, Pérez de Cuéllar agreed, "albeit with misgivings."[62] The butchery began. "They can't believe their luck," remarked a senior aide of Ahtisaari who spoke with South African generals in northern Namibia. "They think they're going on a UN-sponsored turkey shoot."[63] For the first time they were acting with an international mandate, on behalf of the United Nations, hunting an enemy who had entered Namibia openly, without expecting to fight. South African helicopter gunships and warplanes joined the fray. SWAPO fought back, with courage. It was not until April 11 that a truce held. The SWAPO guerrillas were able to return to Angola, but they left behind 316 dead.[64]

SWAPO had sent its fighters into Namibia without consulting Cuba and Angola.[65] Nujoma, Pérez de Cuéllar speculates, "must have felt that SWAPO encampments in Namibia were needed to counter any pressure that the presence of South African encampments in Namibia might exert on the electorate." Perhaps he was also motivated by pride. SWAPO, which had fought with desperate bravery for many years inside Namibia, did not want its guerrillas to return to their country as unarmed refugees, as stipulated for by the UN plan. "SWAPO," a Zambian official had warned in February 1980, "would want to show her supporters that she indeed has fighters who helped to bring about freedom."[66]

After this disastrous beginning, the preparations for the elections, scheduled for the second week of November, began. The settlement plan stipulated that the South African administrator general of Namibia, Louis Pienaar, would retain legislative and executive responsibilities during the transition period. This concession to Pretoria—even though it was stipulated that Pienaar would have to carry out his functions "to the satisfaction" of the special representative of the UN secretary-general[67]—hamstrung the power of the United Nations during the transition. This was most evident in Pretoria's continuing ability to control the Namibian airwaves and its refusal to corral the police.

Radio was the only effective means of mass communication in Namibia, a country with a 60 percent illiteracy rate. Since its creation in 1978, the South West Africa Broadcasting Corporation had been a fierce foe of SWAPO. Ahtisaari's complaints notwithstanding, its coverage of the campaign was "dreadful," one of Ahtisaari's senior aides wrote. It was, a scholar said, "a source of disinformation."[68]

The South West Africa Police Force (SWAPOL) included Koevoet, a 3,000-strong counterinsurgency unit known for its extreme brutality. In May 1989—immediately after the transition had begun—Pienaar announced that Koevoet had been disbanded and its members transferred to other police units. However, the UN noted, the ex-Koevoet members continued to behave "in a violent, disruptive and intimidating manner,"[69] and Ahtisaari demanded that all of them be expelled from SWAPOL. Pienaar refused, and he was supported by the Bush administration.[70]

Pérez de Cuéllar did not give up. In July 1989 he told a press conference in Windhoek: "the continued presence of Koevoet in the police force is like a ghost terrorizing the Namibian people." On August 29 the UN Security Council unanimously approved Resolution 640, demanding that the ex-Koevoet members be dismissed from the police and imposing a September 30 deadline.[71]

The deadline passed. Pérez de Cuéllar continued to demand that the former Koevoet members leave the police force, and Pienaar continued to refuse to expel them.[72]

Through most of October, members of the Security Council sought to draft a resolution that would demand—again—that South Africa comply with the requests of the secretary-general. The challenge was to word it so that the United States and Britain, which insisted on language that would not offend Pretoria, could support it. Finally, on October 31, the Security Council approved a resolution that noted "with deep concern that one week before the scheduled elections in Namibia all the provisions of Resolution 435 . . . are not being fully complied with," and demanded, again, the expulsion of all ex-Koevoet members from the police force.[73] Immediately before the vote, Pienaar announced that all former members of Koevoet had been retired from SWAPOL.[74]

South Africa's transgressions went further. Peter Stiff, a conservative writer with excellent contacts in the armed forces and intelligence services of apartheid South Africa, has lifted a veil on Pretoria's covert operations in Namibia during the transition period. They included widespread wiretapping and bribery, as well as assassinations of members of SWAPO.[75] SWAPO responded with restraint. Even South African officials acknowledged "SWAPO's efforts to avoid a confrontation and violence during the electoral campaign."[76]

From November 7 to 11, 1989, the elections for the Constituent Assembly were held. Ninety-seven percent of the registered voters cast their ballots. The impressive turnout, Pérez de Cuéllar noted, "was testimony to the political maturity of the Namibian people."[77] SWAPO won 57.3 percent of the vote, the Democratic Turnhalle Alliance 28.6 percent. Ahtisaari duly certified that "the electoral process in Namibia has at each stage been free and fair."[78] This was certainly true of the five days of voting, but whether the entire process had been truly "free and fair" given Koevoet, Pienaar's bias, and South African dirty tricks was a question no one wanted to raise. SWAPO had won and its leaders would do nothing that might delay independence. "We shall eat a lot, drink a lot and sing a lot," SWAPO's secretary for foreign affairs, Theo-Ben Gurirab, said. "But then we must get to work." Bitterly, the leader of South Africa's Conservative Party told the press, "What has just happened is the exact opposite of everything South Africa fought for."[79] He was right.

A few days after the elections General Geldenhuys informed Savimbi that SWAPO's victory meant that the SADF would no longer be able to supply weapons to UNITA through Namibia. This supply route had remained active in violation of the New York agreements. "[The aid] will have to cease."[80]

On November 21, 1989, the Constituent Assembly began its work. SWAPO impressed even its foes with its moderation and its willingness to seek reconciliation. The assembly unanimously approved the constitution on February 8, 1990; a week later Nujoma was unanimously elected president. On March 21, 1990, Namibia became independent. Pérez de Cuéllar swore in Nujoma as Namibia's first president. Nujoma made "an admirably conciliatory speech," UN under-secretary Goulding writes. "People sensed," a West German diplomat said, "that it was the beginning of the end of apartheid in southern Africa."[81]

## The Angolan Elections

More than a year after Namibia's independence, the guns fell silent in Angola. In May 1991, President dos Santos and Savimbi signed an agreement that established a cease-fire and stipulated that multiparty elections would be held in late 1992. The agreement ushered in a period of peace—an armed truce—as the MPLA and UNITA, as well as minor parties that sprang up, prepared for the elections. The United Nations was charged with monitoring the cease-fire and observing the country's electoral process.[82]

On September 29 and 30, 1992, the elections took place in the presence of 800 foreign observers who "were struck by the scrupulous fairness of polling," the correspondent of the London *Times* reported. The head of the U.S. liaison office in Luanda told reporters that "the elections went incredibly well."[83] The MPLA won 53.74 percent of the votes in the legislative elections, compared with 34.10 percent for UNITA; dos Santos obtained 49.57 percent of the votes for the presidency, compared with Savimbi's 40.07 percent. Because dos Santos had not reached 50 percent, a second ballot for the presidency was required.

There would be no second ballot. On October 3, when the first results were released showing a majority for the MPLA, Savimbi accused the government of fraud, "'stealing ballot boxes, beating up and deviating polling list delegates and distorting facts and numbers.'" In so doing, the *New York Times* reported from Luanda, "Savimbi also dismissed entirely the views of nearly 800 foreign election observers here that the balloting . . . was generally free and fair." The

*Burger*, which had long supported Savimbi, remarked, "Mr. Savimbi's party, UNITA, which lost the elections, has offered no proof of systematic fraud or intimidation." In the days and weeks that followed, the United Nations and foreign governments tried to persuade Savimbi to accept the verdict of the ballot boxes, but "it was dismayingly clear," wrote Margaret Anstee, who headed the UN mission in Angola, "that nothing whatever could be done to satisfy UNITA, short of a statement, against all evidence, that the elections had been flawed by massive fraud and must be declared null and void."[84]

At the request of foreign diplomats in Luanda, the Angolan National Electoral Council delayed publication of the elections results until UNITA's allegations of fraud had been investigated. The investigations did not support UNITA's claims.[85] On October 17, Margaret Anstee issued a public statement declaring:

> The United Nations considers that while there were certainly some irregularities in the electoral process, these appear to have been mainly due to human error and inexperience. There was no conclusive evidence of major, systematic or widespread fraud, or that the irregularities were of a magnitude to have a significant effect on the results officially announced on 17 October. Nor, in view of their random nature, could it be determined that such irregularities had penalized or benefited only one party or set of parties.
>
> I therefore have the honour, in my capacity as Special Representative of the Secretary-General, to certify that, with all deficiencies taken into account, the elections held on 29 and 30 September can be considered to have been generally free and fair.[86]

"Since I uttered these words," Anstee wrote three years later, "there have been several attempts, instigated by UNITA, to induce me to modify that statement, or even to concede that I was totally mistaken. To this day I remain as convinced as I was in October 1992 that our judgement was the right one. The elections may not have been perfect, but I have yet to see elections that are, even in the most 'developed' countries. And such irregularities as did take place were not on one side only. The only blatant attempt to subvert the sovereign will of the Angolan people, as expressed through the ballot boxes, was that launched by UNITA three days after the elections and sustained for many tragic months afterwards."[87]

In an editorial datelined November 30, 1992, the *Burger* declared, "What should have been a highpoint in Angola—the country's first free, democratic election in its history—has turned into an anticlimax. UNITA has refused to acknowledge its defeat." The International Institute for Strategic Studies of London concluded: Savimbi "prepared to take by force what he had failed to obtain through the ballot box." The country slid back into war.[88]

By the time of the 1992 elections, the U.S. government had no use for Savimbi, and it condemned his refusal to accept the electoral results. In May 1993, President Bill Clinton recognized the Angolan government, and the following September the United States joined in a unanimous vote at the UN Security Council to impose sanctions against Savimbi. But it was too late. Civil war raged again in Angola. By the late 1990s the Angolan government had gained the upper hand against UNITA, but Savimbi continued to fight. Marrack Goulding, who was British ambassador in Angola in 1983–85, wrote in 2001: "The conflict grinds on and will continue to do so until Savimbi is removed from the scene." Goulding was right. The war did not end until the death of Savimbi on February 22, 2002. Goulding continued: "It is important that it should be remembered that he [Savimbi] personifies a lesson that powerful governments need to learn: do not arm and pay and flatter local proxies to fight for your interests in their countries, for those proxies may well become malevolent genies whom you will not be able to put back into the bottle when you no longer need them."[89] The powerful government to which he referred was, of course, the United States.

## CHAPTER 20

# Visions of Freedom

## An American Success Story?

The New York agreements of December 1988 led to the independence of Namibia and the withdrawal of the Cuban troops from Angola. This was precisely what Chester Crocker had promised linkage would deliver. In the United States the liberal press lavished praise on the assistant secretary, whom it had criticized for many years. The *Washington Post* saluted his "splendid achievement," and the *New York Times* proclaimed, "The agreement is a tribute to the skills and endurance of a persistent diplomat, Chester Crocker." Conservative newspapers joined in the praise, with some trepidation. The *Wall Street Journal* wrote, "The American-brokered peace plan is one of the most significant foreign policy achievements of the Reagan administration," and it lauded "the hard-nosed, indefatigable negotiating style of one man, Chester Arthur Crocker"; but it also worried, as did the *Washington Times*, that the agreements might fail to protect Savimbi's interests.[1]

This view—that the New York agreements were the fruit of American skill and persistence—continues to hold sway today. It is forcefully argued in the only important book on Reagan's policy in southern Africa, Crocker's memoir, which is well written and intelligent but relies, unfortunately, on a selective use of the evidence.[2]

U.S., South African, and Cuban documents tell a different story and raise new questions. What was the role played by the United States in southern Africa in the Carter and Reagan years? What does the Angola story tell us about the Soviet-Cuban relationship? Finally, what judgments can be drawn of Cuban policy in southern Africa?

## Chester Crocker and U.S. Policy in Southern Africa

Chester Crocker, that "soft-spoken scholar"[3] who could be quite bossy with Angolan officials, occupies center stage in any discussion of the Reagan administration's policy toward southern Africa. No assistant secretary of state for Africa has served as long as Crocker. None has been as influential. He was able to survive under Secretary of State Haig, and he gained Shultz's trust. He was a tireless and skillful negotiator, and his tactical ability was acknowledged by Cubans, Angolans, Soviets, and South Africans alike. The policy he eloquently defended rested on two pillars: constructive engagement and linkage.

Crocker laid out the intellectual underpinnings of constructive engagement in a 1980 article in *Foreign Affairs*. He argued that by approaching the South Africans with empathy and firmly rejecting the use of sanctions it would be possible to coax them to make concessions to nonwhites at home and pursue a less aggressive policy abroad.[4] Pretoria appreciated the gentle touch of the Reagan administration. In 1987 President Botha told the South African parliament, "President Reagan . . . will always be remembered in South Africa for the contribution he made in proclaiming a down-to-earth policy and trying to maintain that policy toward South Africa."[5]

But did constructive engagement coax Pretoria toward concessions? The evidence indicates that it did not. Instead, the South Africans took advantage of U.S. goodwill to further their foreign policy aims. The decision to blow up the storage tanks in Cabinda in May 1985—destroying U.S. property and killing U.S. citizens—epitomizes the South Africans' understanding of constructive engagement. They resented it. Herman Nickel, Reagan's first ambassador to South Africa, recalls, "In my very first meeting with PW Botha [in March 1982] he said: 'When you talk of constructive engagement what you really mean is that you want to meddle in the internal affairs of my country.' He never budged from this view. He was adamant about it."[6] Therefore, the South Africans refused to reciprocate Reagan's goodwill. Constructive engagement was a one-way street. Nickel captured the essence of the problem when he explained in June 1985 that "our present influence on Pretoria is very low. . . . There is no sign of SA gratitude or even acknowledgment of the Reagan administration's more friendly attitude toward the Pretoria regime."[7] Constructive engagement never worked, and its official demise came in 1986, when the U.S. Congress, overriding Reagan's veto, voted in favor of sanctions against South Africa. When the quadripartite negotiations began in the spring of 1988, constructive engagement was just an unsavory memory. U.S. policy had "turned full circle," the

Johannesburg *Business Day* wrote, "from constructive engagement to destructive disengagement."[8]

What about linkage, which stipulated that South Africa would implement Resolution 435 only if Cuba withdrew its troops from Angola? The reams of South African documents that have been declassified—as opposed to the platitudes Pik Botha showered on U.S. officials—prove that PW Botha and his generals had no intention of implementing Resolution 435. They wanted to bring Savimbi to power in Angola and then, with Savimbi's help, they would crush SWAPO and impose an internal solution in Namibia. This was their policy as the 1988 negotiations began. PW Botha was as interested in reaching a modus vivendi with the MPLA as Reagan was in reaching an agreement with the Sandinistas in Nicaragua. He paid lip service to linkage to mollify the Americans, but he had no intention of subscribing to any settlement that would allow SWAPO to govern Namibia.

Pik Botha and his aides in the Foreign Ministry represented the silent—or quasi silent—opposition within the South African government. They were much more skeptical than was the military about Savimbi's chances of success. Like the military, Pik Botha wanted an internal solution in Namibia, but he was far more aware than were the generals of the pitfalls of imposing one. But if Pik Botha and his cohorts feared alienating the Americans, they feared PW's wrath even more. They did not dare challenge the defense establishment.

Whether Crocker ever believed that Pretoria was negotiating in good faith is an open question. Clearly, he had doubts. The South African ambassador reported from Washington in April 1984 that Crocker was "deeply worried, even depressed," over South Africa's lack of commitment to Resolution 435. And upon landing in Johannesburg the following May, Crocker told Pik Botha that "he had come to South Africa to be reassured."[9] But he never abandoned the idea—or pretense—of linkage. Was it stubborn optimism, naiveté, or the lack of an acceptable alternative? He continued to try to reason with the South Africans while working indefatigably to bring about the withdrawal of the Cuban troops. While Crocker tried to nudge and intimidate the Angolans into accepting the departure of all the Cuban troops from their country, the South Africans sought to forge an internal solution in Namibia. Throughout these years, the SADF crossed the Angolan border at will, in an almost uninterrupted succession of minor raids and air strikes and, at times, major assaults. U.S. intelligence noted Pretoria's "tried and true tactics of thump and talk."[10] In fact, when it came to Angola, the South Africans liked to thump but had no interest in talking. Their idea of a settlement was to replace the MPLA government with

Savimbi. Nor were they interested in talking with SWAPO, preferring instead to thump it.

The Reagan administration did not object to the SADF's minor raids into Angola. At times, however, it vehemently opposed the major attacks. The clearest example of this is in the first half of 1983, when U.S. officials exerted strong pressure to restrain Pretoria because they believed that Luanda was on the verge of agreeing to their demands about the departure of the Cuban troops. At other times, they winked. They clearly thought, as the *Pretoria News* said, "Maybe the only way to bring Angola's rulers to a serious negotiating table is to beat them over the head . . . to kick them into peace talks by the seat of their pants."[11]

The most flagrant example of the wink and nod approach is in late 1987, when Crocker told the South African ambassador that the United States had made sure that the UN Security Council resolution demanding the SADF's withdrawal from Angola did not include any sanctions and "did not provide for any assistance to Angola. That was no accident, but a consequence of our own efforts to keep the resolution within bounds." Crocker explains the logic behind the U.S. stance in his memoirs, pointing out that "we could not officially defend the SADF presence in Angola, but we had no intention of actually pressuring them to leave except as part of a series of mutually reinforcing steps."[12] For Crocker, this meant that the South African juggernaut would force Luanda to agree to send all the Cuban troops home according to a timetable acceptable to Washington and Pretoria. In return, Pretoria would withdraw its troops from Angola and would agree to implement Resolution 435—a concession indispensable for U.S. credibility: since 1981 the Reagan administration had assured the Africans as well as its West European allies that linkage was the fail-proof way to bring about the implementation of Resolution 435. Meeting in late March 1988, Crocker and Pik Botha's aide van Heerden congratulated each other on how clever they were: they had maneuvered the Angolans back to the negotiating table. Van Heerden "drew Dr. Crocker's attention to the change in the strategic balance in southern Angola since 1984. Both UNITA's position and that of the RSA have strengthened considerably. The new realities created by the military situation must be reflected in any agreement." Crocker graciously replied "that the progress made towards CTW [Cuban troop withdrawal] would not have been possible without the role played today by the SADF. They had been a crucial factor and although the United States could not say so publicly should CTW become a reality it would be largely due to their successes in southern Angola."[13]

The joke was on Crocker. Despite years of bitter experience with Pretoria, years of betrayal and abundant evidence that Pretoria had not changed, Crocker failed to understand that the South Africans were not interested in linkage. He wrote in his memoirs that by November 1987 "there was a risk of complete FAPLA collapse in the south of Angola,"[14] but he did not see that a FAPLA collapse would have emboldened the hard-liners around PW Botha, thereby making it less likely that Resolution 435 would be implemented in Namibia. At the June 1988 Cairo meeting, the hard-liners' demands were presented by Pik Botha: "national reconciliation" in Luanda and synchronized withdrawal of the SADF and the Cubans from Angola. Only after national reconciliation was under way in Angola would it be possible to implement Resolution 435—but first, it would have to be revised. These demands turned the U.S. policy of linkage upside down.

Why, then, just a few weeks after the June 1988 Cairo meeting did Pretoria agree to abandon Savimbi and hold free elections in Namibia?

Soviet and South African officials have argued that Gorbachev's new policies influenced the South African government by lessening its fear of Soviet aggression. "The South African representatives told us . . . that the rapid progress [in the 1988 negotiations] would not have been possible without the changes in the international situation wrought by Perestroika," Soviet deputy foreign minister Adamishin writes.[15] But the documents in the South African archives tell another story: for Pretoria, Gorbachev's velvet glove simply hid the iron fist. Soviet aims of world domination had not changed; they were just more cleverly masked in order to better manipulate the West. The South African Intelligence Service warned in August 1988 that "despite the Soviets' more pragmatic approach and willingness to settle regional conflicts . . . by political means, their policy in southern Africa remains consolidating and expanding their influence in the region." The following month—September 1988—the Secretariat of the State Security Council asserted, "Soviet talk about the importance of a political settlement in SA does not signal any lessening of the threat to SA. . . . It is just a new instrument of Soviet foreign policy . . . which has moved beyond traditional military tactics to include also political tactics. This means that the Soviet threat to SA has become more sophisticated and is therefore potentially greater."[16]

There is no evidence in the available South African, Cuban, or U.S. documents that the November 1988 U.S. presidential elections influenced Pretoria's stance in the negotiations. The possibility that the Democratic candidate might win should have spurred South Africa to make concessions, yet Pretoria presented its harshest demands in June 1988—when it seemed quite possible that Michael Dukakis might be the next U.S. president—and softened its position in the weeks that followed, as Dukakis's chances dimmed. Furthermore, the declassified record does not indicate a single instance of the possibility of a Dukakis victory influencing South African decision making. The same is true for the Cubans: there is no suggestion, in the documents I have seen, that the U.S. presidential campaign influenced their negotiating position. "It didn't," their chief negotiator, Jorge Risquet, recalls.[17]

What then forced Pretoria to agree to free elections in Namibia and to abandon Savimbi? By 1988, the South African government faced fierce black resistance, increasing questions about its policies from the country's business elite, disinvestment by foreign firms, and the threat of economic sanctions. South African officials claimed that sanctions, if approved, would be ineffective, but they were worried. "We as a country must be well prepared for any eventuality," South Africa's deputy health minister warned in January 1988, announcing the withdrawal of four major international pharmaceutical companies, "as one cannot but wonder where it will all end." Harsher sanctions, the Johannesburg *Star* lamented in March, were a "virtual inevitability." Crocker disdainfully dismissed as "a piece of political theater" the rising pressure for sanctions in the U.S. Congress, but the South Africans were less complacent. "Sanctions have hurt," Johannesburg's *Business Day* wrote on March 10, 1988. "Since the 1977 arms embargo, the sanctions noose has slowly tightened, but the fact that SA can still breathe is no reason to dare the hangman to do his damnedest. . . . Sanctions can get a lot worse. . . . As sanctions escalate, recession and unemployment will increase social instability."[18]

It was not Gorbachev's new policy or the presidential elections in the United States, it was not constructive engagement nor linkage, that overcame South Africa's resistance. It was, rather, forces that Crocker and the Reagan administration abhorred: black militants in South Africa waving the flag of the ANC, the threat of sanctions, and Fidel Castro.

Crocker himself notes repeatedly in his memoirs that when the quadripartite negotiations began in May 1988, the South Africans had not yet decided to accept a peaceful solution—"South Africa's decision to come to the London meeting in May did not signify that a basic national choice had been made in favor of a settlement," he writes. When the delegations met in July in New York, he adds, "the senior leadership in Pretoria still had taken no basic decisions, and still viewed the . . . talks as, at best, an exploratory process."[19] Why, less than a month later, did Pretoria decide to withdraw unilaterally from Angola?

The answer is abundantly clear in the U.S. and South African archives. It was Cuban military might. Castro's November 15, 1987, decision to send powerful reinforcements to Angola and pursue a more aggressive strategy on the battlefield reversed the military situation. Cuito Cuanavale did not fall. In the south-west, the Cubans advanced within striking distance of the Namibian border. The Cuban air force gained the upper hand in southern Angola and northern Namibia. This changed everything. In late July, the U.S. Joint Chiefs of Staff warned that, if the negotiations deadlocked, "Cuban forces will be in position to launch a well-supported offensive into Namibia." If Pretoria continued to oppose Namibia's independence, a close aide of Foreign Minister Pik Botha warned, it ran "the very real risk of becoming involved in a full-scale conventional war with the Cubans, the results of which are potentially disastrous." The chief of the SADF, General Geldenhuys, was grim: "We must do . . . our utmost to prevent a confrontation."[20] Hence, the New York agreements.

## Crocker's Achievements

The policies of constructive engagement and linkage were naive because they overestimated the U.S. ability to influence South Africa. Crocker's real achievement lies elsewhere: he kept the true Reaganites at bay. A senior South African diplomat pointed out that "there were people in the U.S. government who shared the views of the South African military"[21]: they loathed SWAPO; they were eager to jettison Resolution 435; they wanted to bring Savimbi to power; and they embraced RENAMO, the Mozambican rebel movement.

Crocker disliked SWAPO, but he understood that there was no alternative to Resolution 435—South Africa, despite its military might, was unable to fashion an internal settlement in Namibia that could claim any legitimacy, and U.S. support for a futile attempt would have aroused the wrath of the African countries, and even of U.S. allies, for no practical purpose. He also understood that a UNITA military victory was not possible in Angola, and he helped his government resist the temptation to seek one, despite the true Reaganites' efforts. Less clear is how Crocker saw the future of Angola. Like every other Reagan administration official, he echoed Savimbi's claim that UNITA sought national reconciliation, a claim he and Shultz stolidly repeat in their memoirs. "We had long supported UNITA's goal of political reconciliation," Crocker writes; Savimbi's goal was "national reconciliation in Angola," Shultz asserts.[22] Shultz may have believed it. He spent relatively little time on Angolan matters, and when he met Savimbi in 1986 he was captivated by the charismatic guerrilla chieftain.

It is not credible, however, that Crocker, who focused on Angola and was impervious to Savimbi's charisma (as reams of documents indicate), bought his talk of national reconciliation. In 1986 Crocker told Pik Botha that the United

States "needed to hear more concrete ideas from Dr. Savimbi as to what that term (i.e. national reconciliation) might mean." The CIA was equally in the dark: "UNITA claims that it remains willing to negotiate with the MPLA, but just what Savimbi would accept in a compromise is unclear," it noted.[23] When I asked Crocker, his answer was evasive.

Crocker, however, could not afford the luxury of second guessing Savimbi's intentions or of contemplating Angola's future. Reagan's support for Savimbi was a given that was well above the assistant secretary's pay grade. Herman Cohen, NSC Africa director in 1987–88, pointed out that "we were sort of stuck with him [Savimbi]. He was our Cold War surrogate." Savimbi "was using us and we were using him," Crocker's senior deputy, Chas Freeman, added. What mattered was, as Crocker told South African officials, that "the strategic reversal of the West in Angola in 1975-1976 had to be reversed." The Cubans must leave, and Savimbi—an anticommunist champion—must be supported. The Africa bureau, Jeff Davidow, a senior Crocker aide, said, had "a very pragmatic attitude, almost bloodless. Not much emotion: it was a problem in international relations that had to be solved. Our view was that they were all bad—South Africa, SWAPO, the MPLA, Savimbi. We were, if anything, the only civilizing force that could bring these groups of barbarians to the table."[24]

Crocker's fiercest, most protracted clash with the true Reaganites was not about Angola or SWAPO, but about policy toward Mozambique. "Conservatives, both inside and outside the administration, strongly supported the RENAMO guerrilla movement," Cohen recalls. "There were a lot of them in the Defense Department and the CIA. . . . [In 1987] we [at the NSC] were getting letters from Secretary Weinberger to [National Security Adviser Frank] Carlucci saying RENAMO was the wave of the future, they should be supported." Personal friends wrote to Reagan to express their dismay over the State Department's efforts to bring about a rapprochement with "the communist government of Mozambique." But Crocker and the Africa bureau held the line and Shultz supported them.[25]

The true Reaganites embraced apartheid South Africa, rejected Resolution 435, and sought to overthrow the governments of Angola and Mozambique. Spearheaded by Crocker and his team, a less extreme policy prevailed. The United States accepted Resolution 435 and applied the Reagan doctrine of support to self-professed anticommunist insurgencies in a selective way: against Angola but not against Mozambique. It helped Savimbi but kept RENAMO at arm's length. Even constructive engagement as practiced by Crocker embraced South Africa less wholeheartedly than the true Reaganites demanded.

Given the ideological mind-set of Reagan and many of his supporters, was there any realistic alternative to Crocker's policy? A comparison with the Carter administration is instructive. Obviously there were important differences: Carter abhorred apartheid and cold-shouldered South Africa—"looking back on the Carter era is like trying to recall an unpleasant dream," the South African ambassador in Washington during those years recalled.[26] Carter demanded that Pretoria implement Resolution 435 unconditionally, and while he helped Savimbi, the aid was much more limited than it would become in the Reagan years.

Like Reagan, however, Carter opposed diplomatic relations with Angola as long as the Cuban troops remained there, despite clear evidence that, as the CIA noted, they were "necessary to preserve Angolan independence,"[27] and despite the equally strong evidence that Neto and dos Santos were no one's puppets—not of Havana and not of Moscow. He rejected the State Department's plea to impose sanctions on South Africa when PW Botha refused to implement Resolution 435, and his administration engaged instead in a futile and undignified minuet with Pretoria. Hence, Ambassador McHenry's grim postmortem on January 20, 1981: "The SAG has calculated that it faces no serious threat of international action in the foreseeable future. Certainly the experience of the last two years could only reinforce that conclusion."[28]

## Rewriting History

Reagan's policy toward Angola was cloaked in morality: the United States would right the wrong perpetrated by the Soviet Union and its Cuban proxy in 1975. Crocker lectured Angolan foreign minister M'Binda in January 1988, "It was not us, the United States, who began the foreign involvement in Angola. . . . The Cuban intervention began many months before Angola became independent [on November 11, 1975]. . . . It was not until after Angolan independence that the United States developed a relationship with UNITA." And he told the African ambassadors in Washington a few months later that "the US has never had diplomatic relations with Angola because we thought the decolonization process in that country became illegitimate . . . when foreign (i.e., Cuban) troops installed their favorite faction in power in Luanda."[29]

Crocker was rewriting history. The U.S. covert operation to help UNITA began in July 1975—four months before the independence of Angola. Within a few weeks it had become clear that the MPLA was winning the civil war. "The MPLA has achieved an almost unbroken series of military successes," U.S. intelligence warned in a lengthy report on September 22, 1975. The South African historian of the war explains that "the choice lay between active South African military participation on the one hand and—in effect—acceptance of an MPLA victory on the other." On October 14, 1975, Pretoria, urged on by Washington, invaded Angola. In response, on November 4, Castro ordered his troops to Angola.[30] In plain words: first, the South Africans invaded, encouraged by Washington; then Cuban troops arrived in Angola to repel the South African invasion. Reagan's account stood reality on its head.

As did another tale: that Savimbi was a freedom fighter against Portuguese colonialism. In fact, Savimbi had cooperated with the Portuguese colonial authorities against the MPLA. And yet American journalists and pundits remained stunningly unaware of this reality, even though Portuguese officials—from the deposed prime minister to a slew of generals—had openly discussed Savimbi's collusion in books and in the media, and the relevant documents proving it had been published in the mainstream Portuguese press. U.S. officials seemed oblivious to these facts. Secretary Shultz waxed indignant in a December 1988 cable: "The MPLA persists in treating UNITA as an agglomeration of individual dissidents rather than a nationalist movement with its own *deep credentials in the struggle against Portuguese colonialism* and other foreign occupation and intervention in Angola."[31]

It is instructive to see how former Reagan officials who for so long had strenuously proclaimed Savimbi's desire for national reconciliation dealt with the failed 1992 elections in Angola. In his memoirs, which appeared in 1995, Shultz did not mention the elections. In an ill-tempered op-ed, Crocker suggested that the elections had been flawed—"Claims of foul play (by UNITA and others) before and during the election went unanswered"—and concluded, "Both UNITA and the MPLA bear responsibility for Angola's agony."[32]

The prize for creative dissembling belongs, however, to former NSC official Peter Rodman, who wrote that "U.N. special envoy Margaret Anstee confided to a UNITA official that she had never witnessed a more unfair election, even in Latin America." Rodman's only source for this extraordinary statement that contradicts everything Anstee wrote at the time or later is a transition paper by the Center for Security Policy, a conservative Washington think tank, which referred to "a comment reportedly made by UN special envoy Margaret Anstee to at least one senior UNITA official." The paper offered no evidence for this statement.[33]

The most honest of the lot was Herman Cohen, NSC Africa director in 1987–88, and Crocker's successor as assistant secretary for Africa. In his memoirs he wrote, "I believe emphatically that if UNITA had accepted the results of the elections in good faith, as it had promised, [the agreement reached in May 1991 between the Angolan government and UNITA in the Portuguese town of] Bicesse would have survived. . . . The main reason Angola went back to war was UNITA's refusal to live up to its commitments." Savimbi, he said, "was the master of delay and deceit."[34]

Four days after Savimbi's death, in February 2002, President George Bush received President dos Santos at the White House. Bush expressed America's goodwill toward Angola and urged dos Santos to reach out to all Angolans and bring peace to his devastated country.[35] The U.S. press failed to note the irony of the situation. Instead of lecturing dos Santos, Bush should have asked his forgiveness for the crimes perpetrated by the United States against the people of Angola. On two grounds. First, because the United States had connived with Pretoria in 1975 and throughout the Reagan years; and, second, because the United States had assisted Jonas Savimbi. U.S. officials claimed that Savimbi was a sincere democrat who sought national reconciliation, free elections, and liberation from the Soviet-Cuban yoke. In fact, Savimbi was a terrorist. The Reagan administration pointed out that the MPLA government was corrupt, indifferent to the needs of the population, and repressive. This was true, but the MPLA did not burn its opponents at the stake, much less their wives and children. It repressed dissent but not as cruelly and absolutely as Savimbi, who had imposed a "culture of zero tolerance of dissent and a personality cult that had parallels with those of Mao Tse-Tung and Kim Il-Sung." There was no moral equivalence. Doug Smith, the CIA station chief in Kinshasa from 1983 to 1986, had believed, like many CIA and DIA officers, that Savimbi could overthrow the Angolan government—"his army would grow big enough and strong enough to push the Cubans out." But, he adds, "in retrospect it wasn't a good idea—because of the extent of Savimbi's crimes. He was terribly brutal." Marrack Goulding, the British ambassador in Luanda, characterized Savimbi: "a monster whose lust for power had brought appalling misery to his people."[36]

And so we return to our starting point, and to Mitchell's words, "Our selective recall not only serves a purpose, it has repercussions. It creates a chasm between us and the Cubans: we share a past, but we have no shared memories."[37] In America's memory, the Cubans invaded and occupied Angola as Soviet proxies, while the United States sought to bring peace and democracy to that unhappy country. In America's memory, Reagan's policies of constructive engagement and linkage persuaded South Africa to see reason and agree to the independence of Namibia. This distorts reality. In fact the 1975 South African invasion of Angola, which the Americans encouraged, drew in the Cuban troops. Through linkage the Reagan administration made it easier for South Africa to continue to occupy Namibia and to use it as a springboard to wreak havoc in Angola. U.S. aid helped Savimbi in his war of terror against the Angolan people. It was not Reagan who made the New York agreements possible. It was Fidel Castro.

## The Cuban-Soviet Relationship

Cuban covert operations in Latin America and Africa in the 1960s—small-scale actions involving a limited number of people—were conducted without direct Soviet assistance, as was the dispatch of the Cuban troops to Angola in 1975 and again in 1987, but none of this would have been possible without the military and economic aid that Moscow gave to the island. Cuba's ability to act independently was made possible by the existence of this friendly superpower on which it depended for its economic and military lifeline. This parallels the relationship between the United States and Israel: it is U.S. military and economic support that makes possible Israel's freedom of maneuver. While Havana and Tel Aviv have pursued opposite foreign policies, they have this in common: dependence on a superpower did not translate into being a "client." In his memoirs, Gorbachev wrote: "Castro always maintained his independence, in his views and in his actions. He did not tolerate and did not allow us to give him orders. The Cubans were our allies, not our subordinates."[38]

Fidel Castro complained about a number of Soviet actions, and he did so forcefully with Politburo member Demichev in 1980 and again in 1984. But he also acknowledged that "we could not have survived . . . without the aid that we have received from the Soviet Union in every sphere. . . . This aid has been immense and generous."[39]

Without Moscow, Cuba could not have kept tens of thousands of soldiers in Angola for more than a decade. Without Moscow, the FAPLA would have been virtually unarmed. "The two great achievements of the USSR in Angola," a senior Angolan officer remarked, "were to give the weapons to our army and to aid Cuba." President dos Santos told Castro in December 1988, "The Soviet Union helped Angola and helped Cuba to help Angola."[40]

Where the Soviet Union failed was in military strategy. CIA and Cuban reports, FAPLA and UNITA officers, all agree that Soviet military advice was unsuited to Third World conditions, and to guerrilla and counterguerrilla operations. "The Soviet model of conventional warfare had little flexibility," a former UNITA general remarks. "They would plan the operation on the map; then they wanted to carry out the plan but they were unable to adapt when the situation on the ground diverged from the map."[41]

The Cubans knew very well that they were dependent on the Soviet Union. They were keen to avoid quarrels, but when necessary they stood up to the

Kremlin. They did so in Angola on a regular basis, challenging Soviet strategy there—the Mavinga operations were just the most blatant examples of this clash. No one who reads the minutes of the exchanges between Polo and Konstantin—or Risquet and Varennikov—can have any doubt about how outspoken the Cuban could be and how firm was their refusal to follow Soviet guidance. In November 1975 Castro defied Brezhnev when he sent troops to Angola. In May 1977, the Cubans intervened in defense of President Neto against Nito Alves's revolt, even though they suspected that the Soviets stood behind it. And in November 1987, Castro defied Gorbachev when he decided to push the SADF out of Angola, once for all. Throughout Maniobra XXXI Aniversario, the Cubans conducted their military operations without consulting the Soviets, and in the 1988 negotiations with Americans and South Africans they confined Moscow to the role of junior partner. As Crocker points out, "It was not Soviet pressure which got the parties to the table. We saw no evidence of Soviet arm-twisting. . . . In general Moscow deferred to its allies and, on occasion, hid behind their ample skirts."[42]

What did the Soviet Union gain from its long involvement in Angola? The CIA summed it up: Moscow got "a reliable supporter of Soviet positions in international forums" and the use of naval and air facilities in Luanda. In his memoirs, Crocker wrote that Angola was a lucrative market for Soviet weapons: "The Soviet-Angolan military relationship was by no means a charitable venture on Moscow's part. Devastated Angola suddenly became a major buyer of arms. . . . Some $4.5 billion of arms were supplied to Angola in the first ten years of independence, nearly ninety percent from the USSR."[43]

While it is true that Moscow sold vast amounts of weapons to Angola—worth approximately $6 billion between 1976 and 1988[44]—the Angolans paid in cash only for 10 to 15 percent of the amount; the remaining 85 to 90 percent was given on credit. The debt was not paid during the lifetime of the Soviet Union. Far from being a source of profit, the sale of weapons was, Soviet deputy foreign minister Adamishin writes, a "black hole." Crocker himself acknowledged this in 1988, when he told the South Africans that "the USSR was not benefiting financially from Angola and in return for vast expenses only managed to harvest some fish."[45] Angolan officials told me, "We paid the debt after the collapse of the USSR. The Russians forgave some of the debt, and we paid the rest."[46] I could get no figures but was left with the impression that most of the debt was forgiven.

In their memoirs, most former Soviet officials are critical of Moscow's involvement in Angola, even when they believe that it was morally justified, because it hurt relations with the United States and diverted precious resources that should have been used at home. It was "a serious mistake," wrote Marshal Akhromeyev. "It did not . . . serve the national interest of the Soviet Union," stressed Deputy Foreign Minister Kornienko. "Why, with all our problems, did we have to get involved?" Adamishin asked. "Whether it was just or not, we could not afford it, we had too many problems of our own."[47]

Vladimir Shubin, a former Soviet official and now a prominent scholar, offers a rare contrast to this litany of lamentations. He is unrepentant and proud of what the Soviet Union did in southern Africa. The achievements justified the costs—Moscow helped protect Angola from South Africa and lent crucial assistance to the liberation movements of southern Africa. Armed struggle was a key element in the collapse of white rule in southern Africa, he argues, and it would not have been possible without the weapons provided by the Soviet Union.[48] I agree.

## Cuba's Vietnam?

For the Soviet Union, from 1976 to 1991 southern Africa was but one theater of its foreign policy, and not one of the most important. For Cuba, on the other hand, southern Africa was the locus of the most important foreign policy venture of the Cuban revolution. Fewer than 2,000 Cubans—soldiers and aid workers—had served in missions abroad before 1975. Suddenly, the floodgates opened: between November 1975 and April 1976, 36,000 Cuban soldiers poured into Angola. The number decreased over the next two years, then rose again, to peak at 55,000 in August 1988.

There are obvious similarities between the Cubans' role in Angola and the Americans' role in South Vietnam. Both stayed a very long time. Relative to the population, the death toll was comparable: approximately 58,000 Americans died in Vietnam and 2,000 Cubans in Angola.

There are striking differences, however. The United States created an artificial state in South Vietnam, whereas Cuba intervened in Angola in response to the South African invasion. In Vietnam, the U.S. soldiers bore the brunt of the fighting against the Vietcong and the North Vietnamese. In Angola, the main role of the Cuban soldiers was to act as a shield against an invasion by the troops of the apartheid regime. The Cubans carefully limited their participation in the war against UNITA and constantly reminded the Angolan government that when foreign aid to UNITA ended, so too would Cuba's participation in the fighting against UNITA. "Without foreign aid UNITA becomes an internal problem of Angola," they insisted.[49]

The United States chose South Vietnam's first president, Ngo Dinh Diem, and then brought him down. Throughout their stay in South Vietnam, the Americans showed little respect for the country's sovereignty. The Cubans, however, scrupulously respected the sovereignty of the Angolan government, even though its survival depended on Cuban troops.

And, of course, there was the outcome. The Americans failed to preserve the artificial state of South Vietnam. The U.S. helicopters fleeing from Saigon as the North Vietnamese troops entered the city symbolized the American debacle. Cuba fared very differently. The MPLA government survived. A Cuban official captured the difference succinctly when he told the press, "Ours are not defeated troops, unlike the U.S. troops in Vietnam."[50]

There are no hard data about the reaction of the Cuban soldiers—and the Cuban population at large—to service in Angola. "The general feeling is one of pride," the *Washington Post* reported in February 1976. Two years later, an NSC study concluded, "The average Cuban may not care much about Marxism-Leninism, but the role Cuba is playing in Africa appeals to his sense of nationalist pride." This pride, the NSC expert on Latin America remarked, had even infected the Cuban community in the United States, notorious for its hostility to Castro: "On the issue of Cuban involvement in Africa, their views range from ambivalent to undisguised pride. I suspect this may be reflective of the views of many Cubans in Cuba." In late 1979 the CIA concluded, "Service in Angola remains popular with the youth."[51]

But then came the long, difficult lean years. Only a small percentage of the Cuban soldiers in Angola were attached to FAPLA units fighting against UNITA. The others either manned the defensive line, waiting for a SADF invasion and living in tunnels, or were scattered in military camps throughout the country. It was a hard, monotonous life, with virtually no money, stuck in Angola for two years (only officers had the right to home leave, and this was not always honored). The spell was broken in late 1987, when reinforcements streamed into Angola from Cuba. In the following months the Cuban troops seized the initiative, breaking the SADF's onslaught against Cuito Cuanavale and advancing in the southwest toward the Namibian border. It was, in broad strokes, a return to 1975–76: Cuba against South Africa, with the Cubans pushing back the soldiers of apartheid. Western journalists who went to Cuito Cuanavale were impressed by the morale of the Cuban soldiers. "The ones we spoke to were not senior political officers prepared for our arrival with propagandised briefings," the Johannesburg *Star* wrote, "but ordinary troops waiting for a truck when we stumbled on them." They were eager to go back home, but ready to stay in

Angola "for as long as necessary. We are fighting for a just cause," they told the correspondent of the London *Times*.[52] These fragments are consistent with the impressions I have gathered in two decades of informal conversations in Cuba.

An important feature of Cuban military service probably dampened dissent: no one was obliged to participate in an internationalist mission. The soldiers and reservists who were selected to serve abroad had the right to refuse. A Cuban who did not want to serve in Angola did not have to flee to another country or face jail.

Evidence from the South African archives indicates that the director of Radio Martí and the president of the Cuban American National Foundation, Jorge Más Canosa, visited Savimbi's headquarters in Jamba to create a program on the UNITA radio station that would broadcast appeals "to try and persuade Cubans to desert in favor of settling in the USA, which the Foundation would arrange."[53] If this message was ever broadcast, it was not successful: of the twenty to thirty Cuban soldiers taken prisoner by the SADF or UNITA between 1977 and 1988,[54] only two said that they had deserted, and the *Washington Post* journalist who interviewed them deemed their stories "not entirely credible."[55]

## The Balance Sheet: What Cuba Achieved

There is a tendency, in discussing the Cuban presence in Africa, to focus on the military aspect, and this book has largely followed this approach. But Castro's battalions in the Third World also included the aid workers, and their ranks swelled after 1975 to a total of 70,000—43,257 of whom went to Angola.[56] Cuban primary school teachers went to the Nicaraguan countryside where they taught in improvised classrooms. Cuban doctors went to Tindhouf, in southwestern Algeria, to care for tens of thousands of refugees from the Western Sahara, occupied by Moroccan troops. Other Cuban doctors created and staffed medical faculties in Aden, Bissau, and Jimma (Ethiopia). Doctors, teachers, and construction workers were the flag bearers of Cuba's humanitarian assistance, which was provided free of charge or at very low cost. No other Third World country offered a program of technical assistance of such scope and generosity. The comparison that immediately comes to mind is the U.S. Peace Corps, but with an important difference: Cuba's aid workers included highly skilled professionals—doctors, nurses, engineers, and university professors.

More than 50,000 Africans, Latin Americans, and Asians studied in Cuba on full scholarships funded by the Cuban government between 1976 and 1991.[57] Among them were more than 6,000 Angolans and approximately 2,500 Namibians.[58] In 1996, in French-speaking Conakry, I accompanied a Cuban friend to the Ministry of Agriculture, where many spoke to him in Spanish. He laughed at my surprise—all were graduates of Cuban universities, he explained.

Of the 385,908 Cuban soldiers who served abroad, 337,033 went to Angola.[59] The Americans wanted them out. Their untimely departure would have left Angola at Pretoria's mercy, strengthened the grip of the apartheid regime over Namibia, dealt a heavy blow to SWAPO, and demoralized those fighting apartheid in South Africa. The Cubans stayed, defying Washington, and in 1988 they forced South Africa to accept Namibia's independence and to abandon its dream of installing Savimbi in power.

Their prowess on the battlefield and their skill at the negotiating table reverberated beyond Namibia and Angola. In the words of Nelson Mandela, the Cuban victory "destroyed the myth of the invincibility of the white oppressor . . . [and] inspired the fighting masses of South Africa. . . . Cuito Cuanavale was the turning point for the liberation of our continent—and of my people—from the scourge of apartheid."[60] In late August 1988 the proud SADF was forced to withdraw from Angola by the Cuban army, a Third World nonwhite army. For South Africa's blacks, it signaled the possibility of liberation.

From the mid-1970s American and South African officials had acknowledged that Namibia's independence would have an impact on South Africa. "The way in which self-determination and independence are achieved in Namibia," a U.S. Presidential Review Memorandum noted in 1977, "will have significant consequences for South Africa's domestic situation." In Pretoria, the Secretariat of the State Security Council warned in 1983 that "if SWAPO were to win an election conducted under Resolution 435, this would have an extremely negative impact on every front. A SWAPO victory would propel Black militant groups in South Africa to put even more pressure on the South African government, while right-wing white groups would intensify their criticism of the government. This might lead to a decline in white morale. . . . SWA [Namibia] will immediately enjoy international recognition while the international community will increase its pressure on South Africa to implement universal suffrage."[61]

As the 1988 negotiations came to their conclusion, the South African press stressed the repercussions of the independence of Namibia on South Africa. "At home the government can live with the extra grumbling from the right that will ensue," the Johannesburg *Star* said in a December 15, 1988, editorial. "But it will also face heightened black demands for reform." *Business Day* agreed: "At home there will be . . . renewed black demands for liberation." The *Sowetan*, which had been so careful for so long, dared to be bold: "In Namibia the people have identified SWAPO as their leading organisation," it wrote. "Because South Africa had fears over the power that SWAPO obviously would wield in that country's future, the war went on and on. We have a similar tragic situation in South Africa. Rightly or wrongly the majority of the people of South Africa have identified the banned organisations as their leaders for the future. . . . The history of Namibia and Angola will be instructive to leaders and politicians of the future."[62]

Psychological considerations were very much on the mind of General Geldenhuys when he informed eighteen high-ranking SADF officers in January 1989 that the government would launch a program of dirty tricks to ensure SWAPO's defeat in the forthcoming elections in Namibia. He included a memo by the army's chief of operations itemizing the advantages for South Africa if the Democratic Turnhalle Alliance—Pretoria's client—won the election. The long list included: "This will be a big setback for the ANC's image and morale. . . . It will strengthen the confidence in the SA government's ability to handle the conflict in SA. . . . A victory in the election will mean that we have halted communist expansionism in Africa. . . . This will be a reward for the years of personal and professional sacrifice of the members of the SADF. . . . It will raise the morale of the population of SA and will strengthen its confidence in the future. . . . The SADF's image as a winner will be enhanced."[63] This careful assessment of the likely effects of a SWAPO defeat suggests the profound effect of its victory. In less than two years, apartheid South Africa had suffered two crippling defeats at the hands of nonwhites: its humiliation in southern Angola in 1988, and SWAPO's victory in Namibia in 1989.

I cannot offer an authoritative assessment of the impact of these defeats on the apartheid regime, beyond pointing to Mandela's words about the significance for South Africa of the Cuban victory in southern Angola, and the South Africans' own assessment of the importance of defeating SWAPO in Namibia.

By the time Namibia became independent, in March 1990, apartheid was in its death throes. A month earlier, Frederick de Klerk, who had replaced the ailing PW Botha as South Africa's president, legalized the ANC and the South African Communist Party, and he freed Nelson Mandela. The apartheid government engaged in protracted and difficult negotiations that led in April 1994 to the first elections in the country's history based on universal franchise. Predictably, the ANC swept the polls. A few days later, Mandela was inaugurated president of South Africa. Among the 1,200 guests at his inauguration was Fidel Castro. "No visiting dignitary from princes to premiers, of the 150 countries represented here came close to setting off the buzz that buzzed all day today around a tired-looking ruler of a small island nation in dire economic straits," Paul Taylor, the correspondent of the *Washington Post*, reported from Pretoria. "Fidel Castro had a very good day." He had been, the prominent South African dissident Rev. Allan Boesak told Taylor, "an incredibly loyal friend when the anti-apartheid movement in South Africa needed his help in Angola."[64] Today, in Pretoria's Freedom Park, which opened in 2007, the "Wall of Names" commemorates those who "paid the ultimate price" for South Africa's freedom. The names of the Cubans who died in Angola are inscribed on the Wall. No other foreign country is represented.

## The Balance Sheet: The Costs

Cuba's internationalism came at a price: political, economic and, above all, human. A total of 2,425 Cubans lost their lives, 2,103 of them in Angola.[65] In addition to the lost lives, what Castro called the "human cost"[66] included the sacrifice demanded of millions of Cubans: the hundreds of thousands who spent two years on a distant continent living in difficult conditions far from their loved ones, as well as their families who waited back home. "The cost in human terms is enormous," Castro had told Neto in 1979. "This effort requires great sacrifice for tens of thousands of families who have a son, or a father, or a brother abroad."[67]

Beyond these sacrifices, the assessment of the costs of Cuba's Angolan policy must be more tentative.

First, the economic dimension. Cuba paid the salaries of its troops in Angola which was a significant burden: almost half of the 337,033 Cuban soldiers who served in Angola were reservists who continued to receive the salaries they had been earning in their civilian jobs.[68] The Soviet Union supplied the weapons cost-free. Through 1977 Cuba bore all the other costs (such as food, transportation, and clothing); from January 1, 1978, they were borne by Angola, but often the Angolans failed to meet their obligations, and Havana had to pitch in. Furthermore, Cuba did not charge for its technical assistance, except from 1978 to 1983.

The increases in Soviet economic aid to Cuba after 1975 may have been influenced by the Kremlin's desire to compensate Cuba for its African policy. The answer may lie in sealed boxes in the Cuban and Russian archives. But this element of causality should not be exaggerated. I have found no evidence, for example, that Cuba's decision to provide its technical assistance to Angola cost-free after October 1, 1983, led to any increase in Soviet aid to Cuba. Moreover, Soviet aid decreased slightly from 1986 through 1988, even though the number of Cuban soldiers in Angola increased significantly.

While the Cuban government was generous to Angola, it was not profligate. I have been impressed, sifting through thousands of Cuban documents, by the

Cubans' attempt to minimize hard-currency expenditures. During the 1988 negotiations, for example, Risquet tried to economize on hotel bills, telling Castro that at the May meeting in London, "We [the delegation] . . . were able to stay in the homes of Cubans [who live there], and we saved a lot of money." He was worried, however, about the forthcoming meeting in Cairo, "because only four or five Cubans live there."[69]

Next, the political costs. The dispatch of Cuban troops to Angola hurt Cuba's relations with the United States. In 1975 Kissinger had been ready to normalize relations with Havana—until the Cubans landed in Luanda. Carter's attempt to normalize relations was crippled by the continuing Cuban military presence in Angola. Normalization was out of the question under Reagan, but certainly Cuba's withdrawal from Angola could have tempered the wrath of the Reagan administration.

Given these clear costs, why did Cuba intervene and stay in Angola? In the 1960s, U.S. intelligence analysts occasionally referred to Castro's ego—"his thirst for self-aggrandizement"[70]—as a motivating factor for his foreign policy activism, but the explanations they posited again and again were self-defense and idealism. It was an astute analysis. Self-defense: as U.S. intelligence officials acknowledged, Castro had repeatedly offered to explore a modus vivendi with the United States and had been consistently rebuffed. The American response had been to launch paramilitary operations against Cuba, to attempt to assassinate Castro, and to cripple the island's economy. This led the Cubans to a simple conclusion: if Washington persisted in its aggression, the best defense would be offense—not by attacking the United States directly, to be sure, for that would be suicidal, but in the Third World. Cuba would assist revolutionary forces whenever and wherever possible, thereby gaining friends and weakening U.S. influence.

Self-defense went hand in hand with idealism, what U.S. intelligence correctly called Castro's "sense of revolutionary mission." Castro "is first of all a revolutionary," the chair of the CIA's Board of National Estimates said in September 1963.[71] The men who surrounded Castro shared his sense of mission— "revolution is their *raison d'etre*." As INR director Thomas Hughes wrote in 1964, Castro and his cohorts were "dedicated revolutionaries, utterly convinced that they can and must bring radical change to Latin America some day."[72]

In assessing the motivations of Cuba's policy toward Angola, I see continuity with the 1960s, but also differences. The major difference is that the element of self-defense, so stark in the 1960s, becomes murky. On the one hand, from Havana's perspective, its security and well-being in the 1970s—as in the 1960s— would have been enhanced if the imperialist camp had been weakened. In this broad sense, self-defense may have influenced the decision to send troops to Angola in 1975 and to Ethiopia in 1977. However, Gerald Ford and Jimmy Carter were contemplating normalization of relations with Cuba, and the Cubans knew it, just as they knew that sending troops to Africa would derail the possibility of normalization. Self-defense, therefore, cannot be considered a major factor in Cuba's activism in Africa in the 1970s.

The Cuban perception of a U.S. military threat, which had waned in the 1970s, deepened again in the 1980s. Ronald Reagan's hostility toward the Cuban revolution was as visceral as that of John Kennedy. Until the Iran-Contra scandal exploded in late 1986, the Cubans were haunted by the prospect that the Reagan administration might strike their country, and they were painfully aware of the inadequacy of the Soviet shield. As Castro said, "the Americans . . . can wage a war against Cuba without taking any casualties: they would move their aircraft carriers into position and start bombarding our coasts in twenty different places, and we couldn't do anything about it."[73] This sounds like the 1960s.

Not quite, though. Kennedy and Reagan posed different threats to Cuba. Kennedy was determined to crush the fledgling Cuban revolution, but by the early 1980s very few Americans espoused rollback in Cuba. Castro and his aides recognized that however intensely Reagan might hate Cuba, he was much more likely to strike it for what it did than for what it was. They believed that U.S. military aggression against their country could be triggered by factors that were beyond their control, such as a Soviet invasion of Poland, but they also knew that their own military activities abroad, in Central America and in southern Africa, stoked Washington's fury and increased the danger of U.S. retribution.

Therefore, after the 1960s, self-defense cannot be considered a key motivation of Cuba's activism in Africa. The explanation must be sought elsewhere.

During the Cold War, U.S. policy makers and a phalanx of pundits stuck to a comforting answer: Castro was doing the Kremlin's bidding, he was simply a Soviet proxy. So much evidence to the contrary has emerged over the past two decades that the myth now comforts only the most gullible. But even if we eliminate the Soviet bugaboo, there is always recourse to Castro's monumental ego, to his desire to play a leading role on the international scene.

The point is not whether Castro has a large ego. It is whether this ego significantly shaped Cuba's policy in southern Africa. I have no personal knowledge of Fidel Castro: in nineteen years of research in Cuba, I have never been able to interview him, not for want of trying. Therefore, I must rely on the evidence I have—the more than 15,000 pages of Cuban documents I have amassed for this book (in addition to several thousand I gathered for *Conflicting Missions*), including more than 2,000 pages of transcripts of conversations of Fidel Castro with his brother Raúl and his closest aides. What emerges from these documents is that policy in southern Africa was driven not by Castro's ego, but by his commitment to a cause in which he deeply believed. For Fidel Castro, the struggle against apartheid was "the most beautiful cause."[74]

This conclusion dovetails with that of U.S. intelligence officers, who saw Castro as a leader "engaged in a great crusade," and it echoes Henry Kissinger's assessment when he argued that Castro sent his troops to Angola in 1975 because he "was probably the most genuine revolutionary leader then in power." Castro "places particular importance on maintaining a 'principled' foreign policy," the CIA wrote. "Cuban policy is not free of contradictions. . . . Nevertheless on questions of basic importance such as Cuba's right and duty to support nationalist revolutionary movements and friendly governments in the Third World, Castro permits no compromise of principle for the sake of economic or political expediency."[75]

Obviously, Castro's sense of mission was not the only force shaping his foreign policy, but it was that policy's foundation. Castro felt that "he had a mission to change his country and the world," Leycester Coltman, a former British ambassador to Cuba, argued. This sense of mission—the keynote of Castro's extraordinary life—demands the willingness to sacrifice for the greater good. For Castro, Coltman wrote, "progress was always achieved at a price, often at the price of suffering and bloodshed. . . . The Cuban revolution was not the work of one man or one generation. It was a historical process, started in the independence struggles of the nineteenth century. Thousands had died fighting for it. It was the duty of the present generation to save the Revolution, however arduous the task. Even in capitalist countries, many people looked to Cuba as a beacon of hope. . . . Cuba would not disappoint them."[76] One may agree or disagree with Castro's view of history, but this was certainly Castro's credo in 1959, when he entered Havana in triumph. And it remained his belief over the decades that followed, as he continued to defy Washington's imperial will.

## Visions of Freedom

South Africans, Americans, and Cubans had different visions of freedom for southern Africa. The South Africans claimed they were fighting to stem the communist onslaught. They probably believed it. But they were also fighting for another, more prosaic reason that trumped everything else: to defend apartheid, to uphold racial injustice.

Jimmy Carter wanted to bring about the end of apartheid. And he came out swinging. On his behalf, Vice President Mondale told Prime Minister Vorster in May 1977 that the United States sought majority rule in South Africa, and he uttered those terrible words, "one man, one vote."[77] But it was a grand opening followed by morose silence. Political realities—public opinion in the United States, more pressing problems in southern Africa and throughout the world—stripped the Carter administration of its crusading zeal.

For Namibia, too, Carter wanted freedom. But here, too, the administration's stance was hollow. The United States was the driving force behind Resolution 435—but the resolution left the vital port of Walvis Bay in South Africa's clutches. Worse, Carter shied away from the only weapon that might have forced Pretoria to implement Resolution 435: economic sanctions. Anticommunism trumped the administration's sense of justice: how could the United States slap sanctions on South Africa, Brzezinski successfully argued, when the entire region was threatened by invading Cubans and Soviets?

Carter's vision of freedom for Angola was that the Cuban troops leave the country. The Cold War and imperial hubris trumped logic: Carter approved the presence of French troops in newly independent Djibouti; he applauded the dispatch of French and Belgian troops to save Mobutu's tottering regime; and he knew that the Cuban troops were Angola's only defense against South Africa's aggression. Nevertheless, he demanded that the Cubans leave Angola.

Like Carter, Ronald Reagan wanted to free southern Africa from the communist threat. Unlike Carter, however, he was insensitive to the plight of black South Africans, as even Crocker admitted. Empathy for South Africa's whites replaced Carter's moral indignation, and the "one man, one vote" principle was thrown overboard. In Namibia, the Reagan administration saddled Resolution 435 with linkage, the huge loophole that allowed South Africa to dodge and delay—independence for Namibia would have to wait until the Cuban troops left Angola. In the meantime, Reagan relied on South Africa and on Savimbi—the greatest scourge of the Angolan people.

What about Cuba? What was its vision of freedom in southern Africa? In Angola it supported the government of Agostinho Neto, who was authoritarian, eager to improve the lot of the people, and who lent courageous support to the liberation fighters of South Africa and Namibia. Neto died in 1979, and the government of President dos Santos grew increasingly corrupt and indifferent to the plight of the common people. It had, however, two important pluses: it continued to support the liberation movements in Namibia and South Africa and, for all its faults, it was far better than the alternative, Jonas Savimbi. The Cuban troops did not stay in Angola for more than a decade, however, to keep dos Santos in power. They stayed to defend Angola from South Africa. They stayed to help the ANC and SWAPO. They stayed because the Cuban leaders were convinced that their departure would provide an opportunity for South Africa to impose Savimbi on Angola and a puppet regime on Namibia. They stayed, in other words, to hold the line against apartheid.

I do not know of any other country, in modern times, for which idealism has been such a key component of its foreign policy as for Castro's Cuba. Was it worth it? In terms of Cuba's narrow interests, certainly not. Cuba drew no tangible benefits from its presence in Angola. If, however, one believes that countries have a duty to help other countries—and internationalism is at the core of the Cuban revolution—then the answer is emphatically yes, it was worth it. Any fair assessment of Cuba's foreign policy must recognize its role in changing the course of southern African history despite Washington's best efforts to stop it. There is no other instance in modern history in which a small underdeveloped country has shaped the course of events in a distant region—humiliating one superpower and repeatedly defying the other.

The Cold War framed three decades of Castro's revolutionary zeal, but Castro's vision was always larger than it. For him, the battle against imperialism—his life's raison d'être—was more than the struggle against the United States: it was the war against despair and oppression in the Third World. In July 1991 Nelson Mandela visited Havana and voiced the epitaph to the story of Cuba's aid to Africa during the Cold War. "We come here with a sense of the great debt that is owed the people of Cuba," Mandela said. "What other country can point to a record of greater selflessness than Cuba has displayed in its relations to Africa?"[78]

# *Notes*

NOTE ON CITATIONS

*Documents*

To keep the footnotes as short as possible:

Unless relevant, I do not indicate the place from which the documents originated.

Unless relevant, I list only the two major interlocutors of a memorandum of conversation.

In Cuban documents that identify the sender and addressee by code names, I substitute the real names. In the index, I include the code names with the real names.

I give the page number only if the document is longer than 10 pages. The Oral History Interviews of the Association for Diplomatic Studies and Training are unpaginated.

*Cuban Names*

Cubans have two family names, but generally use only one (usually, but not always, the first) in everyday life. In the text, I follow the common usage, except to distinguish between two people with the same preferred name. In the list of interviews and index, I give the full name.

ABBREVIATIONS

In addition to the abbreviations found in the text, the following source abbreviations are used in the notes.

| | |
|---|---|
| AAD, NSC | African Affairs Directorate, NSC |
| ACC | Archives of the Central Committee of the Cuban Communist Party, Havana |
| *Akten* | Institut für Zeitgeschichte, ed. (on behalf of the German Foreign Ministry), *Akten zur Auswärtigen Politik der Bundesrepublik Deutschland* |
| ALUKA | Digital library of scholarly resources from and about Africa |
| Amconsul | American Consulate |
| Amembassy | American (U.S.) Embassy |
| BC, DHM | Brzezinski Collection, Donated Historical Material |
| BC, NSAd | Brzezinski Collection, National Security Adviser |

| | |
|---|---|
| CC CPSU | Central Committee of the Communist Party of the Soviet Union |
| CECE | Archive of the Ministerio para la Inversión Extranjera y la Colaboración Económica, Havana |
| CF | Archive of the Cuban Armed Forces [Centro de Información de las Fuerzas Armadas Revolucionarias], Havana |
| CHF | Cohen, Herman Files |
| CR | *Congressional Record* |
| CREST | Central Intelligence Agency Records Search Tool, National Archives, College Park, Maryland |
| CWIHP | Cold War International History Project |
| DDR | German Democratic Republic |
| DFA | Archives of the Department of Foreign Affairs of the Republic of South Africa, Pretoria |
| DHL | Dag Hammarskjöld Library, New York City |
| DI | Directorate of Intelligence, CIA |
| DODDC | Department of Defence Documentation Centre, Pretoria |
| DOS | Department of State, United States |
| ed. | editorial |
| EMG | Estado Mayor General |
| ES: MF | Executive Secretariat, Meeting Files |
| ES, NSCCF, Af | Executive Secretariat, NSC, Country File, Africa |
| FIG | Fondazione Istituto Gramsci, Archivio del Partito Comunista Italiano [Archive of the Italian Communist party] |
| FO | British Foreign Office |
| FOIA | Freedom of Information Act |
| FRUS | United States, Department of State, *Foreign Relations of the United States* |
| GRFL | Gerald R. Ford Library, Ann Arbor, Michigan |
| HCFA | U.S. Congress, House, Committee on Foreign Affairs |
| Hqs | headquarters |
| IM | Intelligence memorandum |
| JCL | Jimmy Carter Library, Atlanta |
| JFKL | John F. Kennedy Library, Boston |
| Lake Papers | Papers of Anthony Lake, National Archives |
| LBJL | Lyndon B. Johnson Library, Austin, Texas |
| MAE | Ministère des Affaires Etrangères et Européennes, Direction des Affaires Africaines et Malgaches, Angola, 1973–78, Paris |
| Memcon | Memorandum of conversation |
| MF | Microfiche |
| MINREX | Archives of the Cuban Foreign Ministry, Havana |
| MMCA | Cuban Military Mission in Angola |
| "MMCA—EMG" | Conversation between a senior officer of the Cuban military mission in Angola and a senior officer of the armed forces general staff in Havana. All CF. |
| "MMCA—RPA" | same as above |

| NA | National Archives, College Park, Maryland |
| NIE | National Intelligence Estimate, CIA |
| NSA | National Security Archive, Washington, D.C. |
| NSAd | National Security Adviser |
| NSF | National Security Files |
| NSFCF | National Security File Country File |
| *NYT* | *New York Times* |
| OCI | Office of Current Intelligence, CIA |
| OH | Oral History Interview |
| OS | Oficina Secreta 2do Sec CC PCC [Secret Bureau of the 2nd Secretary of the Communist Party of Cuba], Havana |
| *PP* | United States, General Services Administration, *Public Papers of the Presidents of the United States* |
| PPP | Pre-Presidential Papers |
| PPS | Policy Planning Staff, U.S. State Department |
| PRO | Public Record Office, Kew, Surrey |
| *RDM* | *Rand Daily Mail* (Johannesburg) |
| RG | Record Group |
| RRL | Ronald Reagan Library, Simi Valley, California |
| RSA | Republic of South Africa |
| SAPMO | Stiftung Archiv der Parteien und Massenorganisationen der DDR im Bundesarchiv, Berlin |
| SCFR | Senate Committee on Foreign Relations |
| SecState | secretary of state |
| SNF | Subject-Numeric Files: 1963–73, RG 59, NA |
| SSC | State Security Council of South Africa |
| SVR | Staatsveiligheidsraad, National Archives, Pretoria |
| Tel. interview | Telephone interview |
| Tito Archive | Arhiv Jugoslavije, Arhiv Josipa Broza Tito [Archives of Yugoslavia, Archive of Josip Broz Tito] |
| UNIP | United National Independence Party |
| WHCF | White House Central File |
| WITS | University of Witwatersrand, William Cullen Library, South African History Archive, Johannesburg |
| WOA | Washington Office on Africa |
| *WP* | *Washington Post* |
| WR | weekly report |
| *WSJ* | *Wall Street Journal* |
| *WT* | *Washington Times* |

PROLOGUE

1. Mitchell, "Cold War," p. 67.

2. "Points Made by Dr. Jonas Savimbi during a Meeting on May 28, 1983," Samesprekings met Angola, v. 2, DFA.

3. Goulding, *Peacemonger*, p. 193.

4. Secretariat SSC, "'nasionale Staatkundige en Veiligheidstrategie vir SWA en Angola," Sept. 23, 1983, p. 16, SVR.

5. Bowdler to SecState, Mar. 19, 1977, FOIA.

6. J. Geldenhuys, *Dié*, p. 45.

7. *Daily Telegraph* (London), May 24, 1985, p. 22 (ed.).

8. Sparks, *Tomorrow*, p. 48.

9. CIA, DI, "South Africa: Time Running Out. Revisited," Jan. 10, 1986, p. 2, FOIA.

10. Secretariat SCC, "Strategiese Riglyne: Tov Angola: Nr 22," June 1987, p. 9, SVR.

11. CIA, "Angola Cuba: Some Strains but No New Developments," Apr. 9, 1979, CREST.

12. Reagan, July 9, 1979, broadcast, PPP, ser. 1a, box 36, RRL.

13. National Coalition of Americans Committed to Rescuing Africa from the Grip of Soviet Tyranny, *WT*, Dec. 7, 1984, p. A5.

14. Howard Phillips, *WT*, Dec. 23, 1985, p. A10.

15. "Reunión con el Ministro de Defensa de la URSS en el Ministerio de Defensa," Nov. 27, 1987, p. 18, CF.

16. Gorbachev, *Zhizn'*, 2:421–22.

17. Special NIE, "Soviet Military Support to Angola: Intentions and Prospects," Oct. 1985, p. 7, FOIA.

18. Shevardnadze et al., "Po voprosu kompensazii postavkami iz Sovetskovo Soiuza Respublike Kuba vooruzhenia, kotore mozhet bit' ostavleno kubinskimi voiskami v Narodnoi Respublike Angola," Jan. 31, 1989, enclosed in Politburo meeting, Feb. 7, 1989, NSA.

19. Adamishin, *Beloe Solntse*, p. 204.

20. Akhromeyev, in Akhromeyev and Kornienko, *Glazami*, p. 23; Kornienko, *Kholodnaya voina*, p. 167; interview with Adamishin.

21. V. Shubin, *Hot "Cold War."*

22. Interview with Mendes de Carvalho; Memcon (Castro, dos Santos), Dec. 17, 1988, p. 2, CF.

23. Mandela, July 26, 1991, *Granma* (Havana), July 27, 1991, p. 3.

24. "Indicaciones concretas del Comandante en Jefe que guiarán la actuación de la delegación cubana a las conversaciones en Luanda y las negociaciones en Londres (23-4-88)," p. 5, CF.

CHAPTER 1

1. Shakhnazarov, *Tsena*, p. 384 quoted; Chernyaev, "Diary," entry of 15 Jan. 1989.

2. Gorbachev, *Zhizn'*, 2:425.

3. Memcon (Axen, Risquet), Apr. 14, 1989, p. 4, DY30 IVA 2/20/205, SAPMO. On Gorbachev's visit, see also "Zapiski osnovnovo soderzhania besed M. S. Gorbachev s F. Kastro v Gavane," Apr. 3–4, 1989, p. 38 (courtesy of Sergey Radchenko); Gorbachev, *Zhizn'*, 2:425–29; Memcon (Risquet, Honecker), Apr. 17, 1989, DY30 JIV 958, SAPMO.

4. [Gorbachev,] "Ob itogakh visita Gorbacheva na Kube," Apr. 13, 1989, NSA.

5. Memcon (Castro, dos Santos), Dec. 17, 1988, p. 28, CF.

6. See Akhromeyev and Kornienko, *Glazami*, pp. 250–51; Schoultz, *Infernal*, pp. 425–49.

7. Martí to Manuel Mercado, May 18, 1895, in Martí, *Epistolario*, 5:250. This and the

next five sections of this chapter (until "The Turnhalle Conference") are based on my book, *Conflicting Missions*. Here I will only give the sources of direct quotations.

8. Szulc, *Fidel*, p. 13.

9. "Unofficial Visit of Prime Minister Castro of Cuba to Washington—A Tentative Evaluation," enclosed in Herter to Eisenhower, Apr. 23, 1959, *FRUS 1958–60*, 6:483; Special NIE, "The Situation in the Caribbean through 1959," June 30, 1959, p. 3, NSA.

10. Eisenhower press conference, Oct. 28, 1959, in *PP*, 1959, p. 271; Nancy Mitchell, "Remember the Myth," *News and Observer* (Raleigh), Nov. 1, 1998, p. G5.

11. Schlesinger, *Robert Kennedy*, p. 516.

12. McNamara, in Chang and Kornbluh, *Missile Crisis*, pp. xi–xii.

13. Castro to Khrushchev, Oct. 31, 1962, in Blight, Allyn, and Welch, *Cuba*, p. 491.

14. McCone, memo of meeting with president, Aug. 23, 1962, *FRUS 1961–63*, 10:955.

15. Castro, *Revolución* (Havana), Feb. 23, 1963, p. 4; NIE, "Latin American Reactions to Developments in and with Respect to Cuba," July 18, 1961, p. 5, NSF, NIE, box 8/9, LBJL.

16. CIA, DI, "Cuban Subversive Activities in Latin America, 1959–1968," Feb. 16, 1968, pp. 1–2, NSFCF, box 19, LBJL.

17. "Discurso pronunciado en la reunión consultiva de los Partidos Comunistas y Obreros que se celebra en Moscú," Mar. 3, 1965, p. 3, OS.

18. DOS, "Cuban Presence in Africa," Dec. 28, 1977, p. 4, FOIA.

19. "National Policy Paper—Cuba: United States Policy," draft, July 15, 1968, p. 16, FOIA.

20. Memcon (Raúl Castro, Mengistu), Jan. 7, 1978, p. 61, OS.

21. Hughes to SecState, "Soviet Intentions toward Cuba," Mar. 12, 1965, NSFCF, box 33/37, LBJL.

22. CIA, Board of National Estimates, "Bolsheviks and Heroes: The USSR and Cuba," Nov. 21, 1967, FOIA.

23. I refer to the former French colony as Congo Brazzaville and the former Belgian colony as Zaire.

24. Special NIE, "Cuba: Castro's Problems and Prospects over the Next Year or Two," June 27, 1968, p. 3, NSF, NIE, box 8/9, LBJL.

25. "National Policy Paper—Cuba: United States Policy," draft, July 15, 1968, p. 15, FOIA.

26. José Ramón Machado Ventura, note to author, Havana, July 12, 1995.

27. Hughes to SecState, "Che Guevara's African Venture," Apr. 19, 1965, NSFCF, box 20, LBJL; Che Guevara, "Pasajes de la guerra revolucionaria (Congo)," [Dar-es-Salaam, c. Dec. 1965], pp. 13–14, private collection, Havana.

28. President Luís Cabral, *Nõ Pintcha* (Bissau), Jan. 22, 1977, p. 4.

29. Interview with Víctor Dreke.

30. Quotations from: Denney to SecState, "Cuban Foreign Policy," Sept. 15, 1967, p. 5, Pol 1 Cuba, Subject—Numeric Files: 1963–73, RG 59, NA; Special NIE, "Cuba: Castro's Problems and Prospects over the Next Year or Two," June 27, 1968, p. 3, NSF, NIE, box 8/9, LBJL; CIA, DI, "Cuban Subversive Policy and the Bolivian Guerrilla Episode," May 1968, p. 3, NSFCF, box 19, LBJL; Special NIE, "The Situation in the Caribbean through 1959," June 30, 1959, p. 3, NSA; NIE, "The Situation in Cuba," June 14, 1960, p. 9, NSA.

31. Marcum, *Angolan Revolution*, 1:19.

32. Stewart (British consul, Luanda), "Political Changes in Angola during the Last Year," Jan. 9, 1965, FO 371/181969, PRO.

33. Neto, "A fase actual da nossa luta," in MPLA, "1a Assembleia Regional (1a e 2a Regiões)," Brazzaville, Feb. 22–25, 1968, in Mabeko Tali, *Dissidências*, 1:114.

34. CIA, OCI, "The Angolan Rebellion and White Unrest," Apr. 5, 1963, p. 2, NSF, box 5, JFKL; Hughes (INR) to SecState, "Prospects for Angolan Nationalist Movement," Nov. 5, 1963, p. 19, NSF, box 5, JFKL; Hilsman (INR) to SecState, Aug. 7, 1962, ibid.

35. Lessing, "Bericht über den Besuch des Präsidenten der MPLA, Dr. Agostinho Neto, in der DDR vom 20. bis 23. Mai 1963," p. 5, DY30 IVA 2/20/948, SAPMO; Davidson, *Eye*, p. 224.

36. Carreira, *O pensamento*, p. 31. There is no authoritative biography of Neto. The best is Barradas's sympathetic *Agostinho Neto*.

37. Commission for International Cooperation and Relations of the League of Communists of the Socialist Federative Popular Republic of Yugoslavia, "Angola i Narodni Pokret za Oslobodjenje Angole /MPLA/," Feb. 1971, p. 12, Tito Archive.+

38. Tel. interview with U.S. consul general Killoran; Robert Hultslander, CIA station chief, Luanda, 1975, fax to author, Dec. 22, 1998.

39. Amconsul Luanda to DOS, Nov. 13, 1968, Pol 27 Ang, SNF, NA; Amconsul Luanda to DOS, Jan. 21, 1969, Pol 23–9 Ang, SNF, NA; INR, "Angola: An Assessment of the Insurgency," Sept. 16, 1970, ibid.; Lúcio Lara, "A história do MPLA," n.d., p. 124, private collection, Luanda.

40. Costa Gomes, *Sobre Portugal*, p. 31.

41. Tel. interview with Briggs; annex IV, enclosed in DOS, "United States Policy toward Angola," Dec. 16, 1975, DOS MF 8704129/2; tel. interview with Killoran.

42. Hultslander, fax to author, Dec. 22, 1998.

43. On this point, see the exchange between the author and Jorge Dominguez, a prominent expert on Cuba, in http://www.h-net.org/~diplo/reviews/jcws/jcws2006 .html#gleijeses_one.

44. Spies, *Operasie Savannah*, p. 108. In 1978 the South African Defense Ministry commissioned a study by Professor F. J. du Toit Spies on South Africa's role in the 1975–76 Angolan civil war and gave him access to the closed government archives. His report was approved by a supervisory committee led by an army general and including representatives from the Ministries of Defense and Foreign Affairs and from academia. It was published as *Operasie Savannah. Angola, 1975–1976*. A member of Spies's supervisory committee, Commander Sophie du Preez, also published a book based essentially on the same documentation (*Avontuur in Angola*). These are the only two published accounts based on South African documents.

45. PW Botha, Apr. 17, 1978, RSA, *Hansard—Debates of the House of Assembly*, col. 4852.

46. Ball, *The Past*, p. 374.

47. Dobrynin, *In Confidence*, p. 362; CIA, "Cuban Foreign Policy and Activities Abroad," Feb. 5, 1981, p. 2, ES: MF, box 1, RRL; Kissinger, *Years*, p. 816.

48. That Havana acted independently and challenged Moscow in late 1975 turns conventional wisdom about the relationship between Cuba and the Soviet Union on its

head—so much so that even serious scholars are tempted to ignore the evidence detailed in Cuban and U.S. documents that dovetail with remarkable precision and regularity. See Westad, *Global Cold War*, pp. 234-36, and Gleijeses, *Conflicting Missions*, pp. 367-69; see also the exchange between Westad and Gleijeses on Feb. 19-21, 2007 (h-diplo@ MAIL.H-NET.MSU.EDU).

49. "Indicaciones concretas del Comandante en Jefe que guiarán la actuación de la delegación cubana a las conversaciones en Luanda y las negociaciones en Londres (23-4-88)," p. 5, CF.

50. Kissinger, *Years*, p. 785.

51. Roger Sargent, *RDM*, Feb. 17, 1976, p. 10.

52. *World* (Johannesburg), Feb. 24, 1976, p. 4.

53. "Notas vir minister: Angola en sy invloed op die suiderafrikaanse situasie, met besondere verwysing na SWA," June 1976, p. 19, M, gr. 4, box 172, DODDC.

54. Du Preez, *Avontuur*, p. 21.

55. *Le Monde*, Aug. 17, 1975, p. 3. On Vorster's détente policy, see Anglin and Shaw, *Foreign Policy*, pp. 272-309; Tamarkin, *Zimbabwe*, pp. 20-77; Martin and Johnson, *Struggle*, pp. 115-90; du Pisani, *SWA/Namibia*, pp. 272-80.

56. Burger, "Teeninsurgensie," pp. 187-99, 206-14, 277-97; Ellert, *Rhodesian*, pp. 110-23 (Ellert was a senior Rhodesian intelligence officer); DOS, "South Africa: Policy Review," June 1974, enclosed in Easum and Lord to SecState, June 24, 1974, PPS, box 344.

57. CIA, IM, "South Africa's Policy toward Namibia: A Review of Basic Factors," May 20, 1977, NLC-6-69-10-7-2, JCL.

58. Damara headman Justus Garoeb, *Windhoek Advertiser*, Aug. 28, 1975, p. 1.

59. On the Turnhalle conference, see du Pisani, *SWA/Namibia*, pp. 272-387, and Soggot, *Namibia*, pp. 183-203. Two useful files of documents are "Constitutional Conference in Windhoek," FCO 45/1933, PRO, and "Internal Situation in Namibia," FCO 45/1934, PRO.

60. Du Pisani, *SWA/Namibia*, pp. 293, 378; CIA, Weekly Summary, Aug. 29, 1975, CREST; Peter Katjivivi, SWAPO Western European representative, *Windhoek Advertiser*, Sept. 3, 1975, p. 3.

61. "Presidential Review Memorandum," [early 1977], p. 4, FOIA.

62. CIA, IM, "South Africa's Policy toward Namibia: A Review of Basic Factors," May 20, 1977, p. 2, NLC-6-69-10-7-2, JCL.

63. "Reunión del Comandante en jefe con los políticos para analizar la situación de las tropas cubanas en la RPA," Dec. 9, 1987, pp. 5-6, CF.

64. Castro, in Ramonet, *Cien horas*, p. 367.

65. Memcon (Castro and military commanders of the Cuban military mission in Angola), Sept. 9, 1986, p. 5, CF.

66. "Reunión de análisis de la situación de las tropas cubanas en la RPA, efectuada a partir de las 17:25 horas del 15.11.1987," p. 168, CF.

67. Castro, Dec. 2, 2005, *Juventud Rebelde* (Havana), Dec. 3, 2005, p. 4.

68. Memcon (Fidel and Raúl Castro, Colomé), Oct. 10, 1981, CF.

69. Raúl Castro, in "Primera Reunión con Neto," Apr. 21, 1976, in "Informe al Buró Político del Segundo Secretario del Comité Central del Partido Comunista de Cuba

acerca de su visita a la República Popular de Angola, República Popular del Congo, y República Popular de Guinea, además de su visita a la URSS (19 de abril a 7 junio de 1976)," p. 5, OS.

70. Castro, Dec. 2, 2005, *Juventud Rebelde*, Dec. 3, 2005, p. 4.

71. "Segunda Reunión con Neto," Apr. 22, 1976, in "Informe al Buró Político," pp. 12–13.

72. Risquet to Raúl Castro, June 10, 1976, ACC.

73. Kissinger, NSC meetings, Apr. 7 and May 11, 1976, both National Security Adviser, NSC Meetings Minutes, box 2, GRFL; *Newsweek*, May 10, 1976, p. 51.

74. Embassy of South Africa, "Amerikaanse reaksie op Dr. Kissinger se nuwe Afrikabeleid," May 17, 1976, 1/33/8/3 v. 26 U.S.A. Policy in Africa, DFA. The best analysis of Kissinger's Rhodesia policy is Mitchell, "Race and the Cold War," which will be ready for publication in 2013.

75. See Resolution 385 in www.un.org/documents.

76. See UNSC S/12211, Oct. 15, 1976, and UNSC Official Records, 1963rd meeting, Oct. 19, 1976, DHL.

CHAPTER 2

1. "Presidential Review Memorandum: Rhodesia, Namibia and South Africa," [early 1977], p. 2, FOIA.

2. NSC meeting,"Summary and Conclusions," Mar. 3, 1977, FOIA.

3. "Presidential Review Memorandum," p. 4.

4. Vance, *Choices*, p. 274; "Presidential Review Memorandum," p. 20.

5. Mondale to Carter, Apr. 8, 1977, BC, DHM, box 14, JCL.

6. "Southern Africa—Policy Review," p. 11, enclosed in Dodson to Vice President et al., July 19, 1977, FOIA.

7. NSC meeting, Mar. 3, 1977, p. 6, FOIA.

8. Interview with McHenry. The most important accounts by protagonists of Carter's policy toward Namibia are Vance's *Choices*, pp. 256–57, 272–83, 302–13, and McHenry's OH, but both are, unfortunately, very discreet. My account in this book is based on my article, "Test of Wills." See also Dreyer, *Namibia*, pp. 105–44, and Karns, "Ad Hoc."

9. Vance to Carter, Apr. 6, 1977, NLC-11-1-7-42-5, JCL; Vance, *Choices*, pp. 70–72.

10. José Eduardo dos Santos, in Federal Secretariat for Foreign Affairs, "Izvestaj o zvanicnoj poseti predsednika NR Angole dr. Augustina Neta Jugoslaviji od 22. do 25. aprila 1977," May 12, 1977, p. 4, Tito Archive. On Shaba I, see Gleijeses, "Truth"; Mitchell, "Race and the Cold War," ch. 4.

11. CIA, "Weekly Summary," May 27, 1977, CREST.

12. See Mitchell, "Race and the Cold War," ch. 3.

13. The best discussion of the Carter administration and Mobutu is Pachter, "Our Man." On Mobutu and Angola in 1975, see Gleijeses, *Conflicting Missions*.

14. *NYT*, Mar. 20, 1977, IV:1.

15. Carter's press conference, Apr. 22, 1977, *PP*, 1977, 1:703.

16. W. Smith, *Closest*, p. 121.

17. On Cuba and the Katangans, see Gleijeses, "Truth."

18. Vance, *Choices*, pp. 70–71.

19. Memcon (Garba, Vance, Brzezinski), Mar. 21, 1977, FOIA.

20. Young to Carter, Mondale, Vance, and Brzezinski, May 4, 1977, BC, NSAd (8), Agency, box 22, JCL; interview with Paulo Jorge, who added that he never met Mondale.

21. Frank [no family name] to Vance, July 7, 1977, FOIA.

22. Interviews with Lake (quoted), Moose (quoted), Spiegel (quoted), and McHenry; Brzezinski to Vance, Oct. 17, 1977, NLC-6-4-3-11-6, JCL.

23. Presidential Directive/NSC-6, Mar. 15, 1977, Vertical File: Presidential Directives, JCL. The best studies on U.S.-Cuban relations in the Carter years are W. Smith, *Closest*, pp. 101–237, and Schoultz, *Infernal*, pp. 291–361. For the perspective of the NSC's Cuba expert, see Pastor, "The Carter-Castro Years." For the Cuban perspective, see Ramírez Cañedo and Morales Domínguez, *Confrontación*.

24. DOS, "Cuban Presence in Africa," Dec. 28, 1978, pp. 6–7, FOIA.

25. DOS memo [title sanitized], enclosed in Pastor to Aaron, Aug. 7, 1978, Vertical File—Cuba, JCL; Memcon (Todman, Malmierca), Apr. 27, 1977, MINREX; Risquet to Castro, Feb. 18, 1977, ACC. In early 1977 Angola was the only country in Africa where there were Cuban troops in any significant number. There were also about 1,000 Cuban soldiers in the Congo, but U.S. officials believed, correctly, that this was "directly related to military activities in Angola." ("Soviet, Chinese and Cuban Presence in Sub-Saharan Africa," p. 5, enclosed in "Tanzania, Nyerere; President Visit to US, 1977," [Sept. 1977], FOIA).

26. See Risquet, in "Conversaciones entre representantes del MPLA-PT y el PCC," Dec. 28, 1981, p. 39, ACC.

27. Church to Carter, Aug. 12, 1977, FOIA.

28. Risquet to Neto, [Feb. 1978], pp. 1–2, ACC.

29. Peyronnet to de Guiringaud, May 5, 1977, MAE; Memcon (Castro, dos Santos), Mar. 17, 1984, p. 23, ACC.

30. Memcon (Richmond, Nolan, Castro), pp. 7, 8, 10, 12, enclosed in Richmond to Carter, Dec. 16, 1977, WHCF, box CO-20, JCL.

31. Henze to Brzezinski, June 3, 1980, BC, NSAd, Staff Material, Horn, box 5, JCL. The best discussion of Carter and the Horn is Mitchell's masterful "Race and the Cold War." (See also D. Jackson, *Carter*.) There is no equivalent on Soviet policy in the Horn, but see Mitchell, "Race and the Cold War," and Westad, *Global Cold War*, pp. 250–87.

32. Memcon (Vance, Huang Hua), Aug. 23, 1977, p. 14, FOIA.

33. MINFAR, "Las misiones internacionalistas desarrolladas por las FAR en defensa de la independencia y la soberanía de los pueblos," n.d., p. 65, CF; Castro to Ochoa, Aug. 16, 1977, CF.

34. Brezhnev to Castro, Nov. 27, 1977, CF.

35. Republic of Russia, Ministry of Defense, *Rossiya*, p. 111.

36. Memcon (Castro, Neto), Jan. 24, 1979, p. 23, Consejo de Estado.

37. Brzezinski to Carter, [late Mar. 1977], FOIA; Memcon (Honecker, Castro), Apr. 3, 1977, pp. 20–21, 23, DY30 JIV 2/201/1292, SAPMO.

38. These documents are located in CF; I have copies of all of them.

39. CIA, Weekly Summary, May 28, 1976, CREST; DOS, "Current Foreign Assistance," and "The Case for Continued Assistance," enclosed in Tarnoff to Brzezinski, [May 1978], Warren Christopher Papers, box 16, NA. On the early years of the Ethiopian revolution,

see Ottaway and Ottaway, *Ethiopia*; Lefort, *Éthiopie*; Tubiana, *La révolution*; Tiruneh, *Ethiopian Revolution*; Tareke, *Ethiopian Revolution*.

40. "Síntesis analítica sobre la revolución etiopica. Proposiciones" [Mar. 1977], CF.

41. Henze to Brzezinski, Mar. 1, 1978, BC, NSAd, Staff Material, Horn, box 1, JCL.

42. Amembassy Lagos to SecState, Jan. 16, 1978, FOIA. At the end of Shaba I, Egypt sent a few pilots to Zaire. Saudi Arabia paid the expenses of the Moroccan troops.

43. See Dobrynin, *In Confidence*, pp. 386–90.

44. Garthoff, *Détente*, p. 626; Vance and Warnke to Carter, Aug. 30, 1977, FOIA; Kornienko, *Kholodnaya voina*, p. 174.

45. For the text of the communiqué, see *NYT*, Oct. 2, 1977, p. 16.

46. Kornienko, *Kholodnaya voina*, p. 183.

47. Quotations from Jordan, memo for the president, [c. June 1977], FOIA, and Quandt, *Peace Process*, p. 267.

48. Brzezinski, *Power*, p. 189.

49. "SCC Meeting on Horn of Africa, 2 March 1978," p. 8, FOIA.

50. Brzezinski to President, Mar. 3, 1978, p. 3, BC, DHM, box 28, JCL; Carter, Address at Wake Forest University, May 17, 1978, *PP*, 1978, 1:531.

51. "Response, Presidential Review Memorandum—36: Soviet—Cuban Presence in Africa," Aug. 18, 1978, p. 15, NSA; Pastor to Brzezinski, Sept. 21, 1979, WHCF, box CO-21, JCL.

52. Brzezinski, *Power*, p. 182.

53. Brzezinski to Carter, May 1, 1980, BC, DHM, box 23, JCL.

54. SCC, "The Horn of Africa," Feb. 22, 1978, p. 15, ibid. See also "SCC Meeting on Horn of Africa, Mar. 2, 1978, 12:50–2:25 P.M.," NSA, and Mitchell, "Race and the Cold War." For Brzezinski's less than candid account, see *Power*, pp. 178–90.

55. NSC meeting, Feb. 23, 1978, p. 14, NSA; SCC meeting, Mar. 2, 1978, pp. 12–13, FOIA; SCC meeting, Apr. 7, 1978, pp. 2–3, BC, DHM, box 28, JCL.

56. SCC meeting, May 15, 1978, p. 3, BC, DHM, box 28, JCL.

57. *WP*, May 24, 1978, p. 1; May 25, p. 1.

58. *WP*, June 27, 1978, p. 7.

59. Wicker, op-ed, *NYT*, June 30, 1978, p. 27.

60. NSC meeting, Feb. 23, 1978, p. 14 (emphasis added), NSA; Brzezinski to President, Mar. 3, 1978, p. 4 (emphasis added), BC, DHM, box 28, JCL.

61. Interviews with McHenry and Newsom. On the Reagan administration soliciting aid for the Contras from third countries, see *WT*, June 3, 1987, p. A1; McFarlane, *Trust*, pp. 69–74; Reagan, *Reagan Diaries*, Feb. 12, 1985, 1:425; Gates, *Shadows*, p. 400; Simpson, *Prince*, pp. 114–22.

62. Vance to Carter, June 19, 1978, NLC-128-13-9-14-1, JCL.

63. Tel. interview with Brzezinski.

64. Interview with General Thirion.

65. Herbert Weiss, op-ed, *NYT*, Apr. 29, 1977, p. 51.

66. Braeckman, "La saga," p. 147.

67. See Amnesty International, *Human Rights*, pp. 5, 20; Buyseniers, *L'Église*, pp. 21–44; *NYT*, Apr. 30, 1978, p. 1; *WP*, June 4, 1978, p. 1.

68. Lannon Walker, Mar. 2, 1978, U.S. Congress, House, Committee on International

Relations, *Economic and Military Assistance Programs*, p. 194; *NYT*, May 7, 1978, 3:11. Also "Zaire," in Thornton to Aaron, June 5, 1978, WHCF, box CO-67, JCL.

69. Risquet to Castro, Feb. 21, 1978, ACC.

70. Risquet to Neto, [Feb. 1978], pp. 4–5, ACC.

71. Ibid., pp. 8–9, 11–12.

72. Risquet to Castro, Feb. 21, 1978, ACC; Neto to Risquet, Feb. 21, 1978, ACC.

73. General Yves Gras, in Cohen and Smouts, *La politique*, p. 320. On Shaba II, see Gleijeses, "Truth."

74. Interview with Agramonte.

75. Memcon (Casas, Neto), May 19, 1978, pp. 3–4, ACC.

76. Ibid., pp. 7, 9.

77. Vance to Lane, May 19, 1978, FOIA. Also *NYT*, May 19, 1978, p. 1.

78. *NYT*, May 20, 1978, p. 4; May, 23, p. 14 quoted.

79. Lane to DOS, May 19, 1978, FOIA.

80. Carter, handwritten minutes, 1:30 P.M. meeting, June 2, 1978, Office of the Staff Secretary, box 89, JCL; Brzezinski, in *Meet the Press*, May 28, 1978, DOS *Bulletin*, July 1978, p. 26; interview with Lake.

81. Powell, *WP*, June 14, 1978, p. 1.

82. Kissinger, *NYT*, June 16, 1978, p. 27.

83. Pastor to Aaron, Aug. 7, 1978, p. 1 quoted, and enclosures, Vertical File—Cuba, JCL. The CIA had concluded that "On balance he [Castro] has a fairly good track record for veracity." (CIA, "Shaba, Castro, and the Evidence," June 6, 1978, NLC-6-13-4-13-3, JCL)

84. Memcon (Castro, dos Santos), Mar. 17, 1984, p. 30, ACC.

85. Vance, in Memcon (Gromyko, Vance), May 31, 1978, pp. V-58–V-59, Vertical File: USSR/US Conference, box 2, JCL; Brzezinski, *Power*, p. 209 (emphasis added); Vance, *Choices*, p. 90.

86. Interview with Cutler.

87. *WP*, June 4, 1978, p. 17.

88. *NYT*, July 11, 1978, p. 2.

89. Interview with Wayne Smith.

90. Memcon (Genscher, de Guiringaud), Feb. 6, 1978, *Akten*, 1978, 1:200–202; "NATO Ratstagung in Washington," May 30, 1978, ibid., pp. 844–50.

91. Interview with Claudia Uushona.

92. McGill Alexander, "Cassinga," p. 144. General Alexander's is the only study of the operation based on South African documents and, as such, its only serious military analysis.

93. Memcon (Risquet, Nujoma), May 12, 1978, ACC.

94. MINFAR, "Mensaje trasmitido por el J'RIM Sur," [May 1978,] CF; General Menéndez Tomassevich, "Informe de la Comisión del EM de la MMCA sobre la agresión surafricana al poblado de Cassinga el 4 de mayo de 1978," May 6, 1978, CF.

95. Steenkamp, *Borderstrike!*, p. 90; McGill Alexander, "Cassinga," pp. 146, 155, 185.

96. Memcon (Casas, Neto), May 19, 1978, pp. 7–9, ACC.

97. *Times* (London), May 10, 1978, p. 7.

98. Bwakira, Ortiz-Blanco, and Sellström, "Rapport," pp. 1–2. See also UNICEF Area Office, "Report on a Mission to SWAPO Centres for Namibia Refugees in Angola from

10 to 14 April 1978," Brazzaville, May 2, 1978; Sellström, *Sweden*, 2:349–56; Heywood, *Cassinga*; Truth and Reconciliation Commission of South Africa, *Report*, 2:46–55; Collelo, *Angola*, p. 46. For perspectives that defend Pretoria's handling of the operation, see Steenkamp, *Borderstrike!*, pp. 1–141; Barnard, "Die gebeure"; Breytenbach, *Eagle Strike!*; McWilliams, *Battle*.

99. Brzezinski to Carter, May 8, 1978, NLC-1-6-2-24-6, JCL.

100. My comment on the Western press is based on my examination of the *New York Times, Washington Post, Chicago Tribune, Globe and Mail* (Toronto), *Le Devoir* (Montreal), *Times* (London), *Daily Telegraph* (London); *Le Soir* (Brussels); *Le Monde, Le Figaro* (Paris); *Corriere della Sera* (Milan), *La Stampa* (Turin), *Die Welt* (Hamburg), *Frankfurter Allgemeine*.

101. See UNSC Official Records, 2078th Meeting, May 6, 1978, pp. 1–20, DHL, and Resolutions and Decisions of the Security Council, Resolution 428 (1978) of May 6, 1978, pp. 9–10, DHL.

102. Carter, in "Informal Exchange with Reporters," May 5, 1978, *PP*, 1978, 1:855; Risquet, in Memcon (Risquet, Nujoma), May 12, 1978, pp. 4–5, ACC.

103. *WP*, May 19, 1978, pp. 1, 24.

104. CIA, "Shaba, Castro, and the Evidence," June 6, 1978, NLC-6-13-4-13-3, JCL; "Conversaciones entre representantes del MPLA-PT y el PCC," Dec. 28, 1981, p. 39, ACC.

105. Neto, speech to the 15th Summit of the OAU, July 20, 1978, *Jornal de Angola* (Luanda), July 21, 1978, p. 3.

106. Amembassy Praia to RUEHC/SecState, July 10, 1978, FOIA.

CHAPTER 3

1. Wilkowski to SecState, Jan. 24, 1975, sec. 2, p. 2, DOS MF8802086/2; Lúcio Lara, "A história do MPLA," n.d., p. 94, private collection, Luanda; Moorcraft, *Nemesis*, p. 69; Savimbi, *A Provincia de Angola* (Luanda), Mar. 14, 1975, p. 5. The only informative biography of Savimbi, *Savimbi*, by Fred Bridgland, is undermined by its pervasive pro-Savimbi bias. Five equally biased but far more superficial biographies are Kalflèche, *Savimbi*; Loiseau and Roux, *Portrait*; Vinicius and Saldanha, *Savimbi*; Bréhèret, Sablier, and d'Ormesson, *Savimbi*; Palla and Soares, *Savimbi*. Guerra, *Savimbi*, is very critical of its subject, but equally superficial.

2. Costa Gomes, "Costa Gomes," p. 6; Savimbi to Portuguese authorities, [early Feb. 1972,] in "'Operação Madeira' tenta portugalizar a UNITA," *Expresso* (Lisbon), Nov. 24, 1979, p. 26. *Expresso* published numerous documents in three consecutive issues: Nov. 17, 1979, pp. 18–19; Nov. 24, pp. 25–26; Nov. 30, pp. 8–11.

3. Correia, "Portugal," p. 150.

4. Costa Gomes, *Sobre Portugal*, p. 32; Silva Cunha, *O Ultramar*, pp. 333–34.

5. General Heitor Hamilton Almendra, in Antunes, *A guerra*, 2:738; Costa Gomes, in ibid., 1:118–20; Silva Cunha, *O Ultramar*, p. 334. On Savimbi's collusion with the Portuguese, see also Cabrita Mateus, *A PIDE/DGS*, pp. 199–207, which is based on Portuguese documents and, for more testimonies by Portuguese officials: Caetano, *Depoimento*, pp. 180–81; Correia, *Descolonização*, pp. 37–40; Antunes, *A guerra*, 1:408–9; Guerra, *Memória*, pp. 168–73; Melo, *Os anos*, 1:123–27; Cruzeiro, *Costa Gomes*, pp. 135–36. Also Gleijeses, *Conflicting Missions*, pp. 239–41.

6. Killoran to SecState, Jan. 16, 1975, DOS MF 8802086/2.

7. Guerra, *Memória*, p. 416.

8. General Viljoen, "Notas oor 'n besoek aan Savimbi," Sept. 15, 1975, p. 4 quoted, HS OPS, gr. 1, box 9, DODDC; Spies, *Operasie*, pp. 60–72; du Preez, *Avontuur*, pp. 13–26.

9. SADF, "Op Savannah Beslissings 16 Okt 75," HS OP, gr. 1, box 9, DODDC.

10. "Notas: Mededeling aan leiers van UNITA/FNLA: 25/12/75," ibid., box 11.

11. Interviews with General Thirion (quoted) and UNITA General Nunda. Also Hoof van die Leër, "Waardering in breë trekke van die situasie in die gebied van 101 Taakmag," Feb. 1976, HS OP, gr. 1, box 7, DODDC. The only useful account of Savimbi's activities in the late 1970s is Bridgland's very sympathetic *Savimbi*, pp. 144ff.

12. Quotations from Breytenbach, *Buffalo Soldiers*, p. 148, and *They Live*, p. 187, and from Barlow, *Executive Outcomes*, p. 21. Also Stiff, *Silent War*, pp. 186–204, 234–38; Greeff, *Greater Share*, pp. 86–101; Nortje, *32 Battalion*, pp. 95–124; Bothma, *Die Buffel Struikel*, pp. 72–100.

13. Quotations from Brzezinski to Carter, Aug. 23, 1977, NLC-1-3-5-6-6, JCL, and Memcon (Brzezinski, Han Hsu), Aug. 2, 1977, p. 3, FOIA.

14. S. A. Maonde, Zambian chargé in Beijing, to Zambian foreign minister Mwala, [Aug. 1978], p. 7 quoted, 151 UNIP 7/23/65, UNIP; interview with Nunda; Memcon (Simpson, Chitunda), Mar. 23 and 24, 1982, FOIA.

15. "Saudi Ambassador interview with SUSRIS," Mar. 2, 2006, pp. 9–10, http://www .saudiembassy.net/2006News/Statements/TransDetail.asp?cIndex=590. Also NSC, "Considerations on Regional Conflicts," [1978], FOIA.

16. Quotations from Bridgland, *War*, p. 13, and interview with Nunda. Also Bridgland, *Savimbi*, pp. 256–58, 276; Memcon (Carter, Senghor), June 19, 1978, FOIA; North-South Cluster to Brzezinski, Sept. 1, 1978, NLC-24-100-2-4-8, JCL; Amembassy Lisbon to SecState, May 15, 1979, FOIA.

17. Quotations from W. K. G. Kamwana (Zambian ambassador to Zaire), "Political report no. 2/79," Apr. 5, 1979, p. 11, 152 UNIP7/23/70, UNIP, and from interview with Tonta. Having lost their Zairean rear guard and cut off from external support, the FNLA maquis held out in northern Angola with diminishing strength. While the FNLA's leader, Holden Roberto, abandoned the struggle and relocated to Paris, Tonta led into Angola those who wanted to continue fighting, creating the FNLA-COMIRA. In 1984, after one year of secret negotiations, the FNLA-COMIRA—approximately 1,500 guerrillas and thousands of civilians—rallied the government (interview with Tonta; Júnior, *Forças Armadas*, p. 115). FLEC was never more than a nuisance.

18. Quotations from Far East to Brzezinski, Aug. 7, 1979, NLC-26-1-5-7-0, JCL, and Bridgland, *Savimbi*, p. 273. Also Kamwana, "Political report no. 8/79," Jan. 24, 1980, 154 UNIP7/23/70, UNIP, and interview with Nunda.

19. Stoddard (INR) to Spiegel, "The Angolan Security Situation," July 28, 1978, Lake Papers, box 16.

20. Interviews with South African general Thirion and UNITA general Nunda.

21. Colonel Oelschig to Sunde, June 1988, 1/3/3 v. 3, Cuba: Relations with SA, DFA.

22. On Soviet relations with the MPLA through 1975, see Negin, "V ognennom kolze blokadi," p. 240 quoted; Gleijeses, *Conflicting Missions*, pp. 242–45, 365–72; V. Shubin, *Hot "Cold War,"* pp. 12–66; V. Shubin and Tokarev, "War"; Tokarev, "Kommandirovka"; Westad, *Global Cold War*, pp. 222–27.

23. Department of Foreign Political Affairs, "O stanju u oslobodilackom pokretu Angole i uslovima u kojima deluje," Nov. 20, 1973, Tito Archive; CC CPSU, "O polozhenii v nazionalno-osvoboditelnom dvizhenii v Angole," Dec. 21, 1973, NSA.

24. Negin, "V ognennom kolze blokadi," p. 243; interview with Lúcio Lara. On Yugoslav relations with the MPLA, see Cavosky's pathbreaking "'Yugoslavia's Help.'"

25. Quotations from Columbié to Carlos Rafael Rodríguez, Nov. 17 and Dec. 18, 1975, CF.

26. NSC meeting, July 25, 1975, p. 2, NSAd, NSC Meeting, box 2, GRFL.

27. Dobrynin, *In Confidence*, p. 362; CIA, National Intelligence Daily Cable, Oct. 8, 1976, p. 16, CREST.

28. Westad, "Moscow," p. 27.

29. Memcon (Castro, Honecker), Apr. 3, 1977, p. 36, DY30 JIV 2/201/1292, SAPMO.

30. "Segunda Reunión con Neto," Apr. 22, 1976, in "Informe al Buró Político del Segundo Secretario del Comité Central del Partido Comunista de Cuba acerca de su visita a la República Popular de Angola, República Popular del Congo, y República Popular de Guinea, además de su visita a la URSS (19 de abril a 7 junio de 1976)," p. 14, OS.

31. Republic of Russia, Ministry of Defense, *Rossiya*, p. 104; interviews with the following senior Angolan officers: Ndalu, Ngongo, Kianda, Foguetão; and with the Cubans Risquet, Cintra Frías, Escalante, Fleitas, Rodiles. For accounts by Soviet military personnel who served in Angola, see Tokarev, "Kommandirovka"; Tokarev and G. Shubin, *Vospominaniia uchastnikov*; Tokarev and G. Shubin, *Vospominaniia neposredstvennykh uchastnikov*; Tokarev and G. Shubin, *Veterany*; G. Shubin, *Oral History* and *Kuito-Kuanavale*; Zhdarkin,*"Takovo"*; Kolomnin, *Russkii Spetznaz*; Kuznetsova-Timonova, *Vospominaniia*.

32. Before 1982 there were only six military regions.

33. Barganov, "Mui bili pervimi," p. 17.

34. Memcon (Castro, Neto), Mar. 23, 1977, p. 21, Consejo de Estado.

35. Colomé to Senén [Casas], [Apr. 1977], CF.

36. Memcon (Castro, Honecker), Apr. 3, 1977, pp. 35–36.

37. On Cuban participation in the war against UNITA in the late 1970s, see the candid account of Menéndez Tomassevich and Gárciga Blanco, *Patria*. (General Menéndez Tomassevich was the head of the Cuban military mission in 1977–79.)

38. Barganov, "Mui bili pervimi," p. 12.

39. *Le Soir* (Brussels), May 29–31, 1977, p. 3. The only in-depth discussion of the plot is Mabeko Tali, *Dissidências*, 2:181–227. For Cuban reports that deal with the day of the revolt in Luanda and the Cuban response, see Risquet to Castro, May 27, 1977, ACC; Colonel Bermúdez Cutiño, "Síntesis sobre nuestra participación en los sucesos del 27.5.77," May 31, 1977, CF; Memcon (Raúl Castro, Colomé), May 27, 1977, CF; Colomé to Vice Ministro Primero, May 27, 1977, CF. I have also benefited from interviews with the following Angolan officials: Lúcio Lara, Paulo Lara, Ludi Kissassunda, Onambwe, Xiyetu, Gato, Paulo Jorge; and with the Cubans Moracén and Risquet.

40. Amnesty International, *Imprisonment*, p. 5; Pereira, "Um homem," p. 113. Also Vidal, "Post-Modern," pp. 165–71; Messiant, "Angola, les voies," pt. 1, p. 173.

41. Young, May 12, 1978, in U.S. Congress, SCFR, Subcommittee on African Affairs, *U.S. Policy toward Africa*, p. 32; *Times* (London), Sept. 7, 1983, p. 6.

42. Mabeko Tali, *Dissidências*, 2:207–8; Neto, in Department of Foreign Political Affairs, "Predsednik Neto Razgovarao s Nasim Ambasadorom [2 June 1977]," June 17, 1977, pp. 1–2, Tito Archive; interview with Mendes de Carvalho.

43. "Informe al Buró Político," pp. 125–27.

44. Memcon (Tito, Nascimento), July 20, 1976, p. 6, Tito Archive.

45. Interview with Paulo Jorge. See also Pereira, "Um homem," p. 111.

46. Department of International Relations of the presidency of the CC of the SKJ [League of Communists of Jugoslavia], "Informacija o najnovijem razvoju sovjetsko-angolskih odnosa l predlozi za nasu akciju," Mar. 15, 1977, pp. 2–3, Tito Archive.

47. Raúl Castro to Fidel Castro, June 14, 1977, OS.

48. Neto, in Department of Foreign Political Affairs, "Predsednik Neto razgovarao s nasim ambasadorom [2 June 1977]," June 17, 1977, p. 2, Tito Archive.

49. Peyronnet to de Guiringaud, Oct. 12, 1978, p. 6, MAE; Šašić, in Department of Foreign Affairs, "Unutrasnja Kretanja u Angoli i Netova Poseta Moskvi," Oct. 5, 1977, p. 5, Tito Archive.

50. Department of Foreign Political Affairs, "Predsednik Neto razgovarao s nasim ambasadorom [2 June 1977]," June 17, 1977, p. 2, Tito Archive.

51. Ibid.

52. Department of Foreign Political Affairs, "Uzroci Pokusaja Puca u NR Angoli," June 6, 1977, p. 4, Tito Archive.

53. See Memcon (Tito, Neto), Apr. 23, 1977, p. 10, Tito Archive. Also Federal Secretariat for Foreign Affairs, "Informacija za zvanicnu posetu predsednika Narodne Republike Angole dr. Agostinho Neta SFR Jugoslaviji," Apr. 18, 1977, ibid., and "Izvestaj o boravku jugoslovenska delegacije za finansijska pitanja u NR Angoli od 5. do.11. aprila 1976. g.," ibid.

54. Department of Foreign Political Affairs, "Informacija o Unutrasnjoj i spolnjoj politici NR Angole i Jugoslovensko-Angolskim odnosima," Apr. 20, 1977, p. 5, Tito Archive.

55. Quotations from Tunney, "Angola: Summary of Impressions," enclosed in Tunney to Carter, Feb. 21, 1977, WHCF, box CO-10, JCL; *WP*, Aug. 15, 1982, p. B4; *Economist*, Oct. 10, 1987, p. 39; Safire, op-ed, *NYT*, July 4, 1988, p. 23; Davies, *Constructive Engagement?*, p. 176.

56. "Informe al Buró Político," p. 120.

57. "Septima Reunión con Neto," May 26, 1976, in ibid., pp. 140–42.

58. Ibid., p. 142.

59. Memcon (Casas, Neto), May 19, 1978, pp. 4–5, 10, ACC.

60. "Convenio sobre los principios de colaboración en la rama militar, entre la República de Cuba y la República Popular de Angola," Sept. 14 1978, CF.

61. Interview with Risquet; Memcon (Castro, dos Santos), Mar. 17, 1984, pp. 27, 28, ACC.

62. "Cuban Objectives in Africa," enclosed in Vest to Hibbert, Aug. 11, 1977, FCO 99/22, PRO.

63. Raúl Castro, "Acerca de la necesidad de una masiva ayuda técnica (civil) a RPA," Apr. 23, 1976, CF.

64. *Jeune Afrique*, July 23, 1976, p. 28; "Discussion with Delegates to the World Health

Assembly—Peter G. Bourne, M.D., Geneva, Switzerland, May 1977: Angola," Special Assistant to the President, box 41, JCL.

65. *World* (Johannesburg), June 30, 1976, p. 8; Interagency IM, "Angola: Cuban Interests and Changes in Cuban Personnel Strength," Sept. 1976, pp. 1–3, FOIA.

66. Risquet to Castro, July 13, 1976, ACC; Peyronnet to de Guiringaud, Oct. 12, 1978, p. 5, MAE.

67. Departamento General de Relaciones Exteriores del CC del PCC, "Informe sobre la Colaboración Civil de Cuba con la República Popular de Angola," Nov. 7, 1979, p. 50, ACC.

68. "La colaboración entre Cuba y la República Popular de Angola," June 1979, p. 2, private collection, Havana.

69. Memcon (Farah, Dilowa), [Oct. 1977], p. 5, ACC.

70. My main sources on the living conditions of Cuban aid workers in the late 1970s are interviews with aid workers Gina Rey (quoted), Aleyda Escartín (quoted), Isabel Martín (quoted), Guillermo Domínguez, José Antonio Choy, Serena Torres, Rolando Carballo, Julia León, Rosa Fonseca, Luis Peraza, Nancy Jiménez, and with economic attaché Emiliano Manresa; the diary of Serena Torres, private collection, Havana; the diary of Emiliano Manresa, private collection, Havana; Jiménez Rodríguez, *Mujeres* and *De las mujeres*.

71. Quotations from Manresa diary, July 30, 1977, and from interviews with Manresa, Escartín, Rey, Choy, Domínguez, and Carballo.

72. Interview with Serena Torres. For examples of appeals to extend the stay, and the responses, see *Verde Olivo en Misión Internacionalista* (Luanda), Oct. 7, 1978, p. 4; Oct. 21, p. 4; Dec. 9, p. 1; "Asamblea de Balance del Comité del PCC en la provincia de Zaire, julio de 1978 a marzo de 1979," Mbanza Congo, Apr. 1979, p. 14, private collection, Havana.

73. CIA, "Latin America Review Supplement," Aug. 3, 1978, p. 4, NLC-24-12-2-2-8, JCL.

74. Escartín to her son, Luanda, Mar. 10, 1978, private collection, Havana.

75. Interagency Group—Angola, "Summary of pertinent items from CIA report," Oct. 1979, NLC-6-4-4-15-1, JCL.

76. See Gleijeses, *Conflicting Missions*.

77. My main source is the "Notas del CECE" for the relevant countries, in the archives of the Ministerio para la Inversión Extranjera y la Colaboración Económica.

78. CIA, "Latin America Review Supplement," Aug. 3, 1978, p. 2, NLC-24-12-2-2-8, JCL.

79. "Informe al Buró Político," p. 6.

80. Risquet to Castro, Sept. 23, 1977, ACC.

81. Levy Farah, Oct. 23, 1977, quoted in Departamento General de Relaciones Exteriores del CC del PCC, "Informe sobre la colaboración," pp. 55–57.

82. "Acuerdo especial sobre condiciones generales para la realización de la colaboración económica y científico-técnica entre el gobierno de la República de Cuba y el gobierno de la República Popular de Angola," Nov. 5, 1977, CECE.

83. "Informe de la I sesión de la Comisión Mixta Intergubernamental para la colaboración económica y científico-técnica entre la República de Cuba y la República Popular de Angola," Nov. 5, 1977, CECE.

84. Interview with Risquet; Memcon (dos Santos, Risquet), Oct. 28, 1983, p. 13, ACC.

85. Rodríguez Lompart to Carlos Rafael Rodríguez, Feb. 17, 1984, ACC.

86. "La colaboración entre Cuba y la República Popular de Angola," June 1979, private collection, Havana.

87. Castro, quoted in Manresa diary, Mar. 31, 1977, private collection, Havana.

88. Departamento General de Relaciones Exteriores del CC del PCC, "Informe sobre la Colaboración," pp. 106, 108.

89. Interview with Dr. Miranda; Bender, Sept. 17, 1980, in U.S. Congress, HCFA, Sub-committee on Africa, *United States Policy toward Angola—Update*, p. 33.

90. Castro, June 29, 1971, *Granma* (Havana), June 30, 1971, p. 2.

91. *Granma*, Aug. 3, 1978, p. 1. See also McManus, *Island*, pp. 114–28.

92. Memcon (Neto, Raúl Castro), June 4, 1977, enclosed in Raúl Castro to Fidel Castro, June 8, 1977, CF.

93. Interview with Risquet.

94. CIA, "Latin America Review Supplement," Aug. 3, 1978, p. 3, NLC-24-12-2-2-8, JCL.

95. Embassy of Zambia in Mozambique, "Report no. 3—Mar. 1979," Apr. 26, 1979, p. 7, 152 UNIP 7/23/10, UNIP.

96. "Primera Reunión con Neto," Apr. 21, 1976, in "Informe al Buró Político," pp. 4–5.

97. Risquet to Castro, Dec. 20, 1976, ACC.

98. Memcon (Castro, Honecker), Apr. 3, 1977, p. 41. On Cuba and Guinea-Bissau, see Gleijeses, *Conflicting Missions*, pp. 185–213.

99. "Informe sobre los resultados de la Operación Z-4," Aug. 8, 1977, CF. On the war in Zimbabwe and on ZAPU, see Martin and Johnson, *Struggle*; Sibanda, *Zimbabwe*; Nkomo, *Nkomo*.

100. Memcon (Risquet, Loguinov), Nov. 28, 1978, ACC.

101. "Informe de la disposición del Jefe MMCA para la realización de la Operación 'Z-5,'" Jan. 12, 1978, CF.

102. Menéndez Tomassevich to Vice Ministro Primero de las FAR, Nov. 11, 1978, CF.

103. Interview with Risquet.

104. Burenko, "Trudnii," p. 22.

105. Dirección Inteligencia Militar EMG to Colomé, Oct. 20, 1978, CF.

106. Nkomo, *Nkomo*, p. 177.

107. See Jefe Dirección Inteligencia Militar EMG to Raúl Castro, Sept. 28, 1978, CF; Jefe Dirección Inteligencia Militar EMG to Colomé, Nov. 20, 1978, CF.

108. "Resultado de la investigación realizada sobre la masacre del centro de entrenamiento de Boma por la comisión del EMG (7–12.3.1979)," CF. Also Dirección de Contra Inteligencia Militar, "Parte especial," Feb. 26, 1979, CF; *Jornal de Angola*, Mar. 4, 1979, p. 2; *Verde Olivo en Misión Internacionalista*, Mar. 6, 1979, p. 1.

109. Che Ogara, in "Julio/86 en Habana," pp. 57–58, CF. On the ANC, see Callinicos, *Tambo*, the well-researched biography of the ANC president; Gevisser, *Mbeki*, equally well researched; Barrell, "Conscripts," the best study on the ANC's military strategy through 1986 (see also Barrell, *MK*); Kasrils, *"Armed,"* by a senior member of the ANC's military wing; O'Malley, *Shades*, the outspoken semiautobiographical study of "Mac" Maharaj, a key ANC leader. (Mbeki, Kasrils, and Maharaj were also members of the South African Communist Party.) Ellis and Sechaba, *Comrades*, is a sometimes well-informed book by two unsympathetic authors who "expose" how important, and selfless, was the role of the South African Communist Party in the struggle against apartheid. Adams's

*Comrade Minister* is well documented and sheds light on both the Communist Party and the ANC.

110. *NYT*, Feb. 21, 1976, p. 3.

111. Che Ogara, in "Julio/86 en Habana," pp. 57–58, CF; Kasrils, *"Armed,"* pp. 173–74; interview with Cosmas Sechaba; James Stuart, "Report: Commission of Inquiry into Recent Developments in the People's Republic of Angola," Mar. 14, 1984, p. 3, OAL 2516, WITS.

112. V. Shubin, *ANC*, pp. 186–87; Jefe Dirección Inteligencia Militar EMG to Viceministro Primero, Sept. 11, 1978, CF.

113. Shiriaev, "Tovarish Ivan," p. 27. Shiraev headed the group.

114. V. Shubin, *ANC*, p. 186.

115. Jefe Sección Inteligencia Militar MMCA, "Entrevista sostenida con Oliver Tambo," Sept. 22, 1979, pp. 2–3, CF. For the number of Cuban instructors at Pongo, see García Peláez to Colomé, Aug. 24, 1979, CF.

116. *NYT*, June 2, 1980, p. 1; Lodge, *Mandela*, p. 155.

117. The dearth of documents has hindered research on SWAPO. The two most important books on SWAPO are Leys and Saul, *Namibia's Liberation Struggle*, and Dobell, *SWAPO's Struggle*. Sellström's *Sweden*, 2:233–393, not only illuminates Stockholm's relations with SWAPO but has a wealth of information about SWAPO through the author's privileged access to the Swedish archives; Schleicher and Schleicher cover much the same ground for the German Democratic Republic, though less impressively, in *Die DDR*, pp. 151–229; V. Shubin, *Hot "Cold War,"* pp. 195–235, has useful material on Soviet relations with SWAPO through the 1970s. See also Ansprenger, *Die SWAPO*; Leys and Brown, *Histories*. The memoirs of SWAPO president Sam Nujoma, *Wavered*, are interesting but unreliable.

118. Nujoma, *Wavered*, pp. 228–29; J. Geldenhuys, *Dié*, p. 45.

119. Quotations from "Die situasie in Owambo soos op 21 April 1976," p. 1, B 1.2.3.24.9, WITS; "Militêre bedreiging teen die RSA en SWA: kort termyn: Des 77," June 22, 1976, pp. 8–9, enclosed in Chief of Staff Intelligence to CS (DG Ops), June 24, 1976, HSI AMI, gr. 3, box 602, DODDC; interview with SWAPO commander Lazarus Hamutele. Interviews with SWAPO combatants who were active at the time (see next note) confirm the estimates in the text.

120. Interviews with Nujoma and with SWAPO fighters Malakia Nakandungile, Charles Namoloh (quoted), Mwetufa Mupopiwa, Martin Shalli, Thomas Ilwenya Ilwenya, Patrick M'Mwinga, Alfeus Shiweda Kalistu, Vilho Nghilalulwa, and Wilbard Nauyoma.

121. Casas to Colomé, Jan. 20, 1977, CF.

122. Interview with Dr. Haydée del Pozo.

123. Risquet to Colomé, Oct. 31, 1977, CF.

124. Quotations from interviews with Mutopiwa and Fortun; also interviews with Chibia students Miriam Shikongo, Gabriel Shaanika, Erasmus Tulesheni Naikako, and Esther Moombolah-Goagoses.

125. Memcon (Risquet, Nujoma), June 11, 1978, ACC; Memcon (Risquet, Nujoma), Oct. 5, 1978, quoted, ACC.

126. Interviews with Claudia Uushona (quoted) and Sophia Ndeitungo (both Cassinga survivors); and with Miriam Shikongo, Erasmus Tulesheni Naikako, Esther Moombolah-

Goagoses, and Gabriel Shaanika—all members of the group of Namibian youth who went to Cuba in late 1978; and with Nixon Marcus, a Cassinga survivor who went to the German Democratic Republic (GDR). See also Colina la Rosa, "Estudiantes," pp. 10–11; Kenna, Die "DDR-Kinder." I visited the Namibian schools in Cuba in 1980 and 1981.

The East European country that gave the greatest aid to African Liberation Movements, as well as to Angola and Mozambique, was the GDR. On the GDR and Africa, see Schleicher and Schleicher, Die DDR; Husemann and Neumann, "DDR"; H.-G. Schleicher, "Juniorpartner"; Voss, Wir; Storkmann, Geheime Solidarität; Siebs, Aussenpolitik, pp. 280–306; Heyden, Schleicher, and Schleicher, Engagiert; and (only for the 1960s) Lorenzini, Due Germanie.

127. Quotations from interviews with Nixon Marcus and Sophia Ndeitungo.

128. Interviews with Uushona (quoted), Ndeitungo, Shikongo, Tulesheni Naikako, Moombolah-Goagoses, and Shaanika—all of whom went to the Island of Youth in late 1978—and with Asser Mudhika, one of the teachers.

129. DOS, "Namibia: Turnhalle Constitutional Proposals," enclosed in Tarnoff to Cliff, May 9, 1977, FOIA; CIA, IM, "South Africa's Policy toward Namibia," May 20, 1977, NLC-6-69-10-7-2, JCL; Bowdler to SecState, Mar. 19, 1977, FOIA.

130. Aide-mémoire, enclosed in "Verbatim Minutes: Meeting (Cape Town)," Apr. 7, 1977, ALUKA; interview with McHenry.

131. Memcon (Carter, Waldheim), Oct. 5, 1977, FOIA.

132. Dreyer, "Dispute," p. 509. Also Berat, Walvis Bay.

133. Staatsveiligheidsraaddirektief no. 24, "Totale Strategie vir Walvisbaai," May 24, 1983, p. 4, SVR.

134. CIA, IM, "South Africa's Policy toward Namibia: A Review of Basic Factors," May 20, 1977, NLC-6-69-10-7-2, JCL.

135. DCI PRC Briefing, "Namibia: Status and Prospects (Revised and Updated)," Apr. 9, 1979, CREST.

136. "Abraham du Plessis," Windhoek Advertiser, Aug. 11, 1979, p. 14.

137. Bowdler to SecState, Mar. 19, 1977, FOIA.

138. Helman, Harrop, and Katz to Vance, Oct. 5, 1978, Lake Papers, box 4.

139. Quotations from Risquet to Castro, Sept. 9, 1977, ACC, and Memcon (Risquet, Nujoma), Oct. 12, 1977, ACC.

140. Karis and Gerhart, Protest, p. 315.

141. Memcon (Brzezinski, Fourie), Nov. 11, 1977, FOIA.

142. CIA, IM, "South Africa's Policy toward Namibia: A Review of Basic Factors," May 20, 1977, p. 12, NLC-6-69-10-7-2, JCL.

143. "Letter dated 10 April 1978 from the representatives of Canada, France, Germany, Federal Republic of, the United Kingdom of Great Britain and Northern Ireland and United States of America addressed to the President of the Security Council," UNSC S/12636, Apr. 10, 1978, DHL.

144. Vance, Choices, p. 395.

145. Du Pisani, "On Brinkmanship," p. 9.

146. Donald Norland (U.S. ambassador, Botswana) to SecState, June 23, 1978, FOIA.

147. Castro, Dec. 2, 2005, Juventud Rebelde (Havana), Dec. 3, 2005, p. 4.

148. Quotations from Beliaev, "Osnovnoiie napravleniia," p. 62, and Beliaev, "Vas tam

bit' ne moglo," *Krasnaya Zvesda* (Moscow), Sept. 9, 2000, p. 6. See also Kolomnin, *Russkii Spetznaz*, pp. 47–50, 57–63; DIA, "Soviet Military and Other Activities in Sub-Saharan Africa," Apr. 1984, FOIA; CIA, "Soviet Policy in Southern Africa," Feb. 1985, FOIA; Special NIE, "Soviet Military Support to Angola: Intentions and Prospects," Oct. 1985, FOIA.

CHAPTER 4

1. Vance, *Choices*, p. 275.

2. USMission USUN New York to SecState, June 2, 1978, FOIA.

3. Quotations from Young to SecState, June 8 and 12, 1978, FOIA.

4. SecState to Amembassy Kinshasa, June 20, 1978, FOIA.

5. Quoted in SecState to USDel Secretary, June 16, 1978, FOIA, and SecState to Amembassy Paris, June 21, 1978, FOIA.

6. Amembassy Rome to SecState, June 26, 1978, FOIA.

7. Ibid.

8. Ibid., p. 7 of the copy enclosed in Brzezinski to Vance, June 27, 1978, FOIA.

9. SecState to OAU Collective Priority, July 6, 1978, FOIA.

10. Amembassy Rome to SecState, June 26, 1978, FOIA.

11. SecState to OAU Collective Priority, July 6, 1978, FOIA.

12. Amembassy Rome to SecState, June 26, 1978, FOIA; "Notes of Presentation by Don Petterson to UNA Breakfast for Senate Staff, 9/7/78," 45–29, WOA, Yale University. For Carter's marginal comment, see p. 4 of Amembassy Rome to SecState, June 26, 1978, enclosed in Brzezinski to Vance, June 27, 1978, FOIA.

13. Vance to Carter, "Evening Reading: McHenry Visit to Luanda," [late June 1978], FOIA. Also Moose to Vance, July 3, 1978, Lake Papers, box 17, and McHenry to Vance, enclosed in Moose to Vance, July 8, 1978, ibid., box 16.

14. Amembassy Kinshasa to SecState, Nov. 21, 1978, FOIA.

15. Amembassy Brussels to SecState, Nov. 9, 1978, FOIA.

16. Interview with Moose. Unlike Moose and McHenry, Funk has published his memoirs, *Life*. Unfortunately they are extremely shallow.

17. Quotations from Christopher to President, Nov. 21 and 22, 1978, Plains File, box 39, JCL. See also Amembassy Kinshasa to SecState, Nov. 23, 1978, FOIA, and Vance to President, Nov. 29, 1978, Plains File, box 39, JCL.

18. SecState to Amembassy Lagos, Nov. 25, 1978, FOIA.

19. Amembassy Kinshasa to SecState, Nov. 24, 1978, FOIA.

20. *NYT*, Dec. 13, 1978, p. 9; Vance to President, Dec. 27, 1978, Plains File, box 39, JCL.

21. *Jornal de Angola* (Luanda), Dec. 14, 1978, p. 6. See also *Expresso* (Lisbon), Dec. 16, 1978, p. 9; *NYT*, Dec. 13, 1978, p. 9, and Dec. 14, p. 4; *WP*, Dec. 14, 1978, p. 26.

22. Memcon (Neto, Honecker), Feb. 19, 1979, p. 2, DY30 JIV 2/201/1338, SAPMO.

23. Vance, *Choices*, pp. 275, 305.

24. Neto, quoted in Risquet to Castro, Dec. 5, 1978, [#1], ACC.

25. Memcon (Castro, Neto), Jan. 24, 1979, pp. 16–18, Consejo de Estado; Memcon (Neto, Honecker), Feb. 17, 1979, p. 5, DV30 JIV/597, SAPMO.

26. Neto, quoted in Risquet to Castro, Dec. 5, 1978, [#2], ACC, and in *Jornal de Angola*, Dec. 11, 1978, p. 1.

27. Neto, quoted in Risquet to Castro, Dec. 5, 1978, [#1], ACC; SSC, Mar. 13, 1979, #4,

SVR; Funk to Brzezinski, Feb. 16, 1979, National Security Affairs, Country File, box 3, JCL.

28. Brzezinski to Carter, Sept. 29, 1978, NLC-1-7-9-44-6, JCL; Peyronnet to de Guiringaud, Oct. 12, 1978, p. 13, MAE.

29. See Peyronnet to de Guiringaud, July 6 and Oct. 12, 1978, MAE; *Jornal Novo* (Lisbon), June 21–28, 1978; *Expresso*: June 24, 1978, p. 1 R; July 1, pp. 3–5 R; July 8, p. 3; Feb. 3, 1979, p. 5; Chan and Venancio, *Diplomacy*, pp. 38–43.

30. Fidel Castro, quoted in Diary of Emiliano Manresa, Mar. 31, 1977, private collection, Havana; Raúl Castro, quoted in ibid., June 10, 1977.

31. Dos Santos to Castro, Oct. 28, 1983, p. 4, ACC.

32. "Octava reunión con el Presidente Neto," May 27, 1976, in "Informe al Buró Político del Segundo Secretario del Comité Central del Partido Comunista de Cuba acerca de su visita a la República Popular de Angola, República Popular del Congo, y República Popular de Guinea, además de su visita a la URSS (19 de abril a 7 junio de 1976)," p. 156, OS. Neto "said that he was stunned that Raúl, a top Cuban leader, apologized to Bolingó [the commander in Cabinda], that this was not necessary. I answered that this was part of our attempt to eliminate any tensions in our relations and that we would not spare any effort to achieve this" (ibid., p. 157). On the incident with Bolingó, see also "Septima reunión con Neto," May 26, 1976, ibid., pp. 136–37, and "Situación en la provincia de Cabinda," ibid., pp. 28–31, 38.

33. Interview with Agramonte.

34. Memcon (Castro, Neto), Jan. 24, 1979, p. 40. For a surprisingly good analysis of these January talks between Castro and Neto, see National Intelligence Daily, Feb. 2, 1979, CREST.

35. Memcon (Castro, Neto), Jan. 26, 1979, pp. 4–6, 9, 4, 12, 13–16, 17, Consejo de Estado.

36. Ibid., pp. 37–39.

37. Ministerio para la Inversión Extranjera y la Colaboración Económica, "Historia de la Colaboración entre la República de Cuba y la República de Angola," unpublished manuscript, Havana, 2002, pp. 6, 8–9.

38. Boniface Zulu (Zambian ambassador to Portugal) to Zambian foreign minister Chakulya, # 4/79, Apr. 1979, 153 UNIP 7/23/71, UNIP; *Jornal de Angola*, July 24, 1979, p. 1.

39. Nascimento, in Memcon (Castro, dos Santos), Mar. 17, 1984, p. 64, ACC.

40. Dos Santos to Castro, Oct. 28, 1983, p. 4, ACC.

41. Interview with Julio de Almeida.

42. See Menéndez Tomassevich to Rodiles, Jan. 9, 1979, CF, and "Versión de la reunión con el ministro de defensa de la República Popular de Angola," Jan. 11, 1979, CF.

43. Memcon (Castro, Neto), Jan. 26, 1979, pp. 11–12.

44. "Nota Verbal: Al presidente Antonio Agostinho Neto," Feb. 1, 1979, CF; Memcon (Menéndez Tomassevich, Neto), Feb. 21, 1979, p. 2 quoted, CF.

45. "Besuch des Genossen B. N. Ponomariow, Kandidat des Politbüros und Sekretär des ZK der KPDSU, vom 25–27. Januar 1979," Jan. 31, 1979, p. 15 (quoting Ponomarev), DY30 JIV 856, SAPMO.

46. Memcon (Casas, Neto), May 4, 1979, pp. 1, 3, 5, CF.

47. Quotations from Peyronnet to de Guiringaud, Oct. 31 and 12, 1978, MAE.

48. Amembassy Abidjan to SecState, June 22, 1978, FOIA.

49. Young to Carter and Vance, Mar. 27, 1979, p. 4, FOIA.

50. Neto, Nov. 11, 1978, *Jornal de Angola*, Nov. 12, 1978, p. 4; Neto, Dec. 18, 1978, ibid., Dec. 19, 1978, p. 3.

51. Risquet to Castro, Dec. 29, 1978, ACC.

52. See UNSC Resolution 447, Mar. 28, 1979, in www.un.org/documents, and Maynes and Moose to Newsom, Mar. 27, 1979, Lake Papers, box 5.

53. See Casas to García Peláez, July 16, 1979, CF; García Peláez to Vice Ministro Primero, July 24, 1979, CF; MINFAR, "Cronología de las conversaciones sobre la reducción de tropas cubanas en la R.P.A. por el presidente Agostinho Neto y el ministro de defensa Enrique Tieles Carreira (Iko)," Oct. 17, 1979, CF; MINFAR, "Sobre la situación política actual en la RPA," Nov. 11, 1979, OS.

54. Vance and McHenry to Carter, Oct. 23, 1979, enclosed in Brzezinski to Carter, Dec. 21, 1979, NLC-126-29-39-1-9, JCL.

55. Peyronnet to de Guiringaud, Oct. 12, 1978, p. 13, MAE.

56. CIA, "Angola Cuba: Some Strains but No New Developments," Apr. 9, 1979, CREST.

57. Memcon (Neto, García Peláez), Aug. 30, 1979, enclosed in García Peláez to Colomé, Aug. 31, 1979, CF. The Soviet position on the withdrawal of Cuban troops was that it was a bilateral issue between Angola and Cuba. In fact, however, the Soviets hoped that Cuba would not withdraw any troops (see "Versión de la conversación del día 4.1.79 en la residencia del embajador soviético en la R.P.A.," CF, and Vorotnikov, *Gavana—Moskva*, p. 45).

58. This assessment is based on conversations with Angolan and Cuban officials. I interviewed Lúcio Lara four times in 1997.

59. Crocker, *High Noon*, pp. 137–38. Dos Santos had studied in the Soviet Union in 1963–69, graduating as a petroleum engineer. After leaving the Soviet Union, he went to the MPLA headquarters in Brazzaville and was appointed deputy head of telecommunication services of the FAPLA for the II Military Region (Cabinda). In 1974 he became a member of the MPLA's political bureau. After independence he was briefly Angola's foreign minister, then first deputy prime minister; when the post was abolished in late 1978 he became planning minister.

60. Castro to Buró Político of MPLA, Sept. 15, 1979, CF.

61. "Nota informativa sobre la conversación por la delegación de Cuba a las honras funebres del Presidente Neto con una representación del BP del MPLA-PT," Sept. 18, 1979, enclosed in Aldana to Vorotnikov, Oct. 15, 1979, OS.

62. Castro to Crombet, Oct. 16, 1979, OS; García Peláez to Raúl Castro, Oct. 16, 1979, CF.

63. "Principales ataques de Africa del Sur contra la República Popular de Angola a partir de principios de 1978," [1982], CF; Stiff, *Silent War*, pp. 206–15; Greeff, *Greater Share*, pp. 83–85; Benga Lima, *Percursos*, pp. 218–19.

64. García Peláez, in "Versión conversación con el Presidente de la R.P.A.," Jan. 2, 1980, enclosed in Matas Colombo to Colomé, Jan. 4, 1980, CF.

65. "Versión entrevista sostenida con presidente R.P.A. el sabado 15 de marzo de 1980," CF.

66. Secretariat SSC, "Riglyne vir samesprekings met Angola," Feb. 1980, SVR.

67. Memcon (Casas, Ustinov), May 14, 1981, OS.

68. "Magtiging van SA Weermag operasionele oorgrens-optredes: Angola, Zambië, Zimbabwe, Mosambiek, Botswana, Lesotho, Swaziland," n.d., M, gr. 7, box 515, DODDC.

69. See Steenkamp, *Borderstrike!*, pp. 167–254.

70. See UNSC, Official Records, 2240th Meeting, June 27, 1980, pp. 1–13, DHL.

71. Bender, Sept. 17, 1980, in U.S. Congress, HCFA, Subcommittee on Africa, *United States Policy Toward Angola—Update*, p. 7.

CHAPTER 5

1. See Carlucci to Brzezinski, Mar. 22, 1978; Benes to Brzezinski, Mar. 24, 1978; Brzezinski to Aaron, Mar. 27, 1978 (all BC, DHM, box 10, JCL). Levine, *Missions*, pp. 85–148, is very unreliable.

2. Memcon (Castro, Neto), Jan. 24, 1979, p. 3, Consejo de Estado.

3. Interview with Newsom.

4. Quotations from W. Smith, *Closest*, p. 148, and interview with Pastor.

5. Interview with Newsom.

6. Ibid.

7. Interview with Padrón.

8. Memcon (Newsom, Padrón), June 15, 1978, pp. 5–6 quoted, FOIA; Brzezinski to Carter, June 19, 1978, BC, DHM, box 10, JCL; Brzezinski to Vance, July 7 and 13, 1978, ibid.; Vance to Carter, July 7, 1978, ibid.; Aaron to Brzezinski, July 20, 1978, quoted, ibid.

9. Interview with Newsom.

10. Memcon (Newsom, Padrón), June 15, 1978, pp. 4–6, FOIA.

11. Memcon (Newsom, Aaron, Padrón), Aug. 8, 1978, NLC-24-12-2-9-1, JCL; Christopher to Carter, Aug. 9, 1978, Vertical File, Subject File, box 39, JCL. On the prisoners' release, see W. Smith, *Closest*, pp. 158–60.

12. Memcon (Newsom, Padrón), July 5, 1978, BC, DHM, box 10, JCL.

13. Odom to Brzezinski, June 15, 1977, NLC-12-21-3-10-1, JCL.

14. Christopher and Brzezinski to Carter, Oct. 19, 1978, BC, DHM, box 10, JCL.

15. Interview with Padrón; Newsom's email to author, Aug. 13, 2007.

16. Interview with Stephanie van Reigersberg.

17. Aaron to Carter, Oct. 30, 1978, quoted, BC, DHM, box 10, JCL; Memcon (Newsom, Aaron, Padrón), Oct. 28, 1978, enclosed in Tarnoff to Aaron, Nov. 1, 1978, ibid.

18. Interview with Newsom; Carter, Nov. 8, 1978, BC, DHM, box 10, JCL.

19. Interview with Newsom.

20. Interview with Pastor.

21. Memcon (Tarnoff, Pastor, Castro), Dec. 3–4, 1978, 10:00 P.M.–3:00 A.M., pp. 6–7, Vertical File: Cuba, JCL.

22. *Le Monde*, Nov. 24, 1978, p. 1 (ed.); W. Smith, *Closest*, p. 167.

23. Memcon (Tarnoff, Pastor, Castro), Dec. 3–4, 1978, 10:00 P.M.–3:00 A.M., p. 12, Vertical File: Cuba, JCL.

24. Schoultz, *Infernal*, p. 330. Also Deputy Secretary of Defense to Aaron, Oct. 29, 1978, FOIA, and McAfee to Henze, Oct. 23, 1978, NLC-6-16-2-21-3, JCL.

25. Memcon (Tarnoff, Pastor, Castro), Dec. 3–4, 1978, 10:00 P.M.–3:00 A.M., pp. 2, 5, 9–10, 25, Vertical File: Cuba, JCL.

26. Tarnoff and Pastor to President, "Our Trip to Cuba, December 2–4, 1978," ibid.

27. DOS, "Cuban Presence in Africa," Dec. 28, 1978, p. 19, FOIA.

28. CIA, National Foreign Assessment Centre, "Grenada: Origins and Implications of the 13 Mar. Coup," Apr. 20, 1979, pp. 6, 5, NLC-24-66-6-3-4, JCL.

29. Pastor to Brzezinski, July 19, 1979, NLC-24-13-5-7-9, JCL.

30. Brzezinski to Carter, WR #102, July 6, 1979, BC, DHM, box 41, JCL; Brzezinski to Carter, WR #104, July 27, 1979, ibid.

31. Garthoff, *Détente*, pp. 913–34 (p. 920 quoted) is the best analysis of the crisis. See also Newsom, *Brigade*; Schoultz, *Infernal*, pp. 335–46.

32. Carter, *Faith*, p. 264; Memcon (Castro, Demichev), Jan. 8, 1984, p. 16, Consejo de Estado.

33. Republic of Russia, Ministry of Defense, *Rossiya*, p. 167.

34. Newsom, OH; Vance, *Choices*, p. 362; Turner, *Secrecy*, p. 229.

35. Church, *NYT*, Aug. 31, 1979, p. 2.

36. Brzezinski to Carter, WR #109, Sept. 13, 1979, BC, DHM, box 41, JCL.

37. Brzezinski to Carter, Sept. 4, 1979, NLC-6-16-6-1-2, JCL; Carter, *Faith*, p. 263.

38. Schoultz, *Infernal*, p. 340; Vance, Carter, in DOS *Bulletin*, Oct. 1979, pp. 14–15 and 63–64; *Guardian* (Manchester), Sept. 7, 1979, p. 13.

39. Vance, *Choices*, p. 362; *Pravda* (Moscow), Sept. 11, 1979, p. 1 quoted; Vance to Carter, Sept. 5, 1979 (enclosing Soviet reply), NLC-128-14-11-2-0, JCL.

40. Brement to Brzezinski, Sept. 12, 1979, BC, DHM, box 37, JCL; Garthoff, *Détente*, p. 925.

41. Brzezinski to Carter, Sept. 17, 1979, BC, DHM, box 10, JCL.

42. Brzezinski to Carter, Sept. 19, 1979, ibid.

43. Brzezinski to Carter, Sept. 17, 1979, ibid.

44. Ibid.

45. Ibid.

46. Newsom, *Brigade*, p. 45; Vance to Carter, Sept. 20, 1979, NLC-128-14-11-11-0, JCL.

47. Carter to Brezhnev, Sept. 25, 1979, "USSR-US Conference," Vertical File, box 117, JCL; Brezhnev to Carter, Sept. 27, 1979, ibid.

48. Vance, *Choices*, p. 362; Brzezinski, *NYT*, Sept. 23, 1979, p. 1; Carter, Sept. 25, 1979, *PP*, 1979, 2:1754.

49. Carter, Oct. 1, 1979, *PP*, 1979, 2:1802–6 (p. 1803 quoted).

50. Carter, *Diary*, Sept. 24, 1979, p. 357.

51. Newsom, *Brigade*, pp. 52–53; Brzezinski, *Power*, p. 346; Dobrynin, *In Confidence*, p. 429.

52. Memcon (Castro, Demichev), Jan. 8, 1984, pp. 17, 21, Consejo de Estado.

53. Memcon (Castro, Honecker), May 28, 1980, pp. 2–3, DY30 JIV 2/201/1365, SAPMO; interview with Risquet; Vorotnikov, *Gavana—Moskva*, pp. 69–84 (p. 83 quoted).

54. Yury Andropov, in Mar. 18, 1980, Politburo meeting, CWIHP *Bulletin*, nos. 8–9 (Winter 1996–97): 141.

55. Gates, *Shadows*, pp. 148–49, 251.

56. Wolf, *Spionagechef*, pp. 326, 328; Memcon (Tarnoff, Pastor, Castro), Jan. 16–17, 1980, 4 P.M. to 3 A.M., p. 13, Vertical File: Cuba, JCL.

57. Interview with Pastor. The minutes end with the following: "Note: This was the end of the formal meeting. For the next hour the group chatted informally. A summary

of the contents of that informal conversations follows." The summary has not been declassified.

58. Tarnoff, "Conversation with Castro," Jan. 22, 1980, Lake Papers, box 1.

59. See Vorotnikov, *Gavana—Moskva*, pp. 125–33 (p. 127 quoted).

60. Interview with Risquet.

61. Vorotnikov, *Gavana—Moskva*, p. 108. For a candid description of the reaction of the Cuban leadership to the Soviet invasion of Afghanistan, see ibid., pp. 103–15.

62. Raúl Roa Kouri, Jan. 14, 1980, *Granma* (Havana), Jan. 15, 1980, p. 6.

63. Memcon (Castro, Honecker), May 28, 1980, pp. 30–31.

64. Smith to Secstate, Feb. 20, 1980, NLC-6-14-5-7-8, JCL.

65. Smith to SecState, Mar. 18, 1980, NLC-6-14-5-12-2, JCL.

66. Situation Room to Brzezinski, Apr. 29, 1980, NLC-1-15-2-26-4, JCL.

67. The best discussions of the Mariel crisis are W. Smith, *Closest*, pp. 197–237; Schoultz, *Infernal*, pp. 349–61; Engstrom, *Adrift*.

68. W. Smith, *Closest*, p. 199.

69. Ibid., p. 200.

70. Associated Press report, Oct. 24, 1979, LexisNexis Academic.

71. *Miami Herald*, Feb. 1, 1980, p. 24 quoted; Feb. 2, p. 1; Feb. 17, p. 1; Feb. 27, 3:1; W. Smith, *Closest*, pp. 200–203.

72. Vance to Carter, Mar. 5, 1980, with Carter marginalia, NLC-128-15-3-3-8, JCL.

73. The first time ever that Cubans who fled to the United States in a hijacked boat were indicted was on July 18, 1980, for a July 8, hijacking (*NYT*, July 19, 1980, p. 18).

74. Castro, Mar. 8, 1980, *Granma*, Mar. 10, 1980, p. 4.

75. See Engstrom, "Mariel Boatlift," pp. 142–49; "Cubans at the Peruvian Embassy in Havana," enclosed in Tarnoff to Secretary of Defense et al., Apr. 8, 1980, FOIA.

76. See *Granma*, Apr. 4, 1980, p. 1.

77. W. Smith, *Closest*, p. 210.

78. *La Nación* (San José, Costa Rica), Apr. 17, 1980, p. 1 quoted, and Apr. 18, pp. 1, 4.

79. *Granma*, Apr. 22, 1980, p. 1.

80. Schoultz, *Infernal*, p. 361.

81. Memcon (Richmond, Nolan, Castro), pp. 7–8, enclosed in Richmond to Carter, Dec. 16, 1977, WHCF, box CO-20, JCL.

82. W. Smith, *Closest*, p. 213.

CHAPTER 6

1. My comments on Carter and Rhodesia are based on Nancy Mitchell's superb "Race and the Cold War" and her essay, "Terrorists?" Mitchell's research demonstrates that, while the final agreement was negotiated in England, at Lancaster House, it was the Carter administration, far more than the British government, that made it possible. See also DeRoche, "Standing Firm."

2. Quotations from CIA, National Foreign Assessment Center, "Rhodesia: Looking beyond the April Election," Apr. 2, 1979, pp. 3, 1, FOIA.

3. Mitchell, "Terrorists?" p. 1.

4. See Mitchell, "Race and the Cold War."

5. SCC meeting, Mar. 27, 1978, p. 3, FOIA.

6. Vance and Moose, May 12, 1978, in U.S. Congress, SCFR, Subcommittee on African Affairs, *U.S. Policy toward Africa*, p. 21.

7. See, e.g., the following files: "Commentary on Recent Cuban Activities," FCO 99/23 and FCO 99/160; "Cuban Involvement in the Rhodesian Problem," FCO 36/2217. All PRO.

8. Aaron to Brzezinski, Apr. 13, 1978, BC, DHM, box 10, JCL.

9. Brzezinski to Carter, WR #46, Feb. 9, 1978, FOIA; CIA, "The Soviet Role in Southern Africa," May 30, 1978, FOIA; Pastor to Brzezinski and Aaron, Apr. 24, 1978, BC, DHM, box 28, JCL.

10. Amembassy Maputo to SecState, June 30, 1978, FOIA; Memcon (Vance, Huang Hua), Oct. 3, 1978, p. 10, FOIA; Brzezinski to President, Mar. 3, 1978, BC, DHM, box 28, JCL.

11. Memcon (Tarnoff, Pastor, Rodríguez), Dec. 2–3, 1978, pp. 16–17; Vertical File: Cuba, JCL; Memcon (Tarnoff, Pastor, Castro), Dec. 3–4, 1978, 10:00 P.M.–3:00 A.M., ibid.

12. Pastor to Brzezinski and Aaron, Dec. 19, 1978, ibid.

13. Newsom, Solarz, Oct. 18, 1979, in U.S. Congress, HCFA, Subcommittee on Africa, *U.S. Interests*, pp. 55–56; DOS, "US Reaction to Soviet-Cuban Military Collaboration," [July 1979,] p. 4, enclosed in Dodson to Vice President et al., July 11, 1979, NLC-20-24-6-1-6, JCL.

14. Memcon (Raúl Castro, Samora Machel), Dec. 13, 1977, p. 16, CF.

15. Memcon (Castro, Neto), Jan. 24, 1979, pp. 1–3, 21–23, Consejo de Estado.

16. Special NIE, "The Cuban Foreign Policy," June 21, 1979, p. 12, NLC-6-14-1-2-7, JCL.

17. Memcon (Castro, Neto), Jan. 24, 1979, pp. 19, 25–27.

18. "Zapis besedi s ministrom inostraniikh del Narodnii Respubliki Angola Paulo Jorgi," Feb. 9, 1979, p. 4, NSA. On Soviet relations with ZAPU and ZANU, see Somerville, "Soviet Union"; V. Shubin, *Hot "Cold War*," pp. 151–91; H.-G. Schleicher, "Befreiungs-kampf"; Vorotnikov, *Gavana—Moskva*, pp. 49–50, 147–48.

19. Memcon (Castro, Neto), Jan. 24, 1979, pp. 20, 26.

20. Vorotnikov, *Gavana—Moskva*, p. 143; Chirkin, "S tainoi missiei," p. 133; Martin and Johnson, *Struggle*, p. 317.

21. See BBC Summary of World Broadcasts, Apr. 21 and 23, 1980, LexisNexis Academic.

22. See Solodovnikov, "K istorii," pp. 137–38.

23. *Herald* (Salisbury), Apr. 18, 1980, p. 3.

24. "Talking Points on Southern Africa for Cabinet Meeting 7/10/78," enclosed in Lake to Vance, July 7, 1978, Lake Papers, box 4. On the importance of Walvis Bay, see chapter 3.

25. Interviews with McHenry and Moose; Memcon (Risquet, Nujoma), July 13, 1978, ACC; Peyronnet to de Guiringaud, Oct. 12, 1978, p. 10, MAE.

26. Situation Room to Brzezinski, May 30, 1978, NLC-1-6-4-7-3, JCL.

27. USMission USUN New York to SecState, May 1, 1978, FOIA.

28. INR, Current Reports, July 26, 1978, p. 2 quoted, NLC-SAFE 17 B-12-63-17-4, JCL; Memcon (Carter, Callaghan), July 17, 1978, in *Akten*, 1978, 2:1114.

29. Interview with Gurirab; Mutukwa and Kapoma, "Report on the Security Council debate on 'The Situation in Namibia,'" Aug. 3, 1978, p. 3, 166 UNIP 7/24/8, UNIP. Also "Notes of Presentation by Don Petterson to UNA Breakfast for Senate Staff," July 9, 1978, 45–29, WOA, Yale University.

30. See Resolutions 431 and 432 in www.un.org/documents; for Vance's statement, see UNSC Official Records, 2082nd meeting, July 27, 1978, pp. 3–4 quoted, DHL.

31. *NYT*, July 28, 1978, p. 3; Pik Botha, in UNSC Officials Records, 2082nd meeting, July 27, 1978, pp. 25–26, DHL.

32. Carter to Nyerere, July 13, 1978, Lake Papers, box 4.

33. Urquhart, *A Life*, p. 309.

34. "Report of the Secretary-General Submitted Pursuant to Paragraph 2 of Security Council Resolution 431 (1978) concerning the Situation in Namibia," UNSC Document $/12827, Aug. 29, 1978, DHL.

35. *Burger* (Cape Town), Sept. 2, 1978, p. 1; Sept. 7, p. 1; Sept. 8, p. 12 (ed.).

36. Pik Botha, *Burger*, Sept. 18, 1978, p. 1, and Sept. 20, p. 3.

37. Christopher to President, Sept. 12, 1978, FOIA.

38. Vance to President, Sept. 1, 1978, FOIA; Vance to President, Sept. 2, 1978, NLC-7-20-7-1-4, JCL; Waldheim, in UNSC Officials Records, 2082nd meeting, Sept. 29, 1978, p. 3 quoted, DHL.

39. *Burger*, Sept. 21, 1978, p. 1.

40. *Windhoek Advertiser*, Sept. 21, 1978, p. 1.

41. *Die Republikein* (Windhoek), Sept. 21, 1978, p. 1; *RDM*, Sept. 22, 1978, p. 2.

42. *RDM*, Sept. 22, 1978, p. 12 (ed.).

43. Situation Room to Brzezinski, Sept. 28, 1978, NLC-1-7-9-41-9, JCL.

44. See Resolution 435 in www.un.org/documents.

45. Helman, Harrop, and Katz to Vance, Oct. 5, 1978, Lake Papers, box 4.

46. Memcon (Vance, Mkapa), Oct. 3, 1978, FOIA.

47. *WP*, Oct. 15, 1978, p. 21.

48. [Buitelandse Sake], "New Proposals on South West Africa by Five. South West African and Southern African Strategy," Aug. 14, 1979, pp. 11–12, DFA.

49. Interview with McHenry.

50. Cabinet meeting, Oct. 12, 1978, p. 2, CM (78) 34th, CAB/128/64/14, PRO. For the list of sanctions, see UKMIS New York to FCO, Oct. 5, 1978, enclosed in memorandum by the Secretary of State for Foreign and Commonwealth Affairs, "Namibia," Oct. 11, 1978, CP (78) 100, CAB/129/203/25, PRO.

51. Vance, *Choices*, p. 308.

52. Moose and Lake to Vance, Oct. 5, 1978, Lake Papers, box 4. For the agenda prepared by the NSC, see "NSC Meeting on Africa, October 6, 1978: Agenda," enclosed in Dodson to Vice President et al., Oct. 4, 1978, ibid.

53. NSC meeting, Oct. 6, 1978, FOIA.

54. Ibid.

55. Carter to PW Botha, Oct. 11, 1978, SWA Basic Documents, v. 8, DFA.

56. "Introductory Statement: Prime Minister of South Africa: meeting with Five's Foreign Ministers," Oct. 16, 1978, Samesprekings met Vyf (Pretoria 16–18 Oktober 1978) en daarna, DFA; de Villiers and de Villiers, *PW*, p. 344.

57. Owen, *Time*, p. 377. Also Genscher, *Erinnerungen*, pp. 335–36; Vance, *Choices*, pp. 309–10; "Meetings of Foreign Ministers of the Five with the South African Prime Minister and Foreign Minister in Pretoria on 17 and 18 October 1978," PREM 16/1876,

PRO; "Zu den Namibia-Gesprächen der fünf westlichen Aussenminister mit Südafrika," *Akten*, 1978, 2:1575–79.

58. *WP*, Nov. 4, 1978, p. 14.

59. For the text of the "Joint South African—Western Five Statement" that spelled out the agreement, see DOS *Bulletin*, Dec. 1978, p. 24.

60. Quotations from *WP*, Oct. 19, 1978, p. 1, and Oct. 23, p. 20.

61. Cabinet meeting, Oct. 26, 1978, p. 1, CM (78) 36th, CAB/128/64/16, PRO.

62. *RDM*, Oct. 20 1978, p. 1.

63. *WP*, Oct. 18, 1978, p. 15.

64. Owen to Prime Minister, Oct. 20, 1978, p. 2, PREM 16/1876, PRO; *Times* (London), Oct. 20, 1978, p. 17 (ed.).

65. See Resolution 439 in www.un.org/documents. Quotation from Canada's Ambassador William Barton, speaking on behalf of the Five, UNSC Provisional Verbatim Record, 2098th meeting, Nov. 13, 1978, p. 8, DHL.

66. Vance, *Choices*, p. 310.

67. *Le Monde*, Dec. 8, 1978, p. 6. For an excellent analysis of the terror that surrounded the elections, see Soggot, *Namibia*, pp. 247–58.

68. *Die Republikein*, Dec. 11, 1978, p. 1; *RDM*, Dec. 22, 1978, p. 1.

69. Amembassy Lusaka to SecState, Dec. 4, 1978, FOIA.

70. British ambassador Peter Jay to Prime Minister, Nov. 17, 1978, PREM 16/1876, PRO.

71. SecState to USMission USUN New York, Apr. 18, 1979, FOIA; Carter to PW Botha, Apr. 6, 1979, Lake Papers, box 17.

72. Interview with John (Jay) Taylor.

73. HS OPS, "Strategiese Inligtingsoorsig oor 'n moontlike tweede verkiesing in SWA," Dec. 5, 1978, p. 5, Die Militêre Standpunt tov SWA, DFA.

74. Urquahrt, *A Life*, p. 309.

75. [Buitelandse Sake], "New Proposals on South West Africa by Five. South West African and Southern African Strategy," Aug. 14, 1979, p. 1, Angola 1979, DFA.

76. Vance to Carter, May 7, 1979, NLC-7-29-3-64, JCL.

77. Interview with Moose.

78. "Samesprekings met Eerste Minister tov Hernieude Inisiative tov SWA," Jan. 18, 1980, p. 6, SVR.

79. CIA, DCI Notes,"Congressional Worldwide Briefing: Overview," Feb. 29, 1980, CREST.

80. Sole, "'This Above All,'" p. 430. Also unsigned to secretary DFA, Jan. 9, 1980, 1/156/3 Annexure Jacket 1980, DFA; "Discussion with Minister Bulle in Pretoria," Jan. 11, 1980, ibid.; unsigned, "Persoonlik vir Sekretaris," Feb. 11, 1980, ibid.

81. Chipampata (Zambian high commissioner in Gaborone) to Zambian foreign minister Chakulya, Feb. 27, 1980, UNIP.

82. SSC meeting, Mar. 10, 1980, #4, SVR.

83. SSC meeting, Apr. 14, 1980, #4, and Oct. 9, 1980, #4, SVR.

84. McHenry to SecState, Jan. 20, 1981, FOIA.

85. Interview with McHenry.

86. Hans-Joachim Vergau, in Weiland and Braham, *Peace Process*, pp. 19, 20.

87. *Burger*, Oct. 20, 1978, p. 1 (1st and 3rd quotes) and p. 16 (ed.).

88. See the excellent analysis in D. Geldenhuys, *Diplomacy*, chs. 4 and 7.

89. Interview with Pik Botha.

90. Interview with McHenry.

91. Ibid.

92. Brzezinski to president, WR #94 (emphasis in original), Apr. 12, 1979, BC, DHM, box 41, JCL.

93. Umberto Cardia, "Relazione sul viaggio in Angola e Mozambico (missione Radi)," Sept. 1, 1977, p. 4, Note a Segretería, v. 0304: 0313, FIG.

94. Melvin Hill, president of Gulf Oil Exploration and Production, Sept. 17, 1980, in U.S. Congress, HCFA, Subcommittee on Africa, *United States Policy toward Angola—Update*, pp. 10–12).

95. Christopher to Carter, Apr. 14, 1979, Lake Papers, box 17; Moose, Sept. 30, 1980, in U.S. Congress, HCFA, *Update*, pp. 40, 44, 47; Memcon (Muskie, Jorge), Oct. 7, 1980, Muskie Papers, box 2, NA.

96. Christopher to Carter, Apr. 14, 1979, p. 3, Lake Papers, box 17; Moose, Sept. 30, 1980, in U.S. Congress, HCFA, *Update*, pp. 41, 47.

97. Bender, Sept. 17, 1980, in U.S. Congress, HCFA, *Update*, p. 6.

98. Moose, Sept. 30, 1980, in ibid., p. 42.

99. Quotations from Vance and McHenry to Carter, Oct. 23, 1979, and McHenry to President, Dec. 21, 1979 (both enclosed in Brzezinski to Carter, Dec. 21, 1979, NLC-126-19-29-1-9, JCL).

100. Brzezinski to Carter, Oct. 29, 1979, enclosed in ibid.

101. Moose and Lake to Vance, Aug. 1, 1980, Lake Papers, box 6.

102. Interview with Moose.

103. Vance, "U.S. Foreign Policy: Constructive Change," Harvard University, June 5, 1980, *Vital Speeches of the Day*, July 1, 1980, p. 571; Vance, *Choices*, p. 72.

104. Interviews with Moose (quoted), Marianne Spiegel (quoted), Lake (quoted), and McHenry. Also Young to Carter and Vance, Mar. 27, 1979, FOIA; Harrop and Lake to Vance, Feb. 16, 1979, Lake Papers, box 16; Vance and McHenry to Carter, Oct. 22, 1979, ibid., box 6; Moose and Lake to Vance, Aug. 1, 1980, ibid.

105. Harrop to SecState, Jan. 10, 1979, FOIA; Harrop and Lake to Vance, Feb. 16, 1979, Lake Papers, box 16; Christopher to Carter, Apr. 14, 1979, p. 4, ibid., box 17.

106. Mitchell, "Cold War," p. 67. This essay is the best available analysis of Carter's foreign policy. See also G. Smith, *Morality*; Garthoff, *Détente*, pp. 623–1180; Dumbrell, *Carter*; Strong, *Working*.

107. Mitchell, "Cold War," p. 83.

108. On Carter and the Middle East, see Quandt, *Camp David*. On Carter and China, see Mann, *About Face*, pp. 78–114, and Tyler, *Great Wall*, pp. 229–85.

CHAPTER 7

1. Norman Podhoretz, "Making the World Safe for Communism," *Commentary*, Apr. 1976, p. 1.

2. Reagan, *NYT*, Jan. 29, 1976, p. 21.

3. Reagan, Apr. 3, 1978 broadcast, PPP, ser. 1a, box 22, RRL. Kiron Skinner et al. have published Reagan's radio broadcasts, with, however, a few minor mistakes (see Skinner et al., *Reagan*).

4. Fischer, "Conundrum," pp. 6 (quoting William Schneider, under secretary of state for military assistance and technology) and 3. Also Wolf, *Spionagechef*, pp. 331–32; Dobrynin, *In Confidence*, pp. 522–25; Andrew and Mitrokhin, *World*, pp. 131–33.

5. Reagan, *Reagan Diaries*, Nov. 18, 1983, 1:290.

6. NSC meeting, Feb. 6, 1981, p. 3, ES: MF, box 1, RRL.

7. "An Interview with Ronald Reagan," *WSJ*, May 6, 1980, p. 26.

8. W. Smith, *Closest*, p. 245.

9. Allen, memo for NSC Feb. 11, 1981 meeting, ES: MF, box 1, RRL.

10. NSC meeting, Feb. 6, 1981, ibid.

11. NSC meeting, Feb. 11, 1981, ibid.

12. Reagan, *Reagan Diaries*, Feb. 11, 1981, 1:19; Haig, *NYT*, Feb. 28, 1981, p. 1; Weinberger, *Fighting*, p. 31; McFarlane, *Trust*, pp. 177–78.

13. Glassman, OH; interview with Burt. See also Gillespie, OH.

14. McFarlane, *Trust*, p. 180.

15. Memcon (Castro, Honecker), May 28, 1980, pp. 23–24, DY30 JIV 2/201/1365, SAPMO.

16. "Aktuelle Fragen der Beziehungen der USA zur Republik Kuba," enclosed in Sieber to Honecker, Mar. 4, 1981, DY30, JIV 2/20/197, SAPMO.

17. "Aus der Aussprache mit Genossem Fidel Castro am 14. November 1968 während des Mittagessens im Gürtel von Havanna," pp. 4–5, DY30 IVA 2/20/205, SAPMO.

18. Memcon (Haig, Rodríguez), Mexico City, Nov. 23, 1981, enclosed in Vorotnikov to CC CPSU, Dec. 8, 1981, NSA. The Cuban original was translated into Russian and then the Russian version was translated into English. Both translations (but not the original) are available at the NSA. The quotation in the text is based on the Russian translation. It corrects errors in the English version. For Haig's account, see *Caveat*, pp. 132–36.

19. Reagan, *Reagan Diaries*, Jan. 15, 16, 1982, 1:101.

20. "Draft Talking Points: Approach to Cuba," n.d., Clark, William files, box 2, RRL.

21. Interview with Padrón; Walters, *Mighty*, p. 155; Reagan, *Reagan Diaries*, Mar. 9, 11, 1982, 1:115.

22. "Encuentro con el presidente Samora Machel 1.25.82," pp. 7, 8, CF.

23. DIA, *Handbook*, 1979, pp. 1.5–1.6, 1.10, 2.11, 1.5.

24. Fidel Castro, in Memcon (Castro, Shevardnadze), Oct. 28, 1985, p. 14, Consejo de Estado; Raúl Castro, in Vázquez Raña, *Raúl Castro*, pp. 29, 35.

25. DIA, *Handbook*, 1986, pp. 3.4–3.5; Memcon (Risquet, Mengistu), Dec. 2, 1986, p. 2, ACC.

26. Memcon (Castro, dos Santos), [Sept. 8, 1986], pp. 17, 16, 58–59, CF.

27. "Zapis osnovnovo soderzhania besedi M. S. Gorbacheva s Fidelem Kastro Rus," Mar. 2, 1986, p. 6, NSA.

28. Memcon (Risquet, Gromyko), Dec. 7–9, 1981, pp. 70, 46–47, ACC.

29. Memcon (Casas, Ogarkov), May 14, 1981, OS.

30. Memcon (Ustinov, Ogarkov, Casas), May 20, 1981, OS.

31. CIA, "CIA Long-Range Planning for 1985–90/92. Phase 2," Apr. 1982, p. 11, CREST. The literature on Reagan's policy toward southern Africa is poor. The best secondary

accounts are Massie, *Loosing the Bonds*, and Thomson, *U.S. Foreign Policy*. The most important account by a participant is *High Noon*, by Assistant Secretary of State for Africa Crocker. Written in a lively style, it combines valuable information and shrewd insights with a selective use of the evidence. Also useful are Secretary of State Shultz's *Turmoil*, pp. 1109–29; Chas Freeman's "The Angola/Namibia Accords" (Freeman was principal deputy assistant secretary of state for Africa from 1986 to 1989); senior NSC aide Peter Rodman's *Precious*, pp. 358–99.

32. Clark, in "Besoek van Mnr. Clark aan Suid-Afrika en Suidwes-Afrika: 10–13 Junie 1981," p. 10, Briewe van Minister van Buitelandse Sake en Inligting aan sy Kabinetskollegas oor Suidwes-Afrika—Samesprekinge en vervikkelinge sedert mei 1981 tot desember 1981, DFA.

33. Memcon (Pik Botha, Crocker), Apr. 15/16, 1981, T.5 US/SA relations, WITS.

34. Crocker, "South Africa: Strategy for Change," pp. 346, 349, 350–51.

35. Urquhart, *A Life*, p. 317.

36. Reagan, July 6, 1977 broadcast, PPP, ser. 1a, box 11, RRL; Reagan, Mar. 3, 1981 interview with Walter Cronkite of CBS News, *PP*, 1981, p. 197; Crocker, *High Noon*, pp. 80–81.

37. D'Oliveira, *Vorster*, pp. 44–103; de Villiers and de Villiers, *PW*, pp. 21–22, 27–28; Hagemann, *Südafrika*.

38. "RSA/VSA Verhoudings: Besoek van die Minister van Buitelandse Sake en Inligting aan die VSA, 13–16 mei 1981," p. 17, Briewe van Minister van Buitelandse Sake en Inligting aan sy Kabinetskollegas oor Suidwes-Afrika—Samesprekinge en vervikkelinge sedert mei 1981 tot desember 1981, DFA.

39. "An Interview with Ronald Reagan," *WSJ*, May 6, 1980, p. 26.

40. Haig to President, "Strategy in Southern Africa," Mar. 18, 1981, ES: MF, box 1, RRL.

41. Ibid.

42. Crocker, *High Noon*, p. 66.

43. Handwritten diary of Ronald Reagan, Mar. 24, 1981, courtesy of the Ronald Reagan Presidential Foundation. I asked to see this entry in the original manuscript diary because in the two-volume *Reagan Diaries*, edited by Douglas Brinkley, Neto is mistakenly transcribed as "N.A.T.O." and in the abridged one-volume edition of the diary, also edited by Brinkley, Neto is transcribed as "NATO." This made no sense.

44. NSC meeting, Feb. 6, 1981, p. 4, ES: MF, box 1, RRL.

45. Interview with Thirion; Steward, in "Meeting at Omega of the Angola Group: 7 December 1983," p. 2 quoted (emphasis added), Samesprekings met Angola, v. 4, DFA. See also Weissman, *Deference*, pp. 118–21.

46. Crocker, *High Noon*, p. 67.

47. "Besoek van Mnr. Clark," p. 4.

48. Ibid., pp. 25–28.

49. "RSA/VSA Verhoudings: Besoek van die Minister," p. 19.

50. "Besoek van Mnr. Clark," p. 29.

51. Ibid., pp. 32–33.

52. Fourie, *Brandpunte*, p. 182.

53. "Besoek van Mnr. Clark," p. 36.

54. Quotations from Crocker to SecState, Sept. 22, 1981, NSA, and "Discussions between the Delegations of South Africa and the United States of America in Zurich on 21

September 1981," pt. 2, p. 3, Suidwes-Afrika Dokumentasie, v. 1, DFA. For the exchange of letters, see Haig to Pik Botha: July 5, July 21, and Sept. 10, 1981; Pik Botha to Haig: July 8, July 28, and Sept. 23, 1981 (all in Messages between the South African Minister of Foreign Affairs and Information and the United States Secretaries of State between 14 May 1981 and 3 September 1982, DFA). For the Zurich meeting, see also AmConsul Cape Town to SecState, Sept. 18 and 23, 1981, FOIA; Bremer to Allen, Sept. 24, 1981, ES, NSCCF, Af, box 2, RRL.

55. SSC meeting, Nov. 23, 1981, #3, SVR; Walker to SecState, Oct. 9, 1981, FOIA.

56. Crocker, *High Noon*, p. 43.

57. Urquhart, *A Life*, p. 321.

58. Reagan, July 9, 1979 broadcast, PPP, ser. 1a, box 36, RRL.

59. CIA, "Moscow and the Namibia Peace Process," Apr. 7, 1982, p. 11, FOIA.

60. Crocker, *High Noon*, pp. 43, 66, 93.

61. Wisner, OH; also Thatcher, *Downing Street*, p. 158. For Bonn's Namibia policy in the Reagan years, see Engel, *Afrikapolitik*, pp. 147–84, and Brenke, *Bundesrepublik*; for Canada's, see L. Freeman, *Champion*, pp. 129–233.

62. Antonio Lengue, in Memcon (Sandri, Lengue), Nov. 13, 1981, Estero, v. 0507: 3174, FIG.

63. *Windhoek Advertiser*, Jan. 8, 1985, p. 2 quoted; *Times* (London), Jan. 9, 1985, p. 4, and Jan. 12, p. 4.

64. Pik Botha, May 7, 1988, RSA, *Hansard—Debates of Parliament*, col. 9404.

65. Pik Botha, Apr. 25, 1985, RSA, *Hansard—Debates of the House of Assembly*, col. 4124.

66 Flower, *Serving*, p. 262 quoted; Stiff, *Silent War*, pp. 369–405; Hall and Young, *Leviathan*, pp. 117–20, 125–37; Cabrita, *Mozambique*, pp. 133–204.

67. Military Information Bureau, SADF, "'Platform for Peace'—The History of the Joint Monitoring Commission from the South African Perspective," n.d., p. 4, DFA.

68. SADF Military Intelligence, "Inligtingsvoorligting en verdere optrede nav Op Protea," Sept. 18, 1981, p. 3, OAMI, gr. 10, box 197, DODDC.

69. *Pretoria News*, Aug. 27, 1981, p. 3.

70. Interview with Colonel Barlow.

71. J. Geldenhuys, *Dié*, p. 115; PW Botha, *RDM*, Aug. 27, 1981, p. 1; *Pretoria News*, Aug. 27, 1981, p. 3.

72. Interview with Foguetão, the senior Angolan officer who was the commander of the Fifth Military Region from late 1979 to late 1981. For a list with the names of the Soviet personnel at Ondjiva and Xangongo, based on captured documents, see "Information Relating to Russian Military Involvement in Southern Angola prior to OP Protea," Sept. 1981, OAMI, gr. 10, box 197, DODDC.

73. Petr Khrupilin, "Mena zvali kamarada Pedro: zapiski sovetnika," *Krasnaya Zvesda* (Moscow), Sept. 9, 2000, p. 6; Kolomnin, *Russkii Spetznaz*, p. 188; interview with Kianda.

74. Hoof van Staf Inligting, "Inligtingsvoorligting en verdere optrede nav Protea," Sept. 18, 1981, p. 99, OAMI, gr. 10, box 197, DODDC. See also Khrupilin, "Mena zvali"; Kolomnin, *Russkii Spetznaz*, pp. 77–87; Shkarinenko in Tokarev and G. Shubin, *Veterany*, pp. 71–79. For press reports, see *Burger* (Cape Town), Aug. 31, 1981, p. 1, and Sept. 3, p. 1; *Pretoria News*, Sept. 3, 1981, p. 3; *RDM*, Sept. 13, 1981, p. 1.

75. SADF Military Intelligence, "Effek van Operasie Protea op die SWA Konfliksitu-asie," Sept. 24, 1981, p. 11, OAMI, gr. 10, box 197, DODDC.

76. Quotations from DOS statement, Aug. 26, 1981, in *NYT*, Aug. 27, 1981, p. 10; *RDM*, Aug. 28, 1981, p. 10; *Burger*, Aug. 28, 1981, p. 20 (ed.).

77. *RDM*, Aug. 31, 1981, p. 1; *Star*, Sept. 2, 1981, p. 25; *Burger*, Sept. 2, 1981, p. 18 (ed.). For the Security Council debate, see the minutes of the meetings on Aug. 28–31, S/PV 2296 through S/PV 2300, DHL.

78. Quotations from James, *History*, p. 152; Memcon (Honecker, dos Santos), Oct. 12, 1981, pp. 10–11, DY30 JIV 2/201/1400, SAPMO; interview with Foguetão. The most interesting South African accounts of Protea, Daisy, Super, and Meebos are Breytenbach, *Buffalo Soldiers*, pp. 222–41, and Nortje, *32 Battalion*, pp. 169–85.

79. Memcon (Machel, Risquet), Jan. 25 1982, p. 2, ACC.

80. Dos Santos, in "Notas tomadas de la audiencia concedida por el presidente José Eduardo dos Santos al enviado especial de Cuba el día 3 de enero de 1988," p. 9, CF.

81. Nyerere, in Memcon (Risquet, Nyerere), Jan. 27, 1982, pp. 8–9, ACC; Amembassy Lusaka to SecState, June 6, 1982, FOIA.

82. Interview with Ita.

83. This paragraph is based on interviews with the following senior Angolan officers: Ngongo (quoted); Miranda (quoted), Foguetão (quoted), Paulo Lara, Ndalu, Kianda, Ita, Mendes de Carvalho, Pahama, Correia de Barros.

84. Quotations from interviews with Ngongo and Ndalu, and from MINFAR, aide-mémoire to the Soviet EMG, Aug. 28, 1984, p. 10, CF. Also interviews with the Angolan officers listed in the previous note.

85. Interview with Nunda; MINFAR, aide-mémoire to the Soviet EMG, Aug. 28, 1984, p. 8, CF.

86. Bridgland, *Savimbi*, pp. 293, 279.

87. Interview with Nunda.

88. Interview with Ngongo. Also Gárciga Blanco, "Olivo," pp. 20–24.

89. "Conversaciones entre representantes del MPLA-PT y el PCC," Dec. 29, 1981, pp. 95 and 143, CF.

90. CIA, "Soviet Policy and Africa," Mar. 1981, p. vi, FOIA.

91. Memcon (Risquet, Gromyko), Dec. 7–8, 1981, pp. 23, 9, 54–55, ACC.

92. Risquet to Castro, Dec. 12, 1981, ACC.

93. "Conversaciones," Dec. 29, 1981, p. 143.

94. Ibid., pp. 96–97, 101.

95. Ibid., p. 144.

96. MINFAR, aide-mémoire to Soviet EMG, Aug. 28, 1984, p. 15, CF.

97. "Contenido fundamental de la intervención del primer secretario del CC del PCC, compañero Fidel Castro, en las conversaciones sostenidas en Cuba con la delegación del Movimiento Popular para la Liberación de Angola—Partido del Trabajo (MPLA-PT), encabezada por el compañero Lúcio Lara," Dec. 30, 1981, pp. 171–73, CF.

98. Interview with Risquet.

99. "Declaración de los Ministros de Relaciones Exteriores de Cuba y Angola," Feb. 4, 1982, *Granma* (Havana), Feb. 6, 1982, p. 6.

100. Memcon (Castro, Shevardnadze), Oct. 28, 1985, p. 23, Consejo de Estado.

101. "Conversaciones," Dec. 29, 1981, pp. 107–8.

102. Reagan, *Reagan Diaries*, Jan. 26, 1982, 1:104; SecState to USDel Secretary, Jan. 28, 1982, FOIA. See also Memcon (Haig, Gromyko), Jan. 26, 1982, 10:00 A.M.–12:40 P.M., FOIA, and Memcon (Haig, Gromyko), Jan. 26, 1982, 2:00 to 7:00 P.M., FOIA.

CHAPTER 8

1. CIA, "The Growing Power of Black Labor," June 30, 1981, FOIA.

2. CIA, "South Africa: Prospects for Black Unrest," Dec. 2, 1982, FOIA.

3. "Discussions between the Delegations of South Africa and the United States of America in Zurich on 21 September 1981," pt. 1, p. 2, Suidwes-Afrika Dokumentasie, v. 1, DFA.

4. Secretariat SSC, "Salient Proposals of South African Negotiations with the 'Contact Group' Countries and the United Nations on the Question of South West Africa," June 1983 (emphasis in original), SVR.

5. Haig to Pik Botha, July 21 and Sept. 10, 1981, Messages between the South African Minister of Foreign Affairs and Information and the United States Secretaries of State between 14 May 1981 and 3 September 1982, DFA.

6. "Summary Notes of a Meeting between a South African Delegation and a United States Delegation on the Question of South West Africa: Geneva, May 10–11, 1982," p. 13, SWA/N, v. 3, DFA.

7. "Discussions between the Delegations of South Africa and the United States of America in Zurich on 21 September 1981; Message of the Western Five to the South African Government dated 12 September 1981," p. 4, Suidwes-Afrika Dokumentasie, v. 1, DFA.

8. Memcon (Pik Botha, Walker), Jan. 8 1982, SWA/N, v. 2, DFA; Pik Botha to Haig, Jan. 20, 1982, Messages between the South African Minister of Foreign Affairs and Information and the United States Secretaries of State between 14 May 1981 and 3 September 1982, DFA.

9. "Discussions between South Africa and the United States of America, Pretoria, 17 November 1982," pp. 10, 6–7, SA/USA (Crocker): Pta: 17 Nov. 82, SA/SWA (EM): Windhoek: 19–20 Nov. 82, SA/USA (Washington): 24–26 Nov. 82, DFA; Memcon (Pik Botha, Crocker), Nov. 27, 1982, p. 8, ibid.

10. "Namibia/Angola: Africa Directors' Meeting," Dec. 17, 1982, enclosed in SecState to Amembassy Gaborone, Dec. 18, 1982, FOIA.

11. See SecState to CFR Collective, Mar. 10 and Apr. 14, 1982, p. 2 quoted, NSA; SecState to Amembassy Brussels, Apr. 27, 1982, NSA.

12. Quotations from: Amembassy Kinshasa to SecState, June 7, 1982, p. 4, FOIA; Walters, "Lisbon, Luanda, Rabat, Paris, Istanbul, New Delhi, Bangkok, Hong Kong, Beijing, Tokyo—July 16–Aug. 31, 1982," p. 1, FOIA. Also SecState to Amembassy Lusaka, June 4, 1982, NSA; Memcon (dos Santos, Walters), June 7, 1982, FOIA; SecState to OAU Collective, June 8, 1982, FOIA; Walters to dos Santos, July 1, 1982, FOIA; Shultz to Reagan, Aug. 26, 1982, ES, NSCCF, Af, box 2, RRL.

13. Crocker to SecState, July 28, 1982, FOIA.

14. D. Geldenhuys, *Diplomacy*, pp. 33–42 (p. 41 quoted). As Geldenhuys notes, the Con-

stellation of States was part and parcel of the "total national strategy" that was designed to resist a "total onslaught" on South Africa. The total national strategy "involved the mobilisation of South Africa's total physical and human resources in a national endeavour to thwart the onslaught" (ibid., p. 38; also Stiff, *Warfare*, ch. 5; Pottinger, *Imperial Presidency*, esp. ch. 1).

15. Chipamata to Zambian foreign minister Chakulya, Feb. 27, 1980, p. 5, UNIP.

16. Van Tonder, "Samesprekings met Angola: 7 Des 82," Dec. 6, 1982, H SAW, gr. 2, box 183D, DODDC; Viljoen to Director General Foreign Affairs, Feb. 7, 1983, ibid.; Viljoen to Malan, Feb. 15, 1983, ibid.

17. Viljoen to Director General Foreign Affairs, Feb. 7, 1983, ibid.

18. Ekstein, "Ontmoeting tussen Suid-Afrika en die Kaap Verdiese Eilande: Eiland van Sal, 7 Oktober 1982," ibid.

19. Van Tonder, "Samesprekings met Angola: 7 Des 82," Dec. 6, 1982, ibid. For a list of the previous South African–Angolan meetings, see "Meetings with Angola," Angola VII: Verhoudings/Samesprekings met Angola, v. 1, DFA.

20. Pik Botha, in "Samesprekings tussen die RSA en Angola: 7 desember 1982," p. 4, Angola VII: Verhoudings/Samesprekings met Suid-Afrika, v. 1, DFA. Also "Meeting between South Africa and Angola, Ilha do Sal, Cape Verde, 7 December 1982," ibid.; "S.V.R. se vergadering op 20 Desember 1982: Suid-Afrika se samesprekings met Angola en gebeure daarna," ibid.; "Minutes of a Meeting between South African and Angolan Delegations: Ilha do Sal, 23 February 1983," ibid., v. 2; "Samesprekings tussen Suid-Afrikaanse en Angolese afvaardigings. Ilha do Sal—23 februarie 1983," Samesprekings met Angola, v. 1, DFA.

21. Van Tonder, "Samesprekings met Angola 23 Februarie 1983," Feb. 24, 1983, p. 5, H SAW, gr. 2, box 183D, DODDC.

22. "Versión de la reunión de la delegación cubana con la parte soviética," Feb. 3, 1983, p. 6, CF; Memcon (Risquet, José María), Dec. 17, 1982, p. 1, OS.

23. Steward to Pik Botha, Mar. 11, 1983, Samesprekings met Suidwes-Afrika/Namibië, v. 5 (emphasis in original), DFA.

24. Memcon (Crocker, Fourie, van der Westhuyzen), Mar. 19, 1983, ibid. For Eagleburger's speech, see "Discussions between South African and United States Delegations, Washington DC—17–19 March 1983," H SAW, gr. 2, box 185B, DODDC.

25. Shultz to President, June 6, 1983, ES, NSCCF, Af, box 2, RRL.

26. SSC meeting, May 16, 1983, #4, SVR.

27. Secretariat SSC, "'nasionale Staatkundige en Veiligheidstrategie vir SWA en Angola," Sept. 23, 1983, pp. 1–2, SVR.

28. SWA-GIS, "South West Africa Peoples [sic] Organisation (SWAPO)," Sept. 23, 1983, p. 11, DFA.

29. Pérez de Cuéllar, *Pilgrimage*, p. 299; Crocker, in Memcon (Pik Botha, McFarlane), Aug. 8, 1985, p. 2, Angola, v. 16, DFA.

30. "Report of the Secretary-General concerning the Implementation of Security Council Resolution 435 (1978) and 439 (1978) on the Question of Namibia," Feb. 26, 1979, S/13120, DHL; "Further Report of the Secretary concerning the Implementation of Security Council Resolutions 435 (1978) and 439 (1978) concerning the Question of Namibia," May 19, 1983, S15/776, DHL.

31. See UNSC Resolution 532 of May 31, 1983 in www.un.org/documents.

32. SSC, Aug. 22, 1983, #4, SVR.

33. "Minutes of the Meetings between a South African Delegation and the Secretary-General of the United Nations, Cape Town, 23 and 24 August 1983," p. 10 quoted, Suidwes-Afrika/Namibië, v. 6, DFA; Memcon (PW Botha, Pérez de Cuéllar), Aug. 23, 1983, ibid.

34. Pérez de Cuéllar, *NYT*, Aug. 27, 1983, p. 4; "Further Report of the Secretary General concerning the Implementation of Security Council Resolutions 435 (1978) and 439 (1978) concerning the Question of Namibia," Aug. 29, 1983, p. 6 quoted, UNSC S/15943, DHL. See also Pérez de Cuéllar, *Pilgrimage*, pp. 296–300.

35. Quotations from UNSC Resolution 539, Oct. 28, 1983, in www.un.org/documents, and UNSC Official Records, 2492nd meeting, Oct. 28, 1983, p. 7, DHL.

36. "Samesprekings Crocker en H Leër 18 November 1982," Nov. 25, 1982, p. 4, H SAW, gr. 2, box 183D, DODDC.

37. Cheysson, *Le Monde*, Dec. 9, 1983, p. 1; "Incontro con l'ambasciatore angolano Telmo de Almeida (Roma, 10 gennaio 1984)," Estero, v. 8401: 0111, FIG; *Times*, Dec. 9, 1983, p. 6.

38. Du Pisani, "On Brinkmanship," p. 4; Simon, "Decolonisation," p. 510.

39. Secretariat SSC, "Die omskepping van die Sentrale Regeringsteltsel in SWA/N," Apr. 14, 1982, p. 13, SVR.

40. *Windhoek Advertiser*, Jan. 11, 1983, p. 1; Jan. 18, p. 3; Feb. 23, p. 3.

41. Du Pisani, "On Brinksmanship," p. 7.

42. Interviews with Robinson and Nojoba; *Windhoek Advertiser*, Jan. 4, 1985, p. 3. For the semi-official story of the SWATF, see Snyman, *Beeld*. See also Toase, "South African Army."

43. Interviews with Robinson and Nojoba.

44. See telegrams from Havana, [Oct. 1979,] nos. 741 and 744, NSA; Shubin, *Hot "Cold War,"* pp. 221–22.

45. Interview with general Nakandungile.

46. *Windhoek Advertiser*, Feb. 21, 1983, p. 1; Scholtz, "War," p. 36.

47. Barlow, *Executive Outcomes*, p. 17.

48. For the April meeting in Havana, see "Reunión de las delegaciones de Angola, URSS, SWAPO y Cuba, efectuada en el salón de protocolo, en el Laguito, el día 12 de abril de 1982"; "Reunión de las delegaciones de Angola, URSS, SWAPO y Cuba, efectuada en el salón de protocolo, en el Laguito, el día 13 de abril de 1982," morning and afternoon sessions; "Reunión de las delegaciones de Angola, URSS, SWAPO y Cuba, efectuada en el salón de protocolo, en el Laguito, el día 14 de abril de 1982," morning and afternoon sessions. For the September meeting in Luanda, see "Reunión conjunta entre las delegaciones de Cuba, Unión Soviética, SWAPO y Angola, celebrada en Luanda, el día 7 de septiembre de 1982"; "Reunión conjunta entre las delegaciones de Cuba, Unión Soviética, SWAPO y Angola, celebrada en Luanda, el día 8 de septiembre de 1982"; "Reunión conjunta entre las delegaciones de Cuba, Unión Soviética, SWAPO y Angola, celebrada en Luanda, el día 8 de septiembre de 1982 (Sesión Noche)." All ACC.

49. "Reunión," Sept. 7, 1982, pp. 54, 60–61.

50. "Reunión," Apr. 12, 1982, pp. 53, 33.

51. Ibid., pp. 88, 101–2, 104–7.

52. Nujoma, in "Reunión," Apr. 14, 1982, morning, pp. 41–42; Risquet, in "Reunión," Apr. 13, 1982, afternoon, p. 111; Risquet, in "Reunión," Apr. 14, 1982, afternoon, pp. 33, 40–41, 51; Lara, in "Reunión," Apr. 14, 1982, morning, p. 44; Lara, in "Conversaciónes entre representantes del MPLA-PT y el PCC," Dec. 28, 1981, p. 17, CF.

## CHAPTER 9

1. Quotations from Júnior, *Forças Armadas*, p. 92, and CIA, DI, "Moscow's Response to the Diplomatic Challenge in Southern Africa," May 1984, p. 3, FOIA.

2. For a good overview of the Angolan economy, see the "Quarterly Economic Reviews" of the *Economist Intelligence Unit.*

3. "Versión de la reunión de la delegación cubana con la parte soviética," Feb. 3, 1983, p. 20, CF.

4. "Protocolo entre el gobierno de la República de Cuba y el gobierno de la República Popular de Angola, para el asesoramiento a la unidades de lucha contra bandidos," Sept. 16, 1982, appendix 2, CF.

5. Memcon (Castro, Konstantin Kurochkin), Feb. 11, 1984, p. 22, CF.

6. A town along the Namibe-Menongue road, not to be confused with Savimbi's headquarters in Cuando Cubango, near the Namibian border.

7. Interview with Gárciga Blanco.

8. MINFAR, "Las Misiones Internacionalistas Desarrolladas por las FAR en Defensa de la Independencia y la Soberanía de los Pueblos," p. 50, CF; interviews with Moreno and Serrano.

9. Interviews with Moreno, Serrano, and Risquet.

10. Raúl Castro, in "Conversaciones entre representantes del MPLA-PT y el PCC," Dec. 29, 1981, p. 139, CF. Also Raúl Castro, in "Reunión de análisis de la situación de las tropas cubanas en la RPA, efectuada a partir de las 17:25 horas del 15.11.1987," pp. 117, 120–21, CF.

11. "Situación de la Misión Militar Cubana en Angola," enclosed in "Primera Reunión Cuba—URSS," Feb. 3, 1983, pp. 63–64, CF.

12. "Cuba-URSS," May 18, 1983, in "Tripartita," May 1983, p. 81, ACC.

13. Memcon (Ustinov, Risquet), Sept. 7, 1984, p. 29, ACC.

14. Interview with Risquet.

15. Memcon (Raúl Castro, Andropov), Dec. 29, 1982, pp. 4–13, OS.

16. Interview with Risquet.

17. Memo Telcon (Raúl Castro, Andropov), Jan. 1, 1983, OS.

18. Session of Politburo of CC CPSU, May 31, 1983, CWIHP *Bulletin*, Fall 1994, p. 80.

19. Raúl Castro, in Vázquez Raña, *Raúl Castro*, p. 32.

20. MINFAR, "Misiones internacionalistas militares cumplidas por Cuba, 1963 a 1991," July 1998, pp. 62–64, OS.

21. See "Primera Reunión Cuba—URSS," Feb. 3, 1983, CF.

22. "Apreciación de la situación política y socioeconómica de la República Popular de Angola y propuestas para enfrentarlas," [Mar. 1983], pp. 4, 3, 9, 24, 11–12, 29, CF.

23. "Cuba—URSS," May 18, 1983, in "Tripartita," May 1983, pp. 81, 105–6 (emphasis in original), CF.

24. "Reunión Tripartita URSS—Angola—Cuba," May 18, 1983, in ibid., pp. 136–39.

25. Memcon (Castro, Pedalé, Lúcio Lara), July 29, 1983, p. 2, CF.

26. Del Pino, *General del Pino*, p. 17.

27. My account of the battle of Cangamba is based on MINFAR, "Experiencias de las acciones combativas de Cangamba," Dec. 9, 1983, p. 28 quoted, CF; MINFAR, "Sobre la situación en la región de Cangamba en la RP de Angola," [Aug. 1983], CF; and on the transcripts of the conversations between the military mission and the general staff of the Cuban armed forces in Havana that occurred 2–3 times a day during the Cangamba operation ("MMCA—EMG"). For UNITA's version, see Bridgland, *Savimbi*, pp. 409–11. (The 6,000 figure is from ibid., p. 410.) For a well-documented Cuban account, see Blandino, *Cangamba*.

28. "A Concise History of Operation Moduler (Phase One) May–October 1987," p. 4, JFH, gr. VERS, box 30, DODDC.

29. Castro to dos Santos, Aug. 10, 1983, CF. See also the conversation between Castro and Polo Cintra Frías in "MMCA—EMG," Aug. 10, 1983, 4 P.M., and Castro to dos Santos, Sept. 20, 1983, CF.

30. Polo to Castro, "Mensaje cifrado No. 6095, 6096, 6097 y 6098 procedentes de la MMCA 11.8.83, 0840 horas," CF. For Konstantin's confused account of his differences with the Cubans following the victory at Cangamba, see V. Shubin, *Hot "Cold War,"* pp. 85–88, 90–91.

31. "Análisis de la situación de Angola," Aug. 15, 1983, p. 1, CF.

32. Castro to Polo, Aug. 11, 1983, 3 P.M., CF; Ulises, Polo, in "MMCA—EMG," Aug. 11, 1983, 2 P.M., p. 5.

33. Puente Ferro to Fidel and Raúl Castro, Aug. 11, 1983, CF.

34. Raúl Castro to Puente Ferro, Aug. 11, 1983, CF.

35. Puente Ferro to Raúl Castro, Aug. 11, 1983, CF.

36. D. Lord, *Fledgling*, p. 292.

37. See *Pretoria News*, Aug. 17, 1983, p. 1, and Aug. 20, p. 2.

38. Interview with Risquet.

39. "Análisis sobre la situación de Angola 14.8.83," pp. 1, 6–8, 30, 40–41, 44, CF.

40. "Instrucciones impartidas al compañero Jorge Risquet por el Comandante en Jefe," Sept. 16, 1983, pp. 1, 3, CF.

41. "Reunión con la dirección angolana el 18 de agosto a las 8:30 A.M.," pp. 14, 17, CF.

42. Ibid., pp. 14–15.

43. "Reunión cubano-soviética," Aug. 22, 1983, pp. 6, 11–12, ACC.

44. Blandino, *Cangamba*, p. 268.

45. MMCA, "Resumen anual de la situación militar en la República Popular de Angola: 1984," Feb. 1985, p. 74, CF.

46. Crocker, *High Noon*, p. 175.

47. Fischer, "Conundrum," pp. 13–14 quoted; Gates, *Shadows*, pp. 267–73; Kornienko, *Kholodnaya voina*, pp. 210–33.

48. "Narrative of the Anti-Castro Cuban Operation Zapata," June 13, 1961, p. 23 quoted, enclosed in Taylor to president, June 13, 1961, NSF, box 61A, JFKL; "Narrative of Air Activity," enclosed in memorandum for Lieutenant Colonel Tarwater, Apr. 26, 1961, ibid.

49. MINFAR, "Misiones internacionalistas militares cumplidas por Cuba, 1963 a 1991," pp. 71–77, OS.

50. Memcon (Castro, dos Santos), [Sept. 8, 1986], pp. 18–19, CF.

51. "Documento de trabajo de la sección Africa del CC del PCUS," pp. 1, 2, enclosed in "Reunión cubano-soviética," Aug. 22, 1983, ACC.

52. See Memcon (Colomé, Ulises, Konstantin), Feb. 8, 1984; "Situación político-militar en la República Popular de Angola para el 1ro. de noviembre de 1984," enclosed in Polo to Jefe Secretaría del Ministro de las FAR, Nov. 9, 1984; MMCA, "Resumen anual de la situación militar en la República Popular de Angola: 1984," Feb. 1985, pp. 35–38. All CF.

53. Castro to dos Santos, Sept. 20, 1983, pp. 3, 5–10, CF.

54. For Cuba's earnings in the 1978–83 period, see Ministerio de la Inversión Extran-jera y la Colaboración Económica, "Historia de la Colaboración entre la República de Cuba y la República de Angola," unpublished manuscript, Havana, 2002, p. 64. For the new agreement, see "Acuerdo Especial sobre las Condiciones Generales para la Rea-lización de la Colaboración Económica y Científico-Técnica entre el Gobierno de la República de Cuba y el Gobierno de la República Popular de Angola," Oct. 28, 1983, CECE. For the 4,168 figure, see "Protocolo de la V Sesión de la Comisión Mixta Intergu-bernamental Cubano-Angolana de Colaboración Económica y Científico Técnica," Oct. 23, 1983, p. 2, CECE.

55. Dos Santos to Castro, Oct. 28, 1983, CF.

56. Colonel Oelschig, "South Africa's Involvement with the UNITA organisation," June 1, 1988, 1/3/3 v. 2, Cuba: Relations with South Afrida, DFA.

57. Quotations from Chief of SADF, "OP Seawarrior," May 24, 1985, HS OPS, gr. 9, box 5, DODDC, and General Liebenberg, "OP Cerberus," Oct. 2, 1985, ibid.

58. See *Times* (London), Dec. 2, 1981, p. 6, and Nov. 12, 1982, p. 9; Stiff, *Silent Wars*, pp. 357–58; Bridgland, *Savimbi*, p. 442; Amembassy Pretoria to Amembassy Harare, Nov. 11, 1982, ES, NSCCF, Af, box 2, RRL.

59. SADF, "A Concise History of Operation Moduler (Phase One) May–October 1987," p. 4, JFH, gr. VERS, box 30, DODDC.

60. H SWA 2 to H SAW 3, Feb. 3, 1988, p. 4, M, gr. 7, box 518, DODDC.

61. Memcon (Crocker, Generals Geldenhuys and van der Westhuizen), Aug. 1, 1982, S.W.A./N v. 4, DFA.

62. Eagleburger to Pik Botha, Feb. 15, 1983, H SAW, gr. 2, box 185B, DODDC; "Sa-mesprekings Crocker en H Leër 18 November 1982," Nov. 25, 1982, p. 2, ibid.; "Closing Remarks by Deputy Secretary [sic] Eagleburger," Mar. 19, 1983, ibid.

63. South Africa's Ambassador Fourie to Minister and Director General, Apr. 29, 1983, courtesy of Ronnie Kasrils.

64. Hoof van Staf Inligting, "Komopsplan: Op Askari," Dec. 5, 1983, pp. 4, 5, HS OPS, gr. 9, box 4, DODDC.

65. Viljoen, *RDM*, Dec. 24, 1983, p. 1; DIA, "South Africa—Angola: South African Attacks," Dec. 28, 1983, FOIA. The only useful published account of the operation is R. Lord, "Operation Askari."

66. Different Cuban documents give slightly different figures for the strength of the four brigades. See "Composición de unidades FAPLA en el sur," [Dec. 1983]; "Informe

sobre la situación de la 11 BIR ubicada en Cuvelai," Jan. 13, 1984; "Resultado de la visita efectuada por una comisión de la Misión Militar Cubana en Angola a las tropas cubanas de la Agrupación Sur de la R.P.A.," [Jan. 1984]. All CF.

67. Interviews with Kianda, who was the commander of the Fifth Military Region, and with Ngongo, the FAPLA's deputy chief of staff. Both note that this was the military region with the largest number of Soviet advisers: between fifty and sixty, including those who were attached to the region's Hqs. (The number included the interpreters, who were military officers.)

68. Varennikov, *Nepovtorimoe*, 4:249; V. Shubin, *Hot "Cold War,"* p. 88, quoting Konstantin; interview with Kianda, the commander of the Fifth Military Region.

69. Polo to J' EMG, Dec. 29, 1983, CF. For Konstantin's version of his clashes with Polo during Askari, see V. Shubin, *Hot "Cold War,"* pp. 94–96.

70. Interviews with Kianda, Mendes de Carvalho, Ngongo, Ndalu, Pahama, and Foguetão.

71. Memcon (Risquet, dos Santos), Dec. 30, 1983, pp. 19, 22, CF.

72. Memcon (Risquet, dos Santos), Jan. 22, 1984, p. 5, CF.

73. Quotations from HS OPS, "Sitrap op Askari," [Jan. 1984], p. 1, HS OPS, gr. 9, box 4, DODDC, and Cdr Sektor 10, "Op Plan: Op Askari," Sept. 23, 1983, p. 3, AAN DOK, box 52, DODDC.

74. Konstantin, in Memcon (Castro, Konstantin), Feb. 11, 1984, p. 24, CF.

75. HS OPS, "Sitrap op Askari," [Jan. 1984], HS OPS, gr. 9, box 4, DODDC; "Operasionele Voorligting op Askari," ibid.; H SAW to Minister of Defense, Jan. 5, 1984, M, gr. 5, box 117, DODDC.

76. *RDM*, Jan. 7, 1984, p. 1; *Burger* (Cape Town), Jan. 7, 1984, p. 1. The myth of the two battalions lives on: see, for example, Malan, *My lewe*, p. 262, and Hamann, *Generals*, p. 77.

77. MMCA, "Resumen anual de la situación militar en la Repùblica Popular de Angola: 1984," Feb. 1985, pp. 63–64, CF. On the number of Cubans at Cuvelai, see Polo to Jefe EMG, Jan. 10, 1984, CF.

78. Memcon (Colomé, Ustinov), Jan. 10, 1984, CF.

79. Crocker to SecState, Dec. 31, 1983; Viljoen, *RDM*, Dec. 27, 1983, p. 1. For the Cahama brigade, see "SWA voorligting aan Minister van Verdediging," [Dec. 1983], HS OPS, gr. 9, box 4, DODDC; HS OPS, "Sitrap op Askari," [Jan. 1984], ibid.; H SAW to Minister of Defense, Jan. 5, 1984, M, gr. 5, box 117, DODDC.

80. See UNSC Resolution #546 of Jan. 6, 1984, in www.un.org/documents.

81. *Cape Times*, Jan. 7, 1984, p. 2; Pik Botha, *Beeld* (Johannesburg), Jan. 7, 1984, p. 2.

82. Memcon (Risquet, Varennikov), Jan. 25, 1984, CF; Varennikov, *Nepovtorimoe*, 4:248.

83. Varennikov, *Nepovtorimoe*, 4:272–73.

84. Memcon (Risquet, Varennikov), Jan. 25, 1984, pp. 1–4, CF.

85. Ibid., pp. 6–7.

86. Ibid., pp. 10, 11, 13–14.

87. Ibid., pp. 14, 26, 37. See also Castro to dos Santos, Jan. 7, 1984, CF. In his memoirs, Varennikov writes that he made a spirited defense of Soviet military strategy in Angola (*Nepovtorimoe*, 4:272–76).

88. Military Information Bureau, SADF, "'Platform for Peace'—The History of the Joint Monitoring Commission from the South African Perspective," n.d., pp. 10–11, DFA.

89. "Tripartite Statement," [Feb. 16, 1984,] quoted, Geagte Kollega-Briewe, v. 5, DFA. Also "Summarized Minutes of Discussions between South African and United States Delegations," Jan. 27, 1984, ibid.; "Mulungushi Minute on the Establishment of a Joint South African–Angolan Monitoring Commission," Feb. 14, 1984, ibid.; "Record of a Meeting between Angola, South Africa and the United States on the Establishment of a Joint Monitoring Commission," Feb. 14, 1984, Angola, v. 6, DFA; "First Meeting of the South African/Angolan Joint Monitoring Commission," Feb. 16, 1984, Geagte Kollega-Briewe, v. 5, DFA; Pik Botha, "Drieledige konferensie tussen Suid-Afrika, Angola en die VSA. Lusaka: 16 Februarie 1984," Angola VII: Verhoudings/Samesprekings met Suid-Afrika, v. 2, DFA; "Informele Samesprekings tussen Suid-Afrikaanse en Angolese Afvaardigings," Feb. 17, 1984, Geagte Kollega-Briewe, v. 5, DFA. Also Hill to McFarlane, Jan. 28, 1984, FOIA; SecState to All African Post, Feb. 25, 1984, FOIA; CIA, DI, "Moscow's Response to the Diplomatic Challenge in Southern Africa," May 1984, FOIA.

90. "Información recibida de los compañeros Puente Ferro y general de división Polo el 21-2-84," p. 1, CF.

91. Matlock, *Reagan*, pp. 87–88.

92. Quotations from Crocker to SecState, Mar. 12, 1984, FOIA; CIA, DI, "Moscow's Response to the Diplomatic Challenge in Southern Africa," May 1984, p. 6, FOIA; Stanley Mabizela to SIDA, May 18, 1984, quoted by Sellström, *Sweden*, 2:652. For the text of the Nkomati accord, see *RDM*, Mar. 17, 1984, pp. 2–3. For the ANC and Nkomati, see Barrell, "Conscripts," pp. 332–40, and Callinicos, *Tambo*, pp. 517–19. For a South African perspective by a protagonist, see Heunis, *Inner Circle*, pp. 37–47. For a Mozambican participant, see Veloso, *Memórias*, pp. 154–88. For Mozambique in the 1980s, see Newitt, *History*, ch. 20; Hall and Young, *Leviathan*; Hanlon, *Mozambique*.

93. SecState to All African Diplomatic Posts, Mar. 16, 1984, FOIA.

94. Amembassy Maputo to SecState, Apr. 21, 1984, FOIA; see also Platt to McFarlane, Feb. 5, 1985, FOIA; Stiff, *Silent War*, pp. 377–91; Crocker, *High Noon*, pp. 245–46.

95. *Times*, Mar. 16, 1984, p. 14.

96. Memcon (Castro, dos Santos), Mar. 17, 1984, pp. 43, 29–31, ACC.

97. Ibid., pp. 38–40.

98. Memcon (Castro, dos Santos), Mar. 19, 1984, pp. 51, 55–57, 64–66, 71–73, ACC.

99. Memcon (Risquet, dos Santos) enclosed in "Mensaje cifrado no. 18308 recibido de la RPA el 18.7.87," ACC.

100. "Algunas ideas en cuanto a lo que debe ser nuestra posición en relación al proceso negociador iniciado unilateralmente por la dirección angolana," [Havana, Feb. 1984], p. 5, ACC.

101. Memcon (Castro, Axen), July 26, 1984, p. 5, DY30 IV 2/2.035/41, SAPMO.

CHAPTER 10

1. See Memcon (President dos Santos, General van der Westhuizen), Lusaka, June 25, 1984, Geagte Kollega-Briewe, v. 7, DFA; "Discussions between South Africa and Angola," Lusaka, Apr. 25, 1984, ibid.; "Meeting between South Africa and Angola. Lusaka: 21 May 1984," Angola, v. 8, DFA; Memcon (Pik Botha, Kito Rodrigues), Lusaka, July 2, 1984, Geagte Kollega-Briewe, v. 8, DFA; "Meeting between Lt-Col A M Rodrigues ("Kito"), Minister of the Interior of Angola, and South African Representatives," Lusaka, July 7,

1984, Angola v. 10, DFA; "Verwikkelinge ten opsigte van die vredensinisiatief met Angola," Maputo, Aug. 17, 1984, Geagte Kollega-Briewe, v. 8, DFA; "Meeting between South African and Angolan Delegations. Maputo: 9 May 1985," Angola, v. 15, DFA.

2. "Reunión Bipartita Cuba—URSS," Sept. 5, 1984, p. 26, CF.

3. Memcon (Crocker, Chitunda), Oct. 1, 1984, p. 4, FOIA.

4. "Reunión Tripartita Cuba—URSS—Angola," Mar. 6, 1985, p. 41, CF.

5. CIA, DI, "Moscow's Response to the Diplomatic Challenge in Southern Africa," May 1984, p. 4, FOIA.

6. Quotations from Gromyko, in "Reunión Bipartida Cuba—URSS," Sept. 5, 1984, ACC, and Ilyichev, in "Reunión Bilateral Cuba—URSS," Feb. 20–22, 1985, pp. 17, 19, 15, ACC.

7. "Reunión Bilateral Cuba—URSS," Feb. 20–22, 1985, p. 221, ACC.

8. See text of the Angolan proposal, enclosed in dos Santos to Secretary-General of the United Nations, Nov. 17, 1984, Doc. S/16838, DHL; see text of the South African proposal, enclosed in Conradie to Secretary-General of the United Nations, Nov. 23, 1984, Doc. S/16839, DHL.

9. "Discussions between South Africa and Angola," Lusaka, Apr. 25, 1984, p. 8, Geagte Kollega-Briewe, v. 7, DFA; Memcon (Pik Botha, Crocker), May 25, 1984, p. 3, ibid.

10. See Pik Botha, *Pretoria News*, Mar. 13, 1984, p. 1; Memcon (Pik Botha, Nickel), Mar. 12, 1984, Geagte Kollega-Briewe, v. 6, DFA; Steward, "Luncheon Offered by Ambassador Herman Nickel," Mar. 31, 1984, Angola, v. 8, DFA; "Discussions between South Africa and Angola: Lusaka, 25 April 1984," Geagte Kollega-Briewe, v. 7, DFA; Memcon (Pik Botha, Savimbi), Nov. 15, 1984, Angola, v. 13, DFA; Memcon (Pik Botha, Crocker), Nov. 16, 1984, ibid., v. 14.

11. Wisner, in "Versión de las conversaciones EEUU—RPA," Dec. 3, 1984, first sess., pp. 6–7, ACC. For the reference to Nkomati, see Wisner, in "Conversaciones celebradas entre las delegaciones de Estados Unidos y de Angola," Oct. 16, 1984, morning sess., p. 5, ACC.

12. CIA, DI, "Angola: Prospects for MPLA-UNITA Reconciliation," Feb. 1985, p. 7, FOIA; interview with General Thirion.

13. Secretariat SSC, "'n Nasionale Staatkundige en Veiligheidstrategie vir SWA en Angola," Sept. 23, 1983, p. 6, SVR.

14. Ibid., p. 1.

15. For the group's composition, see "Meeting at Tiger base between the South African group on Angola and Dr Jonas Savimbi," Dec. 7, 1983, Samesprekings met Angola, v. 4, DFA.

16. Quotations from "Agenda vir die samesprekings met Mario op 7 Desember 1983," Dec. 6, 1983, ibid., and "Meeting at Omega of the Angola Group," Dec. 7, 1983, ibid.

17. Interview with Colonel Breytenbach.

18. "Points Made by Dr. Jonas Savimbi during a Meeting on May 28, 1983," Samesprekings met Angola, v. 2, DFA.

19. "Besoek aan Savimbi se Leërhoofkwartier in Angola deur lede van die Angola Gesamentlike Bestuursentrum (AGES), 28 en 29 November 1984," Dec. 2, 1984, pp. 5–6, SVR.

20. "Speech Made by President Savimbi during the Visit of State President P. W. Botha to Jamba on June 22, 1985," pp. 1, 5, 7, Angola, v. 15, DFA; interview with General Thirion.

21. Quotations from interviews with Generals Geldenhuys and Thirion, and Colonel Breytenbach.

22. Interview with General Geldenhuys.

23. See "Details of the Meeting in Vila Nova," Mar. 30, 1988; Colonel Oelschig to Sunde, June 1988; Representative Jamba to Director General Foreign Ministry, June 27, 1988; Deputy Director General—Africa to Director General Foreign Ministry, June 28, 1988. All 1/3/3 v. 2, Cuba: Relations with South Afrida, DFA.

24. Tel. interview with van Heerden; Savimbi, in "Meeting between a South African Delegation and Dr Jonas Savimbi: Jamba, Angola: 29 October 1983," pp. 7–8, enclosed in Steward to Pik Botha, Nov. 7, 1983, Samesprekings met Angola, v. 2, DFA.

25. Bridgland, *Savimbi*, p. 422.

26. Quotations from MMCA, "Resumen anual de la situación militar en la República Popular de Angola: 1984," Feb. 1985, p. 18, CF; "Situación político-militar en la República Popular de Angola para el 1ro. de noviembre de 1984," p. 5, enclosed in Cintra Frías to Jefe Secretaría del Ministro de las FAR, Nov. 9, 1984, CF; Secretariat SSC, "Riglyne vir 'n totale strategie vir Angola," Apr. 1984, p. 2, SVR.

27. Interview with General Thirion.

28. Secretariat SSC, "'n Nasionale Staatkundige en Veiligheidstrategie vir SWA en Angola," Sept. 23, 1983, pp. 6, 12, SVR; interview with General Badenhorst.

29. SSC meeting, Mar. 5, 1984, #4, SVR; Memcon (Pik Botha, Crocker), May 25, 1984, p. 3, Geagte Kollega-Briewe, v. 7, DFA; Steward, in Memcon (Crocker, Savimbi, Geldenhuys), May 29, 1984, p. 9, Angola, v. 7, DFA.

30. "Meeting between a South African Delegation and Dr Jonas Savimbi: Jamba, Angola: 29 October 1983," p. 6, enclosed in Steward to Pik Botha, Nov. 7, 1983, Samesprekings met Angola, v. 2, DFA.

31. Interview with General Badenhorst; Chief of the SADF to Secretary, Secretariat SSC, Oct. 22, 1984, SVR; interview with General Thirion. "Thirion was not taken in by Savimbi" (interview with Colonel Breytenbach).

32. SSC, "Konsepriglyne Nr 22: Totale Strategie vir Angola," July 1984, pp. 2–4, SVR.

33. *Star* (Johannesburg), Sept. 14, 1984, pp. 1, 3.

34. *Burger* (Cape Town), Sept. 14, 1984, p. 1.

35. *Times* (London), Sept. 15, 1984, p. 6; Memcon (Pik Botha, Savimbi), Oct. 28, 1984, p. 1, Angola, v. 12, DFA.

36. Crocker, *High Noon*, p. 196; for Pik Botha's statement, see *RDM*, Mar. 21, 1984, p. 6.

37. Quotations from Steenkamp, *Border War*, p. 118, and Nujoma, *Wavered*, p. 329. On the JMC, see SSC, "Die Veiligheidsituasie soos op 25 April 1984," SVR; Military Information Bureau, SADF, "'Platform for Peace': The History of the Joint Monitoring Commission from the South African Perspective," n.d., DFA; Heitman and Dorning, "Joint Monitoring Commission."

38. Memcon (dos Santos, van der Westhuizen), Lusaka, June 25, 1984, Geagte Kollega-Briewe, v. 7, DFA.

39. Ibid.

40. Venancio da Moura, in "Conversaciones celebradas entre las delegaciones de Estados Unidos y la República Popular de Angola," Oct. 16, 1984, afternoon sess., p. 12, ACC.

41. Stiff, *Silent War*, p. 457.

42. Crocker, *High Noon*, p. 215; Stiff, *Silent War*, p. 458; Melvin Hill, president Gulf Oil Exploration and Production, Sept. 17, 1980, in U.S. Congress, HCFA, Subcommittee on Africa, *United States Policy toward Angola—Update*, p. 10. The best account of this South African operation is Stiff, *Silent War*, pp. 457–69.

43. "The Namibia-Angola Negotiations: Briefing by the Assistant Secretary of State for African Affairs (Crocker), April 19, 1985," DOS Files, doc. 164, p. 326, FOIA.

44. *Pretoria News*, May 23, 1985, p. 1 (quoting SADF statement); *Cape Times*, May 25, 1985, p. 1 (quoting General Viljoen); Malan, May 28, 1985, RSA, *Hansard—Debates of the House of Assembly*, col. 6379; *Pretoria News*, May 29, 1985, p. 1 (quoting du Toit). For the full text of du Toit's press conference, see *Jornal de Angola* (Luanda), May 29, 1985, p. 1. For du Toit's own account, see Soule, *Story*, pp. 1–36.

45. *Daily Telegraph* (London), May 24, 1985, p. 22 (ed.); *Star*, May 25, 1985, p. 1.

46. Bridgland, *Savimbi*, p. 442; UNITA, quoted in *Star*, May 30, 1985, p. 8.

47. *NYT*, May 25, 1985, p. 3.

48. *WP*, June 14, 1985, p. 23.

49. Interview with Pik Botha.

50. Memcons (Pik Botha, Nickel): May 27, 1985; May 28, 1985; June 3, 1985; June 7, 1985. (All Angola, v. 15, DFA)

51. "Extract from Talks with US Delegation, Vienna, 8–9 August 1985," ibid., v. 11.

52. McFarlane, "Meeting with Pik Botha," Aug. 8, 1985, FOIA.

53. For the text of the synthesis paper, see "Basis for Negotiations," Suidwes-Afrika/Namibië, v. 11, DFA.

54. Memcon (Pik Botha, Crocker), Mar. 21, 1985, pp. 3–4, ibid.

55. Ibid, p. 9.

56. Memcon (Crocker, Savimbi, two South African Military Intelligence officers), Feb. 18, 1984, Geagte Kollega-Briewe, v. 5, DFA. Also Pik Botha to Geagte Kollega, Feb. 24, 1984, ibid.

57. Memcon (Pik Botha, Crocker), Nov. 16, 1984, pp. 12, 15, Angola, v. 14, DFA.

58. Memcon (Pik Botha, Crocker), Mar. 21, 1985, p. 10, Suidwes-Afrika/Namibië, v. 11, DFA.

59. Pik Botha, "Samespreking met Dr Chester Crocker," Aug. 31, 1984, p. 5, Geagte Kollega-Briewe, v. 8, DFA.

60. Memcon (Pik Botha, Nickel), Mar. 12, 1984, pp. 3, 6, ibid., v. 6.

61. See Kito to Crocker, May 6, 1985, FOIA.

62. Ringdahl to McFarlane, July 3, 1985, AAD, NSC, box 2, RRL.

63. "South African Response to the United States 'Synthesis' on the Withdrawal of the Cubans from Angola," May 30, 1985, pp. 1, 6–7, Angola, v. 15, DFA.

64. Wisner, in Memcon (Wisner, Chitunda), Nov. 21, 1984, FOIA.

65. Memcon (Crocker, Chitunda), Dec. 5, 1984, FOIA.

66. Crocker, in Memcon (Crocker, Savimbi), Nov. 15, 1984, FOIA; Wisner, in Memcon (Wisner, Chitunda), Nov. 21, 1984, FOIA.

67. Savimbi, in Memcon (Crocker, Savimbi, two South African Military Intelligence officers), Feb. 18, 1984, Geagte Kollega-Briewe, v. 5, DFA; Crocker, in Memcon (Crocker, Savimbi, Geldenhuys), Pretoria, May 29, 1984, p. 7, Angola, v. 7, DFA.

68. Memcon (Crocker, Savimbi, van der Westhuizen), Pretoria, Nov. 15, 1984, p. 3, Angola, v. 7, DFA.

69. Savimbi, in Memcon (Crocker, Savimbi, van der Westhuizen), Cape Town, Feb. 11, 1985, ibid., v. 14.

70. Chitunda, in Memcon (Crocker, Chitunda), Dec. 5, 1984, FOIA; Chitunda, in Memcon (Crocker, Chitunda), Sept. 25, 1984, FOIA; van der Westhuizen, in Memcon (Savimbi, van der Westhuizen), Jamba, Mar. 21, 1985, p. 3, Suidwes-Afrika/Namibië, v. 11, DFA.

71. Memcon (Frasure, Cabelly, Carney, Savimbi), Jamba, Mar. 22, 1985, FOIA.

72. Malan to Pik Botha, June 19, 1985 (enclosing Crocker's letter), Angola, v. 15, DFA.

73. Memcon (Savimbi, Pik Botha), June 6, 1985, ibid.

74. Pik Botha to Lieutenant Colonel Rodriguez, minister of interior of Angola, July 17, 1985, CF.

75. Crocker, *High Noon*, p. 461; Goulding, *Peacemonger*, p. 142.

76. Memcon (Rogers, Steward), Apr. 9, 1984, p. 4, Angola, v. 8, DFA.

77. Brand Fourie to Pik Botha, Apr. 16, 1984, Lusaka Ooreenkoms, DFA; Memcon (Pik Botha, Crocker), May 25, 1984, p. 6, Geagte Kollega-Briewe, DFA.

78. Memcon (Pik Botha, Nickel), Feb. 27, 1984, p. 3, Suidwes-Afrika/Namibië, v. 7, DFA; "Samesprekings met Dr Chester Crocker," Aug. 31, 1984, Geagte Kollega-Briewe, v. 8, DFA.

79. Nickel, in Memcon (Killen, Nickel), Apr. 4, 1985, Suidwes-Afrika/Namibië, v. 11, DFA; PW Botha, Apr. 18, 1985, RSA, *Hansard—Debates of the House of Assembly*, cols. 3783–84.

80. Quotations from "The Namibia-Angola Negotiations: Briefing by the Assistant Secretary of State for African Affairs (Crocker), April 19, 1985," DOS Files, doc. 164, pp. 327–28, FOIA; Ringdahl to McFarlane, July 3, 1985, AAD, NSC, box 2, RRL.

81. *Windhoek Advertiser*, May 22, 1985, p. 1 (also for Savimbi's statement).

82. David Bezuidenhout, chairman of the TGNU, *Windhoek Advertiser*, June 18, 1985, p. 4; "Text of Speech by State President PW Botha on the occasion of the inauguration of the legislative and executive authorities for SWA/Namibia," June 17, 1985, pp. 2–3, 5, SWA/Binnelandse Verwikkelinge, v. 4, DFA.

83. Eglin, PW Botha, Apr. 19, 1985, RSA, *Hansard—Debates of the House of Assembly*, cols. 3818–19, 3909.

84. "Giv Opdrag: Bepaling van steun vir SWAPO in 'n moontlike verkiesing in SWA," Mar. 10, 1985, p. 2, SVR.

85. INR, "China's Policy toward Sub-Saharan Africa," Aug. 20, 1985, p. 4, FOIA. Also Jackson, "China's Third World Foreign Policy," and Stark, *Aussenpolitk*, pp. 217–20.

86. Ambassador Lewis, UNSC Official Records, 2588th Meeting, June 13, 1985, pp. 10–11, DHL.

87. CIA, "The African National Congress of South Africa," July 1986, p. 12, FOIA.

88. Quotations from PW Botha, Jan. 31, 1985, RSA, *Hansard—Debates of the House of Assembly*, col. 311; *Sowetan* (Johannesburg), Feb. 11, 1985, p. 2 (for Zinzi Mandela's words); *RDM*, Feb. 11, 1985, p. 2 (for the text of Mandela's reply); Sparks, *Tomorrow*, pp. 50–51.

89. Sparks, *Tomorrow*, p. 48; Chikane, "Children," pp. 342–43.

90. CIA, DI, "South Africa: Time Running Out. Revisited," Jan. 10, 1986, p. 2, FOIA; CIA, DI, "Africa Review," Feb. 5, 1988, p. 3, FOIA.

91. Gevisser, *Mbeki*, p. 531.

92. O'Malley, *Shades*, p. 202; interview with Ricketts.

93. Ringdahl to McFarlane, July 11, 1985, AAD, NSC, box 1, RRL. See also Barrell, "Conscripts," pp. 376–77, and Stiff, *Silent War*, pp. 470–97.

94. Ringdahl to McFarlane, June 20, 1985, AAD, NSC, box 1, RRL,

CHAPTER 11

1. Crocker, *High Noon*, pp. 255, 263–64. On the antiapartheid movement in the United States, see Borstelmann, *Cold War*; Metz, "Anti-Apartheid"; Culverson, *Contesting*; Nesbitt, *Race*; Massie, *Loosing*; Robinson, *Defending*.

2. Reagan to PW Botha, Jan. 7, 1985, AAD, NSC, box 1, RRL.

3. *WSJ*, Apr. 1, 1985, p. 22 (ed.); Johnson, "The Race for South Africa," *Commentary*, Sept. 1985, p. 32; *Human Events*, July 6, 1985, p. 5; *National Review*, Aug. 15, 1986, p. 14.

4. *National Review*, Feb. 28, 1986, p. 19; *National Security Record*, Sept. 2005, p. 4; *Human Events*, June 29, 1985, p. 3. Newspapers that reflected the views of the hard-line critics include the *Washington Times*, the *Wall Street Journal*, *Human Events*, *Commentary*, the *National Interest*, the *Conservative Digest*, the *National Review*, *Policy Review*, *Reason*, and the *National Security Record*.

5. *Times* (London), Oct. 26, 1986, p. 12; Amembassy Maputo to SecState, Feb. 14, 1985, NSA; Sen. Malcolm Wallop (R-Wyo.), "How U.S. Fails Anti-Communist Liberation Movements," *Human Events*, Apr. 6, 1985, p. 14. On RENAMO, see Vines, *RENAMO*; Geffray, *La cause*.

6. Maggie Gallagher and Charles Bork, "The New Freedom Fighters," *Commentary*, Sept. 1985, p. 61.

7. Wisner to SecState, Oct. 17, 1983, NSA.

8. Ibid.

9. On the Reagan administration and Mozambique, see Crocker, *High Noon*, esp. ch. 10 (p. 247 quoted), and Scott, *Deciding*, pp. 193–212.

10. *WSJ*, Apr. 1, 1985, p. 22 (ed.); Howard Phillips, "U.S. Aiding Marxism in Africa?" *Conservative Digest*, Apr. 1985, p. 19; *National Review*, Mar. 14, 1986, p. 17.

11. National Coalition of Americans Committed to Rescuing Africa from the Grip of Soviet Tyranny, *WT*, Dec. 7, 1984, p. A5.

12. Jack Wheeler, "How UNITA Can Win," *Human Events*, Feb. 8, 1986, p. 18.

13. Quotations from interview with Crocker; Shultz, *Turmoil*, p. 1116; C. Freeman, OH. Because of the dearth of documents, there is no authoritative study of the CIA in the Reagan years, and virtually nothing about its activities in southern Africa. The best accounts are Woodward, *Veil*, and Weiner, *Legacy*, pp. 375–422; see also Persico's sympathetic *Casey*, pp. 172–582, and Prados, *Safe*, pp. 466–579.

14. Interview with Freeman; Gerald Frost, "Why Thatcher Coddles Mozambican Marxists," op-ed, *WSJ*, Aug. 12, 1987, p. 19.

15. *NYT*, Sept. 10, 1985, p. 1; *National Review*, Oct. 4, 1985, pp. 13–14.

16. *WT*, Jan. 31, 1988, p. A9 (ed.).

17. Ambassador to Foreign Ministry, May 5, 1986, 1/33/8/3/ v. 45, USA Policy in Africa, DFA.

18. Ambassador to Foreign Ministry, May 8, 1986, ibid.

19. See the statements of the Chief of the Army and the Chief of the Air Force in *Star* (Johannesburg), May 19, 1986, p. 1.

20. *WSJ*, May 20, 1986, p. 33; *Star*, May 20, 1986, p. 15.

21. [Kasrils], in "Julio/86 en Habana," p. 23, ACC.

22. *Times* (London), May 21, 1986, p. 7; Masire, *Business Day* (Johannesburg), May 20, 1986, p. 3; *Botswana Guardian* (Gaborone), May 23, 1986, p. 6 (ed.); *Star*, May 20, 1986, p. 14. Also Stiff, *Silent War*, pp. 506–23.

23. Secretariat SSC, "Zambië," July 22, 1985, pp. 5–6, SVR; Memcon (Pik Botha, Genscher), Apr. 22, 1986, pp. 7–8, Staatsveiligheidsraadvergadering notule van 26/3/86, DFA. See also Secretariat SSC, "Strategie Nr 18: Botswana," June 1986, SVR, and "Zambië: Politieke Situasie," Dec. 12, 1986, SVR.

24. "The Commonwealth Accord on Southern Africa," Oct. 20, 1985, enclosed in the Commonwealth Group of Eminent Persons, *Mission*, p. 144.

25. See Prinslow, *Stem*, pp. 310–14.

26. Quotations from [Kasrils], in "Julio/86 en Habana," p. 23, and the Commonwealth Group of Eminent Persons, *Mission*, pp. 114–15, 117. See also Callinicos, *Tambo*, pp. 591–94, and Gevisser, *Mbeki*, pp. 533–34.

27. *Business Day*, May 20, 1986, p. 6 (ed.); *Times*, May 20, 1986, p. 17 (ed.).

28. Quotations from interview with Pik Botha; Stiff, *Silent War*, pp. 521–22; *Business Day*, May 21, 1986, p. 5.

29. Nickel, OH.

30. See *Beeld* (Johannesburg), Feb. 7, 1986, p. 1; Papenfus, *Pik Botha*, pp. 400–416.

31. Quotations from Nickel, OH, and from interview with Pik Botha. For PW Botha's rebuke, see RSA, *Hansard—Debates of the House of Assembly*, Feb. 7, 1986, pp. 409–10. For a perceptive portrait of Pik Botha, see Heunis, *Inner Circle*, pp. 18–36.

32. Abramowitz (INR) to Acting SecState, Dec. 23, 1987, p. 3, FOIA.

33. SADF, "Amerikaanse militêre optrede teen Libië: Implikasie vir die RSA," Apr. 22, 1986, 1/33/8/3 v. 45, USA Policy in Africa, DFA; PW Botha to Reagan, Apr. 18, 1986, ibid.

34. Shultz, *Turmoil*, p. 1121.

35. *Human Events*, May 31, 1986, p. 1; Nathan Perlmutter and David Evanier, "The African National Congress: A Closer Look," *ADL Bulletin*, May 1986, pp. 13–14.

36. *Times*, June 13, 1986, p. 8; Commonwealth Group of Eminent Persons, *Mission*, pp. 133, 135–36; CIA, "The African National Congress of South Africa," July 1986, p. 13, FOIA.

37. Crocker, *High Noon*, p. 319; C. Freeman, OH.

38. Reagan, "Remarks to Members of the World Affairs Council and the Foreign Policy Association," July 22, 1986, *PP*, 1986, 2:984–88.

39. Shultz, *Turmoil*, p. 1122; Crocker, *High Noon*, p. 323..

40. *Human Events*, Aug. 2, 1986, p. 1.

41. Shultz, July 23, 1986, in U.S. Congress, SCFR, *Situation*, pp. 81, 83–84, 86, 91.

42. Quotations from "Meeting between the African National Congress and the Ambassador of the United States of America, H.E. Mr. Paul Hare, Lusaka, 30 July, 1986,"

Karis-Gerhart Collection, folder 75, WITS, and "Report of a Meeting between the ANC and Robert Cabelly Special Assistant to Chester Crocker: U.S. Information Office, Lusaka, Sept. 7, 1983," ibid., folder 51. Also interview with Cabelly; Gevisser, *Mbeki*, pp. 486–88,

43. Crocker, *High Noon*, p. 323.

44. *WSJ*, Sept. 16, 1986, p. 28 (ed.).

45. *National Review*, Oct. 24, 1986, p. 17; Shultz, *Turmoil*, pp. 1122–23.

46. "Relations between South Africa and Swaziland are now so good that the SADF does not think that any operation will be conducted in Swaziland without the approval and the cooperation of the Swazi government" (SSC Werkkomitee, Oct. 2, 1985, A-9, Angola, v. 16, DFA).

47. CIA, "Options and Scenarios for South Africa's Actions against Its Neighbors," July 14, 1986, p. 2, FOIA.

48. CIA, "South Africa's Changing Policy Agenda," July 1, 1985, p. 25, FOIA.

49. See L. Freeman, *Champion*, pp. 149–65; Morgenstierne, *Denmark*, pp. 98–119; Eriksen, *Norway*, pp. 193–210; Sellström, *Sweden*, 2:781–94; Soiri and Peltola, *Finland*, pp. 137–54; Gleijeses, "Scandinavia."

50. Smith Hempstone, "Pretoria's Defense Buddy," *WT*, June 19, 1987, p. D3; CIA, "Israel: Military and Nuclear Cooperation with South Africa," [date sanitized], FOIA; de Villiers and de Villiers, *PW*, pp. 293–94. On the military relationship between the two countries, see also Potgieter, "The Secret"; Cockburn and Cockburn, *Dangerous*, pp. 280–312; and esp. Polakow-Suransky, *Alliance*, pp. 53–212.

51. Quotations from CIA, "Israel"; CIA, "Africa Review," Supplement, June 8, 1981, p. 5, FOIA; Hempstone, "Pretoria's Defense Buddy."

52. Public Law 99-440, Oct. 2, 1986, sec. 508 (a), *United States Statutes at Large*, v. 100, 99th Cong., 2nd sess.

53. Maseng to "Dear Friend," Sept. 22, 1986, Green, Max Files, box 5, RRL.

54. Quotations from CIA, "Israel"; *Jerusalem Post*, Mar. 19, 1987, pp. 1, 8; Hempstone, "Pretoria's Defense Buddy."

55. South African Broadcasting Corporation, *Jerusalem Post*, Mar. 22, 1987, p. 1; PW Botha, *Business Day*, Mar. 26, 1987, p. 1.

56. DOS, "Report to Congress on Industrialized Democracies' Relations with and Measures against South Africa," May 12, 1987, pp. 27–29, FOIA.

57. *Jerusalem Post*, Sept. 18, 1987, p. 2; *Burger* (Cape Town), Jan. 7, 1988, p. 14 (ed.); Polakow-Suransky, *Alliance*, p. 204.

58. Reagan, Oct. 24, 1985, *PP*, 1985, 2:1288.

59. *WT*, Oct. 25, 1985, p. A9 (ed.).

60. For Cambodia, see Scott, *Deciding*, pp. 82–111. For the Mujahedin, see Gates, *Shadows*, pp. 319–23, 346–50, 354, and Coll, *Ghost Wars*, pp. 101–5, 124–27. For the Contras, see Leogrande, *Backyard*.

61. In mid-1985 the Reagan administration ordered the closing of most Nicaraguan consulates in the United States. In response to that step, which sought to reduce the flow of Americans traveling to Nicaragua, Managua lifted all visa restrictions for U.S. citizens. The visa requirement was reestablished on July 1, 1989 (*NYT*, June 19, 1989, p. 3).

62. Reagan, *Reagan Diaries*, May 4, 1983, 1:223.

63. Interview with Wolpe.

64. Ismael Martins, "Informe Sumario, 26/9–10/10," [Oct. 1985], p. 2, ACC.

65. Interviews with Fenton and Doug Smith.

66. Interview with Wolpe.

67. Buckley, "Help Savimbi," *National Review*, Feb. 28, 1986, p. 62; Hatch, "Why We Should Aid Savimbi," *WT*, Feb. 7, 1986, p. D2; Worthington, "Angola's Unknown War," *National Review*, Nov. 1, 1985, p. 54.

68. Interviews with Napper, Grove, Cabelly, and Davidow; Grove, *Walls*, p. 222.

69. Hodges, *Angola*, p. 19.

70. Fred Bridgland, "Savimbi et l'exercise du pouvoir," *Politique Africaine*, Mar. 1995, p. 95.

71. *WP*, Jan. 29, 1986, p. 16 (ed.); *Los Angeles Times*, Nov. 12, 1985, p. B4 (ed.).

72. Goulding, *Peacemonger*, p. 181.

73. *Times*, July 30, 1980, p. 7; Bridgland, *Savimbi*, p. 277; Amnesty International, *Imprisonment*, p. 3; Amnesty International, *Angola*, p. 4; Hornsby, "The Man Who Would Rule Angola," *Times*, May 17, 1984, p. 12. For the Feb. 9, 1984, blow-up of the Angolan airliner, see *Cape Times*, Feb. 14, 1984, p. 2, and Feb. 16, p. 2; for the Huambo bombing, see my comments in chapter 12.

74. *NYT*, Apr. 24, 1984, p. 12; *WT*, Jan. 28, 1986, p. A6.

75. Brooke, "Angola's Civil War Reduces a Fertile District to Hunger," *NYT*, Dec. 31, 1984, p. 1.

76. Brooke, "The Cubans in Angola: 'They're Not All Soldiers,'" *NYT*, Jan. 22, 1985, p. 2; Brooke, "Angola's Second City: A Faded Postcard of 1975," *NYT*, Jan. 11, 1985, p. 2.

77. *NYT*, Nov. 12, 1985, p. 34 (ed.); Brooke, "War Turns Angolan Breadbasket into Land of Hunger," *NYT*, Dec. 28, 1985, p. 2. For Lewis, see "Marching for Pretoria," *NYT*, Oct. 31, 1985, p. 27.

78. *Expresso* (Lisbon), Nov. 30, 1979, p. 8.

79. *WP*, Jan. 29, 1986, p. 16 (ed.), emphasis added; Cowell, "Reporter's Notebook: Angola's Rebel Stakes Claim," *NYT*, Apr. 2, 1984, p. 8.

80. Hitchens, "Minority Report," *The Nation*, Dec. 7, 1985, p. 606.

81. Here is a representative sample: "Jonas Savimbi, doctor of philosophy (Lausanne University)," *WP*, July 19, 1981, p. 1; Savimbi "has a doctorate in law and political science" (*NYT*, Dec. 5, 1982, IV:2); Savimbi "holds a Ph.D. from Switzerland's Lausanne University" (*WSJ*, Aug. 20, 1985, p. 28); Savimbi "received a Ph.D. in political and juridical sciences from Lausanne University" (*National Review*, May 9, 1986, p. 29).

82. Bridgland, *Savimbi*, pp. 53, 67.

83. CIA, DI, "Angola: Prospects for MPLA-UNITA Reconciliation," Feb. 1985, p. 4, FOIA; [DOS], "The Reagan Doctrine in Southern Africa—Mozambique," p. 1, enclosed in Platt to Carlucci, Jan. 31, 1987, FOIA.

84. Interview with Fenton.

85. Amembassy Lisbon to SecState, June 15, 1982, S.3, p. 7, FOIA (reporting conversation between Wisner and Morais Cabral); interview with Crocker.

86. Arguably the most important exception was Rep. Stephen Solarz (D-N.Y.), who sharply questioned Savimbi's commitment to political democracy. (See, for example, Solarz, "When to Intervene," and Solarz, Nov. 19, 1985, 99th Cong., 1st sess., v. 131, *CR* E5257.)

87. Interview with Wolpe.

88. Interview with Weissman.

89. For a copy of the letter, see Howard Wolpe Collection, A-1286, box 1, Archives and Regional History Collections, Western Michigan University.

90. Savimbi, "The War against Soviet Colonialism," *Policy Review*, Winter 1986, p. 21.

91. Interview with Weissman.

92. Pepper, Nov. 12, 1985, in U.S. Congress, HCFA, subcommittee on Africa, *Angola: Intervention or Negotiation?*, pp. 70, 72. On the congressional debate about aid to Savimbi, see Weissman, *Deference*, pp. 122–36.

93. I culled the excerpts of Shultz's and Michel's letters quoted in the text from *WT*, Oct. 23, 1985, p. A1, and Oct. 24, p. A9 (ed.). The *Washington Times*'s praise of Michel's letter is from its October 24 edition.

94. Kemp, *WT*, Oct. 24, 1985, p. A1.

95. William Murchison, op-ed, *WT*, Nov. 1, 1985, p. D3; Phillips, *WT*, Dec. 23, 1985, p. A10.

96. Shultz, *Turmoil*, pp. 1118–19.

97. Cabinet office, "Brief on the People's Republic of Angola," July 26, 1983, p. 13, 156 UNIP 7/23/78, UNIP.

98. Ambassador to Pik Botha, Jan. 28, 1986, AMI, gr. 14, box 131, DODDC.

99. Reagan, *Reagan Diaries*, Nov. 8, 1985, 2:538.

100. See ibid., Nov. 12, 1985, 2:539; Shultz, *Turmoil*, p. 1119; Gates, *Shadows*, p. 347.

101. The amount of the aid was classified. The $18 million figure is from Shultz, *Turmoil*, p. 1124.

102. Quotations from interviews with Davidow, Fenton, and Doug Smith.

103. *WT*, Feb. 19, 1986, p. A4; Crocker, Moose, Feb. 18, 1986, U.S. Congress, SCFR, *Angola: Options*, pp. 25, 39; Reagan to Mobutu, Feb. 11, 1986, CHF, box 91630, RRL.

104. CIA, [no title, no date], enclosed in Wettering to Clark, Jan. 27, 1982, FOIA; Grove, *Walls*, pp. 263, 264.

105. Reagan, *Reagan Diaries*, Sept. 23, 1984, 1:385.

106. Grove, *Walls*, p. 272.

107. Reagan letter, enclosed in SecState to Amembassy Kinshasa, May 22, 1986, NSA.

108. Interview with Grove.

109. Interview with Doug Smith; Walters to SecState, May 23, 1986, NSA.

110. Levitsky to Powell, [Feb. 1988], FOIA.

111. Gates, *Shadows*, p. 347; interview with General Nunda. See also Nasionale Intel-ligensdiens, "Die huidige stand van VSA-UNITA-betrekkinge," Mar. 23, 1989, 1/22/2/6/1 UNITA: Relations with USA, DFA.

112. Interviews with Nunda, Cohen, Doug Smith, and Fenton.

113. Interview with Nunda.

114. Interview with General Thirion. For 1975, see Gleijeses, *Conflicting Missions*, pp. 294–99.

115. Memcon (Shultz, Savimbi), Feb. 6, 1986, p. 4 quoted, FOIA; "Dr. Savimbi's Schedule," enclosed in Platt to Poindexter, Jan. 27, 1986, NSA.

116. *WSJ*, Jan. 31, 1986, p. 24. Savimbi's December 1981 visit had been far more modest. He had not met Reagan and had received far less attention from the media and from

Congress. See Memcon (Wolfowitz, Savimbi), Dec. 3, 1981; Memcon (Crocker, Savimbi), Dec. 3, 1981; Memcon (Abrams, Savimbi), Dec. 3, 1981. All FOIA. Also Shipley and Smoak to Viall, Dec. 11, 1981, enclosed in van Tonder to H SAW, Feb. 9, 1982, M, gr. 7, box 462, DODDC, and Windrich, *Guerrilla*, pp. 17–22.

117. Tel. interview with Wisner; *WP*, Feb. 9, 1986, p. 1. On Savimbi's trip, see also Windrich, *Guerrilla*, pp. 43–62; South African ambassador, Washington, to DFA, Feb. 2, 1986, Angola, v. 16, DFA; Memcon (Crocker, Pik Botha), Feb. 13, 1986, Suidwes-Afrika, v. 14, DFA.

118. Dos Santos to Castro, Aug. 14, 1985, p. 5, CF.

119. *WP*, Feb. 1, 1986, p. 15 quoted; *Los Angeles Times*, Jan. 30, 1986, p. C1; Economist Intelligence Unit, "Country Profile: Angola," July 1986, pp. 18–24.

120. *National Security Record*, Sept. 1985, p. 4; Crane, *WT*, Feb. 7, 1986, p. A4.

121. Interview with Wolpe.

122. Quotations from *WT*, Jan. 3, 1986, p. A9 (ed.); *Human Events*, Feb. 8, 1986, p. 4 (the poster); Wheeler, "How UNITA Can Win," *Human Events*, Feb. 8, 1986, p. 18. Shortly thereafter, the administration froze all loans and guarantees from the U.S. Export-Import Bank to American companies doing business in Angola until "Luanda . . . stops making war on UNITA" (*WP*, July 31, 1986, p. 32).

123. *WP*, Jan. 29, 1986, p. 3.

124. Quotations from Steward to Manley, Sept. 25, 1985, Angola, v. 16, DFA, and Stewart to Pik Botha, Sept. 26, 1985, ibid. See also Memcon (Steward, Wisner), Sept. 24, 1985, enclosed in Steward to Manley, Oct. 1, 1985, ibid.

125. PW Botha to Reagan, Oct. 4, 1985, Exchanges: Pres Reagan/Pres Botha, DFA; Pik Botha to Shultz, Nov. 22, 1985, SWA/Angola, v. 1, DFA.

126. SSC, "Totale Strategie vir Angola," Aug. 26, 1985, SVR.

127. Defense Minister Malan et al., "Angola: UNITA Strategie," Nov. 11, 1985, p. 1, H SAW, gr. 4, box 160, DODDC; Pik Botha, in "Samesprekings: Staatspresident met die Kabinet van die Oorgangsregering van Nasionale Eenheid (ORNE) van SWA," May 21, 1986, ALUKA.

128. See PRA, Gabinete do Presidente, Memcon (dos Santos, Armacost), Oct. 22, 1985; PRA, Ministerio das Relações Exteriores, Memorandum, Nov. 5, 1985; "Encontro de Lusaka (27–28 de novembro de 1985)"; "Orientações Gerais sobre as Conversações com os Estados Unidos da America, a teram lugar na Republica Popular de Angola de 8 a 9 de enero de 1986." All private collection, Luanda.

CHAPTER 12

1. Reagan, July 8, 1985, *PP*, 1985, 2:806–7; Shultz, *NYT*, Jan. 26, 1986, p. 10.

2. Shultz, May 23, 1985, DOS *Bulletin*, July 1985, p. 42; *NYT*, June 14, 1985, p. 30 (ed.).

3. "National Security Planning Group Meeting," June 25, 1984, p. 7, NSA. On Reagan and Nicaragua, see Leogrande, *Backyard*. For my assessment, see Gleijeses, "Reagan Doctrine."

4. Memcon (Honecker, Raúl Castro), Apr. 8, 1985, p. 10, DY30 JIV851, SAPMO.

5. Goodsell, "Revolutionary Cuba," *Christian Science Monitor* (Boston), Jan. 29, 1985, p. 14.

6. Interview with Alarcón.

7. Memcon (Castro, Demichev), Jan. 8, 1984, pp. 18–19, 23–24, 25, Consejo de Estado.

8. "Reunión de análisis de la situación de las tropas cubanas en la RPA, efectuada a partir de las 17:25 horas del 15.11.87," pp. 169–70, CF.

9. Quotations from interviews with Padrón, Sánchez-Parodi, and Ferch.

10. Interview with Ferch. See also Ferch, OH.

11. Skoug, OH.

12. Memcon (Castro, Axen), July 26, 1984, pp. 2–3, DY30 IV2/2.035/41, SAPMO.

13. *NYT*, Dec. 15, 1984, p. 1, and Dec. 16, p. E2; Schoultz, *Infernal*, pp. 396–99; Castro, in Ramonet, *Cien Horas*, pp. 382–83; Skoug, *United States*, pp. 57–80.

14. For the Castro interview, see Leonard Downie and Karen DeYoung, "Cuban Leader Sees Positive Signs for Ties in Second Reagan Term," *WP*, Feb. 3, 1985, p. 1; for the White House's reply, see *WP*, Feb. 5, 1985, p. 10, and Reagan's Press Conference, *PP*, 1985, 1:159.

15. Skoug, *NYT*, June 9, 1985, p. 9.

16. *NYT*, May 1, 1985, p. 19.

17. Interview with Skoug.

18. Skoug, OH.

19. Ibid.

20. Williamson, "Cuba/USA Relations," June 25, 1986, Cuba 27606, pt. 9, RG 25, Bibliothèque et Archives Canada/Library and Archives Canada, Ottawa.

21. Schlesinger, op-ed, *WSJ*, June 7, 1985, p. 24. Early on, while Radio Martí was pending in Congress, the Cuban government had warned that if the administration put the radio on the air "we would have to answer because we consider it an aggression against our country" (Carlos Rafael Rodríguez, *NYT*, June 17, 1983, p. 3).

22. Interview with Skoug; Embassy of Canada, Havana, "Cuba's Foreign Policy," July 6, 1987, Cuba 27606, pt. 19, RG 25, Bibliothèque et Archives Canada/Library and Archives Canada, Ottawa.

23. Interview with Kamman.

24. Ibid.

25. Interviews with Kamman (quoted), Ferch, Crocker, and Freeman.

26. Interview with Skoug.

27. Memcon (Castro, Shevardnadze), Oct. 28, 1985, p. 14, Consejo de Estado.

28. Reagan, Oct. 24, 1985, *PP*, 1985, 2:1288; Ortega, *Barricada* (Managua), Oct. 25, 1985, p. 12.

29. Memcon (Castro, Shevardnadze), Oct. 28, 1985, p. 3. Also MINFAR, "Misiones internacionalistas militares cumplidas por Cuba, 1963 a 1991," pp. 61–67, OS.

30. *Barricada*, May 3, 1985, p. 1.

31. Memcon (Castro, dos Santos), Mar. 19, 1984, pp. 71–72, ACC.

32. Interviews with three Cuban primary school teachers who worked in Nicaragua: Nancy Herrera, Dinorah Suarez, and Marina González; interview with Sonia Romero, head of the educational mission in Nicaragua (Dec. 1982–Nov. 1983); Jorge Batista Girbau, "La colaboración educacional cubana en Nicaragua," unpublished manuscript, Havana (this is the source for the figures in the text); Contingente Pedagogico, "Augusto César Sandino," *Memorias*, 1981, n.p.,; Rojas, *El aula*; Jiménez Rodríguez, *Mujeres*, pp. 72–83, and *De las mujeres*.

33. Memcon (Castro, Shevardnadze), Oct. 28, 1985, pp. 3–4.

34. Benjamin Cohen, op-ed, *NYT*, Aug. 8, 1985, p. 23.

35. "Zapiski osnovnovo soderzhania besed M. S. Gorbachev s F. Kastro v Gavane," Apr. 3–4, 1989, p. 11 (courtesy of Sergey Radchenko).

36. Memcon (Honecker, Raúl Castro), Apr. 8, 1985, pp. 2, 5, 6, DY30 JIV851, SAPMO.

37. Castro, "Informe central al tercer Congreso," Feb. 4, 1986, *Granma* (Havana), Feb. 7, 1986, p. 3.

38. *NYT*, Aug. 1, 1985, p. D1.

39. Szulc, op-ed, *Plain Dealer* (Cleveland), Oct. 6, 1985, 1-C.

40. Castro, Dec. 2, 1986, *Granma*, Dec. 5, 1986, p. 6. (The Third Congress was held in two rounds, in February and December 1986.)

41. Politburo meeting, Oct. 23, 1986, in Chernyaev et al., *Politburo*, p. 94.

42. Gorbachev, *Zhizn'*, 2:422–23. See also Medvedev, *Raspad*, pp. 254–55. Unfortunately neither the Russians nor the Cubans have declassified the minutes of the conference or the conversation between Castro and Gorbachev. For Gorbachev's opening speech, see "Niederschrift über das Treffen . . .," *Zeitschrift für Geschichtswissenschaft*, no. 8 (1994): 716–21; for a brief account of the conference, see the memoirs of the East German ambassador to the USSR (Winkelmann, *Moskau*, pp. 250–56), and Gorbachev's report at the Politburo meeting of November 13, 1986, in Chernyaev et al., *Politburo*, pp. 105-7.

43. "Country Report: Cuba, Dominican Republic, Haiti, Puerto Rico," *Economic Intelligence Unit*, no. 4 (1986): 10 quoted. The $4.3 billion figure is from Hernández-Catá, "Fall," p. 25, and includes about $2.3 billion a year in loans, the remainder in trade subsidies.

44. For the 1981 figure, General Casas in Memcon (Casas, Ustinov), May 14, 1981, OS; for the 1986 figure, interview with Tony Pérez, Cuba's ambassador in Ethiopia in 1986–91.

45. *NYT*, Jan. 25, 1984, p. 2.

46. Interview with Tony Pérez.

47. Memcon (Honecker, Risquet), Apr. 17, 1989, p. 16, DY30 JIV 958, SAPMO.

48. *Ethiopian Herald* (Addis Ababa), Dec. 18, 2007, p. 1.

49. *Ethiopian Herald*, Dec. 19, 2007, p. 1.

50. Colonel Rodríguez del Pozo, enclosed in Ochoa to Viceministro Primero, May 27, 1977, p. 5 quoted; "Protocolo de las conversaciones sobre colaboración en la rama de la salud entre los gobiernos de la República de Cuba y Etiopia," May 23, 1977; Ministerio de Salud Pública, "Informe sobre la visita realizada a Etiopía de la delegación del Ministerio de Salud Pública de Cuba, presidida por el ministro, Dr. José A. Gutierrez Muñiz, del 17 al 23 de mayo de 1977." All CF.

51. See *Colaboración Internacional* (Havana), Dec. 1984, pp. 17–18.

52. Interview with Berhanu Dibaba.

53. Interview with Sophia Ndeitungo. There is no good study of foreign scholarship students in Cuba. Some valuable information can be culled from Bestard Pavón, "La colaboración," and from Colina la Rosa et al., "Estudiantes." A few useful articles are in the 1980s issues of *Colaboración* (renamed in 1984 *Colaboración Internacional*). My own understanding has been sharpened by my interviews with the Namibian students Claudia Uushona, Sophia Ndeitungo, Miriam Shikongo, Erasmus Tulesheni Naikako, Esther Moombolah-Goagoses, Gabriel Shaanika, Andreas Niicodemus; with the Ethiopians Berhanu Dibaba, Lemma Hundessa, and Abraham Waldemariam; with the Guineans

Safayo Ba, Moussa Beavogui, Mamoudou Diallo, Mohamed Sadialoiu Sow, Aboubacar Sidiki, Sékou Sylla; with Félix Mandjam Sambú (Guinea-Bissau), Charles Onguemby (Congo Brazzaville), Arkangelo Gur Tong (Sudan), Dexter Ross (San Vicente); with Asser Mudhika, one of the Namibian teachers in the Island of Youth. In 1980 and 1981 I visited Namibian, Nicaraguan, and Mozambican schools in the Island of Youth.

54. Bestard Pavón, "La colaboración," p. 44.

55. This is based on the country notes of the CECE. For Angola, see also "La colaboración cubana en la RPA," table of Jan. 1985, CF.

56. Interview with Alberto González Polanco; country note "R.A.S.D. (Sahara Occidental)," CECE. Also *Colaboración*, Jan. 1983, p. 21, and July 1983, pp. 38–40.

57. Interview with Noemí Benítez. The two best studies on Cuba's technical assistance during the Cold War are Bestard Pavón's well-documented "La colaboración" and Benítez, "La colaboración." See also Díaz-Briquets and Pérez López, "Internationalist."

58. Richard Dowden, "Cubans Retain Low Profile," *Times* (London), Sept. 7. 1983, p. 6.

59. Diary of Feliberto Arteaga, May 9, 1984, private collection, Havana.

60. Interview with Dr. Norberto García Mesa.

61. MINFAR, Sección Especial de Operaciones, "Análisis de las acciones combativas en Zumbe," July 9, 1984, p. 4, CF. The strength of the Angolan militia varied from province to province depending on the abilities and dynamism of the local authorities and the degree of threat from UNITA. With few exceptions, the militia could withstand only minor UNITA attacks (interviews with Pedro Ross, senior Cuban adviser to the militia in 1977–78; Andres Mendes de Carvalho, a senior political commissar of the FAPLA; and Kundi Pahama, governor of the province of Benguela in 1981–86).

62. Bridgland, *Savimbi*, p. 429.

63. MINFAR, Sección Especial de Operaciones, "Análisis de las acciones combativas en Zumbe," July 9, 1984, pp. 10, 15, CF. My account of the battle of Sumbe is based also on interviews with three Cuban aid workers who participated in the fighting: Norberto García, Roberto Domínguez, and Salvador Mateo. For an eyewitness's account, see also González Montero, *Sumbe*.

64."MMCA-EMG," Mar. 29, 1984, 4 P.M., p. 12.

65. Cintra Frías, "Informe sobre el atentado terrorista contra el predio cubano en Huambo," Apr. 20, 1984, CF. *Verde Olivo en Misión Internacionalista* (Luanda), May 1, 1984, p. 1, lists the names and occupations of the Cuban dead. For UNITA's responsibility, see my discussion in chapter 11.

66. Interview with Dr. Lourdes Franco Codinach. Unless otherwise stated, the quotations in the portrait of Dr. Lourdes that follows are from my interviews with her.

67. Interview with Dr. Goliath Gómez.

68. Lourdes to her mother, Benguela, May 8, 1988.

69. Lourdes to her mother, Benguela, Aug. 4, 1988.

70. Lourdes to her mother, Benguela, Mar. 24, 1988.

71. Lourdes to her mother, Benguela, July 20, 1988.

72. Lourdes to her mother, Benguela, July 27, 1988.

73. Interviews with aid workers Gilberto García (quoted), Salvador Mateo (quoted), Gustavo Atencio, Sonia Romero, Serena Torres, Goliath Gómez, Norberto García, Roberto Domínguez, Manuela González. See also Jiménez Rodríguez, Mujeres and De las mujeres.

74. James Brooke, "Cuba's Strange Mission in Angola," *NYT*, Feb. 1, 1987, VI:45. See also Hatzky, "'Os Bons Colonizadores.'"

75. "Situación de la colaboración civil en la RPA," Jan. 1987, CF.

76. Quotations from interview with Serena Torres, and Puente Ferro to Risquet, May 2, 1986, ACC.

77. "Reunión Bilateral Cuba—URSS," Feb. 20–22, 1985, pp. 122–23, 129, 138, CF.

78. "Tripartita Cuba—URSS—RPA," Jan. 27, 1986, pp. 83–84, CF.

79. Kasrils, *"Armed,"* p. 122; interview with Dalmau.

80. Kasrils, *"Armed,"* p. 195.

81. Tensions increased in 1981, when a spy ring led by senior MK commanders was uncovered in Angola, "fueling a movement-wide paranoia about agents and spies" (Gevisser, *Mbeki*, p. 393). The SWAPO leaders were also gripped with anxieties about spies in their midst. This led to a tragic wave of repression; it represents a dark page in the history of that liberation movement. (See Africa Watch, *Accountability*, pp. 68–118; Leys and Brown, *Histories*, chs. 5 and 6; Saul and Leys, "Lubango.")

82. James Stuart, "Report: Commission of Inquiry into Recent Developments in the People's Republic of Angola," Mar. 14, 1984, pp. 10, 16, AL 2516, WITS; interview with Mabaso.

83. Memcon (Castro, Tambo), Mar. 25, 1986, p. 10, Consejo de Estado; interview with Sechaba.

84. Memcon (Castro, Tambo), May 13, 1983, pp. 15, 22, Consejo de Estado.

85. On the mutiny, see above all Stuart, "Report," and D. S. Motsuenyane, "Reports of the Commission of Enquiry into Certain Allegations of Cruelty and Human Rights Abuse against ANC Prisoners and Detainees by ANC members," Aug. 20, 1993, AL 2516, WITS. Also Ellis and Sechaba, *Comrades*, pp. 124–36; Callinicos, *Tambo*, pp. 457–63; Kasrils, *"Armed,"* pp. 248–54.

86. Memcon (Castro, dos Santos), Oct. 25, 1985, p. 43, ACC.

87. Memcon (Castro, Tambo), Mar. 25, 1986, p. 56, Consejo de Estado; Memcon (Risquet, Tambo), Mar. 26, 1986, ACC. Also Callinicos, *Tambo*, p. 601.

88. Memcon (Risquet, Slovo), June 9, 1986, pp. 1, 3, 17, 20, ACC.

89. Memcon (Raúl Castro, Risquet), June 17, 1986, pp. 3–4, 18, 21, CF.

90. "Informe sobre el encuentro entre Oliver Tambo, presidente del ANC y Angel Dalmau—22 de julio de 1986. Asuntos bilaterales," pp. 2, 4–5, ACC. For Castro's offer, see Memcon (Castro, Tambo), Mar. 25, 1986, Consejo de Estado.

91. "Conversación de Dalmau con Oliver Tambo el 22 de julio de 1986 en el sur de la RDA. Aspectos políticos," p. 9, enclosed in Risquet to Castro, July 30, 1986, ACC.

92. *Guardian*, Sept. 1, 1986, p. 19; *Le Monde*, Aug. 30, 1986, p. 3.

93. Castro, Sept. 2, 1986, *Granma*, Sept. 3, 1986, pp. 2–3.

94. Castro to dos Santos, Oct. 16, 1985, pp. 2–3, ACC.

95. Memcon (Castro, dos Santos), Oct. 25, 1985, pp. 65–71, 85, 87, ACC; Memcon (Castro, Shevardnadze), Oct. 28, 1985, pp. 31–32.

96. "Reunión Bilateral Cuba—URSS," Jan. 24, 1986, pp. 9–10, ACC.

97. Ulises Rosales to Raúl Castro, Dec. 28, 1986, CF.

98. "Reunión Bipartita Cuba-URSS," Mar. 10, 1987, pp. 11–12, ACC.

99. No title [document prepared for], "Reunión Tripartita Cuba—URSS—ANC," Sept.

16–17, 1987, p. 32, ACC. See also Dalmau to Risquet, June 11, 1987, ACC; "Cursos impartidos al ANC 1986 y 1987," [Sept. 1987], CF.

100. Interview with Risquet.

101. Risquet, in "Reunión Bipartita Cuba—URSS, 15-9-87 (17:00) sobre el ANC," p. 19, ACC; Risquet to Castro, Sept. 18, 1987, ACC.

102. Quotations from "Informe sobre la visita del presidente del ANC Oliver Tambo (junio 27 a julio 2)," p. 4, enclosed in Padilla to Risquet, July 7, 1987, and from Risquet to Castro, Aug. 22, 1987. See also Education Minister José R. Fernández to Risquet, Jan. 6, 1987, and Risquet to Fernández, Aug. 24, 1987. All ACC.

103. Raymond Nkuku (ANC representative in Cuba) to ANC Secretary General, Sept. 28, 1988, Karis-Gerhart Collection, folder 42, WITS.

104. "Cuba: An Overview," pp. 1–2, enclosed in Charland and Smith to Secretary of State for External Affairs, Jan. 30, 1985, Cuba 24959, RG 25, Bibliothèque et Archives Canada/Library and Archives Canada, Ottawa.

105. Castro, in "Indicaciones concretas del Comandante en Jefe que guiarán la actuación de la delegación cubana a las conversaciones en Luanda y las negociaciones en Londres (23-4-88)," p. 5, CF.

106. Memcon (Raúl Castro, Risquet), June 17, 1986, p. 4, CF.

CHAPTER 13

1. This is the figure given by General Gusev, who headed the military mission from February 1987 to June 1990 (Gusev, *Ishchi*, p. 140). The Angolan and Cuban officers I interviewed (see chapter 3, n. 31) give a slightly lower figure—somewhat more than 1,000.

2. Interview with General Tonta. This paragraph relies also on interviews with the following Angolan officers: Kianda, Ngongo, Ndalu, Ita, Mendes de Carvalho, Correia de Barros, Foguetão, and Paulo Lara.

3. Memcon (Castro, Konstantin Kurochkin), Feb. 11, 1984, p. 1, CF.

4. CIA, DI, "Supporting Allies under Insurgent Challenge: The Soviet Experience in Africa," Feb. 1988, p. 23, FOIA.

5. Interviews with Ita (quoted), Ndalu, Kianda, Ngongo, Mendes de Carvalho, Paulo Lara, and Foguetão.

6. Memcon (Polo Cintra Frías, Konstantin), Mar. 2, 1984, p. 9, CF.

7. Aide-mémoire to Soviet EMG, Aug. 28, 1984, pp. 18–19, CF.

8. Memcon (Castro, Adamishin), Mar. 28, 1988, pp. 61–62, ACC.

9. Interviews with Colonel Breytenbach and General Thirion.

10. "Besoek aan Savimbi se Leërhoofkwartier in Angola deur lede van die Angola Gesamentlike Bestuursentrum (AGES), 28 en 29 November 1984," Dec. 2, 1984, p. 2, SVR.

11. Interview with Nunda.

12. Interviews with Mendes de Carvalho and Pahama.

13. Kolomnin, *Russkii Spetznaz*, p. 99; *Krasnaya Zvezda* (Moscow), Mar. 29, 2001, p. 2.

14. Interview with Polo.

15. Interviews with Generals Ulises Rosales, Polo, Fleitas (quoted), Rodiles (quoted), and Lussón, and with Colonel Escalante, who was Polo's chief of staff in Angola.

16. Interview with Ngongo.

17. Interviews with Ndalu (quoted), Ngongo, Mendes de Carvalho, Paulo Lara, Pa-

hama, Foguetão, Kianda, Tonta, Ita, and Correia de Barros. For the six Cubans, see my n. 15.

18. Interview with Polo.

19. Memcon (Castro, Konstantin), Feb. 11, 1984, p. 1, CF.

20. Ibid., pp. 44, 6–10, 73.

21. For Konstantin's account of his visit to Havana, see V. Shubin, *Hot "Cold War,"* pp. 96–99.

22. Memcon (Castro, Konstantin), Feb. 11, 1984, p. 1, CF.

23. Memcom (Colomé, Ulises, Konstantin), Feb. 8, 1984, pp. 2–4, CF.

24. V. Shubin, *Hot "Cold War,"* p. 99.

25. Malan, "Angola: UNITA Strategie," Nov. 11, 1985, H SAW, gr. 4, box 160, DODDC.

26. Interview with Colonel Barlow.

27. "Versión de la conversación sostenida en el Estado Mayor de la Misión Militar Cubana en Angola, efectuada a las 1600 horas del día 6 de junio de 1984," pp. 30–31, 19, 34, CF.

28. Risquet and Colomé to Fidel and Raúl Castro, [August 1984], pp. 1–6, CF.

29. "Consideraciones a los aspectos planteados por el general de ejército Varennikov, durante su visita a la RPA, agosto de 1984," n.d., pp. 2–3, 9, CF. See also Memcon (Polo, Varennikov), Aug. 12, 1984, CF. In his memoirs, *Nepovtorimoe,* Varennikov does not refer to this second visit to Angola.

30. "Versión de la conversación sostenida en el Ministerio de Defensa de la RPA el 12 de septiembre de 1984," pp. 4 and 5, CF. This meeting had been preceded by another, in the morning, between Soviet and Cuban officers in which they tried, unsuccessfully, to reach a common position (Memcon, [Konstantin, Avila], Sept. 12, 1984, CF).

31. "Versión de la conversación sostenida en Futungo de Velas el 29 de septiembre de 1984," pp. 6, 15, CF.

32. "Versión de la conversación sostenida con el coronel general Konstantin, iniciada esta en el automovil cuando salíamos de la entrevista con el presidente," Sept. 29, 1984, p. 1, CF.

33. "Versión de la conversación efectuada en Futungo de Velas el día 18 de junio de 1984," p. 12, CF.

34. "Versión de la conversación sostenida en la Misión Militar Soviética en la RPA el 23 de octubre de 1984," pp. 13, 7, 8–9, 10, 13, CF.

35. Interview with General Lussón. "When referring to the operation . . . [against Mussende], use the code word 'Berlin'" (Ulises to Polo, Sept. 22, 1983, CF).

36. "Versión de la conversación en el estado mayor de la Misión Militar Cubana en Angola, el 7 de octubre de 1984, a las 11 horas," pp. 15, 18, 15, 18, 19, CF.

37. Interview with Ita.

38. CIA, DI, "Supporting Allies under Insurgent Challenge: The Soviet Experience in Africa," Feb. 1988, pp. v–vi, 1, FOIA.

39. Interview with General Lussón.

40. Dos Santos to Castro, Oct. 28, 1983, CF; Memcon (Ustinov, Colomé), Jan. 20, 1982, OS.

41. Memcon (Akhromeyev, Ulises), Sept. 17, 1984, p. 12, CF; Varennikov, *Nepovtorimoe,* 4:290.

42. Memcon (Akhromeyev, Ulises), Sept. 17, 1984, pp. 1, 14–15, CF.

43. Memcon (Polo, Konstantin), Jan. 10, 1985, pp. 24–25, enclosed in Polo to Rodríguez Cutiño, Jan. 10, 1985, CF.

44. Interviews with Foguetão and Ngongo.

45. Varennikov, *Nepovtorimoe*, 4:290.

46. "Encuentro Tripartito realizado en el Ministerio de Defensa de la URSS el día 28 de enero de 1986," pp. 8, 9, CF.

47. See MMCA, "Informe del desarrollo de las acciones combativas en la dirección 'Cuito Cuanavale—Mavinga,' dentro del marco de la Operación II Congreso del MPLA-PT," Oct. 18, 1985, CF.

48. Breytenbach, *Buffalo Soldiers*, pp. 255–56. For South African accounts of the operation, see ibid., pp. 254–66; Nortje, *32 Battalion*, pp. 213–19; D. Lord, *Fledgling*, pp. 351–58. For a Soviet account, see Gukov, "V Voiushei Brigade," pp. 169–86. (Gukov was a Soviet military adviser who at the time was based at Cuito Cuanavale.)

49. Polo to Jefe EMG, Sept. 17, 1985, CF.

50. "MMCA—RPA," Oct. 17, 1985, appendix 1, CF.

51. Abramowitz to SecState, Sept. 19, 1985, p. 1, FOIA.

52. *WP*, Sept. 24, 1985, p. 27; General Viljoen, *Cape Times*, Sept. 17, 1985, p. 1.

53. Malan, *Star* (Johannesburg), Sept. 21, 1985, pp. 1, 2; Savimbi, *NYT*, Sept. 22, 1985, p. 20.

54. See UNSC Resolution 574, Oct. 7, 1985, www.un.org/documents, and Security Council, Provisional Verbatim Record of the 2617 meeting, Oct. 7, 1985, DHL.

55. *WT*, Oct. 9, 1985, pp. A1 and A6.

56. *Burger* (Cape Town), Oct. 9, 1985, p. 17.

57. Breytenbach, *Buffalo Soldiers*, p. 256.

58. "Encuentro Tripartito realizado en el Ministerio de Defensa de la URSS el día 28 de enero de 1986," p. 6, CF.

59. MMCA, "Informe del desarrollo de las acciones combativas en la dirección 'Cuito Cuanavale—Mavinga,'" Oct. 18, 1985, p. 4 quoted, CF. For the account by a Cuban pilot who participated in the operation, see González Sarría, *Angola*, pp. 65–128; for a South African account, see Venter, *Chopper*, pp. 163–68.

60. Gukov, "V Voiushei Brigade," pp. 177–81.

61. Polo to Jefe EMG, Sept. 30, 1985, CF.

62. Kuzmenko, "Al camarada Pedro María Tonha (Pedalé), Ministro de Defensa de la República Popular de Angola," [Oct. 8, 1985,] enclosed in Avila Trujillo to Ulises, n.d., CF.

63. "MMCA—RPA," Oct. 4, 1985, p. 4.

64. "Resumen especial sobre la República Popular de Angola, semana del 7 al 13 de octubre 1985," p. 7, CF.

65. Polo to Raúl Castro, Oct. 16, 1985, CF. (For Raúl's reply, see "Mensaje cifrado enviado por el Jefe del EMG y aprobado por el ministro FAR al Gral Div Leopoldo Cintra Frías," Oct. 16, 1985, CF.)

66. Quotations from "MMCA—RPA," Oct. 17, 1985, appendix 1, p. 1, and "MMCA—RPA," Oct. 18, 1985, p. 4.

67. Sokolov to Raúl Castro, Nov. 2, 1985, CF.

68. "Síntesis del informe resumen de la 'Operación II Congreso,' realizado por el EMG-

FAPLA, 15-11-85," pp. 19–20, CF; Special NIE, "Soviet Military Support to Angola: Intentions and Prospects," Oct. 1985, pp. 3, 4, 10, FOIA.

69. Lieutenant Colonel Ngongo, Estado Maior General/Posto Comando da Frente Leste, "2° Congreso," Nov. 15, 1985, p. 40, private collection, Luanda. For the casualty figures, see ibid., pp. 21–22.

70. Interviews with Ngongo, Foguetão, Correia de Barros, and Ndalu.

71. Memcon (Castro, Shevardnadze), Oct. 28, 1985, pp. 18, 30, 20, 33, 34, Consejo de Estado.

72. "Reunión Bilateral Cuba—URSS," Jan. 24, 1986, pp. 15–16, CF.

73. "Tripartita Cuba—URSS—RPA," Jan. 27, 1986, pp. 33–34, CF.

74. Quotations from "Versión de la sesión de trabajo realizada entre la delegación cubana y la delegación de la URSS en el Ministerio de Defensa el día 26.1.86," pp. 2 (quoting Ulises) and 14 (quoting General Ilarionov); Memcon (Ulises, Akhromeyev), Jan. 30, 1986, p. 2 (quoting Ulises); Ulises to Akhromeyev, [mid-Feb. 1986], p. 1. See also "Encuentro Tripartito realizado en el Ministerio de Defensa de la URSS el día 28 de enero de 1986," and General Zaitsev to Ulises, Feb. 8, 1986. All CF.

75. Memo Telcon (Castro, Gorbachev), Nov. 15, 1985, OS; Gorbachev, *Zhizn'*, 2:312.

76. Reagan to Gorbachev, Mar. 11, 1985, "To the Geneva Summit," NSA.

77. Memcon (Raúl Castro, Gorbachev), Mar. 20, 1985, OS. Gorbachev told a group of top Soviet officials, "The general impression that the American delegation left is . . . quite mediocre" ("Conference of Secretaries of the CC CPSU," Mar. 15, 1985, p. 4, "To the Geneva Summit," NSA).

78. Memo Telcon (Gorbachev, Castro), Nov. 27, 1985, pp. 3, 8–9, OS. On the Nov. 19–20, 1985, Geneva summit, see "To the Geneva Summit," NSA; Reynolds, *Summits*, pp. 343–400; Garthoff, *Great Transition*, pp. 234–48. For accounts by participants, see Matlock, *Reagan*, pp. 149–69; Gorbachev, *Zhizn'*, 2:11–22; Akhromeyev and Kornienko, *Glazami*, pp. 54–68. On U.S.-Soviet relations in 1985–88, see also Leffler, *Soul*, pp. 338–450; Oberdorfer, *Turn*, pp. 107–326.

79. "Informe Central de Fidel al Tercer Congreso," Feb. 4, 1986, *Granma* (Havana), Feb. 7, 1986, p. 2.

80. Kapto, *Na perekrestkakh zhizni*, p. 407; Gorbachev, *Zhizn'*, 2:422. For Castro's speech at the Congress, see *Granma*, Feb. 27, 1986, p. 8.

81. Chernyaev, *My Six Years*, pp. 51–52.

82. Memcon (Castro, Gorbachev), Mar. 2, 1986, CF. See also "Zapis osnovnovo soderzhania besedi M. S. Gorbacheva s Fidelem Castro Rus," Mar. 2, 1986, NSA.

83. Akhromeyev and Kornienko, *Glazami*, p. 167.

84. Interview with Ulises.

85. "Transcripción de la conversación del Jefe EMG sobre historia de la RPA (el 12.12.87)," p. 33, CF.

86. Gorbachev, *Zhizn'*, 2:421–22.

87. "Encuentro Tripartito realizado en el Ministerio de Defensa de la URSS el día 28 de enero de 1986," pp. 16–17, CF.

88. Memcon (Polo, Konstantin), Apr. 23, 1986, p. 7, CF.

89. Memcon (Polo, Konstantin), July 17, 1986, p. 16 quoted; Memcon (Ochoa, Polo, Konstantin), July 19, 1986; Ochoa to Konstantin, July 1986; Ochoa, "Informe sobre la visita de trabajo en la RPA," July 31, 1986. All CF.

90. Stiff, *Silent War*, pp. 534–35; MINFAR, "Informe sobre sabotajes a barcos e instalaciones en la ciudad de Namibe," [June 1986], CF; *Granma*, June 6, 1986, p. 1.

91. *Pravda*, June 9, 1986, p. 1.

92. See UNSC Official Records, 2693th meeting, June 18, 1986, DHL.

93. Memcon (Castro, Konstantin), Sept. 8, 1986, p. 9, CF.

94. Ibid., p. 15.

95. Ibid., pp. 16–17, 19–20.

96. Ibid., pp. 26–27, 22, 24–25.

97. Ibid., pp. 26–27.

98. Memcon (Castro, dos Santos, Konstantin), Sept. 9, 1986, pp. 3, 6, 7, 27–28, 30, CF.

99. Ibid., pp. 28, 31.

100. Ibid., pp. 28, 29.

101. Memcon (Castro, dos Santos), [Sept. 8, 1986], p. 37, CF.

102. Memcon (Castro, Konstantin), Sept. 8, 1986, pp. 27–28, CF.

103. "Indicaciones concretas del Comandante en Jefe que guiarán la actuación de la delegación cubana a las conversaciones en Luanda y las negociaciones en Londres (23-4-88)," p. 5, CF.

104. Memcon (Castro, dos Santos), [Sept. 8, 1986], p. 2, CF.

105. Memcon (Crocker, Savimbi), Oct. 29, 1986, FOIA.

106. Freeman to SecState, Jan. 2, 1987, FOIA. See also NIE, "Soviet and Cuban Objectives and Activity in Southern Africa through 1988," n.d., FOIA; Júnior, *Forças Armadas*, pp. 113–14.

107. Quotations from interview with Breytenbach; J. Geldenhuys, *Dié*, p. 150; "Interview with Col. F. Oelschig," Sept. 30, 1987, p. 3, enclosed in "A Concise History of Operation Moduler (Phase One) May–October 1987," JFH, gr. VERS, box 30, DODDC; Breytenbach, *Eden's Exiles*, p. 245.

108. Quotations from Cornelissen (NIS) and Cdr. De Beer (SADF), in "Memorandum van die verrigtinge van die staatkundige komitee," Feb. 19, 1987, pp. 5, 7–8, B1.6.2.2, WITS, and from Secretariat SSC, "Konsep Strategiese Riglyne Nr 22: Angola," June 26, 1987, pp. 3–4, SVR. This document replaced the one approved by the State Security Council on August 26, 1985.

109. See PRA, Ministry of Defense, "Relatório da situação político-militar no território da R.P.A.," Mar. 1987, pp. 31–33, private collection, Luanda.

110. Dos Santos, "Não devemos tolerar atitudes que ponham em causa a revolução," *Jornal de Angola* (Luanda), May 1, 1987, p. 3, and "E utópico esperar pelo fim da guerra para corrigir a distorções já detectadas," *Jornal de Angola*, Aug. 18, 1987, p. 3 quoted.

111. Risquet to Castro, Dec. 11, 1985, p. 3, ACC.

112. "Raport Polityczny, Ambasady PRL v Angoli za 1987 rok," p. 11, Polish United Workers' Party Central Committee in Warsaw, 1948–90, Foreign Department, Archiwum Akt Nowych, Warsaw; Bridgland, *War*, p. 14.

113. Allister Sparks, "Toll Rises in Angola's Civil War," *WP*, Mar. 15, 1987, p. 23.

114. Blaine Harden, "12-Year War Starves, Maims Angola's Children," *WP*, Aug. 23, 1987, p. 22; Ned Temko, "Angolan Civilians Bear Brunt of 12-Year War," *Christian Science Monitor*, July 8, 1987, p. 9.

115. Quotations from Memcon (Crocker, Chitunda), Jan. 17, 1985; Gelbard to Crocker,

Feb. 6, 1985; Memcon (Crocker, Savimbi), Feb. 10, 1985; Memcon (Wisner, Chitunda), Mar. 27, 1986. Also Memcon (Crocker, Chitunda), Sept. 25, 1984; Memcon (Crocker, Chitunda), Oct. 1, 1984; Gelbard to Crocker, Jan. 17, 1985; Memcon (Crocker, Chitunda), Feb. 6, 1985. All FOIA.

116. "Raport Polityczny, Ambasady PRL v Angoli za 1987 rok," p. 6, Polish United Workers' Party Central Committee in Warsaw, 1948–90, Foreign Department, Archiwum Akt Nowych, Warsaw.

117. Politburo meeting, Nov. 13, 1986, in Chernyaev et al., *Politburo*, p. 107.

118. "Informe para la Reunión Bilateral Cuba—URSS. Diciembre 1986," Dec. 13, 1986, pp. 1, 10, 11, enclosed in Secretaría del ministro de las FAR, "Nota," [Dec. 17, 1986], CF.

119. Dos Santos to Castro, Feb. 6, 1987, p. 3, CF.

120. Akhromeyev, quoted in Ulises to Raúl Castro, Dec. 28, 1986, CF.

121. "Reunión Tripartita URSS—Angola y Cuba," Mar. 10–11, 1987, p. 30, CF.

122. Ibid., pp. 11, 28–29.

123. Medvedev, *Raspad*, pp. 273–74.

124. Scholtz, "War," p. 43.

125. Memcon (Raúl Castro, Nujoma), Apr. 10, 1987, pp. 24–24a, 36–37, CF.

126. Interview with Puente Ferro.

127. Risquet, in "Bipartita Cuba—URSS," Jan. 10, 1984, p. 44, ACC.

128. Memcon (Castro, M'Binda, Ndalu), Oct. 15, 1987, p. 20, CF.

129. Ibid., p. 22; Risquet, in "Reunión Tripartita URSS—Angola y Cuba," Mar. [10–11], 1987, p. 23. CF.

130. "Reunión Tripartita URSS—Angola y Cuba," Mar. [10–11], 1987, pp. 23, 24, CF.

131. See dos Santos to Castro, Feb. 6, 1987, CF; Malmierca to Risquet, Feb. 19, 1987, ACC; Castro to dos Santos, Mar. 5, 1987, CF.

CHAPTER 14

1. "Reunión Tripartita URSS—Angola y Cuba," Mar. [10–11], 1987, pp. 21–23, CF.

2. SecState to All African Diplomatic Posts, Mar. 16, 1984, p. 8, FOIA; Memcon (Raúl Castro, Gorbachev), Mar. 20, 1985, p. 26, OS.

3. Quotations from DOS memo to Frank Carlucci, "The Reagan Doctrine in Southern Africa: Angola and Mozambique," Jan. 20, 1987, FOIA, and DOS, "The Reagan Doctrine in Southern Africa—Mozambique," enclosed in Platt to Carlucci, Jan. 31, 1987, FOIA.

4. Memcon (PW Botha, Crocker), Jan. 13, 1986, Exchanges Pres Reagan/Pres Botha, DFA.

5. Interview with Colonel Breytenbach.

6. DOS, "The Reagan Doctrine in Southern Africa—Mozambique," enclosed in Platt to Carlucci, Jan. 31, 1987, FOIA.

7. Crocker, *High Noon*, p. 345.

8. The $40 million figure is from Shultz, *Turmoil*, p. 1123.

9. *NYT*, June 7, 1987, p. 20; *Star* (Johannesburg), June 8, 1987, p. 9.

10. Van Tonder, "Besprekingspunte: Staatspresident met Dr Savimbi," May 18, 1987, H SAW, gr 4, box 160, DODDC.

11. Senator Jesse Helms (R-N.C.) to "Dear Chevron Stockholders," Apr. 27, 1987, SWA/Angola, v. 1, DFA.

12. Rodman, *Precious*, p. 385.

13. *CR*, Senate, July 9, 1987, 100th Cong., 1st sess., v. 133, *CR* S9496. Also ibid., July 8, 1987, *CR* S9437.

14. On the Reykjavik summit, see "The Reykjavik File," NSA; Matlock, *Reagan*, pp. 212–36; Gorbachev, *Zhizn'*, 2:25–34; Akhromeyev and Kornienko, *Glazami*, pp. 110–20; Garthoff, *Transition*, pp. 252–99.

15. Politburo meeting, Nov. 13, 1986, in Chernyaev et al., *Politburo*, pp. 109–10.

16. Grachev, *Gorbachev*, p. 200.

17. Gates, *Shadows*, p. 423. See also "The INF Treaty and the Washington Summit: 20 Years Later," NSA.

18. *WT*, Sept. 21, 1987, p. D2 (ed.).

19. "Orden del Ministro de las Fuerzas Armadas Revolucionarias Creando la Agrupación de Tropas del Sur de la Misión Militar de Cuba en la República Popular de Angola," July 24, 1982, CF.

20. Memcon (Castro, dos Santos), July 31, 1987, pp. 76, 62, 33, CF.

21. Memcon (Risquet, Dobrynin), Sept. 18, 1987, pp. 13–14, ACC.

22. Risquet, in "Reunión Tripartita URSS—Angola y Cuba," Mar. [10–11], 1987, p. 20, CF; Castro, in Memcon (Castro, dos Santos), July 31, 1987, pp. 20, 77, CF.

23. See "Samesprekings: Staatspresident met Kabinet van die Oorgangs-Regering van Nasionale Eenheid (ORNE) van SWA," May 21, 1986, Angola, v. 14, DFA; "Verbatim notule van die eerste vergadering van die Gesamentlike Suid-Afrika—Suidwes-Afrika Kabinetskomitee oor Buitelandse Sake en Verdediging: Pretoria, 4 November 1986," DFA; Administrator-General Pienaar to Staatspresident, Aug. 6, 1987, AG aan SP, v. 2, DFA.

24. Nickel to SecState, Mar. 27, 1986, NSA. See also van Wyk, *Dirk Mudge*, pp. 147–60.

25. "SWA: Seminaarspel," Apr. 23, 1986, p. 5, Military Documents, v. 5, DFA.

26. Secretariat SCC: "Steun van politieke partie in geval van verkiesing in SWA," enclosed in "Ovambo: Algemene Toestand gedurende mei 1986," May 20, 1986; "Konsep vir 'n Totale Strategie vir Suidwes-Afrika," [1987]; "Strategie riglyne tov Suidwes-Afrika," Feb. 1987; "Strategie riglyne tov Suidwes-Afrika," Mar. 1987; "Strategie riglyne tov Suidwes-Afrika," June 1987. All SVR.

27. Secretariat SSC, "Konsep vir 'n Totale Strategie vir Suidwes-Afrika," [1987], p. 9, SVR.

28. Memcon (Pik Botha, Kozonguizi), May 21, 1986, pp. 2, 6, 4, SWA/Binnelandse Verwikkelinge, v. 5, DFA.

29. Secretariat SSC, "Strategiese Riglyne vir Suidwes-Afrika," Mar. 1987, p. 11, SVR.

30. Nickel to SecState, Mar. 27, 1986, NSA; Secretariat SSC, "Angola: Huidige strategie," Aug. 1987, SVR.

31. Botha, *Business Day* (Johannesburg), Mar. 26, 1987, p. 1.

32. Perkins to SecState, Apr. 17, 1987, NSA. See also Memcon (Pik Botha, Perkins), May 12, 1987, SWA Basic Documents, v. 16, DFA. Unfortunately, Ambassador Perkins's memoirs (*Mr. Ambassador*) are little more than a litany of self-congratulations.

33. See "Versión Conversaciones RPA/USA, 9/9/87 (20:00 horas)," ACC, and Risquet to Castro, Sept. 9, 1987, ACC.

34. "Continuación conversaciones EE.UU.—RPA. 15/7/87 (17:00)," p. 2, ACC.

35. "15/7/87. Conversaciones Angolano/Norteamericanas, Luanda (10:15 A.M.)," p. 9, ACC.

36. "Conversaciones Angola—Estados Unidos realizada [sic] en Bruselas, Bélgica, el 24 de septiembre de 1987," ACC. On Luanda's desire to join the IMF and the World Bank, see *NYT*, Aug. 26, 1987, p. 23, and Dec. 29, p. 6.

37. Quotations from "Conversaciones entre la RPA y EE.UU., Futungo de Belas, 14.7.87. 16:00—19:40," p. 9; "15/7/87. Conversaciones Angolano/Norteamericanas, Luanda (10:15 A.M.)," p. 11; "Versión de las conversaciones Angola/EEUU. 8/9/87 (16:00 a 19:00 horas)," pp. 5-6, 10. All ACC.

38. "Conversaciones Angola—Estados Unidos realizada [sic] en Bruselas, Bélgica, el 24 de septiembre de 1987," p. 7, ACC.

39. PW Botha, Aug. 14, 1987, RSA, *Hansard—Debates of the House of Assembly*, col. 3823; Malan, Sept. 14, 1987, ibid., col. 5898.

40. M'Binda, in "Conversaciones Angola—Estados Unidos realizada [sic] en Bruselas, Bélgica, el 24 de septiembre de 1987," p. 11, ACC.

41. Memcon (Risquet, Dobrynin), Sept. 18, 1987, pp. 16-17, 22, ACC.

42. Risquet to Castro, Sept. 10, 1987, ACC.

43. "Proposición para la apertura por los angolanos de la sesión del miércoles," [July 15, 1987], ACC.

44. Memcon (Castro, dos Santos), July 31, 1987, p. 60, CF.

45. Interviews with Napper and Freeman. Also Taylor, OH; Cohen, OH. When I asked Crocker about this clash, he was evasive (interview with Crocker).

46. Interviews with Napper and Skoug.

47. Interview with Cabelly.

48. Interviews with Taylor and Skoug.

49. Interview with Freeman.

50. "Versión de las conversaciones Angola/EEUU. 8/9/87 (16:00 a 19:00 horas)," pp. 4, 7-8, ACC.

51. Crocker, in "Conversaciones Angola—Estados Unidos realizada [sic] en Bruselas, Bélgica, el 24 de septiembre de 1987," p. 9, ACC; "The Brussels Formula," n.d., FOIA; Risquet, "Notas para la discusión con la delegación angolana M'Binda—N'Dalu," [Oct. 13, 1987], p. 5, ACC.

CHAPTER 15

1. Gusev, *Ishchi*, p. 144, and MINFAR, "Antecedentes y desarrollo de la maniobra 'XXXI Aniversario del desembarco del Granma,'" p. 1, CF.

2. My discussion about the decision to launch Salute to October is based on interviews with the following Angolan officers: Ndalu, Ngongo, Paulo Lara, Mendes de Carvalho, Miranda, and Ita.

3. Ochoa, "Informe sobre las visitas realizadas a la República Popular de Angola y a la República de Etiopía Socialista en el periodo de 29.6 al 19.7.87," July 24, 1987, pp. 2-3, CF. For Konstantin's arrival in Luanda, see "MMCA—EMG," June 25, 1987.

4. "MMCA—EMG," July 2, 1987, p. 2.

5. Interviews with Ngongo, Ndalu, and Paulo Lara.

6. Interviews with Ndalu, Mendes de Carvalho, and Ngongo.

7. "MMCA—EMG," July 9, 1987, p. 3.

8. There are no scholarly accounts of the campaign, which stretched through Au-

gust 1988. For the official South African perspective, see J. Geldenhuys, *Dié*, pp. 185–212; Malan, *My lewe*, pp. 266–302; Heitman, *War*; Steenkamp, *Border War*, pp. 149–77; D. Lord, *Fledgling*, pp. 394–450. While also biased, Colonel Breytenbach provides a more valuable account in *Buffalo Soldiers*, pp. 272–325. Savimbi's biographer Bridgland describes the campaign "through the eyes of the ordinary South African soldiers who did the fighting" (*War*, p. 1). He is interesting, but unreliable. For a twenty-year-old lieutenant's account, see van der Walt, *Bos Toe!* For the Cuban perspective, see Jiménez Gómez, *Al sur*; Gómez Chacón, *Cuito Cuanavale*; Ricardo Luis, *Prepárense*. Two Cuban Americans have written accounts that are, simply, fantasy: Ros, *La Aventura*, pp. 208–37; Benemelis, *Las guerras*, pp. 253–59. George, *Intervention*, pp. 213–55, is based entirely on secondary sources.

9. *Business Day* (Johannesburg), Sept. 28, 1987, p. 1 quoted; *WT*, Sept. 30, 1987, p. A12; *Beeld* (Johannesburg), Nov. 13, 1987, p. 2. Still today the Konstantin Shaganovitch nonsense is repeated stolidly. See, for instance, Labuschagne, *Secret Service*, pp. 110–12; Hamann, *Days*, pp. 85–89; Nogueira Pinto, *Jogos*, p. 123; Grant MacLean, letter to the editor, *London Review of Books*, Oct. 21, 2004, p. 4.

10. V. Shubin, *ANC*, p. 314.

11. The FAPLA figure is from MINFAR, "Antecedentes," p. 1. The UNITA figure is from Bridgland, *War*, p. 1. For the Soviet military advisers, see Rolando to Silvio, Jan. 4, 1988, CF.

12. Hoof van die SA Leër, "Op Instr 18/87: Op Moduler," June 22, 1987, in Moduler (Historiogram Leër), 309/1, v. 1, pp. 59–49, JFH, gr. VERS, box 14, DODDC.

13. SADF, "A Concise History of Operation Moduler (Phase One) May–October 1987," pp. 1, 34, 35, ibid., box 30.

14. "Magsamestellings en ontplooings," Aug. 27, 1987, pp. 76–75, in Moduler (SITRAP) Historiogram Leër, ibid., box 14.

15. SADF, "Concise History," p. 32.

16. C SADF to C Army, Sept. 7, 1987, in Moduler (Historiogram Leër) 309/1, v. 2, p. 91 quoted, JFH, gr. VERS, box 15, DODDC. Also "Doel van optrede," n.d., in ibid., pp. 15–13; H Leër to SWA GB, Aug. 29, 1987, ibid., pp. 42–41; [SADF,] "Volgorde van gebeure: OP Moduler/Hooper," [1988], p. 3, M, gr. 7, box 515, DODDC.

17. Quotations from Dorning, "Personal Impression of Op Moduler (Phase One) based on a visit to 20 Brigade forward-HQ over the period 19–30 September 1987," Oct. 1987, pp. 5–6, enclosed in SADF, "Concise History" ; SADF, "Concise History," p. 46; Commander Schabort, in "Interview with Cmdts C. Van den Berg and Schabort on the SAAF Role in Op Moduler," Sept. 24, 1987, p. 4, enclosed in ibid.

18. SADF, "Concise History," p. 61.

19. MINFAR, "Transcripción del MC enviado por el oficial enlace del EMG con la RPA el 16.9.87," Sept. 27, 1987, p. 3, CF.

20. Dorning, "Personal Impression," p. 11. See also the daily reports from Task Force Hqs in Rundu to the Commander of the Army for the second half of September in Moduler (SITRAP) (Historiogram Leër), JFH, gr. VERS, box 14, DODDC.

21. *Star* (Johannesburg), Sept. 30, 1987, p. 10 (ed.).

22. Quotations from SADF, "Concise History," pp. 74–76, and SADF, "Volgorde van gebeure: OP Moduler/Hooper," [1988], p. 4, M, gr. 7, box 515, DODDC. See also the daily

reports for Oct. 3 and Oct. 4 from Task Force Hqs in Rundu to the Commander of the Army in Moduler (SITRAP), Historiogram Leër, JFH, gr. VERS, box 15, DODDC.

23. J Geldenhuys, *Dié*, p. 173.

24. *Business Day*, Oct. 5, 1987, p. 2.

25. H Leër to SWA GN, Aug. 29, 1987, in Moduler (Historiogram Leër), 309/1, v. 2, p. 41, JFH, gr. VERS, box 15, DODDC.

26. Castro to Gorbachev, Mar. 3, 1988, p. 9, CF.

27. Interviews with Ndalu (quoted) and Fleitas.

28. Gusev, *Ishchi*, p. 146.

29. See MINFAR, "Informe sobre la situación presentada durante los días 25.9 y 7.10.87 en el frente sudeste," n.d., and MINFAR, "Actividades más importantes realizadas por las FAPLA en la región del río Lomba," n.d. Both CF.

30. Interview with General Thirion.

31. SADF, "Concise History," pp. 71–72.

32. Dorning, "Personal Impression," pp. 21–22. Also H Leër to SAW GM 31, TAK HK Rundu, Oct. 27, 1987, in Moduler Plan (Historiogram Leër), pp. 33–32, JFH, gr. VERS, box 16, DODDC.

33. SADF, "Concise History," p. 72.

34. Ibid., p. 3.

35. Bridgland, *War*, pp. 182–83. See also the daily reports from Task Force Hqs in Rundu to Commander of the Army for October 1987 in Moduler (SITRAP), Historiogram Leër, JFH, gr. VERS, box 15, DODDC.

36. Dorning, "Personal Impression," p. 13.

37. *Beeld*, Oct. 30, 1987, p. 6 (quoting UNITA communiqué), and Nov. 2, p. 2.

38. Bridgland, *War*, p. 211.

39. Interview with Colonel Breytenbach.

40. Geldenhuys, *Star*, Nov. 13, 1987, p. 15; *Beeld*, Nov. 13, 1988, p. 1; *Star*, Nov. 12, 1987, p. 1.

41. *Argus* (Cape Town), Nov. 13, 1987, p. 11.

42. Malan, *Star*, Nov. 13, 1987, p. 15; Malan, *Star*, Nov. 15, 1987, p. 1.

43. Malan, *Burger* (Cape Town), Nov. 16, 1987, p. 1.

44. Interview with General Geldenhuys.

45. *Burger*, Nov. 12, 1987, p. 16 (ed.), and Nov. 16, pp. 1–2; *Beeld*, Nov. 16, 1987, p. 1.

46. UNSC Resolutions 602 of 25 Nov. 1987 in www.un.org/documents.

47. SecState to Amembassy Pretoria, Dec. 5, 1987, FOIA.

48. H Leër to SAW GM 31, TAK HK Rundu, Oct. 27, 1987, in Moduler Plan (Historiogram Leër), pp. 53–52, JFH, gr. VERS, box 16, DODDC.

49. Pik Botha, in "Notule van die derde vergadering van die Gesamentlike Kabinetskomitee van Suid-Afrika en Suidwes-Afrika oor buitelandse sake en verdediging," Nov. 6, 1987, pp. 4, 7, M, gr. 7, box 452, DODDC; H SAW (Geldenhuys) to H Leër (Liebenberg), Nov. 18, 1987, in SADF, "Gesamentlike militêre aksies deur RSA en UNITA teen FAPLA magte in die Sesde Militêre Streek van Angola vanaf Desember 1987 tot Maart 1988," [1988], p. 35, JF Huyser, gr. VERS, box 92, DODDC; Geldenhuys, in SSC meeting, Nov. 30, 1987, #1, SVR; Ngongo, "Tinhamos condições para aniquilar o agrupamento sul-africano," *Jornal de Angola* (Luanda), March 3, 2008, p. 3.

50. Interview with Thirion.

51. SADF, "Gesamentlike," p. 20.

52. Ibid., p. 1. See also the daily reports for Nov. 23–27, 1987, from Task Force Hqs in Rundu to Commander of the Army, in Moduler—SITRAP (Historiogram Leër), 309/1, v. 4, JFH, gr. VERS, box 15, DODDC.

53. General Liebenberg's instructions, Dec. 24, 1987, in SADF, "Gesamentlike," pp. 31–32; H SAW to SWA GM, Nov. 30, 1987, in Moduler Plan (Historiogram Leër), 309/1, v. 3, p. 30, JFH, gr. VERS, box 16, DODDC; H SAW to H Leër, Dec. 11, 1987, quoted, in ibid.

54. Quotations from interviews with Thirion and Hutchinson, and SADF, "Gesamentlike," p. 2.

55. "Reunión de análisis de la situación de las tropas cubanas en la RPA, efectuada a partir de las 17:25 horas del 15.11.1987," p. 84, CF. On the 1987 immigration talks, see Skoug, *United States*, pp. 166–73; Schoultz, *Infernal*, pp. 410–15; Alarcón, "Informe sobre la reunión entre los representantes de Cuba y Estados Unidos del 4 al 6 de noviembre de 1987," MINREX; Alarcón to Malmierca, Dec. 21, 1987, MINREX.

56. CIA, National Intelligence Council, "Fidel and Raúl Castro: Preparing for the Dynastic Succession in Cuba," July 1987, p. 15, FOIA.

57. Vladislav Chirkov, "An Uphill Task," *New Times* (Moscow), Aug. 24, 1987, pp. 16–17; *WT*, Nov. 2, 1987, p. A4.

58. Interview with Risquet.

59. Gorbachev's aide Medvedev writes, "We . . . literally learned only a few hours in advance when Castro would arrive." He speculates that this was due to security considerations, but it was because Castro's decision to attend was made at the last moment. (Medvedev, *Raspad*, p. 257. Castro's speech is printed in *Granma* [Havana], Nov. 6, 1987, p. 3.)

60. Memcon (Gorbachev, Castro), Nov. 6, 1987, pp. 1–2, Consejo de Estado.

61. Gorbachev, *Zhizn'*, 2:423. See also Medvedev, *Raspad*, pp. 257–59, and Kapto, *Na perekrestkakh zhizni*, pp. 400–406, 414–15. Medvedev attended the meeting; Kapto quotes excerpts from the Soviet minutes of the conversation. Both accounts are consistent with the Cuban minutes.

62. Memcon (Gorbachev, Castro), Nov. 6, 1987, pp. 22–23, 6–7, 26, Consejo de Estado.

63. "MMCA—RPA," Nov. 12, 1987, p. 3.

64. Ochoa to Raúl Castro, Nov. 14, 1987, CF. See also the daily reports from Task Force Hqs in Rundu to Commander of the Army for the first half of November in Moduler (SITRAP), Historiogram Leër, JFH, gr. VERS, box 15, DODDC.

65. "MMCA—RPA": Nov. 2, 1987 (p. 5 quoted), Nov. 9, Nov. 12, Nov. 16. Also "Calculos invasión RPA por Africa del Sur para golpe aéreo masivo sorpresivo," Nov. 16, 1987, CF.

66. Castro to Gorbachev, Mar. 3, 1988, CF.

67. Risquet, in Vorotnikov, *Gavana—Moskva*, p. 210.

68. "Reunión de análisis de la situación de las tropas cubanas en la RPA, efectuada a partir de las 17:25 horas del 15.11.1987," CF.

69. Castro to Gorbachev, Mar. 3, 1988, p. 11, CF.

70. "Reunión de análisis," pp. 98, 109, 90, 180.

71. Ibid., pp. 97, 143, 158.

72. Gates, *Shadows*, pp. 420–21.

73. "Reunión de análisis," pp. 51, 67.

74. Ibid., pp. 101, 137.

75. Crocker, *High Noon*, pp. 367–68.

76. MINFAR, "Antecedentes," p. 6. For a list of the men and materiel Cuba sent to Angola during Maniobra XXXI Aniversario, see MINFAR, "Buques Maniobra XXXI Aniversario," CF; MINFAR, "Algunos datos solicitados sobre la operación 'XXXI Aniversario (Refuerzo),'" Dec. 22, 1989, CF.

77. Quotations from Raúl Castro, in "Reunión de análisis," pp. 117, 120, and MINFAR, "Extracto del Resumen de la Maniobra XXXI Aniversario del Desembarco del Granma," Dec. 12, 1989, p. 4. Also Ulises Rosales to Jefe Brigada de Tanques Independiente Plaza, Nov. 18, 1987; Ulises to Jefe Ejército Oriental, Nov. 18, 1987; Ulises, "Para el reforzamiento de las tropas cubanas en Angola," Nov. 20, 1987; Ulises to Jefe del Ejército Occidental, Jan. 27, 1988; Ulises to Jefe Ejército Occidental, [late Feb. 1988]; Ulises to Jefe UM 1011, Apr. 5, 1988. All CF.

78. *Burger*, Dec. 7, 1987, p. 10 quoted (ed.); *Star*, Dec. 10, 1987, p. 4 quoted; *Business Day*, Dec. 7, 1987, p. 1; *Beeld*, Dec. 8, 1987, p. 12 (ed.); *Pretoria News*, Dec. 5, 1987, p. 1. The reinforcements were arriving, but the 50th Division did not go to Angola (interview with Risquet).

79. Castro to dos Santos, enclosed in Castro to Ochoa, Dec. 2, 1987, CF; Memcon (Castro, Slovo), Sept. 29, 1988, p. 15, CF.

80. "Nota verbal al Asesor Principal de las FAR," Nov. 19, 1987, CF.

81. Quotations from Castro to dos Santos, Nov. 22, 1987; dos Santos to Castro, Dec. 2, 1987; Risquet to Castro, Nov. 25, 1987. All CF.

82. "Reunión en el Ministerio de Defensa de la URSS para informar la situación creada en la RPA," Nov. 25, 1987, pp. 9–10, CF.

83. Interview with Ulises.

84. Matlock, *Autopsy*, p. 138.

85. "Reunión en el Ministerio de Defensa de la URSS para informar la situación creada en la RPA," Nov. 25, 1987, pp. 13–14, 17–18, CF. To my intense frustration, in his memoirs of the Gorbachev years, Akhromeyev says not one word about Ulises' November 1987 visit. He focuses almost entirely on U.S.-Soviet arms negotiations and the gradual collapse of the Soviet Union. The memoirs include a few pages on Afghanistan, none on Angola, and only one and a half pages on Cuba. Next to Afghanistan and the United States, Cuba is the country to which he devotes, by far, the most space. (See Akhromeyev and Kornienko, *Glazami*, pp. 210–11.)

86. Kapto, *Na perekrestkakh zhizni*, p. 419.

87. During the Missile Crisis, Yazov, then a colonel, commanded an infantry regiment in eastern Cuba (Yazov, *Udari*, pp. 155–210; Gribkov, *U Kraya*, pp. 86–87, 90).

88. "Reunión con el Ministro de Defensa de la URSS en el Ministerio de Defensa," Nov. 27, 1987, pp. 13, 14, 15, 18, CF.

89. Handwritten notes, [Nov. 27, 1987], CF.

90. Memcon (Ulises, Akhromeyev), Nov. 27, 1987, pp. 1–4, CF.

91. "Nota entregada al Ministro de las FAR el 30.11.87 por el encargado de negocios soviético, compañero Kisiliov," CF.

92. "Nota del Ministro de las FAR sobre la entrevista con el compañero Kisiliov," [Nov. 30, 1987], CF.

93. Fidel Castro to Gorbachev, Dec. 1, 1987, CF.

94. Gorbachev, *Zhizn'*, 2:424.

95. Gorbachev to Castro, Dec. 5, 1987, CF.

96. Castro to Gorbachev, Mar. 3, 1988, pp. 12–13, CF.

97. Risquet to Castro, Dec. 8, 1987, CF.

98. Reynolds, *Summits*, p. 395; Politburo session, Dec. 17, 1987, in Chernyaev et al., *Politburo*, p. 280. On the summit, see "The INF Treaty and the Washington Summit: 20 Years Later," NSA; Matlock, *Reagan*, pp. 271–82; Gorbachev, *Zhizn'*, 2:57–69; Akhromeyev and Kornienko, *Glazami*, pp. 136–45.

99. Castro to Gorbachev, Mar. 3, 1988, p. 15, CF.

100. See "Reunión del Comandante en Jefe," Dec. 3, 1987, p. 10, CF; MINFAR, "Algunos datos solicitados sobre la operación 'XXXI Aniversario (Refuerzo),'" Dec. 12, 1989, CF.

101. "Reunión del Comandante en Jefe," Jan. 4, 1988, p. 24, CF.

102. Kapto, *Na perekrestkakh zhizni*, p. 419; Medvedev, *Raspad*, pp. 274, 275. The Soviets insisted with the invitation, but the Cubans did not budge (MINFAR, "Cronología de las principales actividades de la Maniobra XXXI Aniversario," p. 69, CF).

103. Castro to Ochoa, Jan. 14, 1988, CF.

104. "Reunión del Comandante en Jefe," Dec. 3, 1987, p. 106, CF.

105. Fidel Castro, in "Reunión del Comandante en Jefe," Dec. 4, 1987, p. 20, CF; Raúl Castro, in "Reunión del Comandante en Jefe," Nov. 30, 1987, pp. 17–18, CF.

106. Interview with Risquet; Kapto, *Na perekrestkakh zhizni*, p. 417.

107. Pavlov, *Alliance*, p. 121.

108. "Reunión del Comandante en Jefe," Feb. 1, 1988, p. 138, CF. See also "Indicaciones del Comandante en Jefe, durante análisis de la situación en la R.P.A.," Jan. 23, 1988, CF.

109. "Orientaciones de FC sobre RPA," [Jan. 24, 1988], p. 11, CF.

110. Castro to Gorbachev, Mar. 3, 1988, pp. 15–16, CF.

111. Note to "Compañero Mariscal Ajromeev," pp. 3, 7, enclosed in Memcon (Akhromeyev, Ulises), Feb. 21, 1988, CF.

112. Memcon (Akhromeyev, Ulises), Feb. 21, 1988, p. 7, CF.

CHAPTER 16

1. See MINFAR, "Algunos datos solicitados sobre la Operación 'XXXI Aniversario (Refuerzo),'" Dec. 12, 1989, CF; Castro, July 30, 1998, *Granma* (Havana), Aug. 7, 1998, p. 4.

2. Memcon (Castro, Slovo), Sept. 29, 1988, p. 16, CF.

3. Raúl Castro to Ochoa, Dec. 1, 1987, CF.

4. On Ochoa's career, see MINFAR, "Misiones internacionalistas militares cumplidas por Cuba, 1963 a 1991," pp. 64, 67, OS; Raúl Castro, in Republic of Cuba, *Vindicación*, p. 31. On the nine Cubans in Venezuela, see Báez, *Secretos*, pp. 107–9, 498–99. For the tale that Ochoa had been in Angola in 1975–76, see Oppenheimer, *Final Hour*, p. 71; Raffy, *Castro*, p. 520.

5. Castro to Ochoa, Dec. 2, 1987, CF.

6. "MMCA—EMG," Nov. 30, 1987, pp. 10–11.

7. SADF, "Gesamentlike militêre aksies deur RSA en UNITA teen FAPLA magte in die Sesde Militêre Streek van Angola vanaf Desember 1987 tot Maart 1988," [1988], p. 4, JF Huyser, gr. VERS, box 92, DODDC.

8. Oleg Arkadevich, in Tokarev and G. Shubin, *Veterany*, pp. 109–10.

9. Quotations from MINFAR, "Antecedentes y desarrollo de la maniobra 'XXXI Aniversario del desembarco del Granma,'" p. 6, CF, and Castro to Gorbachev, Mar. 3, 1988, p. 13, CF. Also MINFAR, "Principales acontecimientos ocurridos en Cuito Cuanavale," Feb. 16, 1988, CF. For a detailed Cuban account of military developments in the Cuito Cuanavale area from Nov. 14, 1987, to Aug. 26, 1988, see MINFAR, "Cronología de las principales actividades de la Maniobra XXXI Aniversario," CF. For a detailed South African account, see SADF, "Gesamentlike."

10. [Ulises,] in "Reunión del Comandante en jefe sobre la situación en la RPA 14.1.88," p. 118, CF.

11. SADF, "Gesamentlike," pp. 58, 28, 60.

12. Ibid., pp. 3, 23.

13. Memcon (Castro, Adamishin), Mar. 28, 1988, pp. 79–80, ACC.

14. Geldenhuys, *Le Figaro* (Paris), Apr. 1, 1988, p. 2.

15. Interview with Lieutenant Colonel Hutchinson.

16. Malan, May 16, 1988, RSA, *Hansard—Debates of Parliament*, col. 9932; Geldenhuys, *NYT*, Apr. 20, 1988, p. 11.

17. SADF, "Gesamentlike," pp. 136, 173.

18. *Sowetan* (Johannesburg), Feb. 25, 1988, p. 6 (ed.); Snyder to Crocker, Feb. 26, 1988, FOIA.

19. Jan Raath, "Luanda Forces Braced for South African Onslaught," *Times* (London), Mar. 1, 1988, p. 8, and "Storms of Shells amid the Lilies: Letter from Cuito Cuanavale," *Times*, Mar. 3, 1988, p. 10; *Weekly Mail* (Braamfontein), Mar. 11, 1988, p. 7, and Apr. 22, p. 2.

20. JCS, Apr. 15, 1988, NSA; DIA, May 11, 1988, NSA; SADF, "Gesamentlike," p. 149.

21. SADF, "Gesamentlike," p. 163.

22. Geldenhuys, in SSC meeting, Feb. 15, 1988, p. 2, SVR; Botha, in SSC meeting, Mar. 14, 1988, p. 5, SVR.

23. Breytenbach, *Buffalo Soldiers*, p. 308; JCS, Apr. 15, 1988, NSA. See also Packer (Historiogramer), JFH, gr. VERS, box 29, DODDC, and "Packer SITRAP (van 18-2-88)," [Mar. 1988], ibid., box 30; MINFAR, "Cronología de las principales actividades de la Maniobra XXXI Aniversario," pp. 155–59, CF; "MMCA—EMG," Mar. 23, 24, and 25, 1988.

24. Mandela, *Granma*, July 27, 1991, p. 3.

25. Quotations from Shevardnadze, in Memcon (Shultz, Shevardnadze), Mar. 21, 1988, p. 9, FOIA; Crocker, *High Noon*, p. 385; Adamishin, in Memcon (Shultz, Shevardnadze), Mar. 23, 1988, p. 18, FOIA.

26. Adamishin, *Beloe Solntse*, pp. 96–99. On Adamishin's lack of military experience, interview with Adamishin.

27. Memcon (Castro, Adamishin), Mar. 28, 1988 (See also chapter 13.)

28. Crocker, quoted by Adamishin, in Memcon (Risquet, Adamishin), Mar. 26, 1988, pp. 3, 5, enclosed in Risquet to Castro, Mar. 27, 1988, ACC.

29. Memcon (Castro, Adamishin), Mar. 28, 1988, pp. 48, 47.

30. See MINFAR, "Algunos datos solicitados sobre la Operación 'XXXI Aniversario (Refuerzo),'" Dec. 12, 1989, CF; Risquet, "Conferencia," Dec. 8, 2011, p. 16, ACC.

31. Crocker, *High Noon*, p. 366; Anstee, *Orphan*, p. 177.

32. On South Africa's nuclear weapons program, see Albright, "South Africa"; Reiss, *Bridled Ambition*, pp. 7–43; Venter, *Atom Bombs*.

33. Castro, July 30, 1998, *Granma*, Aug. 7, 1998, p. 5.

34. Interview with Ulises (quoted); Jefe de la Dirección Relaciones Exteriores MINFAR to Ulises, Jan. 25, 1988, and attachments, CF; MINFAR, "Nota informativa," Jan. 29, 1988, CF; "MMCA—EMG," June 1, 1988.

35. Castro to Ochoa and Polo, Mar. 22, 1988, CF; "Proposiciones del EMG para la Operación Antonio Maceo 88," Mar. 24, 1988, p. 2, CF.

36. Interview with General Charles Namoloh.

37. Ochoa to Ulises, Jan. 11, 1988, CF.

38. Interviews with Pedro Ross Fonseca and Felix Johannes.

39. Memcon (Castro, Adamishin), Mar. 28, 1988, pp. 35, 39, 95–96; Castro to Ochoa, Mar. 21, 1988, CF.

40. Quotations from Snyder to Crocker (quoting Rindle), Apr. 7, 1988, FOIA; Bentley (INR) to Kamman, Apr. 28, 1988, FOIA.

41. H SWA 2 to H SAW 5, Apr. 14, 1988, H SAW, gr. 4, box 160, DODDC.

42. "Tendense in Vyf Militêre Streek (MS)," [Apr. 1988,] p. 2, M, gr. 7, box 515, DODDC.

43. Interview with Colonel Breytenbach.

44. Risquet to Castro, Mar. 20, 1988, CF (the general was José Milian).

45. Castro, in "Indicaciones del comandante en jefe durante el analisis de la situación en la RPA," Mar. 22, 1988, CF; Castro to dos Santos, Mar. 31, 1988, p. 4, CF.

## CHAPTER 17

1. Castro, in Memcon (Castro, M'Binda, Ndalu), Oct. 15, 1987, p. 36, CF; interview with Risquet.

2. Memcon (Castro, M'Binda, Ndalu), Oct. 15, 1987, pp. 35, 43, CF.

3. Taylor, aide-mémoire, enclosed in Memcon (Risquet, Taylor), Dec. 25, 1987, ACC. Informed by the Cubans, the Soviets replied, "Taylor's assertion that on the eve of the Washington summit we had an extensive exchange of views with the U.S. about a solution of the situation in southern Africa is not true." There had only been "a general exchange of views about the regional conflicts" on November 17 in Geneva between U.S. under secretary of state Armacost and Soviet deputy foreign minister Yuli Vorontsov. Vorontsov had stated "firmly our full support for the position of Angola in the conversations with the U.S." ("Entregado al Co. Jorge Risquet por el embajador soviético, en la tarde del día 5.1.88," ACC).

4. Memcon (Risquet, Taylor), Dec. 25, 1987, ACC. For the "Brussels formula," see chapter 14.

5. Risquet to dos Santos, Dec. 26, 1987, ACC.

6. "Notas tomadas de la audiencia concedida por el presidente José Eduardo dos Santos al enviado especial de Cuba el día 3 de enero de 1988," ACC; dos Santos to Castro, enclosed in Ochoa to Castro, Jan. 2, 1988, CF.

7. M'Binda to Crocker, [early January 1988], ACC.

8. "Orientaciones de F[idel] C[astro] sobre RPA," Jan. 24, 1988, pp. 13, 6, CF.

9. Dos Santos to Castro, Jan. 11, 1988, pp. 3–4, ACC.

10. Castro to dos Santos, Jan. 23, 1988, pp. 2–5, 6, 7, ACC.

11. Risquet to Castro, Jan. 26, 1988, ACC.

12. Cohen, *Intervening*, p. 247, n. 8.

13. Interview with Cohen. Crocker agrees: "The NSC Africa staff was basically CIA people from the DDO [Deputy Directorate of Operations] side of the agency, rather than the intelligence side." (Interview with Crocker. See also Bishop, OH.)

14. Interview with Cohen.

15. Interviews with Crocker and Freeman.

16. Interview with Cohen; Risquet to Castro, Jan. 28, 1988, p. 5, ACC.

17. "Conversações Angola—Estados Unidos de America realizadas no Futungo de Belas (Luanda) em 28/01/988," pp. 3, 4, private collection, Luanda.

18. "Conversaciones Angola/EEUU, Futungo de Belas, Luanda, 29/1/88," pp. 5–6, ACC.

19. Crocker, *High Noon*, p. 374.

20. "Conversaciones Angola/EEUU, Futungo de Belas, Luanda, 29/1/88," pp. 9, 11–13, ACC.

21. "Conversaciones Angola-Cuba-EEUU realizadas en Futungo de Belas, 29-1-88 (16:40)," pp. 6–7, ACC.

22. Risquet to Castro, Jan. 29, 1988, ACC.

23. Memcon (dos Santos, Risquet), Jan. 30, 1988, enclosed in Risquet to Castro, Jan. 30, 1988, ACC.

24. Castro to dos Santos, Feb. 3 and Feb. 19, 1988 (pp. 4–5 quoted), both ACC.

25. Castro to dos Santos, Mar. 6, 1988, pp. 4–5, ACC.

26. Castro to Risquet, Mar. 10, 1988, ACC; SecState to Amembassy Abidjan et al., Mar. 24, 1988, p. 5, NSA.

27. Interview with Napper.

28. Risquet to Castro, Mar. 9, 1988, ACC.

29. "Conversaciones entre la RPA y los EUA realizadas en Luanda el día 9 de marzo de 1988," p. 22, ACC, and "Conversaciones realizadas entre la RPA y los Estados Unidos del 9 al 11 de marzo de 1988 en Futungo de Belas, Luanda. Tercera Sesión Trilateral, 10.3.88—16:00 horas," p. 7, ACC.

30. "Conversaciones entre la RPA y los EUA realizadas en Luanda el día 9 de marzo de 1988," p. 4, ACC.

31. "Las conversaciones bilaterales realizadas entre la República Popular de Angola y los Estados Unidos del 9 al 11 de marzo de 1988 en Futungo de Velas," Mar. 10, 1988, pp. 2, 3, 5, ACC.

32. Crocker to M'Binda, Mar. 15, 1988, enclosed in Risquet to Castro, Mar. 16, 1988, ACC.

33. "Acta de las conversaciones realizadas entre la RPA y los Estados Unidos del 17 al 18 de marzo de 1988, en Futungo de Belas, Luanda," pp. 10, 16–18, ACC.

34. Risquet to Castro, Mar. 19, 1988, ACC.

35. JCS, Apr. 15, 1988, NSA.

36. Crocker to M'Binda, Apr. 14, 1988, ACC.

37. Crocker, *High Noon*, p. 461.

38. Memcon (Castro, Adamishin), Mar. 28, 1988, pp. 53–54.

39. Gorbachev to Castro, Feb. 25, 1988, CF.

40. Castro to Gorbachev, Mar. 3, 1988, pp. 17–20, CF.

41. Medvedev, *Raspad*, p. 276. Medvedev and Dobrynin arrived in Havana on Feb. 28 and left on Mar. 5. For a detailed account of their visit, see ibid., pp. 259–77.

42. Castro to dos Santos, Mar. 6, 1988, p. 6, CF.

43. Risquet to Castro, Mar. 10, 1988, pp. 5–6, ACC; "Intervención de Jorge Risquet Valdés en el primer punto de la agenda de la reunión de Secretarios de Relaciones Exteriores de los Partidos de la Comunidad Socialista," Feb. 29, 1988, p. 4, ACC.

44. Risquet to Castro, Mar. 19, 1988, pp. 2–4, 10, ACC.

45. Malan, *Burger* (Cape Town), Mar. 7, 1988, p. 1. For PW Botha, see interviews in *WT*, Mar. 14, 1988, p. B8, and *Sunday Telegraph* (London), Mar. 27, 1988, p. 23. For Pik Botha's statement, see *Star* (Johannesburg), Feb. 3, 1988, p. 1.

46. Geldenhuys, "Angola Strategie," Jan. 29, 1988, M, gr. 7, box 518, DODDC; PW Botha, in SSC meeting, Mar. 14, 1988, p. 8, SVR.

47. Quotations from Oelschig to Sunde, June 1988; Sunde to Director General, June 27, 1988; Deputy Director General—Africa to Director General, June 28, 1988. Also Sunde, "Visit to Jamba on 23 and 24 May 1988." All 1/3/3, v. 2 Cuba: Relations with South Africa, DFA.

48. *Star*, Feb. 25, 1988, p. 13 (quoting the government decree).

49. CIA, DI, "Africa Review," Feb. 25, 1988, FOIA.

50. SSC meeting, Mar. 14, 1988, p. 2, SVR; CIA, DI, "South Africa's African National Congress: Weathering Challenges," Mar. 1988, p. 1, FOIA. On the broadening of the ANC's contacts with the West, see Thomas, *Diplomacy*, pp. 199–215.

51. Reagan's news conference, Feb. 24, 1988, *PP*, 1988, 1:255.

52. Rosenberg to Powell, Mar. 31, 1988, Fortier Alison Files, box 3, RRL.

53. *Business Day* (Johannesburg), Mar. 29, 1988, p. 8.

54. *Business Day*, Mar. 9, 1988, p. 1, and Mar. 15, p. 3; UNSC, Provisional Verbatim Record of the 2796th and 2797th meetings, Mar. 8, 1988, morning and afternoon sessions, DHL.

55. "Indicaciones concretas del Comandante en Jefe que guiarán la actuación de la delegación cubana a las conversaciones de Luanda y las negociaciones de Londres (22-4-88)," pp. 2–4, 9, 11, CF.

56. Ibid., pp. 7–8, 11.

57. Ibid., p. 6.

58. "Indicaciones concretas del Comandante en Jefe que guiarán la actuación de la delegación cubana a las conversaciones de Luanda y las negociaciones de Londres (23-4-88)," pp. 13, 7–8, CF.

59. "Indicaciones del Comandante el Jefe durante el análisis de la situación en la RPA, el 27.4.88," p. 1, CF.

60. Interview with Risquet.

61. Risquet to Castro, Apr. 30, 1988, ACC.

62. Risquet to Castro, Apr. 6, 1988, ACC; Nujoma, *Wavered*, p. 374. Also Memcon (van Heerden, Crocker), March 30, 1988, SWA/Angola—Violations, v. 1, DFA.

63. Interview with Gurirab.

CHAPTER 18

1. Brown, *Rise*, p. 507.

2. Politburo meeting, Feb. 25, 1988, in "The Moscow Summit 20 Years Later," NSA.

3. See "The Moscow Summit 20 Years Later," NSA.

4. Matlock, *Reagan*, p. 261.

5. NIE, "Soviet Policy toward Eastern Europe under Gorbachev," May 1988, p. 1, http://www.foia.cia.gov/Reagan.asp.

6. Gaddis, *Cold War*, p. 238.

7. *Burger* (Cape Town), July 14, 1988, p. 2 (quoting van Heerden); Risquet, in "Primera Reunión Cuatripartita celebrada en Londres los días 3 y 4 de mayo de 1988," p. 12, ACC; van Heerden, in "Summary minutes of exploratory discussions held in London on 3 May and 4 May 1988," p. 4, SWA/Angola: Angola talks, v. 1, DFA.

8. Memcon (van Heerden, Savimbi), Apr. 30, 1988, 1/3/3, v. 2, Cuba: Relations with SA, DFA; Crocker, *High Noon*, p. 405; Risquet notes, enclosed in Memcon (Dobrynin, Risquet), May 10, 1988, pp. 3–5, ACC.

9. Memcon (Crocker, Savimbi), May 14, 1988, p. 4, FOIA.

10. *WT*, May 4, 1988, p. F2 (ed.).

11. Abramowitz (INR) to SecState, May 13, 1988, pp. 1–2 (emphasis added), FOIA.

12. H SWA 2 to H SAW 3, May 23, 1988, M, gr. 7, box 518, DODDC.

13. "Reunión del Comandante en Jefe," Dec. 3, 1987, pp. 88, 106, CF.

14. "Reunión del Comandante en Jefe," Dec. 15, 1987, pp. 36, 13, CF.

15. Memcon (Castro, Adamishin), Mar. 28, 1988, p. 76, ACC. See also Adamishin, *Beloe Solntse*, p. 124.

16. *Weekly Mail* (Braamfontein), May 20, 1988, p. 14; Malan, *Star* (Johannesburg), May 17, 1988, p. 1; Geldenhuys, *Star*, May 27, 1988, p. 1.

17. "Sobre los aspectos esenciales de las conversaciones sostenidas entre A. L. Adamishin, viceministro de relaciones exteriores de la URSS y Chester Crocker, secretario adjunto de estado de los Estados Unidos en Lisboa los días 18–19 de mayo [1988]," p. 1, OS.

18. Levitsky to Colin Powell, May 23, 1988, FOIA.

19. Memcon (Crocker, Adamishin), May 29, 1988, FOIA; No title [Information from the Cuban leadership to the Soviet leadership for the Gorbachev-Reagan summit, late May 1988], p. 6, CF; Memcon (Crocker, Adamishin), May 30, 1988, FOIA; Adamishin, *Beloe Solntse*, p. 125.

20. Quotations from interview with Roger Reyes Carrasco and Castro to dos Santos, June 2, 1988, p. 3, CF. See also "MMCA—EMG," June 3, 1988. Cahama's second runway was completed on July 26 (*Verde Olivo en Misión Internacionalista* [Luanda], Aug. 4, 1988, p. 1).

21. Geldenhuys, *Burger*, May 27, 1988, p. 1.

22. *Business Day* (Johannesburg), May 5, 1988, p. 8 (ed.), and June 7, p. 4 (ed.).

23. Bridgland, *War*, p. 344; *Business Day*, June 17, 1988, p. 2; *Times* (London), June 16, 1988, p. 9; *WT*, June 13, 1988, p. A8.

24. Castro to Ochoa, June 7, 1988, quoted, CF; Castro to Ochoa and Polo, June 7, 1988, CF.

25. "Nota verbal al asesor principal del MINFAR," [June 7, 1988], CF.

26. *Burger*, June 9, 1988, pp. 1–2,

27. Interviews with Major Vilho Nghilalulwa (quoted), Major Alfeus Shiweda Kalistu (quoted), General Malakia Nakandungile (quoted); with Generals Charles Namoloh and Martin Shalli, Captain Thomas Ilwenya Ilwenya, and Major Joseph Katangolo.

28. Quotations from General Gleeson, *Namibian* (Windhoek), May 6, 1988, p. 5; *Star*, May 5, 1988, p. 3; General Secretary Dr. Abisai Shejavali, "We Will Not Be Consoled," *Namibian*, Apr. 29, 1988, p. 6. The black banner quote is from *Namibian*, May 6, 1988, p. 1. Next to England, West Germany was the major opponent of sanctions within the European Community (see Engel, *Afrikapolitik*, pp. 185–217, and Brenke, *Die Bundesrepublik*).

29. *WT*, June 20, 1988, p. A7; *Star*, June 17, 1988, p. 8.

30. On SWAPO and the fledgling student and workers' movement, see SWA-GIS, "South West Africa Peoples [sic] Organisation [SWAPO]," Sept. 23, 1983, DFA; Secretariat SSC, "Strategie Riglyne tov Suidwes-Afrika," Mar. 1987, SVR; Bauer, *Labor*, pp. 51–95; Becker, *Namibian Women's*, pp. 183–88; Maseko, "Namibian Student"; Peltola, *May Day*, pp. 167–211; Pakleppa, "40,000 Workers."

31. Secretariat SSC, "Tweemaandelike SWA-verslag vir die tydperk junie en julie 1988," p. 6, SVR; interviews with John Pandeni, secretary-general of the Namibian Food and Allied Workers' Union, and with Hendrick Witbooi.

32. Quotations from *Namibian*: Apr. 22, 1988, pp. 1 and 10 (Malan cartoon), May 27, p. 1; and from *Windhoek Advertiser*, June 27, 1988, p. 3 (quoting Administrator General Luis Pienaar). While the *Namibian* was sympathetic to SWAPO, the *Windhoek Advertiser* loathed it. Nevertheless, both papers provided strikingly similar accounts of military developments across the border in those critical months. Like the *Namibian*, the *Windhoek Advertiser* said that there were "conflicting reports" on the battle of Cuito Cuanavale (Jan. 27, 1988, p. 1). Like the *Namibian*, in the late spring it began reporting the Cuban advance—"there was a serious and dangerous force moving south in Angola" (May 13, p. 3).

33. Malan, May 16, 1988, RSA, *Hansard—Debates of Parliament*, col. 9933.

34. PRA, Gabinete do Presidente, "Conversações realizadas entre a RPA e a RSA em Brazzaville no dia 13.05.988," May 13, 1988, pp. 11 and 13, private collection, Luanda; see also "Summary minutes of the bilateral meeting held in Brazzaville on Friday, 13 May 1988, between delegations from the governments of the Republic of South Africa and the People's Republic of Angola," SWA/Angola: Angola Talks, v. 1, DFA.

35. *Burger*, May 11, 1988, p. 2; Taylor to SecState, May 14, 1988, FOIA.

36. PRA, Gabinete do Presidente, "Conversações realizadas entre a RPA e a RSA em Brazzaville no dia 13.05.988," May 13, 1988, p. 14, private collection, Luanda.

37. [Information from the Cuban leadership to the Soviet leadership for the Gorbachev-Reagan summit, late May 1988], p. 4, CF.

38. *Weekly Mail*, May 20, 1988, p. 14.

39. SecState to AmConsul Cape Town, June 3, 1988, p. 2, FOIA.

40. Castro to dos Santos, May 18, 1988, pp. 2–4, CF.

41. Pik Botha, May 18, 1988, RSA, *Hansard—Debates of Parliament*, col. 10,168; INR, "Peacekeeping in Angola," June 10, 1988, p. 3, FOIA; Renwick, *Diplomacy*, pp. 130, 114; David Villers, *Star*, Nov. 20, 1988, p. 4.

42. [DFA], "Current State of Negotiations between South Africa and Angola," June 15, 1988, SWA/Angola: Angola talks, v. 2, DFA.

43. Tel. interview with van Heerden.

44. SADF, "Angola/SWA Strategie," [June 1988], M, gr. 7, box 518, DODDC. Also SADF, "SAW Konsep voorstelle vir Kubaanse en vreemde magte troepe-ontrekking uit Angola en die implementering van VNVR Res 435/78," [late May or early June 1988], ibid.

45. Arbesú, Castro, in "Reunión con el Comandante en Jefe el 17/6/88," pp. 5–7, 14, 18–19, 17, CF.

46. "Propuesta sudafricana con respecto a la retirada total de las tropas cubanas de Angola y la aplicación de la resolución 435 1978 del Consejo de Seguridad de las Naciones Unidas," June 18, 1988, pp. 2–5, enclosed in "Segunda Reunión Cuatripartita celebrada en el Cairo los días 24 y 25 de junio de 1988," ACC.

47. "Reunión con el Comandante en Jefe el 18/6/88," pp. 23, 14–15, 38, CF. The second Fidel quote is from "Reunión con el Comandante en Jefe (19/6/88)," p. 4, CF.

48. Akhromeyev and Kornienko, *Glazami*, p. 211.

49. Quotations from Gorbachev, *Pravda* (Moscow), June 2, 1988, p. 4; Raúl Castro, in "Reunión 19/6/88," p. 7; Fidel Castro, in "Reunión 17/6/88," p. 19.

50. Fidel Castro, in: "Reunión 18/6/88," pp. 56–57; "Reunión 17/6/88," p. 14; "Reunión 18/6/88," pp. 57–58.

51. Fidel Castro, in "Reunión 18/6/88," pp. 30, 49; Fidel Castro, in "Reunión 17/6/88," p. 4.

52. SSC meeting, June 20, 1988, #10, SVR.

53. "Summary Minutes of a Meeting Held at the U.S. Embassy in Cairo on 24 June 1988 between the South African and U.S. Delegations to the Cairo Talks," pp. 4–6, SWA/ Angola, Angola Talks, v. 2, DFA. Crocker had just told Shultz, "The danger of a major confrontation between South African and Cuban troops is growing" (Crocker to Sec-State, June 21, 1988, FOIA).

54. M'Binda, in "Acta das Conversações Quadripartidas entre a RPA, Cuba, Estados Unidos da América e a Africa do Sul realizadas no Cairo de 24–26.06.988," p. 4, private collection, Luanda; Castro, in "Encuentro del comandante Fidel Castro Ruz con el regimiento de artillería que partiría para Angola. Junio de 1988," p. 15, CF.

55. "Conversaciones RPA-Cuba EEUU-RSA," June 24, 1988, afternoon sess., pp. 16, 18, 21, ACC.

56. "Summary Minutes of a Meeting between the Republic of South Africa, an Angolan/Cuban Delegation and the United States of America as Mediator on the Question of SWA/Namibia and Angola," June 24–25, 1988, ALUKA.

57. "Actividades desarrolladas por la delegación cubana a las conversaciones en el Cairo," [June 27, 1988], ACC. On the Cairo meeting, see also "Conversaciones Cuba-RPA/ EEUU (Reunión Tripartita)," June 24, 1988; "Segunda reunión cuatripartita, celebrada en el Cairo los dias 24 y 25 de junio de 1988"; "Conversaciones RPA-Cuba EEUU-RSA," June 25, 1988, morning session; Memcon (Ulises, Geldenhuys), June 25, 1988. All ACC.

58. "Conferencia de prensa de Jorge Risquet Valdés. El Cairo. 26/8/88," pp. 2–3, in "Conferencias de Prensa de Jorge Risquet," ACC.

59. *Burger*, June 27, 1988, p. 1.

60. SSC meeting, June 20, 1988, #2, SVR.

61. Amembassy Cairo to SecState, June 26, 1988, FOIA.

62. Memcon (Risquet, Crocker), June 26, 1988, pp. 22–23, 26–27, ACC.

63. "Nota del Comandante en Jefe de fecha 26.6.88," quoted, CF;"MMCA-EMG," June 27, 1988; MINFAR, "Cronología de las principales acciones realizadas en Tchipa,"

[July 20, 1988], CF. The SADF first claimed to have killed "about 200 Cuban and Angolan soldiers," then it jacked up the number to 300 (*Burger*, June 29, 1988, p. 1 quoted, and July 1, p. 13).

64. Quotations from Castro to Ochoa and Polo, June 26, 1988, #91, CF, and June 26, 1988, no #, CF.

65. For the SADF estimate, see *Burger*, June 29, 1988, p. 1. For the Cuban estimate, see Ulises to Risquet, June 29, 1988, CF.

66. Quotations from Bridgland, *War*, p. 361 (quoting Colonel Dick Lord), and CIA, "South Africa—Angola—Cuba," June 29, 1988, FOIA. See also MINFAR, "Cronología de la aviación cubana, Maniobra XXXI Aniversario," n.d., p. 94, CF; MMCA, "Informe Cumplimiento de Misión," June 27, 1988, CF.

67. CIA, "South Africa—Angola-Namibia," July 1, 1988, FOIA; DIA, July 1, 1988, NSA.

68. *Namibian*, July 1, 1988, pp. 7, 11 (ed.).

69. Castro to Ochoa and Polo, June 27, 1988, #25398 and #25397, CF.

70. *Burger*, June 29, 1988, p. 1.

71. *Die Kerkbode* (Cape Town), July 8, 1988, p. 4 (ed.); *Star*, July 8, 1988, p. 10 (ed.).

72. *Business Day*, Aug. 10, 1988, p. 4 (ed.); Crocker, *High Noon*, p. 380.

73. Eglin, *Pretoria News*, May 7, 1987, p. 3; Tutu, *Pretoria News*, May 8, 1987, p. 8; CIA, DI, "South African Whites: Resolve in the Face of Pressure," Dec. 1987, p. iii, CHF, box 91630, RRL.

74. *Pretoria News*, Mar. 3, 1988, p. 1; *Business Day*, Mar. 31, 1988, p. 8 (ed.).

75. *NYT*, July 15, 1988, p. 30 (ed.); *Business Day*, July 15, 1988, p. 4 (ed.).

76. Grundy, *Militarization*, pp. 23–25; Stiff, *Silent War*, pp. 219–20.

77. Interview with Colonel Barlow.

78. http://www.joburg.org.za/march2002/sowetan.stm (quoting editor Aggrey Klaaste).

79. Quotations from *Sowetan* (Johannesburg), May 2, 1988, p. 6; June 8, p. 6; June 10, p. 4 (quoting Geldenhuys); June 13, p. 7; July 12, p. 9 (Risquet interview); July 18, p. 7.

80. "Análisis de la posición de Cuba en la próxima ronda de negociaciones en Estados Unidos," [July 4, 1988], pp. 15, 23, 24, ACC.

81. Aldana to Castro, July 11, 1988, CF.

82. Crocker to SecState, July 13, 1988, FOIA.

83. The statement is reprinted in Crocker, *High Noon*, pp. 499–501. For the New York round, see "Reunión Tripartita Nueva York, Cuba—RPA—Estados Unidos, 10-7-88"; "Reunión cuatripartita," July 11, 1988; "Reunión cuatripartita," July 12, 1988; "Ultima reunión," July 13, 1988; "Conversaciones militares en New York"; "Reuniones para lograr una solución al conflicto de la región del suroeste de Africa. Conversaciones entre militares". All ACC. See also South Africa, "Summary Minutes of a Meeting Held in New York on July 11–12, 1988, between a South African Delegation and an Angolan Delegation, Facilitated by a Delegation from the United States," ALUKA.

84. Morejón, "Entrevista con el general van Tonder de la inteligencia militar sudafricana el 12.7.88," ACC.

85. See *Burger*, July 21, 1988, p. 2; *WT*, July 21, 1988, p. B7.

86. Memcon (Crocker, Adamishin), May 30, 1988, p. 5, FOIA; Memcon (Adamishin, Risquet), Mar. 27, 1988, p. 4, ACC; INR, "Peacemaking in Angola," June 10, 1988, p. 4, FOIA; PW Botha, Aug. 24, 1988, RSA, *Hansard—Debates of Parliament*, col. 15508.

87. Interview with Risquet.

88. Alcibiades to Castro, July 11, 1988, CF.

89. Quotations from interview with Napper; Memcon (Dobrynin, Risquet), May 10, 1988, p. 14, ACC; Crocker, *High Noon*, p. 379.

90. Geldenhuys, in Memcon (Ndalu, Ulises, Geldenhuys, Woods), July 12, 1988, 9:00–10:10 A.M., enclosed in "Reuniones para lograr una solución . . . Conversaciones entre militares," p. 17; Geldenhuys, in Memcon (Ndalu, Ulises, Geldenhuys, Woods), July 12, 1988, 15:15–16:15, enclosed in ibid., p. 20.

91. Ulises to Castro, July 13, 1988, CF.

92. Mike Malone to A. Jacquet, enclosed in Jacquet to Pik Botha, July 20, 1988, SWA/Angola, v. 2, DFA.

93. Ulises to Fidel and Raúl Castro, July 22, 1988, #9, CF. My three main sources for the Cape Verde meeting are a forty-five-page folder of cables, which includes the cables quoted in the text ("Reunión de Expertos Militares, Cabo Verde, Julio 22 y 23/1988: cifrados recibidos y enviados"), and two other documents: "Resumen de la Reunión de Delegaciones Militares de Angola, Cuba, y Sudafrica, así como de representantes de Estados Unidos, celebrada los días 22 y 23.7.88 en la Isla de Sal" and "Resultados de las discusiones sobre temas militares celebradas en Cabo Verde, los días 22 y 23 de julio de 1988. All CF. The South Africans have declassified "Summary of Points of Agreement and Others Discussed at the South African and Angolan/Cuban Military Meetings: Sal Island, Cape Verde, July 22–23, 1988," ALUKA, and R. to Malone, "Situation Evaluation," July 27, 1988, 1/3/3 v. 2, Cuba: Relations with SA, DFA.

94. "Indicaciones del Comandante en jefe durante el análisis de la situación en la RPA," July 19, 1988, CF.

95. Ulises to Fidel and Raúl Castro, July 22, 1988, CF.

96. Castro to Ulises, July 23, 1988, #6828 and #6829, CF.

97. Ulises to Fidel and Raúl Castro, July 23, 1988, CF.

98. SSC meeting, July 25, 1988, #5, SVR.

99. SSC meeting, July 27, 1988, #2, SVR.

100. JCS, July 28, 1988, NSA.

101. SADF, "Inligtingswaardering op MPLA/kubaanse militêre intensies in suid—en suidos Angola vir HSAW te bepaal," [July 1988], pp. 5–7, H SAW, gr. 4, box 160, DODDC; Geldenhuys, "Samevatting van notas mbt SAW-operasies in Suid-Angola," Aug. 23, 1988, ibid.

102. On the South African Armed Forces, see Helmoed-Römer, *Armed Forces*; Seegers, *The Military*; D. Lord, *Fledgling*.

103. Geldenhuys, "Samevatting van notas mbt SAW-operasies in Suid-Angola," Aug. 23, 1988, H SAW, gr. 4, box 160, DODDC.

104. Geldenhuys, in SSC meeting, Feb. 15, 1988, #1, SVR.

105. DIA, Aug. 2, 1988, NSA; interview with Geldenhuys.

106. Tel. interview with van Heerden; Crocker, *High Noon*, p. 427.

107. Aldana to Fidel and Raúl Castro, Aug. 1, 1988, ACC.

108. "Minutes of Plenary Meetings Held in Geneva, Aug. 2–5, 1988," ALUKA.

109. *Burger*, Aug. 3, 1988, p. 1; Aug. 4, p. 16 (ed.). "Blast of cold water" is from ibid., Aug. 5, p. 16 (ed.).

110. Aldana to Fidel and Raúl Castro, Aug. 2, 1988, ACC.

111. "Protocol of Geneva," Geneva, Aug. 5, 1988, enclosed in "Conversaciones Quatripartitas RPA/Cuba/RSA/EU, Ginebra. Agosto 2 al 5 de 1988," ACC. See also "Conversaciones telefonicas desde Ginebra, delegación cuatripartita, fecha 2-8-88 al 5.8.88," CF (includes long telephone conversations with Castro); "Cuarta Reunión Cuatripartita, Ginebra, del 2 al 5.8.88," ACC.

112. "Minutes of Plenary Meetings Held in Geneva, Aug. 2–5, 1988," ALUKA.

113. *Burger*, Aug. 9, 1988, p. 1.

114. Press communiqué, *Business Day*, Aug. 9, 1988, p. 1.

115. *Sowetan*, Aug. 11, 1988, p. 8; *Star*, Aug. 11, 1988, p. 8 (ed.).

116. Crocker to Acting Secretary, Aug. 25, 1988, p. 6, NSA.

117. *Burger*, Aug. 31, 1988, p. 18 (ed.); *WT*, Sept. 2, 1988, p. A8.

118. Quotations from *Namibian*, Sept. 2, 1988, p. 11 (ed.); *WP*, Aug. 31, 1988, p. 21; *Windhoek Advertiser*, Aug. 31, 1988, p. 2.

119. Hoof van die SA Weermag, "Regstel van wanpersepsies aangaande die SWA/Angola situasie," Sept. 13, 1988, M, gr. 7, box 462, DODDC.

120. "Copia del cifrado de nuestra embajada en Praga," May 18, 1988; Sánchez to Risquet, Sept. 2, 1988; Fariñas to Risquet, Sept. 8, 1988. All with marginalia from Risquet. All ACC.

CHAPTER 19

1. Brecht, *Der aufhaltsame Aufstieg*, p. 124.

2. Memcon (Risquet, Yakovlev), Oct. 28, 1988, p. 9 quoted, enclosed in Risquet to Castro, Nov. 2, 1988, CF; "Sexta Reunión Cuatripartita, Brazzaville, del 7 al 9 de septiembre de 1988," ACC; "Septima Reunión Cuatripartita, Brazzaville, del 26 al 29 de septiembre de 1988," ACC; Jacquet, "Discussions in Brazzaville 6–9 September 1988," ALUKA.

3. *Burger* (Cape Town), Sept. 19, 1988, p. 1 (quoting Malan); *Namibian* (Windhoek), Sept. 23, 1988, p. 9.

4. See "Chairman's Summary (October 8, 1988)," enclosed in "Reunión Cuatripartita Angola/Cuba/EEUU/RSA, Nueva York, Octubre 6–9 de 1988," pp. 30–28, ACC.

5. "Octavo Encuentro Cuatripartito, Nueva York, del 6 al 9 de octubre de 1988," pp. 3, 5–6, in "Reuniones para lograr una solución al conflicto de la región del suroeste de Africa," ACC.

6. Aldana to Fidel and Raúl Castro, Oct. 9, 1988, enclosed in "Reunión Cuatripartita Angola/Cuba/EEUU/RSA, Nueva York, Octubre 6–9 de 1988," pp. 40–35, ACC. The Castro quote is from "Indicaciones concretas del Comandante en Jefe que guiarán la actuación de la delegación cubana a las conversaciones de Luanda y las negociaciones de Londres (22-4-88)," p. 3, CF. For Reagan's misstatements, see "The President's News Conference," Jan. 29, 1981, and "Toast at a Dinner Hosted by Brazilian President João Baptista de Oliveira Figueiredo in Brasilia," Dec. 1, 1982, both in http://www.presidency.ucsb.edu/ws/.

7. Aldana, *Granma* (Havana), Oct. 11, 1988, p. 1; Castro to Ochoa and Polo Cintra Frías, Oct. 10, 1988, CF; General Willie Meyer, *Star* (Johannesburg), Oct. 13, 1988, p. 4.

8. Ulises to Fidel and Raúl Castro, Oct. 7, 1988, and Aldana to Fidel and Raúl Castro,

Oct. 10, 1988, both enclosed in "Reunión Cuatripartita Angola/Cuba/EEUU/RSA, Nueva York, Octubre 6–9 de 1988," pp. 11, 65, ACC.

9. FBIS, "Trends," Oct. 5, 1988, p. 1, FOIA.

10. Risquet to Castro, Nov. 2, 1988, CF.

11. Memcon (Risquet, Yakovlev), Oct. 28, 1988, CF. Also "Viskazivaniia ob angolskoi situazii," Oct. 28, 1988, enclosed in Yakovlev to CC PCSU, Oct. 29, 1988, NSA.

12. Risquet to Castro, Oct. 28, 1988, CF. The text of the draft letter to Crocker and the final version are in "Visita de Risquet a la URSS (27/30/10/88)," CF. Also Memcon (Risquet, dos Santos), Oct. 27, 1988, CF.

13. Amembassy Moscow to SecState, Oct. 27, 1988, NSA.

14. Memcon (Castro, dos Santos), Dec. 17, 1988, ACC; "Über die Ergebnisse des kurzen Arbeitsbesuchs des Vorsitzenden der MPLA-Partei der Arbeit und Präsidenten der Volksrepublik Angola, José Eduardo dos Santos, in der Sowjetunion," Nov. 4, 1988, p. 2 quoted, DY30 JIV 2/202/49, SAPMO.

15. See "Novena Reunión Cuatripartita, Ginebra, del 11 al 15 de noviembre de 1988," ACC. For the 26 weeks, see "Indicaciones concretas del Comandante en Jefe que guiarán la actuación de la delegación cubana a las conversaciones de Luanda y las negociaciones de Londres (23-4-88)," p. 14, CF.

16. Salomón to Castro, Nov. 15, 1988 (enclosing dos Santos to Castro); Castro to Salomón, Nov. 15, 1988 (enclosing Castro's reply). Both ACC.

17. Memcon (Reagan, Savimbi), June 30, 1988, NSA. Also USMission USUN NY to SecState, June 25, 1988, FOIA; Memcon (Shultz, Savimbi), June 28, 1988, FOIA; Levitsky to Gregg, June 28, 1988, FOIA; Windrich, *Guerrilla*, pp. 77–81.

18. Secretariat SSC, "Angola: huidige situasie en posisie van die betrokke partye by onderhandelingsinisiatiewe," [Summer 1988], p. 15, SVR.

19. Savimbi, *Burger*, Sept. 5, 1988, p. 7.

20. Shultz to Savimbi, enclosed in USDel Secretary in New York to Amembassy Kinshasa, Oct. 7, 1988, NSA. For the complaints of Savimbi's American supporters, and the administration's response, see the documents in WHORM, Subject File, box CO 177, RRL.

21. Interview with Cohen.

22. Crocker to SecState, Nov. 30, 1988, FOIA.

23. Alarcón to Castro, Dec. 3, 1988, #101014 and #101016, both ACC; *Star*, Dec. 5, 1988, p. 17. Also "Onceno encuentro cuatripartito Brazzaville, del 1 al 3 de diciembre de 1988," ACC.

24. *Burger*, Dec. 5, 1988, p. 10 (ed.).

25. Alarcón to Castro, Dec. 1, 1988, ACC, quoting van Heerden.

26. *NYT*, Dec. 5, 1988, p. 8; tel. interview with van Heerden.

27. For the text of the protocol, see Crocker, *High Noon*, pp. 506–11.

28. "Report of the Secretary General," Dec. 17, 1988, quoted, S/20338; UNSC Resolution 626, Dec. 20, 1988, www.un.org/documents; United Nations, *Blue Helmets*, pp. 235–36.

29. SecState to All African Diplomatic Posts, Dec. 30, 1988, p. 6, FOIA.

30. "Informe sobre la visita del presidente del ANC Oliver Tambo (junio 27 a julio 2)," p. 1, enclosed in Padilla to Risquet, July 7, 1987, ACC.

31. Memcon (Castro, Ndalu, van Dunem), Sept. 21, 1988, pp. 29–30, ACC.

32. Interview with Cohen; Reagan, Dec. 16, 1988, *PP*, 1988–89, 2:1634.

33. Aldana to Castro, Dec. 21, 1988, CF.

34. *Granma*, Dec. 23, 1988, p. 7.

35. *Granma*, Dec. 22, 1998, p. 4.

36. Castro, July 26, 1989, *Granma*, July 28, 1989, pp. 3–5.

37. See *Granma*: June 14, 1989, p. 1; June 15, p. 3; June 16, p. 1; June 22, p. 3; June 26, p. 1; June 27, p. 1; June 28, p. 3 (quoted).`

38. Preston, "The Trial," p. 26; General Juan Escalona, in Republic of Cuba, *Vindicación*, p. 297.

39. The Ochoa trial has spawned a cottage industry. Among the many far-fetched explanations of why Ochoa was tried, one is relevant to the subject of this book: Andres Oppenheimer asserts that Ochoa and Castro had clashed over military strategy in Angola. Ochoa "simply ignored the most absurd orders," and he implemented "his own battle plans" (Oppenheimer, *Final Hour*, pp. 83, 86). This, of course, makes no sense: Castro directed the campaign from Havana, and all his orders were executed, to the letter. Furthermore, the key man on the ground was Polo, not Ochoa.

40. "Síntesis del Informe del Ministro de las FAR, general de ejército Raúl Castro Ruz, ante el Tribunal de Honor convocado para analizar la conducta del general de división Arnaldo Ochoa Sánchez," June 25, 1989, in *Granma*, June 26, 1988, pp. 1–2; *NYT*, June 28, 1989, p. 2.

41. See the testimonies of Jorge Martínez, Antonio Rodríguez (quoted p. 116), Ochoa (quoted pp. 76, 88), Patricio de la Guardia, and Eduardo Delgado, in Republic of Cuba, *Vindicación*, pp. 68, 76, 88, 94–99, 109, 116, 263, 282.

42. General Escalona, in ibid., p. 300. I was unable to gain access to the pretrial depositions and other unpublished documents. Therefore, my estimate is approximate.

43. For the formal interviews, see Gleijeses, *Conflicting Missions*, p. 509, and the list of interviews in this book.`

44. Pérez de Cuéllar, *Pilgrimage*, p. 324. Also United Nations, *Blue Helmets*, pp. 234–38.

45. "Orientaciones de FC sobre RPA," Jan. 24, 1988, p. 23, ACC; Memcon (Castro, dos Santos), Dec. 17, 1988, p. 31, CF.

46. "Ubicación de los colaboradores cubanos," Nov. 4, 1988, CF.

47. Figures from Bestard Pavón, "La colaboración," p. 44.

48. Memcon (Castro, dos Santos), Dec. 17, 1988, p. 80, CF.

49. Castro, Jan. 29, 1989, *Granma*, Feb. 1, 1989, p. 3.

50. Vergau, *Verhandeln*, p. 85.

51. Risquet to Castro, Dec. 22, 1988, ACC.

52. Aldana to Castro, Dec. 21, 1988, ACC; *Granma*: Jan. 25, 1989, p. 1; Feb. 4, p. 2; Feb. 17, p. 1.

53. Memcon (Risquet, Yakovlev), Jan. 29, 1989, enclosed in Risquet to Castro, Jan. 31, 1989, ACC.

54. UNSC Resolution 632 of Feb. 16, 1989, www.un.org/documents; "Further Report of the Secretary-General concerning the Implementation of Security Council Resolutions 435 (1978) and 439 (1978) concerning the Question of Namibia," Jan. 23, 1989, S/20412, DHL.

55. On the Namibian elections see Leistner and Esterhuysen, *Namibia*; Ansprenger, *Freie Wahlen*; Harlech-Jones, *A New Thing?*; Cliffe, *Transition*; O'Lynn, *Namibia*, pp. 315–79; Weiland and Braham, *Peace Process*; National Democratic Institute for International Affairs, *Nation Building*; Howard, *UN Peacekeeping*, pp. 52–87; and, by participants, Pérez de Cuéllar, *Pilgrimage*, pp. 307–17; Goulding, *Peacemonger*, pp. 139–75; Thornberry, *A Nation*; United Nations, *Blue Helmets*, pp. 203–29.

56. *Burger*, Apr. 1, 1989, p. 1, and Apr. 5, p. 12 (ed.).

57. "Report of the Secretary-General Concerning the Implementation of Security Council Resolution 435 (1978) and 439 (1978) on the question of Namibia," Feb. 26, 1979, S/13120, DHL.

58. Goulding, *Peacemonger*, p. 152.

59. This is not to say that there were no SWAPO guerrillas in Namibia before March 31, 1989. Since the mid-1970s large numbers of fighters had infiltrated into the country every year, particularly during the rainy season, when the vegetation offered more cover. A SADF report in April 1988 had noted, "The infiltration for 1988 is now in full swing," and another, the following August, had said that "SWAPO's terrorist attacks in SWA are steadily increasing." ("Verwikkelinge in SWA en Angola 18 Maart tot 14 April [1988]," p. 3, SWA/Angola, v. 2, DFA; HS OPS to Mil Sek, Aug. 18, 1988, M, gr. 7, box 515, DODDC).

60. Pérez de Cuéllar, *Pilgrimage*, p. 311.

61. Ibid., p. 308.

62. Ibid., p. 311.

63. Thornberg, *A Nation*, p. 98.

64. Gerhard Roux, spokesperson of the Administrator General, *Burger*, May 13, 1989, p. 3.

65. See "Zapiski osnovnovo soderzhania b'esed M.S. Gorbachev s F. Kastro v Gavane," Apr. 3–4, 1989, p. 38 (courtesy of Sergey Radchenko), and Memcon (Risquet, Axen), Apr. 18, 1989, DY30 IV2/2.035/41, SAPMO.

66. Pérez de Cuéllar, *Pilgrimage*, p. 312; Chipampata (Zambian ambassador to Botswana) to Zambian Foreign Minister Chakulya, Feb. 27, 1980, p. 7, 079 UNIP 7/1/1/19, UNIP.

67. "Further Report of the Secretary-General concerning the implementation of Security Council Resolutions 435 (1978) and 439 (1978) concerning the question of Namibia," Jan. 23, 1989, p. 12, S/20412, DHL. "Settlement plan" meant Resolution 435 plus the additional agreements and "informal understandings" that were negotiated in subsequent years (Goulding, *Peacemonger*, p. 143).

68. Thornberg, *A Nation*, p. 286; Howard, *UN Peacekeeping*, p. 69.

69. United Nations, *Blue Helmets*, p. 223. Stiff, *Covert War*, and Hooper, *Koevoet*, are sympathetic to Koevoet, but include useful information.

70. *Burger*, June 22, 1989, p. 2, and July 11, p. 13 (quoting U.S. Assistant Secretary of State for Africa Herman Cohen).

71. Pérez de Cuéllar, *Burger*, July 22, 1989, p. 2; UNSC Resolution 640 of Aug. 29, 1989, in www.un.org/documents.

72. "Report of the Secretary-General on the Implementation of Security Council Resolution 640 (1989) Concerning the Question of Namibia," Oct. 6, 1989, S.20883, DHL; *Windhoek Advertiser*, Oct. 11, 1989, p. 1.

73. UNSC Resolution 643 of Oct. 31, 1989, in www.un.org/documents.

74. *Burger*, Nov. 1, 1989, p. 21.

75. Stiff, *Warfare*, pp. 375–412.

76. "SWA: Situasie mbt die implementering van resolusie 435 (1989): Augustus 1989 tot September 1989," n.d., p. 20, SWA/Angola, v. 1, DFA.

77. "Further Report of the Secretary General concerning the Implementation of Security Council Resolution 435 (1978) concerning the Question of Namibia," Nov. 14, 1989, p. 3, S/20967, DHL.

78. *Windhoek Advertiser*, Nov. 15, 1989, p. 3.

79. *Burger*, Nov. 15, 1989, p. 1 (quoting Gurirab), and Nov. 16, p. 2 (quoting Andries Treurnicht).

80. Memcon (Geldenhuys, Savimbi), Nov. 23, 1989, 1/22/3 v. 33, DFA.

81. Goulding, *Peacemonger*, p. 174; Vergau, *Verhandeln*, p. 90.

82. On the 1992 elections, see Anstee, *Orphan*; Goulding, *Peacemonger*, pp. 176–88; United Nations, *Blue Helmets*, pp. 238–44; Cohen, *Intervening*, pp. 87–116; Messiant, "Angola, les voies"; Albuquerque, *Angola*, pp. 175–222.

83. *Times* (London), Oct. 5, 1992, p. 9; Jeffrey Millington, head of the U.S. Liaison office, *NYT*, Oct. 2, 1992, p. 3.

84. *NYT*, Oct. 4, 1992, p. 15; *Burger*, Oct. 10, 1992, p. 8; Anstee, *Orphan*, p. 235.

85. See United Nations, *Blue Helmets*, p. 244.

86. Anstee's statement, quoted in "Further Report of the Secretary-General on the United Nations Angola Verification Mission (UNAVEM II)," Nov. 25, 1992, p. 6, S/24858, DHL.

87. Anstee, *Orphan*, p. 238.

88. *Burger*, Nov. 30, 1992, p. 10 (ed.); International Institute for Strategic Studies, *Strategic Survey, 1992–93*, p. 206. For an authoritative account of how Angola plunged back into war, see Anstee, *Orphan*, pp. 199–544. While the MPLA comes in for its share of criticism, Anstee's verdict is unequivocal: "It was UNITA's actions since the elections that had precipitated the crisis. . . . It was UNITA that had started the aggression" (ibid., p. 349). This was also the verdict of the international community: see, e.g., "Further Report of the Secretary-General on the United Nations Angola Verification Mission (UNAVEM II)," Jan. 21, 1993, UNSC S/25140, DHL, and UNSC Resolutions 804 of Jan. 29, 1993, 811 of Mar. 12, 1993, and 834 of June 1, 1993, in www.un.org/documents. For UNITA's perspective, see Africano, *L'UNITA*.

89. Goulding, *Peacemonger*, p. 197. The best overall discussion of this last period of Angolan history is Hodges, *Angola*. See also *Last*, by Paul Hare, the U.S. special representative for the Angolan peace process from 1993 to 1998; *Memórias*, by UNITA official Alcides Sakala; *Executive Outcomes*, by Eeben Barlow, a former SADF officer who fought for the Angolan government in 1993–95; *Angola Unravels*, by Human Rights Watch. Good journalistic accounts are Maier, *Angola*; Brittain, *Death*; and Albuquerque, *Angola*, pp. 223–364. For a valuable scholarly analysis, see Messiant, "Angola."

CHAPTER 20

1. *WP*, Dec. 26, 1988, p. 24 (ed.); *NYT*, Dec. 15, 1988, p. 38 (ed.); *WSJ*, Dec. 21, 1988, p. 14 (ed.); Dec. 22, p. 16 quoted; *WT*, Dec. 19, 1988, p. E2 (ed.); Dec. 21, p. F1; Dec. 23, p. F1.

2. Crocker, *High Noon*.

3. Jim Hoagland, op-ed, *WP*, July 17, 1988, p. 19.

4. Crocker, "South Africa: Strategy for Change."

5. PW Botha, Aug. 13, 1987, RSA, *Hansard—Debates of the House of Assembly*, col. 3765.

6. Interview with Nickel.

7. Ringdahl to McFarlane, June 20, 1985, AAD, NSC, box 1, RRL.

8. *Business Day* (Johannesburg), Dec. 22, 1987, p. 4 (ed.).

9. Brand Fourie to Pik Botha, Apr. 16, 1984, Lusaka Ooreenkoms, DFA; Memcon (Pik Botha, Crocker), May 25, 1984, p. 6, Geagte Kollega-Briewe, DFA.

10. INR, "South Africa: The Resurrection of Thump and Talks," June 26, 1985, AAD, NSC, box 1, RRL.

11. *Pretoria News*, Dec. 29, 1983, p. 16 (ed.).

12. SecState to Amembassy Pretoria, Dec. 5, 1987, FOIA; Crocker, *High Noon*, p. 388.

13. Memcon (van Heerden, Crocker), Mar. 30, 1988, pp. 13, 15, SWA/Angola—Violations, v. 1, DFA.

14. Crocker, *High Noon*, pp. 360–61.

15. Adamishin, *Beloe Solntse*, p. 131 quoted; Saunders, "Ending," pp. 264, 267.

16. "Nasionale Inligtingswaardering 1988," [Aug. 1988], p. 5, SVR; Secretariat SSC, "USSR-pogings tot bewerkstelliging van 'n houdingsverandering in die RSA," Sept. 1988, p. 4, SVR.

17. Interview with Risquet.

18. Deputy National Health Minister Veldman, *Business Day*, Jan. 18, 1988, p. 2; *Star* (Johannesburg), Mar. 13, 1988, p. 12; Crocker to Armacost, enclosed in SecState to USDel Secretary, Aug. 27, 1988, FOIA; *Business Day*, Mar. 10, 1988, p. 6 (ed.).

19. Crocker, *High Noon*, p. 405.

20. U.S. Joint Chiefs of Staff, July 28, 1988, NSA; Mike Malone to A. Jacquet, enclosed in Jacquet to Pik Botha, July 20, 1988, SWA/Angola, v. 2, DFA; Geldenhuys, "Samevatting van notas mbt SAW-operasies in Suid-Angola," Aug. 23, 1988, H SAW, gr. 4, box 160, DODDC.

21. Tel. interview with van Heerden.

22. Crocker, *High Noon*, p. 463; Shultz, *Turmoil*, p. 1119.

23. Crocker, in Memcon (Pik Botha, Crocker), Feb. 13, 1986, p. 3, Angola, v. 16, DFA; CIA, DI, "Angola: Prospects for MPLA-UNITA Reconciliation," Feb. 1985, p. iii, FOIA.

24. Cohen, OH; interview with Freeman; Crocker, in "Discussions between South Africa and the United States of America, Pretoria, 17 November 1982," p. 10, SA/USA (Crocker): Pta: 17 Nov 82, SA/SWA (EM): Windhoek: 19–20 Nov 82, SA/USA (Washington): 24–26 Nov 82, DFA; interview with Davidow.

25. Cohen, OH; Henry Salvatori to Reagan, June 11, 1987, WHORM, Subject File, box CO 108, RRL.

26. Sole, "'This above all,'" p. 417.

27. CIA, "Angola, Cuba: Some Strains but No New Developments," Apr. 9, 1979, CREST.

28. McHenry to SecState, Jan. 20, 1981, FOIA.

29. Crocker, in "Conversaciones (28-1-88)," pp. 4–5, enclosed in Risquet to Castro, Jan. 29, 1988, ACC; SecState to All African Diplomatic Posts, Nov. 23, 1988 (quoting Crocker), FOIA.

30. Quotations from INR, "Angola: The MPLA Prepares for Independence," Sept. 22, 1975, NSA; Spies, *Operasie*, p. 82. For a detailed account, see Gleijeses, *Conflicting Missions*, pp. 266–72, 300–308.

31. SecState to All African Diplomatic Posts, Dec. 30, 1988, pp. 6–7 (emphasis in the original), FOIA. See also my discussion in chapter 11. In 1988, U.S. scholar William Minter attempted to break the wall of silence in the United States with *Operation Timber*, a collection of Portuguese documents translated into English that detailed Savimbi's cooperation with the colonial authorities. The book was ignored by the *New York Times*, the *Washington Post*, and the other newspapers that had waxed eloquent about Savimbi's nationalist credentials. In fact, Minter noted, "there were definitely no reviews in the major press" (Minter's email to author, June 11, 2010). My own research confirms this.

32. Shultz, *Turmoil*; Crocker, op-ed, *WP*, Oct. 13, 1993, p. 21.

33. Rodman, *Precious*, p. 398; Center for Security Policy, "Democracy in Angola: Executed under a White Flag?" Transition Brief #92-T-143, Washington, D.C., Nov. 18, 1992, p. 2.

34. Cohen, *Intervening*, pp. 123, 121.

35. Bush, Feb. 26, 2002, Weekly compilation of Presidential Documents, v. 38, no. 9, Mar. 4, 2002, p. 300.

36. Hodges, *Angola*, p. 19; interview with Doug Smith; Goulding, *Peacemonger*, p. 193.

37. Mitchell, "Remember the Myth," *News and Observer* (Raleigh), Nov. 1, 1998, p. G5.

38. Gorbachev, *Zhizn'*, 2:421.

39. Vorotnikov, *Gavana—Moskva*, pp. 125–33; Memcon (Castro, Demichev), Jan. 8, 1984, p. 27 quoted, Consejo de Estado.

40. Interview with Mendes de Carvalho; Memcon (Castro, dos Santos), Dec. 17, 1988, p. 2, CF.

41. Interview with Nunda.

42. Crocker, *High Noon*, p. 423.

43. Special NIE, "Soviet Military Support to Angola," Oct. 1985, p. 7, FOIA; Crocker, *High Noon*, p. 52.

44. Shevardnadze et al., "Po voprosu kompensazii postavkami iz Sovetskovo Soiuza Respublike Kuba vooruzhenia, kotore mozhet bit' ostavleno kubinskimi voiskami v Narodnoi Respublike Angola," Jan. 31, 1989, enclosed in Politburo meeting, Feb. 7, 1989, NSA. The dollar figure in 1988 dollars.

45. Adamishin, *Beloe Solntse*, p. 204; Crocker, in "Summary Minutes of a Meeting Held at the U.S. Embassy in Cairo on 24 June 1988 between the South African and U.S. Delegations to the Cairo Talks," p. 4, SWA/Angola, Angola Talks, v. 2, DFA.

46. Interviews with Paulo Jorge (quoted) and Paulo Lara.

47. Akhromeyev, in Akhromeyev and Kornienko, *Glazami*, p. 23; Kornienko, *Kholodnaya voina*, p. 167; interview with Adamishin. Also Brutents, *Tridtsat' let*, pp. 213–16; Dobrynin, *In Confidence*, pp. 360–66, 403–07.

48. V. Shubin, *Hot "Cold War."*

49. Memcon (dos Santos, Risquet), Jan. 30, 1988, enclosed in Risquet to Castro, Jan. 30, 1988, ACC.

50. Aldana, *Granma* (Havana), Oct. 11, 1988, p. 1.

51. *WP*, Feb. 22, 1976, p. 18; NSC, "Response, Presidential Review Memorandum—36: Soviet/Cuban Presence in Africa," Aug. 18, 1978, pt. 1, p. 20, NSA; Pastor to Brzezinsky and Aaron, June 8, 1978, FOIA; Interagency Group—Angola, "Summary of Pertinent Items from CIA Report," Oct. 1979, NLC-6-4-4-15-1, JCL.

52. *Star*, Mar. 6, 1988, p. 12; *Times* (London), Mar. 3, 1988, p. 10.

53. Memcon (van Tonder, Savimbi), Mar. 30, 1988, 1/22/2/3, DFA.

54. See MINFAR, "Nota sobre información del PMIM," Dec. 29, 1983; MINFAR "Mensaje enviado por el Jefe EM-MMCA el 10-2-86" and "Proyecto de mensaje cifrado a la MMCA," n.d., both enclosed in Ulises to Risquet, Feb. 13, 1986; Castro to dos Santos, Aug. 31, 1988; Aldana to Castro, Dec. 22, 1988, #12101 and #12119. All CF. Also *Granma*, Apr. 1, 1989, p. 1.

55. Richard Harwood, *WP*, July 23, 1981, p. 20.

56. Ministerio de la Inversión Extranjera y la Colaboración Económica, "Historia de la Colaboración entre la República de Cuba y la República de Angola," unpublished manuscript, Havana, 2002, p. 3.

57. The total number of foreign students who studied on the Island of Youth was 50,727 (Colina la Rosa et al., "Estudiantes," p. 6). A few thousand more went directly to Cuban universities.

58. Ministerio de la Inversión Extranjera y la Colaboración Económica, "Historia de la Colaboración," p. 27.

59. MINFAR, "Misiones internacionalistas militares cumplidas por Cuba, 1963 a 1991," table I, OS.

60. Mandela, July 26, 1991, *Granma*, July 27, 1991, p. 3.

61. "Presidential Review Memorandum: Rhodesia, Namibia and South Africa," [early 1977], p. 4, FOIA; Secretariat SSC, "'nasionale Staatkundige en Veiligheidstrategie vir SWA en Angola," Sept. 23, 1983, p. 16, SVR.

62. *Star*, Dec. 15, 1988, p. 10 (ed.); *Business Day*, Dec. 14, 1988, p. 4 (ed.); *Sowetan* (Johannesburg), Dec. 15, 1988, p. 6 (ed.).

63. "Vordele vir die RSA as ons die verkiesing wen," enclosed in Geldenhuys, "Instruksies en riglyne vir beplanning en uitvoering," Jan. 23, 1989, H SAW, gr. 4, box 160, DODDC.

64. *WP*, May 11, 1994, p. 25.

65. To be precise, 317 of the 2,425 died in Cuba as a result of their service abroad (229 because of their service in Angola) (MINFAR, "Misiones," table #2).

66. Memcon (Castro, dos Santos), Mar. 19, 1984, ACC.

67. Memcon (Castro, Neto), Jan. 26, 1979, pp. 14, 17, Consejo de Estado.

68. MINFAR, "Misiones," table #1. Reservists serving in Angola numbered 158,852; 18,295 of the 41,730 soldiers in Ethiopia, and 2,582 of the 7,145 who served in other countries were reservists (ibid.).

69. "Reunión con el Comandante en Jefe el 18/6/88," p. 45, CF.

70. Denney (INR) to SecState, "Cuban Foreign Policy," Sept. 15, 1967, p. 4, Pol 1 Cuba, Subject—Numeric Files: 1963–73, RG 59, NA.

71. Ibid., p. 5; Sherman Kent to DCI, Sept. 4, 1963, NSC 145-10001-10126/205, John F. Kennedy Assassination Collection, RG 263, NA.

72. DOS, Policy Planning Council, "Caribbean: Cuba" (draft outline), Feb. 13, 1964, p. 6, NSFCF, box 26/29, LBJL; Hughes to SecState, "Cuba in 1964," Apr. 17, 1964, pp. 10–11, FOIA.

73. "Reunión de análisis de la situación de las tropas cubanas en la RPA, efectuada a partir de las 17:25 horas del 15.11.1987," p. 170, CF.

74. Castro, in "Indicaciones concretas del Comandante en Jefe que guiarán la actuación de la delegación cubana a las conversaciones en Luanda y las negociaciones en Londres (23-4-88)," p. 5, CF.

75. NIE, "The Situation in Cuba," June 14, 1960, p. 9, NSA; Kissinger, *Years*, p. 785; Special NIE, "The Cuban Foreign Policy," June 21, 1979, p. 6, NLC-6-14-1-2-7, JCL.

76. Coltman, *The Real Fidel Castro*, pp. 219, 280.

77. See Memcon (Mondale, Vorster), May 19, 1977, FOIA, and the brilliant analysis of Nancy Mitchell in "Race and the Cold War."

78. Mandela, *WP*, July 28, 1991, p. 32.

# Bibliography

ARCHIVES
*Angola*
Private collections, Luanda

*Canada*
Bibliothèque et Archives Canada/Library and Archives Canada, Ottawa

*Cuba*
Centro de Información de las Fuerzas Armadas Revolucionarias [Center of
    Information of the Armed Forces], Havana
Comité Central del Partido Comunista de Cuba [Central Committee of the
    Communist Party of Cuba], Havana
Consejo de Estado [Council of State], Havana
Ministerio de Relaciones Exteriores [Ministry of Foreign Affairs], Havana
Ministerio para la Inversión Extranjera y la Colaboración Económica [Ministry of
    Foreign Investment and Economic Cooperation], Havana
Oficina Secreta 2do Sec CC PCC [Secret Bureau of the 2nd Secretary of the
    Communist Party of Cuba], Havana,
Private collections, Havana

I have posted a large selection of these documents on a website hosted by the Cold
War International History Project of the Woodrow Wilson International Center for
Scholars at digitalarchive.org.

*France*
Ministère des Affaires Etrangères [Ministry of Foreign Affairs], Paris.

*German Democratic Republic*
Stiftung Archiv der Parteien und Massenorganisationen der DDR im Bundesarchiv
    [Archive of the Political Parties and Mass Organizations of the German Democratic
    Republic in the Federal Archives], Berlin

*Italy*
Fondazione Istituto Gramsci, Archivio del Partito Comunista Italiano
   [Archive of the Italian Communist Party], Rome

*Poland*
Archiwum Akt Nowych [The Central Archives of Modern Records], Warsaw

*South Africa*
Department of Defence, Documentation Centre, Pretoria
Department of Foreign Affairs, Pretoria
National Archives, Pretoria
University of Witwatersrand, William Cullen Library, South African History
   Archive, Johannesburg

*United Kingdom*
Public Record Office, Kew, Surrey

*United States*
Jimmy Carter Library, Atlanta, Georgia
Gerald R. Ford Library, Ann Arbor, Michigan
Lyndon B. Johnson Library, Austin, Texas
John F. Kennedy Library, Boston, Massachusetts
National Archives, College Park, Maryland
National Security Archive, Washington, D.C.
Ronald Reagan Library, Simi Valley, California
Records of the Washington Office on Africa, Divinity School Library,
   Yale University, New Haven, Connecticut
Howard Wolpe Collection, Archives and Regional History Collections,
   Western Michigan University, Kalamazoo, Michigan

*Yugoslavia*
Arhiv Jugoslavije, Arhiv Josipa Broza Tito [Archives of Yugoslavia, Archive of
   Josip Broz Tito], Belgrade

*Zambia*
United National Independence Party archive, Lusaka

NEWSPAPERS
Unless otherwise noted, the newspapers are dailies, and the place of publication is the
capital city.

*Angola*
*Jornal de Angola*: July 1977; July 1978–July 1979; 1987
*A Provincia de Angola*: Oct. 1974–June 1975

*Belgium*
*Le Soir*: 1977–78

*Botswana*
*Botswana Guardian* (weekly): May 1986

*Costa Rica*
*La Nación*: Apr. 1980

*Cuba*
*Colaboración* (from 1984 *Colaboración Internacional*) (quarterly): 1980–89
*Granma*: June 1971; 1975–91.
*Juventud Rebelde*: Dec. 1985; Dec. 1988
*Verde Olivo en Misión Internacionalista* (Luanda): Apr. 1978–July 1979

*Ethiopia*
*Ethiopian Herald*: Dec. 2007

*France*
*Jeune Afrique* (weekly): 1976–79
*Le Monde*: 1975–79; July 1980; 1985–86; Oct.-Dec 1987; Apr. 1989, Sept.–Nov. 1992

*Guinea-Bissau*
*Nõ Pintcha*: (three times a week): Aug. 1975–Dec. 1983

*Israel*
*Jerusalem Post*: Mar. 1987; Sept. 1987; Feb.–Apr. 1988

*Namibia*
*Die Republikein*: Sept.–Dec. 1978
*Namibian* (weekly): 1988–89
*Windhoek Advertiser*: June–Dec. 1975; July–Dec. 1978; Aug.–Dec. 1980; 1983; 1985; 1988–89

*Nicaragua*
*Barricada*: Feb.–May 1985; Oct. 1985

*Portugal*
*Diário de Notícias*: Nov. 1983; May 1985
*Expresso* (weekly): 1975–80; 1984–86
*Jornal Novo*: June–Dec. 1978

*South Africa*
*Argus* (Cape Town): Sept. 1985; Nov. 1987
*Beeld* (Johannesburg): Nov. 1983–Feb. 1984; 1986–88
*Burger* (Cape Town): Sept–Dec. 1978; 1981–89; Oct.–Nov. 1992
*Business Day* (Johannesburg): 1986–88
*Cape Times*: 1981; 1984–85
*Die Kerkbode* (Cape Town, weekly): July 1988
*Pretoria News*: Aug. 1981; Nov. 1983–Sept. 1984; May–Sept. 1985; May 1987–Mar. 1988
*Rand Daily Mail* (Johannesburg): 1975–76; 1978–79; 1981–84; Apr. 1985
*Sowetan* (Johannesburg): Oct. 1987–Dec. 1988

*Star* (Johannesburg): Sept. 1984–Dec. 1988; Sept.–Nov. 1992; May 1994
*Weekly Mail* (Braamfontein, weekly): 1987–88
*World* (Johannesburg): Nov. 1975–Aug. 1976

*United Kingdom*
*Guardian* (Manchester): Aug.–Sept. 1979; Aug. 1986
*Times* (London): 1976–88; Apr. 1989, Sept.–Nov. 1992

*United States*
*Atlanta Constitution*: Aug. 1985–Mar. 1986
*Baltimore Sun*: Aug. 1985–Mar. 1986
*Christian Science Monitor* (Boston): 1975–92
*Cleveland Plain Dealer*: Aug. 1985–Mar. 1986
*Commentary* (New York, monthly): 1976–88
*Conservative Digest* (monthly): 1984–88
*Human Events* (weekly): 1984–88
*Los Angeles Times*: Aug. 1985–Mar. 1986
*Miami Herald*: Oct. 1979–Mar. 1980
*National Review* (New York, fortnightly): 1984–88
*National Security Record* (monthly): 1984–88
*New York Times*: 1975–92
*Policy Review* (quarterly): 1984–88
*Reason* (Los Angeles, monthly): 1984–88
*Wall Street Journal* (New York): 1975–92
*Washington Post*: 1975–92
*Washington Times*: 1985–88

*Zambia*
*Zambia Daily Mail*: May 1986

*Zimbabwe*
*Herald*: Apr. 1980; May–Sept. 1986

INTERVIEWS
I give only the position(s) held by the interviewee that are relevant for this book.

*Angola (All the interviews were in Luanda)*
Correia de Barros, Manuel. Senior FAPLA officer. Nov. 19, 2007
De Almeida, Julio. Deputy Minister of Transports, 1976–83. Nov. 22, 2007
Foguetão (Pedro Benga Lima). Senior FAPLA officer. Nov. 22, 2007
Gato (Ciel da Coinceção Cristovão). Senior FAPLA officer. Jan. 13, 1997
Ita (Mário Plácido Cirilo de Sá). Senior FAPLA officer. Nov. 19, 2007
Jorge, Paulo. Foreign Minister, 1977–83. Nov. 28, 2007
Kianda (Salviano de Jesus Sequeira). Senior FAPLA officer. Nov. 25, 2007
Lara, Lúcio. MPLA leader. Jan. 9, 11, 15, and 29, 1997
Lara, Paulo. Senior FAPLA officer. Nov. 18 and 26, 2007
Ludi Kissassunda (Rodrigues João Lopes). Senior MPLA official. Jan. 21, 1997

Mendes de Carvalho, Andres. Senior FAPLA officer. Nov. 22 and 29, 2007

Miranda, Tozé. Senior FAPLA officer. Nov. 26, 2007

Ndalu (António dos Santos França). Senior FAPLA officer. Chief of Staff of the FAPLA, 1982–91. Nov. 30, 2007

Ngongo (Roberto Ramos Monteiro). Senior FAPLA officer. Deputy Chief of Staff of the FAPLA, 1983–89. Nov. 24, 2007

Nunda (Geraldo Sachipengo). UNITA general and member of UNITA's political bureau. Nov. 23, 2007

Onambwe (Henrique Santos). Senior MPLA official. Jan. 25, 1997

Pahama, Kundi. Senior FAPLA officer. Governor of the province of Benguela, 1981–86. Nov. 30, 2007

Tonta (Afonso Castro). General, Chief of Staff, FNLA, 1975–78; leader of FNLA-COMIRA, 1979–83. Nov. 19, 2007

Xiyetu (João Luis Neto). Senior FAPLA officer. Jan. 18, 1997

*Cuba (Unless otherwise noted, the interviews were in Havana)*

Agramonte Sánchez, Manuel. Ambassador to Angola, 1977–79. June 25, 2004; Dec. 19, 2006

Alarcón de Quesada, Ricardo. Deputy foreign minister. June 6, 2005

Atencio Sariol, Gustavo. Physician. Aid worker in Angola, 1986. Dec. 19, 2006.

Benítez y de Mendoza, Noemí. Deputy minister of the Ministerio para la Inversión Extranjera y la Colaboración Económica, 1986–2002. July 20, 1995

Carballo Torres, Rolando. Professor. Aid worker in Angola, 1977–80. Dec. 14, 2006

Choy López, José Antonio. Architect. Aid worker in Angola, 1977–80. Dec. 20, 2006

Cintra Frías, Leopoldo (Polo). Commander of the Cuban troops in southern Angola (ATS), Nov. 1982–July 1983; head of the Cuban military mission in Angola, July 1983–Sept. 1986; commander of the ATS, Dec. 1987–Jan. 1989. July 15, 2005; July 22, 2010

Dalmau Fernández, Angel. Official at the Cuban embassy in Angola, 1978–80; senior staffer of the Central Committee of the Cuban Communist party working on southern Africa, 1980–90. July 13, 2007

Del Pozo Jerez, Haydée. Military doctor. Angola, 1976–77. May 11, 2005

Domínguez Eorge, Roberto. High school teacher. Aid worker in Angola, 1983–84. Mar. 16, 2007

Domínguez Espinosa, Guillermo. University professor. Aid worker in Angola, 1979–81. Dec. 18, 2006

Dreke Cruz, Víctor. Deputy to Che Guevara in Zaire in 1965; head of the Cuban military mission in Guinea and Guinea-Bissau, 1967–68. July 11, 1994

Escalante Colá, Amels. Military officer. Angola, 1982–85. Dec. 6, 2005

Escartín Fernández, Aleyda. Teacher. Aid worker in Angola, 1976–80. May 20, 2005

Fleitas Ramírez, Gustavo. General. Head of the Cuban military mission in Ethiopia, 1982–84; head of the Cuban military mission in Angola, 1986–87; deputy commander of the Cuban troops in southern Angola, 1987–88. Dec. 22, 2006

Fonseca Dorado, Rosa. Teacher. Aid worker in Angola, 1976–78. Luanda, Nov. 27, 2007

Fortun del Sol, Feliberto. Teacher. Aid worker in Angola, 1976–78. Jan. 22, 2005

Franco Codinach, Lourdes. Physician. Aid worker in Angola, 1987–88. June 1, 6, 8, 2005; Nov. 26, 2005; Dec. 1, 2005; Mar. 22, 2007; July 21, 2010

García Espinosa, Gilberto. University professor. Aid worker in Angola, 1983–84. Dec. 13, 2006

García Mesa, Norberto. Physician. Aid worker in Angola, 1982–84. Dec. 19, 2006

García Peláez, Pedro. General. Head of the Cuban military mission in Angola, 1979–81. Dec. 19, 2006

Gárciga Blanco, José Angel. Military officer. Angola, 1977–79, 1981–83. Dec. 13, 2006; Nov. 23, 2011

Gómez Reina, Goliath. Physician. Aid worker in Angola, 1986–87; Dec. 1, 2005

González Marrero, Manuela. Aid worker in Angola, 1985–89. Mar. 22, 2007

González Polanco, Alberto. Physician. Aid worker in Tindhouf, 1979–80. June 23, 2007

González Tendero, Marina. Primary school teacher. Aid worker in Nicaragua, 1981–83. June 21, 2007

Herrera Toriza, Nancy. Primary school teacher. Aid worker in Nicaragua, 1979–81. July 8, 2007

Jiménez Rodríguez, Limbania (Nancy). Aid worker in Angola, 1976–79. Mar. 19, 2007; July 16, 2010

León Lacher, Julia. Architect. Aid worker in Angola, 1978–79. Dec. 20, 2006

Lussón Battle, Antonio Enrique. Military officer. Angola, 1982–84, 1988–89. Dec. 21, 2006

Machado Ventura, José Ramón. Minister of Public Health, 1960–68. Note to the author, July 12, 1995

Manresa Porto, Emiliano. Economic attaché of the Cuban embassy in Angola, 1976–79. July 10, 2007; Luanda, Nov. 30, 2007

Martín González, Isabel. Nutritionist. Aid worker in Angola, 1976–79. July 15, 2007; Luanda, Nov. 28, 2007

Mateo Trujillo, Salvador. University professor. Aid worker in Angola, 1982–84. Mar. 18, 2007

Moracén Limonta, Rafael. Military officer. Angola, 1975–77. Luanda, Jan. 12 and 30, 1997

Moreno Hernández, Juan. Journalist. Military officer in Angola, 1977–80. Dec. 6, 2006

Padrón González, José Luis. Senior Castro aide, late 1970s to mid 1980s. July 7, 2007

Peraza Cabrera, Luis. Physician. Aid worker in Angola, 1976–78. July 5, 1994

Pérez Herrero, Tony. Ambassador to Ethiopia, 1986–91. May 26, 2005

Puente Ferro, Rodolfo. Ambassador to Angola, 1983–87. June 2, 2005

Rey Jiménez, Gina. Architect. Aid worker in Angola, 1976–78. May 28, 2005

Reyes Carrasco, Roger. Military officer. Angola, 1987–88. Jan. 22, 2004

Risquet Valdés, Jorge. Head of the Cuban civilian mission in Angola, 1975–79; Castro's point man for Africa, 1981–90. Jan. 10, 2004; Mar. 18 and May 25, 2005; Dec. 18, 2006; July 5 and Dec. 4, 2007; July 11, 2010; Nov. 26, 2011; Santo Domingo, D.R, Mar. 22, 2012

Rodiles Plana, Samuel. General. Deputy head of the Cuban military mission in Angola, 1978–80; chief of staff of the military mission, 1987–89; head of the military mission, 1989–91. Dec. 21, 2006

Romero Alfau, Sonia. Teacher. Head of Cuban teachers in Nicaragua, 1982–83; head of Cuban teachers in Angola, 1984–85. Dec. 15, 2006

Rosales del Toro, Ulises. General. Chief of the General Staff and first deputy minister of defense, 1981–96. July 12, 2005

Ross Fonseca, Pedro. Military officer. Angola 1988. Jan. 19, 2006

Ross Leal, Pedro. Senior adviser of the Angolan militia, 1977–78. Luanda, Nov. 25, 2007

Sánchez-Parodi Montoto, Ramón. Head of the Cuban Interests Section, Washington, D.C., 1977–89. July 15, 2007

Serrano Reyes, Carlos Manuel. Electrician. Soldier in Angola, 1981–83. Jan. 14, 2006

Suárez Valdés, Dinorah. Primary school teacher. Aid worker in Nicaragua, 1979–82. July 1, 2007

Torres Peñalver, Serena. Nurse. Aid worker in Angola, 1976–77, 1983–85. May 11 and 16, 2005


*Namibia (Unless otherwise noted, the interviews were in Windhoek)*

Gurirab, Theo-Ben. SWAPO's permanent observer at the United Nations. Nov. 13, 2007

Hamutele, Lazarus. SWAPO commander. Nov. 15, 2007

Ilwenya, Thomas Ilwenya. SWAPO fighter. Nov. 15, 2007

Johannes, Felix. SWAPO fighter. Nov. 12, 2007

Katangolo, Joseph. SWAPO fighter. Nov. 16, 2007

Marcus, Nixon. Cassinga survivor; scholarship student in the German Democratic Republic, 1979–90. Nov. 18, 2007

M'Mwinga, Patrick. SWAPO fighter. Nov. 16, 2007

Moombolah-Goagoses, Esther. Scholarship student in Cuba, 1978–93. Nov. 16, 2007

Mudhika, Asser. Teacher in one of the Namibian schools in Cuba, 1980–86. Nov. 17, 2007

Mupopiwa, Mwetufa. SWAPO fighter. Nov. 13, 2007

Nakandungile, Malakia. SWAPO commander. Nov. 11, 2007

Namoloh, Charles. SWAPO commander. Nov. 15, 2007

Nauyoma, Wilbard. SWAPO fighter. Nov. 18, 2007

Ndeitungo, Sophia. Cassinga survivor; scholarship student in Cuba, 1978–94. Nov. 13, 2007

Nghilalulwa, Vilho. SWAPO fighter. Nov. 14, 2007

Niicodemus, Andreas. Scholarship student in Cuba, 1980–86. Nov. 18, 2007

Nojoba, Karel. Military officer in the South West Africa Territory Force. Nov. 17, 2007

Nujoma, Sam. President of SWAPO. Nov. 15, 2007

Pandeni, John. Labor union leader. Nov. 17, 2007

Robinson, John. Military officer in the South West Africa Territory Force. Nov. 14, 2007

Shalli, Martin. SWAPO commander. Nov. 12, 2007

Shaanika, Gabriel. Scholarship student in Cuba, 1978–89. Nov. 15, 2007

Shikongo, Miriam. Scholarship student in Cuba, 1978–91. Nov. 17, 2007

Shiweda Kalistu, Alfeus. SWAPO fighter. Nov. 14, 2007

Tulesheni Naikako, Erasmus. Scholarship student in Cuba, 1978–82. Nov. 14, 2007

Uushona, Claudia Grace. Cassinga survivor; scholarship student in Cuba, 1978–84. Havana, Jan. 16, 2004; June 20, 2005

Witbooi, Hendrick. Vice-President of SWAPO. Nov. 17, 2007

*South Africa (Unless otherwise noted, the interviews were in Pretoria)*

Badenhorst, Witkop. General. Dec. 12, 2007

Barlow, Eeben. Military officer. Oct. 22 and Dec. 6, 2007

Botha, Pik. South Africa's foreign minister. Dec. 15, 2007

Breytenbach, Jan. Military officer. George, Oct. 27–28, 2007

Geldenhuys, Jannie. General. Chief of the army, 1980–85; chief of the armed forces, 1985–90. Dec. 5 and 8, 2007

Hutchinson, Les. Military officer. Dec. 5, 2007

Mabaso, Bongani Cyril. ANC fighter. Dec. 11, 2007

Ricketts, Patrick (Blahz). ANC fighter. Dec. 4, 2007

Sechaba Setsubi, Cosmas. ANC fighter. Dec. 4, 2007

Thirion, Chris. General. Dec. 6, 2007

Van Heerden, Neil. Deputy Director General of the South African Foreign Ministry, 1985–87; Director General of the South African Foreign Ministry, 1987–92. Tel. interview, Dec. 14, 2007

*United States (Unless otherwise noted, the interviews were in Washington, D.C.)*

Briggs, Everett. Consul general, Luanda, 1972–74. Tel. interview, June 28, 1999

Brzezinski, Zbigniew. National security adviser, 1977–81. Tel. Interview, Sept. 6, 2012

Burt, Richard. Director, State Department's Bureau of Political-Military Affairs, 1981–83. Aug. 7, 2012

Cabelly, Robert. Special assistant of the Assistant Secretary of State for Africa, 1981–89. Aug. 14, 2012

Cohen, Herman. Africa Director, NSC, 1987–89; Assistant Secretary of State for Africa, 1989–93. May 8, 2006

Crocker, Chester. Assistant Secretary of State for Africa, 1981–89. May 18, 2009

Cutler, Walter. Ambassador to Zaire, 1975–79. Mar. 6, 1995

Davidow, Jeff. Director, Office of Southern African Affairs, Department of State, 1984–86. Tel. interview, Aug. 29, 2012

Fenton, Daniel. CIA analyst, southern Africa branch, 1981–93. Aug. 17, 2012

Ferch, John. Head of the U.S. Interests Section in Cuba, 1982–85. Fairfax, Va., Mar. 2, 2007

Freeman, Chas. Principal Deputy Assistant Secretary of State for Africa, 1986–89. June 23, 2009

Grove, Brandon. U.S. ambassador to Zaire, 1984–87. Aug. 14, 2012

Hultslander, Robert. CIA station chief, Luanda, 1975. Fax to the author, Dec. 22, 1998

Kamman, Curtis. Head of the U.S. Interests Section in Cuba, 1985–87. June 4, 2007

Killoran, Tom. Consul general, Luanda, 1974–75. Tel. interviews, Apr. 7 and 10, 1998; Sept. 14, 1998

Lake, Anthony. Director Policy Planning Staff of the State Department, 1977–81. May 9, 2006

McHenry, Donald. U.S. deputy representative to the United Nations, 1977–79; U.S. ambassador to the United Nations, 1979–81. Sept. 15, 2005

Moose, Richard. Assistant Secretary of State for Africa, 1977–81. Alexandria, Va., Oct. 19, 2005

Napper, Larry. Deputy Director, Office of Southern African Affairs, Department of State, 1986–88. Tel. interviews, Aug. 9 and 20, 2012

Newsom, David. Undersecretary of State for Political Affairs, 1978–81. Charleston, Va., May 18, 2007

Nickel, Herman. Ambassador to South Africa, 1982–86. Tel. interviews, July 23 and 27, 2012

Pastor, Robert. Latin America Director, NSC, 1977–81. Nov. 8, 2006

Skoug, Kenneth. Director of the State Department's Office of Cuban Affairs, 1982–88. Alexandria, Va., May 15, 2012

Smith, James Douglas. CIA station chief in Zaire, 1983–86. Tel. interview, Aug. 31, 2012.

Smith, Wayne. Director of the State Department's Office of Cuban Affairs, 1977–79; chief of the U.S. Interests Section in Cuba, 1979–82. Mar. 1, 1995

Spiegel, Marianne. Africa specialist, Policy Planning Staff of the State Department, 1977–81. Sept. 19, 2006

Taylor, John (Jay). Political counselor, U.S. embassy in South Africa, 1977–80; head of the U.S. Interests Section in Cuba, 1987–90. Arlington, Va., Apr. 20, 2006

Van Reigersberg, Stephanie. State Department interpreter. Sept. 13, 2007

Weissman, Stephen. Staff member (1979–86) and then staff director (1987–91) of the House Foreign Affairs Committee's subcommittee on Africa. Apr. 20. 2006.

Wisner, Frank. Principal Deputy Assistant Secretary of State for Africa, 1982–86. Tel. interview, Aug. 13, 2012

Wolpe, Howard. Chair of the House Foreign Affairs Committee's Subcommittee on Africa, 1982–92. May 31, 2007

*Other*

Adamishin, Anatoly (Soviet Union). Deputy foreign minister in charge of Africa south of the Sahara, 1986–90. Washington, D.C., Apr. 2, 2008

Ba, Safayo (Guinea). Scholarship student in Cuba, 1972–79. Conakry, Apr. 22, 1996

Beavogui, Moussa (Guinea). Scholarship student in Cuba, 1973–79. Conakry, Apr. 17, 1996

Diallo, Mamoudou (Guinea). Scholarship student in Cuba, 1973–79. Conakry, Apr. 19, 1996

Dibaba, Berhanu (Ethiopia). Scholarship student in Cuba, 1979–90. Havana, Dec. 15, 2006

Gur Tong, Arkangelo Kuech (Sudan). Scholarship student in Cuba, 1986–99. Havana, June 29, 2005

Hundessa, Lemma (Ethiopia). Scholarship student in Cuba, 1978–88. Tel. interview, Feb. 3, 2007

Mandjam Sambú, Félix (Guinea-Bissau). Scholarship student in Cuba, 1973–85. Bissau, Apr. 26, 1996

Onguemby, Charles (Congo Brazzaville). Scholarship student in Cuba, 1964–77. Havana, Dec. 14, 2000

Ross, Dexter (San Vicente). Scholarship student in Cuba, 1983–88. Havana, Mar. 14, 2007

Sadialiou Sow, Mohamed (Guinea). Scholarship student in Cuba, 1974–81. Conakry, Apr. 22, 1996

Sidiki, Aboubacar (Guinea). Scholarship student in Cuba, 1972–77. Conakry, Apr. 20, 1996

Sylla, Sékou (Guinea). Scholarship student in Cuba, 1974–81. Washington, D.C., July 16, 1996

Waldemariam, Abraham (Ethiopia). Scholarship student in Cuba, 1979–85. Washington, D.C., Apr. 6, 2007

## WORKS CITED

Adamishin, Anatoly. *Beloe Solntse Angoly*. Moscow: Vagrius, 2001.

Adams, Simon. *Comrade Minister: The South African Communist Party and the Transition from Apartheid to Democracy*. Huntington, N.Y.: Nova Science, 2001.

Africa Watch. *Accountability in Namibia: Human Rights and the Transition to Democracy*. New York: Africa Watch, 1992.

Africano, Manuel. *L'UNITA et la 2e guerre civile angolaise*. Paris: L'Harmattan, 1995.

Akhromeyev, Sergei, and Georgi Kornienko. *Glazami marshala i diplomata: kriticheskii vzglyad na vneshniuiu politiku SSSR do i posle 1985 goda*. Moscow: Mezhdunarodnie Otnosheniya, 1992.

Albright, David. "South Africa and the Affordable Bomb." *Bulletin of the Atomic Scientists* 50:4 (July 1994): 37–47.

Albuquerque, Carlos. *Angola. A cultura do medo*. Lisbon: Livros do Brasil, 2002.

Amnesty International. *Political Imprisonment in the People's Republic of Angola*. New York: Amnesty International, Mar. 1984.

———. *People's Republic of Angola: Background Briefing on Amnesty International's Concerns*. New York: Amnesty International, 1983.

———. *Human Rights Violations in Zaire*. London: Amnesty International, 1980.

Andrew, Christopher, and Vasili Mitrokhin. *The World Was Going Our Way: The KGB and the Battle for the Third World*. New York: Basic Books, 2005.

Anglin, Douglas, and Timothy Shaw. *Zambian Foreign Policy: Studies in Diplomacy and Dependence*. Boulder, Colo.: Westview, 1979.

Ansprenger, Franz. *Freie Wahlen in Namibia: Der Übergang zur staatlichen Unabhängigkeit*. Frankfurt am Main: Peter Lang, 1991.

———. *Die SWAPO. Profil einer afrikanischen Befreiungsbewegung*. Mainz: M. Grünewald, 1984.

Anstee, Margaret. *Orphan of the Cold War: The Inside Story of the Collapse of the Angolan Peace Process, 1992–93*. New York: St. Martin's Press, 1996.

Antunes, José Freire. *A guerra de África (1961–1974)*. 2 vols. Lisbon: Temas e Debates, 1996.

Báez, Luis. *Secretos de Generales*. Havana: Editorial SI-MAR, 1996.

Ball, George. *The Past Has Another Pattern: Memoirs*. New York: Norton, 1982.

Barganov, Vladimir. "Mui bili pervimi." In Andrei Tokarev and Gennady Shubin, eds., *Vospominaniia uchastnikov i ochevidsev voiny v Angole 1975–2002 gg.* Moscow: Memories, 2008, pp. 5–20.

Barlow, Eeben. *Executive Outcomes: Against All Odds.* Alberton, South Africa: Galago, 2007.

Barnard, Leo. "Die gebeure by Cassinga, 4 Mei 1978: 'n Gevallestudie van die probleme van 'n militêre historikus." *Historia* (South Africa) 41:1 (1996): 88–99.

Barradas, Acácio, ed. *Agostinho Neto. Uma vida sem tréguas, 1922–1979.* Luanda: Seguros & Pensões, 2005.

Barrell, Howard. "Conscripts to Their Age: African National Congress Operational Strategy, 1976–1986." Ph.D. diss., University of Oxford, 1993.

———. *MK: The ANC's Armed Struggle.* Harmondsworth: Penguin Books, 1990.

Bauer, Gretchen. *Labor and Democracy in Namibia, 1971–1996.* Athens: Ohio University Press, 1998.

Becker, Heike. *Namibian Women's Movement 1980 to 1992: From Anti-Colonial Resistance to Reconstruction.* Frankfurt am Main: IKO-Verlag für Interkulturelle Kommunikation, 1995.

Beliaev, Valeri. "Osnovnoiie napravleniia deiatelnosti sovetskovo voennovo sovetnicheskovo apparata v Narodnoi Respublike Angola v konze 1980-x—nachale 1990-x godov." In L. I. Sannikov and Cristovão Bragança, eds., *40 Let Vmeste/40 Anos juntos 1961–2001.* Moscow, 2002, pp. 61–65.

Benemelis, Juan. *Las guerras secretas de Fidel Castro.* Miami: Fundación Elena Mederos, 2002.

Benga Lima, Pedro (Foguetão). *Percursos Espinhosos (Memórias).* Luanda: Instituto Nacional do Livro y do Disco, 2007.

Benítez y de Mendoza, Noemí. "La colaboración economica y científico-técnica de Cuba a los paises de Africa." Unpublished manuscript, Havana, Mar. 1985.

Berat, Lynn. *Walvis Bay: Decolonization and International Law.* New Haven: Yale University Press, 1990.

Bestard Pavón, Elías. "La colaboración de Cuba con los paises de Africa Subsahariana (1959–1988)." M.A. thesis, Instituto Superior de Relaciones Internacionales, Havana, 1989.

Bishop, James. "Oral History Interview." The Foreign Affairs Oral History Collection of the Association for Diplomatic Studies and Training, Washington, D.C., 1995.

Blight, James, Bruce Allyn, and David Welch, eds. *Cuba on the Brink: Castro, the Missile Crisis and the Soviet Collapse.* New York: Pantheon Books, 1993.

Borstelmann, Thomas. *The Cold War and the Color Line: America's Race Relations in the Global Arena.* Cambridge, Mass.: Harvard University Press, 2001.

Bothma, L. J. *Die Buffel Struikel: 'n Storie van 32 Bataljon en sy mense.* Bloemfontein: Handisa Media, 2006.

Braeckman, Colette. "La saga du Shaba." *La Revue Nouvelle*, Feb. 1979, pp. 141–50.

Brecht, Bertolt. *Der aufhaltsame Aufstieg des Arturo Ui.* Berlin: Suhrkamp, 1965.

Bréhèret, Yves, Édouard Sablier, and Olivier d'Ormesson. *Savimbi. Demain la liberté.* Paris: Nouvelles Éditions Latines, 1988.

Brenke, Gabriele. *Die Bundesrepublik Deutschland und der Namibia-konflikt*. Munich: Oldenbourg Verlag, 1989.

Breytenbach, Jan. *Eagle Strike! The Controversial Airborne Assault on Cassinga, 04 May 1978*. Sandton, South Africa: Manie Grove, 2008.

———. *Buffalo Soldiers: The Story of South Africa's 32 Battalion, 1975–1993*. Alberton, South Africa: Galago, 2002.

———. *Eden's Exiles: One Soldier's Fight for Paradise*. Cape Town: Queillerie, 1997.

———. *They Live by the Sword*. Alberton, South Africa: Lemur, 1990.

———. *Forged in Battle*. Cape Town: Saayaman and Weber, 1986.

Bridgland, Fred. *The War for Africa: Twelve Months That Transformed a Continent*. Gibraltar: Ashanti, 1990.

———. *Jonas Savimbi: A Key to Africa*. New York: Paragon House, 1987.

Brittain, Victoria. *Death of Dignity: Angola's Civil War*. Trenton, N.J.: Africa World Press, 1998.

Brown, Archie. *The Rise and Fall of Communism*. New York: HarperCollins, 2009.

Brutents, Karen. *Tridtsat' let na staroi ploshchadi*. Moscow: Mezhdunarodnie Otnoshenia, 1998.

Brzezinski, Zbigniew. *Power and Principle: Memoirs of the National Security Adviser, 1977–1981*. New York: Farrar, Straus and Giroux, 1983.

Burenko, Anatoly. "Trudnii, no iskliuchitelno vazhnii period zhizn." In Andrei Tokarev and Gennady Shubin, eds., *Vospominaniia uchastnikov i ochevidsev voiny v Angole 1975–2002 gg.* Moscow: Memories, 2008, pp. 21–26.

Burger, Frederik Johannes. "Teeninsurgensie in Namibië: Die Rol von die Polisie." M.A. thesis, Universiteit van Suid-Afrika, 1992.

Buyseniers, Rob. *L'Église Zaïroise au service de quelle nation?* Brussels: Association pour la formation, la recherche et l'information sur le centre de l'Afrique, 1980.

Bwakira, Nicolas, Juan Ortiz-Blasco, and Tor Sellström. "Rapport Conjoint des Réprésentants du Haut Commissaire des Nations Unies pour les refugiés et de l'Organisation Mondiale de la Santé sur leur visite à Cassinga et aux refugiés Namibiens." Luanda, May 30, 1978.

Cabrita, João. *Mozambique: The Tortuous Road to Democracy*. Basingstoke: Palgrave, 2000.

Cabrita Mateus, Dalila. *A PIDE/DGS na guerra colonial (1961–1974)*. Lisbon: Terramar, 2004.

Caetano, Marcello. *Depoimento*. Rio de Janeiro: Distribudora Record, 1974.

Callinicos, Luli. *Oliver Tambo: Beyond the Engeli Mountains*. Cape Town: David Philip, 2004.

Carreira, Iko. *O pensamento estratégico de Agostinho Neto*. Lisbon: Dom Quixote, 1996.

Carter, Jimmy. *White House Diary: Jimmy Carter*. New York: Farrar, Straus and Giroux, 2010.

———. *Keeping Faith: Memoirs of a President*. New York: Bantam Books, 1982.

Cavosky, Jovan. "'Yugoslavia's Help Was Extraordinary': Yugoslavia's Political and Material Assistance and the MPLA's Rise to Power, 1961–1975." *Journal of Cold War Studies*, forthcoming.

Chan, Stephen, and Moises Venancio. *Portuguese Diplomacy in Southern Africa, 1974–1994.* Johannesburg: South African Institute of International Affairs, 1996.

Chang, Laurence, and Peter Kornbluh, eds. *The Cuban Missile Crisis, 1962: A National Security Archive Documents Reader.* New York: New Press, 1992.

Chernyaev, Anatoly. *My Six Years with Gorbachev.* University Park, Pa.: Pennsylvania State University Press, 2000.

———. "The Diary of Anatoly Chernyaev," 1985–89. National Security Archive, Washington, D.C.

Chernyaev, Anatoly, et al., eds. *V Politburo TSK KPSS: Po zapisiam Anatoliia Cherniaeva, Vadima Medvedeva, Georgiia Shakhnazarova (1985–1991).* Moscow: Alpina Biznes Buks, 2006.

Chikane, Frank. "Children in Turmoil: The Effects of the Unrest on Township Children." In Sandra Burman and Pamela Reynolds, eds., *Growing Up in a Divided Society: The Contexts of Childhood in South Africa.* Evanston, Ill.: Northwestern University Press, 1986, pp. 333–44.

Chirkin, Venyamin. "S tainoi missiei v Zheneve i Londone." In Institute of Africa, ed., *Afrika v vospomonaniyah veteranov diplomaticheskoi sluzhby.* Moscow: XXI Vek-Soglasie, 2000, pp. 124–33.

Cliffe, Lionel, with Ray Bush et al. *The Transition to Independence in Namibia.* Boulder, Colo.: Lynne Rienner, 1994.

Cockburn, Andrew, and Leslie Cockburn. *Dangerous Liaison: The Inside Story of the U.S.-Israeli Covert Relationship.* New York: HarperCollins, 1991.

Cohen, Herman. *Intervening in Africa: Superpower Peacemaking in a Troubled Continent.* New York: St. Martin's Press, 2000.

———. "Oral History Interview." The Foreign Affairs Oral History Collection of the Association for Diplomatic Studies and Training, Washington, D.C., 1996.

Cohen, Samy, and Claude Smouts, eds. *La politique extérieure de Valéry Giscard d'Estaing.* Paris: Association Française de Science Politique, 1985.

Colina la Rosa, Juan, et al. "Estudiantes Extranjeros en la Isla de la Juventud." Unpublished manuscript, Havana, 2004.

Coll, Steve. *Ghost Wars: The Secret History of the CIA, Afghanistan and Bin Laden, from the Soviet Invasion to September 10, 2001.* London: Penguin Books, 2004.

Collelo, Thomas, ed. *Angola: A Country Study.* Washington, D.C.: GPO, 1991.

Coltman, Leycester. *The Real Fidel Castro.* New Haven: Yale University Press, 2003.

Commonwealth Group of Eminent Persons. *Mission to South Africa: The Commonwealth Report.* Harmondsworth: Penguin Books, 1986.

Correia, Pedro Pezarat. "Portugal na hora da descolonização." In António Reisp, ed., *Portugal contemporaneo,* vol. 6. Lisbon: Publicações Alfa, 1992, pp. 117–70.

———. *Descolonização de Angola: a jóia da coroa do império portugués.* Lisbon: Inquéerito, 1991.

Costa Gomes, Francisco da. "Costa Gomes conta tudo." *Expresso* (Lisbon), Oct. 8, 1988, supplement, pp. 4–11.

———. *Sobre Portugal: diálogos com Alexandre Manuel.* Lisbon: A Regra do Jogo, 1979.

Crocker, Chester. *High Noon in Southern Africa: Making Peace in a Rough Neighborhood.* New York: Norton, 1992.

———. "South Africa: Strategy for Change." *Foreign Affairs* 59:2 (Winter 1980): 323–51.

Cruzeiro, Maria Manuela. *Costa Gomes, o último marechal: entrevista de Maria Manuela Cruzeiro*. Lisbon: Notícias, 1998.

Culverson, Donald. *Contesting Apartheid: U.S. Activism, 1960–1987*. Boulder, Colo.: Westview, 1999.

Davies, J. E. *Constructive Engagement? Chester Crocker & American Policy in South Africa, Namibia and Angola*. Athens: Ohio University Press, 2007.

Davidson, Basil. *In the Eye of the Storm: Angola's People*. Harmondsworth: Penguin Books, 1974.

Del Pino, Rafael. *General del Pino Speaks: An Insight into Elite Corruption and Military Dissension in Castro's Cuba*. Washington, D.C.: Cuban American National Foundation, 1987.

DeRoche, Andrew. "Standing Firm for Principles: Jimmy Carter and Zimbabwe." *Diplomatic History* 23:4 (Fall 1999): 657–85.

De Villiers, Dirk, and Johanna de Villiers. *PW—A Biography of South Africa's President PW Botha*. Cape Town: Tafelberg, 1984.

Díaz-Briquets, Sergio, and Jorge Pérez López. "Internationalist Civilian Assistance: The Cuban Presence in Sub-Saharan Africa." In Sergio Díaz-Briquets, ed., *Cuban Internationalism in Sub-Saharan Africa*. Pittsburgh: Duquesne University Press, 1989, pp. 48–77.

Dobell, Lauren. *SWAPO's Struggle for Namibia, 1960–1991: War by Other Means*. Basel: Schlettwein, 2000.

Dobrynin, Anatoly. *In Confidence: Moscow's Ambassador to America's Six Cold War Presidents*. Seattle: University of Washington Press, 1995.

D'Oliveira, John. *Vorster—the Man*. Johannesburg: Ernest Stanton, 1977.

Dreyer, Ronald. *Namibia and Southern Africa: Regional Dynamics of Decolonization 1945–90*. London: Kegan Paul International, 1994.

———. "Dispute over Walvis Bay—Origins and Implications for Namibian Independence." *African Affairs*, no. 83 (Oct. 1984): 497–510.

Dumbrell, John. *The Carter Presidency: A Re-evaluation*. Manchester: Manchester University Press, 1993.

Du Pisani, André. *SWA/Namibia: The Politics of Continuity and Change*. Johannesburg: Jonathan Ball, 1985.

———. "Namibia: On Brinkmanship, Conflict and Self-interest—The Collapse of the UN-Plan." *Politikon* 8:1 (June 1981): 1–16.

Du Preez, Sophia. *Avontuur in Angola. Die verhaal van Suid-Afrika se soldate in Angola 1975–1976*. Pretoria: J. L. van Schaik, 1989.

Ellert, Henrik. *The Rhodesian Front War: Counterinsurgency and Guerrilla Warfare, 1962–1980*. Gweru, Zimbabwe: Mambo Press, 1993.

Ellis, Stephen, and Tsepo Sechaba. *Comrades against Apartheid: The ANC and the South African Communist Party in Exile*. Bloomington: Indiana University Press, 1992.

Engel, Ulf. *Die Afrikapolitik der Bundesrepublik Deutschland 1949–1999: Rollen und Identitäten*. Hamburg: LIT Verlag, 2000.

Engstrom, David. *Presidential Decision Making Adrift: The Carter Administration and the Mariel Boatlift*. Lanham, Md.: Rowman and Littlefield, 1997.

———. "The Carter Administration's Response to the Mariel Boatlift." Ph.D. diss., University of Chicago, 1992.

Eriksen, Tore Linné, ed. *Norway and National Liberation in Southern Africa.* Uppsala: Nordiska Afrikainstitutet, 2000.

Ferch, John. "Oral History Interview." The Foreign Affairs Oral History Collection of the Association for Diplomatic Studies and Training, Washington, D.C., 1991.

Fischer, Benjamin. "A Cold War Conundrum: The 1983 Soviet War Scare." CIA, Center for the Study of Intelligence, 1997, http://www.cia.gov/csi/monograph/coldwar/source/htm.

Flower, Ken. *Serving Secretly: An Intelligence Chief on Record; Rhodesia into Zimbabwe, 1964 to 1981.* London: John Murray, 1987.

Fourie, Brand. *Brandpunte: Agter die skerms met Suid-Afrika se bekendste diplomaat.* Cape Town: Tafelberg, 1991.

Freeman, Chas. "Oral History Interview." The Foreign Affairs Oral History Collection of the Association for Diplomatic Studies and Training, Washington, D.C., 1995.

———. "The Angola/Namibia Accords." *Foreign Affairs* 68:3 (Summer 1989): 126–41.

Freeman, Linda. *The Ambiguous Champion: Canada and South Africa in the Trudeau and Mulroney Years.* Toronto: University of Toronto Press, 1997.

Funk, Jerry. *Life Is an Excellent Adventure: An Irreverent Personal Odyssey.* Victoria, B.C.: Trafford, 2003.

Gaddis, John Lewis. *The Cold War: A New History.* New York: Penguin Press, 2005.

Gárciga Blanco, José Angel. "Los primeros de Olivo. Mayo de 1981 a julio de 1983." Unpublished manuscript, Havana.

Garthoff, Raymond. *The Great Transition: American-Soviet Relations and the End of the Cold War.* Washington, D.C.: Brookings, 1994.

———. *Détente and Confrontation: American-Soviet Relations from Nixon to Reagan.* Rev. ed. Washington, D.C.: Brookings, 1994.

Gates, Robert. *From the Shadows: The Ultimate Insider's Story of Five Presidents and How They Won the Cold War.* New York: Simon and Schuster, 1996.

Geffray, Christian. *La cause des armes au Mozambique: Anthropologie d'une guerre civile.* Paris: Karthala, 1990.

Geldenhuys, Deon. *The Diplomacy of Isolation: South African Foreign Policy Making.* New York: St. Martin's Press, 1984.

Geldenhuys, Jannie. *Dié Wat Gewen Het: Feite en fabels van die bosoorlog.* Pretoria: Litera, 2007.

Genscher, Hans-Dietrich. *Erinnerungen.* Berlin: Wolf Jobst Siedler Verlag, 1995.

George, Edward. *The Cuban Intervention in Angola, 1965–1991: From Che Guevara to Cuito Cuanavale.* London: Frank Cass, 2005.

Gevisser, Mark. *Thabo Mbeki: The Dream Deferred.* Johannesburg: Jonathan Ball, 2007.

Gillespie, Charles. "Oral History Interview." The Foreign Affairs Oral History Collection of the Association for Diplomatic Studies and Training, Washington, D.C., 1995.

Glassman, Jon David. "Oral History Interview." The Foreign Affairs Oral History Collection of the Association for Diplomatic Studies and Training, Washington, D.C., 1997.

Gleijeses, Piero. "A Test of Wills: Jimmy Carter, South Africa, and the Independence of Namibia." *Diplomatic History* 34:5 (Nov. 2010): 853–91.

——. "Scandinavia and the Liberation of Southern Africa." *International History Review* 27:2 (June 2005): 324–31.

——. *Conflicting Missions: Havana, Washington, and Africa, 1959–1976.* Chapel Hill: University of North Carolina Press, 2002.

——. "Truth or Credibility: Castro, Carter, and the Invasions of Shaba." *International History Review* 18:1 (Feb. 1996): 70–103.

——. "The Reagan Doctrine and Central America." *Current History*, Dec. 1986, pp. 401–4, 435–37.

Gómez Chacón, César. *Cuito Cuanavale: Viaje al centro de los héroes.* Rev. ed. Havana: Verde Olivo, 2009.

González Montero, Orlando. *Sumbe: las alturas de las antenas.* Bayamo, Cuba: Ediciones Bayamo, 2006.

González Sarría, Eduardo. *Angola: Relato desde las alturas.* Havana: Editorial de Ciencias Sociales, 2003.

Gorbachev, Mikhail. *Zhizn' i reformy.* 2 vols. Moscow: Novosti, 1995.

Goulding, Marrack. *Peacemonger.* Baltimore: Johns Hopkins University Press, 2002.

Grachev, Andrei. *Gorbachev.* Moscow: Vagrius, 2001.

Greeff, Jack. *A Greater Share of Honour.* Ellisras, South Africa: Ntomeni Publications, 2001.

Gribkov, Anatoly, et al. *U kraya yadernoi bezdny.* Moscow: Gregori-Peidzh, 1998.

Grove, Brandon. *Behind Embassy Walls: The Life and Times of an American Diplomat.* Columbia: University of Missouri Press, 2005.

Grundy, Kenneth. *The Militarization of South African Politics.* Bloomington: Indiana University Press, 1986.

Guerra, João Paulo. *Savimbi, Vida e Morte.* Lisbon: Bertrand Editora, 2002.

——. *Memória das Guerras Coloniais.* Oporto, Portugal: Afrontamento, 1994.

Gukov, Danial. "V Voiushei Brigade." In Andrei Tokarev and Gennady Shubin, eds., *Vospominaniia neposredstvennykh uchastnikov i ochevidtsev grazhdanskoi voiny v Angole. Ustnaia istoriia zabytykh voin.* Moscow: Memories, 2009, pp. 105–86.

Gusev, Petr. *Ishchi svoiu sud'by: vospominania nachal'nika shtaba PrikVO (1951–2001).* Ishevsk: Udmurtia, 2004.

Hagemann, Albrecht. *Südafrika und das "Dritte Reich": Rassenpolitische Affinität und machtpolitische Rivalität.* Frankfurt am Main: Campus Verlag, 1989.

Haig, Alexander. *Caveat: Realism, Reagan, and Foreign Policy.* New York: Macmillan, 1984.

Hall, Margaret, and Tom Young. *Confronting Leviathan: Mozambique since Independence.* London: Hurst, 1997.

Hamann, Hilton. *Days of the Generals: The Untold Story of South Africa's Apartheid-era Military Generals.* Cape Town: Zebra Press, 2001.

Hanlon, Joseph. *Mozambique: Who Calls the Shots?* Bloomington: Indiana University Press, 1991.

Hare, Paul. *Angola's Last Best Chance for Peace: An Insider's Account of the Peace Process.* Washington, D.C.: United States Institute of Peace, 1998.

Harlech-Jones, Brian. *A New Thing? The Namibian Independence Process, 1989–1990*. Windhoek: EIN Publications, 1997.

Hatzky, Christine. "'Os Bons Colonizadores': Cuba's Educational Mission in Angola, 1976–1991." *Safundi* 9:1 (Jan. 2008): 53–68.

Heitman, Helmoed-Römer. *War in Angola: The Final South African Phase*. Gibraltar: Ashanti, 1990.

———. *South African Armed Forces*. Cape Town: Buffalo Publications, 1990.

Heitman, Helmoed-Römer, and W. A. Dorning. "The Joint Monitoring Commission." *Militaria* (Pretoria) 18:1 (Aug. 1988): 1–25.

Hernández-Catá, Ernesto. "The Fall and Recovery of the Cuban Economy in the 1990s: Mirage or Reality?" In Association for the Study of the Cuban Economy, ed., *Cuba in Transition*, vol. 10. Miami, 2000, pp. 24–38.

Heunis, Jan. *The Inner Circle: Reflections on the Last Days of White Rule*. Johannesburg: Jonathan Ball, 2007.

Heyden, Ulrich van der, Ilona Schleicher, and Hans-Georg Schleicher, eds. *Engagiert für Afrika: Die DDR und Afrika II*. Münster: Lit Verlag, 1994.

Heywood, Annemarie. *The Cassinga Event*. Windhoek: National Archives of Namibia, 1994.

Hodges, Tony. *Angola: Anatomy of an Oil State*. Bloomington: Indiana University Press, 2004.

Hooper, Jim. *Koevoet. Die mens en die oorlog*. Pretoria: Unibook, 1989.

Howard, Lise. *UN Peacekeeping in Civil Wars*. Cambridge: Cambridge University Press, 2008.

Human Rights Watch. *Angola Unravels: The Rise and Fall of the Lusaka Peace Process*. New York: Human Rights Watch, 1999.

Husemann, Bettina, and Annette Neumann. "DDR-VR Angola: Fakten zur bildungspolitischen Zusammenarbeit von 1975 bis 1989." In Ulrich van der Heyden, Ilona Schleicher, and Hans-Georg Schleicher, eds., *Engagiert für Afrika: Die DDR und Africa II*. Münster: LIT Verlag, 1994, pp. 158–78.

Institut für Zeitgeschichte, ed. (on behalf of the German foreign ministry). *Akten zur Auswärtigen Politik der Bundesrepublik Deutschland, 1977–80*. Munich: R. Oldenbourg Verlag, 2008–11.

International Institute for Strategic Studies. *Strategic Survey, 1992–93*. London: Routledge, 1993.

Jackson, Donna. *Jimmy Carter and the Horn of Africa: Cold War Policy in Ethiopia and Somalia*. Jefferson, N.C.: McFarland, 2007.

Jackson, Steven. "China's Third World Foreign Policy: The Case of Angola and Mozambique, 1961–93." *China Quarterly*, no. 142 (1995): 388–422.

James, Martin. *A Political History of the Civil War in Angola 1974–1990*. New Brunswick, N.J.: Transaction Publishers, 1992.

Jiménez Gómez, Rubén. *Al sur de Angola. Memorias de un soldado que no combatió*. Havana: Verde Olivo, 2002.

Jiménez Rodríguez, Limbania. *De las mujeres y sus memorias*. Havana: Verde Olivo, 2011.

———. *Mujeres sin Fronteras*. Havana: Editora Política, 2008.

Júnior, Miguel. *Forças Armadas Populares de Libertação de Angola: 1o Exército Nacional (1975–1992)*. Lisbon: Prefacio, 2007.

Kalflèche, Jean-Marc. *Jonas Savimbi: Une autre voie pour l'Afrique*. Paris: Éditions Criterion, 1992.

Kapto, Alexandr. *Na perekrestkakh zhizni: politicheskie memuary*. Moscow: Sozialno-politicheski zhurnal, 1996.

Karis, Thomas, and Gail Gerhart. *From Protest to Challenge*. Vol. 5: *Nadir and Resurgence, 1964–1979*. Bloomington: Indiana University Press, 1997.

Karns, Margaret. "Ad Hoc Multilateral Diplomacy: The United States, the Contact Group, and Namibia." *International Organization* 41:1 (Winter 1987): 93–123.

Kasrils, Ronnie. *"Armed and Dangerous": My Undercover Struggle against Apartheid*. Oxford: Heinemann, 1993.

Kenna, Constance, ed. *Die "DDR-Kinder" von Namibia—Heimkehrer in ein fremdes Land*. Göttingen: Klaus Hess Verlag, 1999.

Kissinger, Henry. *Years of Renewal*. New York: Simon and Schuster, 1999.

Kolomnin, Sergey. *Russkii Spetznaz v Afrike*. Moscow: Eksmo, 2005.

Kornienko, Georgi. *Kholodnaya voina: svidetel'stvo ee uchastnika*. Moscow: Mezhdunarodnie Otnoshenia, 1994.

Kurochkin, Konstantin. "Osnovnoiie napravleniia deiatelnosti sovetskovo voennovo sovetnicheskovo apparata v Narodnoi Respublike Angola v nachale 1980-x godov." In L. I. Sannikov and Cristovão Bragança, eds., *40 Let Vmiestie/40 Anos juntos 1961–2001*. Moscow: n.p., 2002, pp. 19–21.

Kuznetsova-Timonova, Alexandra, et al., eds. *Vospominaniia veteranov voiny v Angole i drugikh lokal'nykh konfliktov*. Moscow: Memories, Izdatel I. B. Belyi, 2011.

Labuschagne, Riaan. *On South Africa's Secret Service: An Undercover Agent's Story*. Alberton, South Africa: Galago, 2002.

Leffler, Melwyn. *For the Soul of Mankind: The United States, the Soviet Union, and the Cold War*. New York: Hill and Wang, 2007.

Lefort, René. *Éthiopie: la révolution hérétique*. Paris: Maspero, 1981.

Leistner, Erich, and Pieter Esterhuysen, eds. *Namibia 1990: An Africa Institute Country Survey*. Pretoria: Africa Institute of South Africa, 1991.

Leogrande, William. *Our Own Backyard: The United States in Central America, 1977–1992*. Chapel Hill: University of North Carolina Press, 1998.

Levine, Robert. *Secret Missions to Cuba: Fidel Castro, Bernardo Benes, and Cuban Miami*. New York: Palgrave Macmillan, 2001.

Leys, Colin, and Susan Brown, eds. *Histories of Namibia: Living Through the Liberation Struggle*. London: Merlin Press, 2005.

Leys, Colin, and John Saul, eds. *Namibia's Liberation Struggle: The Two-Edged Sword*. Athens: Ohio University Press, 1995.

Lodge, Tom. *Mandela: A Critical Life*. New York: Oxford University Press, 2006.

Loiseau, Yves, and Pierre-Guillaume de Roux. *Portrait d'un révolutionnaire en général: Jonas Savimbi*. Paris: La Table Ronde, 1987.

Lord, Dick. *From Fledgling to Eagle: The South African Air Force during the Border War*. Johannesburg: South Publishers, 2008.

Lord, R. S. "Operation Askari (a Sub-commander's Retrospective View of the Operation)." *Militaria* 22:4 (1992): 1–12.

Lorenzini, Sara. *Due Germanie in Africa: La cooperazione allo sviluppo e la competizione per i mercati di materie prime e tecnologia*. Florence: Edizione Polistampa, 2003.

Mabeko Tali, Jean-Michel. *Dissidências e Poder de Estado: O MPLA perante si próprio (1962–1977)*. 2 vols. Luanda: Nzila, 2001.

McFarlane, Robert, with Zofia Smardz. *Special Trust*. New York: Cadell and Davies, 1994.

McGill Alexander, Edward. "The Cassinga Raid." M.A. thesis, University of South Africa, 2003.

McHenry, Donald. "Oral History Interview." The Foreign Affairs Oral History Collection of the Association for Diplomatic Studies and Training, Washington, D.C., 1993.

McManus, Jane. *Cuba's Island of Dreams: Voices from the Isle of Pines and Youth*. Gainesville: University Press of Florida, 2000.

McWilliams, Mike. *Battle for Cassinga: South Africa's Controversial Cross-Border Raid, Angola 1978*. Solihull (UK): Helion, 2011.

Maier, Karl. *Angola: Promises and Lies*. Rivonia: William Waterman Publications, 1996.

Malan, Magnus. *My lewe saam met die SA Weermag*. Pretoria: Protea, 2006.

Mann, James. *About Face: A History of America's Curious Relationship with China, from Nixon to Clinton*. New York: Knopf, 1998.

Marcum, John. *The Angolan Revolution*. 2 vols. Cambridge, Mass.: MIT Press, 1969 and 1978.

Martí, José. *Epistolario*. Vol. 5. Havana: Centro de Estudios Martianos, 1993.

Martin, David, and Phyllis Johnson. *The Struggle for Zimbabwe: The Chimurenga War*. London: Faber and Faber, 1981.

Martín Blandino, Jorge. *Cangamba*. Havana: Verde Olivo, 2006.

Maseko, Sipho. "The Namibian Student Movement: Its Role and Effects." In Colin Leys and John Saul, eds., *Namibia's Liberation Struggle: The Two-Edged Sword*. Athens: Ohio University Press, 1995, pp. 115–32.

Massie, Robert. *Loosing the Bonds: The United States and South Africa in the Apartheid Years*. New York: Doubleday, 1997.

Matlock, Jack. *Reagan and Gorbachev: How the Cold War Ended*. New York: Random House, 2004.

———. *Autopsy of an Empire: The American Ambassador's Account of the Collapse of the Soviet Union*. New York: Random House, 1995.

Medvedev, Vadim. *Raspad: Kak on nazreval v "Mirovoi Sisteme Sotsialisma."* Moscow: Mezhdunarodnie Otnoshenia, 1994.

Melo, João de, ed. *Os Anos da Guerra 1961–75: Os Portugueses em Africa*. 2 vols. Lisbon: Dom Quixote, 1988.

Menéndez Tomassevich, Raúl, and José Angel Gárciga Blanco. *Patria Africana*. Havana: Editorial de Ciencias Sociales, 2006.

Messiant, Christine. "Angola: entre guerre et paix." In Roland Marchal and Christine Messiant, *Les chemins de la guerre et de la paix*. Paris: Karthala, 1997, pp. 157–208.

———. "Angola, les voies de l'ethnisation et de la décomposition." Part 1, *Lusotopie*, nos. 1–2 (1994): 155–210, and Part 2, *Lusotopie* (1995): 181–212.

Metz, Steven. "The Anti-Apartheid Movement and the Formulation of American Policy toward South Africa, 1969–1981." Ph.D. diss., Johns Hopkins University, 1985.

Minter, William, ed. *Operation Timber: Pages from the Savimbi Dossier*. Trenton, N.J.: Africa World Press, 1988.

Mitchell, Nancy. "Race and the Cold War: Jimmy Carter in Africa." Forthcoming.

———. "The Cold War and Jimmy Carter." In Melvyn Leffler and Odd Arne Westad, eds., *Cambridge History of the Cold War*. Cambridge: Cambridge University Press, 2010, 3:66–88.

———. "Terrorists or Freedom Fighters? Jimmy Carter and Rhodesia." In Sue Onslow, ed., *Cold War in Southern Africa: White Power, Black Liberation*. London: Routledge, 2009, pp. 177–200.

Moorcraft, Paul. *African Nemesis: War and Revolution in Southern Africa (1945–2010)*. London: Brassey's, 1990.

Morgenstierne, Christopher. *Denmark and National Liberation in Southern Africa*, Uppsala: Nordiska Afrikainstitutet, 2003.

National Democratic Institute for International Affairs. *Nation Building: The UN and Namibia*. Washington, D.C.: National Democratic Institute for International Affairs, 1990.

Negin, Oleg [pseudonym, real name Oleg Nazhestkin]. "V ognennom kolze blokadi." In V. Karpov, ed., *Vneshyaya Razvedka*. Moscow: XXI Vek-soglasie, 2000, pp. 234–56.

Nesbitt, Francis. *Race for Sanctions: African Americans against Apartheid, 1946–1994*. Bloomington: Indiana University Press, 2004.

Newitt, Malyn. *A History of Mozambique*. London: Hurst, 1995.

Newsom, David. "Oral History Interview." The Foreign Affairs Oral History Collection of the Association for Diplomatic Studies and Training, Washington, D.C., 1991.

———. *The Soviet Brigade in Cuba: A Study in Political Diplomacy*. Bloomington: Indiana University Press, 1987.

Nickel, Herman. "Oral History Interview." The Foreign Affairs Oral History Collection of the Association for Diplomatic Studies and Training, Washington, D.C., 1989.

Nkomo, Joshua. *Nkomo: The Story of My Life*. London: Methuen, 1984.

Nogueira Pinto, Jaime. *Jogos Africanos*. Lisbon: Esfera dos Livros, 2008.

Nortje, Piet. *32 Battalion: The Inside Story of South Africa's Elite Fighting Unit*. Cape Town: Zebra, 2003.

Nujoma, Sam. *Where Others Wavered: The Autobiography of Sam Nujoma*. London: Panaf Books, 2001.

Oberdorfer, Don. *The Turn: How the Cold War Came to an End; The United States and the Soviet Union, 1983–1990*. London: Jonathan Cape, 1991.

O'Lynn, Bryan. *Namibia: The Sacred Trust of Civilization*. Windhoek: Gamsberg Macmillan, [2003].

O'Malley, Padraig. *Shades of Difference: Mac Maharaj and the Struggle for South Africa*. New York: Viking, 2007.

Oppenheimer, Andres. *Castro's Final Hour: An Eyewitness Account of the Disintegration of Castro's Cuba*. New York: Simon and Schuster, 1992.

Ottaway, Marina, and David Ottaway. *Ethiopia: Empire in Revolution*. New York: Africana, 1978.

Owen, David. *Time to Declare*. Rev. ed. Harmondsworth: Penguin Books, 1992.

Pachter, Elise Forbes. "Our Man in Kinshasa: U.S. Relations with Mobutu." Ph.D. diss., Johns Hopkins University, 1987.

Pakleppa, Richard. "40,000 Workers Stayaway in Namibia." *South African Labour Bulletin* 13:6 (Sept. 1988): 15–23.

Palla, Maria Antónia, and João Soares. *Savimbi: um sonho africano*. Lisbon: Edições Nova Atica, 2003.

Papenfus, Theresa. *Pik Botha and His Times*. Pretoria: Litera, 2010.

Pastor, Robert. "The Carter-Castro Years: A Unique Opportunity." In Soraya Castro and Ronald Pruessen, eds., *Fifty Years of Revolution: Perspectives on Cuba, the United States, and the World*. Gainesville: University Press of Florida, 2012, pp. 237–60.

Pavlov, Iuri. *Soviet-Cuban Alliance: 1959–1991*. New Brunswick, N.J.: Transaction Publishers, 1994.

Peltola, Pekka. *The Lost May Day: Namibian Workers Struggle for Independence*. Helsinki: Finnish Anthropological Society, 1995. Pereira, Moutinho. "Um homem nos alicerces do mundo." In Acácio Barradas, ed., *Agostinho Neto: Uma vida sem tréguas, 1922–1979*. Luanda: Seguros & Pensões, 2005, pp. 91–113.

Pérez de Cuéllar, Jávier. *Pilgrimage for Peace: A Secretary-General's Memoir*. New York: St. Martin's Press, 1997.

Perkins, Edward, with Connie Cronley. *Mr. Ambassador: Warrior for Peace*. Norman: University of Oklahoma Press, 2006.

Persico, Joseph. *Casey: The Lives and Secrets of William J. Casey: From the OSS to the CIA*. New York: Viking, 1990.

Petterson, Don. "Oral History Interview." The Foreign Affairs Oral History Collection of the Association for Diplomatic Studies and Training, Washington, D.C., 1996.

Polakow-Suransky, Sasha. *The Unspoken Alliance: Israel's Secret Relationship with Apartheid South Africa*. New York: Pantheon Books, 2010.

Potgieter, Thean. "The Secret South African Project Team: Building Strike Craft in Israel, 1975–79." *Scientia Militaria* 32:2 (2004): 119–45.

Pottinger, Brian. *The Imperial Presidency: P. W. Botha the First 10 Years*. Johannesburg: Southern Book Publishers, 1988.

Prados, John. *Safe for Democracy: The Secret Wars of the CIA*. Chicago: Ivan R. Dee, 2006.

Preston, Julia. "The Trial that Shook Cuba." *New York Review of Books*, Dec. 7, 1989, pp. 24–31.

Prinsloo, Daan. *Stem uit die Wilderness: 'n Biografie oor oud-pres. PW Botha*. Mosselbaai, South Africa: Vaandel, 1997.

Quandt, William. *Peace Process: American Diplomacy and the Arab-Israeli Conflict since 1967*. Washington, D.C.: Brookings, 1993.

———. *Camp David: Peace Making and Politics*. Washington, D.C.: Brookings, 1986.

Raffy, Serge. *Castro, l'infidèle*. Paris: Fayard, 2003.

Ramírez Cañedo, Elier, and Esteban Morales Domínguez. *De la confrontación a los intentos de "normalización": La política de los Estados Unidos hacia Cuba*. Havana: Editorial de Ciencias Sociales, 2011.

Ramonet, Ignacio. *Cien Horas con Fidel: Conversaciones con Ignacio Ramonet*. Rev. ed. Havana: Ediciones del Consejo de Estado, 2006.

Ramos Montero, Roberto (Ngongo). "Angola na via pela paz y reconciliação." In L. I. Sannikov and Cristovão Bragança, eds., *40 Let Vmiestie/40 anos juntos 1961–2001*. Moscow: n.p., 2002, pp. 141–44.

Reagan, Ronald. *The Reagan Diaries Unabridged*. Edited by Douglas Brinkley. 2 vols. New York: HarperCollins, 2009.

Reiss, Mitchell. *Bridled Ambition: Why Countries Constrain Their Nuclear Capabilities*. Washington, D.C.: Woodrow Wilson Center Press, 1995.

Renwick, Robin. *Unconventional Diplomacy in Southern Africa*. New York: St Martin's Press, 1997.

Republic of Cuba. *Vindicación de Cuba*. Havana: Editora Política, 1989.

Republic of Russia, Ministry of Defense. *Rossiia (SSSR) v lokalnykh voinakh i voennykh konfliktakh vtoroi poloviny XX veka*. Moscow: Kuchkovo Pole and oligrafresursy, 2000.

Republic of South Africa. *Hansard—Debates of Parliament* and *Hansard—Debates of the House of Assembly*, 1976–1988. Pretoria

Reynolds, David. *Summits: Six Meetings That Shaped the Twentieth Century*. New York: Basic Books, 2007.

Ricardo Luis, Roger. *Prepárense a vivir: crónicas de Cuito Cuanavale*. Havana: Editora Política, 1989.

Robinson, Randall. *Defending the Spirit: A Black Life in America*. New York: Dutton, 1998.

Rodman, Peter. *More Precious than Peace: The Cold War and the Struggle for the Third World*. New York: Charles Scribner's Sons, 1994.

Rojas, Marta. *El aula verde*. Havana: Unión de Escritores y Artistas de Cuba, 1982.

Ros, Enrique. *La Aventura africana de Fidel Castro*. Miami: Ediciones Universal, 1999.

Sakala, Alcides. *Memórias de um guerrilheiro: os ultimos anos de guerra em Angola*. Lisbon: Dom Quixote, 2005.

Saul, John, and Colin Leys. "Lubango and After: 'Forgotten History' as Politics in Contemporary Namibia." *Journal of Southern African Studies* 29:2 (June 2003): 333–53.

Saunders, Chris. "The Ending of the Cold War and Southern Africa." In Artemy Kalinovsky and Sergey Radchenko, eds., *The End of the Cold War and the Third World: New Perspectives on Regional Conflicts*. London: Routledge, 2011, pp. 264–76.

Schleicher, Hans-Georg. "Befreiungskampf Zimbabwe: Höhen und Tiefen der DDR-Afrikapolitik." In Ulrich van der Heyden, Ilona Schleicher, and Hans-Georg Schleicher, eds., *Engagiert für Afrika: Die DDR und Afrika II*. Münster: Lit Verlag, 1994, pp. 49–72.

———. "Juniorpartner der Sowjetunion: Die DDR im südlichen Afrika." In Michael Behrens and Robert von Rimscha, eds., *Südafrika nach der Apartheid*. Baden-Baden: Nomos, 1994, pp. 59–74.

Schleicher, Ilona, and Hans-Georg Schleicher. *Die DDR im Südlichen Afrika: Solidarität und Kalter Krieg*. Hamburg: Institut für Afrika-Kunde, 1998.

Schlesinger, Arthur. *Robert Kennedy and His Times*. New York: Ballantine, 1979.

Scholtz, Leopold. "The Namibian Border War: An Appraisal of the South African Strategy." *Scientia Militaria* 34:1 (2006): 19–48.

Schoultz, Lars. *That Infernal Little Cuban Republic: The United States and the Cuban Revolution.* Chapel Hill: University of North Carolina Press, 2009.

Scott, James. *Deciding to Intervene: The Reagan Doctrine and American Foreign Policy.* Durham, N.C.: Duke University Press, 1996.

Seegers, Annette. *The Military in the Making of Modern South Africa.* London: Tauris, 1996.

Sellström, Tor. *Sweden and National Liberation in Southern Africa.* 2 vols. Uppsala: Nordiska Afrikainstitutet, 1999 and 2002.

Shakhnazarov, Georgi. *Tsena Svobody: reformatsiia Gorbacheva glazami ego pomoshchnika.* Moscow: Rossika Zevs, 1993.

Shiriaev, Biacheslav. "Tovarish Ivan." In Andrei Tokarev and Gennady Shubin, eds., *Vospominaniia uchastnikov i ochevidsev voiny v Angole 1975–2002 gg.* Moscow: Memories, 2008, pp. 27–33.

Shubin, Gennady, ed. *Kuito-Kuanavale. Neizvestnaia voina: memuary veteranov voini v Angole.* Moscow: Memories, 2008.

———, ed. *The Oral History of Forgotten War: The Memoirs of Veterans on the War in Angola.* Moscow: Memories, 2007.

Shubin, Vladimir. *The Hot "Cold War": The USSR in Southern Africa.* London: Pluto Press, 2008.

———. *ANC: A View from Moscow.* Bellville, South Africa: Mayibuye Books, 1999.

Shubin, Vladimir, and Andrei Tokarev. "War in Angola: A Soviet Dimension." *Review of African Political Economy,* no. 90 (Dec. 2001): 607–18.

Shultz, George. *Turmoil and Triumph: My Years as Secretary of State.* New York: Charles Scribner's Sons, 1993.

Sibanda, Eliakim. *The Zimbabwe African People's Union, 1961–1987: A Political History of Insurgency in Southern Rhodesia.* Trenton, N.J.: Africa World Press, 2005.

Siebs, Benno-Eide. *Die Aussenpolitik der DDR 1976–1989: Strategien und Grenzen.* Padeborn: Ferdinand Schöningh, 1999.

Silva Cunha, Joaquim Moreira da. *O Ultramar, a nação e o "25 de Abril."* Coimbra: Atlantida, 1977.

Simon, David. "Decolonisation and Local Government in Namibia: The Neo-Apartheid Plan, 1977–83." *Journal of Modern African Studies* 23:3 (1985): 507–26.

Simpson, William. *The Prince: The Secret Story of the World's Most Intriguing Royal, Prince Bandar bin Sultan.* New York: HarperCollins, 2006.

Skinner, Kiron, Annelise Anderson, and Martin Anderson, eds. *Reagan, in His Own Hand.* New York: Free Press, 2001.

Skoug, Kenneth. "Oral History Interview." The Foreign Affairs Oral History Collection of the Association for Diplomatic Studies and Training, Washington, D.C., 2000.

———. *The United States and Cuba under Reagan and Shultz: A Foreign Service Officer Reports.* Westport, Conn.: Praeger, 1996.

Smith, Gaddis. *Morality, Reason, and Power: American Diplomacy in the Carter Years.* New York: Hill and Wang, 1986.

Smith, Wayne. *The Closest of Enemies: A Personal and Diplomatic History of the Castro Years.* New York: Norton, 1987.

Snyman, P. H. R. *Beeld van die SWA Gebiedsmag.* Pretoria: SA Weermag, 1989.

Soggot, David. *Namibia: The Violent Heritage.* New York: St. Martin's Press, 1986.

Soiri, Iina, and Pekka Peltola. *Finland and National Liberation in Southern Africa.* Uppsala: Nordiska Afrikainstitutet, 1999.

Solarz, Stephen. "When to Intervene." *Foreign Policy*, no. 63 (Summer 1986): 20–39.

Sole, Donald. "'This above all': Reminiscences of a South African Diplomat." Unpublished manuscript, 1989, Cory Library, Rhodes University, Grahamstown, South Africa.

Solodovnikov, V. G. "K istorii ustanovleniia diplomaticheskikh otnoshenii mezhdu SSSR u Simbabwe." In Institute of Africa, ed., *Afrika v vospominaniiakh veteranov diplomaticheskoi sluzhby.* Moscow: XXI Vek-Soglasie, 2000, pp. 134–74.

Somerville, Keith. "The Soviet Union and Zimbabwe: The Liberation Struggle and After." In Craig Nation and Mark Kauppi, eds., *The Soviet Impact in Africa.* Lexington, Mass.: Lexington Books, 1984.

Soule, Allan, Gary Dixon, and René Richards. *The Wynand du Toit Story.* Johannesburg: Hans Strydom Publishers, 1987.

Sparks, Allister. *Tomorrow Is Another Country: The Inside Story of South Africa's Road to Change.* Chicago: University of Chicago Press, 1995.

Spies, F. J. du Toit. *Operasie Savannah. Angola, 1975–1976.* Pretoria: S. A. Weermag, 1989.

Stark, Christoph. *Die Aussenpolitik der Volksrepublik China in Afrika von 1969 bis 1983, unter besonderer Berücksichtigung des südlichen Afrika.* Frankfurt am Main: Peter Lang, 1990.

Steenkamp, Willem. *Borderstrike! South Africa into Angola.* Durban: Butterworths, 1983.

———. *South Africa's Border War, 1966–1989.* Gibraltar: Ashanti, 1989.

Stiff, Peter. *The Covert War: Koevoet Operations in Namibia 1979–1989.* Alberton, South Africa: Galago, 2004.

———. *Warfare by Other Means: South Africa in the 1980s and 1990s.* Alberton, South Africa: Galago, 2001.

———. *The Silent War: South African Recce Operations, 1969–1994.* Alberton, South Africa: Galago, 1999.

Storkmann, Klaus. *Geheime Solidarität: Militärbeziehungen und Militärhilfen der DDR in die "Dritte Welt."* Berlin: Ch. Links Verlag, 2012.

Strong, Robert. *Working in the World: Jimmy Carter and the Making of American Foreign Policy.* Baton Rouge: Louisiana State University Press, 2000.

Szulc, Tad. *Fidel: A Critical Portrait.* New York: Avon Books, 1987.

Tamarkin, M. *The Making of Zimbabwe: Decolonization in Regional and International Politics.* London: Frank Cass, 1990.

Tareke, Gebru. *The Ethiopian Revolution: War in the Horn of Africa.* New Haven: Yale University Press, 2009.

Taylor, John. "Oral History Interview." The Foreign Affairs Oral History Collection of the Association for Diplomatic Studies and Training, Washington, D.C., 2003.

Thatcher, Margaret. *The Downing Street Years.* New York: HarperCollins, 1993.

Thomas, Scott. *The Diplomacy of Liberation: The Foreign Relations of the ANC since 1960*. London: Tauris, 1996.

Thomson, Alex. *U.S. Foreign Policy towards Apartheid South Africa, 1948–1994: Conflict of Interests*. New York: Palgrave Macmillan, 2008.

Thornberry, Cedric. *A Nation Is Born: The Inside Story of Namibia's Independence*. Windhoek: Gamsberg Macmillan, 2004.

Tiruneh, Andargachew. *The Ethiopian Revolution, 1974–1987: A Transformation from an Aristocratic to a Totalitarian Autocracy*. New York: Cambridge University Press, 1993.

Toase, Francis. "The South African Army: The Campaign in South West Africa/ Namibia since 1966." In Ian Beckett and John Pimlott, eds., *Armed Forces and Modern Counter-Insurgency*. New York: St. Martin's Press, 1985, pp. 190–221.

Tokarev, Andrei. "Kommandirovka v Angolu." *Aziya i Afrika sevodnya*, no. 2 (2001): 36–41.

Tokarev, Andrei, and Gennady Shubin, eds. *Veterany lokal'nukh voin i mirotvorchenskikh operatsii OON vspominaiut*. Moscow: Memories, 2010.

———, eds. *Vospominaniia neposredstvennykh uchastnikov i ochevidtsev grazhdanskoi voiny v Angole. Ustnaia istoriia zabytykh voin*. Moscow: Memories, 2009.

———, eds. *Vospominaniia uchastnikov i ochevidsev voiny v Angole 1975–2002 gg.* Moscow: Memories, 2008.

Truth and Reconciliation Commission of South Africa. *Report*. 5 vols. Cape Town: Truth and Reconciliation Commission, 1998.

Tubiana, Joseph, ed. *La révolution éthiopienne comme phénomène de société: témoignages et documents*. Paris: L'Harmattan, 1990.

[Turki Al-Faisal.] "Saudi Ambassador Interview with SUSRIS." Mar. 2, 2006, pp. 9–10, http://www.saudiembassy.net/2006News/Statements/TransDetail.asp?cIndex=590

Turner, Stanfield. *Secrecy and Democracy: The CIA in Transition*. Boston: Houghton Mifflin, 1985.

Tyler, Patrick. *A Great Wall: Six Presidents and China*. New York: Public Affairs, 1999.

United Nations. *The Blue Helmets: A Review of United Nations Peace-Keeping*. New York: United Nations Department of Public Information, 1996.

United States Congress, House, Committee on Foreign Affairs, SubCommittee on Africa. *Angola: Intervention or Negotiation?*, 99th Cong., 1st sess. Washington, D.C.: GPO, 1986.

———. *Namibia Update*. 96th Cong., 2nd sess. Washington, D.C.: GPO, 1981.

———. *United States Policy toward Angola—Update*. 96th Cong., 2nd sess. Washington, D.C.: GPO, 1980.

———. *U.S. Interests in Africa*. 96th Cong., 1st sess. Washington, D.C.: GPO, 1980.

United States Congress, House, Committee on International Relations. *Economic and Military Assistance Programs in Africa*. 95th Cong., 2nd sess. Washington, D.C.: GPO, 1978.

United States Congress, Senate, Committee on Foreign Relations. *Situation in South Africa*. 99th Cong., 2nd sess. Washington, D.C.: GPO, 1986.

———. *Angola: Options for American Foreign Policy*. 99th Cong., 2nd sess. Washington, D.C.: GPO, 1986.

United States Congress, Senate, Committee on Foreign Relations, Subcommittee on Africa: *U.S. Policy toward Africa*. 95th Cong., 2nd sess. Washington, D.C.: GPO, 1978.

United States, Defense Intelligence Agency. *Handbook on the Cuban Armed Forces*. Washington, D.C.: Defense Intelligence Agency, 1986.

———. *Handbook on the Cuban Armed Forces*. Washington, D.C.: Defense Intelligence Agency, 1979.

United States, Department of State. *Foreign Relations of the United States*, 1958–1976. Washington, D.C.: GPO, 1991–2012.

United States, General Services Administration. *Public Papers of the Presidents of the United States*, 1959–1988. Washington, D.C.: GPO, 1960–1990.

Urquhart, Brian. *A Life in Peace and War*. New York: Harper and Row, 1987.

Vance, Cyrus. *Hard Choices: Critical Years in America's Foreign Policy*. New York: Simon and Schuster, 1983.

Van der Walt, Nico. *Bos Toe! 'N Storie oor die laaste fase van die Grensoorlog soos beleef deur 'n junior offisier van 32-Bataljon*. Pretoria: N. van der Walt, 2007.

Van Wyk, At. *Dirk Mudge: Reënmaker van die Namib*. Pretoria: J. L. van Schaik, 1989.

Varennikov, Valentin. *Nepovtorimoe*. Vol. 4. Moscow: Sovestskii pisatel, 2001.

Vázquez Raña, Mario. *Raúl Castro: Entrevista al periodico El Sol de México*. Havana: Editorial Capitán San Luis, 1993.

Veloso, Jacinto. *Memórias em Voo Rasante*. Maputo: António José Correia Paulo, 2006.

Venter, Al J. *How South Africa Built Six Atom Bombs*. Gibraltar: Ashanti, 2008.

———. *The Chopper Boys: Helicopter Warfare in Africa*. Johannesburg: Southern Book Publishers, [c 1994].

Vergau, Hans-Joaquim. *Verhandeln um die Freiheit Namibias. Das diplomatische Werk der westlichen Kontaktgruppe*. Baden-Baden: Nomos, 2006.

Vidal, Nuno. "Post-Modern Patrimonialism in Africa: The Genesis and Development of the Angolan Political System, 1961–1987." Ph.D. diss., King's College, London, 2002.

Vines, Alex. *RENAMO: From Terrorism to Democracy in Mozambique?* London: James Currey, 1996.

Vinicius, Marco, and Maria João Saldanha. *Jonas Savimbi: Um desafio à dictadura comunista em Angola*. Lisbon: Edições Armasilde, 1977.

Vorotnikov, Vitaly. *Gavana—Moskva: pamiatnye gody*. Moscow: Fond imeni I. D. Sytina, 2001.

Voss, Matthias, ed. *Wir haben Spuren hinterlassen! Die DDR in Mosambik*. Münster: Lit Verlag, 2005.

Walters, Vernon. *The Mighty and the Meek: Dispatches from the Front Line of Diplomacy*. London: St Ermin's Press, 2001.

Weiland, Heribert, and Matthew Braham, eds. *The Namibian Peace Process: Implications and Lessons for the Future*. Freiburg: Arnold Bergstrasser Institut, 1994.

Weinberger, Caspar. *Fighting for Peace: Seven Critical Years in the Pentagon*. New York: Warner Books, 1990.

Weiner, Tim. *Legacy of Ashes: The History of the CIA*. New York: Doubleday, 2007.

Weissman, Stephen. *A Culture of Deference: Congress's Failure of Leadership in Foreign Policy*. New York: Basic Books, 1995.

Westad, Odd Arne. *The Global Cold War, Third World Interventions and the Making of our Times*. New York: Cambridge University Press, 2006.

———. "Moscow and the Angolan Crisis, 1974–1976: A New Pattern of Intervention." Cold War International History Project *Bulletin*, nos. 8–9 (Winter 1996–97): 21–37.

Windrich, Elaine. *The Cold War Guerrilla: Jonas Savimbi, the U.S. Media, and the Angolan War*. New York: Greenwood, 1992.

Winkelmann, Egon. *Moskau, das war es: Erinnerungen des DDR-Botschafters in der Sowjetunion, 1981–1987*. Berlin: Edition Ost, 1997.

Wisner, Frank. "Oral History Interview." The Foreign Affairs Oral History Collection of the Association for Diplomatic Studies and Training, Washington, D.C.,1998.

Wolf, Markus. *Spionagechef im geheimen Krieg: Erinnerungen*. Munich: List, 1997.

Woodward, Bob. *Veil: The Secret Wars of the CIA, 1981–1987*. New York: Simon and Schuster, 1987.

Yazov, Dmitri. *Udari sudbi. Vospominaniia soldata i marshala*. Moscow: Paleia Mishin, 1999.

Zhdarkin, Igor. *"Takovo ne bilo dazhe v Afgane": Vospominaniia uchastnika voini v Angole (1986–1988 gg.)/"We Did Not See It Even in Afghanistan": Memoirs of a participant of the Angolan War (1986–1988)*. Moscow: Memories, 2008.

# Index

*Note*: Cuban documents identify some people by secret code names (see Note on Citations, p. 527). I give these secret names in the index followed by a cross-reference to the real name. Some Angolans were always called by their noms de guerre. For these individuals, I list their noms de guerre, followed by their real names in parentheses.

troops, 77–79; and quadripartite nego-
tiations, 443–45, 447–49, 460–61, 472,
474, 478–80, 483–84, 486–87, 489; and
South West Africa People's Organiza-
tion, 100, 112, 202, 209–12, 250–51, 335.
*See also* Askari; Carter administration:
and Angola; Cuba; Neto; Operation
Salute to October; Operation Second
Congress; Protea; Shaba I; South
Africa: and Angola

Anstee, Margaret, 428, 501, 512, 608
(n. 88)

Arbenz, Jacobo, 19

Arbesú Fraga, Antonio, 317, 319

Argentina, 9

Armacost, Michael, 596 (n. 3)

Arteaga Pérez, Feliberto, 327

Askari, 231–33

Badenhorst, Witkop, 248

*Bahía de Nipe*, 23

Bakaloff (Ernesto Gomes), 76

Baker, Howard, 408

Baker, James, 169

Bakongo, 26

Ball, George, 29

Barbarito (code name). *See* Dos Santos,
José Eduardo

Barganov, Vladimir, 72

Barroso Hipólito, Abel, 66

Bay of Pigs, 19

Belgium, 56

Bender, Gerald, 84, 118, 160

Benguela, 329

Benítez y de Mendoza, Noemí, 327

Berbera, 164

Beukes, Herbert, 285

Biko, Steve, 95

Bilak, Vasil, 481

Black, Manafort, Stone and Kelly, 310

Blumenthal, Michael, 152

Boesak, Allan, 521

Boma, 86, 87

Boris, 366, 454

Botha, Pik, 11, 178, 179, 181–85, 202, 233,
248, 287, 288–89; 313; and PW Botha,
288–89; and Cabinda raid, 253–54; and
Namibia, 148, 154–56, 158, 206, 260,
386, 402; and 1988 negotiations, 445,
460–62, 465–66, 472, 478, 488; and
1984–85 negotiations, 242, 244, 250,
255–56, 311; and Nkomati pact, 237–38;
and Reagan administration, 230; and
Savimbi, 247; and Zimbabwe, 286.
*See also* Angola; South African Foreign
Ministry

Botha, PW, 11, 29, 117–18, 149, 179, 182,
186, 201, 250, 389, 504; and domestic
politics, 197, 263, 292; and Israel, 295;
and Maniobra XXXI Aniversario, 425,
465; and May 1986 raids, 287–89; and
Namibia, 150, 152–54, 155, 157, 260–62,
387; and 1988 negotiations, 440,
445–46, 461, 467, 476; and Operation
Moduler, 398, 400–401; and Reagan,
312, 504; and Savimbi, 244–50; and
Soviet Union, 473. *See also* South
African Defence Force

Botswana, 38, 94, 201, 264, 286, 293, 335

Bowdler, William, 92

Brademas, John, 163

Brazil, 9, 70, 76, 297

Brecht, Bertolt, 482

Breytenbach, Jan, 67, 245–46, 345, 356,
372, 380, 399, 425, 430

Brezhnev, Leonid, 30, 34–35, 45, 48, 70,
71, 75, 76

Briggs, Everett, 28

Britain, 22, 36, 38, 118, 140, 185, 188, 233,
297, 367, 447. *See also* Contact Group

Brooke, James, 301, 333

Broomfield, William, 163

Brown, Harold, 51, 152

Brzezinski, Zbigniew, 12, 49, 51–53, 62,
99, 101, 104, 163; and Angola, 42,
159, 161–62; and Cuba, 46, 50, 57–59,
119–22, 124–25, 134, 140, 151–52, 158.
*See also* Soviet Brigade

Buchanan, John, 163
Buchanan, Pat, 283, 290, 291
Buckley, William, 298
Buffalo Battalion, 67, 209
Bulgaria, 176, 452
Bureau of Intelligence and Research of the U.S. Department of State (INR). *See* U.S. intelligence services
Burt, Richard, 169–70
Bush, George H. W., 513

Cabelly, Robert, 251, 292, 299, 391, 441, 484
Cabinda raid, 251–54
Caetano, Marcelo, 66
Cahama, 187, 188, 231, 428, 455
Caiundo, 231
Callaghan, James (Jim), 60
Calueque, 468
Cambodia, 443, 451
Canada, 38, 188, 293. *See also* Contact Group
Cangamba, 221–24
Carballo Torres, Rolando, 81, 258
Carlucci, Frank, 382, 408, 436–37, 510
Carrazo, Rodrigo, 137
Carreira, Iko, 26, 54, 78, 110, 111, 114, 116, 117, 190, 367
Carter, Jimmy, 10, 12, 47, 62, 133, 136, 139, 163–65; and Angola, 98, 100; and Cuba, 41, 52, 120, 121, 123–25, 134, 158, 523; and Namibia, 148, 154; and southern Africa, 511, 524–25. *See also* Carter administration; Soviet Brigade
Carter administration: and Afghanistan, 133; and Angola, 41–43, 98–103, 112–13, 117, 158–63; and Cuba, 43–45, 49–51, 106, 119–26; and Horn of Africa, 45–47; and Namibia, 37–39, 92–96, 102, 146–58; and Rhodesia, 37–39, 139–45; and Savimbi, 51–53, 68, 99, 101, 310; and South Africa, 37, 92–96, 117, 118, 152; and South West Africa People's Organization, 100; and Soviet Union,

47–49; and Zaire, 53. *See also* Carter, Jimmy; Mariel; Shaba I; Shaba II; Soviet Brigade
Casas Regueiro, Senén, 56–67, 72, 78, 90, 111–12, 117, 176–77
Casey, William, 283–84, 308–9, 310, 408
Cassinga massacre, 60–62, 96, 117, 118, 150
Castro Ruz, Fidel, 23, 30, 85, 86, 119, 141, 216, 227, 340–41, 426; and Afghanistan, 134–35; and African National Congress, 73, 335, 337; and Angola, 34, 84, 96, 105, 106, 111, 116, 243; and Brezhnev, 13, 34; and Cangamba, 221–25; and Carter administration, 125–26; and Demichev, 132, 134, 315; and dos Santos, 238–41, 335, 338–39, 347, 368–71, 384–85, 390, 411, 460–61; and Ethiopia, 144; and Gorbachev, 17, 324, 361, 362–64, 403–7, 414–18, 423, 444–45, 464, 514; and Kurochkin, 347, 368–71; and Latin America, 20–21, 23, 322–23; and Mengistu, 325; and Namibian students in Cuba, 495; and Neto, 72–73, 103, 106–8, 110, 142; and Neto's succession, 115–16; and Nicaragua, 320–21; and 1988 negotiations, 431–40, 443–45, 447–49, 462–65, 472, 474, 484–85, 490; and offensive in southwest Angola, 362–65; and People's Armed Forces for the Liberation of Angola, 72–73, 195, 221, 228–29; and Reagan, 175; and Reagan administration, 174, 227, 316–17, 319, 404; and Shevardnadze, 320–21, 329, 360–61; and South Africa, 34, 338–41, 443; and South West Africa People's Organization, 73; and Soviet military mission in Angola, 73, 344–45, 360; and Soviet Union, 19–22, 71, 170, 452, 464–65, 492, 514–15; and technical assistance to Angola, 229, 434, 494; and United States, 18–19, 170. *See also* Cuba; Maniobra XXXI Aniversario; Mariel; Shaba II; Soviet Brigade

Castro Ruz, Raúl, 21, 142, 190, 215, 341; and African National Congress, 336; and Andropov, 216–18, 316; and Angola, 35, 71, 75, 78, 79, 85, 105, 114, 192, 194, 215, 350, 547 (n. 32); and Askari, 234–35; and Cangamba, 233–34; and Gorbachev, 361; and Latin America, 322; and Machel, 379–80; and Maniobra XXXI Aniversario, 407, 410, 414, 418, 421; and 1988 negotiations, 463; and Nujoma, 376–77; and Ochoa, 493; and Reagan administration, 315; and South Africa, 336; and Soviet Union, 22, 414, 418, 464

Central Intelligence Agency (CIA). *See* U.S. intelligence services

Chernenko, Konstantin, 176, 236–37

Chernyaev, Anatoly, 363

Chevron, 310, 311, 381

Cheysson, Claude, 207

Chibia, 91

Chiles, Lawton, 382

China (People's Republic of), 9, 67, 68, 150, 171, 217, 262, 451

Chirkin, Venyamin, 145

Chitunda, Jeremias, 242, 257

Choy López, José Antonio, 81

Christopher, Warren, 101, 122, 148, 160, 163

Church, Frank, 43, 128

Cintra Frías, Leopoldo (Polo), 13, 236; and Askari, 231, 233; and Cangamba, 222–23; and Kurochkin, 235, 345–54, 367; and Maniobra XXXI Aniversario, 419, 422, 428, 468–69, 485. *See also* Operation Salute to October; Operation Second Congress

Ciskei, 250

Civiletti, Ben, 137

Clark, Dick, 52

Clark, William, 178, 181–82, 256, 283

Clark amendment, 51, 62, 296, 304

Clinton, Bill, 502

Cohen, Herman, 309, 436, 491, 510, 512

Colby, William, 70

Colombia, 173

Colomé Ibarra, Abelardo, 192–93, 224–26, 233, 348, 350, 492

Coltman, Leycester, 524

Columbié Álvarez, Arquimedes, 70

Comprehensive Anti-Apartheid Act, 294

Congo Brazzaville, 24, 108

Conservative party (of South Africa), 198, 470, 500

Constructive engagement, 178, 292–93, 504–5

Contact Group: and Carter administration, 92–96, 103–4, 113, 146–58, 497; and Reagan administration, 185, 198–200, 205–7, 212, 262

Correia de Barros, Manuel, 359

Costa Gomes, Francisco da, 65, 66

Cowell, Alan, 302

Crane, Phil, 311

Crocker, Chester, 13, 178, 179–81, 204–5, 207, 226, 230, 279, 311, 312, 409, 503–12; and Adamishin, 426–27, 455, 473; and National Union for the Total Independence of Angola, 374; and 1988 negotiations, 434–42, 453, 467–68, 472, 474, 478, 480, 483–84, 488; and 1984–85 negotiations, 236, 242, 244, 252, 254–55; and 1987 negotiations, 380, 388–92; and 1992 elections in Angola, 512–13; and Nkomati pact, 238; and Reagan, 290–92; and Savimbi, 257–59, 299, 303, 307, 372, 452, 488; and South Africa, 178, 233, 260–61, 285, 401, 469; and Soviet Union, 515. *See also* Linkage; Reagan administration

Crombet Hernández-Baquero, Jaime, 116

Cuando Cubango, 222, 348

Cuangar, 192

Cuba: and Afghanistan, 134–35; and Africa, 23–24, 324, 495; and African National Congress, 87–89, 92, 334–41, 490; and Algeria, 23; and Angola, 28–29, 63, 71–73, 77–79, 97, 105–6, 109–11,

176–77, 194–96, 213–16, 218, 242–43, 377–78, 494; and Askari, 232–33; and Cangamba, 221–24, 225–26; and Carter administration, 38, 43–45, 119–26, 143–44; and Cassinga massacre, 60–62; and Cuban economy, 323–25, 340; and Cuito Cuanavale, battle of, 406, 422–26; and defensive line in Angola, 110–11, 187, 188, 214, 228; and differences with USSR about military strategy in Angola, 344–54, 359, 366–71; and Ethiopia, 324–26, 341; and Grenada, 226–27; and Horn of Africa, 45–47, 49; and January 1988 negotiations, 431–38; and Latin America, 321; and Lusaka agreement, 236, 238–39; and March 1988 negotiations, 439–42; and March 1987 tripartite meeting, 374–76, 379; and May 1983 tripartite meeting, 219–21; and Mozambique, 143–44; and Namibia, 142, 496; and Nicaragua, 218, 315, 320–21; and 1987 negotiations, 379, 384–85, 389–92; and Nito Alves coup, 74–77; and Operation Salute to October, 393–94; and Operation Second Congress, 355, 358–59; and People's Armed Forces for the Liberation of Angola, 190–91, 195, 219–21; and policy in southern Africa, an assessment, 508–9, 513, 516–24, 525–26; and Protea, 189; and Reagan administration, 170–76, 216–18, 227, 314–20, 404; and Rhodesia, 141; and scholarship program for foreign students, 326, 495, 516–19; and Shaba I, 44; and South West Africa People's Organization, 90–92, 94–95, 209–12, 475, 495; and Soviet Union, 70–71, 192–94, 234–36, 323–24, 341, 404, 409–14, 418, 473, 514–15; and Sumbe, 327–28; and technical assistance abroad, 326–27, 518; and technical assistance to Angola, 79–85, 105–6, 108–9, 220, 327–34, 494; and Zimbabwe African National Union, 144–45; and Zimbabwe African People's Union, 86–87, 92, 144–45. *See also* Castro Ruz, Fidel; Maniobra XXXI Aniversario; Mariel; Quadripartite negotiations; Shaba II

Cuban American National Foundation, 305, 318

Cuito Cuanavale (town), 348–49, 393–94

Cuito Cuanavale (battle of), 399–493, 406–7, 422–26

Cunene (province), 187, 189, 209, 427–28

Cutler, Walter, 59

Cuvelai, 231

Czechoslovakia, 91, 147, 150, 428, 452

Dahlak islands, 164

Dalmau Fernández, Ángel, 334, 336–37

Darushenko, Oleg, 405

Davidow, Jeff, 299, 510

Davies, J. E., 77

Dayan, Moshe, 294

DeConcini, Dennis, 436

De Klerk, Frederick, 520

De la Guardia Font, Tony, 123

Del Pino, Rafael, 221, 223

Del Pozo Jerez, Haydée, 90

Delta (camp), 67

Demichev, Petr, 132, 134, 315

Democratic Turnhalle Alliance (DTA), 94, 149, 154, 155, 156, 184, 207, 259–60, 499, 520

Denmark, 294

Dibaba, Berhanu, 326

Diggs, Charles, 163

Djibouti, 102

Dobrynin, Anatoly, 70, 129, 132, 168, 339, 444–45, 474

Domínguez Espinosa, Guillermo, 81

Dorning, W., 396, 397, 398, 399

Dos Santos, José Eduardo, 15, 105, 114, 116, 117, 135, 189, 225, 347, 373, 548 (n. 59); and Askari, 232–34; and Cangamba, 222–23; and Fidel Castro, 229, 238–41, 338–39, 368–71, 384–85, 390,

411, 494; and military strategy, 350–51, 353, 357; and 1988 negotiations, 431–35, 438–39, 441, 442, 444–45, 461, 486–87; and Operation Salute to October, 394, 398; and Reagan administration, 200; and South Africa, 242, 251; and Soviet Union, 220–21, 514

Dreke Cruz, Víctor, 25, 495

Dukakis, Michael, 507–8

Du Pisani, André, 33

Du Plessis, Abraham, 94

Du Toit, Wynand, 252–53

Eagleburger, Lawrence, 230

Eastern Europe, 164, 451

Easum, Donald, 47

Eglin, Colin, 261, 470

Egypt, 47, 51, 68, 126, 164, 516 (n. 42)

Eisenhower, Dwight, 19, 24

El Salvador, 126, 168

Enders, Thomas, 170

Eminent Persons Group (EPG), 286–88, 290

Enrique (code name). *See* Aldana Escalante, Carlos

Eritrea, 325

Escartín Fernández, Aleyda, 81, 82

Ethiopia, 45–47, 82, 109

Farah Balmaseda, Levy, 83

Fascell, Dante, 163

Fenton, Daniel, 297–98, 303, 307, 309

Ferch, John, 317, 319–20

Finland, 294

Fischer, Oskar, 134

Fleitas Ramírez, Gustavo, 346, 398

Foguetão (Pedro Benga Lima), 189, 191, 353–54, 357, 359

Ford, Gerald, 10, 36, 48, 70, 166, 523

Ford administration, 28, 36

Fortun del Sol, Feliberto, 91

Fourie, Brand, 182

France, 36, 38, 41, 47, 56, 67, 68, 102, 118, 188, 297, 367, 447. *See also* Contact Group

Franco Codinach, Lourdes, 328–32

Fraser, Malcolm, 287

Freeman, Charles (Chas), 284, 290, 391, 436, 510

Front for the Liberation of the Enclave of Cabinda (FLEC), 68, 539 (n. 17)

Frontline States (FLS), 38, 94, 96, 143, 146, 147, 198, 335

Funk, Jerry, 101

Gabon, 68

Gaddis, John Lewis, 452

Garba, Joe, 42

García, Calixto, 492

García Espinosa, Gilberto, 332

García Mesa, Norberto, 327

García Peláez, Pedro, 113, 114

García Ramírez, Ernesto, 424

Gárciga Blanco, José Angel, 214

Garthoff, Raymond, 48, 127, 129

Gates, Robert, 309, 383

Geldenhuys, Jan, 187, 207, 230, 372, 445, 500, 509, 520; and military situation in 1988, 424–25, 455–57, 459, 471; and 1988 negotiations, 472, 474–78, 489; and Operation Moduler, 397, 399, 400, 402–3, 407; and Savimbi, 246–47, 249

Geneva summit, 382

Genscher, Hans-Dietrich, 153, 185

German Democratic Republic (GDR), 91, 176, 251, 428, 452, 545 (n. 126)

Giscard d'Estaing, Valéry, 60, 121

Glassman, Jon, 169

Gleeson, Ian, 458

Gómez Reina, Goliath, 330

González Polanco, Alberto, 326–27

Goodsell, James Nelson, 315

Gorbachev, Mikhail, 443–44, 450–52; and Afghanistan, 382–83, 451; and Fidel Castro, 17, 361, 362–64, 405–6, 414–17, 443–44, 514; and Cuba, 14, 323–24; and 1988 negotiations, 432, 486; and Reagan, 361–62, 417

Goulding, Marrack, 259, 300, 497, 500, 502, 513

Mozambique, 8, 82, 86, 94, 109, 140, 143, 201–2, 243, 335, 379–80; and Nkomati pact, 237–38

Mozambique National Resistence (RENAMO), 186, 238, 281, 380

Mudge, Dirk, 94, 207–8

Mugabe, Robert, 143, 145

Mulondo, 231

Mupopiwa, Mwetufa, 91

Muskie, Edmund, 160

Muzorewa, Abel, 139, 156

Nakandungile, Malakia, 209, 457

Namibe (port), 110, 116, 212

Namibe (province), 187

Namibia, 10–11, 31, 154, 201, 207–8, 259–62, 457–59; and 1989 elections, 496–500. *See also* Carter administration; Linkage; South Africa; South West Africa People's Organization

Namoloh, Charles, 90, 429

Napper, Lawrence (Larry), 299, 390, 391, 439–41, 474

Nascimento, Lopo do, 75, 98, 99, 100

National Front for the Liberation of Angola (FNLA), 26, 27, 28, 68, 539 (n. 17)

National Party (of South Africa), 156, 197, 460–67

National Party of South West Africa, 33, 94

National Union for the Total Independence of Angola (UNITA), 26, 28, 65–69, 111, 116, 176, 192, 195, 213, 247–48, 372, 482, 490; and Cangamba, 221–24; and Cuito Cuanavale, battle of, 399–400, 403, 423; and Operation Salute to October, 394–96, 398; and Operation Second Congress, 354–57; and quadripartite negotiations, 445; and South Africa, 381; and Sumbe, 327–28; and terrorism, 300–302, 328, 372–74. *See also* Savimbi, Jonas

Nazhestkin, Oleg, 69

Ndalu (António dos Santos França), 191, 233, 346, 350, 359, 393–94, 398; and

1988 negotiations, 432, 437–38, 472, 475, 478, 484

Ndeitungo, Sophia, 326

Neto, Agostinho, 26–27, 61, 65, 68, 86, 114, 194; and Carter administration, 97–99, 101, 103, 106–7, 112–14; and Fidel Castro, 106–8; and Cuba, 35, 77, 78, 80, 103–8, 111–14, 116, 547 (n. 32); and Namibia, 113–14, 146–47; and South Africa, 103–4, 112–14; and South West Africa People's Organization, 103–4, 114. *See also* Nito Alves coup; Shaba II; Soviet Union

Newsom, David, 52, 119–24, 128, 132, 142

New York Agreements, 491–92

Nghilalulwa, Vilho, 457

Ngongo (Roberto Ramos Monteiro), 190, 191, 192, 346, 350, 354, 359, 394

Nicaragua, 126, 168, 171, 173, 176, 320–21, 451, 574 (n. 61)

Nickel, Herman, 253–54, 256, 260, 264, 288, 385–86, 387, 504

Nigeria, 38, 41, 42, 94, 189

Nito Alves coup, 73–77

Nixon, Marcus, 91

Nixon, Richard, 166

Nkomati pact, 237–38, 243, 244

Nkomo, Joshua, 86, 87, 104, 143

Nojoba, Karel, 208

North Korea, 176

North Vietnam, 82

Norway, 294

Novo Catengue, 88, 89

Nujoma, Sam, 90, 91, 94, 95, 96, 104, 146, 184, 206, 210–11, 376, 497, 498, 500

Nunda (Geraldo Sachipengo), 68, 191, 192, 309, 345

Nyerere, Julius, 39, 148, 189

Obasanjo, Olusugun, 287

Obey, David, 163

Ochoa Sánchez, Arnaldo, 367, 393, 406–7, 411–12, 428–29, 468–69, 485; and trial, 492–94

Oelschig, Fred, 372, 446

raid, 253–54; and Cuba, 167–74, 316–20; and Grenada, 226–27; and Israel, 295; and January 1988 negotiations, 431–39; and Joint Chiefs of Staff, 425, 442, 476; and Libya, 289, 314; and Maniobra XXXI Aniversario, 455, 465–66; and March 1988 negotiations, 439–42; and Mobutu, 307–8; and Mozambique, 281, 284; and Mozambique National Resistence, 281, 284; and Nicaragua, 296, 314–15, 574 (n. 61); and 1984–85 negotiations, 242–44, 254–55; and Protea, 188–89; and Savimbi, 245, 257, 305–10, 380, 437; and South Africa, 233, 259, 264, 284–85, 290, 293, 367, 401, 499; and southern Africa, 177–85, 504–14; and Soviet Union, 226, 382–83, 407–8, 426, 450–51. *See also* Linkage; Quadripartite negotiations

Regan, Donald (Don), 283, 408

Renwick, Robin, 461

Reston, Tom, 57

Reyes Carrasco, Roger, 455

Rey Jiménez, Gina, 80, 81

Reykjavik summit, 382, 418

Reynolds, David, 417

Rhodesia, 33, 139–44, 146, 177, 186. *See also* Smith, Ian; South Africa

Rindle, Fred, 424, 429

Ringdahl, Philip, 436

Risquet Valdés, Jorge, 24, 63, 109, 133, 175, 176; and African National Congress, 89, 335–36, 340; and Angola, 35, 80, 82–84, 195, 213, 215, 224–25, 242–43, 373; and Askari, 232, 234–35; and dos Santos, 241, 411, 430; and Eritrea, 325; and January 1988 negotiations, 431–39; and Ligachev, 417; and Maniobra XXXI Aniversario, 407–9; and March 1988 negotiations, 439–42; and military strategy in Angola, 349, 351, 361; and Neto, 43, 54–56, 86; and New York agreements, 491–92; and 1987 negotiations, 379, 385, 389, 392; and Nujoma, 62, 91, 95; and quadripartite negotia-

tions, 444–45, 447–49, 452–53, 462–63, 466–68, 472, 483, 485–86, 522; and South West Africa People's Organization, 60, 210–12; and Soviet Union, 134, 192–94, 218–20, 225–26, 473, 496

Roberto, Holden, 26, 539 (n. 17)

Robinson, John, 208

Rodiles Plana, Samuel, 346

Rodman, Peter, 381, 512

Rodríguez Rodríguez, Carlos Rafael, 57, 124, 135, 141, 170–72, 405

Romania, 452

Rosales del Toro, Ulises, 223, 348, 353–54, 361, 366, 409, 410–14, 419–20, 454, 474–75, 484

Ross Fonseca, Pedro, 429

Ross Leal, Pedro, 580 (n. 61)

Rundu, 446, 480

Sadat, Anwar, 67

Safari Club, 67–68

Safire, William, 77

Safonov, Leonid, 473

SALT II treaty, 47, 127, 130, 131, 133

Sánchez-Parodi Montoto, Ramón, 317, 462–63

Sandinistas, 168, 176

São Tomé, 108

Šašić, Nikola, 75, 76, 77

Saudi Arabia, 47, 51, 67, 68, 284, 516 (n. 42)

Savimbi, Jonas, 10, 12, 27, 42, 65–69, 110, 191, 298–304, 310, 482, 487, 502, 512–13, 576 (n. 116); and PW Botha, 487; and Cabinda raid, 253; and Cangamba, 224; and Carter administration, 50–52, 161; and Crocker, 257–59, 372, 487, 488; and 1986 trip to U.S., 310, 436; and 1992 Angolan elections, 500–502; and Operation Salute to October, 397, 400; and Operation Second Congress, 356–67; and South Africa, 244–50, 261, 381, 400; and U.S. press, 297–303. *See also* South African Defence Force

Schlesinger, Arthur, Jr., 19, 318–19

Schmidt, Helmut, 60

South West Africa Territory Force (SWATF), 208, 417, 457, 470

Soviet Brigade, 126–33

Soviet Union, 164–65, 450–52; and Afghanistan, 133–35, 177, 382–83, 426, 443, 451, 460; and African National Congress, 87–89; and Angola, 28, 69–73, 80, 96–99, 187, 192–93, 227, 243, 514–16; and Carter administration, 47–49; and Cuba, 20–22, 70–71, 96, 170, 192–94, 344–54, 361, 365–67, 404, 409–14; and Ethiopia, 46; and Lusaka agreement, 236; and Maniobra XXXI Aniversario, 418–20, 428, 454–55, 457, 515; and March 1987 tripartite meeting, 374–76, 379; and military mission in Angola, 71–73, 343–44; and Namibia, 147, 150, 244, 249, 496; and Nicaragua, 451; and 1988 negotiations, 436, 442–45, 460, 464, 473–74, 478, 485–86, 515; and People's Armed Forces for the Liberation of Angola, 190–91, 194–95, 219–21, 227, 394–95; and Reagan administration, 166–67, 226, 407–8, 426, 456; and Savimbi, 181–83; and South West Africa People's Organization, 90, 184, 209–12, 353; and Zimbabwe African National Union, 145; and Zimbabwe African People's Union, 87, 145. *See also* Nito Alves coup; Soviet Brigade

Soweto, 88, 157

Sparks, Allister, 263

Spiegel, Marianne, 42, 162

Steenkamp, Willem, 61

Steward, David (Dave), 180, 245, 248, 312

Steyn, M. T., 154

Stiff, Peter, 251, 288, 499

Sullivan, Michael, 356

Sumbe, 327–28

Sunde, John, 446

Swaziland, 186, 201, 293, 335

Sweden, 70, 76, 185, 294

Symms, Stephen (Steve), 382

Szulc, Tad, 322

Tambo, Oliver, 89, 287, 335, 337, 340

Tanzania, 38, 94, 108

Tarnoff, Peter, 42, 124, 125–26, 134, 141

Taylor, John (Jay), 155, 391, 432–33, 442

Taylor, Paul, 520

Tchamutete, 60

Thailand, 451

Thatcher, Margaret, 143, 158, 185, 284, 286–87, 291

Thirion, Chris, 53, 67, 180, 244, 246, 248–49, 309, 345, 398, 402, 403

Tito, Josip Broz, 75

Todman, Terence, 43

Togo, 68

Tonta (Afonso Castro), 343

Torres Peñalver, Serena, 81, 333

Transitional Government of National Unity, 261, 385–86

Transkei, 179, 250

"True Reaganites," 283; and Crocker, 282–83, 453; and National Union for the Total Independence of Angola, 453; and Savimbi, 488; and southern Africa, 280–84, 509–10; and Soviet Union, 383–84

Tunney, John, 77

Turkey, 161

Turnhalle conference, 33, 34, 92

Turki Al-Faisal, 67

Turner, Stansfield, 51, 128

Tutu, Desmond, 470

Umkontho We Sizwe (MK), 87–89, 264, 334, 335

United Nations Security Council Resolution 385, 93, 95

United Nations Security Council Resolution 431, 147

United Nations Security Council Resolution 432, 147

United Nations Security Council Resolution 435, 149, 181–82, 185, 198, 205–6, 236, 241, 251

United Nations Security Council Resolution 439, 153

Xangongo, 116, 187

Yakovlev, Alexander, 485–86, 496
Yazov, Dmitry, 411–14, 415
Young, Andrew, 37, 38, 42, 74, 98, 112, 152, 154, 162
Yugoslavia, 77, 91, 171

Zablocki, Clement, 163
Zaire, 24, 44, 53, 108, 201, 213, 397. *See also* Mobutu Sese Seko; Shaba I; Shaba II

Zaitsev, Alexei, 410, 457
Zambia, 31, 38, 89, 94, 140, 186, 201–2, 210, 286, 307
Zimbabwe, 186, 189, 201–2, 286, 337
Zimbabwe African National Union (ZANU), 87, 139, 141, 143
Zimbabwe African People's Union (ZAPU), 39, 86–87, 139, 141, 143

Piero Gleijeses, *Visions of Freedom: Havana, Washington, Pretoria, and the Struggle for Southern Africa, 1976–1991* (2013).

Lien-Hang T. Nguyen, *Hanoi's War: An International History of the War for Peace in Vietnam* (2012).

Tanya Harmer, *Allende's Chile and the Inter-American Cold War, 1970–1973* (2011).

Alessandro Brogi, *Confronting America: The Cold War between the United States and the Communists in France and Italy* (2011).

Gregg Brazinsky, *Nation Building in South Korea: Koreans, Americans, and the Making of a Democracy* (2007).

Vladislav M. Zubok, *A Failed Empire: The Soviet Union in the Cold War from Stalin to Gorbachev* (2007).

Stephen G. Rabe, *U.S. Intervention in British Guiana: A Cold War Story* (2005).

Christopher Endy, *Cold War Holidays: American Tourism in France* (2004).

Salim Yaqub, *Containing Arab Nationalism: The Eisenhower Doctrine and the Middle East* (2003).

Francis J. Gavin, *Gold, Dollars, and Power: The Politics of International Monetary Relations, 1958–1971* (2003).

William Glenn Gray, *Germany's Cold War: The Global Campaign to Isolate East Germany, 1949–1969* (2003).

Matthew J. Ouimet, *The Rise and Fall of the Brezhnev Doctrine in Soviet Foreign Policy* (2003).

Pierre Asselin, *A Bitter Peace: Washington, Hanoi, and the Making of the Paris Agreement* (2002).

Jeffrey Glen Giauque, *Grand Designs and Visions of Unity: The Atlantic Powers and the Reorganization of Western Europe, 1955–1963* (2002).

Chen Jian, *Mao's China and the Cold War* (2001).

M. E. Sarotte, *Dealing with the Devil: East Germany, Détente, and Ostpolitik, 1969–1973* (2001).

Mark Philip Bradley, *Imagining Vietnam and America: The Making of Postcolonial Vietnam, 1919–1950* (2000).

Michael E. Latham, *Modernization as Ideology: American Social Science and "Nation Building" in the Kennedy Era* (2000).

Qiang Zhai, *China and the Vietnam Wars, 1950–1975* (2000).

William I. Hitchcock, *France Restored: Cold War Diplomacy and the Quest for Leadership in Europe, 1944–1954* (1998).